# The Last Hundred Yards

# The Last Hundred Yards

*The NCO's Contribution to Warfare*

*Illustrated*

H.J. Poole

*Foreword by
William S. Lind*

**Posterity
Press**

Published by Posterity Press, P.O. Box 5360, Emerald Isle, NC 28594
www.posteritypress.org

Copyrights © 1994, 1995, 1996, 1998 by H.J. Poole

Protected under the Berne Convention. All rights reserved. No part of this book may be reproduced or utilized in any form or by any means, electronic or mechanical, including photocopying or recording by any information storage-and-retrieval system without full permission in writing from the publisher. All inquiries should be addressed to Posterity Press, 102 Inlet Court, Emerald Isle, NC 28594-2011.

*Cataloging-in-Publication Data*

Poole, H.J., 1943-
    The last hundred yards.
    Includes bibliography and index.
    1. Infantry. 2. Infantry drill and tactics. 3. Firepower.
    4. Military history. 5. Military art and science.
    6. Military education. 7. United States Marine Corps.
I. Title.                                                  ISBN 0-9638695-2-3
1996    356'.1    Library of Congress Catalog Card Number 94-67181

This publication contains copyrighted material from other sources. Permissions to use this material are contained in the "source notes" that precede the "endnotes" at the back of the book. This material may not be further reproduced without the consent of the original owner. Additionally, every effort has been made to reach all the owners of copyrighted material. Any who may have been missed should identify themselves now to negotiate the appropriate permission agreements.

Cover art © 1995 by Michael Leahy

Edited by Dr. Mary Beth Poole and proofread by Martha B. Spencer
Fourth printing in the United States of America, July 2002

*This book is dedicated to the enlisted Vietnam War dead of G/2/5, 1st Marine Division. May the tactical experience, for which they paid so dearly, help future generations of American infantrymen.*

**GRUNT**

Term of affection used to denote that filthy, sweaty, dirt-encrusted, footsore, camouflage-painted, ripped-trousered, tired, sleepy, beautiful little son of a b— who has kept the wolf away from the door for over two hundred years.
— H.G. Duncan, *Green Side Out* © 1980

# Contents

Figures and Tables — ix

Foreword — xiii

Preface — xv

Acknowledgments — xix

**Part One: *The Shortfall in Recorded Knowledge***

    Chapter 1: *The Anatomy of Small-Unit Victory* — 3

    Chapter 2: *Operate on Blind Luck or Win Consistently* — 9

    Chapter 3: *Improving One's Chances for Success* — 15

    Chapter 4: *Old Habits May Get in the Way* — 21

    Chapter 5: *A Different Style of Warfare May Be Necessary* — 25

    Chapter 6: *Perhaps the Role of the Small Unit Must Change* — 39

    Chapter 7: *Another Outlook on When to Advance and When to Hold* — 43

    Chapter 8: *Reassessing the Role of the Weapons* — 51

**Part Two: *Techniques from the NCO Corps***

    Chapter 9: *Successfully Traversing a Battlefield* — 61

    Chapter 10: *Point Men* — 85

    Chapter 11: *Patrols That Look for Trouble* — 91

    Chapter 12: *Winning Chance Contact* — 101

    Chapter 13: *Evening Up the Odds with Indirect Fire* — 119

    Chapter 14: *The Great Equalizer — Close Air Support* — 133

    Chapter 15: *Counterambushing* — 151

    Chapter 16: *The Ultimate Ambush* — 159

Contents

| | |
|---|---|
| Chapter 17: *When Prepared Enemy Positions Are Encountered* | 173 |
| Chapter 18: *The Daylight Attack Is the Hardest* | 177 |
| Chapter 19: *Attack at Night to Save Lives* | 201 |
| Chapter 20: *The Safest Way to Attack — Short-Range Infiltration* | 225 |
| Chapter 21: *Defend Only to Reestablish Momentum* | 251 |
| Chapter 22: *Surviving the Unthinkable — NBC Attack* | 273 |
| Chapter 23: *The Unbeatable Urban Defense* | 283 |
| Chapter 24: *What the Urban Attacker Must Know to Stay Alive* | 313 |
| Chapter 25: *Getting Ready to Meet the Test* | 339 |
| Chapter 26: *What All of This May Mean to the Big Picture* | 349 |
| Appendix A: *Inventory Test* | 357 |
| Appendix B: *Guidelines for a Free-Play Exercise* | 369 |
| Appendix C: *Eulogy to a Fallen Platoon Leader* | 371 |
| Appendix D: *Eulogy to a Fallen Staff Sergeant* | 373 |
| Notes | 375 |
| Glossary | 389 |
| Bibliography | 393 |
| About the Author | 395 |
| Name Index | 397 |

# Tables and Figures

**TABLES:**

Chapter 1: *The Anatomy of Small-Unit Victory*

| | | |
|---|---|---|
| 1.1: | What May Be Required to Win at Low Cost | 4 |

Chapter 18: *The Daylight Attack Is the Hardest*

| | | |
|---|---|---|
| 18.1: | The Daylight Assault Sequence | 184 |
| 18.2: | The Speed Assault Technique | 196 |

Chapter 19: *Attack at Night to Save Lives*

| | | |
|---|---|---|
| 19.1: | The Night Assault Sequence | 214 |

Chapter 20: *The Safest Way to Attack — Short-Range Infiltration*

| | | |
|---|---|---|
| 20.1: | The Short-Range Infiltration Sequence | 240 |

Chapter 22: *Surviving the Unthinkable — NBC Attack*

| | | |
|---|---|---|
| 22.1: | The Immediate-Action Drill for Nuclear Attack | 276 |
| 22.2: | The Drill for Residual Radiation | 277 |
| 22.3: | The Immediate-Action Drill for Chemical/Biological Attack | 279 |
| 22.4: | The Modification to the Drill for a Solitary Blood Agent | 280 |

**FIGURES:**

Chapter 9: *Successfully Traversing a Battlefield*

| | | |
|---|---|---|
| 9.1: | Where to Travel Relative to the Military Crest | 64 |
| 9.2: | Using a Microterrain Horizon to Spot Enemy at Night | 69 |
| 9.3: | Using an Artificial Horizon to Spot Enemy at Night | 69 |
| 9.4: | Map Error | 70 |
| 9.5: | Resecting off Well-Placed Illumination Rounds | 72 |
| 9.6: | Triangulation | 73 |
| 9.7: | Aiming Off | 73 |
| 9.8: | Patrol Objectives Must Be Chosen Carefully | 75 |
| 9.9: | The Disadvantages of Always Dead Reckoning between March Objectives | 76 |

## Tables and Figures

| | | |
|---|---|---|
| 9.10: | First, See How Many Attack Points Are Available | 77 |
| 9.11: | Plan to Follow Linear Terrain Features and Avoid Obstacles or Danger Area | 78 |
| 9.12: | Choose the Legs before the Checkpoints | 79 |
| 9.13: | With a Route Card, the Navigator Can Focus on the Enemy | 80 |
| 9.14: | For Speed, Use the Bump Method at Caution Area | 82 |
| 9.15: | Use Polaris to Determine Latitude | 84 |

Chapter 11: *Patrols That Look for Trouble*

| | | |
|---|---|---|
| 11.1: | An Alternative to Standard Patrolling Technique | 96-100 |

Chapter 12: *Winning Chance Contact*

| | | |
|---|---|---|
| 12.1: | The Typical Chance Encounter | 105 |
| 12.2: | Chance-Contact Technique | 106-108 |
| 12.3: | The Unit That Can "Fire and Move" Has the Edge in Chance Contact | 110 |
| 12.4: | A Situation Requiring Fire and Movement | 111 |
| 12.5: | Fire-and-Movement Technique | 112-114 |
| 12.6: | An Opportunity for a Hasty Flanking Attack | 116 |
| 12.7: | The Hasty Flanking Attack | 117 |
| 12.8: | When an Enemy Force of Superior Strength Is Encountered | 118 |

Chapter 13: *Evening Up the Odds with Indirect Fire*

| | | |
|---|---|---|
| 13.1: | The Keys to Adjusting Fire | 124 |
| 13.2: | The Usual Firing Method Works Well Against Soft Area Targets | 128 |
| 13.3: | It Takes a Different Procedure to Hit a Distant Hardened Target | 129 |
| 13.4: | Precision Fire Could Replace Rushing Machinegun Bunkers | 130 |
| 13.5: | Still Another Technique Is Required to Hit a Moving Target | 131 |
| 13.6: | School of Infantry Fire Support Card Used by 2nd LAV Battalion in the Gulf War | 132 |

Chapter 14: *The Great Equalizer — Close Air Support*

| | | |
|---|---|---|
| 14.1: | Rotary-Wing Close Air Support | 141-143 |
| 14.2: | Fixed-Wing Close Air Support | 145-149 |

Chapter 15: *Counterambushing*

| | | |
|---|---|---|
| 15.1: | A Typical Daytime Counterambush Scenario | 154 |
| 15.2: | The Counterambush Technique in the Daytime | 155 |
| 15.3: | A Common Nighttime Counterambush Opportunity | 157 |
| 15.4: | The Counterambush Technique at Night | 158 |

Chapter 16: *The Ultimate Ambush*

| | | |
|---|---|---|
| 16.1: | Choosing a Good Ambush Site Is the Key | 166 |
| 16.2: | Occupying the Ambush Site with No Wasted Motion | 167 |
| 16.3: | The Ambush That Can Handle Any Force from Any Direction | 169 |
| 16.4: | The Enemy Can't Tell What Happened, and the Ambushers Get Away | 170-171 |

Chapter 18: *The Daylight Attack is the Hardest*

| | | |
|---|---|---|
| 18.1: | The Situation Often Encountered during a Daylight Attack | 187 |
| 18.2: | Preregistering the Objective is *Not* Part of the Plan of Attack | 188 |
| 18.3: | Use the Artillery and Base of Fire Only to Mask Envelopment Noise | 189 |
| 18.4: | When Facing Barbed Wire, Creep Smoke near the Intended Breach | 190 |
| 18.5: | The Situation at the End of the Envelopment Route | 191-192 |
| 18.6: | The Daytime Assault Sequence | 193-194 |
| 18.7: | The Speed Assault Technique | 197-198 |
| 18.8: | It Is Much Simpler to Use an Airstrike as the Deception | 200 |

Chapter 19: *Attack at Night to Save Lives*

| | | |
|---|---|---|
| 19.1: | The Situation Often Encountered During a Night Attack | 216 |
| 19.2: | The Inside Edge of the Barbed Wire is the Probable Line of Deployment | 217 |
| 19.3: | The Night Assault Sequence | 218-222 |
| 19.4: | A Night Attack Alternative for an Objective without Barbed Wire | 224 |

Chapter 20: *The Safest Way to Attack — Short-Range Infiltration*

| | | |
|---|---|---|
| 20.1: | Short-Range Infiltration Route Possibilities | 228 |
| 20.2: | How the Military Crest Helps the Short-Range Infiltrator | 229 |
| 20.3: | The Oriental Infiltration Technique | 230 |
| 20.4: | Locating Soft Spots during the Day with Short-Range Infiltration | 233 |
| 20.5: | The Teams That Can't Get Close, Fall In behind Those That Can | 234 |
| 20.6: | Once within Grenade Range, It's Easy to Force Open a Gap | 235 |
| 20.7: | The Gap Can Be Easily Widened | 236 |
| 20.8: | Unsuccessful Infiltration Teams Can Still Serve a Useful Purpose | 241 |
| 20.9: | The Linkup at the Rendezvous Point between Successful Teams | 242 |
| 20.10: | If Possible, the Subsequent Attack Should Use Explosives Only | 243 |
| 20.11: | The Safest Way to Escape Is Silently | 244 |
| 20.12: | The Sound of Small Arms Would Be the Signal for the Outside Teams to Act | 246 |
| 20.13: | The Outside Team Is in a Good Position to Force Open a Gap in the Lines | 247 |
| 20.14: | Telling the Inside Group Where the Foothold Is Located | 248 |
| 20.15: | The Entire Force Makes Good Its Escape | 249 |

Chapter 21: *Defend Only to Reestablish Momentum*

| | | |
|---|---|---|
| 21.1: | The Case for Preregistration in the Defense | 254 |
| 21.2: | The Fire Support Terrain Sketch Shortens Reaction Time | 255 |
| 21.3: | Anti-Armor Ambushes in Series to Delay Enemy Tanks | 258-260 |
| 21.4: | Stopping Infiltrators Requires Attention to Microterrain | 263 |
| 21.5: | How the Military Crest Affects the Placement of the Fighting Holes | 264 |
| 21.6: | The Wrong Way to Establish a Perimeter Defense | 265 |
| 21.7: | A Perimeter Defense That Will Stop Infiltrators | 266 |
| 21.8: | Stopping Infiltrators Takes Staying Hidden | 271 |

Chapter 22: *Surviving the Unthinkable — NBC Attack*

| | | |
|---|---|---|
| 22.1: | It Takes Practice to Counter a Surprise Chemical Attack | 280 |
| 22.2: | The Deliberate-Decontamination Station | 282 |

Tables and Figures

Chapter 23: *The Unbeatable Urban Defense*

| | | |
|---|---|---|
| 23.1: | Moving Pockets of Resistance | 289-291 |
| 23.2: | The M-16 Can Cover Machinegun Dead Space in Urban Terrain | 293 |
| 23.3: | Every Man is a Tank Killer in an Urban Setting | 294 |
| 23.4: | Maneuver Warfare Options for a City Defense Scenario | 296-298 |
| 23.5: | The Soft-Urban-Defense Technique | 299-305 |
| 23.6 | Retrograde Movement along a City Street | 306 |
| 23.7: | An Alternate Technique for Moving Backward in Urban Terrain | 307 |
| 23.8: | Inside Barriers Give the Defender an Edge | 308 |
| 23.9: | Escape Routes Permit the Defender to Win | 309 |
| 23.10: | The All-Around Room Defense | 310-311 |

Chapter 24: *What an Urban Attacker Must Know to Stay Alive*

| | | |
|---|---|---|
| 24.1: | How to Employ the Machineguns without Curtailing Momentum | 318 |
| 24.2: | A Typical City Block along a Platoon Avenue of Advance | 321 |
| 24.3: | Options for Moving along a City Street with Momentum | 322 |
| 24.4: | The Mid-Block Technique | 323-328 |
| 24.5: | What the Platoon Often Faces at the End of the Block | 330 |
| 24.6: | The Intersection-Crossing Technique | 331-334 |
| 24.7: | Move between Buildings without Facing Fire in the Street | 335 |
| 24.8: | Hallways Are Kill Zones Too | 336 |
| 24.9: | The Floors of Multistory Buildings Must Be Cleared Twice | 337 |

# Foreword

The greatest weakness of the maneuver warfare movement in the United States Marine Corps has been its failure to address the Non-Commissioned Officer (NCO) corps.

As one of the founders of that movement, I have been aware of this failure for many years, and I share the responsibility for it. But, I also understand why it has occurred. Quite simply it takes an NCO to speak effectively and credibly to other NCO's.

Here, in *The Last Hundred Yards*, Gunnery Sergeant H.J. Poole, USMC (Ret.), does exactly that. He translates the concepts of maneuver warfare into the tactics and techniques which are rightly the focus of NCO's and Staff NCO's.

The Non-Commissioned Officer must be a master of techniques, and also a teacher of techniques. This is no less true in maneuver warfare than in attrition warfare. As I wrote in 1985 in my *Maneuver Warfare Handbook*, "It cannot be said often enough that excellence in techniques is vitally important in maneuver warfare."

But, the techniques of maneuver warfare are often different from those of attrition warfare, as *The Last Hundred Yards* correctly argues. For example, in attrition warfare, the assault is based on two elements, and the purpose is to take the objective. In maneuver warfare, the assault uses three elements, and the purpose is to pass through the objective and continue to advance deep into the enemy's rear. Normally, the largest of the three elements is the exploitation element.

*The Last Hundred Yards* is the most detailed, most complete look at techniques in maneuver warfare. No FMFM even comes close, although the *MCI Warfighting Skills Program* does take a useful look at the subject. That alone should make this book of prime interest to any NCO or Staff NCO.

But, the value of the book goes beyond techniques. It also addresses tactics. In modern war, the NCO must be a first-rate technician, but he must also be more than that. He must be a tactical-decision maker who employs combined arms.

This may seem like a radical step to those NCO's who have grown up in today's Marine Corps. Seldom, in training, are Marine NCO's or Staff NCO's allowed to make tactical decisions; and "combined arms" usually refers to artillery and aircraft, which are controlled at higher levels (though the NCO may request support from either, he does not control them). But, it merely describes what German corporals, leading *Stosstruppen*, were doing routinely by 1918. They were deciding where and how to engage the enemy (and where not to) in attacks with unlimited objective, and they were employing combined arms in the form of the light machinegun and the trench mortar, both of which were squad weapons by that time.

Since 1918, the battlefield has not grown more amenable to centralized control; quite the contrary. Particularly in operations like those in Somalia or Haiti, an NCO may find himself making decisions with operational or even strategic effects. The fact that Marine Corps' training seldom allows NCO's or Staff NCO's to make decisions beyond the level of techniques is a fault in that training, not a reflection of combat realities.

*The Last Hundred Yards* is a book about making tactical decisions, as well as employing effective, modern techniques. Most important, it is a book about integrating tactics and techniques. Techniques are the "tools" an NCO has at his disposal; tactics is the art of selecting the right tools for the particular job at hand. While the techniques themselves may be formulas, the art of selecting the right techniques can never be done by formula, because each situation is different. This book shows the NCO the right way to use techniques in his tactics, and makes clear the distinction between the two.

Correctly, Gunny Poole has made extensive and knowledgeable use of history in researching and explaining his topic. His example here should encourage other NCO's to study military history. It is not a subject reserved to officers and civilians interested in the military art.

But, to the study of history, the author of *The Last Hundred Yards* has added something that previously has been missing in works on maneuver warfare: the experience of a Marine Staff NCO. Gunny Poole's experience includes combat in Vietnam, plus many years of helping train Marine infantrymen. From that experience he has gathered the observations and lessons which, when combined with the lessons of history, make this book the extraordinary resource that it is.

The Marine Corps, and only the Marine Corps among the American armed services, has begun the long and difficult task of changing from an attrition style of warfare to maneuver warfare — from the French way of war to the

## Foreword

German. It can only succeed if the maneuver warfare way of thinking becomes deeply rooted at the level where most tactical decisions are actually made, in the NCO corps. *The Last Hundred Yards* is the first book that gives NCO's the knowledge and understanding they need to make that transition. As such, it is a book of immense importance, and a fitting tribute to all the NCO's who have paid in blood for the lessons it so aptly distills.

WILLIAM S. LIND

# Preface

U.S. Marine enlisted men have always enjoyed their fair share of self-esteem. But, as they face more destructive weapons on the modern battlefield, their capacity for *self-reliance* has become more critical to their survival. So much so, that today's Marine Corps is redefining the role of its infantry *Non-Commissioned* Officers (NCO's) and revamping its small-unit infantry tactics. One famous U.S. general has gone so far as to imply that, in the close-quarter combat necessary to neutralize modern weaponry, the proper role of the NCO is that of tactical-decision maker:

> The last hundred yards in combat is the purview of the non-commissioned officer.[1]

This viewpoint is not difficult to substantiate. Many enlisted infantrymen spend almost half their careers in rifle companies. They experience numerous billet assignments and countless field exercises. By the time they become NCO's, many have spent years where the "rubber (of their commanders' decisions) meets the road." By the time they become senior Staff NCO's (SNCO's), many have operated under a wide assortment of battlefield conditions and have become quite familiar with the most common. These experienced enlisted infantrymen have mastered the execution phase of small-unit tactics, in much the same way that career mechanics master the performance of car repair. For this reason, NCO's are often called the "technicians" of tactics — their "tricks of the trade" being the ways to accomplish the various actions that make up any tactical maneuver. In other words, they've become experts in the *detail of execution*. But, experts must be fully utilized. A U.S. Army general noticed that the tactical technicians were underused in Vietnam:

> The Army was successful in developing the military statesmen, staff planners, and management experts, but it had neglected the "military mechanics." The results were beginning to show in the units.[2]
> 
> —Gen. A. Collins U.S. Army (Ret.)

Just as automotive mechanics become highly skilled at diagnosing car problems, so too do infantry NCO's become adept at assessing tactical situations. Not only have they personally experienced many of the circumstances, but they have also realized the cost of ignoring subtle differences in each. They have learned that stormy nights can either hinder tactical coordination or enhance surprise. Because the ground to their immediate front has always been their priority, they have developed a unique appreciation for microterrain. Having themselves filled the shoes of riflemen and fire team leaders, they have unique insight into the *training status* of the "troops-available" aspect of the "combat situation." And having participated in countless range details with every weapon organic to the infantry battalion, they understand how each weapon will perform under the "fire-support-available" aspect. In short, NCO's are a little-used but excellent source of information about a dimension of the situation that is often overlooked — the *detail of the situation*. Only by meshing precisely with existing circumstances, will a tactical decision normally succeed. Without compensating for the subtle differences in situational variables, a field commander could logically arrive at a tactical solution that won't work. His NCO's could provide him with the missing situational detail.

This expertise in the detail of both situation and execution should qualify most infantry NCO's *to make sound tactical decisions*. Again, the mechanic comparison serves to illustrate the point. When a mechanic encounters a bolt in a tight space under a car, what tool he chooses and how hard he twists it, establishes how easily the bolt comes out. For small units, tactical maneuvers are like tools. When a platoon encounters enemy on the battlefield, what tactical maneuver it chooses and how well it executes that maneuver, establishes how easily the enemy is defeated. Just as a mechanic's level of experience affects his choice of tools and how to use them, so too does a platoon's collective experience affect its choice of tactical maneuvers and how to execute them. In the average platoon, the NCO's and SNCO's provide most of the collective experience. For this reason, they should participate in most of the tactical decisions. This should in no way challenge the authority of their officers. After all, commissioned and non-commissioned officers share the same responsibilities in combat. If the lieutenant is wounded, the platoon sergeant takes over. When both work together, better decisions result. This brain trust can be further enhanced by including the squad leaders. The enduring satisfaction that comes from making a situationally correct decision, and then having that decision fully supported during its execution, far outweighs the temporary insecurity that may come from soliciting the advice of subordinates. On the other hand, it is courting disaster to rely on one's personal impressions to provide the solution to a complex scenario and then not consider whether one's subordinates have the skills to execute that solution.

Throughout this century, other countries have capitalized on the tactical expertise of their infantry NCO's. By the end of 1917, the Germans had not only put their NCO's in charge of the units spearheading their ground attacks,[3] but also of the autonomous forts comprising their front lines of defense.[4] Their success is indelibly etched in the Allied casualty totals for 1918.

U.S. infantry units have only just recently begun to rely more on the tactical-decision-making ability of their NCO's. American SNCO's have never had the opportunity as a group to commit their tactical insights to writing. They have had to pass along these insights to the next generation of infantrymen by word of mouth. The published guidelines on how to conduct fire team, squad, and platoon tactics are, for the most part, the broad conclusions of commissioned officers with a year or two of rifle company experience. The tragedy is that every time a seasoned NCO or SNCO leaves the Service, much of what he has learned about situational detail and the tricks of the trade of tactical execution goes with him. Field Marshal Zhukov — the Allied commander who turned the tide in World War II — said this about organizations in which NCO's are not fully trusted:

> My many years in the Army have demonstrated that wherever confidence in NCO's is lacking... you have... no really combat-worthy units.[5]
> — Georgi K. Zhukov

Because NCO knowledge has not been systematically retrieved, the U.S. Armed Forces have not learned as much about small-unit tactics as they should have. Before World War II, Chesty Puller — a prior-enlisted Marine veteran of nine years of small-unit combat in Haiti and Nicaragua — noticed a void in what should have been available in writing on small-unit warfare:

> Puller often heard these officers [his instructors] admit that they did not know the answers he was constantly seeking. In truth, it seemed that little had been written about his favorite topic — limited, small-scale combat.[6]

To a U.S. infantryman actively engaged in a losing effort, this shortage of reference material can be quite unsettling. With a combat commission from Korea, Lt.Col. D.H. Hackworth was no stranger to war when called to serve in Vietnam. After two tours, he pointed out that U.S. knowledge on small-unit infantry tactics had *not* been significantly enhanced by the longest war in U.S. history:

> Almost fifteen years since the tragic, inevitable fall of Saigon, there has been no major, honest post mortem of the war. There have been critiques dealing with the big picture... but none has addressed the lessons learned the hard way, at the fighting level, where people died and the war was in fact, lost.[7]

With their quip "Remember the basics," famous Americans have continually warned of the consequences of ignoring tactical *detail*. For infantrymen, the basics have been categorized as "shoot," "move," and "communicate." While, on the surface, these may look like simple concepts, in truth they are very complex. The enemy is not going to sit still while someone shoots at him, will kill whomever he sees moving, and can gain an insurmountable advantage by just correctly guessing his opponent's intentions. Perhaps it was a mistake to refer to these crucial skills as basics in the first place. One would assume that the basics would be covered during basic training, or boot camp. In actuality, other military fundamentals — history and traditions, customs and courtesies, wearing of the uniform, close-order drill, marksmanship, discipline — are, for the most part, what is covered during basic training. The finer points of shooting, moving, and communicating must be learned by trial and error (sometimes the hard way) or from an experienced NCO. They are not basics in the sense of being elementary — something to be endured as a young infantryman and then outgrown. They are basics in the sense that no infantry unit can operate effectively without them. They are the *detail of execution*. And, with each departing generation of infantry NCO's, much of what it takes for a unit to perform the simplest of tactical maneuvers *is lost*.

Yes, many of the skills that individuals and small units need in combat are described somewhere in the towering stacks of historical literature. But, these descriptions are so sparsely sprinkled throughout what are predominantly discussions about large units, that they are *inaccessible* to the average infantryman. Only by dedicating thousands of man-hours to a computer hunt, could a researcher identify meaningful trends.

And, yes, a significant amount of basic knowledge is presented in the manuals. But, here again, it is presented piecemeal in scores of locations. Furthermore, what is presented is *seldom comprehensive*. Whenever a discussion on something basic can be found (like how to crawl unnoticed through the enemy's barbed wire), only a few sentences are allocated to it. This does little to raise one's confidence that he could actually perform this function in combat. He also wonders how comprehensive the discussion can be, when only one way of doing the activity is offered, and generally without referencing the literature.

The recent FMFM 1 — *Warfighting* — contains the central precepts for winning battles at minimal cost. But the larger FMFM's on small-unit combat must be rewritten in the same professional style (with historical literature referenced). FM 21-75 — *Combat Training of the Individual Soldier and Patrolling* — provides young infantrymen with many important skills, but where is the manual on how to walk point? Point men perform the most dangerous job in war and affect the outcome of enemy contact every bit as much as the overall unit leader.

Some say that the formal schools cover what the manuals omit. They are correct — to the extent that enlisted instructors are allowed to teach the same subject long enough to discover what's missing from the manuals, and to fill the void with common sense. But, all too often, instructors must teach verbatim from a handful of manuals and then change jobs before becoming comfortable with their subject matter. Without a wide assortment of military publications and historical references, the novice instructor can only do so much.

What NCO's know collectively about small-unit tactics extends far beyond what is in the manuals. It is what has been learned by generations of NCO's trying to adapt the one (official) way of doing things to more than one set of circumstances. It is also how to deal with unique circumstances for which the book solution does not compensate. This common sense of the NCO corps is unwritten, yet still alive around the campfires. It is every bit as valuable as what is in the manuals:

> *Basic Field Manual* [italics added] knowledge is fine, but it is useless without common sense. Common sense is of greater value than all the words in the book.[8]
> — Col. Amor Le R. Sims
> 7th Mar. CO on Guadalcanal

There is nothing inherently wrong with the one way of doing each maneuver described in the manuals. The problem is that the manuals *lack detail in situation and execution.* In other words, they don't specify under which circumstances, or with which pre-existing skills, the one way will work. Because this detail is missing, overeager practitioners of the book solution sometimes make poor decisions. They forget that this one way was probably never intended as "doctrine" that had to be obeyed every time, but rather as "broad guidance" that would work under ideal conditions. In truth, it is only one way to handle a unique combination of circumstances (which are for the most part *unspecified* and long since forgotten). Small-unit leaders who don't realize this, may not only make illogical tactical decisions, but also become totally predictable in combat:

> The central ideas of an army is *[sic]* known as its doctrine, which to be sound must be based on the principles of war, and which to be effective must be elastic enough to admit of mutation in accordance with change in circumstances. In its ultimate relationship to human understanding this central idea or doctrine is nothing else than common sense — that is action adapted to circumstances.[9]
> — Maj.Gen. J.F.C. Fuller

Without NCO advice on situational variables, military commanders may become intimidated by the unlimited number of combinations possible. They may underestimate the effect of subtle differences in these variables and consider the "book solution" to be applicable most of the time. Or, they may overestimate the effect of these subtle differences, and consider it futile to prepare for any particular set of circumstances — i.e., *futile to train.* The small unit that too faithfully follows the method in the book will eventually attempt it under the wrong conditions. Furthermore, the unit may have difficulty surprising any enemy who has read their book. On the other hand, the unit that doesn't prepare for any particular scenario will take too long to decide what to do (automatically sacrificing surprise and momentum), and then not have the teamwork to execute what it does decide to do. When considered in this context, enlisted one-liners, like "Forget the book" or "Out here you've got to learn fast," seem less insubordinate:

> The ordinary soldier has a surprisingly good nose for what is true and what is false.[10]
> — Rommel

Because, as a group, infantry NCO's enjoy vast experience, they can easily identify probable combat scenarios and through trial and error develop tactical solutions to those scenarios. Such solutions are called "techniques." The squad that can develop the best techniques, and then combine them to counter a unique set of circumstances in combat, has a decided edge over the one that can't. Any infantryman who has averaged three hours of sleep a night for months on end, and then tried to capture the momentum from a strong opponent, realizes the limits to impromptu problem solving under duress. In actuality, most small-scale combat is won or lost months before the battle — *during training.* What this training should consist of, can best come from the NCO corps.

It remains to be seen how badly the U.S. Armed Forces may have hurt themselves by not systematically recording the collective tactical knowledge of their NCO's. If the famous general's observation about the purview of the NCO is correct, the disturbing implication is that the U.S. military may have retrieved little of what young Americans need successfully to cross the "last 100 yards" in combat. And if, by chance, the "next 100 yards" falls under the purview of the NCO as well, U.S. infantry tactics as a whole may be less than perfect. Without NCO input, the tactics may have outlived their usefulness.

# Preface

This book contains many techniques from the NCO corps, and how and when they might be combined to facilitate standard U.S. infantry tactics. It also discusses how to alternate these techniques to become less predictable. What has been intended is an easily accessible reference on, and starting point for further research into, small-unit infantry tactics. A Chinese military scholar by the name of Sun Tzu alluded to the importance of small-unit knowledge as early as 350 B.C.:

He who knows how to use both large and small forces will be victorious.[11]
— Sun Tzu

The techniques herein have been generated by consensus opinions from the forty or so U.S. Marine NCO's and SNCO's who attended each of the Camp Lejeune Platoon Sergeant Courses between 1986 and 1991, and the 3rd Marine Division Combat Squad Leader Courses during 1992 — roughly 1200 NCO's in all. The method of collection was simple. The student body was asked in the classroom to identify promising solutions to common situations, and then again in the field to identify refinements to those solutions. While most of the techniques were developed in the forested coastal plain of eastern North Carolina, the vast majority of them worked equally well in the precipitous and heavily jungled terrain of Okinawa.

Many of the common-sense insights of these career enlisted infantrymen closely parallel the tenets of an ancient style of warfare that has recently gained popularity in the United States — "maneuver warfare." This is significant, because it has been hypothesized that only through its NCO's can any infantry organization fully adopt maneuver warfare. Several years of research have gone into supporting this hypothesis.

Why hasn't more small-unit tactical knowledge been recorded for easy access by U.S. infantrymen? Were the founders of their military heritage somehow lacking? Or, has this oversight in learning occurred despite everyone's best efforts? The final chapter will provide a possible answer to this mystery, and discuss how other nations have successfully dealt with the same problem.

To appreciate fully the contribution that U.S. infantry NCO's could make to the body of recorded tactical knowledge (part two of the book), it will first be necessary to discuss the shortfall that has occurred without their systematic input (part one). Everyone has been affected to some degree by this shortfall in recorded knowledge. Before beginning the chapters, the reader should take the inventory test in appendix A. For NCO's without formal instruction in maneuver warfare, a score of 50 is satisfactory, 60 is good, 70 is excellent, and 80 is outstanding. Seasoned staff NCO's and officers score about 10 points higher. If the reader cannot agree with some of the answers to tactical questions, he should not become discouraged. Many of the questions are designed to gauge receptivity to a style of warfare quite different from the one traditionally practiced by most U.S. infantrymen. In other questions, the situation may be inadequately described to permit agreement on the answer. After all, there are no right or wrong answers in tactics, just many thought-provoking questions. The test is only intended as a way to stimulate further interest in the book and to gauge its impact.

# Acknowledgments

To the United States Marine Corps rightly belongs the credit for this contribution to small-unit infantry tactics. Without the dynamic learning environment that existed in Marine Corps infantry schools from 1986 to 1992, this work would not have been possible.

None of the ideas presented herein are original; all have come from other people. Most of the tactical techniques have been developed by Marine infantry NCO's and SNCO's. In WWII, their predecessors were forced to deal with what could best be described as worst-case scenarios. The only way to root the die-hard Japanese from their holes on those tiny islands in the Pacific, was to go directly at them in broad daylight. But, in the early eighties, to compensate for the combat power disadvantage that the Marines were expected to encounter on future battlefields, General Al Gray and his civilian adviser Bill Lind began to emphasize what has since come to be known as "maneuver warfare." This is a style of warfare that relies more heavily on the element of surprise. It helped Allied forces to attain a quick and relatively bloodless victory in the Gulf War.

Some traditionalists have had trouble accepting the looser control parameters of maneuver warfare. And, as is always the case with professionals, their concerns are partially justified. Some situations do take a more traditional approach. But, at the same time, many others can be solved *at less cost* by following the new way of thinking. There is no reason why both points of view cannot coexist in harmony. All that is needed is a better understanding of which conditions might favor one warfare style over the other. Then, any difference of opinion could only provide a healthy stimulus for additional learning.

There is a body of knowledge that allows the opposing viewpoints to coexist. It comes from the segment of military society that prides itself on supporting the decisions of every commander—the NCO corps. Passed along verbally from one generation to the next is an *expertise in tactical detail* that has played no small part in the establishment of the proud heritage of the United States Marine Corps. The collective experience of NCO's in handling every conceivable combination of wartime circumstances provides a framework in which *both* styles of warfare can play important roles. In an effort to reconcile the opposing viewpoints and to shed more light on the situations in which maneuver warfare can work, this book provides a brief glimpse into this immense body of knowledge.

*Semper fidelis*

# Part One

## The Shortfall in Recorded Knowledge

[Marine Corps general-to-be] Puller often heard these officers [his instructors] admit that they did not know the answers he was constantly seeking. In truth, it seemed that little had been written about his favorite topic — limited, small-scale combat.
— Burk Davis, *Marine* © 1962

# 1 The Anatomy of Small-Unit Victory

- To Americans, what constitutes a "military victory"?
- What does it take to defeat an enemy at any cost?
- What else does it take to defeat that enemy at minimal cost?

(Sources: FM 23-30 (1988), p. 5-3; FM 7-8 (1984), p. 3-28)

## WHAT EVERY U.S. INFANTRY LEADER WOULD LIKE TO LEARN BEFORE GOING TO WAR

The annals of warfare are filled with the exploits of armies, divisions, and regiments — not the separate actions of squads, fire teams, and riflemen. For the small-unit leader to learn more about his wartime role from the literature, he must examine a concept universal to units of every size — *what it takes to win*. Of course, winning means different things to different people. To Sun Tzu in 350 B.C., it meant more than just defeating the enemy:

> Only when the enemy could not be overcome by these [political] means was there recourse to armed force, which was applied so the victory was gained: (a) in the shortest possible time; (b) at the least possible cost in lives and effort; (c) *with infliction on the enemy of the fewest possible casualties* [italics added].[1]

In any civilization, defeating an enemy at too great a cost no longer constitutes "winning":

> Throughout American history, from Antietam to Hamburger Hill, a victory won with too many lives was not a victory at all.[2]

Wars are won with battles, and battles with engagements. Leaders of every rank must strive to determine what it takes to win *engagements* at low cost. (See table 1.1.)

1. **JUST DEFEATING AN ENEMY MINIMALLY TAKES THE FOLLOWING:**

   A. *TACTICS*:

   (1) SOME TACTICAL KNOWLEDGE.
   (2) ACCURATE ASSESSMENT OF THE INITIAL SITUATION.
   (3) LOGICAL DECISION MAKING.
   (4) DECISIVENESS.
   (5) A LOCALIZED COMBAT POWER ADVANTAGE.
   (6) SOME SEMBLANCE OF CONTROL.

   B. *LOGISTICAL ASSETS*:

   C. *PERSONNEL ASSETS*:

   (1) THE WILL TO FIGHT.
   (2) SOME TRAINING.
   (3) TEAMWORK.
   (4) SOME LEADERSHIP.

2. **FOR WINNING AT LOW COST, THERE ARE ADDITIONAL REQUIREMENTS:**

   A. *(UNDER) TACTICS:*

   (7) STATE-OF-THE-ART TACTICAL KNOWLEDGE.
   (8) AUTHORITY TO MAKE COMMON-SENSE DECISIONS AT EVERY ECHELON WITHIN THE UNIT.
   (9) MINIMIZING THE NUMBER OF ACTIONS TAKEN WITHOUT THINKING.
   (10) ALLOWING SUBORDINATES TO OBEY HUMAN SURVIVAL INSTINCTS.
   (11) FLEXIBILITY TO AN EVER CHANGING SITUATION.
   (12) MAKING AS SMALL A TARGET AS POSSIBLE.
   (13) CONSISTENTLY SURPRISING THE ENEMY.
   (14) EXPLOITING SUCCESS TO KEEP THE FOE OFF BALANCE (MOMENTUM).

   C. *(UNDER) PERSONNEL ASSETS:*

   (5) WELL-FOCUSED PERSONNEL.
   (6) TROOPS WITH THE MOVEMENT SKILLS TO UTILIZE EXISTING COVER.
   (7) TROOPS WITH THE SHOOTING SKILLS TO COVER THE MOVEMENT OF OTHERS BY FIRE WHEN NECESSARY.
   (8) SPECIALIZED TRAINING FOR THOSE WHO NEED IT TO SURVIVE.
   (9) ENOUGH TRAINED PERSONNEL TO ROTATE DANGEROUS BILLETS.
   (10) APPROPRIATE ASSIGNMENT OF PERSONNEL.
   (11) PAIRING UP OF PERSONNEL AS WITH POLICEMEN.
   (12) A LEADERSHIP STYLE THAT PERMITS SUBORDINATES TO REACT QUICKLY TO UNFORESEEN DANGERS.

*Table 1.1: What May Be Required to Win at Low Cost*

## JUST DEFEATING AN ENEMY CAN CARRY WITH IT A HEFTY PRICE TAG

Vanquishing an enemy takes people — either well-trained people or a large number of people. After all, a battle is nothing more than a series of engagements, and each engagement a series of small-unit contacts. How many personnel it takes to defeat an enemy at every level is inversely proportional to how much training those personnel have received. In fact, the solutions to all tactical situations necessarily depend on the training status of the individuals and subordinate units involved. Often the optimal tactical solution is not viable simply because of the training deficiencies within the unit. Having been heavily deployed in recent years, most U.S. infantry units have had little time to devote to individual and small-unit training. The recent Gulf War didn't adequately test this aspect of their training readiness. Because the struggle ended so quickly, most of the individuals and small units never got the chance to show what they could do. Latent deficiencies in individual and small-unit training can have dire consequences in future combat:

> Unit commanders must be taught that just maneuvering about doesn't win the fight. It helps, but it is well-trained troops — each one doing his individual part as well as possible — that make the team function efficiently and win in battle.[3]
> —Gen. A. Collins U.S. Army (Ret.)

> Success in battle is dependent on the coordinated effort of small units.... Other things being equal, the army with the best trained small units will prevail. Even when other things are not equal, the army with skilled soldiers and determined small units will sometimes defeat bigger and better equipped armies.... The modern Israeli army is a good example of the former; the Viet Cong and North Vietnamese armies are good examples of the latter. The importance of small-unit training to mission accomplishment cannot be overemphasized.[4]

> Generally the bigger the exercise the poorer the training at the small-unit level.[5]

Historically, U.S. forces have tried to minimize their casualties by using overwhelming firepower. Unfortunately, against a well-prepared adversary (in all but level desert terrain) no quantity of bombs or shells can limit friendly casualties. Minimizing one's cost takes *surprising* that adversary; and, for surprising enemy soldiers, there is no substitute for having properly trained *individuals* and *small units* of one's own. There is abundant evidence to suggest that, for U.S. forces over the years, this aspect of their training has been less than optimal:

> Since 1941 . . . our forces were not as well trained as those of the enemy, especially in the early stages of the fighting. After the buildup of forces, when we went on the offensive, we did not defeat the enemy tactically. We overpowered and overwhelmed our enemies with equipment and fire power.[6]
> —Gen. A. Collins U.S. Army (Ret.)

## WINNING AT LOW COST INVOLVES SOME CONTROVERSIAL TRADEOFFS

Some of the factors that permit winning at low cost compete with each other. In other words, what is done without careful consideration to enhance one factor, can create a shortfall in another. How much *control* must be applied to individuals and small units appears to be at the center of the debate.

First, there is the tradeoff between "control" and "tactical knowledge." Whenever a military organization endorses any particular set of tactical maneuvers as doctrine, it discourages common sense in tactical decision making and sanctions a status quo in tactical knowledge. Standardized tactics can't even keep pace with weapons technology, much less a rapidly changing contingency situation. After memorizing tactical doctrine, a novice decision maker may be tempted to discount any situational variable that doesn't mesh precisely with his perception of the "book solution." If his subordinates subsequently risk telling him that his decision violates common sense, he may feel his authority threatened. At this point, he will only compound the problem by tightening his control.

Tactical knowledge is best served by continual study and experimentation under loose control. Knowledge and training are inseparably linked. Tactical knowledge does not drive training, tactical knowledge *derives* from training. For this reason, training cannot be controlled through standardization without limiting the growth of tactical knowledge. Only when small units are allowed to experiment in the field, can they experience the full range of situational variables and the greatest growth in their tactical expertise. Some military thinkers have gone so far as to connect combat casualties from friendly fire to training that has been too highly controlled:

> But the main problem of friendly fire casualties [in Vietnam] — unrealistic and oversupervised training was never solved.[7]

Then, there is the competition between "control" and "surprise/momentum." In a cruel paradox of war, the level of control necessary to minimize losses *from friendly fire over the short term* invariably sacrifices the surprise and momentum needed to minimize casualties *from hostile fire over the long term:*

> Two [of the] fundamental lessons of war experience are — never to check momentum, never to resume mere pushing.[8]
> — Liddell Hart

The differences between Gulf and Vietnam Wars serve to illustrate the point. In the Gulf War, the overwhelming swiftness of Allied thrusts into Kuwait would not have been possible if their rates of advance had been tightly controlled. In the process, a few Allied armored vehicles were hit by friendly fire. On the other hand, in Vietnam, all movement and firing were closely controlled. Not surprisingly, the war progressed more slowly. The Gulf War had a much higher percentage of casualties from friendly fire than did the Vietnam War, but it also had a much lower overall casualty count and much happier outcome.

Too much control at the small-unit level can be costly as well. For example, trying to control a small unit through detailed orders and standardized procedures may help to prevent shooting accidents, but it also gives the enemy more time to prepare for what is almost totally predictable:

> Safety first is the road to ruin in war.[9]
> — Winston Churchill

Finally, there is the conflict between "control" and "flexibility." In extended combat, the enemy will invariably change the situation to his advantage after the battle has been joined. Too much control can stifle the reaction by friendly forces to that change. When subordinates believe that they must follow orders or rehearsed drills "to the letter," their missions and very lives are in jeopardy. For example, if an opposition machinegun unexpectedly opens up from the flank during an attack, the subordinates may be tempted to ignore the machinegun fire and continue forward as ordered or rehearsed.

Of course, some degree of control is always necessary. How can a commander minimally coordinate his subordinates, if those subordinates don't at least keep him apprised of their actions? In the U.S. Armed Forces, the infantryman's psychological makeup and turnover rate make a certain amount of control unavoidable:

> Positive characteristics generally attributed to American fighting men are initiative, creativity, independence of action, and a high level of technical competence.... Americans are ... undisciplined.... They have little respect for authority, are oriented to individual freedom rather than group or collective accomplishments.[10]
> — Gen. A. Collins U.S. Army (Ret.)

To be most effective, small units require a form of control that interferes as little as possible with their tactical knowledge, surprise/momentum, and flexibility.

## WINNING AT LOW COST REQUIRES CAREFUL MANAGEMENT OF PERSONNEL ASSETS

Leadership, training, and the assignment of personnel are *interdependent* functions within every infantry unit; the first two cannot be maximized without fine tuning the third. The unit needs teamwork to win in war. When trying to surprise an enemy force, the unit is only as strong as its weakest member. If someone cannot be trained to do a particular task, no amount of leadership will guarantee that he can accomplish that task in combat; he must be reassigned to another task. Then, just as with policemen in large cities, infantrymen must be paired off with their buddies to enhance their proficiency and survivability on the battlefield.

U.S. infantry NCO's have *traditionally* shouldered much of the responsibility for leadership, training, and assignment of personnel within their units. Only for the last twenty-five years or so, have commissioned officers encroached upon these traditional roles of the NCO:

> Charging the NCO with responsibility for training the young soldier builds a close relationship between the NCO and his subordinates. This kind of relationship is critical and vital in combat because the NCO learns about the capabilities of his subordinates.[11]

> [L]eadership is so much a part of the conduct of training that at times it is difficult to tell where one stops and the other starts.[12]

> The gunnery sergeant ... is the principal enlisted assistant to the company commander in supervising the training of the company.[13]
> — FMFM 6-4

> A considerable part of our duties will be concerned with assigning men to jobs or recommending that they be reassigned.... [B]esides having the right man in the right place, you should have a trained replacement for every key man.[14]
> — *Handbook for Marine NCOs*

When SNCO's and NCO's are again allowed to perform their traditional training, leadership, and personnel-assignment roles, the cohesion within the units will improve. Cohesion is generally acknowledged to be the driving force behind a unit's "will to fight." Without it, no unit can win consistently. It has been said that men fight for each other more than for any other reason:

> My first wish would be that my military family, and the whole army, should consider themselves as a band of brothers, willing and ready to die for each other.[15]
> — George Washington

> The strength of a fighting outfit is the mutual respect of all its members of whatever rank.... [S]tudents of military history have often tried to determine why some men fight well and others run away. It never seemed to me that ideological motives or political or moral concepts had much to do with it. If I could get any of my men to discuss a matter so personal as their honest reaction to combat, they would tell me that they fought, though admittedly scared, because "I couldn't let the other boys down" or "I couldn't look chicken before Dog Company."[16]
> — General Maxwell Taylor

Of course, a soldier's will to fight is also influenced by his heritage. He tries to live up to the example set by his predecessors, as well as to the expectations of his peers. Further, his will to fight depends on how much influence his NCO's have over him. The German Army came close to winning WWII largely because of the strength of its NCO corps. In Korea, the U.S. Army found its fighting ability enhanced by placing more reliance on its NCO's:

(Source: FM 21-6 (1975), cover)

> Strengthening the prestige of non-commissioned officers within the combat arms contributed more directly than anything else to an uplift of the fighting power of the army.[17]
> — S.L.A. Marshall

## WHERE CERTAIN COMPROMISES MIGHT PERMIT VICTORY AT LOWER COST

Until American NCO's are allowed to perform the *majority* of training, leadership, and personnel-assignment functions within their respective units, this country may have trouble defeating a strong enemy in difficult terrain at any cost. Only by permitting NCO's to perform their optimal roles, will U.S. commanders stand much of a chance of curing the other symptoms of overcontrol.

For example, there are ways to maintain adequate control in combat without sacrificing the element of surprise. Perhaps the most obvious is *to decentralize tactical control* — to let subordinates make the tactical decisions. The Germans discovered this while trying to turn the tide of WWI. According to Major Bruce I. Gudmundsson USMCR, author of *Stormtroop Tactics*, German commanders eventually realized that they had greater success when they let their squad leaders do the thinking:

> In the new tactics, the NCO became a leader and tactical-decision maker.[18]
> — MCI 7401

Of course, for tactical control to be successfully decentralized, subordinates must receive adequate individual and small-unit training. If they understand their commander's intent well enough, fewer orders will be necessary to control them. If they have rehearsed two or three tactical techniques for each expected situation, and their leader knows what these techniques are, fewer signals will be necessary as well. Then, even when communication is lost during the heat of battle, the leader still has a general idea of what his elements are doing. This is probably the original intent of the "battle drill":

> ... Battle drill teaches small units to react quickly and with some semblance of order without lengthy instructions....
> ... When a formation has been ordered and taken, it may and frequently should be modified to meet the specific situation; but even if modified, the commander's decision has been quickly converted into action by battle drill.[19]
> — Gen. A. Collins U.S. Army (Ret.)

Like football players, rifle squad members can receive a short play designator in a huddle, exercise personal initiative to overcome unexpected threats, and still successfully interact as a team. Of course, only plays that could be quickly tailored to existing circumstances would do them much good. If their plays were further to depend more on secrecy and deception than on complex instructions and signaling, the elusive element of *surprise* might even be within reach. Running several of these situational hybrids in tandem could produce *momentum:*

> Rapid and forceful action [of a battle drill] will often surprise an enemy and throw him off balance.[20]

As a unit's ability to surprise an opposition force improves, so too does its leader's ability to control that unit. For example, it's much easier to control a squad about to surprise an opponent's defensive lines than a squad that has just been prematurely discovered. There are certain squad techniques with which the military leader can achieve both adequate control and victory at low cost. But, before he can discover what they are, he must thoroughly investigate what role the element of chance may play in winning.

# 2     Operate on Blind Luck or Win Consistently

- Do the Laws of Probability apply to small-unit combat?
- How could tactical procedures persist that are unlikely to succeed?
- What type of training might enhance a squad's chances for success?

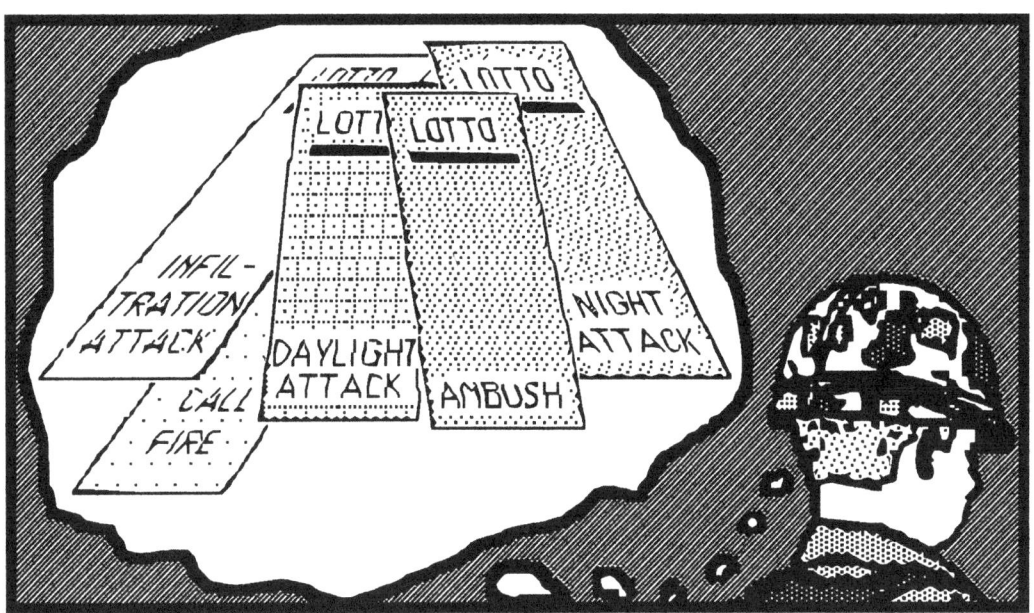

(Source: MCO P1500.44B, p. 9-49)

### DO THE RULES OF CHANCE APPLY TO SMALL-UNIT COMBAT?

The Laws of Probability apply to every variety of human endeavor. Just as a football team has "odds" of winning before a game, so does a rifle squad before an enemy encounter.

At the small-unit level, encounters follow distinct patterns. While a few circumstances may vary, the broad scenarios do not. For this reason, how well a small unit will do during any particular type of engagement *can be foretold*. To improve its chances for success, the unit must accurately predict unique circumstances, and then prepare for them in advance. At whatever point, the unit stops preparing for what may lie ahead, it forces itself to rely on "blind luck." In other words, its chances of coping with unforeseen circumstances are at best 50-50. If that unit *mistakenly* believes itself to be "fully trained," or just better trained than its adversary, it may have difficulty winning even half of its encounters. For centuries, great military leaders have warned against relying on blind luck in combat:

> If you are lucky and trust in luck alone, even your successes reduce you to the defensive; if you are unlucky you are already there.[1]
> — Frederick the Great

First of all, no infantryman or small unit is ever fully trained. Training is something that must be continuous.

As expected battlefield conditions change, so too must learning. Overreliance on the "book solutions" in itself constitutes a shortfall in training, because it minimizes the importance of the unique aspects of each situation. Blind faith in standard operating procedures doesn't even constitute being well trained.

Fortunately, for a small unit, the unique aspects of each situation are not nearly as complex as those for a large unit. In low-intensity conflicts, the most probable types of small-unit encounters are a matter of historical record. A squad-sized patrol, for example, will either make chance contact, be ambushed, or run into a prepared enemy position. The squads that actively prepare for these three eventualities will have a better chance in combat than those that don't. Just by experimenting in the field with appropriate reactions, squads can *improve their chances for success*. By then experimenting under "worst-case" scenarios, those squads can learn how to counter the most challenging of conditions. This should also empower them to handle "less severe" combinations of the same variables. After this type of "training," the squads will be better able to influence their own chances for success on the battlefield. The victor of the 10-month Franco-Prussian War had this to say about luck:

> Luck in the long run is given only to the efficient.[2]
> — Field Marshal von Moltke

To be sure, the mathematical probabilities for each small-unit maneuver have never been precisely calculated, but *they nevertheless exist*. Because they exist, and because all battles are just a composite of squad contacts, warfare as practiced by professionals must necessarily be based on the Laws of Probability. That's why military leaders talk about "taking calculated risks" in war. Under the most common conditions, certain courses of action have better chances for success than others.

Of course, the best way to increase one's odds of winning on the battlefield is to fight, and to encourage one's subordinates to fight, only when existing circumstances coincide with the level of preparation. In other words, when one can choose when and where to fight, his methods will have a higher probability of success.

## TO WHAT EXTENT HAVE AMERICANS PLAYED THE ODDS IN COMBAT HISTORICALLY?

Americans have traditionally based their chances for success in battle on the quality and quantity of ordnance fielded, and not on the training or tactical procedures involved:

> In my judgment our forces were not as well trained as those of the enemy, especially in the early stages of the fighting. After the buildup of forces, when we went on the offensive, we did not defeat the enemy tactically. We overpowered and overwhelmed our enemies with equipment and fire power.[3]
> — Gen. A. Collins U.S. Army (Ret.)

There are standardized squad procedures in practice to this day that have low probability of success under the most common of combat conditions. For example, U.S. forces are taught to conduct standup assaults against ambushers less than 50 yards away. An enemy could position his ambush 40 yards from the kill zone, and then stretch communications wire at knee level across his front. What chance would U.S. forces have against the enemy's automatic weapons then? Perhaps hitting the ground and crawling behind cover would make a better counterambush procedure. After all, there are some limits to what courage can accomplish:

> Defense and congressional officials make statements on the capability of current forces. Most often they overstate the case, whatever they are trying to prove. If it is a matter of shortfalls, these can generally be accommodated by a belief that even if the enemy is stronger, one red-blooded American can beat seven, five, or at least three of any other nationality. How well these claims withstand objective scrutiny is written in the history of United States battle casualties.[4]
> — Gen. A. Collins U.S. Army (Ret.)

## WHY TACTICS WITH HIGHER PROBABILITIES FOR SUCCESS ARE SOMETIMES IGNORED

For a variety of reasons, tactical knowledge does not build upon itself, like other forms of knowledge. U.S. platoons are still trained in a daylight attack method that has remained unchanged for over fifty years. Somewhat unsettling is the realization that potential adversaries now have a grenade launching machinegun (the equivalent of the U.S. MK-19) that would make this traditional method of attack extremely dangerous.

The most perplexing of the reasons for this slow growth in tactical knowledge involves the interrelationship between strategy, the operational art (campaigning), and tactics:

> Thus as strategy is the discipline of making war, and tactics is the discipline of fighting and winning in combat, we can describe the operational level of war as the discipline of campaigning.[5]
> — FMFM 1-1

While all three levels of decision making are important to winning wars, military theorists sometimes err by relegating tactics to a wholly supporting role. This way of thinking can be counterproductive, because it fails to acknowledge the opportunities that tactical initiative can create:

> What the strategic plan demands, operational art must supply. Likewise, tactical objectives must slavishly submit to the operational plan, or they become disastrously inappropriate. But when the lower planning levels are elevated and emphasized above the higher, we produce ineffective, and often bloody diversions.[6]

On the surface, this line of reasoning obeys most of the Rules of Logic, but some fairly credible war veterans see more harm in *not* authorizing tactical initiative at the lower levels:

> NCO's must love initiative and must hold what ground they [have] gained to the utmost. It often happens that a sergeant or even a corporal may decide a battle by the boldness with which he seizes a bit of ground and holds it.[7]
> — Gen. "Blackjack" Pershing
> Commander of AEF in WWI

Not surprisingly, the senior members of an infantry organization spend most of their time learning, writing about, and performing their unique function in that organization. Occasionally, that function will involve strategy or campaigning. Unfortunately, the lower ranking personnel on whom these seniors submit fitness reports are tempted to share the same priorities. In the process, *small-unit infantry tactics* often receive insufficient emphasis. In U.S. military periodicals, articles pertaining to landing-force or regimental procedures far outnumber those discussing small-unit tactical techniques. Between wars, infantry companies spend an inordinate amount of time supporting major exercises and satisfying requirements from higher headquarters. As campaigning appears to be everyone's first priority, small-unit infantry leaders mistakenly assume that maintaining the status quo in their area of responsibility — squad and platoon tactics — is not only acceptable, but virtually required. In wartime, this type of thinking can equate to the squandering of tactical opportunities that do not mesh precisely with operational or strategic plans.

Then, there are many societal, economic, and political reasons why tactical knowledge may not grow as rapidly it should. One wonders to what extent the fiscal pressures of a free enterprise system might affect the equation. Would arms manufacturers wholeheartedly embrace infantry tactics that all but eliminated the need for "high-tech" weapons and mountains of ammunition, or would they do everything within their power to promote their products? Would their lobbyists be any less powerful than those of the NRA? Perhaps that's what President Eisenhower was talking about in 1961:

> In the councils of government we must guard against the acquisition of unwarranted influence, whether sought or unsought, by the [U.S.] military-industrial complex. The potential for the disastrous rise of misplaced power exists and will persist.[8]
> — Dwight D. Eisenhower
> (final address as President)

For highly progressive Western societies, pride of invention or authorship can sometimes get in the way of learning. Americans hear continually how "underdeveloped" nations, like Russia and China, have had to copy U.S. weapons technology. Some might see dishonor in extracting ideas from other nations' infantry tactics.

Then, there's the propaganda that accompanies any war. The foe is always a heartless and mindless automaton. How could he possibly be capable of independent action on the battlefield, much less of effective tactics? "Stormtroop tactics" should evoke interest in how German squads were able to break the deadlock of trench warfare in WWI. Instead, for all but history buffs, it conjures up distasteful images of brown-shirted Nazis. When Senator McCarthy started seeing communists under every rock in the early 1950's, he made it difficult for Americans to admit that a country with the wrong political beliefs might nevertheless have valuable tactical ideas. By stereotyping a former adversary, Americans could easily overlook an important milestone in the evolution of tactics.

Even giving a sister organization with the same manuals credit for knowing anything can be difficult. Pride in one's unit can help to build cohesion, but it can also stand in the way of learning. Learning must always take priority over pride. How readily a military organization can assimilate new information establishes how easily its component elements can acquire new knowledge. The Germans of WWI are generally credited with developing the application parameters that define modern infantry tactics. Here's how they did it:

> The German Army of 1914 was the most decentralized [in terms of control] in Europe....
> Free from all but the most general supervision and relieved, by a promotion system based on strict seniority, of the need to constantly please superiors, the German battalion or company commander was free to train his troops according to his own lights.[9]

To some extent, human nature may impede the assimilation of tactical knowledge. It is only natural to attribute greater expertise in small-unit infantry tactics to whichever nation wins any particular war. Of course, many factors contribute to winning a war. There are wealthy nations that have been victorious in war despite substandard infantry tactics, and poor nations that have been defeated in war despite advanced infantry tactics.

For example, by 1918, the Germans had line infantry squads that could penetrate Allied defense lines almost at will. Fortunately, by this time, the Allied defense lines existed in such great depth that the German squads could seldom reach the last one without growing weary:

> The failure of the German Army in 1918 was not a failure of German tactics at the squad, platoon, company, battalion, regimental, division, or even army level, but a failure of German operational art, German strategy, and German national policy.[10]

If a U.S. infantryman were to come to the mistaken conclusion that his manuals contained everything the Germans, Russians, Orientals, and even his own predecessors had learned about infantry tactics in the past, he might regard "old ideas" and even "old military men" as superfluous. What he may not realize is that his manuals contain, for the most part, what he must *minimally* know to defeat an enemy operating under a combat power *disadvantage*. Those who do not read beyond what's in the manuals may have trouble handling an adversary more powerful than themselves. They may also get the opportunity to relearn some of the lessons of history.

But "older" does not always mean "better" in the context of tactical expertise. Pure novices can have better overall perspective than those who have come to regard any particular way of doing things as the best way. Unfortunately, in the U.S. military, the opinions of newcomers are seldom actively solicited and often considered disruptive. In a permissive society, every generation appears to be less disciplined than the last. This apparent lack of discipline is too often used as an excuse to squelch original ideas and valuable initiative. It has been said that many of the young men who won the Battle of Britain bordered on being societal outcasts before World War II. Seasoned infantry leaders eventually realize that their most vocal personnel also have the greatest capacity for initiative. Before a leader can accurately assess the worth of subordinates who occasionally question tactical decisions, he must make sure those decisions *obey common sense*.

Some military leaders unintentionally create a status quo in tactical knowledge by using established procedure to build discipline. While orderly conduct is very important to any military organization, the type of discipline that does the most good in combat is *self-discipline* (namely, what each soldier does when his superiors aren't around). Self-control cannot always be elicited. It must at some point be voluntarily given. There is a subtle yet important difference between learning how to accomplish what one is told and developing self-discipline.

These are only some of the reasons why a number of low-probability tactical procedures may have survived. One wonders if legality or morality could also have been at issue.

## IS IT LEGAL TO STACK THE ODDS OF WINNING AT MINIMAL COST IN ONE'S FAVOR?

Perhaps the Laws of War or traditional values have prevented Americans from stacking the odds (tactically) in their favor. For example, during the Civil War, operating behind enemy lines was considered to be less honorable than frontal attack. Of course, those who worked behind the lines did not totally agree with this perception:

> It is just as legitimate to fight an enemy in the rear as in the front. The only difference is in the danger.[11]
>
> — John S. Mosby

In his graduation address to the Naval Academy Class of 1962, one U.S. President went so far as to imply that two of the best ways to win small-unit encounters at minimal cost — ambush and infiltration — are somehow immoral:

> There is another type of warfare — new in its intensity, ancient in its origin — war by guerrillas, subversives, insurgents, assassins; war by ambush instead of by combat, by infiltration instead of aggression, seeking victory by eroding and exhausting the enemy instead of engaging him.[12]
>
> — President J.F. Kennedy

While it is unknown in what context the President made these remarks, and while it is possible that he was using other than standard meanings for the words "ambush" and "infiltration," it is still troubling that he would deride two of the best tools for swift and decisive small-unit victory at minimal cost. Why couldn't these tools be used militarily without any political subversion? Slowly and methodically slugging it out with massed weaponry does little to reduce casualty totals. Moral theologians might prefer a way of waging war that creates fewer casualties on *both sides*. Chapter 5 will discuss such a way. Foot soldiers seldom understand the political ramifications of a war, and every death *on either side* is a tragedy:

> [T]he hypothesis of legitimate defense, which never concerns an innocent but always and only an unjust aggressor, must respect the principle that moralists call the *principium inculpatae tutelae* (the principle of nonculpable defense) [italics from original]. In order to be legitimate, the "defense" must be carried out in a way that causes the least damage and, if possible, saves the life of the aggressor.[13]
>
> — Pope John Paul II

Has dislike for the foreign policies of other nations so prejudiced the American viewpoint on other matters? Is it possible that a nation with less than acceptable foreign policy, might nevertheless have cost-efficient infantry tactics? While preemptive strikes are considered less than good form prior to a formal declaration of war, surprise attacks during the course of that war in no way violate international law. Basically, any activity that is not specifically disallowed by the Geneva Conventions is "legal." Taking an opponent by surprise from the blind side, and locally outnumbering him, both qualify:

> Examples of legitimate ruses are: surprises; ambushes; the feigning of attacks, retreats, or flights; the simulation of quiet or inactivity; ... transmitting false or misleading signals and telegraph messages for the enemy to pick up, or lighting camp fires where there are no troops or leaving tents in position when troops have been moved away from them; making use of the enemy's signals, bugle and trumpet calls, watchwords and words of command; pretending to communicate with troops or reinforcements which have no existence; moving landmarks; the use of dummies to simulate troops and weapons.[14]
> — *Modern Law of Land Warfare*

Certainly, there are a few tactical rules that must be obeyed. Two are not pretending to surrender oneself and always letting the enemy surrender when he so chooses:

> [Disallowed are] treacherous request for quarter, and the treacherous simulation of death, wound, or sickness or surrender, for the purpose of putting the enemy off his guard and then attacking him. . . . It is particularly forbidden to kill or wound an enemy who having laid down his arms, or no longer having the means to resist, has surrendered at discretion.[15]
> — *Modern Law of Land Warfare*

The restrictions on weapons are more complicated. Those for silent and flame weapons are continually debated. Of course, any weapon that can be employed silently helps to maintain the element of surprise. At one time, Force Reconnaissance Marines carried "grease guns" (.45 caliber submachineguns) with "cans" (silencers) attached.[16] If the legality of these silencers has since come into question, perhaps crossbows (with conventional arrows) would suffice. All incendiary devices are in the gray area of legality. Yet, they are still used in one form or another on every battlefield. Without flamethrowers, the Germans in Europe and the Marines in the Pacific could not have as successfully attacked the formidable enemy fortifications they faced. Here's what the Geneva Conventions had to say about the legality of weapons:

> [I]t is particularly forbidden to employ arms, projectiles, or material calculated to cause unnecessary suffering. Examples of weapons and missiles prohibited under the general rule are poison and poisoned weapons, lances with barbed heads, irregularly shaped bullets, projectiles filled with broken glass, the scoring of the surface of bullets, the filing off of the end of their hard case, the smearing on them of any substance likely to inflame a wound, and the use of chain shot, crossbar shot, red-hot balls, and the like, in cannons.[17]
> — *Modern Law of Land Warfare*

## HOW U.S. INFANTRYMEN COULD INCREASE THEIR ODDS FOR TACTICAL SUCCESS

Most military leaders agree that doing nothing to prepare an infantry squad for combat also does little to enhance its chances for success. Most can also agree that providing guidance that is too restrictive may cause the squad to disregard unforeseen circumstances. The answer must lie somewhere in between. Small-unit leaders are trained to compare possible courses of action while making tactical decisions in combat. Why couldn't they also be encouraged to compare solutions to common combat scenarios during field rehearsals? If these rehearsals were conducted with simulated casualty assessment procedures, poorly conceived solutions would quickly be discarded. If casualty assessment personnel or apparatus were not available, participants could simply be asked whether or not they would have survived the tactical maneuver. The squad leaders could then create "play books" of three or four high-percentage moves for each of the general situations expected in combat. As long as the officers could choose the scenarios and stay apprised of what had been learned, what difference would it make if the squads developed slightly different techniques? In the process, the squads might even regenerate some long-forgotten master stroke. Successful squads would brag about their methods, and unsuccessful squads would copy those ideas. The end result would be dynamic parity, instead of inflexible standardization. Officers would only have to check squad techniques for mutual compatibility and then use them to form promising platoon and company techniques. At every level, leaders would have a number of prerehearsed choices that they could combine to handle projected scenarios. Those leaders would also have a frame of reference from which to estimate the relative prospects of their tactical options. That means that when they went to war, they could avoid courses of action that did not *assure victory at acceptable cost*. This has been the Oriental way of war for as long as anyone can remember:

> The expert commander strikes only when the situation assures victory.[18]
> — Sun Tzu

If the calculations made in the temple before a battle indicate victory, it is because careful calculations show that your conditions for a battle are more favorable than that of your enemy; if they indicate defeat, it is because careful calculations show that favorable conditions for a battle are few. With more careful calculations, one can win, with less one cannot. How much less chance of victory has one who makes no calculations at all! By this means, one can foresee the outcome of a battle.[19]
— Sun Tzu

Therefore the victories of good warriors are not noted for cleverness or bravery. Therefore their victories in battle are not flukes. Their victories are not flukes because they position themselves where they will surely win, prevailing over those who have already lost.[20]
— Sun Tzu

Strike to win, strike only if success is certain, if not, then don't strike.[21]
— General Vo Nguyen Giap
North Vietnamese Cmdr.

## THE FOOTBALL ANALOGY PROVIDES VALUABLE INSIGHT INTO HOW SQUADS CAN WIN CONSISTENTLY IN COMBAT

Seasoned infantrymen (like Lt.Col. Ernie Cheatham after the Battle of Hue City) have likened squad combat to a freewheeling game of football. In both, the participants must bypass or locally overpower their opponents to reach an objective location. In both, teamwork is important. And, in both, victory usually belongs to whichever side can capture the momentum.

But, the comparison is by no means perfect. Football has many rules that are strictly enforced. Combat has a few rules, but they are subject to interpretation and seldom enforced. Because of the greater level of violence, in combat one's behavior is influenced to a greater extent by a different of kind of rules — the Rules of Human Nature. And, for whichever side is surprised or off balance, their effects are predictable.

It is true that on a battlefield the players are shooting at each other, but they usually have somewhere to take cover as well. It is easier to surprise an opponent at night in vegetated and rolling terrain, than it is in the daytime on an unobstructed and flat gridiron with boundaries. In combat, the opponent's greater susceptibility to the Rules of Human Nature should more than adequately compensate for his freedom to violate the other rules.

To keep from becoming predictable in combat, the U.S. infantry squad must practice its reactions to various contingency situations before entering a war zone. To create predictability in the opponent, the squad must do the innovative more quickly than the opponent can analyze its actions. Because of the mind-numbing effect of enemy contact, the way to accomplish both goals at once is to rehearse plays that can be combined quickly to handle the situation at hand. The key is having *enough good plays* and permitting *enough initiative* in their execution. That squads would develop different plays is a benefit, not a discrepancy. By so doing, they are lessening their predictability. To be sure, the football analogy only applies to the extent that replacement personnel get to practice the plays, and then modify them as necessary in combat.

Just as coaches must play the odds to win consistently in football, so too must small-unit leaders play the odds to win consistently in combat. That the odds are at best only approximate and then likely to change, is not at issue. At issue is the fact that situational trends do occur in small-unit combat, *particularly when the small unit gets to decide when to fight,* and that certain ways of handling these trends enjoy more success than others. Even the much belabored "chaos" or unstructured "friction" of combat creates participant predictability. The combatants are too highly stressed to deviate much from the way they were trained. One must look closely at a typical small-unit encounter to see how the odds for handling it at minimal cost might be enhanced.

(Source: FM 21-6 (1975), p. 30)

# 3. Improving One's Chances for Success

- What is small-unit contact like?
- What does history disclose about how to win such an encounter?
- How can a squad's tactics be altered to improve its odds of winning?

(Source: FMFM 22-100 (1983), p. 41)

## WHAT SMALL-UNIT CONTACT IS LIKE

Most enemies rely heavily on the element of surprise to enhance their chances for survival. And, to make themselves smaller targets, they use all available cover and concealment. This type of adversary can seem almost *invisible* to an infantryman having to contend with the stress and fatigue of prolonged combat. After the Marines had fought 22,000 Japanese for 36 days on the eight-square-mile chunk of barren volcanic ash that was Iwo Jima, many commented on seldom seeing their adversary:

> Seldom on Iwo, from D-Day until the battle was over, did you see the enemy — just the sights and sounds of deadly fire from his weapons.[1]

One moment, the infantryman is walking through a secluded forest glen quietly minding his own business, and the next moment all hell breaks loose. The air is filled with deadly shards of metal coming from who knows where. The only way to escape them is to take cover. Loud explosions and cries of the wounded add to the confusion. Strange feelings of isolation and helplessness replace what was once confidence. Even seasoned leaders forget much of what they have learned. Their portfolio of tactical options is suddenly reduced to just two — whether to move or to stay put. And their thoughts of moving all focus on how to do so without exposing themselves:

> This wasn't the Hollywood version of men going into battle [on Iwo Jima]....

They move in small units; fire teams scamper, one man at a time, in a low, running crouch from one hole to another, from one ravine to another, from one burned-out bunker to another. Live troops win battles, and cover is the key to survival. When a man has no cover, he doesn't stand, he crawls. Only when it is thought an area is secure and cleared of enemy will men move in anything like a Hollywood style formation, even then, they are vigilant, wary, and keep distance between each other.[2]

Because most men have difficulty thinking clearly under the stress and shock of combat, small units tend to *fight the way they train*. If they haven't practiced any tactical techniques at all and try to solve each situation on its own merits, they react tentatively. If they have practiced just one technique for each category of occurrence, they use that one technique whether it meshes with the unique circumstances or not. And, if that one technique has a low probability of success under the most prevalent circumstances, they start to feel unlucky, and then eventually begin to act unlucky. Only when a unit practices *several high-probability* moves for each event (under realistic combat conditions), can it maximize its chances for success in combat.

## WINNING SUCH AN ENCOUNTER

To win any type of competition, one must act *decisively*. Team-sports enthusiasts will agree that a winning attitude can often be the deciding factor in a close contest. Unfortunately, to avoid risking defeat, coaches and military leaders alike sometimes fail to pursue decisive victory. President Lincoln relieved a couple of generals during the Civil War for doing just that. Of course, because of what modern weapons can accomplish, acting decisively means something quite different today than it did during General Grant's era. To win consistently on a modern battlefield, an infantry unit must use logical yet unpredictable plays, while retaining the flexibility to modify those plays as conditions change. The unit's composite elements must execute each play as a team, while retaining the prerogative to deviate from that play to handle unforeseen circumstances.

To win at minimal cost, a unit must maximize surprise/momentum to demoralize and beat decisively its opponent. In small-unit combat (as in football), teamwork, momentum, and nonpredictability can be achieved concurrently by having a choice of prerehearsed plays.

## THE COMPLEXITY OF A COMBAT SITUATION

As it relates to combat, the term "situation" encompasses many variables. The acronym METT-TSL (mission, enemy, terrain and weather, troops and fire support available, time, space, and logistics) only delineates the broad categories of these variables. Each category has many facets. Disregarding a seemingly inconsequential circumstance can invalidate an otherwise logical solution. One must continually study the possibilities.

A combat situation is an elusive and moving target. Seldom can military intelligence or reconnaissance accurately assess it ahead of time. Its composite circumstances will only become fully apparent as the battle unfolds, and then they will change. Providing highly detailed instructions to subordinates before a battle can make it hard for them to uncover the subtle nuances of the situation and properly react to them. Small units must prepare for combat in a different way. No combat situation ever exactly repeats itself; but for small units, situations often follow patterns.

## WHAT IT TAKES TO ANALYZE A COMBAT SITUATION ACCURATELY

While making tactical decisions, small-unit leaders may be tempted to rely on their personal knowledge of the enemy and terrain. This may work for a while, if no other variables are involved, and if their subordinates can execute the decisions well enough. But, those in charge cannot expect through leadership and communications skills to get poorly trained personnel satisfactorily to execute complicated schemes of maneuver. The leader must stay apprised of his unit's training deficiencies. The most frequently overlooked aspect of the situation is the *training status* of the troops available. Decisions made without this vital information often can't be properly executed. To win consistently in battle, the leader must carefully prepare his unit ahead of time, and then readily acknowledge whatever deficiencies may still exist:

> Therefore a victorious army first wins [during its preparation phase] and then seeks battle; a defeated army first battles and then seeks victory.[3]
> — Sun Tzu

The search for deficiencies must be constant. Rommel conducted a full-blown training program during his most hectic months in North Africa:

> Probably our most fundamental and important advantage over the enemy in North Africa was that when my army arrived in Africa in 1941, it was in a better position to benefit from further training on modern lines than were the British.[4]
> — Rommel

> Officers and NCO's must continually train their troops.... [T]he commander must be at constant pains to keep his troops abreast of all the latest

Improving One's Chances for Success

tactical experience and developments, and must insist on their practical application. He must see to it that his subordinates are trained in accordance with the latest requirements. The best form of "welfare" for the troops is first-class training, for this saves unnecessary casualties.[5]
— Rommel

[F]everish training was going on among the forces detailed for the attack.[6]
— Rommel

And, Field Marshal Slim pushed the Japanese out of India/Burma, largely because of his in-theater training:

Training in Ranchi was continuous and progressive. There were infantry battle schools, artillery training centres, cooperation courses with the R.A.F., experiments with tanks in the jungle, classes in watermanship and river crossing, and a dozen other instructional activities, all in full swing. Our training grew more ambitious until we were staging inter-divisional exercises over wide ranges of country under tough conditions. Units lived for weeks on end in the jungle and learned its ways. We hoped we had finally dispelled the fatal idea that the Japanese had something we had not.[7]
— Field Marshal Bill Slim

Accurately assessing a combat situation takes the input of one's subordinates. A leader cannot be everywhere at once. When a leader makes decisions without group input, he is doing so with only partial information. Furthermore, no lone decision maker can simultaneously weigh all the variables of a complex situation, even when he knows what they are. Weighing all the variables again takes group effort. That is why group decision making is so valuable in combat. The North Vietnamese used it without adversely affecting their war effort. U.S. leaders must also listen to their subordinates. Not doing so in war carries with it a terrible price tag. Still, as in football, the combat leader cannot solve each situation from scratch with a group of free thinkers. He and the group must do their thinking ahead of time, and then rehearse well-conceived plays in which team members are allowed to exercise some initiative. Only then, can the right balance be struck between control and surprise/momentum.

**HISTORY'S LESSONS ON ENEMY CONTACT**

The literature contains trends that could be loosely construed as guidelines for when and how to attack:

*1. A unit cannot successfully "fire and move" against a prepared enemy position:*

. . . The [second-generation] tactics that evolved during this time [1870-1914] . . . were called skirmisher tactics or . . . fire and movement. . . .
When the European Powers went to war in 1914, few anticipated that second-generation tactics would soon be obsolete. . . . As World War I began, these weapons [quick-firing artillery and machineguns] confirmed what some suspected: skirmisher tactics did not work in frontal attacks against prepared positions.[8]
— MCI 7401

The skirmish line [in tactics of the same name] advanced in a series of alternating rushes. Part of the line rushing forward 50-100 meters, went to ground, and took cover. By fire, that unit then supported the rush of an adjacent unit.[9]
— MCI 7401

*2. As weapons technology has advanced, the maneuver element has had to present a smaller target. It has had to become smaller in composition and to operate more in defilade:*

The new [third-generation] tactics departed from the broad, linear assault. Instead, small [squad-sized] columns of stormtroopers used terrain to infiltrate the enemy's defense.[10]
— MCI 7401

*3. In difficult terrain, no amount of firepower will dislodge a good defender:*

The Soviets relearned through practical experience [in Afghanistan] the lesson learned by the

(Source: FM 22-100 (1983), p. 133)

Americans in Korea: that troops dug in and defending mountainous terrain are almost impossible to dislodge with indirect fire.[11]

*4. An attacker minimally needs a 3 to 1 manpower advantage over a defender:*

Second Marine Division, had only about 6,000 men for the attack [on Tarawa]. That is much less than the three-to-one ratio required by doctrine.[12]

Consequently, the art of using troops is this. When ten to the enemy's one, surround him. When five times his strength, attack him. If double his strength, divide him. If weaker numerically, be capable of withdrawing.[13]
— Sun Tzu

*5. Built-up areas should be bypassed whenever possible. In urban terrain, the attacker may need as much as a 10 to 1 manpower advantage:*

The worst policy is to attack cities.[14]
— Sun Tzu

If troops are attacking cities, their strength will be exhausted.[15]
— Sun Tzu

### GIVING SMALL-UNIT ATTACK METHODS A BETTER CHANCE FOR SUCCEEDING

To succeed consistently in war, a unit must practice "battle drills." To avoid becoming predictable, the unit must have *more than one* battle drill for each category of event. These drills can also function as *courses of action on which to base decisions*. Familiarity with several courses of action could expedite the decision-making process in minds numbed by the shock of combat.

While the manuals generally contain only "one way" to solve each broad category of combat situation, their writers probably never intended for this one way to be used all the time. The ways were undoubtedly designed as *guidelines,* to be practiced in peacetime to build teamwork, but not to be continually replicated in war. Perhaps, it's time to develop some high-percentage variations to the tactical methods that have been mistakenly construed as doctrine. Then, these variations could be used as alternative solutions. To make viable modifications to standard tactical procedures, one must concentrate on six prerequisites for victory at minimal cost from the first chapter:

*1. Accommodation for frequently recurring situational variables.*

*2. Focus on the enemy.*

*3. Flexibility to a changing situation.*

*4. Surprise (through stealth, speed, or deception) and momentum.*

*5. Controlling subordinates only to the extent that surprise and momentum are not sacrificed.*

*6. Localized combat power advantage.*

### ACCOMMODATION FOR FREQUENTLY RECURRING CIRCUMSTANCES

For small units, combat situations can easily be categorized: attack, defense, ambush, counterambush, etc. In each category, certain circumstances occur more often than others. For example, there are covered routes that lead to within assaulting distance of most objectives. If the avenue of approach are large, like streambeds or dry washes, the defenders can cover them by observation and fire. However, if the avenues are shallow and numerous, the defenders can seldom prevent short-range infiltration.

The Principles of War are historical guidelines on how to handle recurring circumstances and should be followed whenever possible. Murphy's Law — "What can go wrong, will go wrong" — is also a valuable guideline.

### FOCUS ON THE ENEMY

Respect for one's enemy is crucial to success on the battlefield. He is not a coward, he is not stupid, and he probably has comparable weaponry. A military force that focuses more on itself than on its adversary, succeeds less often in combat. For example, only a small percentage of U.S. ambushes in Vietnam succeeded. With the benefit of perfect hindsight, one can now identify the problem. Ambushers were sent to trail junctions that appeared on published maps. Only the most foolhardy of Viet Cong would travel through such a place. The typical U.S. ambush patrol made little attempt to disguise its departure from friendly lines. Local VC could have easily observed and followed the patrols into position. They could have marked the ambushed trails in much the same way that railroad signalmen mark occupied train tracks.

Soldiers from non-industrialized nations can often see better in the woods than city-born Americans. While practicing walking point in a vegetated draw with Marines, a soldier from Belize spotted human silhouettes at three times the distance that any American could.[16] One wonders what might happen to an American who had to patrol against him. This problem has been noted before:

There must be training in difficult observation, which is needed for the offense. It is my observa-

tion [on Guadalcanal] that only 5% of the men can really see while observing.[17]
— Col. Merritt A. Edson

## FLEXIBILITY TO A CHANGING SITUATION

Having the ability to detect and then react to a changing situation can have great value in war. What the manuals contain is mostly technique, not doctrine. This technique is merely a framework around which to build common-sense solutions. For example, if a maneuver element were to run into stiff resistance, it could simply switch roles with its support element:

> However, your main effort must remain flexible. If the attack of the main effort bogs down while a supporting element finds unexpected success, then you will shift your main effort to the supporting element.... The main effort must remain fluid at all times.[18]
> — MCI 7401

Or, if the element of surprise were irretrievably compromised during an attack, the maneuver element could pull back and try another avenue of approach later:

> He who knows when he can fight and when he cannot will be victorious.[19]
> — Sun Tzu

Not enough flexibility can constitute a severe handicap. An example from Vietnam will serve to illustrate the point. In war, the side that suffers from a disadvantage in combat power must regularly split into small groups to get close enough to attack any lucrative target in force. It must establish well-stocked and lightly defended infiltration routes. In Vietnam, these routes could have been located by simply plotting on a map all the enemy contacts and supply cache discoveries, and then connecting the dots with lines that ran radially outwards from lucrative targets. Unfortunately, few field commanders were ever told to ambush these probable microfilament ends of the Ho Chi Minh Trail. In early 1967 west of Gio Linh, a fully camouflaged and heavily traveled cobblestone road was found running south out of the DMZ and stopping 100 yards short of the east-west trail used by the U.S. units. This location had seen so much contact that it had been nicknamed the Three Gateways to Hell. Instead of being allowed to ambush the cobblestone road, the discovering unit was moved several miles away to join another operation that accomplished little.[20] Less structure and more flexibility to a changing situation might have netted some NVA anti-aircraft guns that night.

During an attack, two-man teams and fire teams will also identify lightly defended gaps and lucrative targets. The plan of attack must not be so restrictive as to prevent them from exploiting these opportunities. Optimal flexibility comes from training individuals and small-units well, giving them broad guidance, and then letting them run. If they are regularly issued "mission-type" orders, they will not have to deviate from those orders to obey common sense.

## SURPRISE (THROUGH STEALTH, SPEED, OR DECEPTION) AND MOMENTUM

Surprise is so important to limiting friendly casualties that, without a good chance of it, no attack should be contemplated. On the other hand, successes made possible through surprise, should be exploited:

> I approve all methods of attacking provided they are directed at the point the enemy army is weakest and where the terrain favors them the least.[21]
> — Frederick the Great

> There is only one principle of war and that's this. Hit the other fellow, as quick as you can, and as hard as you can, where it hurts him the most, when he ain't looking.[22]
> — Sir William Slim

> Since I joined the Marines, I have advocated aggressiveness in the field and constant offensive action. Hit quickly, hit hard and keep right on hitting. Give the enemy no rest, no opportunity to consolidate his forces and hit back at you. This is the shortest road to victory.[23]
> —Gen. H.M. "Howlin' Mad" Smith

Outdated is the belief that, by keeping an enemy's head down, one can attack him without risk. How hard would it be for that enemy to rig a periscope? When Americans appear in his wire fifty feet away, what keeps him from command detonating a claymore, calling for mortars on a preregistered target, throwing grenades, or firing his AK-47 at arm's length — all from the relative safety of his fighting hole? Daylight standup charges for more than 50 meters are a vestige of the bloody past. To avoid risk, the attacker must surprise his opponent. Of course, a certain amount of surprise may be lost during any attack. Still, one can compensate for this loss of surprise — through deception:

> All warfare is based on deception. Therefore, when capable of attacking, feign incapacity; when active in moving troops, feign inactivity. When near the enemy, make it seem that you are far away; when far away, make it seem that you are near.[24]
> — Sun Tzu

All maneuver elements must do everything within their power to avoid drawing attention to themselves. They must refrain from using colored pyrotechnics as alternate signals. These pyrotechnics can give away their position at the most critical time. A more appropriate signal might be a sight or sound occurring infrequently in nature, an assault method step only visible from the rear, the relative positioning of a maneuver element leader, or (with enough masking noise) a well-placed explosion.

Issuing detailed instructions to attackers gives defenders longer to prepare. Formal orders must be simplified and reserved for deliberate attacks against particularly difficult objectives. For most deliberate attacks, units well rehearsed in effective techniques only need mission-type orders. For hasty attacks, they need little more than the play designators in a football huddle.

### CONTROLLING SUBORDINATES ONLY TO THE EXTENT THAT SURPRISE AND MOMENTUM ARE NOT SACRIFICED

Personnel should become so familiar with their leader's intent that they can be trusted to act on their own initiative. They should never be required to ask permission to respond to crisis situations. Seconds count in close combat. Subordinates must be trusted to act appropriately and only required to inform their leaders of decisions that might affect others. Mistakes will happen, but well-trained units can absorb them and still win. For example, requiring a point man to ask for instructions every time he sees his enemy counterpart is the equivalent of issuing him a death sentence:

[A]ttempts to control men in combat easily undermine initiative.[25]
— FMFM 1-3

The only control that a small-unit leader needs in combat is knowledge of the techniques developed by his subordinates, and timely feedback on the major decisions made by those subordinates. Of course, this takes a streamlined and secure signaling system.

### LOCALIZED COMBAT POWER ADVANTAGE

A localized combat power advantage is necessary to *guarantee* victory over a prepared enemy position. An infantry unit should minimally have a three-to-one manpower advantage at the point of attack. That means that a rifle squad should not attack more than four enemy soldiers at any given time. History is replete with examples of attacks failing simply because they were conducted piecemeal. Throughout the Battle of Antietam, the Confederates were badly outnumbered. The Federals might have won, if they had just attacked en masse:

On September 16 [1862], both armies massed near Sharpsburg. McClellan initially enjoyed an almost 4:1 advantage in infantrymen but did not attack. By midday . . . the Union still had an advantage of slightly over 2:1. . . . At dawn on the 17th . . . began the savage fighting which remains the single bloodiest day in American history. Confederate and Union forces mauled each other in three essentially separate engagements. Twenty thousand Union infantrymen, over two divisions, were never committed.[26]

I always make it a rule to get there first with the most men.[27]
— Nathan Bedford Forrest

The principles of war could for brevity be condensed into a simple word "concentration."[28]
— Liddell Hart

While any part of the element of surprise is still intact, firing and moving across the last 50 yards of open ground during an assault constitutes attacking piecemeal. Furthermore, it puts the attacking force in harm's way longer.

### SPECIFICS ON HOW TO INCREASE ONE'S ODDS FOR SUCCESS AT THE SMALL-UNIT LEVEL

The first three chapters have clearly shown that small units enjoy the best chance of winning at minimal cost when they are allowed to think for themselves and to surprise the enemy. These units must continually develop new techniques for what they expect to encounter in combat, and they must permit their members to exercise initiative in the execution of these techniques.

Part two will discuss how alternative tactical methods can be developed from standard procedures. These methods won't be the only way to operate, nor will they categorically be the best way; they will just be examples of what can result from a different way of thinking and a different way of training. When techniques vary between units, those units are less predictable. For this reason, the techniques *should not* be all the same, only minimally compatible in the eyes of the parent-unit commander. While part two will undoubtedly add to what has been written so far about small-unit tactics, its real purpose is to reinforce the thought process that is required to develop sound techniques. In other words, the thought process is more important than any particular technique it may produce. Yet, one wonders if the American frame of reference on small-unit tactics can support the change. For this reason, the next few chapters are dedicated to reassessing and supplementing this frame of reference. There are more tactical choices available than many U.S. infantrymen have been led to believe.

# 4. Old Habits May Get in the Way

- Is there more to the story?
- Is trying to annihilate one's enemy the best way to win?
- In combat, is it helpful to use detailed instructions and signaling?

(Source: FM 7-11B1/2 (1978), p. 1-I-A-9)

## WHATEVER ONE ACCEPTS ON FAITH INFLUENCES HOW HE THINKS

Adults learn within the context of what they already know. Ideas that are too far removed from their personal frames of reference are hard for them to accept. Unfortunately, when one gets dropped into a hot landing zone on his first day in combat, it's often too late for him to learn any more. For this reason, infantrymen must continually reassess and expand their frames of reference. When one's survival is at stake, the "other way" can hold as much appeal as the "established way."

What adults "know" comes primarily from two sources: (1) what they have been told, and (2) what they have experienced personally. They sometimes have difficulty keeping the two sets of ideas separated — becoming convinced that what they have been told is true, even though they have never personally experienced it. When their outside advice comes from a single source and is not corroborated by other evidence, their point of view can be somewhat less than universally correct. At some point in their lives, most adults come to the realization that what they have heard from any one source may not have been the entire story. Sources have many reasons for not disclosing every facet of an issue. One is to propound more convincingly their perspective. Infantrymen can't afford to harbor points of view that aren't well founded. They need continually to reassess their viewpoints and expand their frames of reference to encompass infantry knowledge from around the world and across the centuries.

How to slightly modify standard small-unit tactical techniques to create useful alternatives has already been discussed. But knowing what to do and being able to do it are two different things. Old habits can be hard to break. At issue are the dynamics of change, not the sincerity of one's forefathers. To perform small-unit tactics with a high probability of success and a low cost in casualties, many U.S. infantrymen may have *to change how they think*. Because of the very nature of combat, the "rightness" or "wrongness" of choices can seldom be established before they're made, and then they change. It should come as no surprise then, that the *exact opposite* of what Americans have been doing may also be a valid choice. One must look at some of the most common dilemmas facing today's combat decision makers, to see if any old habits may be in need of reassessment.

U.S. small-unit leaders face the same heart-rending choices that their national strategists do: (1) whether to protect the status quo or to take the risks to win decisively, (2) whether to focus inwards to eliminate mistakes or on the enemy to keep pace with a changing situation, (3) whether to follow predictable established procedures or surprise-producing alternatives, (4) whether to use complex instructions and signaling to enhance control or to use simplified versions to permit momentum, and (5) whether to try to destroy the enemy or merely to break his will to resist. How Americans have previously dealt with each of the above-listed dilemmas may provide valuable insight into how they think.

## PROTECT THE STATUS QUO OR TAKE THE RISKS NECESSARY TO WIN DECISIVELY?

Protecting the status quo can be easier than changing it. To take action, one risks making a mistake. In training exercises, U.S. patrols can be surprisingly non-aggressive during enemy contact. They usually react in one of the following ways: (1) report the enemy sighting to higher headquarters, (2) call in supporting arms that will take too long to arrive, (3) set up a hasty ambush through which the opponent has little chance of moving, (4) envelop immediately to where the foe was never headed, or (5) take the adversary under small-arms fire from ineffective range.

The perfectly human aversion to closing with a dangerous adversary is undoubtedly at the root of the problem. Not surprisingly, winning consistently requires a more decisive and therefore more aggressive response (more on that later).

## FOCUS INWARDS TO PREVENT MISTAKES OR ON THE ENEMY TO KEEP PACE WITH A CHANGING SITUATION?

Professionals of all types try to minimize errors. Unfortunately, trying too hard to do so in the military profession has some serious tradeoffs: initiative, ability to surprise one's adversary, perspective on the overall picture, and learning (just to name a few).

In battle, the "all ready on the right, all ready on the left" syndrome also gives the enemy a chance to get ready. Control that is too tight stifles momentum.

Moreover, focusing inwards takes valuable energy away from accurately assessing the enemy situation. After all, how productive could perfectly executing the solution to the *wrong problem* really be? Sun Tzu went so far as to quantify the odds for each approach:

> When you are ignorant of the enemy but know yourself, your chances of winning and losing are equal.[1]
>
> — Sun Tzu

Key to an infantryman's ability to react to whatever confronts him, is his authority to exercise some initiative. If he is worried about violating orders or making a mistake, he may hesitate (perhaps a second too long) to display this initiative. On the battlefield, a "zero-defect" mentality has little value:

> If people are afraid of making mistakes . . . ; they will not take risks and they will not exercise initiative. Furthermore, they will not win in war.[2]

In combat, the leader must personally supervise only those actions that jeopardize the overall mission, and then allow subordinates to exercise initiative (and make a few mistakes) on everything else. Those subordinates must be able to identify mistakes as they happen without fear of punishment, or the same mistakes will happen again.

Moreover, attempting to eliminate mistakes during infantry training does little to facilitate learning. New tactical knowledge can often only be gained through the experimentation that inevitably leads to a few mistakes. Many of these so called mistakes are in actuality warning signals that the original procedures were inconsistent with the level of training of the participants or some other aspect the situation. Furthermore, correcting mistakes on the spot is one of the best ways to achieve long-term retention of what has been learned.

One can often predict an enemy's intentions by viewing the terrain from his perspective and then attempting to think like he does. But, this takes continually focusing on one's adversary.

## PREDICTABLE ESTABLISHED PROCEDURES OR SURPRISE-PRODUCING ALTERNATIVES?

Trying too hard to follow the "book" while solving battlefield situations makes one fairly predictable, even to enemies who haven't read the book. To surprise an adversary consistently, and thus to keep him off balance, one must mix in some alternative methods. These don't have to be drastically different from what's in the book; often it's enough just to vary the amount of speed, stealth, or deception with which the standard method is executed.

What units will do initially in wartime is what they have trained to do in peacetime. In the past, U.S. forces have had to learn quickly after reaching the war zone. At Kasserine Pass in North Africa and to a lesser extent during the first few weeks at Guadalcanal, this learning process was painful. Standardizing what subordinates practice in peacetime may make those subordinates easier to control, but it does not help them to learn the alternative techniques needed to develop momentum in battle. All available time must be dedicated to experimenting with individual and small-unit tactics. Famous Americans have pointed this out throughout history, but (for whatever reason) their advice has largely gone unheeded. The former commander of a Marine Raider Battalion on Guadalcanal offered this advice to the trainers at home:

> If I had to train my regiment over again, I would stress small group training and the training of the individual....
> Our basic training is all right.... In your training put your time and emphasis on the squad and platoon rather than on the company, battalion and regiment.
> In your scouting and patrolling,... have the men work against each other. Same thing for squads and platoons in their problems....
> ... With proper training, our Americans are better [than the Japanese], as our people can think better as individuals. Encourage your individuals and bring them out.[3]
> — Col. Merritt A. Edson

## COMPLEX INSTRUCTIONS AND SIGNALING FOR CONTROL OR SIMPLIFIED VERSIONS FOR MOMENTUM?

Because thousands of combinations of circumstances are possible in combat, some infantry leaders feel no responsibility to prepare for any given scenario. Perhaps the same people also consider detailed orders to be a necessary evil. There are those who would disagree. Rommel experienced intense combat in North Africa and still managed to conduct a full-blown training program throughout the campaign. U.S. Marines rehearsed heavily in Saudi Arabia right before the Gulf War. There is always time to rehearse, and doing so eliminates the need to use as many detailed instructions.

That human beings are always trying to structure the chaos of battle, may be at the root of the problem. This all too human tendency creates a whole series of associated dilemmas: (1) whether to follow through on preconceived notions or to shift the focus of main effort as the situation changes, (2) whether to follow orders to the letter or to exercise initiative to meet an unforeseen threat, and (3) whether to set off a colored pyrotechnic to shift the "base of fire" or to keep the maneuver element hidden with a more subtle signal. The temptation to control the situation must itself be controlled, or it can do more harm than good. Sun Tzu had definite opinions on the subject:

> Sun Tzu's theory of adaptability to existing situations is an important aspect of his thought. Just as water adapts itself to the conformation of the ground, so in war one must be flexible; he must often adapt his tactics to the enemy situation.[4]

It only takes seconds to ask for the opinions of subordinates. By doing so, one can make more accurate decisions and enjoy more support during the execution phase of those decisions. Complex instructions are, at best, premature during what is usually an inaccurate assessment of the situation. Further, they confuse subordinates, drain their initiative, and even undermine their willingness to take responsibility for their actions.

On the other hand, poorly planned signaling can do more than just waste precious time or confuse subordinates; it can actually compromise the location of the maneuver element. The alternate signal to shift supporting fires must be discreet. Signals are important, but like orders, they can usefully be simplified.

(Source: FM 7-8, p. J-8)

The Shortfall in Recorded Knowledge

(Sources: FM 22-100 (1983), p. 113; FM 7-8 (1984), p. 3-28)

### TRY TO DESTROY THE ENEMY OR MERELY BREAK HIS WILL TO RESIST?

When hatred for the enemy turns into a determined effort to exterminate him, whatever moral cause precipitated the battle is quickly diluted. Of course, some enemies (like the Japanese in WWII) prefer death to surrender. With them, the Marines had little choice.

At the small-unit level, only for someone like Sgt. York, it is easy to get a numerically superior force to *surrender*. But striving systematically to eliminate one's enemies, not only makes the battle harder to win, but also more costly. The enemy seldom complies without taking someone with him. Sun Tzu preferred winning with as little actual fighting as possible:

To capture the enemy's entire army is better than to destroy it; to take intact a regiment, a company or a squad is better than to destroy them.[5]

### GUIDELINES FOR RESOLVING THESE DILEMMAS DURING SMALL-UNIT COMBAT

The manuals and history books do *not* contain definitive guidelines on how squads can resolve such dilemmas during combat. This knowledge resides only in the collective experience of the NCO corps. But, to fully appreciate the value of this knowledge, many U.S. infantry leaders must first acknowledge a frame of reference quite different from their own.

# 5   A Different Style of Warfare May Be Necessary

- Is there a style of warfare different from the one Americans use?
- To what extent have the armies of other nations used it?
- Has anyone ever figured out how to use it at the small-unit level?

(Sources: FMFM 1-3B (1981), p. 4-19; FM 90-10-1 (1982), p. B-4)

### THERE'S ANOTHER STYLE OF FIGHTING QUITE DIFFERENT FROM THE AMERICAN WAY

Every time the external threat to America lessens, the U.S. military budget gets cut. The budget cuts result in fewer "man-days" to spread between end strength and training. Because numbers of people must be reduced gradually, *shortfalls in training* often result. Rather than funding a well-trained standing army, American society apparently prefers to base its defense on the advanced weaponry and munitions it can mass produce in time of war. Then, out of professed regard for the lives of its soldiers, that society freely expends that ordnance.

Forced to operate under these fiscal pressures, the U.S. military establishment has come to rely on what is commonly known as "attrition" or "methodical" warfare. With this style of warfare, one tries to *destroy* his enemy by going directly at him with overwhelming firepower. Not surprisingly, heavy concentrations of enemy make the most lucrative ground attack objectives. Unfortunately, when an armed force relies on firepower to win, it only requires infantrymen who can operate their weapons and follow orders. Although intentions have always been good, results have not always matched expectations:

> ... [This has been] the American way of war — the willingness of Americans to expend firepower freely to conserve human life. . . .
>
> The proclivity to conserve lives in combat has been made all the more difficult by a parallel

distinction of the American military tradition — the distrust of large standing armies. Reliance on the citizen soldier to fight its wars has customarily given America a strong militia — but a less strong military. It has meant that *American armies have had to learn to fight by fighting* [italics added]. Firepower lessened the price of this education. Americans learned as early as the Civil War that firepower steeled and coalesced unsteady troops....

In its major wars, the United States has been willing (and rich enough) to compensate its material wealth for what it lacked in preparedness for war. Once mobilized, American war industry in the 20th Century overwhelmed its enemies with weaponry.[1]

The U.S. can no longer muster its combat power quickly enough to stop a determined aggressor at the other end of the world. For this reason, military planners have been reconsidering an ancient style of warfare that can compensate for a deficiency in combat power. A commander who follows this alternative style of warfare attempts to *demoralize* his opponent by bypassing that opponent's strengths. The commander does not need a firepower advantage, but he does need small units that can secretly maneuver around enemy strongpoints. Not surprisingly, this style of warfare is vastly different from the attrition style in both intent and method. Of late, it has been called "maneuver" or "common-sense" warfare. Because it contrasts so dramatically with the traditional style of operating, some Americans have had difficulty accepting its validity.

## SOME U.S. COMMANDERS HAD TO BYPASS ENEMY STRENGTH OUT OF NECESSITY

Great American generals, who found themselves at an overall combat power disadvantage, have occasionally had to bypass enemy strength on a grand scale. Lee sent Jackson on a forced march around the Union forces at Chancellorsville, MacArthur went around Rabaul during his WWII island-hopping campaign, MacArthur risked dangerous tides to attack the North Korean Army from the rear at Inchon, and most recently General Schwarzkopf sent the bulk of his forces on an end run around the main Iraqi defense line in the Gulf War.

Other gifted American leaders have bypassed enemy strength by attacking not only where, but also *when,* the enemy was the weakest. For example, George Washington crossed the Delaware on Christmas night; Stonewall Jackson moved so quickly in the Shenandoah Valley that he could take on the Union Forces one at a time; and (after his Normandy breakout) Patton kept the Germans off balance across the breadth of France. The difference between the two sets of examples is just one of scale.

Attacking an enemy force along a narrow frontage when least expected, is almost the same as bypassing that force's two halves.

*(Source: FM 22-100 (1973), p. 1-3)*

Just because a conflict between regiments or armies has degenerated into a set-piece battle, doesn't mean that there is no longer any room for maneuver, or that there is no longer any chance to bypass an opponent's strength. Two men crawling up a muddy ditch between enemy fighting holes at 2:00 A.M. qualifies. Again, it's just a matter of scale. American history contains several examples of bypassing enemy strength at the smaller scale as well: (1) American Revolutionaries waging guerrilla war against the British in 1776, (2) Texans spiking Santa Anna's cannons outside the Alamo during their "war of independence," (3) American Indians creeping into settler camps, and (4) Confederate guerrillas like John Mosby operating behind Union lines in the Civil War. In the Gulf War, small groups of reconnaissance Marines probed for mines in the darkness to establish paths between strongpoints in the main Iraqi defense line.

Of course, even on a small scale, circumventing enemy strength need not entail operating silently and sparing the enemy harm. The Minutemen sniped at the British columns returning from Concord to Boston in 1775.[2]

## THIS TYPE OF COMMON SENSE HAS BEEN PRACTICED THROUGHOUT WORLD HISTORY

Because of the high stakes involved, common sense has always played a role in war. As early as 350 B.C., the Chinese military philosopher Sun Tzu expounded (in his classic, *The Art of War)* on the advantages of bypassing enemy strength:

> An army may be likened to water: water leaves dry the high places and attacks hollows; an army turns from strength and attacks emptiness.[3]
> — Sun Tzu

> The supreme art of war is to subdue the enemy without fighting.[4]
> — Sun Tzu

Moreover, Sun Tzu's tactical beliefs appear to have taken their inspiration from *much older* religious philosophies. Most Eastern religions implicitly promote common sense in all human endeavor; they do so by seeking "ultimate reality." The most popular — Buddhism — originated in India around 550 B.C. and then quickly spread into southern China. By 700 A.D., it had been widely accepted throughout *Southeast Asia,* Tibet, Mongolia, China, *Korea,* and *Japan.*[5] Early Buddhism was *not* a religion in the sense that it promoted deity worship; it was simply a way of life. It preached overcoming hardships of every kind through selfless action, exercise of will power, self-examination, and search for truth:

> The sixth [step in the Eightfold Path] is Right Effort: one must *exercise will power* if he would succeed. The seventh is Right Awareness: one must *constantly examine one's behavior* and, like a patient in psychoanalysis, trace it to its cause, trying to understand and remove the cause of misdeeds. The eighth and final step on the Path is Right Meditation: one must *ponder often and deeply on ultimate truth* if one is to find salvation [italics added throughout].[6]

Taoism originated in China even earlier (around 600 B.C.) and became the state "religion" for a time. It promoted self-realization through *patience, simplicity, and nature's harmony.*[7] Perhaps this is why Oriental soldiers have always been so good at *penetrating enemy lines by stealth.* Deception would come easily to anyone who could fathom the confusing paradoxes of Taoism. Sun Tzu's writings on warfare bear the unmistakable fingerprint of a Taoist thinker:

> In my opinion, the importance of understanding the Taoist element of *The Art of War* can hardly be exaggerated. Not only is this classic of strategy permeated with the ideas of great Taoist works such as the *I Ching (The Book of Changes)* and the *Tao-te Ching (The Way and Its Power),* but it reveals the fundamentals of Taoism as the ultimate source of all the traditional Chinese martial arts.[8]

In other words, Sun Tzu didn't invent common-sense warfare; he merely wrote about how Asians have always viewed warfare. Of course, the Orientals don't have a monopoly on stalking skills. All societies, at some point in their history, have practiced avoiding enemy strength in that way. At the start of this century, the Boers successfully employed frontier skills against the British:

> The year 1902 saw the high point of German enthusiasm for "Boer tactics." In that year, infantry units of the Guard Corps held demonstrations where the Guardsmen crept rather than charged into mock battle.[9]

When the Germans got embroiled in the bloody trench fighting of early WWI, they found another way to bypass enemy strength. While the Allies turned to new technology in the form of the *tank* to break the deadlock of the trenches, the Germans developed *new infantry tactics.* Having watched the Boers and the Japanese at the beginning of the century, they understood how to close with an enemy by stealth. And, having endured lengthy artillery barrages since 1914, they also knew how to use exploding shells to mask other sounds. They correctly deduced that a few artillery rounds in an Allied trench would not alert its occupants to the possibility of German assault troops *seconds* behind. If the assault troops could cross no man's land before the rounds were fired, and if the artillery could fire accurately without adjustment, such an attack might be possible. Detailed maps of that part of Europe and customized firing tables for each artillery piece made pinpoint artillery fire without preregistration feasible for the Germans.[10] Times of limited visibility, shellholes, and shallow ditches (for communications wire), made it possible for small groups of assault troops to crawl across no man's land without being detected. Behind a pinpoint barrage of short duration, a squad-sized unit could move forward, bangalore the barbed wire, and jump into an Allied trench at the exact instant the shelling was scheduled to shift. After bayoneting whoever was initially encountered, the squad could then "roll up" the trench with grenades — all without compromising the element of surprise. The Allied soldiers manning other parts of that sector thought the grenade explosions were all part of the artillery barrage. By the Spring of 1918, *every* frontline German infantry squad knew how to accomplish this feat.[11] Because they adopted revolutionary defense techniques as well, the Germans are generally credited with developing the expanded or "modern" version of maneuver warfare:

> The essential elements of the tactics that Rohr developed in the course of these experiments were (1) the replacement of the advance in skirmish lines with the surprise assault of squad-sized "stormtroops," (2) the use of supporting arms . . . coordinated at the lowest possible level . . . to suppress the enemy during the attack, and (3) the clearing of trenches by rolling them up with troops armed with hand grenades.[12]

Over the years, other countries have adopted this alternative style of warfare. If they couldn't find an unmanned place to attack, they simply attacked a narrow sector *when* their opponent was least prepared. For example, in the underreported six-month set-piece battle between Russia and Japan in Manchuria in 1939, both sides were skilled at attacking on a small scale when their opponent was weakest. One night, both sides attempted to attack each other's prepared positions with an interesting result. The Russians assaulted a Japanese position, believing that they had achieved surprise. Unfortunately, the bulk of the Japanese forces had departed that position on an attack of their own. These forces conducted a hasty defense from the Russians' flank, and then successfully counterattacked. "This type of night fighting was the soul of the Imperial Japanese Army."[13]

In May of 1940, the Germans again used what they had learned in WWI. All they needed to defeat Fort Eban-Emael — the linchpin of the Belgian defense line — was a few combat engineers:

> ... The German heavy artillery fired, not in a vain attempt to destroy the fort, but to create craters in the flat terrain....
>
> When darkness fell, the German engineers crossed, in rubber boats, an artificial lake that separated them from Eban-Emael. Using the shellholes made by their own guns for cover, they crept forward. At dawn, flamethrowers sent streams of burning oil onto the embrasures from which the machineguns responsible for the close defense of the fort were expected to fire. Reeling from the heat and blinded by the smoke, the machinegunners failed to see the small team that had rushed forward with a huge shaped charge. A few seconds later, the charge went off.... Other explosions followed.... By the end of the morning, the fort was defenseless and surrendered.[14]

Throughout WWII, the Germans and Russians took turns outmaneuvering each other across the steppes of Russia on scales both large and small. After all, Zhukov, who was to lead the Russians from Moscow to Stalingrad and then on to Berlin, had been the victor of the war with the Japanese in Manchuria in 1939.

In the early fifties, the North Koreans and Chinese showed a remarkable ability to appear in large numbers in places where they weren't supposed to be. They had somehow learned how to avoid American reconnaissance and interdiction efforts. The Marines encountered ten times their number at the Chosin Reservoir. A few hundred miles to the South, the Viet Minh were about to encircle an entire French army at Dien Bien Phu.

In more recent times, guerrilla forces in Vietnam exploited chinks in a superpower's armor to accomplish what few had believed possible. The British attacked almost exclusively at night in the Falklands.

## WHICH STYLE OF WARFARE IS THE LEAST COSTLY?

Not only is maneuver warfare effective in overcoming a manpower disadvantage, but it is also effective in *reducing casualties*. After all, successfully attacking an objective with a limited number of troops, and coming away from a successful attack with the same number of troops standing, are similar concepts. Neither is possible without cost-effective technique.

The relatively higher cost of attrition warfare is not always easy to recognize. When the goal is to kill enemy, success in that endeavor is subject to exaggeration. Reassuring reports, like "Though the friendly cost was high, the enemy's cost was higher," are all too common. Throughout this century, Americans have been told that their adversaries (who have regularly used maneuver warfare) have been uncaring about the lives of their soldiers. There is considerable evidence to the contrary:

> As the depth of the German defense increased and the cost of defending the front line grew greater, the emphasis in German tactics [in WWI] changed. Instead of trying to hold on to a piece of terrain whatever the cost, the key feature of the German defense became the timely counterattack.[15]
>
> The IJA [Imperial Japanese Army] founded its battle doctrine on bold offensive operations.... The IJA relied on the infantry as its main battle force.... [T]acticians had to guarantee that the attacking Japanese infantry reached the enemy positions with a minimum of friendly losses.[16]
> — Leavenworth Papers No. 2
>
> Soviet regulations before the outbreak of war in 1939 recognized that "night operations will be common under modern warfare conditions to exploit surprise, reduce losses, and disorganize the enemy."[17]
> — Leavenworth Papers No. 6

*Attacking where the enemy isn't will always be less costly than attacking where he is.* Additionally, maneuver warfare provides the opportunity to bring hostilities to a rapid conclusion, and thereby lessens the cost in the long run. By design, maneuver warfare conserves limited resources — *to include human life:*

> Battles are won by slaughter and maneuver. The greater the general, the more he contributes in maneuver, the less he demands in slaughter.[18]
> — Winston Churchill

Why has not this alternative style of warfare been used more often in the West? Possibly, because *over the short term,* to only partially trained personnel, it appears more dangerous. For a U.S. infantryman, crawling up on an enemy machinegun bunker entails excessive risk. For a Gurkha or North Vietnamese scout, it doesn't. The difference is in training and perception. One can either take those risks while trying to close with the bunker undetected, or during an extended standup assault. The way that subjects the attacker to the fewest bullets is the safest. Maneuver warfare is not more dangerous, it just involves different risks and requires more skill:

> Now both advantage and danger are inherent in maneuver.[19]
> — Sun Tzu

But, sneaking up on one's opponent can be no more dangerous than running through a steady stream of machinegun bullets. Furthermore, the tactical option most likely to succeed, or even most safe, may not be the one most comfortable for the novice to perform. It isn't difficult to prove that maneuver warfare at the small-unit level is *safer over the short term,* as well as over the long term. *Selectively* penetrating enemy lines at night by stealth and deception is obviously less dangerous than *collectively* going after those lines in broad daylight with guns blazing. If *just one* defender can still fire his automatic weapon during a traditional assault, he can single-handedly defeat an entire unit. On the first day at the Somme, a single German machinegun decimated two British battalions. No amount of small-arms or supporting-arms fire can kill or suppress every defender. The *only* way to control all defenders is to enter the objective before any realize what's going on. The catch is that doing so takes specialized individual and small-unit training.

Although opposites in many ways, both maneuver and attrition warfare are valid under appropriate circumstances. Attrition warfare may even cost less on rare occasions. Still, for every combat situation, both options should be considered, and their costs carefully weighed.

### TO WHAT EXTENT IS MANEUVER WARFARE ACCEPTED IN THIS COUNTRY TODAY?

Out of habit, or more probably to simplify the job of training and leading independence-minded Americans, many infantry leaders *of all ranks* still resist maneuver warfare. Some call it "light-infantry tactics," with the inference that "heavy- or mechanized-infantry tactics" are always preferable. Some refer to it as the alternative to "conventional warfare." This is a particularly unfortunate choice of words, because it implies that maneuver warfare somehow violates the U.S. code of honor. Some claim that, as in sports, an army should never try to compete with an opponent at his own game. This might make sense, if the final casualty count were not at stake. Others see maneuver warfare as simply a variation of the traditional style.

In truth, even the details of execution for maneuver warfare are drastically different from those for the traditional style. To practice maneuver warfare, traditional thinkers may have to make a conscientious effort to view the world differently. Over the years, those with the most to lose — the riflemen — have often suspected the existence of another way of doing things. That's where familiar epithets, like "Forget the book" and "Out here you've got to learn fast," came from.

Much of what has been written (in English) about maneuver warfare has been philosophical and couched in the terminology of large units. The worth of this alternative way of fighting was proven at the large-unit level during the Gulf War. Yet, how American infantry *squads* might best contribute to this new style of warfare is still under discussion. Perhaps, the legendary common sense of the NCO corps could be harnessed as part of that answer.

### A CLOSER LOOK AT ATTRITION (OR METHODICAL) WARFARE

In attrition warfare, bringing one's firepower to bear on the enemy is the ultimate goal, and maneuver is only a means to that end. The offensive mission is to locate, close with, and destroy the adversary. That usually means closing with that adversary by the most direct route to take full advantage of one's fire superiority. Objectives are generally pieces of elevated terrain from which better to direct one's fire. Massive logistical support is required to replenish the huge quantities of ammunition expended. Whatever amount of time is needed methodically to destroy the enemy is used. The focus is inward.[20] This inward focus enhances coordination and helps to keep friendlies from shooting each other. Control is centralized to reduce confusion, and authority to act must often be requested from higher headquarters. Personnel are required to concentrate on complicated orders and signals.

The defensive mission in attrition warfare is to destroy the enemy before he can cross the Forward Edge of the Battle Area (FEBA). Again firepower is the key, and most of the other particulars of execution are the same as for the offense.

### THE SPECIFICS OF THE MANEUVER WARFARE DIFFERENCE

In maneuver warfare, the emphasis is on maneuver. Firepower is considered important only to the extent that it facilitates maneuver. The overall offensive mission is to win decisively by getting the enemy to surrender. This is accomplished by bypassing and collapsing him *on every scale.* That means moving through "gaps" in the enemy's defenses to attack his "center of gravity." This process is often referred to as "infiltration" or "soft-spot tactics."

Terrain also has worth to whatever extent it facilitates maneuver. Attack objectives are no longer hilltops from which to employ firepower, but more often command, communications, transportation, and logistics hubs.

When killing becomes necessary to permit maneuver, it is done efficiently. To employ the concept of "combined arms," a unit must fire its weapons in tandem — the first making the enemy vulnerable to the second. For example, a U.S. squad might fire small arms at an enemy patrol passing an abandoned building, and then command detonate the building.

There is no logistical advantage required to conduct maneuver warfare, because there isn't that much shooting. This means lighter loads, fewer resupply requirements, and less cost.

In maneuver war, the emphasis is on operating at a "higher tempo" than the enemy expects. This often means moving quickly, both to evade enemy fire and to keep the enemy off balance. However, it can also mean moving *slowly*, as long as the enemy doesn't expect the move.

The focus is outward on the enemy, and a few mistakes (like outdistancing one's logistical support or shooting at a friendly unit) are accepted as unavoidable. Control is decentralized, and every subunit (or individual) is encouraged to display the initiative needed to react successfully to the local threat. The emphasis is on training personnel well enough ahead of time that they can follow their commanders' intents in combat after receiving only broad guidance. Of course, subunit leaders must still keep their commanders informed of any actions that might affect adjacent units.

"Mission-type" orders replace "five-paragraph" orders to shorten reaction time and to stimulate initiative. These orders generally contain only a brief statement of the situation, the commanders' intents (goals) to two levels above that of the recipient, the recipient's mission, which sister unit has been named as the "focus of main effort" in the commander's bid to win the engagement decisively, and sometimes a few signals.

In the defense, maneuver warfare relies initially on ambushing to weaken one's opponent and then on counterattacking to defeat that opponent decisively. Holding ground from which to employ one's firepower sometimes gives way to moving backwards.

## MORE ON SOFT-SPOT TACTICS

With soft-spot tactics, one attacks "gaps" (enemy weaknesses), while avoiding "surfaces" (enemy strongpoints) and "fire sacks" (enemy traps that have been made to look like gaps). The whole idea is to save one's energy for attacking the logistics and control apparatus that controls the enemy's will to resist. In attrition warfare, a unit operates under the "command push" system — it is told how to attack based on what is known about a particular objective. Sometimes it hits a gap, and sometimes it doesn't, depending on the reconnaissance effort. In maneuver warfare, a unit operates under the "recon pull" system — it often forgoes preliminary reconnaissance, and instead relies on its forward attack elements to discover a gap. When a forward element finds such a gap, the other elements fall in behind it. Where no gap exists, the forward elements create one by force. Either way, the parent unit follows the path of least resistance.

The difficulty with which a defender can observe during periods of limited visibility, hear during heavy weather or shelling, recognize deceptions through his fatigue and shock, and detect intruders in uneven ground or heavy foliage, all present opportunities for the attacker. That attacker can exploit these opportunities almost as easily as he can exploit the total absence of an opponent. In other words, any weakness whatsoever can constitute a soft spot. Infantrymen of every nation share the same frailties: (1) they don't understand microterrain well enough to position themselves where they can counter short-range infiltration; (2) when new to an area, they see and hear things that are not there; (3) after being rebuked for bothering their superiors several nights in a row, they fail to report things that are there; (4) if the dampness of a particular location threatens their personal comfort, they avoid occupying that location; (5) some are invariably drowsy by 4 A.M.; and (6) when the sun first warms the earth around them, many more are either asleep or away on personal business.

These defensive weaknesses can be exploited by an attacker at minimal risk to himself. If the defensive lines cross a marshy area, the attacker can slither in undetected. If the defender has thermal imaging, but isn't sitting on the military crest of his hill, the attacker can crawl to within grenade range of him. If the defender is positioned correctly and only has Night Vision Goggles (NVG's), the attacker can make his move after the moon has set on a rainy night (NVG's need some residual light to operate effectively). In full moonlight, a North Vietnamese Army (NVA) scout camouflaged to look like a bush, could crawl within grenade range of an *alert* U.S. defender *positioned correctly*. The enemy soldier's movements were so slow that they became imperceptible to the naked eye under those lighting conditions. On moonless night, that NVA scout could move right past the American sentry without being detected.

American "grunts" have no societal inadequacy that prevents them from attacking this way. Furthermore, the same ingenuity that occasionally puts them at odds with established procedure, makes them masters of deception. If ideas like bangaloring the barbed wire as part of an artillery attack (as the German's did in WWI and the NVA did at Con Thien in 1967) are buried too deeply in the literature, they must be reinvented. A favorite ploy of Marines is to have an Amphibious Tracked Vehicle (Amtrac) simulate tank noises on the far side of an objective. With enough imagination, there is no limit to how many soft spots can be created through deception.

## WHO ORIGINATED THESE APPLICATION PARAMETERS FOR MANEUVER WARFARE?

Who first learns to *apply* a very old military philosophy to modern battle is difficult to ascertain. Groups of infantrymen widely separated by time and geography can independently arrive at the same common-sense conclusions. They can do so through experimentation in peacetime, or through "survival of the smartest" in wartime. The Germans of WWI are generally credited with developing the application parameters for post-machinegun maneuver warfare.

Late in 1917, after Ludendorff had assumed operational control of the German Army from Falkenhayn, three manuals were published that made a radical departure from established procedure. These manuals provided the philosophical framework for what is today called maneuver warfare. They promoted the infiltration tactics that had evolved from Captain Rohr's stormtroop squad attack technique of 1915, and a controversial elastic-defense method proven effective in 1917. The first manual described how infantry squads could be trained to penetrate Allied lines at minimal risk to themselves:

> Within a few days [of taking over the German Army — September 1916] Ludendorff was converted to the idea that stormtroopers should become the model for the rest of the German infantry.[21]

> For leaders at the company level and below, the chief reference was the second edition of the *Training Manual for Foot Troops in War*.... It expressed, for the first time in an official document, Ludendorff's command that every German infantryman be trained as a stormtrooper and described exercises ... to help commanders attain this goal.[22]

On 26 January 1918, *Attack in Position Warfare* was published for the commanders of units larger than battalion size. It talked of a battle *mission* type of orders that told subordinates what to do, but not how to do it. The work pointed out that "each attack offers opportunities for self-designated activity and mission-oriented action *[initiative]*, even down to the level of the individual soldier."[23]

Shortly thereafter, *The Attack in Trench Warfare* described success on the battlefield in terms of a *focus of main effort* and *commander's intent*.[24] So, it would seem that the core ideas for modern infantry tactics have been in existence for at least seventy-five years. Could the Germans could have gotten their ideas from an even older source?

Sun Tzu's views were published in Paris about the time of the American Revolution. Yet, for Europeans, the Napoleonic successes with "total warfare" and Clausewitz's treatment of them, probably overshadowed Sun Tzu's work for the remainder of the nineteenth century. At the turn of the century, the Boers displayed an ability to close with the British without being seen. Yet, they were probably not following tactical precepts, but rather just exercising common sense.

There is one way the Germans might have borrowed their ideas from elsewhere. They could have gotten them from the Japanese! After all, by 1917, they had provided Japan with military advisers for some forty-five years.[25] These advisers had observed Japanese ground troops in action against the Russians in 1904-1905:

> Beginning in 1904, the debate over Boer tactics [in the German armed forces] was revived by reports coming from the German officers observing the battles of the Russo-Japanese War.... The Japanese, they noted, had responded to their unacceptable losses in the early battles of the war by attacking in more open formations, with more space between individuals, and greater freedom for platoons and squads to move independently.[26]

> Japanese strength ... lay in small units and the epitome of Japanese doctrine was embodied in small-unit tactics. Night attacks ... and the willingness to engage in hand-to-hand combat were the hallmarks of the Japanese infantryman. Indeed such tactics were very successful against Soviet infantry [in 1939].[27]
> — Leavenworth Papers No. 2

If the Germans did get their ideas from the Japanese, from what source could the Japanese have gotten them? American history books describe Japan as an isolationist nation until 1854. Perhaps Japan was more open to its Eastern neighbors than it was to the West. In fact, the literature shows that much of what would become Japanese culture originated on the Asian mainland:

> ... [The Orient has] technology, ... commercialism, and traditional ways of thought and behavior. All Asian societies show these contrasts and tensions. Alone among them, Japan has made the tensions dynamic — producing enormous social energy, stability, and the capacity to absorb change....

> Around the start of the Christian era in Europe, Mongoloid people invaded Japan through Korea and organized themselves into small clans.... The leaders of these clans were men of vision. In 552 A.D., Buddhist missionaries arrived from Korea. [Japanese] Amato rulers, sending emissaries to see the *T'ang* Court in China, realized the deficiencies of their society. Thus began a long history of judicious selective borrowing by the Japanese people....

> For four centuries (9th - 13th), first one then another established warlord ... [became] military dictator or shogun. ...
>
> The burgeoning Japanese spirit began to absorb another important influence. The Buddhist teaching of Zen brought from China offered enlightenment ..., an immediate perception of unlimited reality. ... They [the ways to achieve enlightenment] pursue a Taoist paradox from China — "To seek the universal rhythm, find a stillness in movement. ... All ways require great self-discipline and long *training in technique.* [They require] order, harmony, balance, *without false symmetry.* ... The aim is to transcend technique. Enter at one stroke," says a Zen master. The property which all Zen ways of enlightenment have in common is their difficulty. Their emphasis on training, self-discipline, and commitment to action had great appeal to the warriors.28
> — "Asian Insights"
> Film Australia Documentary

The T'ang dynasty ruled imperial China during its most vigorous and creative age — 618-907 A.D.29 As both Buddhism and Taoism had become well established in China by this time, their tenets undoubtedly influenced the thinking of T'ang military scholars. How these scholars interpreted Sun Tzu's work was incorporated into its subsequent publications, in much the same way as forewords are added to modern books. In other words, T'ang military scholars helped to write what is recognized today as *The Art of War*:

> During the eleventh century his comments on the text together with the remarks of ten respected T'ang and Sung commentators were collated in an "official" edition.30
> — Gen. Samuel B. Griffith

Finally, Zen Buddhism was introduced into Japan from China (about 1200 A.D.) during the Sung dynasty.31 By disturbing coincidence, the methods that Zen Buddhists developed to perceive "reality" (according to the Australian documentary) closely resemble the methods with which German stormtroopers and Marine NCO's learned to resolve real-world combat situations. They all trained in techniques that provided the "stillness of movement and the harmony of action to enter their respective objectives at one stroke." Further, they all "avoided false symmetry" so as to "transcend their techniques." There is also a good match between the precepts of maneuver warfare and the paradoxes of Taoism — e.g., attack without appearing to attack, defend without appearing to defend, do other than what is expected, etc. The unsettling inference is that Japanese squads and platoons may have instinctively known how to perform something similar to maneuver warfare as early as *1200 A.D.* Mainland Orientals may have had the capability to apply the core precepts of maneuver warfare — soft-spot tactics, surprise and momentum, flexibility and initiative, attacking an enemy's center of gravity, etc. — as early as *350 B.C.*:

> To advance irresistibly, push through their *gaps* [italics added].32
> — Sun Tzu

> Attack when they are unprepared, make your move when they do not expect it.33
> — Sun Tzu

> A speedy victory is the main object in war. If this is long in coming, weapons will be blunted and morale depressed.34
> — Sun Tzu

> When the speed of rushing water reaches the point where it can move boulders, this is the force of *momentum* [italics added].35
> — Sun Tzu

> Sun Tzu advocated that one should take the *initiative* and be *flexible* in fighting a war. Try to grasp the *crux of the battle* and attack where the enemy feels invulnerable, thus bringing about a *decisive change* [italics added throughout].36

## HAS MANEUVER WARFARE EVER BEEN USED AGAINST U.S. FORCES?

American Indians, Confederates, and Boxers notwithstanding, the U.S. encountered its first opponent skilled at maneuver warfare during WWI. In the Jacobsbrunnen Raid of 3 November 1917, Germans captured 11 Americans while suffering 9 wounded and 1 captured themselves. They began with two separate diversions nearby: (1) a feigned raid supported by artillery, and (2) an artillery barrage by itself. Five minutes later, they shelled the point of attack with precision, bangalored the wire, and then leapt into the trench as the shelling stopped to the complete surprise of the U.S. defenders.37 By the time Marines entered the fray to blunt the German Spring Offensive of 1918, *all* participating German infantry squads were using infiltration tactics that had evolved from the stormtroop techniques of the year before.38 In other words, German line infantry squads could keep going along paths of least resistance through successive Allied positions; they didn't have to stay on line with each other:

> In the spring of 1918, the Germans embarked on a major offensive.... The new offensive doctrine called for ... assault units to infiltrate enemy

weak spots and drive deep into his rear to disorganize his defense. The tactics worked well....
Modern infantry tactics are rooted in German defense-in-depth and infiltration tactics.[39]
— MCI 7401

Moreover, for the Germans, an elastic defense in depth replaced the standard linear defense.[40] For a Western nation, this was a significant departure from established procedure, because small units were allowed to *pull back* on their own initiative.

By the time U.S. troops augmented White Russian forces right after WWI, their Red Russian adversaries may have already been proficient in maneuver warfare. After all, the Russians had inflicted 160,000 casualties on the Japanese in Manchuria before losing the Russo-Japanese War of 1904-1905.[41] By 1917, they had elite assault units similar to the German stormtroopers.[42] Unlike the Germans, however, they were either unwilling or unable to pass this assault unit skill along to their line infantry squads.

Shortly thereafter, with the possible help of German advisers, a future adversary of the U.S. in the Pacific reassessed its infantry tactics and control structure:

By 1920 IJA [Imperial Japanese Army] tacticians realized the need to disperse infantry formations in order to reduce losses when attacking a defender who possessed the lethal firepower of modern weapons. The revised 1925 edition of the *Infantry Manual* emphasized tactics designed to allow the attacker to reach the enemy defender's position.[43]
— *Kwantung Army*

... These included infantry cooperation with other combat arms, ... night fighting and maneuver, ... increased reliance on the independent decision-making ability of junior officers and *non-commissioned officers* [italics added]. ...

By the 1930's, IJA planners realized more than ever that the Japanese army could not fight a war of attrition against the ever growing might of the Soviet Union. Consequently, they designed and refined their tactics to wage a short war fought to a quick and decisive conclusion. ... The goal ... was to encircle the enemy.[44]
— Leavenworth Papers No. 2

The tactics employed to achieve that end relied on the unit mobility, initiative, concentration of forces, night attack and movement, and close cooperation between artillery and infantry.[45]
— *Kwantung Army*

Coupled with the spiritual or psychological values of offensive spirit ... such tactics produced one of the finest infantry armies in the world. ...
It was an army ... that tried to use doctrine to compensate for materiel deficiencies.[46]
— Leavenworth Papers No. 2

America's future Cold-War adversary was fine tuning its infantry tactics as well. Pre-WWII Russian manuals stressed concepts reminiscent of maneuver warfare:

Surprise has a stunning effect. Therefore all troop action must be accomplished with the greatest secrecy and speed. Swiftness of action in combination with organization, skillful maneuver, and ability to adapt to the terrain ... are the basic guarantees of success in battle.[47]
— Red Army Fld.Serv.Regs.[1936]

When Japan and Russia came to blows in Manchuria in 1939, each got the opportunity to test its maneuver warfare skills against an equally proficient opponent. Although an edge in armor and logistics finally tipped the scales in favor of the Russians, it was only their skill in small-unit maneuver warfare that kept them in the fight:

Soviet doctrine, they [the Japanese] felt, was too inflexible and the Russian character too rigid to adapt quickly to Japanese tactics which stressed surprise and maneuver.[48]
— Leavenworth Papers No. 2

These [Japanese] scouts were discovering ... another shift in Soviet tactics. The enemy forward line was the weakest point of a position defended in width and depth. Japanese attackers could easily reach and break through that defense, but then they would encounter hardened defenses with interlocking bands of fire [and preregistered artillery fire]. ... Japanese scouts also overheard the sounds of hammers, picks, saws, and other construction tools indicating that the Soviets were building new fortifications [probably a Soviet deception].

But, the Soviet defenses were no longer linear like those encountered at Chang-kufeng/Lake Khasan. Instead, the enemy placed his automatic weapons in depths 500 to 1000 meters behind the initial defensive line. This enabled Soviets to provide punishing covering fire in lanes while Soviet troops withdrew to new fighting positions.[49]
— Leavenworth Papers No. 2

In the early forties, the Russians got a chance to operate at an armor and supporting-arms disadvantage themselves across the vast expanses of Western Russia. Perhaps through their Asian heritage, they had acquired considerable "sapper" or short-range infiltration skills:

In World War II, as in preceding wars, the Russian soldier demonstrated that he was closer to nature than his West European counterpart. This was hardly surprising since most of the Russian soldiers were born and raised far from big cities.... The Russian was able to move without a sound and orient himself in the darkness.... [He] performed particularly well as a night observer. Stern discipline and self-constraint enabled him to lie motionless for hours and observe the German troops at close range without being detected.... Infiltration by small detachments, as well as by larger units up to an entire division, was probably the most effective Russian method of night combat.... Time and again their troops slipped through a lightly held sector during the night and were securely behind the German front by the next morning.[50]

— DOA Pamphlet 20-236

In WWII, the Germans continued to refine the same precepts they had pioneered 20 years earlier. They launched lightning-fast "blitzkriegs" through gaps seized with small-scale infiltration attacks. Germans masquerading as Americans initiated the Battle of the Bulge.

On the other side of the world, the Japanese were refining their warfighting skills as well — in the Pacific. After all, they had used German advisers and "followed German military methods" since 1871.[51] Their ability to surprise an opponent that is still a painful memory for many Americans. They used short-range infiltration tactics against the Marines on Guadalcanal. One night a Marine platoon caught 9 of them trying to slip through their lines.[52] For whatever reason, Marine commanders apparently deduced that every infiltrator was a sniper. Major General Vandegrift's Chief of Staff estimated that hundreds of Japanese had gotten through friendly lines, but saw little incongruity in the fact that only one Marine had been killed by a sniper.[53] Most of these infiltrators were probably reconnaissance scouts for subsequent attacks, and forward observers for naval gunfire:

Japs [on Guadalcanal] who have infiltrated signal to each other with their rifles by the number of shots.[54]

— One NCO to Chesty Puller

A lot of these Japs who infiltrate have radios. Think of this advantage in respect to artillery, mortar fire, location of troops, etc.[55]

— Another NCO to Chesty Puller

Other infiltrators were after command centers and possibly ammunition dumps:

Small groups of enemy that have infiltrated may appear any place. On Guadalcanal a three-man enemy patrol attacked the First Marine CP [Command Post].[56]

— FMFRP 12-9

To force open gaps through which follow-on forces could move, the Japanese also employed night attacks across narrow frontages. These attacks were hauntingly reminiscent of the ones perfected by German stormtroopers in WWI. General Vandegrift's Chief of Staff noticed that, "When given his choice, he [the Japanese] operates exclusively at night;...he attacks on a very narrow front, practically en masse."[57] The similarities to maneuver warfare do not end with the Japanese offensive method:

[T]hey [the Japanese] have surprised us by being in a defensive position on the reverse slope of a ridge.[58]

— Marine Plt.Sgt. F.T. O'Fara

Whether the Japs will continue to fight as they do now, I don't know. They defend on the low ground in the jungle.[59]

— Col. Merritt A. Edson

When we first got here the Japanese fooled us as they like to place their machineguns on the reverse slope of the ridge, shooting upwards.[60]

— CO, 3rd Bn., 164th Infantry

I was in one advance when the Japs let us come through and then rose up out of covered fox holes and shot us in the back.[61]

— Sergeant O.J. Marion

Not all the Marines who faced the Japanese later in the Pacific War would agree that their opponents were using maneuver warfare. They might point out that defending a location "to the death" is inconsistent with maneuver warfare. Perhaps, the Japanese would have pulled back more often, if there had been anywhere to go on those tiny islands, or if a tunnel or trench had connected every hole with a fallback position. And maybe the Japanese would have pulled back more if a strict interpretation of their code of honor — Bushido (Way of the Samurai) — had not grown out of their severe losses in the Russo-Japanese War of 1904-1905.[62] Too strict a code of honor might hamper one's ability to execute a maneuver warfare defense. This should serve as a warning to those Americans who see dishonor in pulling back when outnumbered. Old-timers might argue that shouting "banzai" and charging U.S. positions is inconsistent with maneuver warfare. Some who were there claim that the Japanese would not shout this signal to assault until they had been discovered close to U.S. lines. This may have been just another example of the Japanese code of honor adversely affecting their execution of what was essentially a maneuver warfare offense. After all, there are contemporary maneuver warfare enthusiasts who have yet to conclude that a standup assault should be conducted quietly after diverting the enemy's attention. Again, this should serve as a warning to American commanders who might want to continue an attack after surprise had been irretrievably compromised.

After analyzing Japanese tactics on an island with ample room for maneuver, Guadalcanal's commander identified the warfare style as "unconventional" and told the Marines back home how to prepare for it:

> My message ... to the troops training for this type of warfare is to go back to the tactics of the French and Indian days.[63]
> — Maj.Gen. Vandegrift

The founder of the Marine Raiders already understood how to conduct this "new" style of warfare:

> A thin force from the Marine 2nd Raider Battalion, foraging behind enemy lines [on the island of Guadalcanal], killed more than 500 Japanese. They were led by Col. Evans Carlson, a maverick who had marched as an observer with Mao Zedong's [Mao Tse-tung's] 8th Route Army and transfused Mao's guerrilla tactics to his own troops along with a motto that stressed unity and spirit. Gung ho — work together ... Marines who fought future wars in Korea and Vietnam mouthed it still, unaware that this inspirational slogan was taken from a Communist.[64]

In the early fifties, the North Koreans got the chance to exhibit their prowess in this alternative style of warfare. After all, their ancient culture had endured lengthy occupations by both Chinese and Japanese. If by 1950, the North Koreans had not learned maneuver warfare from their Oriental occupiers, they had learned it from their Soviet military advisers. When large Chinese Communist forces suddenly appeared around the Chosin Reservoir late in 1950, it came as quite a surprise to the Marines. The Chinese Communists had become adept at long-range infiltration. Chesty Puller noticed that the Communist expertise extended to *small-scale combat* as well:

> I'm afraid we haven't recognized the most important lesson from Korea. The Communists have developed a totally new kind of warfare.... This is a total warfare, yet small in scope, and it's designed to neutralize our big ... weapons. Look at Vietnam. The French outnumbered the Communists two to one, yet they were massacred.[65]
> — Chesty Puller

> My prayer now is that our leaders, knowing that we have no war machine, will evacuate Korea completely, have a thorough house cleaning, and then rebuild a real war machine before becoming involved in another war. May God give us wisdom and common sense![66]
> — Chesty Puller

Then, there was the Vietnam experience — America's longest war. By the mid-sixties, Americans were painfully aware of the very real threat posed by Communism and publicly opposed to any form of political subversion. Unfortunately, they still had to endure a tragedy of semantics — they encountered the term "guerrilla warfare." Because a Communist government was involved, they jumped to the conclusion that guerrilla warfare was an immoral and cowardly alternative to conventional warfare. They forgot that guerrilla warfare could be waged without political subversion and that in 1776 their forefathers did just that. What would maneuver warfare look like, if only a few soldiers comprised the maneuver element? These few soldiers would hit and run, refuse to stand and fight, lure opponents into traps, ambush, infiltrate, etc. Could it be that instead of facing a doped-up, maltreated, and ignorant Third-World militia in Vietnam, U.S. forces were actually facing a flexible and opportunistic opponent thoroughly trained in maneuver warfare at the small-unit level? Individuals and small units certainly have ample opportunity to exercise initiative in guerrilla warfare. Could a dictatorial regime maintain political control and still decentralize tactical control? What if that regime required each soldier (of any rank) to report immediately any mistake he personally witnessed? The evidence that guerrilla warfare is nothing more than maneuver warfare practiced at the small-unit level is overwhelming:

> ... [T]he basis for guerrilla discipline must be the individual conscience. With guerrillas a discipline of compulsion is ineffective....
> In guerrilla warfare select the tactic of seeming to come from the east and attacking from the west; avoid the solid, attack the hollow; attack; withdraw; deliver a lightning blow; seek a lightning decision.
> ... [I]f we cannot kill the enemy troops, we can capture them. The total effect of many local successes will be to change the relative strengths of the opposing forces.[67]
> — Mao Tse-tung
> (printed in 1941 "Gazette")

Commander-in-Chief Vo Nguyen Giap ... skillfully adapted Mao Tse-tung's Chinese model for a revolutionary army to the situation in Vietnam.[68]

To exploit the American problems, Vinh [Hanoi's liaison with its headquarters in the South] emphasized, the question of strategy and tactics were all-important. "In a war of position, they can defeat us," he said. "But with our present tactics, we can win and they will be defeated."

In pursuing their strategy of protracted warfare the North Vietnamese relied on precepts summed up in Mao Tse-tung's maxim, "The strategy of guerrilla war is to pit one man against ten, but the tactics are to pit ten men against one." In other words, the North Vietnamese and Viet Cong, although numerically inferior, had to discover the weaknesses in allied formations and defenses and then mass for attacks on smaller concentrations of enemy troops or lightly defended posts. Then their tactics emphasized surprise, speed, and elusiveness, and they chose not to fight unless they had the advantage in numbers.69

Just because American forces have never practiced maneuver warfare at the small-unit level, doesn't mean that it's impossible to do. And, just because other armies have political commissars with which to subvert local populaces, doesn't mean that their small-unit infantry tactics are necessarily "bad" as well. The NVA and Viet Cong would keep their defensive formations hidden until the last moment. More than one U.S. unit got lured into a trap resembling a fire sack. Additionally, the enemy displayed great proficiency at sapper style infiltration. During the five months that one Marine lieutenant spent at base camps in Vietnam, he encountered enemy infiltrators reconnoitering these camps from the inside on two separate occasions.70 Early one morning in 1966, several hours after seeing what looked like an enemy soldier wriggling through the protective wire at Dong Ha, the young officer personally spotted the first infiltrator. While inspecting the ground just outside the wire, he saw a black figure run behind a low hillock some 50 yards away and disappear. The intruder must have dived down a spider hole, but that hole could never be located. In early 1968 inside the 27th Marines compound southwest of Da Nang, the same lieutenant narrowly missed seeing another infiltrator. On a dimly lit path to his billeting area, he ran into a friend who had just bumped into a small black figure who subsequently clotheslined himself on someone's wash before running off into the night. Occasionally captured were maps of U.S. installations so detailed that they could have only been made by infiltrators. That U.S. troops underestimated their adversary's ability to infiltrate their defenses almost at will has a perfectly logical explanation. After all, any self-respecting infiltrator is also an accomplished "exfiltrator," and timing devices for explosives are not that hard to fabricate. One wonders how many of the ammunition dumps that went up did so with the help of an infiltrator instead of a lucky mortar round. For whatever reason, it would appear that the NVA had small-unit tactics *more advanced* than those of U.S. forces. Here's how the enemy commander described these tactics:

Relying on two cardinal principles of the art of war, secrecy and surprise, they [the NVA] would strike when and where the enemy was the most vulnerable.... Giap had repeatedly argued that a commitment to big-unit warfare was inappropriate against an enemy with vastly superior mobility and firepower.71

**Apply Various Forms of Combat**
In any war, after having concentrated large and powerful forces in the right direction and at the right time, we must also solve an equally important question, which is to choose and make full use of the most appropriate *form of combat*. Only by so doing can we create the necessary strength on the battlefield to win victory....

These were campaigns of *large-scale combined attacks by various armed services* in which many large strategic army columns equipped with modern weapons and war means and having high mobility were utilized to attack the enemy over vast areas and within a short period of time, at a very high tempo and with definite objectives in mind. During these campaigns our army carried out very extensively *the strategic splitting and large-scale encirclement of the enemy forces. It suddenly attacked their nerve centers to wipe out and disintegrate all their important defense complexes*....

In Hue our army did not attack the outposts in the outer defense perimeter but rapidly carried out the strategic splitting of enemy forces, made deep thrusts into their rear, upsetting their battle array, then encircled, split, attacked and wiped them out in their inner defense perimeter....

**Lure the Enemy into Committing Errors**
Surprise is a very important factor in war. In many cases it has a decisive effect upon the success or failure of a battle. To use the surprise factor to defeat the enemy is a major problem in military art. This is the art of catching the enemy by surprise as to the direction, targets and time of our attack, the forces fielded and the forms of combat used by our side. From one battle to another, we must create surprise in the most varied ways in order to cause repeated and even bigger surprises to the enemy. We must use skillful stratagems to deceive the enemy and cause them to make a wrong assessment of our intentions. At the same time, we must quickly take advantage of and aggravate these errors in order to cause them ever greater surprises and eventually defeat them completely [bold print and italics from original throughout].72

— Gen. Vo Nguyen Giap
(from *How We Won the War*)

A Different Style of Warfare May Be Necessary

(Source: "Preventive Maintenance: M203 and M79 Grenade Launcher" (pamphlet reproduced by U.S. Army Armor School, Fort Knox, Kentucky)

As the Vietnam War dragged on, a few U.S. commanders — like Lt.Col. D.H. Hackworth — tried to imitate NVA tactics in an attempt to win more consistently and at lower cost. Even their ideas distinctly resemble the central precepts of maneuver warfare:

> [T]he only way to defeat the present enemy in the present war *at a low cost in friendly casualties* [italics added] was through adopting the enemy's own tactics, i.e. "out G-ing the G [Guerrilla]" through surprise, deception, cunning, mobility..., imagination, and familiarity with the terrain.[73]

In summary, there is considerable evidence to suggest that *every major adversary the United States has faced **since the turn of the century** has been skilled in maneuver warfare at the small-unit level:*

> Modern tactics are third-generation tactics.... Infiltration tactics were used successfully by the Chinese in the Korea War, by the North Vietnamese in the Vietnam War, and by the British in the Falklands.[74]
> — MCI 7401

Maybe it's time for Americans to develop more small-unit tactical expertise of their own. According to Liddell Hart, young officers in Chiang Kai-shek's army also mistakenly thought Sun Tzu's ideas outmoded by advances in technology:

> He [a Chinese military attaché] replied that while Sun Tzu's book was venerated as a classic, it was considered out of date by most of the younger officers, and thus hardly worth study in the era of mechanized weapons.[75]

Could there be a lesson here for U.S. infantrymen? Could Sun Tzu's ideas actually be *the way to counter ongoing advances in weapons technology?* Perhaps, because 2300 years after their inception, those ideas continue to shape military thought throughout Asia and Eastern Europe:

> "The Art of War" has had a profound influence throughout Chinese history and on Japanese thought; it is the source of Mao Tse-tung's strategic theories and of the tactical doctrine of the Chinese armies. Through the Mongol-Tartars, Sun Tzu's ideas were transmitted to Russia and became a substantial part of her oriental heritage. "The Art of War" is thus required reading for those who hope to gain a further understanding of the grand strategy of these two countries today.[76]
> — Gen. Samuel B. Griffith

# 6 Perhaps the Role of the Small Unit Must Change

- *How can U.S. infantry squads best contribute to maneuver warfare?*
- *Can self-discipline and self-criticism replace centralized control?*
- *Can the opposing styles of warfare be mixed?*

(Source: FM 22-100 (1983), p. 36)

### WHAT IT TAKES TO CONDUCT MANEUVER WARFARE AT THE SMALL-UNIT LEVEL

Practicing maneuver warfare under the widest assortment of circumstances entails allowing squad-sized (and smaller) units to operate independently. Discipline can often be enhanced by decentralizing control. On the other hand, troops who are seldom allowed to think for themselves will always appear headstrong.

The Asian armies have known how to employ small units in maneuver warfare for at least sixty and perhaps hundreds of years. That means that they have allowed their small-unit leaders to exercise initiative in the absence of orders. It also means that these small-unit leaders have occasionally made mistakes and taken actions inconsistent with their commander's intent. Yet, these Oriental armies have never suffered from major disciplinary problems. With enough training, American soldiers can do the same thing.

One would guess that maneuver warfare at the fire team or squad level might resemble Maoist guerrilla tactics. It would involve surprising the enemy on both offense and defense, and then shifting location before that enemy could properly react. It would also involve stringing such contacts together in series to keep the enemy off balance. Some assume that it always takes speed to develop momentum. This is not true. All that is required is for the next action to occur before the enemy stops thinking about the last one. Any action that the enemy considers to be untimely qualifies, no matter how long it takes. When two men spend eight hours crawling 100 yards through enemy lines to place a demolition charge in an ammunition dump, are they not blowing up the dump before their adversary expects it? If the intruders rig the explosives with a timer and then sneak back out, they can probably do the same thing to the fuel dump the next night. To practice maneuver warfare at the small-unit level, infantrymen must also have patience. For Americans, this will take special training:

> Men should receive training in *patience* [italics from original]. Our national character is foreign to this idea. We are an impetuous people. Training in patience is needed.[1]
> — "Lessons Learned" from *Fighting on Guadalcanal*

Of course, speed is very important to small-unit warfighting too. For the unit attempting to cross open ground in the daytime, speed is often the wiser choice. A running assault can succeed, if the enemy's attention can somehow be diverted.

In an apparent contradiction of terms, it would seem (from the German experience in WWI) that small units can best *prepare for maneuver warfare* by rehearsing *formulas of action* ahead of time. Only through rehearsal, can they acquire enough speed (or patience) to do what is required before the enemy expects it:

> Although the German infantry at Cambrai . . . were organized and equipped for . . . attack "with limited objectives," they did not have the advantage of being able to prepare for weeks . . . for an advance of a few hundred meters. Once the first trench system was reached, there was no time for a detailed reconnaissance. . . . The decision to attack, and the approach used was decided instantly, on the basis of a quick look at a large-scale map and a hasty analysis of the situation. Painstaking preparation and repeated rehearsal had been replaced by rapid improvisation and the almost instinctive execution of battle drills.[2]

But, unlike the formulas associated with attrition warfare, these formulas would *not* have to be strictly adhered to in combat. Rather, they should lend themselves to modification to fit an ever changing situation. They should be technique, *as opposed to doctrine*. The "father" of maneuver warfare in the Marine Corps freely acknowledges that techniques are crucial to this alternative style:

> While maneuver warfare cannot be done by formula, some formulas may be helpful in doing it. As already noted, techniques are formulas . . . and they are very important to maneuver warfare.[3]
> — Bill Lind

Moreover, the best way to keep tactical techniques current with the ever-changing threat is to permit subunits to *regenerate* them continually. If every commander simply keeps himself informed of the techniques developed by his subordinates, he can decentralize control and still loosely regulate what goes on in combat.

Many formulas at the squad level or below could actually serve the best interests of maneuver warfare. Line infantry squads trained in stormtroop tactics were the spearheads of the German Spring Offensive of 1918. All that prevented these squads from breaking through the Allied defensive network was its extreme depth and the seemingly endless supply of men to man it. Many believe that contemporary American enlisted men have the potential to duplicate the German accomplishment. However, as Bill Lind points out, the "system" has been slow to agree with this optimistic assessment of American youth:

> Although combat experience should indicate otherwise, the rifle squad currently occupies a relatively minor place in . . . tactical thought. Squad level training and doctrine seem to suggest that the squad has little independent tactical value. The squad has been relegated to the role of subunit whose movements are closely controlled by the platoon commander. Considered in terms of maneuver warfare, this attitude is disastrous . . . (maneuver warfare demands that the squad assume a primary tactical role).[4]
> — Bill Lind

One wonders what type of technique might lend itself to modification as the situation changes. In a paradox of Oriental proportions, a technique with enough steps to handle a worst-case scenario might qualify — if its steps were *optional*, and if these steps could be performed in any order. A unit executing only those steps absolutely required by the unfolding situation, could remain flexible to unforeseen circumstances and better surprise its adversary. Of course, the steps themselves would also have to be somewhat *provisional* in nature to permit individual initiative, but they could still be executed fairly methodically. That means they could be rehearsed. With such a technique, a small unit could neutralize any threat — unforeseen or otherwise — as it started to restrict maneuver:

> Ensure that both plan and dispositions are flexible — adaptable to circumstances. Your plan should foresee and provide for a next step in case of success or failure, or partial success — which is the most common case in war. Your dispositions (or formation) should be such as to allow this exploitation or adaption in the shortest possible time.[5]
> — Liddell Hart

This means that some maneuver warfare techniques might look fairly complicated, and might even resemble "immediate-action drills" during rehearsal. Yet, these would be quite different from the techniques of attrition warfare. They wouldn't have to be put into practice precisely as rehearsed.

Maneuver warfare techniques for worst-case scenarios could usefully augment the attrition warfare techniques in the manuals. Each would be a collection of separate procedures to overcome the most prevalent conditions and threats in combat. The procedures would not have to be executed in any particular order, or, in fact, at all. Such procedures could be easily mixed and matched to handle any situation. For example, to penetrate a defensive perimeter, a squad might have to neutralize a machinegun emplacement with its shoulder fired "bunker buster" (SMAW) and breach protective barbed wire with its bangalore torpedoes. Whether these steps would be necessary, and in what order, would depend on how close the squad could get to the objective without being discovered, and on when the machinegun and barbed wire were encountered. In actual combat, this information is not always available ahead of time. In fact, most defenders attempt to hide their automatic weapons and obstacles. By rehearsing the steps before the battle, the attacking unit could ensure that its members had the teamwork to accomplish those steps. The intricacies of operating each weapon notwithstanding, employing both SMAW and bangalore in tandem takes teamwork. Rising up to fire a SMAW while a bangalore is going off can be detrimental to one's health, and trying to detonate a bangalore from inside the backblast area of a SMAW can be equally distressing. A well-rehearsed unit could combine steps from its various techniques to handle whatever situation were encountered. The author of *The Maneuver Warfare Handbook* staunchly endorses the employment of techniques:

> Some Marines accuse spokesmen for maneuver warfare of incorrectly deemphasizing the importance of techniques.... Any such deemphasis would indeed be incorrect. Excellence in techniques is highly important in *any* [italics from original] style of warfare.... Maneuver warfare demands excellence in techniques, but it demands more: creativity and originality in selecting from among and combining techniques.[6]
> — Bill Lind in MCI 7401

Combat veterans understand the subtle difference between learning automatic reflexes and preparing to survive. The authors of U.S. manuals may well have intended for their methodical small-unit techniques to be used in a maneuver warfare context. Still, what is intended, and how it is perceived at the bottom of a tall control structure, are not always identical. The original intent of any manual, unless clearly spelled out, may not reach the line infantry squad. Just one overeager disciplinarian or novice trainer anywhere in the long chain of command can turn what may have been intended as productive tactical guidance into counterproductive tactical edicts — rules that must be obeyed every time, no matter what the cost.

Of course, any technique has more utility when practiced under the circumstances for which it was designed. The small unit that is *allowed to choose when and where to fight,* can make any technique work for a while. But for that technique to succeed consistently, it must in no way inhibit the unit's ability to react to the unexpected.

## TO PRACTICE MANEUVER WARFARE, UNITS MUST REPLACE CENTRALIZED CONTROL WITH PERIODIC SELF-CRITICISM

Unit leaders must overcome the temptation to perceive every enemy encounter as a victory. Doing so makes it more difficult to improve. If the leaders can admit occasionally to doing poorly, and analyze why, they can upgrade their tactics in time to help win the war.

Contemporary U.S. fire teams spend most of their limited field training time practicing the formations with which to execute uniformly the decisions of their superiors. The only way they can make a mistake is not to follow whatever manual is available or not to do exactly what they have been told. Little, if any, importance is attributed to what they might learn from the situation or from each other. The North Vietnamese had a different way of controlling their fire teams that did not squelch initiative. Their concept of *Kiem thao* may provide some insight into how U.S. forces might decentralize tactical control and still maintain good order:

> As much as the [three-man] cells constituted a "home," they were a prison as well since the members had to watch each other and criticize any untoward behavior either military or political.... In *Kiem thao* sessions, the soldiers offered judgments of their comrades and listened to evaluations of their own performances. The meetings sometimes featured discussions of tactics from the unit's recent engagements or suggestions ... sent from the army command. *Kiem thao* sessions could become extremely heated and emotional. For some soldiers the sessions were especially traumatic, as they heard their weaknesses and failings denounced publicly and then had to respond to those charges.[7]

While the Communists encouraged their soldiers to "rat" on each other both tactically and politically, Americans could encourage theirs only to offer constructive tactical criticism. The worst that might happen would be additional insight into how to improve U.S. tactics.

## CAN OPPOSITE STYLES OF WARFARE BE COMBINED SUCCESSFULLY?

Few would disagree that either style of warfare will work under ideal circumstances. Further, different styles of warfare might work during subsequent phases of the same tactical evolution. For example, maneuver warfare might be needed to get close to an objective, and then attrition warfare to penetrate its barbed wire. The opposition forces in Vietnam were adept at both styles of warfare and able to shift easily between them as the situation dictated. This ability to switch styles was abundantly obvious at the large-unit level; in fact, Giap's writings in the early sixties discuss it in some depth:

> As the power balance shifts in favor of the Communists, guerrilla warfare gives way to a war of mobility, using regular forces, but without fixed battle lines. In the final stages, this is combined with some positional warfare.[8]
> —Gen. Vo Nguyen Giap
> *Peoples War - Peoples Army*
> (published in U.S. in 1962)

That small NVA units could switch at will between styles of warfare is evident from the photographs. In one picture, enemy soldiers are seen assaulting on line in the daytime. Their assault appears to be fairly methodical in nature, except that few, if any, North Vietnamese soldiers are actually firing their small arms.[9] The enemy's plan of attack undoubtedly came straight out of the maneuver warfare play book. Separate elements probably rendezvoused near their objective before dawn, and then at first light assaulted (without shooting) right behind what the defenders believed to be just another mortar barrage. Because the occasional NVA frontal assault from short range closely resembled what U.S. units practiced regularly from any distance, and because NVA units quickly abandoned whatever ground they had captured, many U.S. leaders were deceived. They believed their subordinates not only evenly matched, but also winning the war:

> ... In battle, 10 [NVA] soldiers might attempt to isolate and rush 2 or 3 enemy. Whether assaulting a fixed position or laying an ambush, the North Vietnamese rigidly adhered to a tactic known as "one slow, and four quick." Slow meant meticulous methodical planning ... with reconnaissance, sand table exercises ..., and rehearsals. During the planning period logisticians sent ammunition, food, and medical supplies to be cached near the intended battlefield. Only when all was in readiness did the infantry embark on its four "quicks": movement, attack, battlefield policing, and withdrawal.
>
> ... The infantry moved in dispersed groups to the battle area, joining in formation only at the scene. With ambush parties positioned on the flanks to intercept any relief effort, the unit launched the ambush or attack. The action often came at night or in bad weather when U.S. air activities were reduced. In combat the North Vietnamese closed with the defenders as tightly as possible sometimes engaging in hand-to-hand fighting so that tactical air power or artillery could not be called against them. The soldiers tried to bring down the spotter planes of the Forward Air Controller who located targets for fighter aircraft....
>
> When the tactical objectives had been met, or if the attack was failing, the NVA began to break contact. As they did so, they continued to pepper the enemy with rifle fire as any abandoned weapons were collected. After wounded and dead, in that order, had been evacuated ... the NVA fell back in the order of heavy weapons, infantry, reserve elements, and flank guards. A rear guard often remained on the battlefield to keep the enemy pinned down and slow any pursuit. The preplanned route of withdrawal always differed from the path of advance, and an alternate route led in yet another direction.[10]

U.S. infantrymen should formulate some guidelines on when to use this other style of warfare themselves. The temptation is to say that a localized combat power advantage would justify attrition warfare, whereas a disadvantage would make maneuver warfare more attractive. However, America's policy to limit casualties may make maneuver warfare the preferred alternative even when there is no combat power advantage.

Unfortunately, at the small-unit level, a certain amount of closing with the enemy is unavoidable and so too is a certain amount of attrition warfare. The final stages of assault techniques may have to be somewhat methodical, albeit quieter; but the initial and follow-up stages can still be based on maneuver warfare precepts. But when the two styles can most productively be combined must wait until the American viewpoint on "when to advance and when to hold" is examined.

# 7 Another Outlook on When to Advance and When to Hold

- What are the relative merits of attacking and defending?
- How many new options for each has maneuver warfare created?
- Can opposing styles of warfare be mixed to solve a single situation?

(Sources: FM 23-30 (1988), p. 2-6; FM 90-10-1 (1982), p. B-4)

**TO CAPTURE THE MOMENTUM, A UNIT MUST KNOW WHEN TO HOLD ITS GROUND, AND WHEN TO ADVANCE**

The American way of war has been to defend to the death every line drawn in the sand and to attack with guns blazing, every concentration of enemy. To fight this way takes an overwhelming combat power advantage. Sometimes, it is more effective and less costly to let the enemy cross that line, and then to attack his logistics train with very little firing. All can agree that any tactical technique will have more value when its practitioner has loose guidelines on when to attack or defend. What those guidelines might be has troubled military thinkers for centuries. Some prefer to sidestep the issue altogether.

Professional infantrymen can't sidestep it. When a U.S. patrol bumps into its enemy counterpart on the battlefield, it must rapidly make a decision that will influence every subsequent decision — whether to advance, hold its ground, or give way. In other words, it must decide whether to attack, defend, or retreat. One is tempted to advise prospective patrol members always to attack. Doing so will give them a chance at achieving momentum and winning conclusively. According to Sun Tzu, a good defense can keep a unit from getting beaten, but it can't by itself permit that unit to win decisively:

Invincibility lies in the defense; the possibility of victory in the attack.[1]
— Sun Tzu

However, winning football coaches persist in attributing as much of their success to a strong defense, as to momentum. One wonders if there might be some link between the two. *Webster's* says that momentum is "the force with which a body moves against resistance."2 In other words, a unit can't have momentum without moving forward. Momentum belongs to the side that has just attacked successfully, and then attacks again. But, it also belongs to the side that has just defended successfully, and then counterattacks. A strong defense can interrupt an enemy's impetus, thereby creating an opportunity to attack. So, in terms of establishing momentum, a strong defense can be important. Football teams and rifle squads need proficiency at both offense and defense. It might be interesting to compare the relative merits of these opposing courses of action.

## THE RELATIVE STRENGTHS AND WEAKNESSES OF THE DEFENSE

Defenders have some distinct advantages over attackers. They can often choose where to fight. For this reason, they are more familiar with the terrain, and can enhance that terrain with manmade obstacles. Additionally, they have stationary platforms from which to fire; and they are less exposed and harder to shoot.

But, defenders don't have momentum. They are generally forced to react to whatever their attackers do, instead of having the opportunity to initiate decisive actions of their own. They are often "ripe for the picking" by well-trained attackers. In fact, a steady diet of defense tends to weaken one's focus and attitude — and ultimately his survivability. Forced to defend too often, even brave men become hesitant to venture into "the unknown," and at that point become easy to surprise:

> An army that thinks only in defensive terms is doomed. It yields initiative and advantage in time and space to the enemy — even an enemy inferior in numbers. It loses the sense of the hunter, the opportunist.3
> — Gen. Sir David Fraser

If unhealthy attitudes can result from too much defense, one wonders if they might also result from being too conservative on offense, or being too cautious during patrolling. By established procedure, American patrols move along straight lines between objectives, practice stealth to a fault, treat any opening wider than a few yards as a danger area, and plan in-route rally points for those personnel who could get cut off from the main body. Although these practices may be appropriate for highly secretive missions, they are not so for missions that require mixing it up with the enemy. In fact, a steady diet of them could severely damage one's confidence. To the individual rifleman, bored by the slow movement and constant stops, and tired of "humping" his heavy load across ravines and swamps, the methods might unnecessarily drain the energy he needs to handle chance contact.

Of course, a strong defense can periodically inflict a tremendous loss in human life on an overzealous offense. But, few purely defensive battles have been won decisively. The attackers may be severely hurt, as the Federals were at Fredericksburg during the Civil War, but they are not out of contention. Their momentum is at best temporarily blunted. To have real worth, this break in enemy momentum must be exploited by a counterattack. President Lincoln instinctively understood this, and after Gettysburg chided General Meade for not pinning the Confederate Army against the Potomac. The counterattack is what initiates friendly momentum, but it must sometimes be delayed so as not to become too predictable.

## THE PROS AND CONS OF THE ATTACK

Attacks can be decisive in war. They can surprise an enemy, and they can exploit success. If there is any room for maneuver, they can be rapidly conducted in series to demoralize an enemy into surrendering. Attacks such as these saved many lives in the Gulf War.

Small units can also move quickly from one attack objective to another — simply by alternating well-rehearsed attack techniques. The speed that can be generated this way, has long been recognized as an asset in war:

> Speed is the essence of war. Take advantage of the enemy's unpreparedness; travel by unexpected routes and strike him where he has taken no precautions.4
> — Sun Tzu

Being outnumbered does not preclude the use of a good attack technique. A small unit can defeat a larger unit by tackling its component parts separately. All that is needed is a localized combat power advantage for each separate engagement. Of course, it helps when each enemy subunit can be attacked without alerting its sister subunits to the danger. Stonewall Jackson's "foot cavalry" moved so quickly in the Shenandoah Valley that they could tackle individually, separate components of the same force:

> We must make this campaign an exceedingly active one. Only thus can a weaker country cope with a stronger; it must make up in activity what it lacks in strength.5
> — Stonewall Jackson

Of course, by attacking, a small unit also becomes more vulnerable to enemy fire. Even successful assaults result in minor casualties. As the training status of an attacking unit continually erodes, its commander is tempted to tighten the control over his subordinates at the expense of their initiative. Where the terrain conceals mutually supporting defensive positions and provides no room for maneuver, an attacking unit can also have great difficulty establishing momentum. That was the predicament Marines faced on those tiny islands in the Pacific.

## WHAT TO DO *INITIALLY* WHEN A "MOVEMENT TO CONTACT" RESULTS IN "CONTACT"

When a unit on the move unexpectedly encounters enemy, there is an important, albeit short, transition period. It is not discussed in the manuals as part of the movement-to-contact phase, nor as part of the attack phase, but it still happens. Because there is no written guidance on what to do, small units tend to react tentatively to confrontation; and their reactions can become more defensive than offensive in nature. As a result, the units usually forfeit the opportunity to seize the momentum. What might be a more appropriate response?

The Laws of the Wild provide a useful source of information on the subject. In the woods, the size of the opponent doesn't seem to be the deciding factor. When confronted by a larger predator, even the smallest animal will puff itself up and lunge forward, as if to attack. Perhaps small units in chance encounters should do the same thing. If they were rapidly to deploy their full strength on line and move forward, they could initially capture the momentum and better observe enemy weaknesses. If the terrain provided little cover or the enemy were dug in, that forward movement could be discontinued.

## HASTY VERSUS DELIBERATE ATTACKS

Attacking faster than the enemy expects, is the essence of momentum. That means that a unit should probably employ as many hasty attacks, and as few deliberate attacks (those carefully planned), as possible. But, hasty attacks can only be run successfully against gaps. They cannot be conducted against enemy fire in terrain that does not offer adequate cover.

"Bounding overwatch" is a U.S. Army method for leapfrogging forward when enemy contact is imminent. After making contact this way, sister units might be tempted to continue leapfrogging in the attack. In other words, every time one ran into resistance, others would move forward to outflank the opposition. If only two units were involved, this type of procedure might be very effective. The two units would be running what amounted to hasty flanking attacks in series. Whenever withering fire or a large open area blocked their advance (when the gaps ran out), the units could initiate an attack by fire alone, a reconnaissance for a subsequent deliberate attack, or a withdrawal.

## DELIBERATE-ATTACK OPTIONS FOR SMALL UNITS

There are three deliberate-attack options for small units: (1) daylight attack, (2) night attack, and (3) short-range infiltration or "sapper" attack. Note that *long-range* infiltration has not been included. When an infantry squad goes three miles out of its way to avoid an enemy strongpoint as a part of its parent-unit's long-range infiltration plan, its actions in no way constitute an "attack." Its actions more closely resemble a "movement to contact" or "raid patrol." To a rifle squad, attacking means getting up close and personal.

Because it is easier to see one's opponent in the daytime, the daylight attack facilitates killing enemy — the goal of attrition warfare. Unfortunately, because that opponent can also see his attacker more easily, the daylight attack is the most costly of the deliberate-attack options.

At night, an attacking unit at least enjoys some measure of concealment. Unfortunately, U.S. squads and platoons have little experience in attacking at night *by themselves*. In fact, U.S. doctrine discourages night attacks against barbed wire, or with artillery preparation.

Other countries use the short-range infiltration or sapper attack. During such an attack, small elements of the same unit move by stealth through narrow gaps in enemy lines. Because these elements are attempting to bypass the enemy's gunpits, this type of attack pursues the goal of maneuver warfare. And, because these elements have the prerogative to turn back, it is also the least costly of the deliberate-attack options. While few active-duty personnel have ever conducted this type of attack in combat, thousands of veterans have defended against it. Perhaps they could help to refine promising offensive techniques.

Of the three deliberate-attack options, the short-range infiltration most closely resembles maneuver warfare. But, it takes specially trained sappers to penetrate enemy barbed wire *by stealth*. Without them, an attacking unit must force open its gaps. Sometimes one gap that can be enlarged will be enough. It doesn't take an entire company to seize a few enemy holes. This is fortunate, because only a squad-sized unit can usually get close enough to attack those holes by surprise. That is what the German stormtroop squads were doing in WWI — seizing gaps to be used by follow-on forces. Two highly trained men can do the same thing! Americans have learned this the hard way from their Oriental opponents.

## WHEN DEFENDING IS THE THING TO DO

The defense is most productively used to interrupt enemy momentum, but it can also provide vital security during breaks in the action. In maneuver warfare, the defense is implemented secretly and in a way that allows shifting back to the offense in a hurry. U.S. patrols traditionally fan out into 360-degree perimeters every time they stop. Just stopping in trace can actually form a stronger defense. When those carrying the automatic weapons are already positioned near the front and rear of the column, the others can create an impregnable defense by just alternately facing outward. Now, the unit can protect either end of its linear formation with automatic-weapons fire, and can mass all of its firepower to either side of the line. Perimeter defenses cannot do that. Additionally, stopping in trace makes less of a noise and movement signature. Furthermore, from the linear formation, the unit can more easily attack to one flank or shift position.

Successfully defending interrupts the enemy's momentum. But this temporary respite goes for naught, if it is not exploited at some point with a counterattack. In other words, an opponent cannot be kept off balance for long without applying some pressure. Furthermore, defending with a counterattack mentality is much less debilitating psychologically. Even the cost-effective elastic defense used by the Germans in WWI was counterattack oriented. It forever changed the appearance of the battlefield and the delineation between the offense and defense:

> As the depth of the German defense increased and the cost of defending the front line grew greater, the emphasis in German defensive tactics changed. Instead of trying to hold on to a piece of terrain whatever the cost, the key feature of the German defense became the timely counterattack to destroy the attacker at the moment *when he was most off balance*. By the end of 1917, the long thin trenches filled with riflemen standing shoulder to shoulder at parapets had been replaced with a checkerboard system of concrete bunkers and small forts that sheltered individual platoons, squads, and machinegun teams. Additional squads, platoons and companies were sheltered in larger bunkers behind the front line in readiness to mount small counterattacks against local breakthroughs. Like stormtroop leaders, the *NCO's in command of these small forts* often had to make decisions in the absence of orders. "The position of the NCO as group (squad) leader," wrote Ludendorff in his memoirs, "thus became more important. *Tactics became more and more individualized.*"
>
> The bulk of the defender's combat power, however, lay not in the concrete forts but rather remained thousands of meters to the rear of the forward positions [out of artillery range].... As more and more of the troops involved in the defensive battle found themselves in the counterattack forces, the *distinction between attack and defense blurred* [italics added throughout].6

The defense developed by the Germans in WWI bears a striking resemblance to what the Marines encountered on Iwo Jima. It's very doubtful that the resemblance is coincidental.

## THE MANY DEFENSE OPTIONS

Until maneuver warfare was officially endorsed as a viable alternative to attrition warfare, U.S. forces only had one way to defend. They would establish a rigid line and dare anyone to cross it. How well this type of defense works depends largely on the imagination and the wherewithal of the enemy. For Saddam Hussein, it worked well against Iranians with standard munitions and traditional tactics, but less well against Americans with "smart" weapons and (large-scale) maneuver warfare tactics. Unless deployed in depth, the traditional defense has two significant weaknesses: once established, it freezes the defender in place; and once breached, it offers no further protection.

Maneuver warfare provides some attractive alternatives for less than ideal circumstances — e.g., when friendly infantry must face enemy armor supported by artillery and air. The principal options are as follows: (1) the strongpoint defense, (2) the reverse-slope defense, (3) ambushes in series, (4) the soft or elastic defense, (5) the defense in depth, and (6) defending an area from a different location altogether. Implicit in all of these options is a timely counterattack.

In the "strongpoint defense," infantry units man pockets of resistance to channelize the enemy into prearranged killing zones. These pockets should be impervious to tank attack. For example, in rural terrain they might be located on steep hills covered by adult trees. With this type of defense, the antitank assets are often placed *behind* the front lines to destroy enemy tanks that have been funneled into the kill zones.

In the "reverse-slope defense," the defending unit stays hidden behind the crest of a hill to escape enemy observation and fire. Only sentry posts and supporting-arms observers man the crest. This type of defense is most often used in gently rolling terrain, where grazing fire beyond grenade range is possible uphill. In the classic example, "squares" of British infantry were placed on the reverse slopes of the rolling terrain at Waterloo to escape the notice of Napoleon's artillery observers.

"Ambushes in series" weaken and disorganize an enemy, and consequently make him more vulnerable to counterattack. For example, anti-armor ambushes in series can slow down opposition tanks long enough for friendly fixed-wing aircraft to arrive on station.

The "soft or elastic defense" is the most controversial of the maneuver warfare options, because it allows front-line units to fall back under pressure. Upon close examination, some of the combat film footage from the island campaigns in the Pacific shows small groups of Japanese *moving backwards* at a diagonal. The cameras might have shown more of this "pulling back," if they could have seen into the vast network of tunnels and trenches that linked the Japanese positions. How poorly the Japanese code of honor meshed with this display of common sense might serve as a warning to others. Defensive lines must sometimes bend to keep from breaking. Americans discovered this during the Civil War. The soft defense also served the Germans well during WWI:

> In response to the Somme offensive, the German high command published a document.... [T]his document ... became the German defensive doctrine for the rest of the war.... The controversial principle was the one not requiring the defender to hold ground at all costs.... They could withdraw as the situation dictated. This sparked opposition.... [H]owever ... the new defensive tactics proved extremely effective when put into practice. Most officers who criticized the principle later came to support it.[7]

While the "defense in depth" is one of the traditional Fundamentals of the Defense, it must also be identified as a maneuver warfare option. The soft defense is particularly effective when combined with a defense in depth, for then it becomes the bait with which to entice an attacker into a trap reminiscent of a fire sack. Once an enemy force has attacked through such a trap, the defenders on the flanks at the point of entry can counterattack across the opening to effect an encirclement.

"Defending a location from somewhere else" is the last option. It's a good way to defend a barren piece of key terrain without exposing oneself to enemy fire. This type

(Source: FM 22-100 (1983), pp. 139, 160)

of defense would be particularly devastating to an attacker with a strict code of discipline and an inflexible scheme of maneuver. One has visions of a machinegun opening up unexpectedly from the flank of a frontally assaulting unit, and of the attacking infantrymen ignoring the fire from their flank so as better to follow their instructions. At Gettysburg, much of the damage to Pickett's Charge was done from locations other than the copse of trees at which it was aimed.[8]

More recently, the hard-pressed Russians used all the maneuver warfare options to stop the German juggernaut at Stalingrad, and thus to turn the tide of WWII:

> This is when he [General Paulus] decided to strike head-on at his enemy's strongest point . . . the tractor factory, the ordnance plant, and the . . . Red October steel works. . . . [B]ut the Russians, though heavily outnumbered, remained their masters in the technique of house-to-house fighting. They had perfected the use of "shock groups," small bodies of mixed arms . . . who gave one another support in lightning counterattacks; and they had developed the creation of "killing zones," houses and squares heavily mined, to which the defenders knew all the approach routes, where the German advance could be canalized.[9]

## BEING ABLE TO SHIFT OVER TO THE OFFENSE IN A HURRY

The members of a small unit must be able to receive an *offensive* play in a *defensive* huddle, and then launch a surprise attack of their own at the very moment their opponent falters. By so doing, they can exploit a temporary break in his momentum. This type of maneuver was commonplace during the American Civil War. The most famous example was probably at Gettysburg on Little Round Top when Colonel Chamberlain's 20th Maine counterattacked as their ammunition ran out.[10] Their success was just as much a turning point of the Civil War as was Pickett's defeat a day later.

## THE APPROPRIATE STYLE OF WARFARE FOR VARIOUS DEFENSIVE SITUATIONS

If the decision is to defend, the style of warfare seems to depend largely on the threat. Against an adversary with a tank or supporting-arms advantage, one of the maneuver warfare options would be generally more effective than a traditional rigid defense. At least, that's the way Germans and Russians stopped each other on the Eastern Front during World War II. When facing a tank or supporting-arms threat, the defender doesn't want to disclose his position until the last moment. He must also be ready either to break contact or to cuddle up with his attacker (as the NVA did in Vietnam). On the other hand, against unsupported human-wave assaults and infiltrators, the attrition warfare defense works just fine in open terrain (at least it did for the Marines in the Pacific, Korea, and Vietnam). Of course, even with a traditional defense, a few maneuver warfare tricks never hurt:

> The Japanese night attacks, of course, have limited objectives; and sometimes withdrawing after dark as much as fifty yards will fool them and they won't know where you are.[11]
> — Col. Merritt A. Edson

## THE STYLE OF WARFARE FOR VARIOUS OFFENSIVE SITUATIONS

If the decision is to attack, the best style of warfare is the one that will create the fewest casualties. When the attacker has unlimited assets and the defender has nowhere to hide (as was the case during the initial stages of the Gulf War), an assault by fire alone can sometimes get the job done. But, when closing with that defender becomes necessary to win decisively, it is best done secretly. That's the only way to escape harm from the enemy's advanced weaponry.

There are a number of ways to hide from, and to fool, the enemy during an attack. In the Gulf War, the Iraqis outnumbered the Allies in troops by roughly 2 to 1, in tanks by 4700 to 3500, and in artillery pieces by some undisclosed number. Furthermore, much of the enemy artillery had better range. With mobile Scud missiles and chemical/biological munitions, the Iraqis posed quite a threat. To counter this threat, the Allies needed an end run around the left flank, and a whole host of supporting attacks and deceptions. There were efforts to blind the enemy (by limiting his reconnaissance), to cripple his communications, to isolate him, to fix him in place, and generally to demoralize and confuse him. Because many of these ruses can also be incorporated into *small-scale combat,* a closer look at them may prove useful.

As the Allied Forces arrived in Saudi Arabia, they were intentionally arrayed opposite the Kuwaiti border. On seeing this, the Iraqis extended their fortified defense line only slightly west of the Kuwaiti border. Then, a large Allied naval amphibious force was positioned in the Persian Gulf opposite Kuwait City. This force was periodically exercised in mock landings with plenty of media attention. On seeing this, the enemy concentrated on improving his coastal defenses.

The Iraqis had limited reconnaissance capability, so their air force was neutralized early in the game to permit Allied forces to change location without being seen. Additionally, the Iraqi command-and-control network was continually disrupted, and the bridges into Kuwait kept down to limit resupply and reinforcement. A naval bombardment was maintained along the shore line of Kuwait to convince the Iraqis that an amphibious landing was imminent. The Iraqi defense lines along the southern border of Kuwait were also pounded by airstrikes and artillery. It was hoped that the defenders would think that Allied ground forces would move to reinforce their amphibious landings near Kuwait City by the most direct route.

However, when the main ground attack came, the majority of Allied forces had secretly shifted to the west and were poised to make an end run around the Iraqi defense line. The offensive was initiated by two U.S. Marine task forces hitting the center of the line to "fix in place" the majority of the Iraqi units. It was by no accident that one of these task forces attacked through a small segment of the border that runs north and south (instead of east and west). It was assumed that this segment of the lines would be more lightly defended and that the attack would look as if it were headed for the beach. Shortly thereafter, a third (Saudi) task force attacked up the coast. By so doing, it not only outflanked the coastal defenders, but also furthered the amphibious-assault deception. Even after the end run had reached deep into the Euphrates valley, mine-clearing operations continued in the waters off Kuwait City. Again, this was to keep the Iraqis worried about the amphibious assault that would never come.

The Marine thrusts at the center of the Iraqi line were accomplished in a manner consistent with maneuver warfare. They were aimed at Iraqi unit boundaries, initiated with short-range infiltration in total darkness, and intended only to seize gaps large enough to permit passage of task forces. But, the Marines did more than just fix in place the heaviest concentration of Iraqi forces. Their Light Armored Vehicles (LAV's) performed some feints into Kuwait before the main attack started. As the Iraqis came out to defend against what they thought were full-fledged armor attacks, the LAV's saw some heavy action. So much so, that some new traditions for the Marine Corps were written in the process. Interestingly, most of the LAV's were commanded by NCO's, and one SNCO claimed later to have controlled all the supporting arms for his unit — some 250 airstrikes and 300 artillery missions over the course of two days.[12]

The main attack in the west was reminiscent of Col. Chamberlain's "swinging gate" on Little Round Top. Notably, the Allies were smart enough *not* to tackle the enemy forces occupying Kuwait City. Instead, they let them escape under cover of darkness, and then destroyed them (from the air) on the road back to Baghdad.

Historically, armies of this size have seldom clashed without both being severely mauled. Allied casualty totals were nothing short of miraculous. Yet, it is still somewhat disquieting to think about the tens of thousands of young Iraqi soldiers — mostly conscripts with little understanding of political issues — that the preliminary bombardment must have killed.

Only against soft and disorganized targets can an attrition warfare style of ground assault achieve comparable results. However, most NCO's will point out that there may be an exception to this rule. When a unit has no choice but to force open a gap in a prepared position (one that is entrenched and surrounded by barriers), it must do so *methodically*. That is to say when a unit does not have the time or specially trained personnel to infiltrate a prepared position, it must systematically deal with whatever threats are encountered. It must usually overcome sentry posts, barbed wire, claymore mines, and machineguns — in that order. This is undoubtedly why the battle-tested Marines of WWII persisted in making methodical small-scale attacks to dislodge diehard Japanese from their bunkers.

## MIXING STYLES OF WARFARE IN DEFENSIVE COMBAT

To defend against every possible enemy threat, it makes perfect sense to mix styles of warfare. The traditional rigid defense was designed to stop human-wave assaults. With careful attention to where the fighting holes are placed, it can also stop enemy sappers. But, to counter tanks or supporting arms, it must be kept hidden until the last moment. The normal two-man sentry post must be replaced with an armor-killer team capable of adjusting supporting-arms fire. The members of this armor-killer team must build "spider holes," so that they can evade the enemy infantrymen who normally precede tanks. After the enemy soldiers have passed safely overhead, the friendly personnel can emerge from their holes, kill a tank, and then hide again. Or, each armor-killer team can escape down a preestablished route of egress after another team distracts the enemy. Either way, the enemy would have no way of knowing that there was a large defensive position nearby. When the parent unit sprang its trap, it might have to break contact to escape the enemy tank or supporting-arms counterpunch. Most Vietnam veterans have personally experienced what maneuver warfare tricks can do to a well-supported attack.

## COMBINING STYLES OF WARFARE IN THE OFFENSE

Determining how best to combine styles of warfare in the offense is not as easy. In general, it takes a small unit and a maneuver warfare thought process to get close enough to a prepared enemy position to assault it at low cost. Courage and pride (as with Pickett's charge at Gettysburg) cannot guarantee success in the assault. As was referenced in a previous chapter, infantrymen can't even successfully "fire and move" (rushes covered by fire up parallel lanes) against a prepared enemy position.

To stand much of a chance against such a position, the attacking unit must reach assaulting distance (50 meters or so) without being detected. This takes stealth. Then, it

## The Shortfall in Recorded Knowledge

must assault when the defender isn't looking. Sometimes, this takes deception and speed. Other times, it takes sappers crawling in slow motion. In fact, the legendary courage of U.S. fighting men might be better channelled into this alternative way of assaulting. If the NVA successes in Vietnam are any indication, well-trained sappers can penetrate defensive lines at little risk to themselves. Although fully alerted on the night of 26 August 1966 at Cam Lo, the U.S. Marine defenders could do nothing about the first wave of enemy sappers:

> They [the NVA] snuck on through before we ever illuminated the area.... [A]s you know, they're real proficient at moving at night...very silently, very slowly and very patiently.... [The NVA] did get through even though our people were waiting for them. They crawled in between the holes, and our people never even realized that they passed through their positions.[13]
> —Lt.Col. "Blackjack" Westerman
> CO, 1st Battalion, 4th Marines

Occasionally, circumstances will not permit a short-range infiltration attack. If the unit can get close enough to its objective undetected, it can succeed with a fairly traditional assault. But, for an upright assault to stand the best chance, it must incorporate *deception, stealth, and speed*. For it to work, the members of the unit must have penetrated enemy obstacles undetected, have some illumination, and have a 3:1 manpower advantage at the point of attack. By moving quickly to achieve rough alignment, and then limiting their fire to "double taps" at confirmed targets, they can even preserve some measure of surprise. While this edge is still intact, the fire-and-movement type of assault needlessly squanders it. Fire and movement constitutes attacking piecemeal and leaves members of the assault in harm's way longer. Of course, once all surprise has been forfeited inside the enemy's barbed wire, fire and movement becomes the only option.

### IT TAKES NCO EXPERTISE TO MIX STYLES OF WARFARE

The advanced infantry skills being discussed here — building spider holes, sneaking up to within 50 yards of an alert defender, aligning and shooting on the run, etc. — are *not* in common practice in the U.S. military today. The NCO's are the ones best qualified to develop this kind of detail in tactical execution. How best to employ the weapons organic to the rifle company, also falls within their area of expertise.

# Reassessing the Role of the Weapons

- Can all targets be successfully engaged the same way?
- Are weapons useful for anything other than killing?
- What problems could be resolved by tactics requiring less shooting?

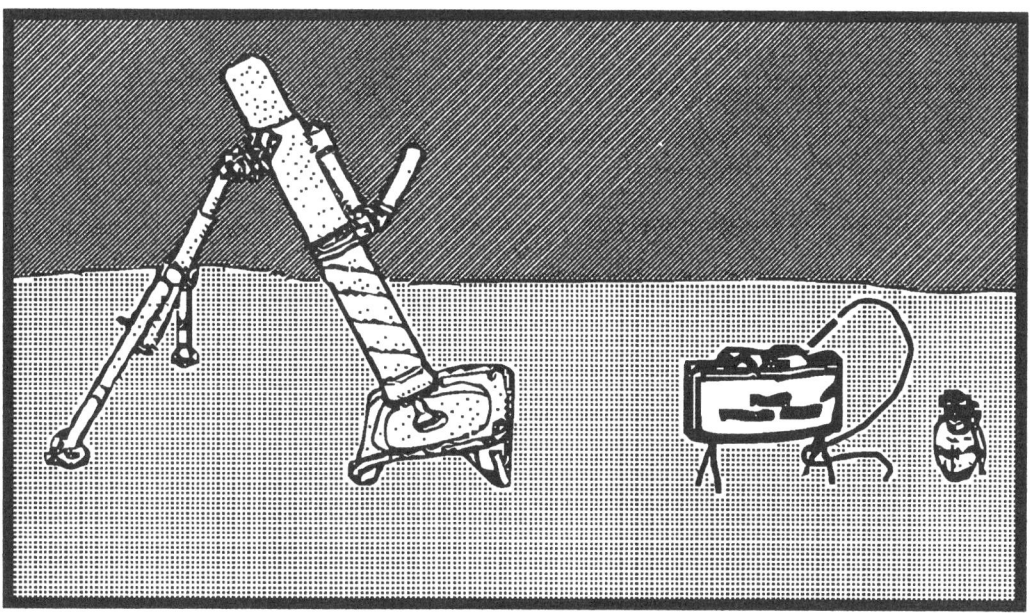

(Sources: FM 23-30 (1988), p. 1-8; MCO P1500.44B, p. 14-18; FM 90-5 (1982), p. 4-13)

**THE ROLE THAT WEAPONS
*USED TO* PLAY IN WARFARE**

No search for the shortfall in small-unit tactical knowledge would be complete without reassessing what is known about weapons employment. If there is a deficiency here, it may be due to an overreliance on the one firing method in the manuals or the advertising claims of the arms manufacturers. Basing one's opinions on these two sources alone could lead to several incorrect assumptions: (1) that weapons are only useful for killing, (2) that shooting one's weapons always helps to win in battle, and (3) that "high-tech" weapons are always the best.

Weapons can often better facilitate maneuver *by not killing,* but rather by masking noise, creating deception, marking, signaling, illuminating, and *remaining silent.* Using one's weapons too freely in war can actually detract from one's ability to win. Doing so takes ammunition that is hard to carry and time consuming to resupply. An infantry unit that requires a lot of ammunition automatically forfeits speed and momentum. Furthermore, weapons make noise when fired. This distinctive noise can compromise the element of surprise. Finally, too much firing can sometimes kill the wrong people.

In maneuver warfare, an army doesn't depend on its firepower to win. For this reason, its weapons — high-tech or otherwise — have less influence on the outcome. Theoretically, an armed force with no tanks or airplanes at all, can still win. What happened in Vietnam should lend credence to this assertion. At the small-unit level, older battle-tested weapons can be more valuable than their technologically advanced replacements. When lightly armored PT-76 tanks made a rare appearance in Vietnam at Lang Vei in 1968, Special Forces personnel sorely missed their old 3.5-inch rocket launchers. Pointblank fire from the newer M72 Light Assault Antitank Weapons (LAAW's) could do nothing more than break the track on one tank.[1] Rifles mass produced in stamping mills can also have more value than rifles carefully machined. Their less precise tolerances enable them to resist jamming when dirty. Of course, there are some high-tech weapons that could be of great value to small maneuver elements — e.g., man-portable laser designators and "smart" munitions. Yet, for whatever reason, line infantry squads are not afforded the opportunity to use them.

The manuals don't stress that different shooting techniques are required to kill (as opposed to scare) different targets. Further, the arms manufacturers don't widely publicize that every type of ordnance has unique limitations. U.S. infantrymen who base their opinions solely on these two sources might have a significant shortfall in what they know about the role of weapons in warfare.

## HOW WELL CAN SUPPORTING ARMS REALLY KILL?

To what extent each supporting arm can accomplish its traditional role of killing depends on the circumstances. To be sure, massive artillery bombardments took a frightful toll in the open trenches of early WWI. Still, the equally heavy rolling barrages that led the infantry attacks across no man's land, could not kill enough of the defenders to guarantee a breakthrough. In fact, throughout this century, Western commanders have chased the fleeting dream that heavy ordnance could do enough damage to dug-in defenders to protect attacking infantry. Only a few commanders have resisted its lure:

> Unlike the German commanders at Soissons, however, Rohr [the inventor of stormtroop tactics] avoided the seductive thought that artillery could do the infantry's work for it.[2]

If the machinegun had never been invented, artillery might have retained its power to prepare the way for infantry. But the machinegun was invented, and it changed warfare forever. If just *one* machinegunner survives the preparatory artillery barrage, he can single-handedly stop a well-organized infantry assault. Corporal Al Schmid and Gunnery Sergeant John Basilone proved that again at Guadalcanal against some of the best infantry the world has ever known:

> Dearly outnumbered, they held in the misnamed Battle of the Tenaru River, killing scores of enemy . . . as they made one heedless rush after another. One Marine, Al Schmid, was blinded by grenade fragments. Lifting his heavy machinegun, Schmid continued to pump fire as his foxhole mate, disabled in both legs, told him where to aim the weapon.[3]

Against defenders well dug in with overhead cover (as were the Japanese later in the Pacific War), even heavy calibers and quantities of ordnance can achieve little. At the coral atoll of Tarawa, 3500 tons of aerial bombs and naval shells were put onto the one-square-mile islet of Betio immediately before the landings. That equates to about two and half pounds of explosive per square yard and does not include what was delivered for days before and after the landing:

> It is 6:20 A.M. before carrier-based Dauntless, Avenger, and Hellcat aircraft roar overhead. They drop 500 tons of bombs. . . . [It is] 6:22 A.M.: The naval bombardment opens, lasting nearly 90 minutes, littering every foot of the atoll with fragments from 3000 tons of shells.[4]

Two years later, the volcanic island of Iwo Jima was heavily plastered before and after the landing. Finally, an outspoken corporal noted the disadvantages of too much bombardment:

> Patrick Couplet, a twenty-five-year-old Fifth Division corporal from New Brunswick, New Jersey, put it more succinctly: "All the bombardment did was let the Nips know we were coming at them again. It stirred them up like a hornet's nest, and the sonsab— were waiting in their caves and bunkers to kill more Marines just as they had every . . . day since we landed."[5]

Because of the tremendous visual effect of heavy shelling, one naturally assumes that there is always a commensurate effect on the enemy. Unfortunately, the correlation does not always exist. After every war, statistics are published on how many tons of explosives and thousands of bullets were needed to kill each enemy soldier, but the lesson never seems to sink in:

> A study done by the operational research office of Johns Hopkins University shortly after the Korean War concluded that many thousands of rounds of artillery were necessary to kill a single enemy in such circumstances [dug into mountainous terrain].[6]

Killing a target that is *not* dug in can prove difficult as well. Novice observers tend to trust what they personally see over the mathematical certainty of ballistics. A mortar man accustomed to engaging targets at short range may be tempted to use the "one-round-adjustment" procedure against a distant enemy tank. In the desert, heat shimmer will make the tank look closer than it really is, and the mortar man can expend scores of rounds without ever getting near his target. Even without heat shimmer, he may still have difficulty. If his round hits a piece of metallic junk or slightly elevated ground in front of the tank, it may look like a direct hit and reason to stop firing. If the mortar man had chosen the successive-bracketing method instead, he could have mathematically assured himself of a hit (possibly with less visual effect).

Choosing the appropriate weapon must necessarily be the first step in killing any target. Each weapon (and the round it delivers) has its own limitations. Certain types of ordnance will be more effective on that particular target than others.

Mortars are the quickest of the supporting arms to bring to bear, but they don't pack much punch and have the least amount of ammunition. For this reason, they are often reserved for immediate-suppression missions against soft targets. Once infantry companies receive portable laser designators, they could use British laser-guided 81mm mortar rounds against enemy armor.

Artillery packs a bigger punch and has more ammunition, but it also risks more equipment when located by counterbattery radar. One wonders how much preparatory artillery fire could be expected prior to a contemporary infantry attack. The High Explosive (HE) standard sheaf with "quick" fuzing is not well enough concentrated to hurt a well-dug-in enemy. More effective against enemy soldiers in open trenches are "variable-time" (airburst) munitions, and against those with overhead protection are "fuze-delay" munitions. It has traditionally taken infantry assaults to silence machinegun bunkers. Precision fire from highly accurate artillery pieces (like the old 8-inch howitzers) can perform the same mission at less cost. Sadly, few 8-inch howitzers are still around.

(Source: FM 22-100 (1983), p. 84)

Naval guns have impressive calibers and quantities of ammunition. They even produce less of a trajectory signature. Still, because they must compensate for an unstable firing platform, they are also less accurate against preregistered targets and along the gun-target line in general. Ships are more vulnerable to enemy air attack. During the Falklands War, a British destroyer had to abort the preparatory fire for the Goose Green attack:

> ... [At Goose Green] Bob Ash, an artillery forward observer, met a request for a fire mission with an unhappy shrug: "We just haven't got the rounds." Mortar ammunition had run out altogether. . . .
> . . . and Sea *Arrow* was compelled to retire. She had continued to provide support for two hours after first light, long after she was intended to retire to the safety of the San Carlos anchorage. But now, at last, she was ordered to go. There would be no more naval gunfire support for 2 Para [2nd Parachute Battalion].[7]

"Smart" weapons are those that can be guided onto their targets. While expensive, they should nevertheless be made available to small units on the battlefield. In the Falklands, the British initiated several of their deliberate attacks with Milan missiles aimed at Argentinean machinegun bunkers.[8] With a portable laser designator, an infantry squad could operate far behind enemy lines with impunity. If the squad leader were careful to call in supporting arms from behind him on a diagonal, he could safely eliminate any threat he was facing with a 155mm "Copperhead" or laser-guided aircraft missile.

Against heavy armor, the weapon of choice has always been fixed- or rotary-wing Close Air Support (CAS). Regrettably, with the advent of surface-to-air handheld missiles and faster aircraft, accuracy with "dumb" bombs has suffered. Even a 500-pounder from an F/A-18 fighter-bomber that lands within 100 yards of its target may not do much damage to a main-battle tank with reactive and hardened armor. An expensive smart bomb might have gotten the job done, if the F/A-18 or the unit on the ground had carried its own laser designator. A dumb 1000-pounder might also have done the trick, if the tank hadn't gotten too close to the friendly infantry while the plane was en route. On a large and active battlefield, close air support can take a long time to arrive. This is not anyone's fault per se — there are just numerous contacts going on at any given time, and not enough planes to handle them all.

Against armor, naval guns and artillery are quicker alternatives. Particularly when the battleships are out of mothballs, naval gunfire can provide a significant deterrent to tank attack. They automatically produce a long narrow sheaf along the gun-target line — an ideal way to disrupt an enemy tank column moving against a coastal city. If the ship were to align itself with the occupied stretch of road, the fire for effect from just one gun would automatically cover a large portion of the tank column. It was discovered in the Gulf War that the Dual Purpose Improved Conventional Munitions (DPICM) for artillery are also highly effective against tanks. Apparently, their shape charges are powerful enough to penetrate the top armor of the older models.

## ENHANCING THE KILLING POWER OF THE WEAPONS

With the procedure of "combined arms," maneuver warfare practitioners maximize the killing power of their limited weaponry. To escape the effects of the first weapon in a combined-arms attack, the enemy must subject himself to the effects of a second. Of course, great leaders have always known how to use weapons in combination:

> Puller saw Japanese swarming from a circular ravine in the jungle growth — an old crater. Puller called for an artillery concentration. . . . When the mortar fire drove the Japanese up the slopes of their crater, they emerged into the field of fire from his machineguns, which cut down scores of the small figures. When the tide flowed back into the crater the mortars opened [up] once more, within a few minutes the slaughter was compete and the enemy unit had ceased to exist as an effective force.[9]

Many combined-arms procedures are taken for granted. In the traditional defense, claymores and mortar registrations cover dead space in machinegun final protective fires. When one considers deception as a weapon, he can come up with some interesting tactical techniques. For example, a few rifle shots could cause the members of an enemy patrol to jump into a ditch lined with well-hidden punji stakes or command-detonated claymores.

## THE CASE FOR PREREGISTRATION

As interest in maneuver warfare has grown, so too has reluctance to preregister with indirect-fire weapons. Some are concerned that preregistering around a defensive position compromises its location, and that preregistering on top of an offensive objective provides advanced warning of the attack. They point out that, without preregistering, the German's were able to produce pinpoint artillery fire during WWI. What they may not realize is that the Germans could only do so because they had totally reliable maps and customized firing tables for each artillery piece:

> . . . Many of the artillery pieces scheduled for the offensive were transported to firing ranges

behind the lines. There they were test fired to determine the "peculiarities" of each gun and each was provided with a set of firing tables customized by a professional mathematician. . . .

A critical element in the success of the German plan to fire without registration was the quality of the maps in the hands of the artillery officers. This problem was solved by a stroke of luck — the battlefield over which the German infantry would attack had been the rear of the German position in France from late 1914 until the middle of 1917. This area had been made the subject of many precise surveys and from this raw material, first-class maps were made and issued to the artillery.[10]

Preregistration is still required because most maps contain significant "map error." Only with an accurate initial barrage, can one kill a moving target. Such a barrage is usually only possible with a registration point nearby. A defender can only achieve enough surprise and accuracy to hurt a mobile attacker, when he preregisters along his entire defensive frontage.

A registration signature can be disguised through timing and deception. A defensive frontage can be registered in such a way that the rounds look like Harassing and Interdiction (H&I) fires. An offensive objective can be registered *after* the maneuver element has moved into assaulting distance. Only then, can the maneuver force leader determine whether or not he will even need an artillery deception. From just outside an enemy's wire, he can better place the fire where it will do him the most good.

## THE WAYS OF EMPLOYING EACH WEAPON ARE ENDLESS

There is not just one way to use each weapon. There are many. The "best" way is situational, just as in tactics. The challenge is to match the way of using the weapon with the circumstances. One must be familiar with the alternative techniques for employing weapons organic to the rifle company, and what conditions might justify their use.

When shooting a 60mm mortar against a linear enemy formation, there is no need for an optical sight. If the mortar is moved to a location on line with the linear formation and sighted in along its bore, a perfect sheaf can be attained by merely spinning the elevation knob between rounds. On other occasions, precious moments can again be saved by not using the optical sight. It is quicker to sight in along the bore, rapidly position the tube at a cant estimated to achieve the proper range, and then drop a round. After seeing where the round lands, the mortar man can then spin the elevation knob enough turns to ensure a bracket with the second round. Between successive rounds, he can then halve the number of turns of the

(Source: FM 5-103 (1985), p. 4-12)

wheel until the bracket is shortened enough to justify a "fire for effect." When opposing mortar crews meet on a battlefield, whichever crew puts rounds on target first, wins.

The M203 grenade launcher can be registered like a mortar. Only required are a few aiming stakes and some entries on a range card.

Shoulder-launched Multipurpose Assault Weapons (SMAW's) should always accompany maneuver elements into combat. During an assault, they must be available to bust bunkers harboring enemy automatic weapons. Even when the SMAW's can't totally silence those weapons, they can cause enemy gunners to "blink" long enough for riflemen to get within grenade range.

In the defense, AT-4 "tank killers" should initially be employed *forward* of friendly lines in anti-armor ambushes. Tanks that are allowed to get too close to those lines can do some real damage.

The most destructive, yet underused, weapon on the table of equipment for the rifle company is the machinegun. Some credit the machinegun for bringing the Marines out of the Chosin Reservoir during the Korean War. On defense, its power to stop human-wave assaults has been well documented since the Battle of the Somme in WWI. Yet, established procedure disallows its use until the enemy's final assault. This is ostensibly to keep its location secret. Why couldn't it fire earlier under circumstances that did not compromise its position, or from a temporary location? A machinegun on a tripod with a Traversing and Elevation mechanism (T&E) can fire into the defiladed area near the end of its trajectory the same way an indirect-fire weapon can. Then, an observer with binoculars can adjust the fire from the dust of the impacting rounds. If no tracers are used, the enemy may have a hard time figuring out where the gun is located. At night, a machinegun might be temporarily positioned high on a hill or manmade structure. From there, its tracer fire could be walked onto an approaching enemy force by a listening post with a radio. While the gun team would have to move, the listening post would not. A good machinegunner can shoot without disclosing his position, even while firing his Final Protective Line (FPL). He does so by removing the tracers from his ammunition belts, positioning his weapon behind sandbag cloth curtains, and only firing when an enemy automatic weapon does likewise.

In the daytime, the machineguns do not belong with the maneuver element. They are too vital to the survival of the unit. The guns belong in a supporting role away from the objective. From there, they can better handle surprise enemy initiatives from the flanks. Once a "base of fire" has been activated, machinegun teams can alternate moving forward to improve accuracy, enhance deception, and expedite final displacement to the objective.

At night, the machineguns *should* accompany the maneuver element to just outside the enemy wire. From there, experienced gunners can fire safely over the heads of crawling attackers. Of course, it never hurts to have a few trees on which to steady the gun barrels.

While Squad Automatic Weapons (SAW's) definitely belong on the assault, they must be fired sparingly while surprise is intact. Theirs is a supporting role. They must only suppress enemy automatic-weapons fire if the assault is discovered. Any enemy, who is adjacent to the point of attack and hears a long burst from an overeager SAW gunner, will realize immediately that a ground assault is underway. He may have an automatic weapon of his own. On Iwo Jima, SAW's would have been fired into the embrasures of active enemy machinegun bunkers while Marines crawled closer to toss satchel charges:

> Other heroes took his [Gunnery Sergeant "Manila John" Basilone's] place that day on Iwo Jima. One was Tony Stein....
> ...Stein spotted a pillbox holding up the advance and went for it. His weapon was a one-of-a-kind machinegun fired from the hip....
> The husky corporal called it his "stinger," and it was unique. Stein had been an apprentice toolmaker before enlisting in 1942, and used his skills to fashion it from a scrounged machinegun from the wing of a wrecked Navy fighter plane. Spewing bullets in rapid bursts, the "stinger" and its gung-ho triggerman pinned the Japanese inside the pillbox while Savage finished them off with a demolitions charge.[11]

Although not officially sanctioned for the job, SAW's could also hurt lightly armored aircraft. The massed fire from a unit's M249's would create a curtain of steel through which even a supersonic jet might have trouble flying. A SAW has a considerably higher rate of fire than a machinegun.

Even the lowly rifle can perform some interesting feats on the battlefield. In urban terrain, a rifleman can cover dead space in a machinegun's FPL with plunging fire from an upstairs window. In rural terrain, a running rifleman can hesitate to "snap shoot" a confirmed target with a "double tap." He watches where the first round hits, and then walks the next round onto the enemy's torso. A rifleman who can combine quickly moving with accurate shooting can better preserve the element of surprise during an assault. He has more chance of survival than one who depends on heavy fire to keep his adversary's head down and then walks toward him. A traditional assault makes too much noise — noise that can attract unwanted attention from the flanks.

For sheer killing power in relation to weight, there is no equal to the claymore. Unlike any other weapon system available to the squad, the claymore mine produces hundreds of lethal projectiles over a considerable distance *without any warning*. If there is even a split second of advance notice during an ambush, the enemy can drop to the ground and crawl away unharmed. That is why claymores, and not closed-bolt weapons, should be used to initiate ambushes. Claymores sound to the enemy like booby traps or artillery rounds. This happy coincidence can keep secret not only the location, but also the very existence, of the claymore operators.

To the enemy, a hand grenade sounds to the like a mortar or booby trap. By removing the spoon slowly, one can prevent its telltale noise. Furthermore, a grenade can be used with precision against a distant target. All it takes is a former quarterback or pitcher atop a steep hill or a tall building. Molotov cocktails helped to kill scores of Soviet tanks during the 1956 Budapest Uprising:

> Once or twice the Russians attempted to penetrate into the small streets, but these proved fatal for them: it was too easy to drop any number of Molotov cocktails from the higher floors, and one small street became a cemetery of Russian tanks.[12]

### USING WEAPONS ONLY TO KILL CARRIES WITH IT A TRADEOFF

When used for killing, weapons (supporting arms in particular) endanger friendlies. Even armies that focus inward take many casualties from friendly fire during wartime. Some estimates from Vietnam were quite high:

> As our [U.S. Army] study shook out, the fact became inescapable that a staggering 15 to 20 percent of all U.S. casualties in Vietnam were caused by friendly fire.[13]

On the other hand, if an armed force were to focus outward (such as in maneuver warfare), it could expect to have less control over its maneuver elements. One would expect that an even higher percentage of casualties from friendly fire might result. Yet, this conclusion is based on an unfounded assumption — that there will be just as much shooting. With maneuver warfare, there won't be; there will be only enough to permit maneuver. At the small-unit level (better to surprise the enemy), units will no longer fire until absolutely necessary. They will silently approach their adversary, instead of relying on sister units to keep his head down. Their bases of fire may be directed at terrain *other than* the objective, and used *only* to mask sounds coming from the envelopment route. Of course, *less shooting translates into fewer casualties from friendly fire*. This reduction in the overall potential for mistakes could more than offset the few errors that might result from less control. And, if Americans aren't shooting at their foes as much, the foes won't be shooting back as much either. That means fewer casualties still. In the final analysis, maneuver warfare is safer than attrition warfare over both short and long term.

## WEAPONS CAN BE USED FOR MANY PURPOSES OTHER THAN KILLING

Killing large numbers of enemy is by no means the acme of military skill:

Therefore those who win every battle are not really skillful — those who render others' armies helpless without fighting are the best of all.[14]
— Sun Tzu

Trying to demoralize or confuse an enemy can be less dangerous than trying to kill him. Once an infantryman understands this, he will also realize that his weapons can be used for purposes other than killing. For example, they can be used for masking noise, creating deceptions, screening, marking, signaling, and illuminating.

Armies have used indirect fire to mask the sounds of their own movement and to divert their opponent's attention for as long as there have been mortars and artillery:

Shelling [in Manchuria in 1939] ... helped to distract Jap attention by drowning out sounds of Soviet troop movements all of which were accomplished at night.[15]

Indirect fire can cover the sound of bangalore torpedoes as well. The Germans used this deception during the Jacobsbrunnen Raid of 1917.[16] Indirect fire against a target *other than the attack objective* can also divert the defenders' attention. With a little smoke mixed in for screening, it can even prevent another enemy unit from helping to defend the objective from long range.

To mark close-air-support targets, an observer usually needs mortars or artillery. But, with an assortment of colored-smoke rounds, the M203 grenade launcher is also well suited for targets within 300 meters. Intersecting bands of machinegun tracers marked targets for night bombers during the Marines' breakout from the Chosin Reservoir.

In fact, the M203 grenade launcher, may be more useful for signaling and illumination than for killing. When the maneuver element leader experiences radio failure at the end of the envelopment route, he could place a white-smoke round on another avenue of approach as an alternate signal to shift the artillery and base of fire. If the foe could distinguish it at all from the smoke in the preparation fire, his attention would be diverted from the actual point of attack.

In fact, signaling can be accomplished with any weapon. On Guadalcanal, Japanese infiltrators used rifle shots to signal, possibly after their radios had failed:

Japs [on Guadalcanal] who have infiltrated signal to each other with their rifles by the number of shots.[17]
— Best NCO to Chesty Puller

One M203 illumination round can simultaneously signal the assault for a night attack, shut off the base of fire, silhouette the enemy, and facilitate alignment of the assaulting elements. Furthermore, it can do all of these things without alerting the enemy. The enemy would assume that it was one of their own. If anything, the illumination round would draw attention away from the point of attack. Signaling with a white-star cluster during a night attack, would look to the enemy like one of their own illumination pop-ups had malfunctioned.

At night, properly placed illumination rounds can both blind enemy night vision devices and cover movement that would otherwise be visible to the naked eye. An artillery flare swinging on its parachute in the breeze creates moving shadows in vegetated terrain. These shadows can, in turn, conceal the movement of men. Patrol leaders who could reset off artillery illumination rounds would never get lost again. In the Falklands, the British used overhead tracer fire to help their troops land navigate at night.

## WEAPONS CAN ALSO BE USED TO DECEIVE AN ENEMY

Because weapons are so often used to kill in combat, there are many opportunities for tactical deception. Consider the following examples.

After subjecting an attack objective to intense bombing, an infantry unit could safely cross the defender's cleared fields of fire by having the aircraft make another low-level pass without dropping any bombs (a dry run).

*The Shortfall in Recorded Knowledge*

On any battlefield, there are scores of artillery and mortar barrages that are not followed up with ground assaults. This permits softening up ground attack objectives without entirely compromising the element of surprise. The bombardment need not kill anyone on the objective as long as it freezes the defenders in place, and masks the sound of the maneuver force sloshing up the envelopment route or blowing bangalores in the wire. When a few smoke rounds are added in, the defenders may assume that their poor visibility has been caused by spotting rounds, malfunctioning White Phosphorous (WP) rounds, or just burning grass; but they won't be able to see the personnel emplacing bangalores or transiting holes in the barbed wire. Without killing, artillery could make the daylight attack much less hazardous.

Instead of keeping the defenders' heads down for the duration of the attack, the base of fire might only shoot to mask the sound of unavoidable small-arms fire in the envelopment route. The limited amount of ammunition available to the base of fire would no longer present a problem. Most support elements can't carry enough ammunition to fire continuously during a typical envelopment anyway. Combat loads could be cut in half. Firing for whatever reason only serves to compromise the element of surprise. If just one enemy soldier can still function his automatic weapon, he can stop the assault cold.

## SOMETIMES NOT USING ONE'S WEAPONS AT ALL IS THE ANSWER

Infantry units can't carry enough ammunition to execute back-to-back traditional attacks without resupply. This severely limits their ability to establish momentum. Just trying to carry enough ammunition saps the strength of unit members. According to S.L.A. Marshall, if a soldier's load in the approach march is any heavier than one third of his body weight, he must be given a chance to rest before he can participate in the attack.[18] Fatigue and fear are inseparably linked.[19] While it is difficult to see how being tired could make one fearful, it is not hard to see how being overloaded might make one less willing to exercise initiative. These dilemmas could be resolved by simply adopting tactics that did not entail as much shooting!

## IT TAKES NCO'S TO DESIGN EFFECTIVE WEAPONS AND TACTICS

That new weapons don't always live up to expectations should come as no surprise. During heavy fighting at Dai Do in Vietnam, the men of 2nd Battalion, 4th Marines felt the need to swap their M16A1's for AK-47's:

Worst of all, most of the M16 rifles in the rifle companies had malfunctioned and were discarded in favor of captured AK-47 assault rifles. In fact, when I visited Golf Company I saw only one M16 rifle. It was carried by Captain Vargas, the company commander.[20]
— B.Gen. W. Weise USMC (Ret.)

The M16A2 rifle is an improvement over the M16A1, but the M203 grenade launcher attachment more easily breaks than its M79 predecessor. The new barrel latch is the problem. Further, there is no white-smoke round for the M203. Firing a white-smoke-canopy round at the ground for screening leaves much to be desired. With some masking noise, an ordinary white-smoke round could isolate an objective without disclosing its source. It would look to the foe like a spotting round from a distant mortar, and would not forewarn him of ground attack.

Which infantry weapon to use, and how to use it, can be discussed at great length by theoreticians. At some point these theories must be put to the test. They can either be put to the test in combat at a price, or beforehand. As the technicians of both tactics and weapons, the NCO's are the logical source for this advice.

Every weapon malfunctions occasionally. This malfunction can have a decided influence on one's mission and survival. How much a weapon can fire before becoming damaged, and how often it must be cleaned, are all things that its operator must know. Just as a rifle's propensity to jam must affect the actions of a rifleman, so too must the limitations of organic weapons influence the tactics of a unit. Tactics and weapons are mutually dependent concepts; one can't be analyzed without the other. Most of what affects small-unit tactical decision making has been covered. At issue now is how techniques collectively generated by the NCO corps could help U.S. forces to fill the shortfall in recorded knowledge and prepare for the challenges of the next millennium.

# Part Two

## Techniques from the NCO Corps

The last hundred yards in combat is the purview of the non-commissioned officer.
— Unidentified American general

 # Successfully Traversing a Battlefield

- How can a land navigator remain focused on the enemy?
- While planning a route, how can he take full advantage of terrain?
- While on the move, how can he best keep track of his location?

(Source: FM 90-6 (1980), pp. 1-4, 1-5)

### ONE NEEDS MORE THAN MODERN TECHNOLOGY TO LAND NAVIGATE

There now exists a computerized module with which to determine one's location on the earth's surface. It depends for its bearings on radio signals from known points. The most advanced version works off satellite transmissions. Unfortunately, it must have a direct line of sight with several satellites at once. This only happens reliably where a tree branch does not obstruct the line of sight to one of the moving satellites — namely, in a field or desert. In heavily wooded terrain, the module must often be moved to open ground. Moreover, not enough satellites exist to cover every part of the world 24 hours a day. The version that uses earthbound signals has even greater limitations. Now, hills can also interrupt line of sight, and the module must often be moved to higher ground. Additionally, transmitters must be positioned at known points in enemy territory prior to each opposed landing or advance. Like radios, both versions of the module are delicate and apt to fail in combat. They are expensive and not standard issue to small units. This creates additional problems, because the maps will *not always agree* with the computer. An infantry squad at a map-generated grid coordinate cannot strictly depend on accurate fire from an artillery battery at a computer-generated grid coordinate. In heavily jungled and precipitous terrain, where the distance to an explosion cannot be accurately ascertained by ear, this discrepancy could increase the risk of "short rounds."

*Techniques from the NCO Corps*

Yet, the limitations of the module are not the real reason why small-unit leaders must still learn to land navigate. They must do so to *focus properly on the enemy and to take tactical advantage of the terrain:*

Know the ground, know the weather, and your victory will be complete.[1]
— Sun Tzu

## FOCUSING ON THE ENEMY WHILE MOVING

When small-unit leaders are not expert at land navigation, they must struggle to find their way around. This struggle can sometimes be so intense as to divert their attention away from higher priorities — namely, the enemy. During the execution phase of any tactical evolution, infantrymen must concentrate on their adversary. They cannot be preoccupied with the fear of being lost. They must be at home in their environment — utilizing natural terrain features as they would streets and street signs while driving their car, and watching for hints of enemy activity as they would for incongruous actions by oncoming motorists. Like drivers, they must be able almost instinctively to move toward their destinations, so that they can better concentrate on their opposition. A British fighter ace once was heard to say that he took his Spitfire up for a couple of hours of flying practice before every mission over Germany, because in combat the last thing he wanted to worry about was how to fly his airplane.

For any type of warrior, well-founded self-confidence is his strongest weapon. The infantryman's very survival depends on whether or not he considers himself the "big bear of the woods." The ease with which he can move through those woods affects this level of self-confidence.

Early Native Americans showed what light infantry can accomplish with the right amount of land navigational skill. The war party that could spot its adversary's sign, follow it, and then attack from an unexpected quarter, had the highest longevity. More recently, British Commonwealth personnel relied on similar skills to defeat the Communists in Malaysia in the early sixties. Conversely, contemporary infantrymen who have difficulty finding their way around in the field, should not brag too loudly about their fighting ability.

Focusing on one's enemy takes actively looking for him. Continually looking down at maps, compasses, or electronic gadgetry detracts from this effort. The proper level of focus involves spotting abnormalities in one's natural surroundings. One can best do this by using terrain features as aids to land navigation.

## TAKING TACTICAL ADVANTAGE OF THE TERRAIN WHILE ON THE MOVE

Successfully transiting an active battlefield is not simply a problem of navigation; it is also one of tactics. Planning to move haphazardly or along straight lines between march objectives makes adequate provision for neither, as it ignores changes in terrain. Ideally, a land navigator includes in his route not only ground that acts as an aid to navigation, but also ground that facilitates winning chance contact. If he wants to avoid contact, he chooses terrain that will hide him. If he wants to make contact, he picks terrain from which he can more easily spot his foe. On other occasions, he might prefer ground that permits stealth or speed. Whatever the land navigator's unique requirements, he must ensure that most of the countryside along his route provides some *tactical advantage.*

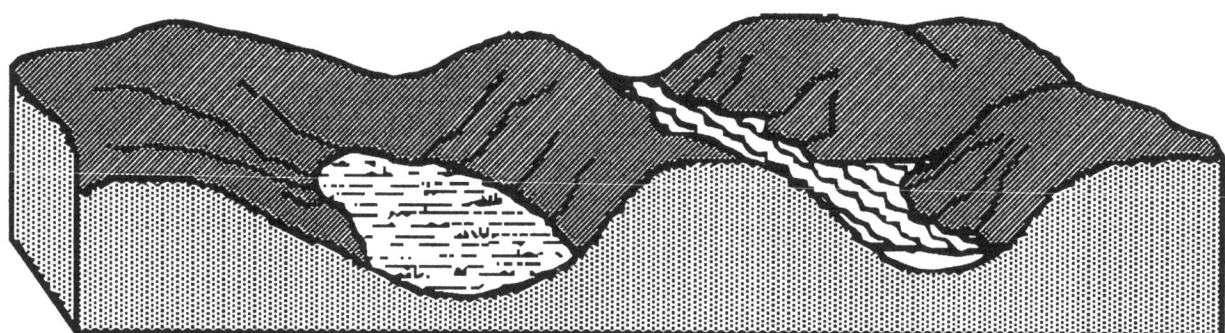

(Source: FM 21-76 (1970), p. 49)

Unless terrain features are utilized as *navigational aids* during simulated combat, infantrymen never fully realize their tactical value. Nor, do they see any benefit from moving along certain features rather than others. Land navigation can't be practiced in peacetime without taking into consideration an enemy threat. Doing so builds bad habits that can prove costly in war.

## TERRAIN THAT AFFORDS TACTICAL BENEFIT

During any movement, there is a chance of enemy contact. The importance of the terrain to winning that contact cannot be overemphasized. The unit with the best ground usually wins. Buford's choice of Cemetery Hill to block Lee's invasion of Pennsylvania, and Warren's insistence that Little Round Top anchored the Union position, made a critical difference at Gettysburg and ultimately in the American Civil War. The same principle holds true for squad-sized encounters. Regrettably, as Americans have become more a society of city dwellers, familiarity with rural terrain has suffered. The "observation and fields of fire" afforded by an area are established by its ground relief and foliage. The amount of "cover" depends on the abundance of manmade structures, trees, rocks, and depressions; while the amount of "concealment" is a function of all of these things in combination with weather and lighting conditions. To move across a battlefield with any hope of consistently winning chance contact, a unit must have a leader with an in-depth knowledge of terrain. Further, this knowledge must extend to "microterrain." A one-foot rise in the ground can hide an infantryman or block a bullet. General Lou Walt credited much of his success in combat to what he learned about microterrain from Chesty Puller:

> Being under Puller in Basic School did more for me than anything I experienced until I got to Guadalcanal. He taught us the use of terrain like a master, how to use the tiniest bit of cover to our advantage.[2]
> — Lou Walt

In peacetime, troops can often become indifferent to microterrain. Without real bullets whizzing past their heads, they have little motivation to learn how to use the tiny folds in the ground.

Terrain that is favorable for winning chance contact is terrain that provides cover and concealment from direct-fire weapons, without sacrificing observation and fields of fire. Cover and concealment are enhanced by heavy vegetation, whereas observation and fields of fire are enhanced by the lack of it. When contact occurs, the friendly unit would prefer to find itself just inside a tree line, and its foe in the middle of a large field. When confronting a larger unit, there is no substitute for being in heavy cover oneself, while one's opponent has to contend with a complete lack of cover. Under these circumstances, automatic weapons can usually keep an adversary of any size at bay.

Another valuable piece of real estate from the standpoint of chance contact is the "military crest" on sloping ground. This is any place from which a person can face downhill and see the surface of the earth out to beyond grenade range. On any given hill, the military crest may be near the base on one side and near the top on another. Further, some sides of the hill may have more than one military crest. In a meeting engagement, the unit that occupies the military crest can quickly move into defilade and produce grazing fire out to beyond grenade range. This gives the unit a decided edge. (See figure 9.1 for how to move relative to a military crest.)

## TERRAIN THAT OBSCURES FROM VIEW A UNIT MOVING THROUGH IT

To escape detection while crossing a flat open area in bright sunshine or moonlight, a person must crawl. If crawling destroys his momentum, he can run across the opening to limit his time of exposure. In starlight, he can both hide and maintain some momentum by remaining upright and moving *slowly* across the opening. In partial light, his opponent cannot distinguish vague shapes and slow movement from normal background images.

Deep shadows near patches of bright moonlight will also hide a man. While attempting to compensate for the bright light nearby, the human eye has difficulty seeing into the shadows.

Artillery illumination rounds will sometimes help to obscure human movement. In forested terrain, flares swinging from airborne parachutes create dancing shadows that make movement on the ground harder to identify. Furthermore, the bright light from those flares will temporarily blind any opposition soldier wearing Night Vision Goggles (NVG's).

Certain types of terrain will even hide infiltrators from thermal imaging. It must provide either defilade or heavy vegetation. Of course, heavy vegetation can be difficult to negotiate without making noise.

## TERRAIN THAT CAN BE FOLLOWED WITHOUT ANY SOUND SIGNATURE

Heavy brush and dry leaves are difficult to cross silently. Of course, the only sound that matters is the one that stands out above the background noise. After dark in the Equatorial jungle, normal conversation is indistinguishable above the din of animal and insect noises. An artillery barrage or passing helicopter can just as easily drown out the sound of twigs snapping.

Damp foliage underfoot is quieter than dry; but, when crossed by infantrymen, extremely wet ground makes a

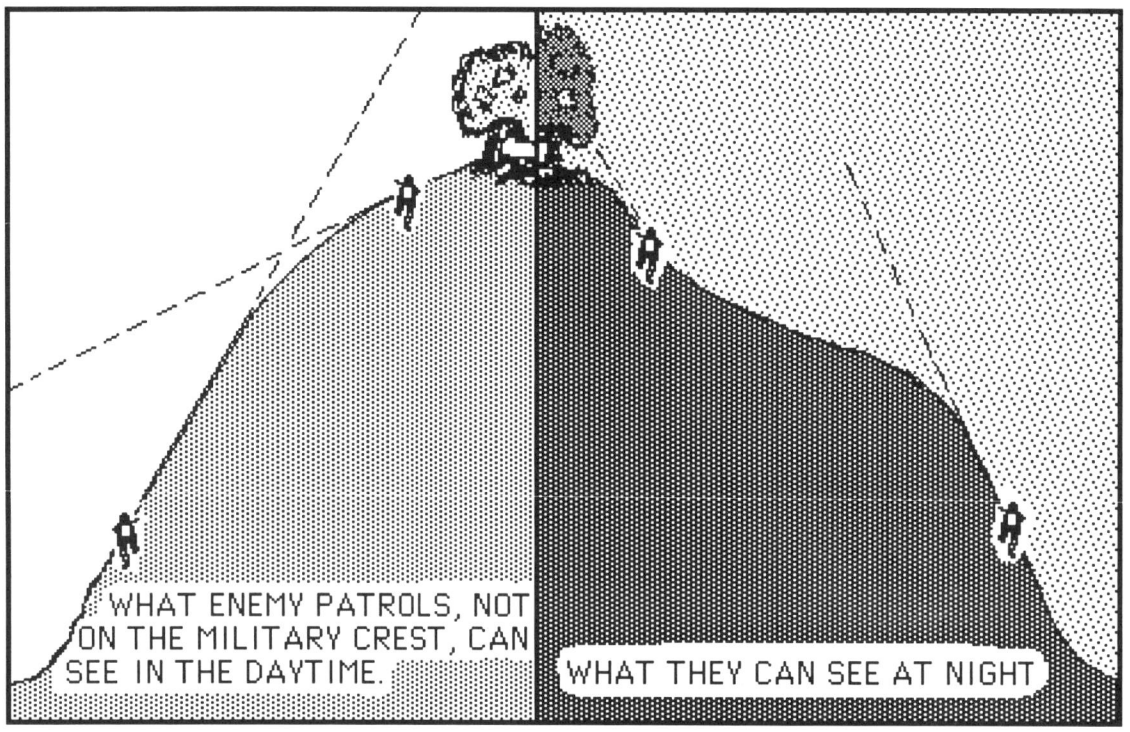
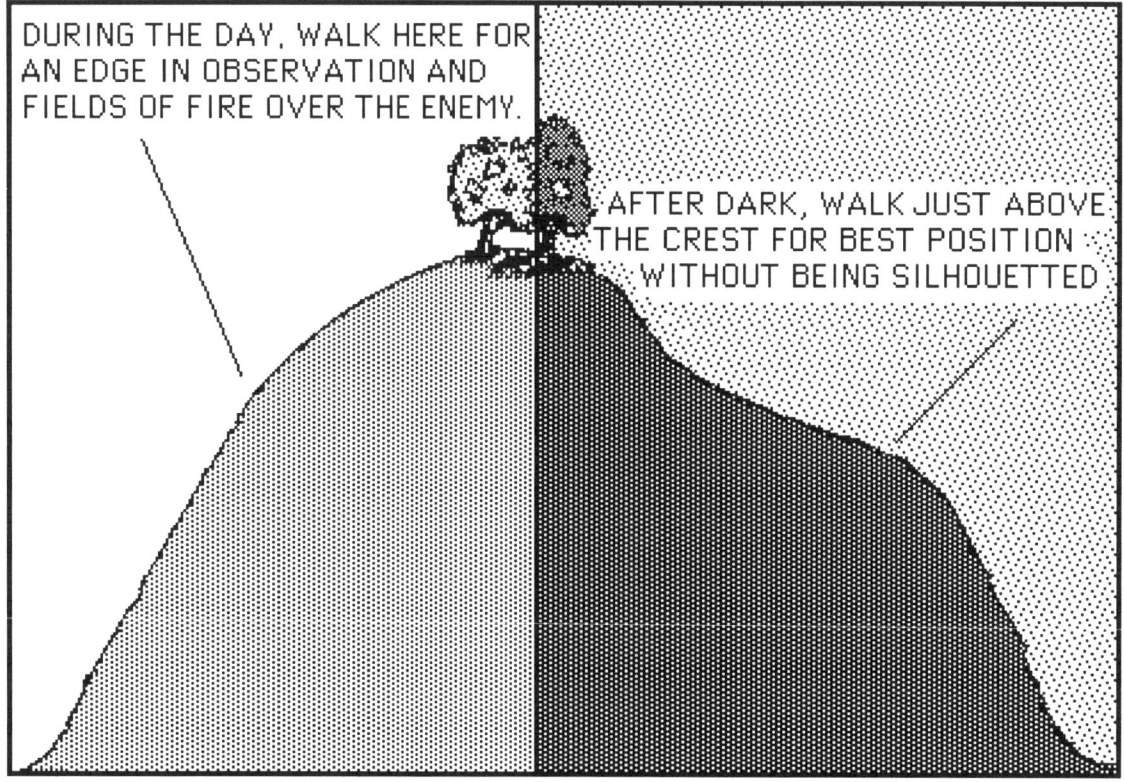

Figure 9.1: Where to Travel Relative to the Military Crest

characteristic slogging sound. Luckily, rain drops hitting a defender's helmet will prevent him from hearing all but the loudest sounds of movement around him.

Third-World militia are particularly adept at detecting subtle differences in background noise. To escape detection, U.S. infantrymen must familiarize themselves with the changes that will occur in background noise as human beings move through or occupy different types of terrain. Often, animals or insects will either make a particular sound or stop emitting any sound whatsoever.

## SPEED COULD SOMETIMES USEFULLY REPLACE THE TRADITIONAL PACE

Traditionally, a rather slow and stealthy type of movement has been the trademark of U.S. patrols and approach marches. While this deliberate type of movement is certainly hard to spot, makes minimal noise, and facilitates carrying heavy loads of ammunition, it doesn't contribute much to momentum. The U.S. preoccupation with stealth regularly extends to having all hands get down every time their unit pauses, and to having advance elements carefully reconnoiter the far side of every opening in the woods, however small.

While this is undoubtedly the best type of movement for certain circumstances, it is inappropriate for others; and interesting alternatives exist. Just as a solitary man must sometimes dash upright across an open area to limit his time of exposure, so too must a whole patrol sometimes use *speed as a type of security*. What makes most of the noise is the gear, and gear can be taken off or silenced. Even heavily laden men can move quickly without being heard as long as there is enough background noise from stormy weather, nocturnal wildlife, artillery explosions, passing helicopters, tracked vehicles, or small-arms fire.

Speed might be useful for moving through sparse cover, or over hard and unobstructed ground. It might also be appropriate for outflanking an enemy or eluding his supporting arms. In Vietnam, small columns of NVA regularly *ran* in from the mountains to attack major U.S. installations. They needed speed to cross the cultivated coastal plain over paddy dikes and trails without being targeted by U.S. supporting arms. By the time artillery observers got their missions cleared, the enemy had usually moved out of sight. Because these NVA columns zigzagged as they ran, it was difficult even to adjust preregistered fire onto them. Copses of bamboo and trees would obscure them from view. While obscured, they could sidestep the fire simply by changing direction.

If an enemy patrol's flank security element were to spot a quickly passing U.S. infantry patrol, it probably couldn't get the sighting corroborated in time to do anything about it. Additionally, a fast moving target is more difficult to shoot. Any hunter can attest to that.

The NVA combined speed with an understanding of camouflage and lighting conditions. They made their approach "runs" at dusk dressed like bushes. Seen through a heavy spotting scope from one of the small hilltops that dotted the Vietnamese coastal plain, they made quite a sight.

This is just one of many ancient military skills that may not have made the transition into modern American thought. For guidelines on how and when to utilize speed on patrol, one may have to depend on historical works like *The Last of the Mohicans*. The commander of the Marines on Guadalcanal was perfectly sincere when he gave this training advice:

> [G]o back to the tactics of the French and Indian days. This is not meant facetiously. Study their tactics and fit in our modern weapons, and you have a solution. I refer to the tactics . . . of the days of ROGERS' RANGERS.[3]
> — Archibald Vandegrift

An example of when and where to alter one's speed exists in nature. The hunted, like the deer, moves slowly through thick foliage and quickly through thin. The slow hunter (like the python) lies in ambush for its quarry; whereas the quick hunter (like the cheetah) stalks and then rushes its prey.

Some terrain permits both moving quickly and winning chance contact. For example, in wooded terrain, the type of firebreak made by a ditching machine provides both an unobstructed path and good cover. Additionally, it's not normally considered to be a conduit for travel, and is therefore seldom ambushed. A shallow draw can serve the same purpose.

## TERRAIN THAT CAN BE TRAVERSED QUICKLY

Paths, edges of roads, fence lines, power lines, and tree lines are all common linear terrain features that can be followed quickly. Yet, when considering patrol routes, leaders often rule these linear terrain features out as being too dangerous. This is unfortunate, because many can be followed safely — simply by altering movement security procedures. These procedures will be discussed later. There are also less common conduits for movement. In forested coastal plains, firebreaks and sparsely wooded areas certainly qualify. In precipitous rain forests, streambeds and ridge lines often provide the answer. Naturally, the more obstacles and "danger areas" a unit can avoid along its route, the more quickly it can move.

## TO PLAN A ROUTE, ONE MUST CONSIDER SEVERAL IMPORTANT FACTORS AT ONCE

First, the route must match the mission. A unit attempting to make contact with its adversary will require a route quite different from one attempting to avoid contact. Making contact requires passing through likely conduits of enemy movement and locations that afford good observation of the battlefield. Avoiding contact requires moving through terrain that has abundant concealment and no channelizing effect on the enemy.

Once the mission has been considered, terrain availability dictates route. Terrain can provide tactical advantage and function as an aid to navigation. To rely on supporting arms, a unit must closely monitor its whereabouts while on the move. Still, it must do so without incurring a tactical disadvantage. Routes should not normally be planned between major landmarks (like road or trail junctions), because these landmarks invite ambush. The U.S. patrols that ambushed major trail junctions in Vietnam rarely saw the NVA forces that moved continually through their areas of responsibility. For route markers, combat travelers should choose less conspicuous, yet still distinguishable, terrain combinations like where trails cross draws.

Routes should not normally be plotted through danger areas (like fields of elephant grass) or obstacles (like marshes). Crossing these obstructions can not only be slow and tiring, but can also invite ambush. Friendly units must be given a wide berth as well!

Route selection is further complicated by maps that don't accurately depict what's on the ground. Just to keep from getting lost, one must plan to pass close to unique terrain features that clearly show on aerial photographs (like the sharp bends in a road). That's why land navigation has been called an "art," as opposed to a "science." As with any art, it must be practiced to be retained. One cannot practice this art without first learning how to plan a route properly.

## PLANNING TO TRAVERSE A LARGE OBSTACLE CARRIES WITH IT A HEFTY PRICE TAG

If speed is important in war, then so too is avoiding obstacles. Even a series of small obstacles can slow a unit down. For example, a unit can move almost twice as fast along a firebreak as it can through heavy brush. Large obstacles like steep ravines or swamps can make 200 yards seem like 2 miles. Although traversing obstacles can sometimes be tactically advantageous, doing so routinely can be counterproductive. It is slow, noisy, and so tiring as to sometimes make the unit incapable of handling enemy contact on the far side:

> The man whether tired or frightened suffers a loss of muscular function and has a pervading feeling of physical weakness.[4]
> — S.L.A. Marshall

Whether to avoid an obstacle depends on the circumstances. But, unless crossing the obstacle helps to surprise an enemy, the obstruction should be bypassed.

## THE PROBLEMS ASSOCIATED WITH PLOTTING ROUTES THROUGH LARGE DANGER AREAS

A danger area is one in which *an entire unit can be destroyed in an instant*. A good example is the long axis of a road or trail. Another is a large field. A few enemy soldiers feigning fear and retreating across an area covered with tall but spindly vegetation has suckered more than one U.S. unit to its death. Elephant grass, sugar cane, and tall weeds will not stop bullets. The whole idea is to preclude having to cross any ground known to be a danger area, because to cross it safely, one must sacrifice either surprise or momentum.

## THE RISKS ASSOCIATED WITH PLANNING A ROUTE TOO CLOSE TO A FRIENDLY UNIT

During movement, patterns must be avoided at all cost. That means not using the same route twice. It also means returning to one's patrol base by a route different from the one used to depart. Even sentry posts have been ambushed for using the same route too often.

Of course, patrol leaders should study their parent-unit's daily patrol overlay to see which sister units may be operating in the same general vicinity. Well-meaning units occasionally stray from their approved routes. Easiest to forget, are the two-man sentry posts in the patrol's path.

## ROUTES SHOULD FOLLOW TERRAIN THAT FACILITATES WINNING CHANCE CONTACT

To maintain cover and concealment, units should plan to move through mature forests, boulder-strewn slopes, shallow ditches, etc. To maintain adequate observation and fields of fire, they should plan to skirt breaks in the vegetation (like roads, firebreaks, or bodies of water), and to pass over elevated terrain. When hilltops are not available, tall trees will suffice. They did for the Japanese at Guadalcanal and for the NVA at Ia Drang. It is particularly hard to spot enemy observers in trees, because humans do not normally look for each other in trees. To improve their powers of observation in the daytime, units should plan to walk along the military crests of *ridge lines* and *fingers*.

Night patrols could plan to move more through low areas or *draws*. Doing so would not only conceal their movement, but also increase their powers of observation. Enemy soldiers would be silhouetted against the unobstructed sky and easy to spot from below. Of course, shallow draws would provide cover with the least risk. The low ground in microterrain also has value at night. Security elements (whether moving or stationary) can see better at night when located in slight depressions or near

Successfully Traversing a Battlefield

the bases of slight rises in the terrain. By putting their heads to the ground and looking up, they can easily pick out enemy soldiers who are now silhouetted against a natural horizon. (See figure 9.2.) At the same time, these security elements become almost invisible to their adversaries. Upright human beings tend only to see other upright human beings.

Of course, low ground offers a skilled enemy the same advantage at night. Therefore, a good case can also be made for friendlies patrolling during hours of darkness just above the military crests of fingers and ridge lines. Friendly patrols should avoid barren high ground at all cost. (Refer back to figure 9.1.)

From reflected starlight, *roads* appear white at night and can thus function as false horizons. The unit that moves parallel to, but barely within sight of, a road can spot enemy units moving along the road's edge without being seen itself. The same holds true for *edges* of bodies of water. All the terrain features italicized above are linear; they could easily be incorporated into a zigzag patrol route. (See figure 9.3.)

### DURING ROUTE SELECTION, ONE MUST COMPENSATE FOR MAP INACCURACIES

Maps for most of the world (except parts of Europe) contain inaccuracies. Many are outdated — not only in decade depicted, but also in preparation technology. Such maps create many problems for military units:

(Source: FM 7-8 (1984), p. B-4)

Inaccurate maps meant inaccurate [artillery] fire, and the maps in Vietnam were notoriously bad. Topographic surveys, inherited from the Japanese and the French, were so unreliable that points on the ground were commonly misrepresented on the map by a quarter-mile or more. Manmade structures and roads had long since disappeared or been moved since the maps were printed, causing terrible confusion for unwary soldiers who relied on temporary features for navigation.[5]

Even recently published maps contain "map error" with respect to the exact shape of permanent terrain features. This type of map error does not result from the age of the map, but rather from the process by which the map was made. Most maps come from the photographs taken during a few passes by an airplane. While these photos are somewhat distorted by the different angles at which they are taken, they are still manually pieced together by a technician. To help this technician put the collage of photos into better perspective, a surveyor occasionally traverses the area once or twice. Finally, the map maker sits down and with his pen creates what he thinks the terrain looks like. Significant errors can result. If aerial photos are pieced together incorrectly, hundreds of yards of terrain can simply vanish. If tree cover obscures ground relief from the camera, the map will show draws and fingers of the wrong length, or hills of the wrong height. Smaller draws, fingers, and hills won't show at all. (See figure 9.4.) Recent technological advances make identifying minor changes in elevation below the leaf canopy possible, but many decades will pass before the world can be totally remapped using this procedure.

## USING TERRAIN FEATURES TO DETERMINE DIRECTION AND DISTANCE

To land navigate, one doesn't need a compass and a "pace count." To the extent that maps accurately reflect what exists on the ground, the terrain itself provides an adequate means by which to measure direction and distance.

Every tall/pointed feature that exists on both map and ground, can provide direction to the land navigator. By plotting azimuths to widely separated landmarks, the navigator can pinpoint his location on a map. Of course, there aren't always elevated features visible. Artillery illumination rounds can serve the same purpose — even during the daytime.

On the other hand, common linear features (like fingers, draws, roads, trails, power lines) can also provide direction to the navigator. Such a feature can be broken down into a series of straight linear segments, each of which has a unique grid azimuth. This grid azimuth can be easily converted into a magnetic azimuth. Then, the navigator could quickly doublecheck with a compass each linear route segment he encountered on patrol. Naturally occurring linear terrain features are safer to travel along than manmade ones — because of their relative abundance. On the other hand, streambeds and river/lake banks meander and change location so often that their map depictions are not dependable.

Additionally, straight segments of linear terrain features represent straight-line distances. These distances can be easily measured by using a map's "bar scale." Unfortunately, distances computed this way are somewhat less reliable than the directions. If a map shows a finger bending after 200 meters, that finger may actually bend anywhere between 150 meters and 250 meters.

## THE ESTABLISHED WAY TO LAND NAVIGATE IS "DEAD RECKONING"

U.S. infantrymen are taught to move along straight lines between march objectives — i.e., to "dead reckon." Although useful under certain circumstances, this navigational method has many limitations.

Each direction is obtained by measuring the grid azimuth of the line connecting the start point and march objective on the map, and then converting this grid azimuth to a magnetic azimuth. Map error near either end of the line can throw off the computation. Compass error can also make a difference. Military compasses are hard to read, sensitive to magnetic fields or metal nearby (including ammunition magazines and electronic wristwatches), and usually a bit out of calibration. In theory, over a thousand meter patrol leg, a three-degree error in azimuth should only cause a navigational mistake of about 50 meters. Unfortunately, even in relatively flat and lightly forested terrain, the actual miss can be much greater than that. The error must be compounded somehow as the navigator rechecks his compass after moving around each obstruction.

The established procedure for determining distance is the "pace count." The average man takes 60 double steps every 100 meters. Again, implicitly prerequisite to the pace count technique, is ideal terrain. The terrain to be crossed on patrol must be identical to the that through which the land navigator has measured his pace count. Obviously, this only happens when both contain only flat and unobstructed terrain, and when lighting conditions are identical. Furthermore, maps can't possibly depict all the detail in the microterrain. Therefore, terrain that is not totally level or unobstructed invariably yields a pace count that is inconsistent with the map distance.

Because an aerial photograph show's only the tops of the trees, it cannot always differentiate between high ground with short trees and low ground with tall trees. Even for terrain without tree cover, the photograph cannot show all the folds in the ground, nor can the map maker include them in his drawing. Most military maps

Successfully Traversing a Battlefield

Figure 9.2: Using a Microterrain Horizon to Spot Enemy at Night
(Sources: FM 7-11B1/2 (1978), p. 2-III-E-8.2; FM 5-103 (1985), p. 4-4; FM 22-100 (1983), p. 22)

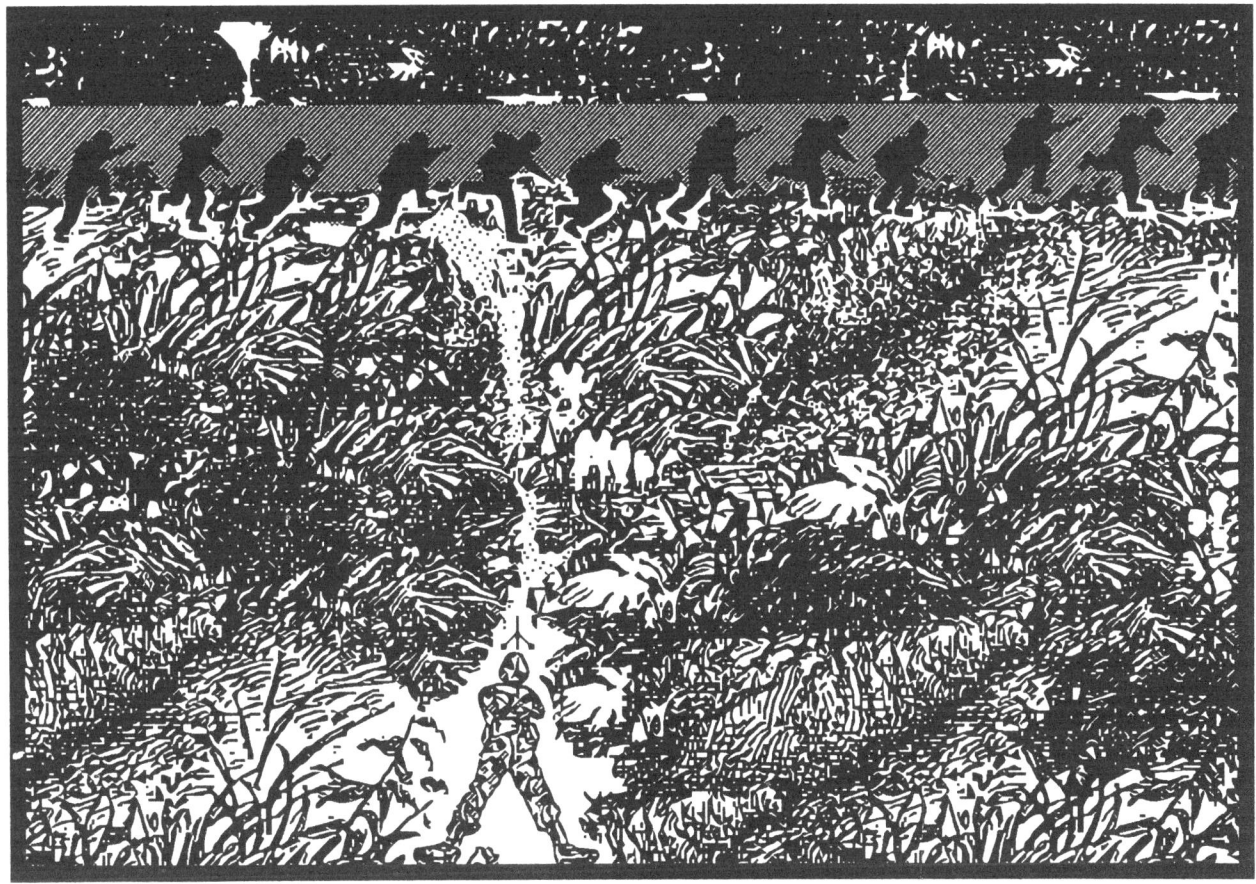
Figure 9.3: Using an Artificial Horizon to Spot Enemy at Night
(Sources: FM 7-11B1/2 (1978), p. 2-III-E-8.2; FM 90-10-1 (1982), pp. B-3, B-4; FM 5-103 (1985), p. 4-4)

Techniques from the NCO Corps

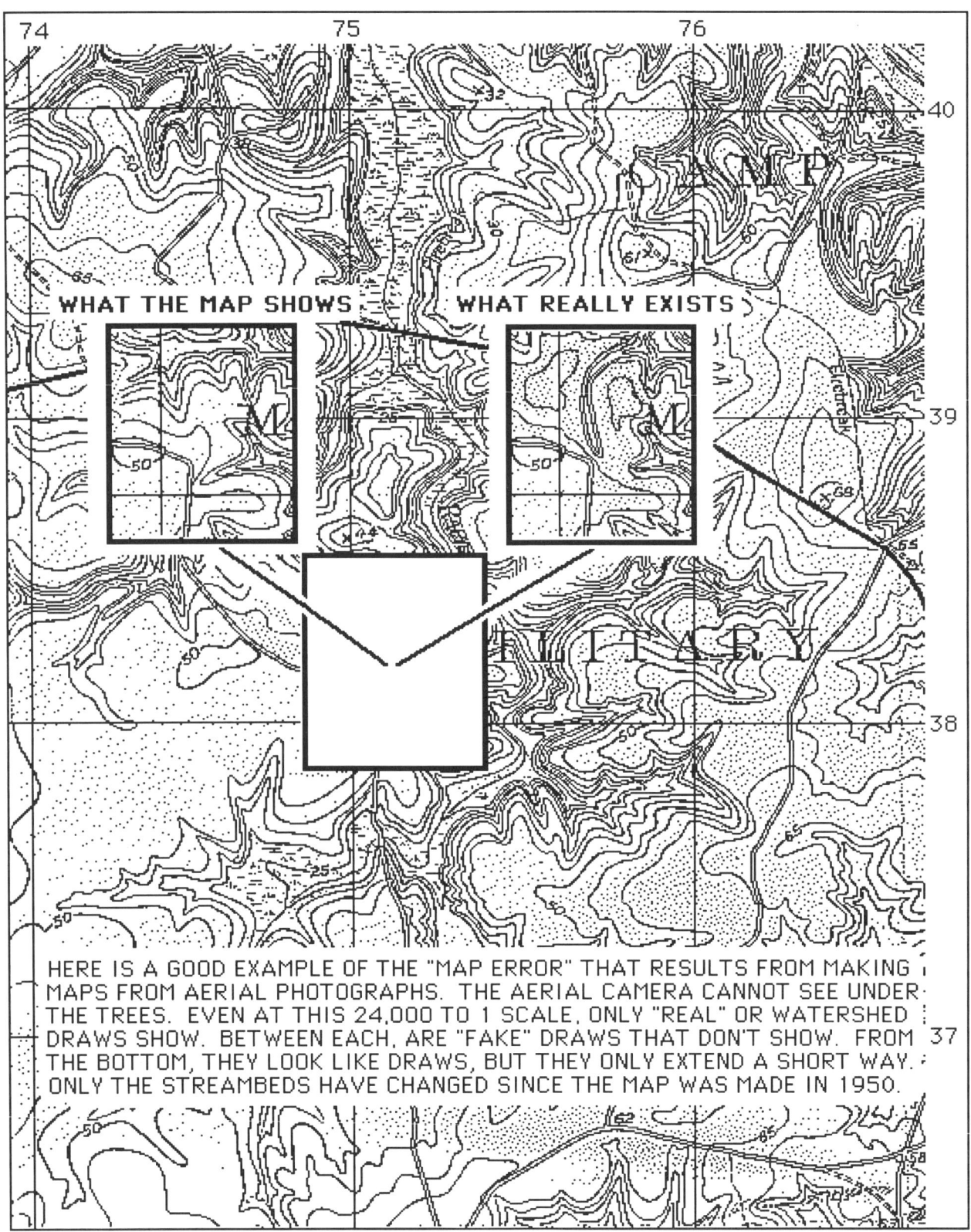

Figure 9.4: Map Error
(Source: U.S. Dept. of Interior, "Jacksonville South Quadrangle," 1:24,000)

are drawn at a scale of 1:50,000. This means that one inch on the map equates to 50,000 inches or 1400 yards on the ground. That's about 3/4 of a mile. Even if the map maker knew the detail throughout this great expanse of real estate, he could not adequately depict it in a single inch of map space. One at a time, each undulation in the ground might produce only a slight pace count error. But collectively over a long distance, hundreds of undulations could produce a significant inaccuracy in distance estimation. Even under ideal conditions, pace counts are only approximate — affected by everything from the pacer's load to his degree of caution. Using some other method to determine distance — e.g., identifying terrain features along the way — does not alter the fact that "straight-line" navigation constitutes dead reckoning. Because of the many sizable depressions in the ground that do not show up on any given map in densely foliated terrain, it is very difficult correctly to identify the draws encountered. Ultimately, in most parts of the world, dead reckoning over a long distance denies the navigator a reliable means of keeping track of his precise location. That means that he can't quickly summon supporting arms in case of trouble.

Additionally, dead reckoning makes little provision for the successful handling of enemy contact. Straight-line navigation ignores the fact that large obstacles and danger areas may exist between one's start point and march objective. Scaling the sides of deep ravines, slogging through swamps, and climbing over piles of jumbled logs makes even well-conditioned troops with reasonable loads too tired to handle chance contact. Under these conditions, merely enduring the hardships of the trip becomes more the goal than overcoming an opponent.

Similarly, planning to travel directly through a danger area (like an overgrown field) is courting disaster. Even pine saplings are not sturdy enough to stop .50-caliber machinegun bullets.

## THE MORE USEFUL ALTERNATIVE — "TERRAIN ASSOCIATION"

There's another way to land navigate — namely, to "terrain associate." This is a lesser-known but more valuable way to change location in combat. As military objectives are often associated with terrain features, using such features as navigational aids helps a unit to accomplish its mission. For example, if the intersection of a streambed and a road were considered a good defensive security patrol objective, the easiest way to find it would be to follow either the road or the streambed. *In essence, terrain association involves following a zigzag pattern of linear terrain features to reach one's final destination.* Each linear terrain feature is further broken down into a series of straight segments. Each segment now has a unique direction and length with which it can be associated. While on the move, this unique "fingerprint" can be doublechecked with a compass and distance estimation technique for each successive segment. *In other words, with terrain association, the terrain itself is employed as the primary means of determining one's direction and distance, whereas the compass and distance estimation techniques are used only as backups.* This enables the combat navigator to focus more completely on his surroundings.

Across uneven and partially obstructed terrain, an infantryman can estimate distance in small increments and then keep track of the total. He can do so, because he has often walked to the 50-, 100-, or 200-yard line at the rifle or pistol range. To remember how far he has traveled, he has only to save pebbles in his pocket.

The zigzag path a person uses to terrain associate may cover slightly more map distance than the straight lines he would require to dead reckon. Yet, because the zigzagging often involves less cumulative change in elevation, the actual distance traveled on the ground may be comparable. Additionally, with the zigzagging, fewer obstacles and danger areas are generally encountered.

In dead reckoning, the route checkpoints are chosen first. In terrain association, *the route legs are picked before the checkpoints.* Straight segments of the linear terrain features serve as the legs. The ends of the legs automatically become checkpoints. Of course, each checkpoint has unique characteristics — e.g., "the end of a finger," "the junction of a draw with another running NW," or "a bend from 30 to 45 degrees in a finger." These checkpoints are often of the "intersection-of-line" variety. This is the only type that describes an exact location that can be found easily. Unlike hard-to-find "point" checkpoints, intersection-of-line checkpoints occur in such abundance that there is little chance they will be ambushed. For example, in most rural locales there are many more intersections of draws with roads than there are abandoned buildings. Friendly patrols could more safely use the culverts at these locations for checkpoints.

## OTHER TECHNIQUES AVAILABLE

The most useful of the supporting methods is that of the *attack point*. An attack point is any location that the navigator is certain that he can find. Good examples are distinct bends in roads and places where major watersheds pass underneath roads. In other words, aerial photographs can't miss them. A well-conceived route includes as many of these attack points as possible, even when it must be lengthened to do so. The more attack points the land navigator includes in his route, the less chance he has of getting confused by map error. By reducing his chances of getting lost, he can also better utilize his supporting arms in case of trouble. Furthermore, his chances of finding a specific location are greatly enhanced by having an attack point nearby. *Because of map limitations, attack points are crucial to land navigation.*

# Techniques from the NCO Corps

*Reference points and lines* are terrain features not directly in the path of the navigator, but still useful as navigational aids. By watching point features, a navigator can monitor his position relative to them. This is nothing more than subconsciously *resecting* off the features. Previously occupied known locations and artillery illumination rounds can also be used as reference points from which to resect. (See figure 9.5.)

*Triangulation* is a variation of one-point resection. Here, the navigator measures azimuths to the same known point from a couple of different locations. By keeping track of the distance and direction traveled between those locations, he creates a unique triangle (with all three angles and one side known). When he computes the lengths of the other sides, his exact location at the corner of the triangle becomes evident. No mathematical expertise is required, only a little trial-and-error exercise on a map with three pieces of string. (See figure 9.6.)

*Collecting features* are linear terrain features that intersect the route of march. They tell the navigator how far he has gone. The method can be usefully expanded to include other changes in ground relief — for example, a bend in a finger also tells the navigator how far he has gone. *Limiting features* are similar to collecting features, except that their function is to tell the navigator that he has gone too far.

The *deliberate-offset* or *aiming-off* method involves moving along a straight line so as intentionally to miss a march objective. When that objective is located on a linear terrain feature roughly perpendicular to the approach route, the navigator can aim off so that he will know which way to turn when he reaches the linear feature. For example, when the march objective is the NW corner of a low hill surrounded by tall vegetation, the navigator that aims initially for the center of the hill has more chance of finding his objective, than the one who aims for the corner of the hill and risks walking past it. (See figure 9.7.)

## CHOOSING AMONG THE VARIOUS TECHNIQUES

Mission affects technique selection more than any other factor. Does the unit want enemy contact en route or not? Dead reckoning avoids "lines of drift." In other words, it prevents units on the move from being channelized by terrain. By so doing, it theoretically hampers enemy efforts to interrupt that movement. Of course, at the same time, it hampers a friendly unit's chances of finding enemy. If a unit using dead reckoning were to make contact, it would probably do so under a tactical disadvantage at some danger area or obstacle. For these reasons,

**Figure 9.5: Resecting off Well-Placed Illumination Rounds**
(Sources: FM 7-11B1/2 (1978), p. 3-II-A-4.2; OPNAV P 34-03 (1960), p. 40)

dead reckoning is most productive when there are no danger areas or obstacles in the way, and when the unit is not trying to make enemy contact. For example, a patrol wanting to reconnoiter a fuel dump on the far side of level forest might use dead reckoning. The chances of meeting an enemy patrol along any particular straight line through that forest would be slim.

On the other hand, dead reckoning would be counterproductive for any mission that required mixing it up with the enemy (like that of a defensive security patrol). The security patrol has a better chance of finding enemy by following the natural avenues of approach to its own perimeter. Of particular interest would be the watershed system for the draws leading to the perimeter.

### TECHNIQUE MAY VARY FROM LEG TO LEG

There are many techniques for land navigation. Just like the map or compass, each method has its own limitations. Different legs in the same route may require different techniques. Knowing which to use at any given time can only be learned through practice. Without practice, infantrymen will get lost in combat. And, when they do, they will be as much at risk from friendly fire, as from enemy fire.

### THE MECHANICS OF PLOTTING A ROUTE AND WHY A ROUTE CARD IS ADVISABLE

Great care should be taken while plotting march objectives on a map. It's easy to plot an objective in the wrong place, simply by misreading the grid line designators at the edge of the map or forgetting the basic rule for plotting/reading grid coordinates — "right and up."

Once the route has been carefully considered and plotted, the length of each straight leg can be measured. By extending each leg with a straight edge, its azimuth can next be determined with a square protractor. Finally, conversion of these azimuths from grid to magnetic completes the information necessary to fill out a "route card."

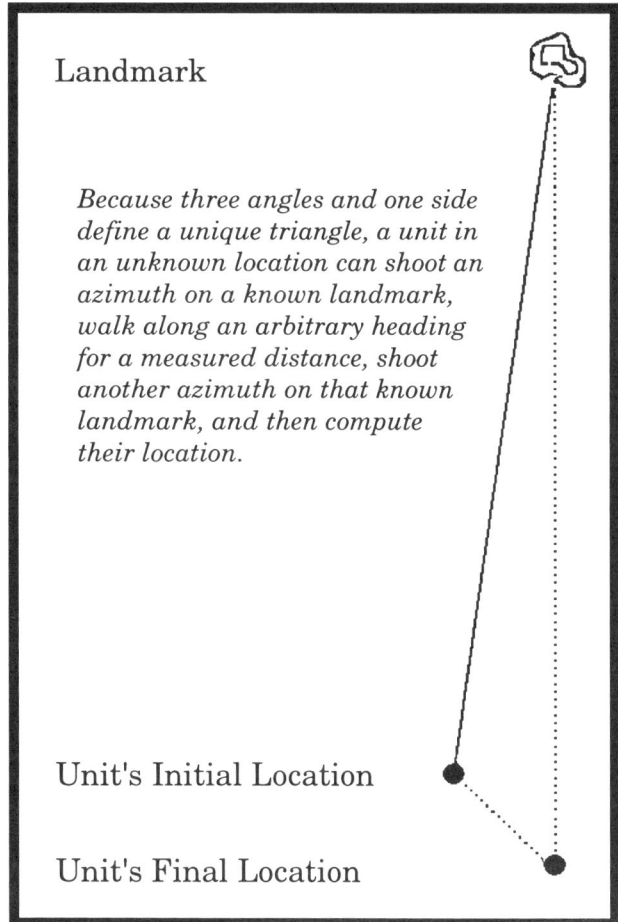

Figure 9.6: Triangulation

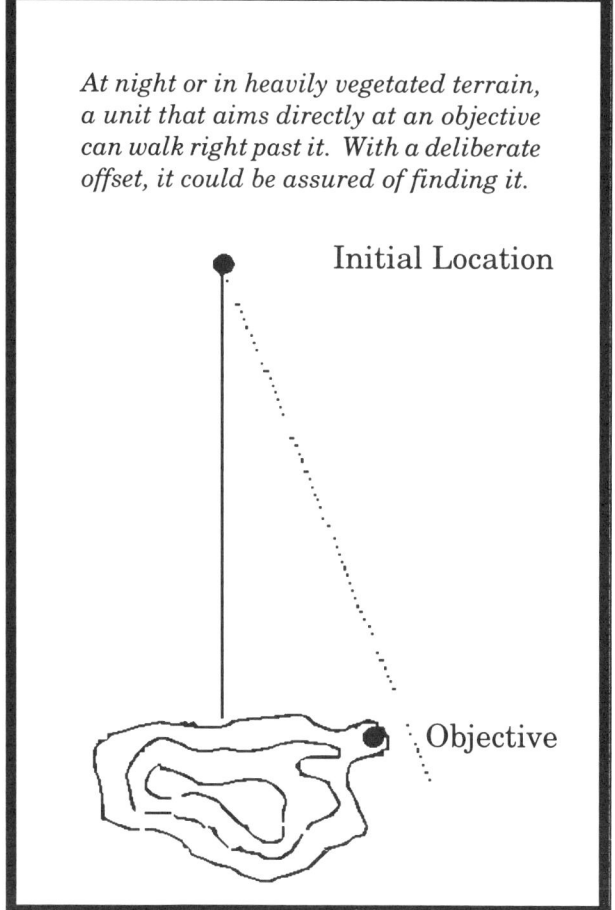

Figure 9.7: Aiming Off

*Techniques from the NCO Corps*

When utilized during the execution phase of land navigation, the route card permits the navigator to focus on his surroundings, instead of his map.

| TYPE OF LINEAR TERRAIN ON LEG | DIRECTION (DEGREES MAGNETIC) | DISTANCE (METERS) | CHECKPOINT DESCRIPTION/# |
|---|---|---|---|
| Draw | 300 | 200 | Jnct SE draw/#1 |
| None | 280 | 100 | End NW finger/#2 |
| Finger | 330 | 250 | Finger bend/#3 |
| Finger | 285 | 400 | Hilltop/#4 |

*Now, instead of continually referring to his map and compass, the navigator can take a quick look at his route card and compass at the beginning of each leg. As long as what he sees on the ground matches what he sees on the card and compass, he is on course. (Figures 9.8 through 9.13 show the planning process for a typical patrol.)*

(Source: FM 22-100 (1983), p. 66)

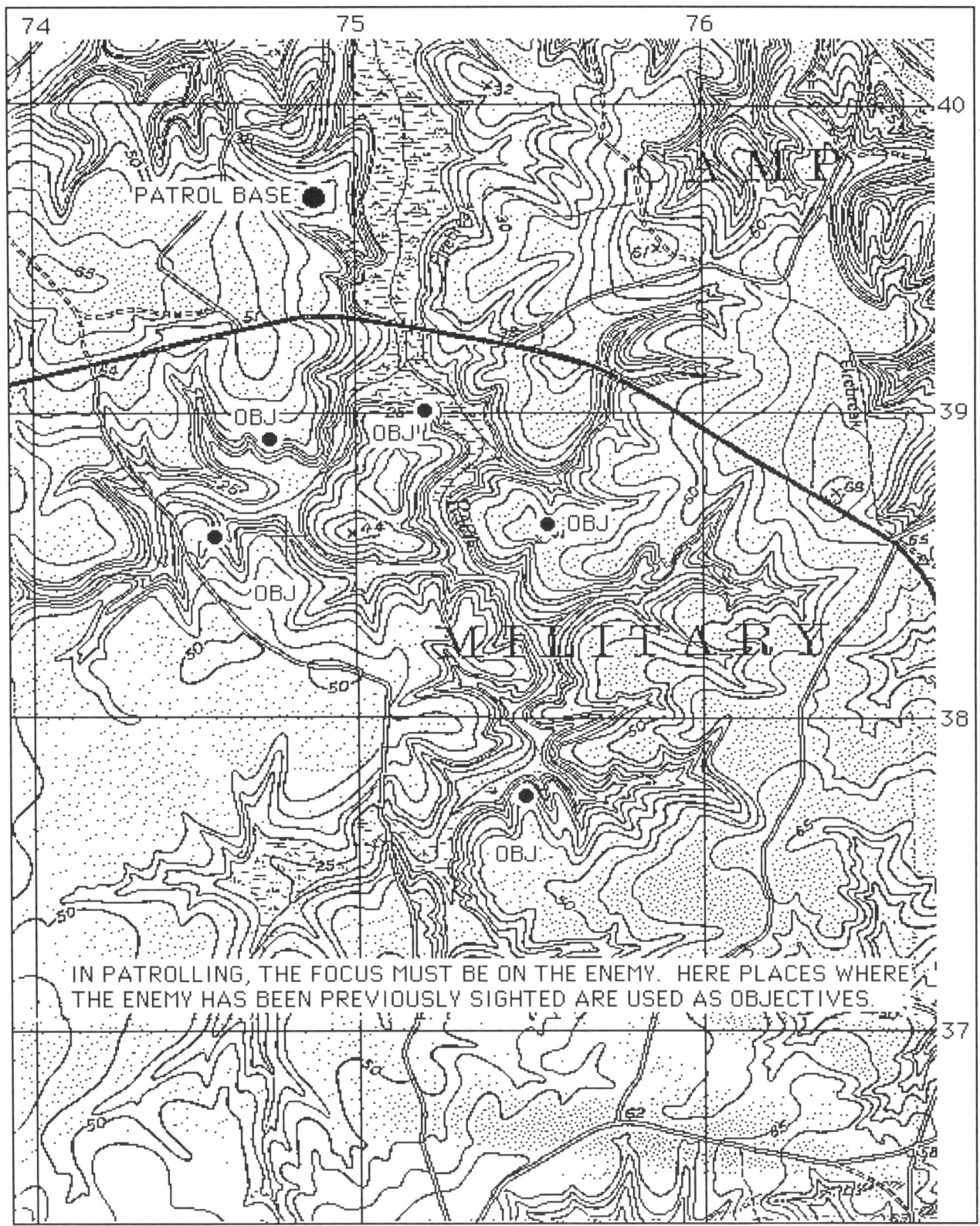

*Figure 9.8: Patrol Objectives Must Be Chosen Carefully*
(Source: U.S. Dept. of Interior, "Jacksonville South Quadrangle," 1:24,000)

Techniques from the NCO Corps

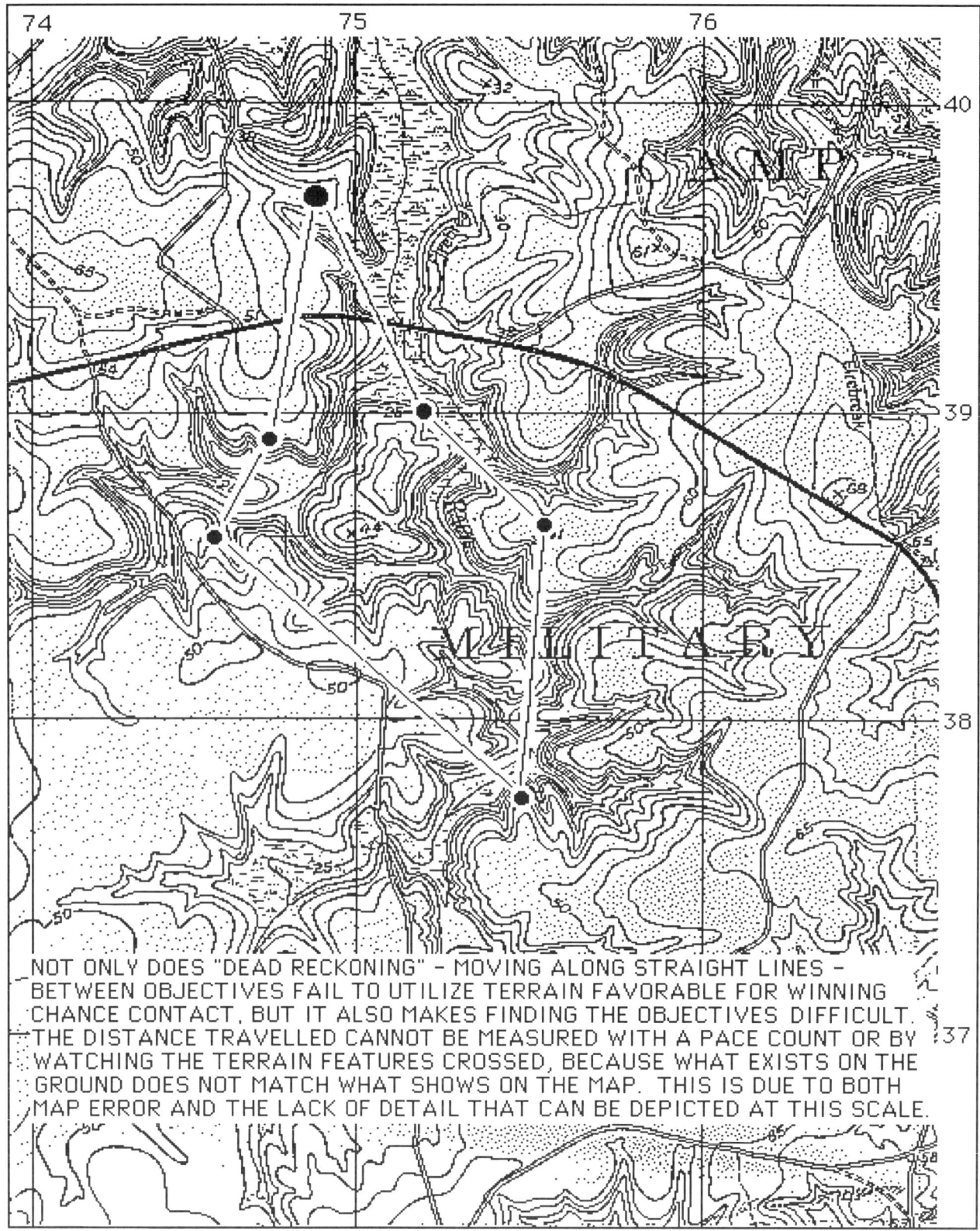

Figure 9.9: The Disadvantages of Always Dead Reckoning between March Objectives
(Source: U.S. Dept. of Interior, "Jacksonville South Quadrangle," 1:24,000)

*Successfully Traversing a Battlefield*

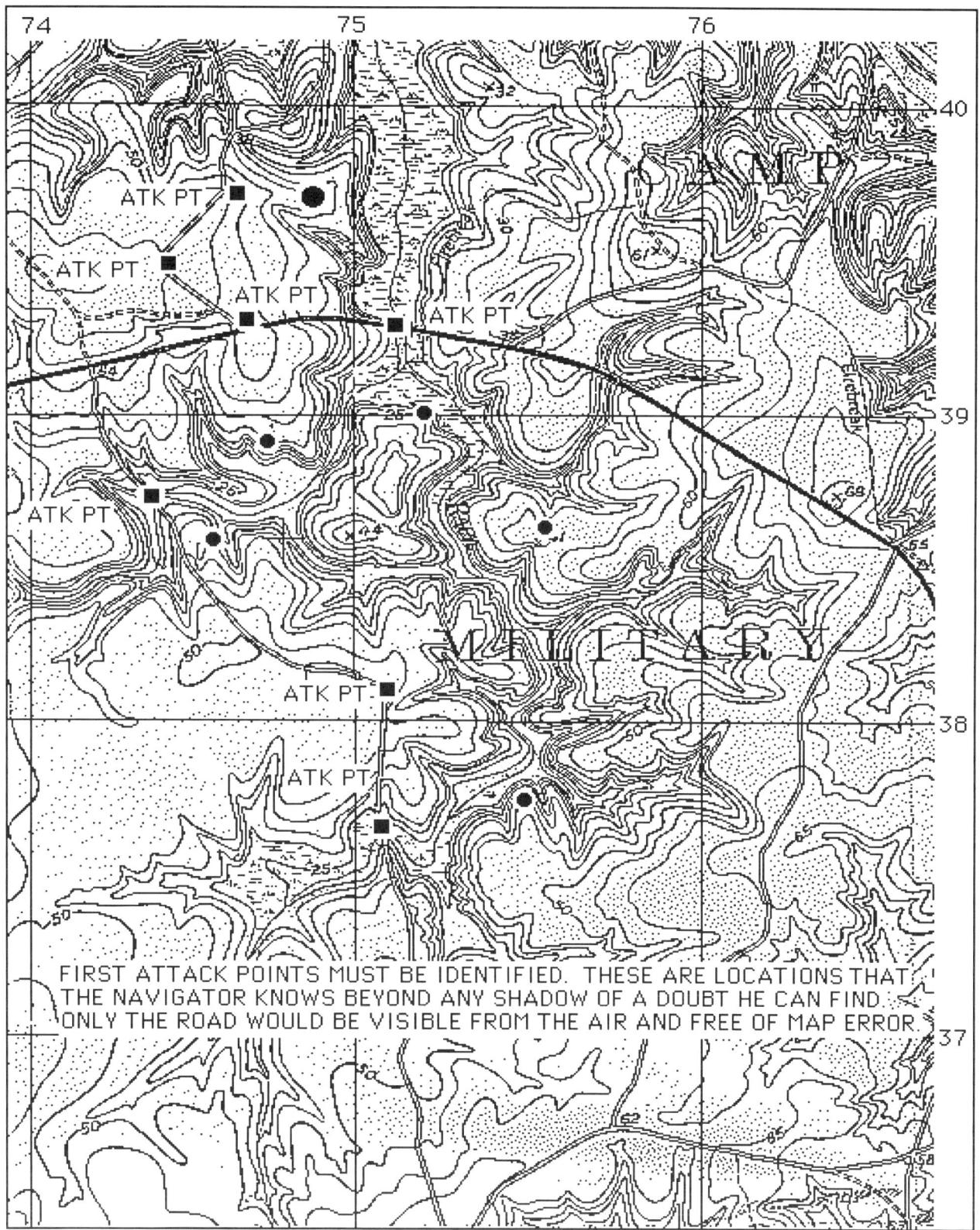

*Figure 9.10: First, See How Many Attack Points Are Available*
(Source: U.S. Dept. of Interior, "Jacksonville South Quadrangle," 1:24,000)

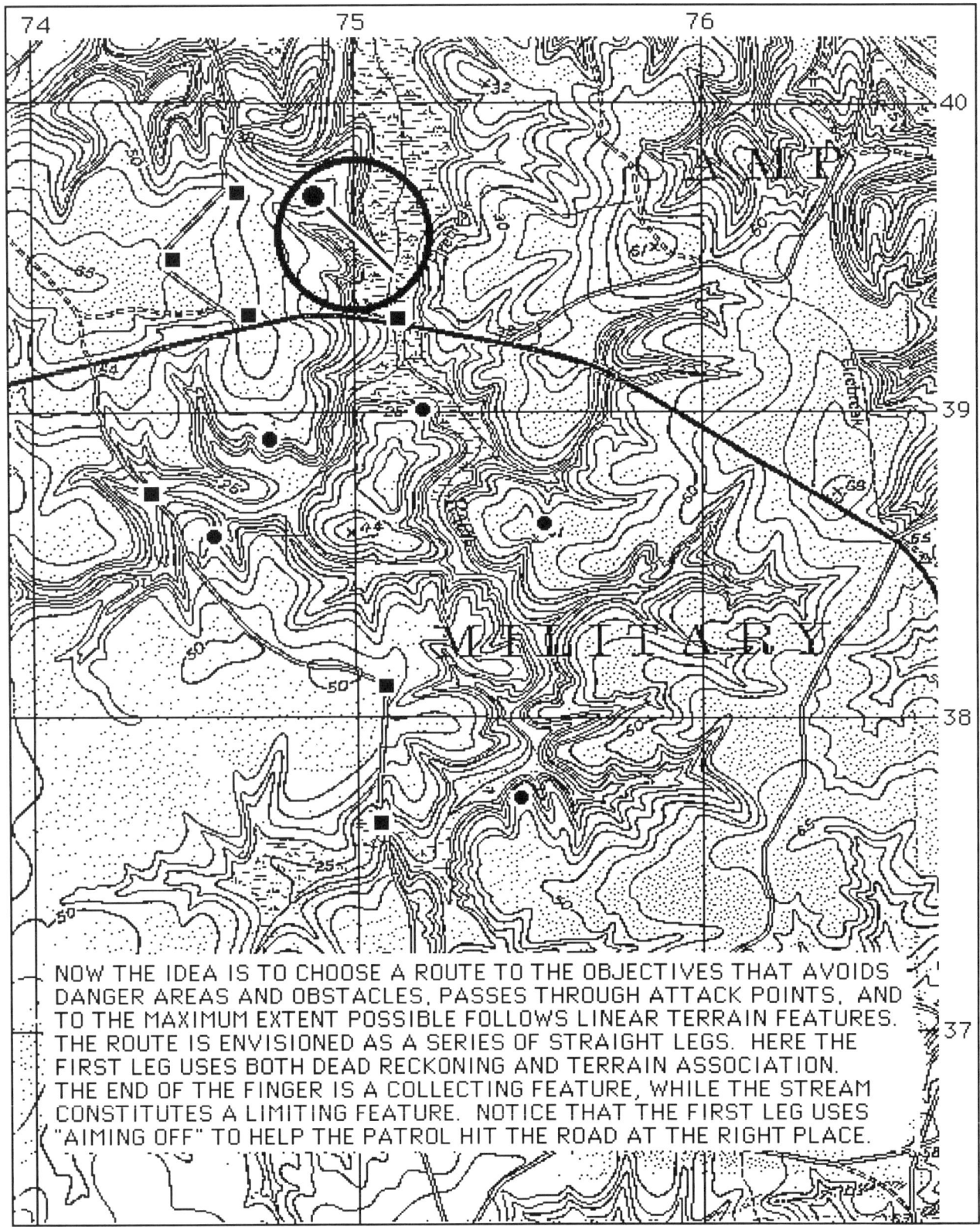

Figure 9.11: Plan to Follow Linear Terrain Features and to Avoid Obstacles or Danger Areas
(Source: U.S. Dept. of Interior, "Jacksonville South Quadrangle," 1:24,000)

*Successfully Traversing a Battlefield*

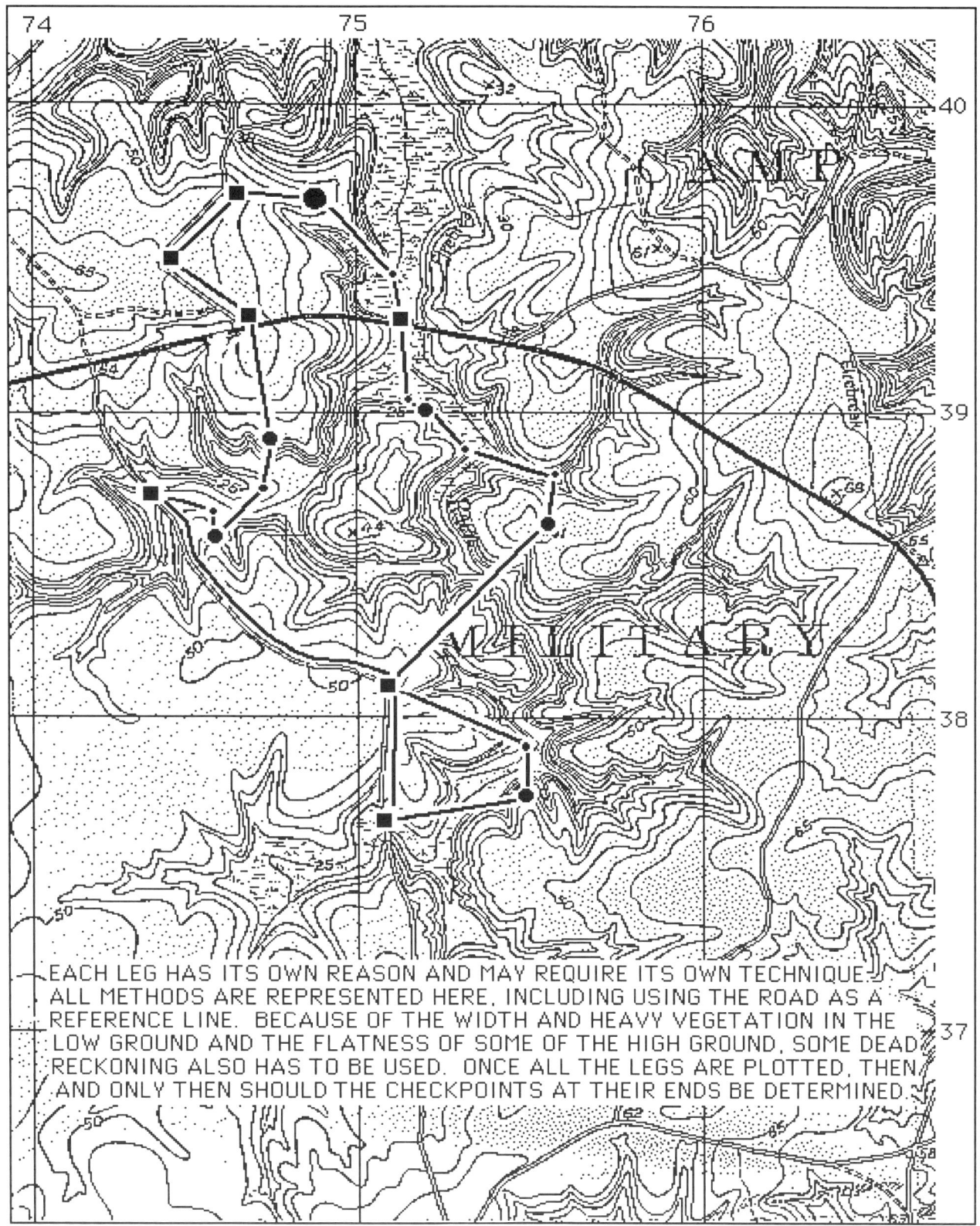

*Figure 9.12: Choose the Legs before the Checkpoints*
(Source: U.S. Dept. of Interior, "Jacksonville South Quadrangle," 1:24,000)

79

| ROUTE CARD | | | |
|---|---|---|---|
| NEXT LEG DESCRIPTION | LEG DIRECTION | LEG LENGTH | CHECKPOINT DESCRIPTION/# |
| MOSTLY FINGER | 144° MAG | 350M | STREAM/#1 |
| STREAMBED | SOUTHERLY | 200M | STREAM GOES UNDER ROAD/#2 |
| MOSTLY STREAMBED | 188° MAG | 250M | HILL MASS/#3 |
| RIDGE LINE | EASTERLY | 100M | HILL'S NE POINT/#4 |
| RIDGE LINE | SOUTHEASTERLY | 200M | HILL'S EASTERNMOST POINT/#5 |
| MOSTLY STREAMBED | 120° MAG | 250M | WHERE THE MAIN DRAW TURNS NORTH/#6 |
| MOSTLY DRAW | 190° MAG | 150M | NEAR HILLTOP/#7 |
| DEAD RECKONING IN MIXED TERRAIN | 231° MAG | 700M | DOGLEG IN ROAD/#8 |
| DEAD RECKONING ACROSS HIGH GROUND | 122° MAG | 400M | HILLS EASTERNMOST POINT/#9 |
| DEAD RECKONING ACROSS LOW GROUND | 188° MAG | 185M | TOP OF FIRST FINGER ENCOUNTERED/#10 |
| DEAD RECKONING IN MIXED TERRAIN | 260° MAG | 400M | STREAM GOES UNDER ROAD/#11 |
| PARALLEL TO ROAD | NORTHERLY | 400M | DOGLEG IN ROAD/#12 |
| PARALLEL TO ROAD | NORTHWESTERLY | 900M | STREAM GOES UNDER ROAD/#13 |
| STREAMBED | EASTERLY | 200M | FIRST BIG SOUTHERLY DRAW/#14 |
| DRAW | 188° MAG | 100M | UP FORK TO RIGHT/#15 |
| DRAW | 48° MAG | 200M | EAST END OF FIRST FINGER CROSSED/#16 |
| DEAD RECKONING ACROSS LOW GROUND | 10° MAG | 180M | TOP OF FIRST FINGER ENCOUNTERED/#17 |
| DEAD RECKONING ACROSS HIGH GROUND | 358° MAG | 350M | ROAD JUNCTION/#18 |
| PARALLEL TO ROAD | NW THEN NE | 600M | SECOND BEND/#19 |
| DEAD RECKONING | 98° MAG | 250M | HOME/#20 |

A SIMPLE ROUTE CARD ALLOWS THE SQUAD LEADER (WHO IS ALSO THE NAVIGATOR) TO KEEP HIS EYES AND HIS MIND ON THE TERRAIN. NOW, INSTEAD OF BEING PREOCCUPIED WITH HIS MAP, HE CAN SPOT ENEMY AND USE THE TERRAIN TO HIS TACTICAL ADVANTAGE.

*Figure 9.13: With a Route Card, the Navigator Can Focus on the Enemy*

## THE SMALL-UNIT LEADER MUST BE ROUTE PLANNER AND LONG-RANGE NAVIGATOR

Until about twenty years ago, small-unit leaders were encouraged to do their own navigating. Then, the responsibility was shifted to junior (and often inexperienced) personnel on point, referring to them as the "navigational team." Intentions were good and junior enlisted personnel gained vital land navigation experience, but there were some adverse consequences as well.

Point men were distracted from their primary function of watching for enemy. Instead of remaining within sight of the leader, they started going beyond where they could be easily supported by the main body, and they became hard to retrieve in case of contact from the rear. In short, teamwork and the minimal amount of control necessary to run a patrol, suffered. Through inactivity, many leaders lost the ability to practice the art of land navigation. When a navigational team gets lost, everyone in the unit quickly learns about it, and the confidence of the unit as a whole plummets. When a leader gets lost, he can sometimes keep it from the rest of the unit and turn the mistake into a less predictable scheme of maneuver. Still, he should always rely on a second in command to doublecheck his navigation. The proper role for the point men is only to choose the route to their immediate front:

Use the point for security and not for navigation.[6]
— FMFM 6-7

## THE DANGERS OF DEPARTING AND REENTERING FRIENDLY LINES

Too long spent departing friendly lines, hesitating near them after departure, moving parallel to them, or waiting near them for permission to reenter, can be extremely dangerous.

When enemy scouts can see patrols leaving friendly lines, they can easily ascertain where the patrols are headed. They also know the location of the gate in the barbed wire and the path through the mine field. Among other things, they will be cognizant of a very lucrative ambush site. More than one U.S. unit has been ambushed within full view of its parent-unit compound.

## WHEN AN AREA LACKING IN COVER IS UNEXPECTEDLY ENCOUNTERED EN ROUTE

Unexpected danger areas — those not showing on maps or remembered from previous patrols — can be negotiated in a number of ways: (1) going around them, (2) crossing them after posting security on the near side, (3) sending people across a few at a time, and (4) crawling through them along slight depressions in the ground.

However, there are problems associated with treating every opening, however small, as a danger area. To the rifleman on patrol, constantly stopping to cross small openings seems like a series of defensive maneuvers. So

(Source: FM 90-5 (1982), p. 2-12)

much so, that stopping to investigate every opening wide enough to hold four men in column, can adversely affect a squad's morale. Small openings are better classified as "caution areas" to be dealt with quickly on all but highly secretive missions. If they can't be bypassed, they can be quickly and safely crossed by using the "bump method." Before crossing, each buddy team waits for the next two men in column to advance to the edge of the opening, face outboard, and cover their movement. (See figure 9.14.)

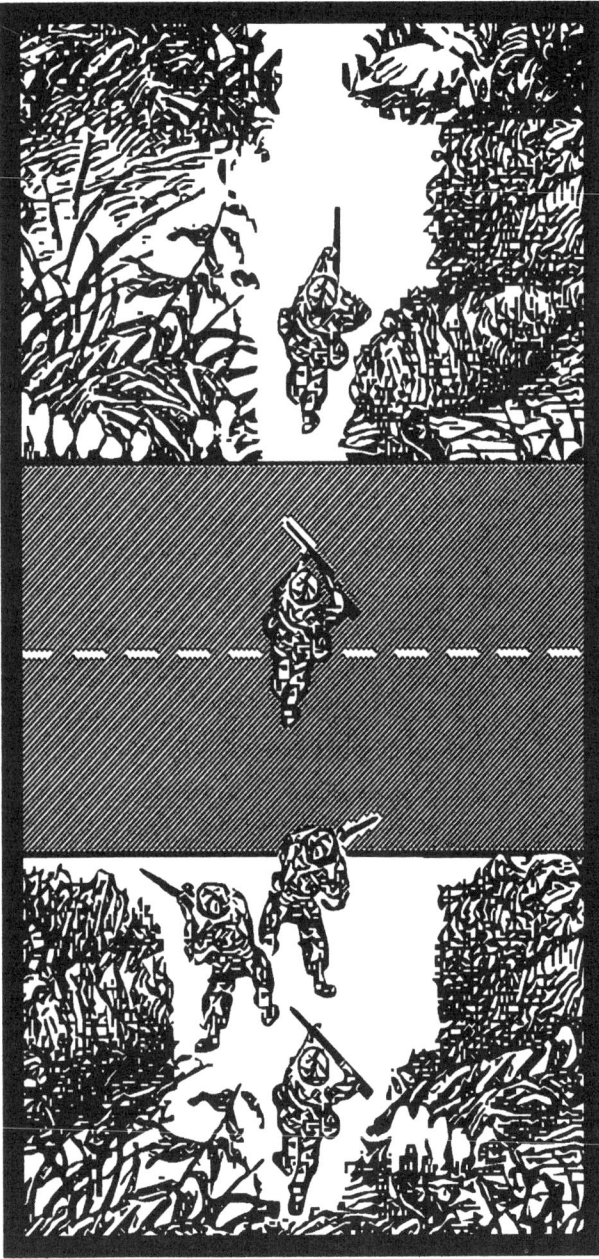

**Figure 9.14: For Speed, Use the Bump Method at Caution Areas**
(Source: FM 5-103 (1985), pp. 4-4, 4-6)

The "box recon" style of crossing a danger area has proven counterproductive. It not only makes momentum virtually impossible to achieve on the move, but it also violates one of the basic axioms of combat: Never send a two-man security team beyond view of the main body. Impatient point men will split up to accomplish the box-shaped search pattern more quickly. That violates two more rules: (1) Never operate alone, and (2) Never move unobserved towards a person with a loaded weapon.

For any large (bona fide) danger area that can't be bypassed, there are other options that are both quicker and safer. One of the best is to send a two-man point team across to check only the *edge* of the far side. Enemy forces beyond that edge can't see well enough to be a threat. When enemy forces occupy the edge, they must withhold their fire until the two-man team gets almost across or endure a pounding by supporting arms. All the crossing team has to do is to zigzag quickly or crawl deliberately across the last 50 yards.

When large open areas are crossed a few men at a time, they no longer pose a danger to the unit as a whole. That means that they don't have to be crossed slowly. If the unit's leader requires speed to maintain momentum, he can send a few men at a time across the opening. By so doing, he no longer risks losing his whole unit to a single burst of machinegun fire.

The proper deployment of movement security elements can effectively eliminate what is potentially a danger area — e.g., sending one's point element up to the next bend in a trail before allowing the main body to walk a long straight section. Too much hesitation at danger areas contributes to an overly defensive mentality.

## DEALING WITH UNFORESEEN OBSTRUCTIONS

Most U.S. infantrymen have only been taught how to move around an obstacle using the "90-degree-offset" method. There's another way to bypass an obstruction — whether obstacle or danger area — without losing one's bearings. First, the navigator chooses a distinctive steering point on the far side of the obstruction — e.g., a dead oak tree on the far side of a mangrove swamp. Then, he walks around the swamp until he reaches the tree and estimates the straight-line distance traveled.

A unit can avoid small obstructions by following the "path of least resistance" — for example, animal trails or firebreaks. When these natural conduits for movement occur in abundance, they can be relatively safe to use for establishing momentum. In a jungle replete with deep ravines and thick underbrush, the only way to approximate speed is by following the ridge lines or streambeds. Without doing so, a 300-meter envelopment can take hours. When these paths of least resistance do not occur in abundance, they channelize the unit. At this point, they become dangerous. That's why it was so risky to walk along a paddy dike into an enemy stronghold in Vietnam.

## TRICKS FOR NIGHT LAND NAVIGATION

To land navigate effectively at night, one must rely more on dead reckoning. Any azimuth can be put on a compass in the dark by counting clicks of the bezel ring, but following that azimuth can be disconcerting. With a military compass, the major component still visible — the luminous north arrow — is invariably pointing in a direction different from that being traveled. This can confuse those too familiar with following arrows.

Limiting features and the deliberate-offset (aiming-off) method gain utility at night as well. Falling into a chilly stream sends an unmistakable message to the navigator that he has overshot his objective. If a location on the stream to one side of the objective is aimed at initially, the search process can be greatly simplified.

Terrain association has its place at night, but only prominent terrain features are still visible — notably, roads and waterways. Night routes can usefully parallel these features. To terrain associate along fingers and draws in total darkness, the navigator must rely on senses other than vision. He must differentiate changes in elevation and degrees of dampness underfoot. For example, he can follow the crest of a finger by merely avoiding any downhill movement to either side. Similarly, by not moving uphill, he can follow the bottom of a draw. Further, he can usually identify draws large enough to show on a map — they will have traces of runoff water at their bottoms. If the march objective happens to be in a side draw along a streambed, the navigator can find it by walking along the stream's bank until he feels dampness under foot.

Finally, the whole issue of concealment during movement changes after dark. Any area bathed in bright moonlight becomes a caution area, whereas any area devoid of vegetation but in heavy shade may still effectively conceal moving men.

## EVERY LAND NAVIGATOR OCCASIONALLY GETS LOST

Every land navigator periodically loses his way. The difference between a novice and an expert is what he does about it. The novice tends to panic whereas the expert does not. The expert has several options with which to reorient himself: (1) using a cloverleaf search pattern to investigate surrounding terrain; (2) backtracking to the

(Sources: FM 7-11B1/2 (1978), p. 3-II-A-4.2; OPNAV P 34-03 (1960), p. 40)

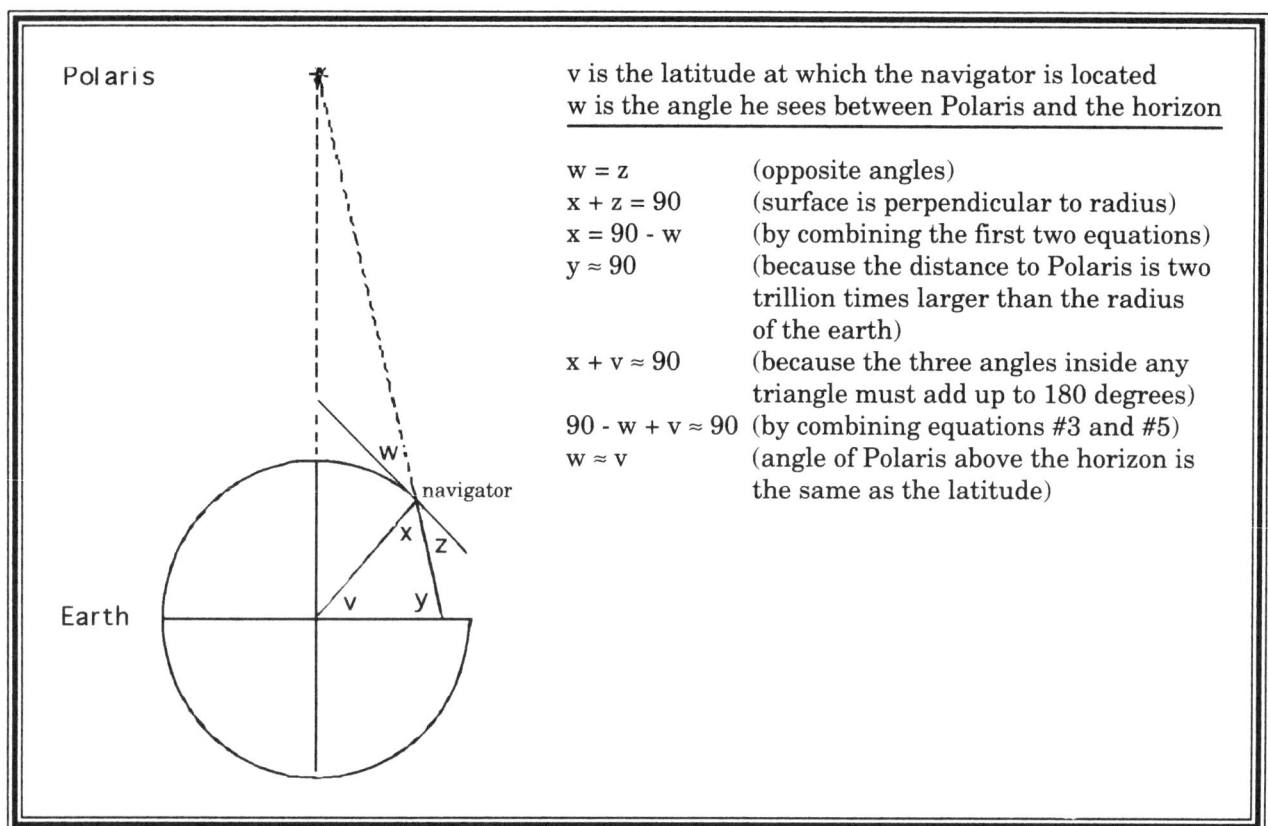

Figure 9.15: Use Polaris to Determine Latitude

(Source: MCOP 1550.44D (1983), p. 13-29)

last known checkpoint and trying another route to his march objective; or (3) shooting an escape azimuth to a known collecting feature and then moving to a different attack point from which to proceed.

Land navigators must be aware of the temptations they face while lost. One of the biggest is overuse of the same technique. Confidence is crucial to successful land navigation. Once one's confidence has been sacrificed, no amount of effort can salvage the situation. The key to locating any particular point on the ground is approaching it from several different directions with a variety of methods, until any two attempts produce the same result.

Losing a compass is no excuse for staying lost. The "watch," "shadow-tip" and "Polaris" field expedient methods of determining direction make compasses unnecessary in clear weather. When heading north or south at night, the angle that Polaris makes with the horizon closely approximates one's latitude on the map. If the earth's surface is obstructed at the horizon, this angle can be easily determined using a square protractor and plumb line. (See figure 9.15.)

Still, what about the point men? They will have to perform short-range land navigation on their own. How can this be accomplished concurrently with their security responsibilities?

# 10 — Point Men

- *How important to an infantry unit on the move, are its point men?*
- *What must point men know to survive?*
- *How can point men be selected and trained?*

(Source: FM 21-75 (1967), p. 8)

### THE LOST ART OF WALKING POINT

Occasionally, a history book will make a fleeting reference to someone called a point man. The expression has an exciting ring to it. One pictures a strong young infantryman out in front of his unit adeptly handling whatever might occur. Sadly, more often than not, whatever might occur handles him. And, as he becomes a casualty, so too does the forward vision of his unit. While blinded to the enemy situation, the unit can no longer make an appropriate response. Nevertheless, the term "point man" continues to hold a particular (albeit often fatal) fascination for wartime enlistees eager to experience history. The penalty for a mistake "on point" is frequently death.

The point man is often written about in the third person — as the first casualty of a meeting engagement. When a live point man can be found, he talks about being put on point without any special training and has difficulty putting into words what he was forced to learn through trial and error. Of the skills essential to winning small-unit combat, his are the most obscure. What he does, or fails to do, affects the outcome of a meeting engagement as much as what the unit leader does. Yet, the point man's job is not described in detail in any U.S manual or formal-school handout. To learn more about what point men do, one must rely on conversations with war veterans and young infantrymen who have walked point during some training evolution. Further, one must enjoy researching the basics.

## WHY ARE THE POINT AND OTHER MARCH SECURITY BILLETS SO VITAL

Security men (to include those at flank and rear) are the eyes and ears of a unit on the move. Whatever they sense or fail to sense constitutes most of what the unit leader knows about the local situation. A patrol without proficient point men is like a snake without eyes or teeth, and has about the same survivability in a world of predators. In the majority of cases where units have been surprised and hurt while on the move, highly skilled local security elements could have prevented the tragedy.

To be effective, security men must be able to detect both additions and deletions to the normal background sights, sounds, and smells. At times, they must pass this information along quickly and silently to the unit leader. At other times, they must have the self-confidence, training, and authority to initiate contact with the enemy.

## DETECTING INCONSISTENT SIGHTS, SOUNDS, AND SMELLS

All the senses come into play while walking point. The normal five are used to detect inconsistencies in one's natural surroundings. An experienced point man often has a "sixth sense" with which he can detect danger. This sixth sense may be partially based on his ability to think like the enemy, but Jim Corbett (the famous hunter of man-eating tigers) would credit his guardian angel.

Visible signs of trouble can be grouped into three categories: (1) human occupancy, (2) booby traps, and (3) residual NBC attack. Any rapid motion can portend the presence of enemy. A lack of synchronization in the movement of leaves or grass can mean the same thing. When an opponent uses tall vegetation for helmet camouflage, the tips of that vegetation move every time he changes the position of his head.

To spot enemy fortifications or soldiers, point men must learn to look *through* the foliage closest to them. In other words, they must focus on the ground and horizons behind that foliage. Deer hunters seldom see the full shape of their quarry. They only see the horizontal lines of back and belly, or shape of the head. Horizontal lines and head shapes occur infrequently in nature. Point men could look for the distinctive inverted "V" of a man's legs, outline of his head and shoulders, aperture of his bunker, or straight edge of his trip wire or weapon barrel. Weapons are seldom adequately camouflaged so as not to impede their functioning.

Point men must also look for subtle differences in the shape, color, and texture of the foliage. Barely perceptible variations in color and rigidity could mean that the vegetation had been recently cut and is starting to wilt. Of course, dew on the plants at the wrong time of day, dead animals, or swarms of insects would warn of residual chemical or biological contamination.

How point men might best detect the enemy after sundown is a separate issue. In Korea, colorblind personnel were sometimes used as roving listening posts, because they could differentiate between the various textures and shades of gray. People with average capabilities must use special techniques to see at night. One method is to use peripheral vision to spot slightly darker shapes that would not otherwise be visible. Another way is to cup one's fingers around each eye to concentrate whatever dim light may be surrounding an object, while excluding the light reflecting off the things around it. Finally, one can put his head to the ground to create additional natural horizons against which to silhouette the enemy.

Muffled noises can also reveal the presence of one's adversary. First, there are the sounds that he makes on his own — e.g., coughs, hiccups, the soft jangling of gear, the click of a weapon coming off "safe," etc. Then, there are the sounds that he makes as he interacts with his environment — e.g., the thud of a weapon against the earth, the crack of a twig underfoot, the sloshing of boots over wet ground, the swishing of water being parted, the rustling of dry leaves being crawled through, etc. Skilled woodsmen can learn the location of an intruder from the warning sounds of birds and other animals.

Odors can also tell a story. The smell of smoke is a dead giveaway of humans nearby. Brand new individual

(Source: FM 7-8 (1984), p. E-10)

equipment in large quantities has a distinctive odor as well. It has been said that, in Vietnam, the NVA could detect Americans from the soap they used. Korean War veterans could smell the garlic in the perspiration of their North Korean and Chinese adversaries. Of course, many chemical agents also give off distinctive odors.

When visibility is low, the sense of touch becomes important to a point man. Broken twigs, matted grass, and depressions in the ground all speak of the passage of human beings to the skilled tracker. With a supple twig, the point man can detect a trip wire across his path.

### IDENTIFYING THE ABSENCE OF NORMAL BACKGROUND SIGHTS AND SOUNDS

What *can't* be detected will also serve as a warning. Foliage that should be there, but isn't, portends of trouble. When animal and insect sounds are inexplicably missing or just momentarily interrupted, the enemy can't be far off. The prospective point man must study how background noises change when human beings are introduced to the equation. He may discover, for example, that crickets will not sing.

### POINT MEN MUST BE IN A POSITION TO COMMUNICATE QUICKLY AND SILENTLY WITH THE LEADER OF THE PATROL

Point men must transmit what they have learned about the situation *directly* to the overall commander of the unit on the move. The commander need not act on this information until his subordinate-unit leaders have had the chance to do so, but learning the situation firsthand helps him to keep from undoing his subordinates' good work later. For this reason, the leader of any unit is more effective when he walks near the front of that unit. The point and flank security teams can then utilize sign language to communicate directly with that leader. The published repertoire of sign language is far short of what is actually required on patrol. Patrol members who don't make up a few signals of their own cannot converse silently or operate effectively. This has been noted before:

> We have developed signals in our Battalion which are not recorded in any text book. I recommend that your troops do the same.[1]
> — Unidentified "old" NCO
> from 2/7 on Guadalcanal

Prerequisite to the use of arm-and-hand signals is an unobstructed line of sight. That means that security men must either remain within view of the main body or carry radios. Most units do not have extra radios, so security men must learn to walk where they can just barely see the main body. Then, by altering their distance as the vegetation thickens or thins, they can automatically accomplish their mission. If the foe can't see the main body, he can't aim his weapons well enough to hurt it. If extra radios are available, keying handsets in code (with the radios on "squelch") is preferable to talking.

The point men should relay to the unit leader what they have learned about the situation and how they plan to circumvent the obstacles and danger areas in their path. As the long-range navigator for the unit, the leader must in turn establish the general direction of march. Both must be able to carry on a conversation without having to speak or change location.

### SECURITY MEN MUST HAVE AUTHORITY TO ACT ON THEIR OWN INITIATIVE

At night, when an upright point man sees another human being coming toward him from the front, he must act. He must shoot, and he must shoot quickly. Any hesitation — whether from discomfort at the thought of killing another human being, from uncertainty about the rules of engagement, or from just being overconditioned to following orders — can cost him his life. Only when the point man is certain that he has not been seen by his adversary, can he consider any other course of action. For example, while prone or behind a tree, he can sometimes signal for a hasty ambush. There may be one exception to the rule. An upright point man who detects an enemy soldier in a prone or sitting position, can sometimes drop to the ground and crawl away unharmed. The reasons for this strange phenomenon are unclear. The enemy soldier may be waiting for instructions, less than fully alert, or just shocked by the sighting. He may be part of a reconnaissance patrol, and as such not interested in enemy contact. Or, he may be flank security for an ambush, and as such hesitant to scare off the main body.

In the daytime, the point man's response to seeing enemy can be quite different. When a well-concealed point man sees an enemy patrol moving at a diagonal across his front, he can signal for his unit to come on line with him facing the enemy. His doing so in no way usurps the authority of his leader; it merely puts his leader in a better position to choose from his various tactical alternatives. In other words, for the leader effectively to use his point men, he must delegate authority. However, this delegation of authority should not extend to matters that might prove distracting, like long-range navigation.

After being thoroughly indoctrinated in obeying orders at boot camp, young infantrymen could benefit from some training in decision making before being put on point. Unfortunately, novice leaders are often reluctant to relinquish any control of their units on the move. Their point men may not be delegated enough authority to save their own lives. Leaders who cannot see what is going on up front should not try to decide what their point men should do. A well-trained unit can absorb the occasional mistake of a point man. To employ surprise and momentum in war, the commander must delegate authority to well-trained point men, as well as small-unit leaders.

## POINT MEN MUST HAVE QUICK-KILL SKILLS

The "eye, muzzle, target" method of scanning for enemy is one way to put rounds on target quickly. The shooter never acquires an actual sight picture; he merely aligns the rear sight, front sight, and target. Then, from the impact of his first round, he can tell where to put the second. This is called a "double tap." Just by affixing a small piece of white tape or cloth to his front sight, he can fire fairly accurately on the darkest of nights.

Ideally, a point man should have some way of defending himself silently. If a rifle with a "silencer" somehow violates the Geneva Conventions, perhaps a crossbow with conventional arrows would not. As a last resort, the point man must be able to dispatch his opponent with grenades only. Grenades will not disclose his presence to that opponent's comrades, because they make the same sound as mines, booby traps, and mortar shells.

## ONLY THOSE WITH SPECIAL ABILITIES SHOULD BE ALLOWED TO WALK POINT

It is unknown what percentage of U.S. infantrymen have the natural ability to survive on point. One can only, on a case-by-case basis, attempt to identify those who *do not*. Infantrymen can be tested for vision, hearing, and reflex action. How much experience each has had in the requisite environment should also be a qualifying factor. Country boys who had to hunt for a living might do better in the woods; whereas city kids who had to patrol their neighborhoods might do better in urban terrain.

To identify promising point men, units should use what has been referred to as a "Gurkha Trail." Human-silhouette targets are placed in the bushes at various distances from the trail. Then, the number of targets spotted by those walking up the trail is used as a measure of their ability to detect enemy. By introducing various sounds and smells along the trail, the other senses can be evaluated as well. It may be possible to estimate how easily a prospective point man can focus on the situation, justify killing another human being, and make a split-second decision under duress. This, after all, is essentially what the "good-guy" and "bad-guy" targets help to ascertain at a quick-kill firing range.

The practice of putting rulebreakers on point makes little sense. Even using someone who is preoccupied with a past mistake or "Dear John" letter, is tantamount to sending him to his death. Furthermore, even a well-focused point man can only concentrate for so long. Because point men must be rotated frequently in combat, more than the required number must be trained.

## COMPOSITION OF THE SECURITY TEAM

Point *man* is really a misnomer. On point, two men have a better chance of survival. Partners can cover each other, just as policemen do. Further, two heads are better than one. That means two men at each of the security locations — point, flank, and rear. Patrols often violate this common-sense rule at the flanks and rear. Well-intended written guidance about one "security" fire team per squad is often taken too literally. Even for a lone squad, it takes *two* fire teams to run 360-degree security on the move.

Furthermore, the two men must be pals. They must be partners on liberty as well as in training — knowing each other's every idiosyncrasy. The NVA put three men in their smallest tactical element and made sure one was highly experienced:

> Another mainstay of Communist control was the three man cell. Each soldier was part of such a cell, and the trio worked, marched and fought together.... The appointed cell leader was often a combat tested veteran.... "If a cell member split from his cell during combat," one soldier said, "our actions would become uncoordinated and casualties higher."[2]

## AN EFFECTIVE FORMATION FOR THE SECURITY TEAM

The security team at any position most effectively walks in a slightly offset column formation. This permits the lead man to watch the area to his immediate front for trip wires and signs of enemy, while the rear man scans the area farther out. During the day, the rear man tries to look *through* the foliage at the terrain and horizons beyond. At night he uses night vision goggles, if available.

## HOW POINT, FLANK, AND REAR SECURITY TEAMS MOVE

Security elements must be allowed to decide how to move over the ground *to their immediate front*. Having this prerogative is crucial to their survival. The only control that must be exercised over them directly, is that of long-range navigation. *Their prior training* and occasional counseling provides the rest of the control — indirectly. They have been trained to stay barely within view of the main body. Even in the desert, their distance from the main body should not exceed 200 meters, because beyond that distance they cannot be reinforced quickly enough. The leader who continually motions for his security elements to move in or out, not only misunderstands his role, but endangers his men by diverting their attention and curtailing their initiative.

(Source: FM 7-8 (1984), p. G-4)

How the security elements are trained will govern how they react to enemy contact. The point team is the only one that requires any guidance from the leader whatsoever. One team member has to look back periodically at the leader to receive long-range navigational guidance and to share what has been learned about the situation. The point team must have already received formal instruction in how various types of terrain affect route selection. They must know how to handle small danger areas and obstacles, how to maximize observation without sacrificing cover and concealment, etc. — i.e., everything in the last chapter. Additionally, they should try to remain in the shadows as they move — whether by day or by night. When they can't advance without losing visual contact with the main body (like when turning a corner on a trail or cresting a hill), they must wait for the main body to catch up. This is not only for their own protection, but also to help the main body react to "contact rear." Guadalcanal Marines learned about contact rear:

> When we move around on these jungle trails, we have learned to have men at the rear of each platoon who . . . can get their weapons into action quickly to help overcome ambush fire from the rear.[3]
>
> — Plt.Sgt. J.C.L. Hollingsworth
> *Fighting on Guadalcanal*

When forced by circumstances to use trails or relatively open terrain, the main body and rear security element must follow the same axiom of relative positioning. In other words, the patrol leader must sometimes wait for rear security to catch up; and rear security must sometimes hang back to keep the main column from coming under automatic-weapons fire from the rear. Accordingly, in most types of terrain, a patrol's movement must necessarily be *somewhat jerky*. The waiting periods should be used to listen and watch for unwanted company.

Throughout history, patrol leaders with maneuver warfare thought processes have let their rear security elements *stalk* the main body:

> Grouped in their three-man cells, they [the North Vietnamese] marched in a column with one trio walking point fifty meters ahead and three other men stalking an equal distance behind.[4]

Flankers operate most effectively without guidance. Those who encounter large clearings should temporarily rejoin the main body, for their deployment now serves no useful purpose and the open ground might prevent their reinforcement. Those who encounter obstructions that obscure them from the main body (like tall bramble bushes) must also return to the central column. When two flankers did just that at the Three Gateways to Hell in Vietnam in early 1967, it probably saved their lives.[5] An enemy squad was dug in on the far side of the bush. An automatic weapon did subsequently fire blindly through the bush at the U.S. patrol, but it didn't hurt anyone.

A unit with effective security can traverse a "danger area" quicker than one without it. In fact, because danger areas are by definition places where an *entire* patrol can be wiped out *in an instant,* they are seldom encountered by patrols that can conduct proper movement security.

## IT TAKES TRACKERS TO PRACTICE MANEUVER WARFARE

Point men can provide the tracking capability vital to maintaining contact with the enemy. Without that contact, there is no momentum; and without momentum, there is no victory. The British defeated the Communists in Malaysia largely because of their proficiency in spotting enemy sign and tracking it to its source.

Much of the mantracking expertise in the United States today resides in the native American community, the U.S. Border Patrol, and volunteer search and rescue units. One of the most popular techniques is the Step-by-Step Method.[6] It has three rules: (1) Don't advance beyond the last footprint found; (2) Don't destroy a clearly identifiable footprint; and (3) Use a sign-cutting stick — one showing the length of the subject's stride. The best time to track is when the sun is rising or setting. Then, footprints between the tracker and sun are automatically sidelighted, and the shallowest of soil indentations clearly outlined by shadow. During midday, prints can be shaded from the direct rays of the sun and sidelighted with a mirror. At night, they can be sidelighted with a red flashlight on a stick. For the footstep that does not leave a clear imprint, the tracker must rely on other "signs of passage": (1) the depression in the ground from a stepped-on twig, (2) dirt stuck to the bottom of a trod-upon plant surface, (3) the bruise on a low growing leaf, (4) a broken twig, (5) bent grass, (6) intertwined vegetation, (7) the moss or bark dislodged from a root, (8) the wet underside of an overturned stone or dead leaf, (9) the lighter and nonshiny underside of an inverted live leaf, (10) buds or berries knocked from a small bush, (11) a pebble pressed into the ground, (12) a stone dislodged from its socket, (13) the soil made more reflective by compression, (14) a scuff mark on hard ground, (15) soft dirt transferred to a rock, (16) dust or dew brushed from a plant, (17) flattened rabbit pellets, (18) a disturbed ant hill, (19) a broken cobweb, (20) an imprint in the dew or frost, (21) wet marks on the far side of a stream or puddle, (22) the collapsed side of a trench or slope, and (23) discarded material. It often takes testing to determine the age of a track — e.g., watching how long it takes bent grass to right itself. However, when cracks or bruises in that grass are still green, the tracks are relatively recent. And, when water has not yet reentered a footprint in the swamp, that print is fresh. Other indicators of a track's age are grass springback, rain pockmarks, superimposed leaves or animal tracks, and wind erosion. Enemy soldiers often wear distinctive footgear. By counting the number of footprints in an average pace and dividing by two, one can determine how many enemy have passed by.

It would take an entire fire team on point to both track an enemy force and maintain proper security. The lead man would be the tracker. Two others could follow at his heels to watch for trouble at short range and tracks leading off to either side. Finally, the rear man would watch for enemy soldiers at long range.

### WHEN AN ENEMY SENTRY IMPEDES MANEUVER, STALKING SKILLS HELP

In stalking, the whole idea is to approach one's quarry without being heard or seen. For this reason, the best time to stalk is just before dawn. Then, the stalker's underfooting is softened by the dampness of the night, and the victim's view is impaired by the ground fog and twilight of the morning. Of course, stalking is much easier for the point man who is camouflaged to blend in perfectly with his background. Then, he must remember only to move when the enemy's gaze is averted. The point man who is less well camouflaged must keep some obstruction (like a tree or bush) between him and his quarry.

### FINALLY, POINT MEN SHOULD KNOW HOW TO BREACH ENEMY BARRIERS

Point men must become totally familiar with the barbed wire, mines, booby traps, early warning devices, and other obstacles that may block their path. To pass undetected through these obstacles, they must have formal sapper training. To neutralize the barriers that cannot be silently breached, they must have expertise in bangalore torpedoes for rural terrain and wall-breaching charges for urban terrain.

Every rifle squad should have at least two security teams trained in short-range infiltration. *Only then, will their parent organization have the wherewithal to employ maneuver warfare at the small-unit level.*

(Source: FM 22-100 (1973), p. 9-7)

### TRAINING POINT MEN

Only those who show a natural propensity for walking point should be trained to do so. The Gurkha Trail can provide both testing and training. Sensory perception and decision-making drills can be added for expected combinations of microterrain, visibility, and threat. Moving targets and live ammunition can provide realism and a way to increase reflex speed. A graduate from point man school should have demonstrated proficiency in the following skills: (1) sensory perception, (2) night vision, (3) arm-and-hand signals, (4) reconnaissance, (5) stalking, (6) tracking, (7) sapper techniques, (8) demolitions, (9) quick-kill methods, and (10) tactical decision making. The importance of these skills to winning in combat must never be underestimated:

> Let us remember the great part that is played by the infantry soldier in war.... It is not generally considered that he requires any very high training, and yet his training in the correct use of ground and his rifle, in the dire stress of battle, is more complicated and more difficult than that of any other arm of the service.[7]

# 11 Patrols That Look for Trouble

- Which patrols should actively seek out enemy contact?
- How could different methods of route selection and movement help?
- How might a maneuver warfare patrol be organized and conducted?

(Sources: FM 7-70 (1986), cover, p. 4-20; FM 90-6 (1980), p. 1-4)

### WHAT DOES A TRADITIONAL COMBAT PATROL DO, IF NOT LOOK FOR TROUBLE?

U.S. infantrymen are by nature quite daring. Yet, they are trained to patrol in a way that gives them little opportunity to encounter their adversary. As a result, few have had enough experience in handling chance contact.

U.S. patrols are trained to "dead reckon" between march objectives. A patrol that travels along a straight line through heavily wooded terrain teeming with enemy patrols will generally see no one. Stealth, concealment, and the Laws of Probability all contribute to this strange phenomenon. The American patrol's best opportunity to see its enemy counterpart is at the landmarks too often chosen as checkpoints, and at the danger areas too often located between the landmarks. In both instances, the U.S. patrol will normally be at a tactical disadvantage. As was discussed in chapter 9, the patrol that uses the dead-reckoning method of route selection spends most of its time on ground devoid of tactical value. By having to negotiate slowly every obstacle and clearing, its members have difficulty maintaining the frame of mind necessary to win chance contact.

Still, route selection is only one of the challenges facing the U.S. patrol. If the squad members are fortunate, they are briefed on *one* established procedure for handling enemy contact during the patrol order, and then given 5 minutes before leaving to *discuss* that one procedure (in the name of rehearsal). When this one tactical procedure is used after inadequate practice, in deference to the situation, and against an enemy who knows what that procedure is, the results can be less than satisfactory. On the other hand, without some sort of established procedure, the squad could not react quickly enough to win. Perhaps, instead of just one procedure, the squad needs *several* techniques that can be mixed and matched to fit the situation. Perhaps, as long as these techniques are continually rehearsed, they do not need to be standardized.

The writers of the manuals may have intended that standard patrolling procedure be used only for missions requiring absolute secrecy. During such missions, contact with the enemy would be counterproductive. The standard procedure, after all, is not bad for getting into position undetected prior to a deliberate attack or ambush. It is certainly appropriate for reconnaissance missions. But, it is less appropriate for a patrol which, for whatever reason, wants to make contact with the enemy.

## WHEN LOOKING FOR TROUBLE IS CRUCIAL TO MISSION ACCOMPLISHMENT

There are times when a patrol must seek out its adversary to accomplish its mission. Consider the defensive security patrol, for example. When a proficient attacker can mass undetected just outside the wire of a proficient defender, the attacker can usually prevail. That is one of the lessons of history. The defender must somehow prevent that attacker from massing near his wire in the first place. He must employ aggressive patrolling to disrupt the momentum of the attacking force, and to prevent composite elements of that force from rendezvousing near his perimeter. After World War II, the Marine Corps Schools Command credited much of the Marines' success against Japanese attacks in the Pacific to aggressive patrolling:

> Japanese night attacks in the Solomon Islands Campaign proved abortive in most cases and cost them many casualties. This was due not only to an alert defense, but also to the fact that aggressive patrolling by day kept enemy reconnaissance at a distance.[1]
> — FMFRP 12-9

Has a returning defensive security patrol that saw nothing, really accomplished its mission, when its zone of responsibility was all the while teeming with well-hidden enemy? Perhaps the security patrol could have made more of a contribution to the defense, if it had actively sought out the enemy force and caused it to deploy early. Attacking a numerically larger force does not necessarily spell disaster:

> I was too weak to defend, so I attacked.[2]
> — Robert E. Lee

## HISTORICAL PRECEDENTS FOR DEFENSIVE SECURITY PATROLS THAT SEEK OUT ATTACKING UNITS

When the armies of Japan and Russia squared off in Manchuria in 1939, both were skilled at small-unit maneuver warfare. Two-man security patrols operated just forward of Japanese lines, much as roving sentry posts might. One night, these Japanese scouts (as they were called) shadowed Russian infiltrators and got their own machineguns moved to a location from which the Russians could be taken under enfilade fire.[3] For many years afterwards, the Japanese used this engagement as their model for countering short-range infiltration:

> Speed and surprise were the hallmarks of this action. The Japanese viewed it as proof of their doctrine of attack inculcated in platoon leaders' ranks *and below* [italics added]. It came to be regarded as a classic example of plugging infiltration gaps on an extended front.[4]
> — Leavenworth Papers No. 2

In the early sixties, tracking skills helped small British Commonwealth patrols to defeat the Communists in Malaysia. Perhaps, the British army had finally come of age.

## ROUTES TO USE WHILE SEEKING ENEMY CONTACT

Prerequisite to making enemy contact, is finding one's adversary. Crucial to making *successful* enemy contact, is finding oneself on good ground at the time.

There are several ways of accurately guessing where that adversary will be. In a guerrilla war, one can learn a lot from the S-2 map showing the history of his area of operations. To mass enough strength to attack a lucrative target, the guerrillas have to stockpile supplies along preestablished infiltration routes. Enemy soldiers are observed, supply caches uncovered, and skirmishes fought along each of these routes. To predict what the enemy will do in a conventional war, each unit must develop a short-term historical map of the area it occupies. By properly debriefing patrols, the unit leader can easily find signs of enemy activity to plot on the map. After all, that enemy needs to reconnoiter his objective before every attack. If a friendly daytime patrol sees a few enemy soldiers at a particular location, an evening patrol might discover an enemy attack force at the same place. The odds of spotting enemy can be further enhanced by patrolling covered routes between the original sighting and the defensive perimeter. Trying to think like the enemy is the key to locating him. If one were trying to attack his own defensive perimeter, where would he place his "base of fire"? What envelopment route would he take? What would he use for a rendezvous point and infiltration lanes? Where would he position his scouts to keep the perimeter under surveillance?

1st Lt. W.L. Roach USMCR used an interesting formula for making contact on patrol in Vietnam. Having grown up on the mean streets of the south side of Chicago, he reasoned that abandoned buildings would be a good place to find people after dark. While the other squads in A/1/4 unsuccessfully ambushed trail junctions south of Chu Lai in 1967, Lt. Roach and his platoon *roved* along the approaches to an abandoned village and surprised several enemy soldiers. (See appendix C.)

For the patrols wanting contact, *locations with good views* must be incorporated into their routes. Hilltops, edges of large clearings, and ends of straight trails, all meet this criterion in the daytime. At night, the bases of elevated terrain provide natural horizons against which to silhouette one's adversary. Roads, water, and other light-colored objects provide artificial horizons.

(Source: FM 21-76 (1970), p. 29)

## MOVEMENT TECHNIQUES FOR THIS ALTERNATIVE STYLE OF PATROLLING

In nature, a predator's speed greatly influences how it hunts. Slower predators hunt from ambush, sometimes with a partner to drive the prey into the trap. Quicker predators stalk and then rush their victims. All freeze in place occasionally — to look and to listen. All plan to pass through locations that their quarries frequent, and other locations that offer good views without sacrificing concealment. Not surprisingly, some of these tactics in nature also work in combat. In Vietnam, one Army battalion intentionally established a fire base in the most dangerous part of its area of responsibility. Just before being attacked one evening, it fell back just slightly so it could usurp the enemy's momentum. After conducting a successful defense, it tracked the enemy to its base camp. There, it established ambushes at every exit, and bombed the camp to drive the enemy out (killing 148 enemy at a loss of 8 friendlies wounded). To capture momentum, the battalion then used intelligence gathering from its ambushes to locate another enemy base camp. This time, a rifle company was inserted by helicopter to drive the camp's occupants into preestablished ambush sites (killing 113 at a loss of 4 wounded).[5]

With more speed, a patrol can muster more martial spirit, cover more ground, make more enemy contact, and generate more surprise/momentum. Of course, moving quickly usually entails a column formation with one's flank security pulled in. Yet, operating point and rear security properly would still create a somewhat jerky motion. During the short halts, patrol members could remain upright behind trees alternately facing outboard. While the point was waiting for the main body to move (and vice versa), the time could be productively spent looking and listening. While large danger areas and obstacles could be circumnavigated, small openings could be crossed two at a time using the "bump method" described in chapter 9. A patrol's quickness provides a type of security, because it limits exposure time and startles the opponent. Picture several members of an enemy patrol spotting (from a distance and through heavy underbrush) several members of a quickly moving friendly patrol. The enemy soldiers probably couldn't get the sighting confirmed by their leaders quickly enough to do much about it. At twilight, the sighting might only last a few seconds. Furthermore, the moving target would be hard to hit.

Lighting conditions and thickness of vegetation establish how quickly animals move in the wild. In the daytime, a deer moves slowly through heavy underbrush, and quickly through thin. A contact patrol may also have to vary its speed as the amount of concealment along its route changes:

Where a deer can cross, a soldier can cross.[6]
— Field Marshal A.V. Surorov

Techniques from the NCO Corps

(Source: FM 22-100 (1973), Studies 4)

## FORMATIONS FOR CONTACT PATROLLING

Decentralized control and improved mobility are the hallmarks of maneuver warfare. Giving fire teams their own radios and allowing them to patrol separately, but close enough together for mutual support, accomplishes these goals. Three fire teams could leave a defensive perimeter in column with the expectation of being observed doing so. Then, one could secretly drop off to shadow the others during the rest of the patrol. Or, two fire teams could "exfiltrate" the perimeter and wait to shadow a decoy patrol made up of the squad leader, other fire team, and attachments. Whichever group made contact first could return fire and assume the role of decoy. The closest other group could move to outflank and surprise the enemy, while the third group moved to block the enemy's probable avenue of retreat. Then, the fire team attacking the enemy's flank would assume the role of decoy, giving the original decoy the opportunity to slip away and change roles. Against a numerically superior foe, a series of diversions can be extremely helpful.

To use this alternative style of patrolling, fire team leaders would need considerable skill in land navigation and tactics. They would also need complete familiarity with the area being patrolled. The distance between fire teams would vary, depending on the amount of concealment available. In heavy jungle, the fire teams might have to stay within 50-100 meters of each other at all times. In more open terrain, they could walk farther apart, but never more than 200 meters to stand any chance of reinforcing each other in case of trouble. (See figure 11.1 and stand by for imminent contact.)

(Source: FM 7-11B1/2 (1978), p. 2-II-B-3.3)

Techniques from the NCO Corps

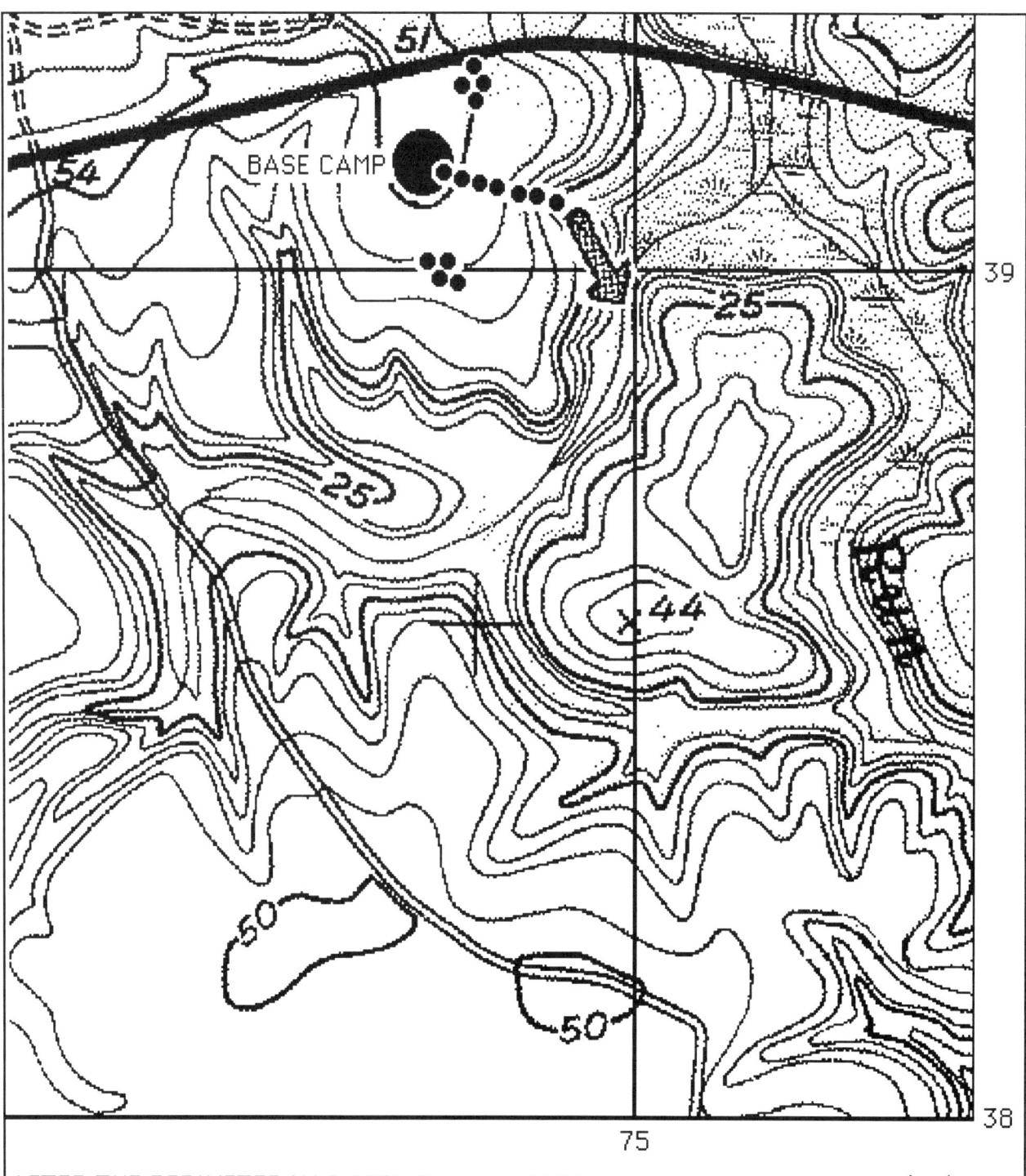

Figure 11.1: An Alternative to Standard Patrolling Technique
(Source: U.S. Dept. of Interior, "Jacksonville South Quadrangle," 1:24,000)

Patrols That Look for Trouble

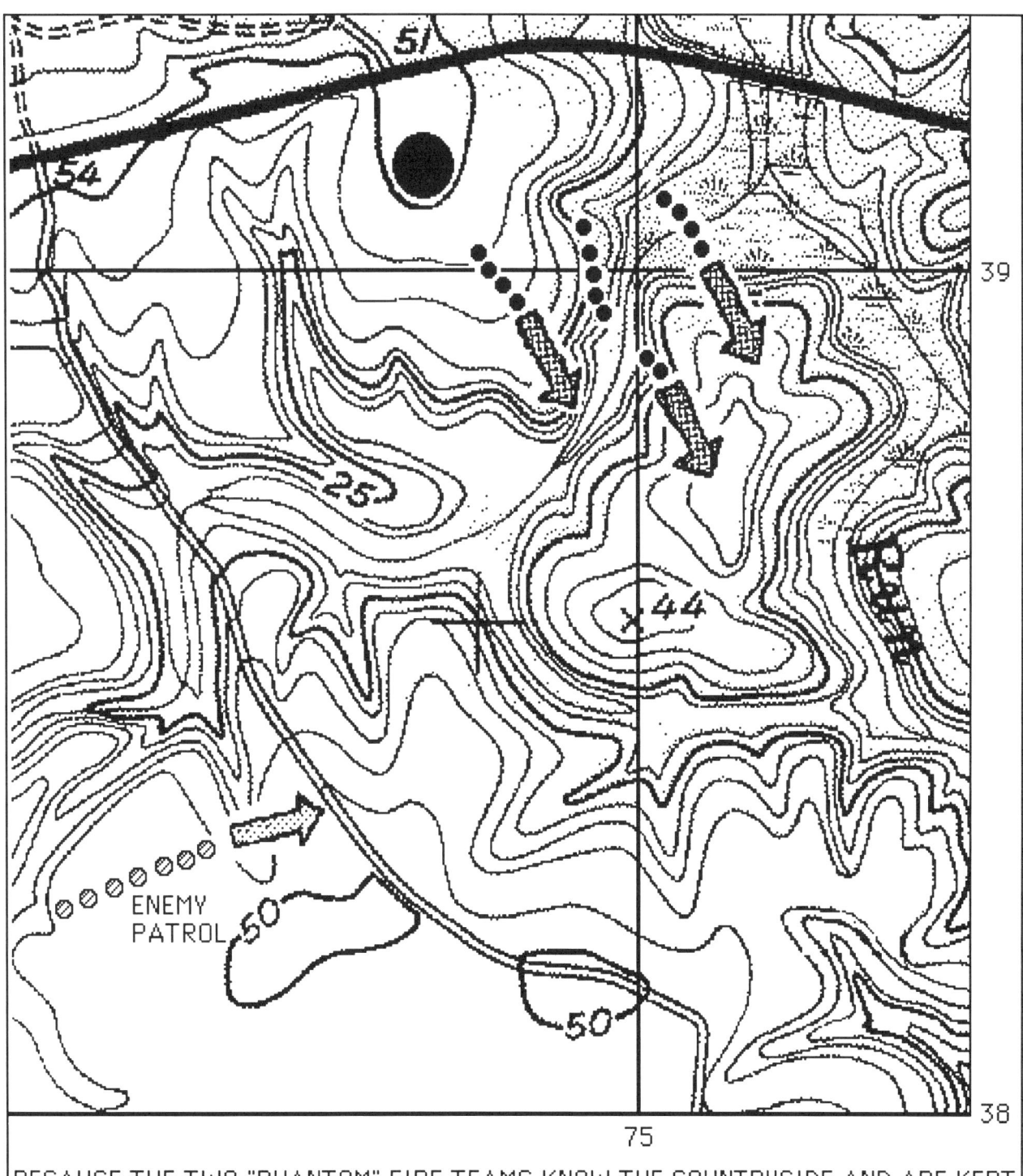

Figure 11.1: An Alternative to Standard Patrolling Technique (Continued)
(Source: U.S. Dept. of Interior, "Jacksonville South Quadrangle," 1:24,000)

Techniques from the NCO Corps

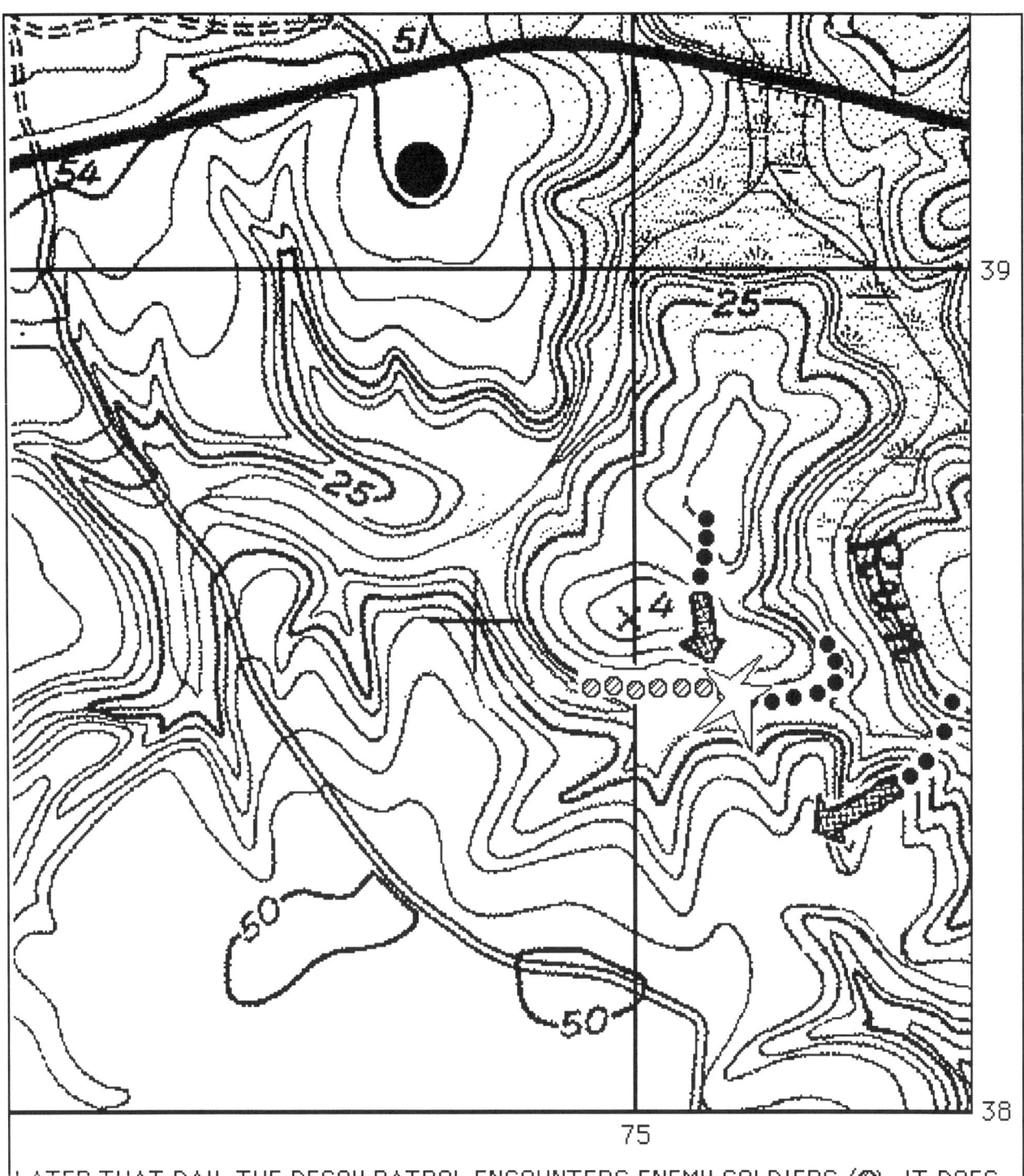

LATER THAT DAY, THE DECOY PATROL ENCOUNTERS ENEMY SOLDIERS (Ø). IT DOES DOES NOT ATTACK BUT "DEMONSTRATES" TO HOLD THE ADVERSARIES' ATTENTION. THE PHANTOM FIRE TEAMS ARE INFORMED OF THE SITUATION AND MOVE TO HELP.

Figure 11.1: An Alternative to Standard Patrolling Technique (Continued)
(Source: U.S. Dept. of Interior, "Jacksonville South Quadrangle," 1:24,000)

Patrols That Look for Trouble

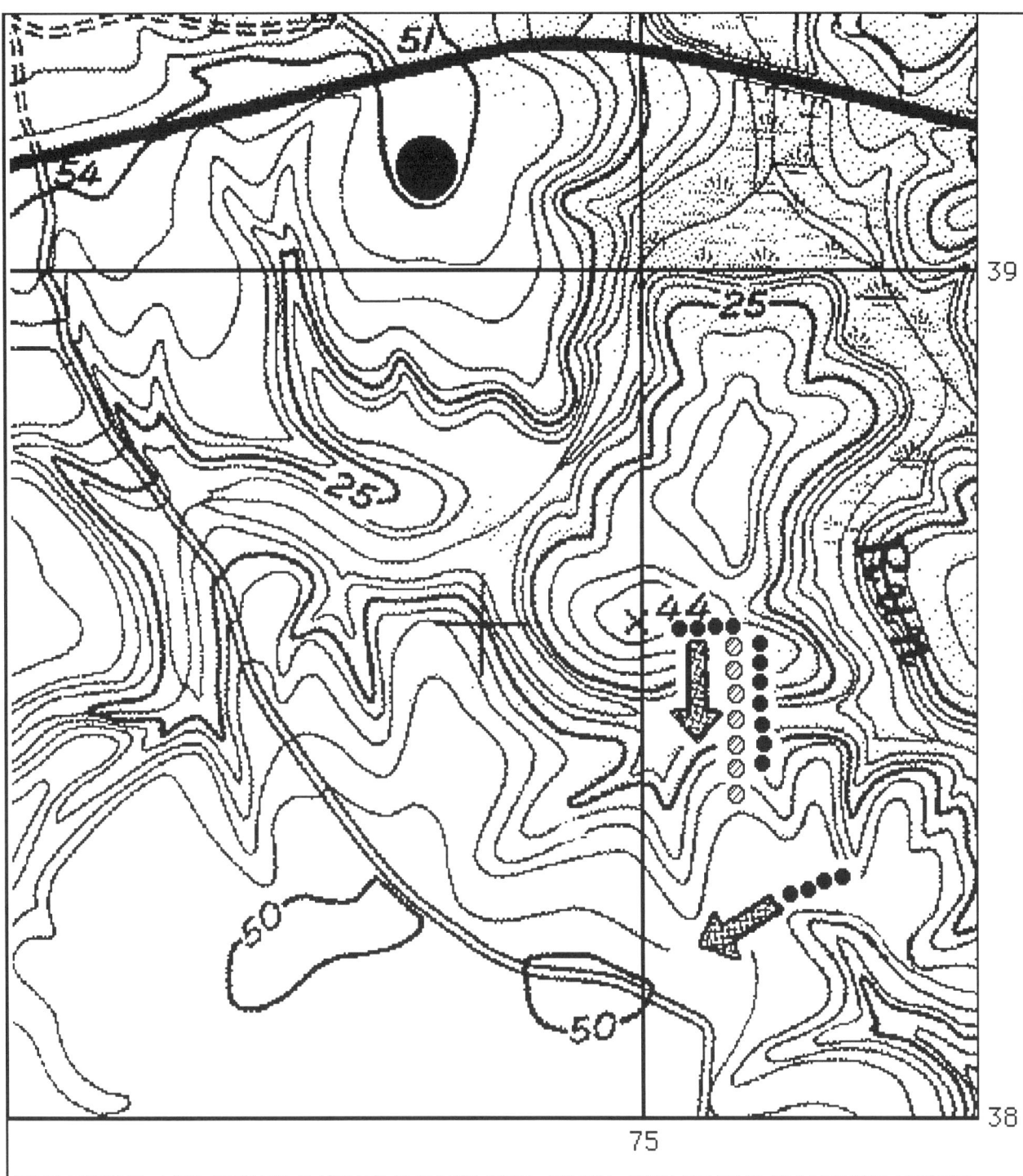

THE ENEMY AND DECOY PATROLS FACE OFF. THEN, ONE OF THE PHANTOM UNITS ATTACKS BY "FIRE AND MOVEMENT," WHILE THE DECOY PATROL FIRES JUST AHEAD OF IT. THE OTHER PHANTOM UNIT MOVES TO AMBUSH THE ENEMY'S ESCAPE ROUTE.

Figure 11.1: An Alternative to Standard Patrolling Technique (Continued)
(Source: U.S. Dept. of Interior, "Jacksonville South Quadrangle," 1:24,000)

*Techniques from the NCO Corps*

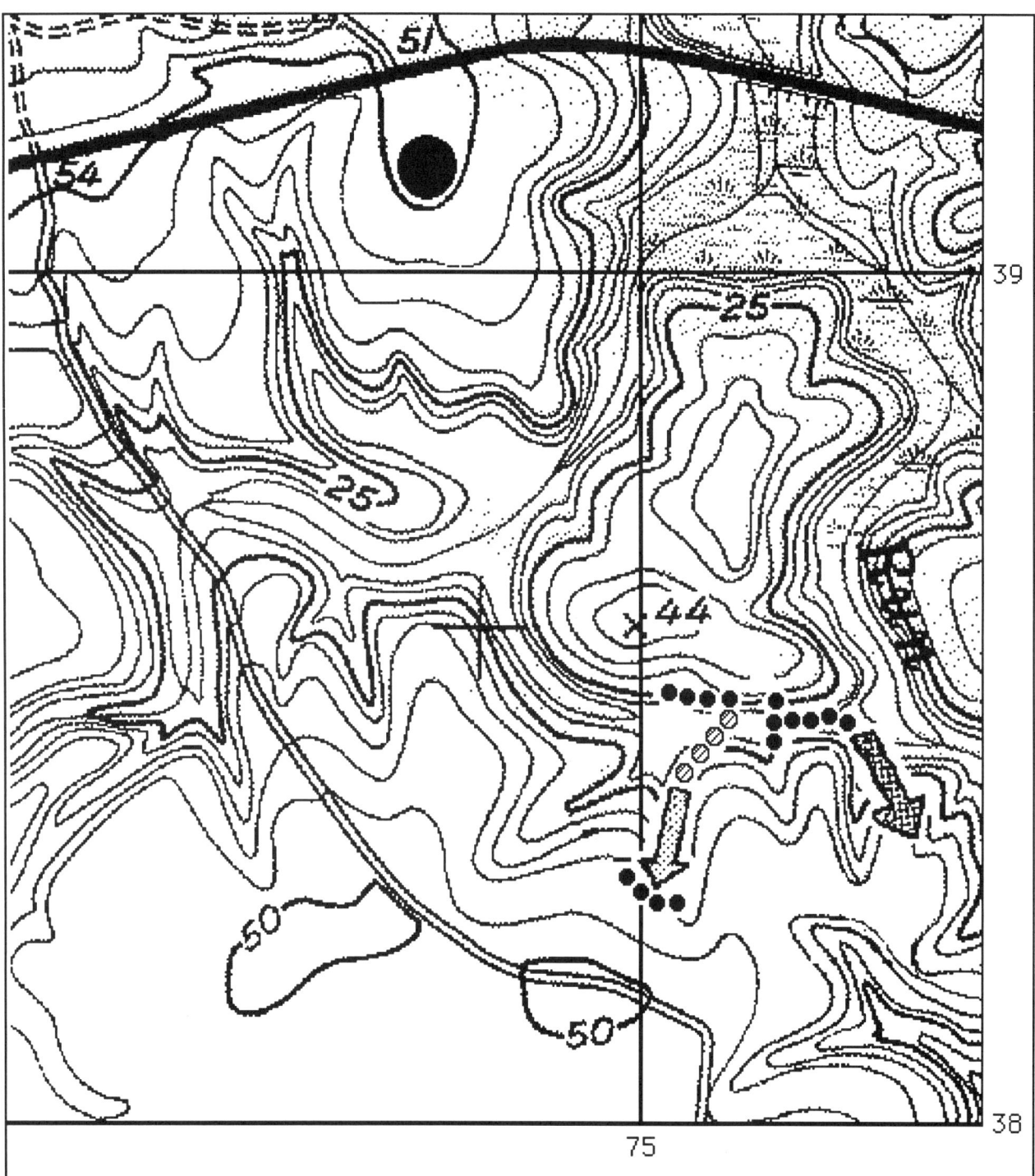

AS THE ATTACKING TEAM GETS THE BEST OF THE ENEMY, THE ORIGINAL DECOY MELTS INTO THE UNDERBRUSH - THE TWO HAVE SWITCHED ROLES. THE ORIGINAL PHANTOM NOW IS THE DECOY AND TAKES OVER PATROLLING RESPONSIBILITIES. WHAT'S LEFT OF THE ENEMY UNIT HAS ONE MORE SURPRISE IN STORE FOR THEM.

*Figure 11.1: An Alternative to Standard Patrolling Technique (Continued)*
(Source: U.S. Dept. of Interior, "Jacksonville South Quadrangle," 1:24,000)

# 12 ⎯⎯ Winning Chance Contact

- Should there be an automatic response to chance contact?
- What's the most effective way to "fire and move"?
- Must a signal stop the "base of fire" during a hasty flanking attack?

(Sources: FM 22-100 (1983), p. 185; FM 90-10-1 (1982), pp. B-3, B-4)

### INTO THE UNKNOWN

A "chance contact" is an accidental encounter between opposing forces on the move. How is it handled? Some manuals prefer not to say. Others talk about breaking contact to resume one's original mission. Still others promote an aggressive, but uniform response.

A defensive security patrol must know how to attack its opponent during chance contact. After all, making contact is its implicit mission. One would suspect that other types of patrols would have better odds of surviving if they too knew how to attack when all else had failed.

Successfully attacking during chance contact would logically entail some sort of thought process. After all, each set of circumstances would be different. However, the majority of U.S. infantry trainees become convinced that the best way to handle every chance contact (or every ambush for that matter) is to run an Immediate-Action (IA) Drill. Their favorites are contact "front," "rear," "right," and "left." These are hasty attacks that are conducted precisely the same way each time. All entail shouting, shooting, and moving upright. Thinking is not required. The trainees are told that the squad must be able to react instantly. Soon the uninitiated start to talk about their "instant reflexes," as if their training has somehow relieved them of the requirement to think.

That a unit must always react instantaneously to chance contact is simply *not true*. U.S. units in Vietnam regularly found themselves assaulting *prepared enemy positions* after reacting instantly to what they initially believed to be chance contact. What happened then was predictable. To attack successfully during a chance encounter, a unit must take action *only* before the enemy expects it. The squad that fades into the landscape for a few moments of tactical decision making seldom forfeits its chance to capture the momentum. The problem has been that it doesn't take initiative at the small-unit level to conduct attrition warfare, only tight control.

For whatever reason, not much is written in English about chance contact. Chesty Puller spoke of the problem before WWII, and others have spoken of it since. But, to this day, little emphasis has been put on learning more about how to handle this type of encounter. Most rifle squads do not get the opportunity during field training exercises to arrive by trial and error at what the manuals fail to discuss. While on patrol, they spend so much time sneaking around that they seldom see aggressor patrols, much less try to attack them.

## U.S. UNITS NEED AN ALTERNATIVE TO THEIR TRADITIONAL IMMEDIATE-ACTION DRILL

For U.S. infantrymen, exploiting enemy contact generally boils down to an IA drill, and that drill usually concludes with a standup frontal assault. It establishes momentum, but at what cost? IA drills can be conducted quickly, but they telegraph friendly intentions.

Definitely worthy of consideration is the logical follow-up to the U.S. Army's "bounding-overwatch" method of movement to contact. Part of the unit could fix the enemy in place, while other parts moved forward on the flanks. Operating this way might help to establish momentum, but the enemy could see the flank elements coming. And, if those elements turned to attack, they would risk shooting each other. For the bounding-overwatch sequel to work on patrol, the fire teams would need their own radios and familiarity with the terrain. That way, they could travel separately and still properly coordinate the flanking attacks.

To the typical infantry squad with just one radio, the IA drill seems suicidal, and the sequel to bounding overwatch risks coordination problems. Without more realistic guidelines, their reaction to enemy contact during force-on-force training evolutions leans more toward breaking contact, sending a report to higher headquarters, asking for instructions, calling for slow-to-arrive supporting arms, or establishing an improbable hasty ambush. All of these responses sacrifice momentum, cause little damage to the enemy, and erode self-confidence. U.S. patrols are reluctant to close with what may prove to be the advance element of a larger force. Even when they decide to attack, they often delay direct confrontation — by enveloping to intercept. What are the chances that a friendly patrol could accurately guess where an enemy patrol was headed and then get there first? If the enemy is taken under fire to fix him in place, he is forewarned of an impending attack. U.S. infantrymen need another attack technique specifically designed for chance contact.

Perhaps, one could combine the strengths of existing procedures to create a more realistic solution. To consider chance-contact circumstances too varied to justify any method whatsoever is to abandon the idea of seizing the momentum. Determining what to do on a case-by-case basis takes too long. The side that's the least prepared is also the least decisive.

## SOME PREREQUISITES FOR A NEW WAY TO HANDLE CHANCE CONTACT

Any alternative procedure would first have to satisfy the definition of a technique. It would *not* be used in every situation. It would lend itself to modification as circumstances warranted. It would be another course of action with which a squad could become familiar, and throughout which, initiative could be exercised:

When in doubt, do the innovative.[1]
— Gen. Al Gray USMC (Ret)

The new method must capture the momentum from the outset. The unit must move directly at the enemy. There are ways to compensate for any size differential:

Sun Tzu attached great importance to gaining the initiative in any confrontation.[2]

Units at all levels must be active against the enemy. Squad and platoon leaders often face situations that are sketchy. Be aggressive! As a young troop leader in World War I, Lieutenant Erwin Rommel was the epitome of aggressiveness. Frequently, he faced vague situations where a decision was critical. Usually he decided to attack! Rommel forced the enemy to react to him. If you can be fast, do something he doesn't expect, and knock him off balance, then you are likely to succeed.[3]
— MCI 7401

When the situation is obscure, attack.[4]
— Col.Gen. Heinz Guderian

We are outnumbered, there's only one thing to do. We must attack.[5]
— Admiral Cunningham
(before attacking Italian Fleet at Taranto in 1940)

The new method could incorporate stalking the enemy initially. That would mean *no shooting or shouting.* This is the way to enhance one's combat power without increasing the danger. Of course, to have this option, the security men must spot the enemy without being seen themselves. Moving quietly toward one's adversary is not a revolutionary idea:

> My opinion is that there ought not to be much firing at all. My idea is that the best mode of fighting is to reserve your fire till the enemy get [you] — or you get them — to close quarters.[6]
> — Stonewall Jackson

The new method could require all personnel to come on line before opening fire. That way, they could not mask each other's fires. Each must be permitted to move to that line by the quickest and safest route under the circumstances. It's poorly advised to establish a pattern for them to obey every time.

The method should virtually guarantee doing some damage to the enemy. One confirmed kill per contact is sufficient to preserve a unit's self-confidence. Moving closer to the enemy should help to accomplish this goal.

Finally, the method must allow each infantryman leeway on how to move forward once on line with his comrades. He is the one who can best assess how to cross the ground to his immediate front, and he is one who can best determine when the enemy's attention has been diverted.

Yet to be determined is how this new technique could be run against a larger opponent. Without an answer to that question, the method will have few takers.

## HOW IMPORTANT IS ENEMY SIZE?

Bigness in combat has more to do with momentum, terrain, and weaponry than with numbers of personnel. Concentrated effort, the machinegun, and supporting arms brought the Marines out of an encirclement by ten times their number at the Chosin Reservoir. Eight years of long-range patrolling in Haiti and Nicaragua had to give Chesty Puller insight into the importance of enemy size during a meeting engagement. He liked to move forward, no matter what his opponent's size. His first action in charge of twenty-five Haitian Gendarmerie revealed an intuitive understanding of how to handle chance contact:

> About 4:00 P.M., without warning, Lewis stumbled into his first fight of his career — and proved his instinct for combat. The pack train was ambling around a wooded bend..., when it met an oncoming Caco band of about a hundred, equally surprised, and in the same formation. Puller spurred his horse and yelled: "Charge! Attack! Vite (Hurry)!"[7]

Chesty Puller's fondness for hasty frontal attacks against surprised opponents may have led some to believe that he preferred frontal attacks under every circumstance. In all probability, he simply had a well-founded appreciation for momentum:

> You go get 'em. In the end you'll save lives. There are times when you'll have to flank, but don't forget that the shortest distance between two points is a straight line.[8]
> — Chesty Puller

When confronted by a large predator, even a small animal will attack to throw his adversary off balance. The small animal does not have to follow through. The predator knows that the attack was more than just a bluff:

> What counts is not necessarily the size of the dog in the fight, it's the size of the fight in the dog.[9]
> — Dwight D. Eisenhower

While closing with an opposing force by the shortest route, a U.S. squad could easily find itself at a disadvantage from the standpoint of terrain or firepower. The new technique will entail moving straight at the enemy force without concern for its ultimate size. If the enemy's combat power proves too formidable, the friendly unit can always stop to even up the odds with supporting arms.

## WHEN ONE'S COVER RUNS OUT

*Terrain is everything.* When a unit, or any of its parts, discovers open terrain to its front while attacking during chance contact, it must cease moving forward. When the friendly unit's cover runs out, the new chance-contact technique must promote attacking by fire only.

(Source: FM 7-11B3 (1976), p. 2-VII-C-4.4)

This provision must also apply to individuals. When only partial cover is available, only those individuals who can move to the next piece of cover in their lanes within three seconds should do so. That is how long it takes an enemy soldier to draw a bead on a moving target. If a person does not have additional cover just ahead in his lane, he must either temporarily change lanes or stop moving forward altogether.

## THE NEW TECHNIQUE TO PRACTICE FOR CHANCE CONTACT

The security team member (whether point, flank, or rear) who first spots enemy soldiers has three options: (1) to shoot them to save his life, (2) to point out their location to his friends in the main body, or (3) to signal for a hasty ambush. Generally, the last option will only work when the opposition is approaching along the same trail being used by the friendly unit. When the security man chooses either of his first two options, those in the main body must follow the same procedure — moving by whatever route provides the best speed, cover, and subunit integrity to a position on line with that security man.

The leader moves to the center of the line. If his unit has yet to be detected, he gives the signal for the line to move forward by stalking. If his unit has already been seen, and, if the terrain offers enough cover, he gives the signal for the line to advance by "fire and movement" — a series of roughly parallel one-man rushes individually covered by fire. The leader aims for the center of what's visible of the enemy unit, and everyone else guides on him in a ragged line. In other words, no one gets too far ahead of him. Each person doesn't have to keep the leader in sight at all times to accomplish this, but only to stay close to the next person in line on the side toward the leader.

When the stalking unit is spotted, it automatically begins to fire and move. It does so until overrunning the enemy (using grenades at the finish), unless part of the line is forced by lack of cover or enemy fire to stop moving forward. This management by exception helps the unit to maintain its momentum. All the while, only well-aimed shots are being taken at well-defined targets. This helps the unit to preserve whatever surprise remains intact and to kill at least one enemy soldier.

If a major portion of the line runs out of cover, any subordinate-unit leader can pass the word for the entire line to stop. Then, the overall leader has several prerogatives: (1) to send that part of the line still having cover forward on a hasty flanking attack, (2) to attack by fire alone, or (3) to conduct a retrograde movement under his umbrella of supporting arms. The combination of open terrain and automatic-weapons fire should be enough to foil any counterattack. (See figures 12.1 and 12.2.)

(Sources: FM 7-11B1/2 (1978), p. 2-II-C-4.2; FM 22-100 (1983), p. 113; MCO P1500.44B, p. 12-66)

Winning Chance Contact

Figure 12.1: The Typical Chance Encounter
(Sources: FM 7-8 (1984), p. 3-28; FM 5-103 (1985), p. 4-6; FM 7-70 (1986), p. 4-20; FM 7-11B1/2 (1978), pp. 2-II-A-1.2, 2-IV-B-10.2; MCI 03.66a (1986), p. 2-9; FMFM 6-7 (1989), p. 1-13)

Techniques from the NCO Corps

Figure 12.2: Chance-Contact Technique
(Sources: FM 7-8 (1984), p. 3-28; FM 5-103 (1985), pp. 4-6, 4-38; FM 7-70 (1986), p. 4-20; FM 7-11B1/2 (1978), p. 2-II-A-1.2; MCI 03.66a (1986), p. 2-9)

Figure 12.2: Chance-Contact Technique (Continued)
(Sources: FM 7-8 (1984), p. 3-28; FM 7-70 (1986), p. 4-20; FM 7-11B1/2 (1978), p. 2-II-A-1.2; MCI 03.66a (1986), p. 2-9)

*Figure 12.2: Chance-Contact Technique (Continued)*
(Sources: FM 7-8 (1984), p. 3-28; FM 5-103 (1985), pp. 4-6, 4-38; FM 7-70 (1986), p. 4-20; FM 7-11B1/2 (1978), pp. 1-I-A-8, 2-II-A-1.2, 2-II-A-5.2, 2-IV-B-10.2; FM 22-100 (1983), p. 84; MCI 03.66a (1986), p. 2-9; FMFM 6-7 (1989), p. 1-13)

## BECAUSE THE TECHNIQUE IS MANAGED BY EXCEPTION, THE LEADER HAS TIME TO REQUEST A SUPPORTING-ARMS BACKUP

What unit members do after receiving the signal to execute this technique, depends largely on the situation. Control is, for the most part, decentralized. Because the technique is managed by exception, the leader has time to do other things.

When one takes on a potentially larger enemy, it's wise to have a big stick handy. It can take a while to get an indirect-fire mission cleared and the proper settings put on the guns. As soon as the small-arms shooting starts, the leader should request an "immediate-suppression" mission on a "preplanned" target or grid coordinate *behind* the enemy. For safety, he should choose a target beyond danger-close range of his own unit. Then, if the opposition force turns out to be too formidable, he can summon sufficient fire power to even up the odds within two or three minutes.

## HOW TO STALK AND TO FIRE AND MOVE ON LINE

"Stalking on line" and "firing and moving on line" are basically the same maneuver. Both entail individuals moving forward while their partners cover them with their rifles. During stalking, all friendly fire is withheld. For either option to succeed, all movement must be *individual* and *random*. The world has long recognized the advantages of decentralizing control in this way:

> At the Imperial Maneuvers of 1902 [at the height of the interest in Boer tactics], German infantry was observed working . . . in . . . skirmish lines, each rifleman moving from one covered position to another as an individual.[10]

Each man must be allowed to assess the situation to his immediate front, and then to decide *for himself* how and when to move. However much control is deemed essential must be achieved beforehand through long hours of practice in all types of terrain. This is probably the hardest technique for a small unit to learn. The core maneuver element is the two-man team. Each team has its own lane. These lanes must be roughly parallel (inexperienced troops choose lanes that all converge on whatever part of the enemy unit is currently visible). Team members should be close buddies. They will have to take turns moving and covering each other by fire.

The one covering is responsible for suppressing the fire of any enemy soldier in his lane — whether that fire is directed at his team or not. If he can shoot safely in proximity to his moving partner, he does so. His only real limitation is that he cannot normally shoot at any target outside his own lane.

The man on the move can be partially upright or completely prone (namely, crawling). He goes from one covered position to the next. There is no such thing as fire and movement without cover. When the one moving gets to the next object solid enough to fend off a bullet, he stops. He *does not* "hit and roll," because doing so serves no useful purpose. It merely disorients him and subjects him to more enemy fire. He only moves forward, when he can make it to the next piece of cover within three seconds. His quickest route to that cover is usually a straight line, but he may sometimes prefer a zigzag that for while keeps a tree trunk between him and his greatest perceived threat. When he incorrectly estimates the time of his run, he can hit the deck and crawl the rest of the way, or he can zigzag a bit to throw off his foe's aim. When the distance to the next piece of cover is too great for any attempt, he and his partner must crawl in *behind* a team in an adjacent lane and advance (without firing). Then, once past the area devoid of cover, they should return to their own lane. (See figures 12.3, 12.4, and 12.5.)

## ANOTHER TECHNIQUE FOR INVESTIGATING POSSIBLE ENEMY ACTIVITY ON THE FLANKS

Column and line are the same formation headed in different directions. The ease of transition between the most rapid (column) and the most powerful (line) should be exploited to build momentum. When a contact patrol in column sees something suspicious on one side, it can do a flanking movement as in marching and then stalk on line to that side. If nothing is found, another flanking movement will aim the patrol in the original direction of march.

## THE CHANCE-CONTACT TECHNIQUE CONSTITUTES A VALUABLE TRANSITION BETWEEN PHASES OF THE ATTACK

The chance-contact technique does not start out as an attack per se. For this reason, it constitutes a way to handle the transition period between the movement-to-contact and attack phases of offensive combat. Theoretically, the stalking motion can automatically evolve into fire and movement. In all probability, the unit will be forced by lack of cover or enemy fire to halt its forward progress at some point. Then, its leader has as another option — a hasty flanking attack. His launching of this flanking attack marks the beginning of the attack phase.

It's clear why this technique has great value to the period of transition between the first two phases of offensive combat. After all, what is ultimately at stake is momentum. A unit familiar with this technique can move forward while thinking about how to attack. Doing one's thinking at a standstill for long automatically sacrifices momentum. Furthermore, getting closer to the enemy helps unit leaders accurately to assess the situation.

Techniques from the NCO Corps

TRAINING TWO-MAN BUDDY TEAMS TO "FIRE AND MOVE" GIVES THEM MORE SURVIVABILITY IN COMBAT. THEY MUST KEEP AN IMPENETRABLE OBJECT BETWEEN THEMSELVES AND THE PERSON TRYING TO SHOOT AT THEM, AND TO EXPOSE THEMSELVES FOR NO LONGER THAN THREE SECONDS AT A TIME. FOR THE MAN MOVING, THAT MEANS RUSHING OR CRAWLING TO THE NEXT OBSTRUCTION IN THE TEAM'S ASSIGNED LANE. IF, IN THE PROCESS, HE CAN KEEP A TREE, ROCK, OR SLIGHT RISE BETWEEN HIM AND FOE IN HIS LANE, SO MUCH THE BETTER. IT DOES NO GOOD TO "HIT AND ROLL." THERE IS NO SUCH THING AS "FIRE AND MOVEMENT" ACROSS TOTALLY FLAT AND UNOBSTRUCTED GROUND. IF THE NEXT BIG PIECE OF COVER CAN'T BE REACHED WITHIN THREE SECONDS, THE TEAM HAS FOUR CHOICES: CRAWL THROUGH THE MICROTERRAIN, RISK ONE "ZIGZAG" IN THEIR RUSH, FALL IN BEHIND A TEAM IN AN ADJACENT LANE, OR STAY PUT. TO STALK AN ENEMY FORCE ON LINE, "FIRE AND MOVE" WITHOUT FIRING.

Figure 12.3: The Unit That Can "Fire and Move" Has the Edge in Chance Contact
(Sources: FM 22-100 (1983), p. 84; FM 7-70 (1986), p. D-24)

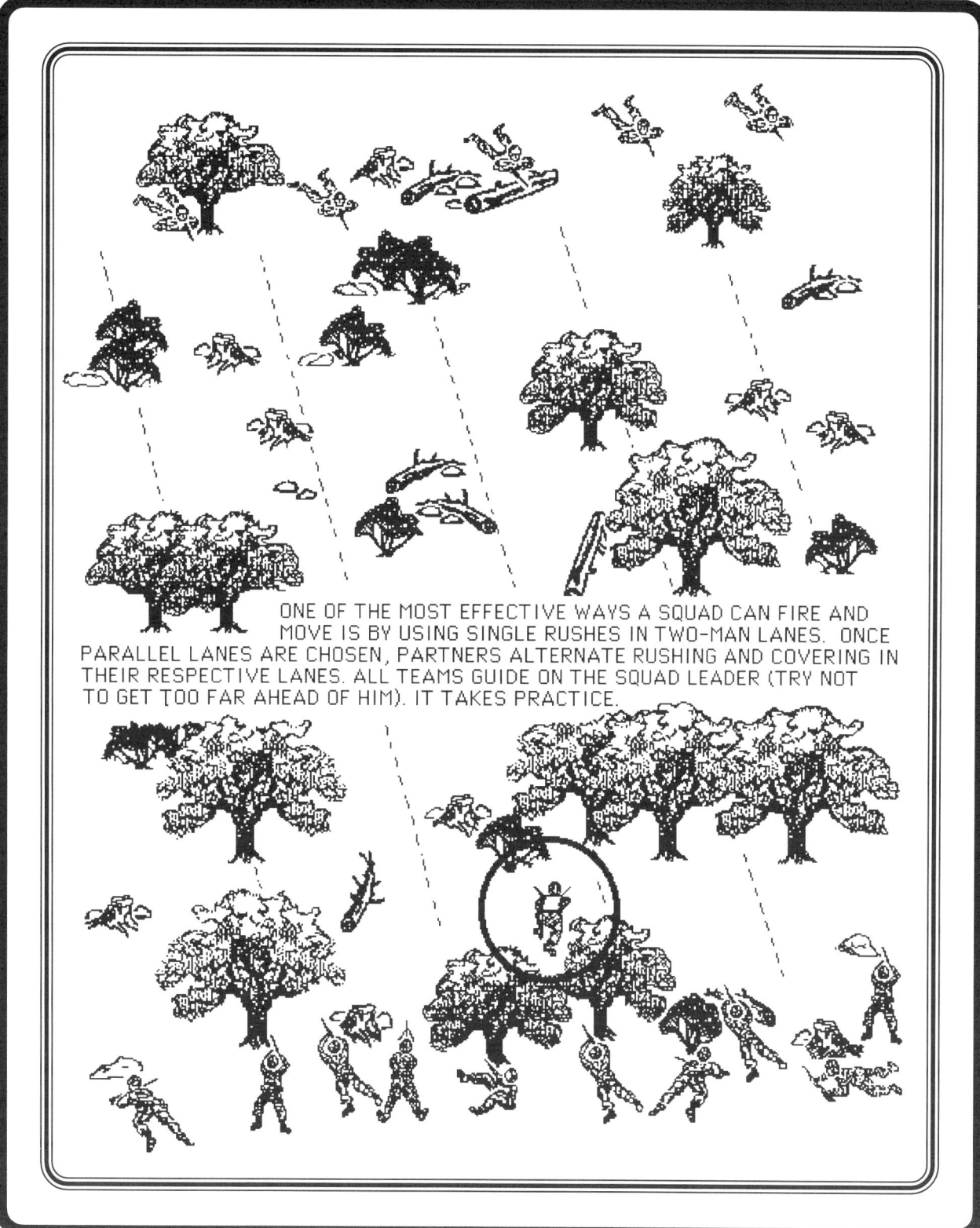

Figure 12.4: A Situation Requiring Fire and Movement
(Sources: MCI 03.66a (1986), p. 2-8; FM 22-100 (1983), p. 66; FM 7-70(1986), p. 4-20; FM 7-11 (1978), p. 2-III-E-8.2; FMFM 6-7 (1989), p. 1-13; FM 5-103 (1985), p. 4-6)

Techniques from the NCO Corps

Figure 12.5: Fire-and-Movement Technique
(Sources: FM 22-100 (1983), p. 66; FM 7-70 (1986), p. 4-20; FM 7-11 (1978), p. 2-III-E-8.2; FMFM 6-7 (1989), p. 1-13; FM 5-103 (1985), pp. 4-6, 4-38; FM 23-30 (1988), p. 2-8)

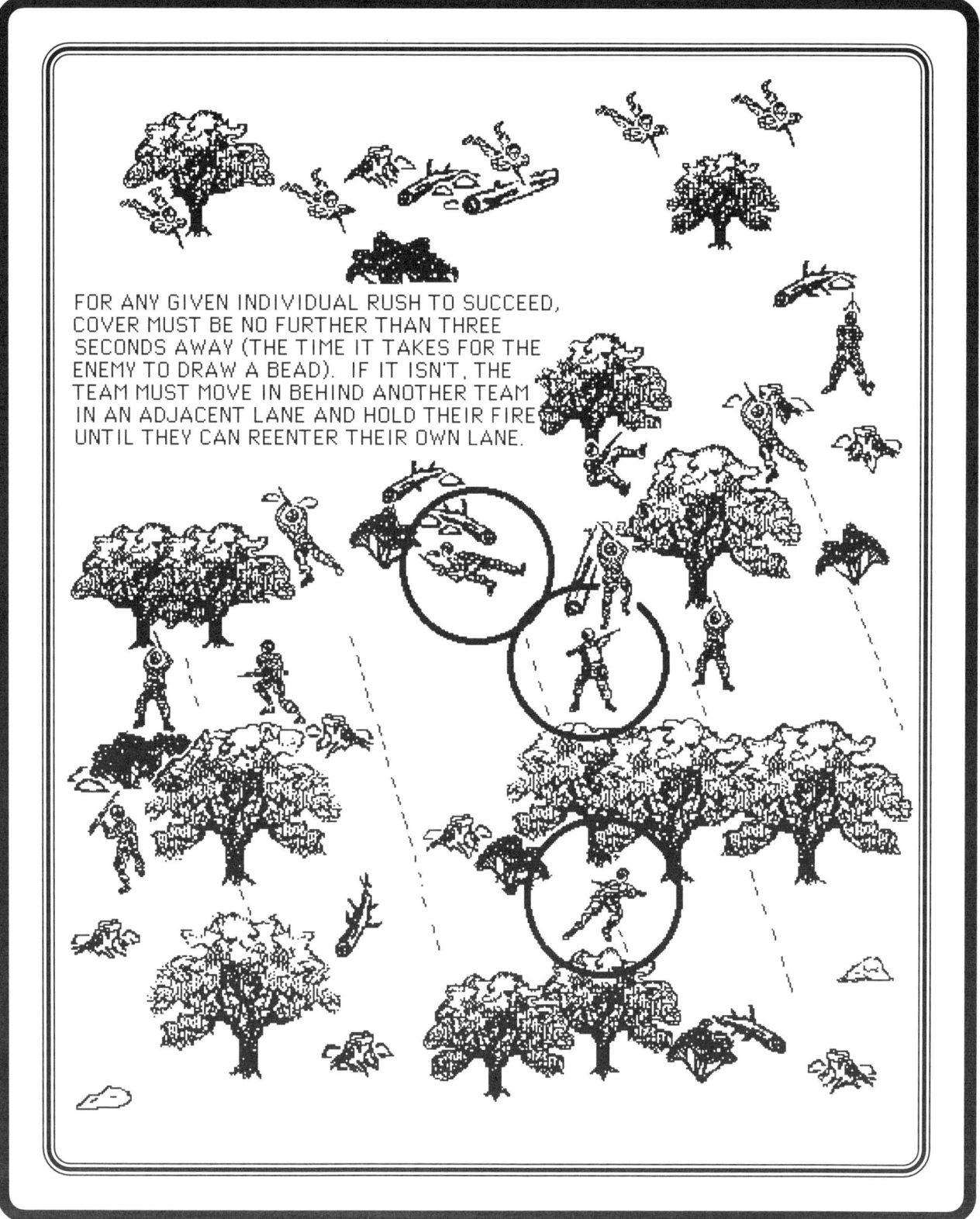

Figure 12.5: Fire-and-Movement Technique (Continued)
(Sources: MCI 03.66a (1986), p. 2-8; FM 22-100 (1983), pp. 66, 84; FM 7-70 (1986), p. 4-20; FM 7-11 (1978), p. 2-III-E-8.2; FMFM 6-7 (1989), p. 1-13; FM 5-103 (1985), pp. 4-6, 4-38; FM 7-11B3 (1976), p. 2-VII-C-4.4)

Techniques from the NCO Corps

*Figure 12.5: Fire-and-Movement Technique (Continued)*
(Sources: MCI 03.66a (1986), pp. 2-8, 2-9; FM 22-100 (1983), pp. 66, 84; FM 7-70 (1986), p. 4-20; FM 7-11 (1978), p. 2-III-E-8.2; FMFM 6-7 (1989), p. 1-13; FM 5-103 (1985), pp. 4-6,4-38; FM 7-11B3 (1976), p. 2-VII-C-4.4)

## FOLLOW-UP OPTIONS

As long as the ratio of combat power remains favorable, the chance-contact technique can easily evolve into an attack. Depending on how much cover is available, this can be a frontal attack by fire and movement, a hasty flanking attack, or an attack by fire alone. Once surprise has been lost, the final assault by fire and movement will probably require grenades.

When the combat power ratio becomes unfavorable, an immediate-suppression call for fire from supporting arms can balance it. The other options are to request reinforcements, to fire and move backwards, or to defend. The last two are dangerous but not impossible with the proper employment of one's automatic weapons.

Adding the chance-contact method to one's tactical toolbox could not only help to reduce casualties outright (as Chesty Puller pointed out), but also to preserve the pride so crucial to a unit's overall survivability.

## HOW TO FIRE AND MOVE SAFELY WITH GRENADES

Grenades are required to win an assault by fire and movement. To throw a grenade safely, one *cannot* have another friendly unit member in front of him in any lane.

Personnel must be tested ahead of time on their ability to throw grenades. Only those qualified should be allowed to do so during any type of assault.

## THE HASTY FLANKING ATTACK THAT DOESN'T REQUIRE A SIGNAL TO SHIFT FIRES

When the on-line forward-moving unit is forced to stop by lack of cover at any point along its front, it can run a hasty flanking attack. Part of the line can crawl in column to either side, and then secretly move to a position from which to launch an assault at right angles to the fire coming from the other part of the line. The leader of the maneuver force positions himself at the end of the assault line closest to, and *within view of,* the "base of fire." Then, no signals to shift fires are necessary. Those in the base of fire can clearly see the leader of the maneuver element and lead him with their fire. By guiding on him, the other members of the maneuver force can also stay behind that fire. This is a high-momentum move reminiscent of the sequel to bounding overwatch. With practice, it can become a lethal weapon. If surprise can be maintained, the assault will consist of a ragged line of running men. If not, it will be accomplished by fire and movement. (See figures 12.6 and 12.7.)

## WHEN THE ENEMY IS TOO BIG TO HANDLE

When the friendly force in a chance contact discovers its opponent to be too strong, it must compensate for the imbalance in combat power with a larger weapon — i.e., supporting arms. (See figure 12.8 for a preview of what indirect fire can do.)

(Sources: FM 5-103 (1985), p. 4-7; FM 7-8 (1984), p. 3-1; FM 7-11B1/2 (1978), p. 2-II-A-5.2; FM 90-10-1 (1982), p. E-18)

*Figure 12.6: An Opportunity for a Hasty Flanking Attack*
(Sources: FM 22-100 (1983), p. 84; FM 7-70 (1986), p. 4-20; FM 7-11B1/2 (1978), pp. 2-II-A-5.2, 2-IV-B-10.2; MCI 03.66a (1986), pp. 2-8, 2-9; FM 5-103 (1985), pp. 4-6, 4-38; FM 7-8 (1984), p. 3-28)

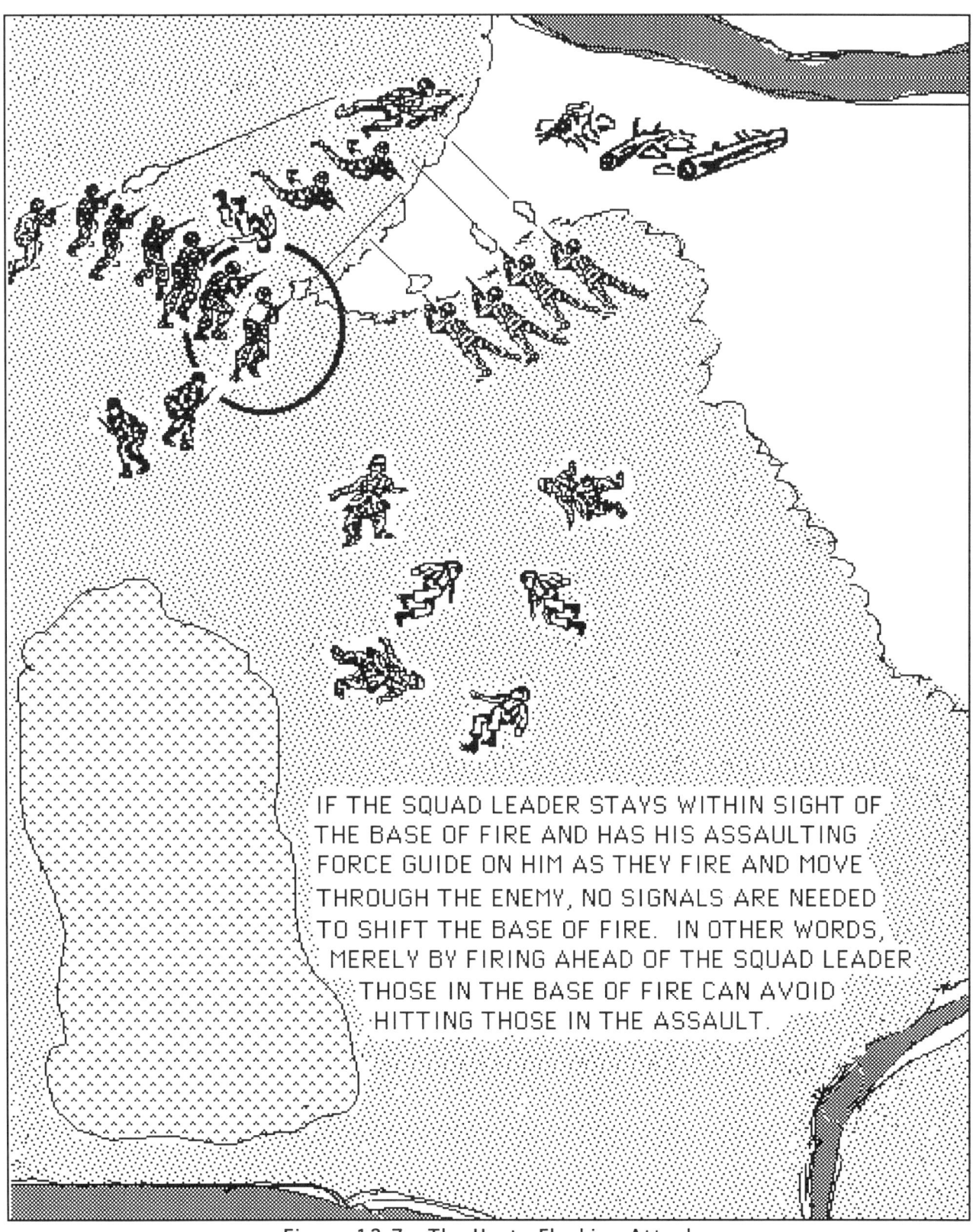

Figure 12.7: The Hasty Flanking Attack
(Sources: FM 22-100 (1983), p. 84; FM 7-70 (1986), p. 4-20; FM 7-11B1/2 (1978), pp. 2-II-A-5.2, 2-IV-B-10.2; MCI 03.66a (1986), p. 2-8; FM 5-103 (1985), p. 4-6; FM 7-8 (1984), p. 3-28)

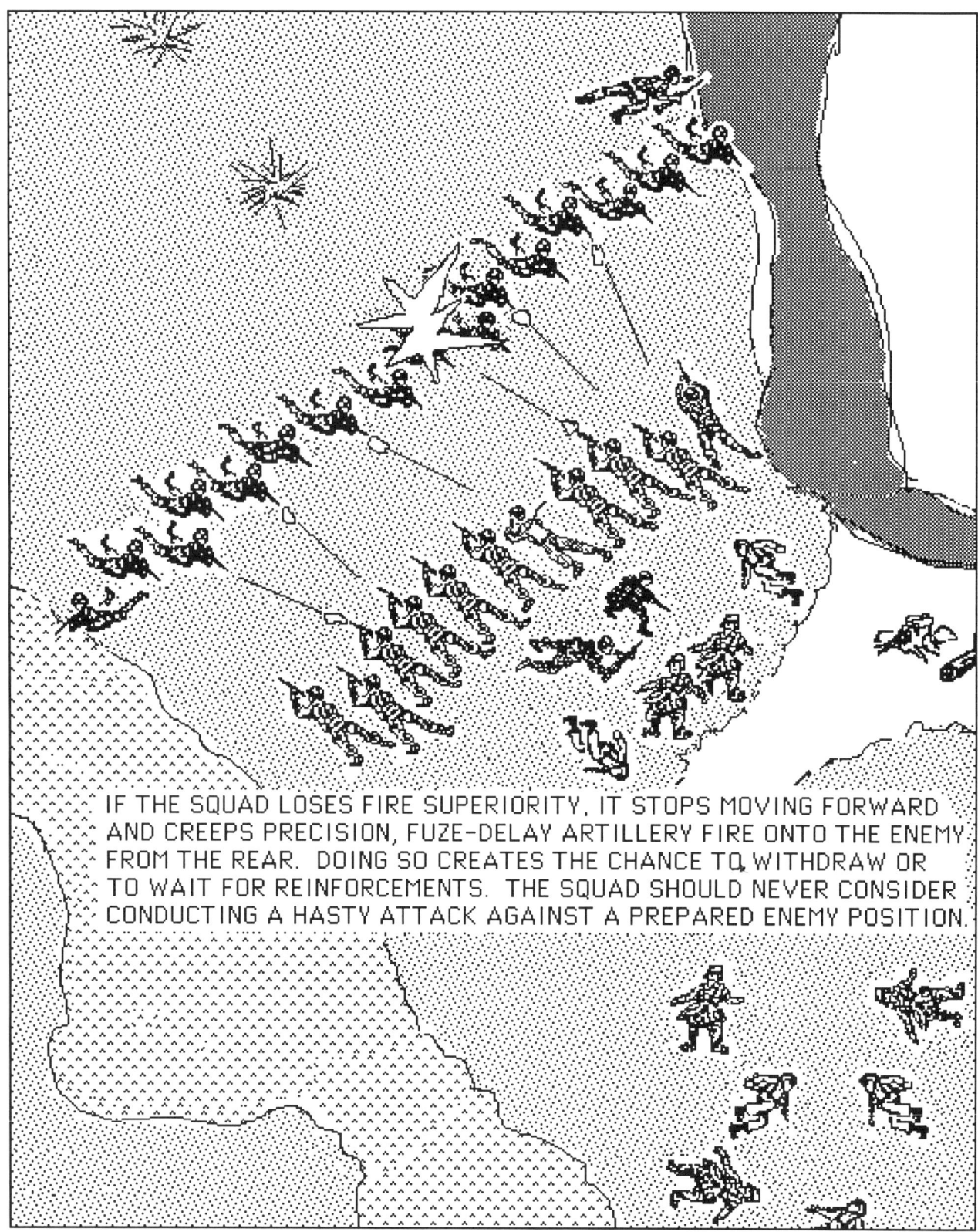

Figure 12.8: When an Enemy Force of Superior Strength Is Encountered
(Sources: FM 22-100 (1983), p. 84; FM 7-70 (1986), p. 4-20; FM 7-11B1/2 (1978), pp. 2-II-A-5.2, 2-IV-B-10.2; FMFM 6-7 (1989), p. 1-13; MCI 03.66a (1986), p. 2-8; FM 5-103 (1985), p. 4-6)

# 13 Evening Up the Odds with Indirect Fire

- How can the wind be used to expedite the process of adjusting fire?
- Can a nearby machinegun bunker be silenced with artillery shells?
- How can one best use indirect fire to hit a moving target?

(Source: FM 22-100 (1973), p. 2-11)

## ONE SOLUTION TO BEING OVERCOMMITTED

"Establishing and maintaining contact" is one of the Principles of Offensive Combat. It keeps the enemy off balance and reveals his weaknesses. From the standpoint of maneuver warfare, "exploiting enemy weaknesses" is the central precept in the Principles of War. Small infantry units must have the self-confidence to use the chance-contact technique from the last chapter against an opponent of unknown size. The enemy unit's size doesn't matter, as long as the friendly unit is carrying a *large enough weapon*. Supporting arms would qualify.

He who knows how to use indirect fire can even up a size differential in a hurry. One can imagine what several accurately placed artillery shells could do to a numerically superior, but equally surprised, enemy. History is replete with examples of uncovered infantry forces being annihilated by artillery fire.

If the decision is to "attack in a different direction," indirect fire can make this possible as well. At the Chosin Reservoir in Korea in late 1950, it helped the 1st Marine Division to break out of an encirclement by a force ten times their number. At Ia Drang in late 1965, it helped a U.S. infantry battalion to rescue its forward elements from the clutches of two NVA regiments:

> The lesson of Ia Drang was that the pivotal factor in the tactical contest would be firepower. If the Americans could bring artillery and air power to bear quickly and effectively, the advantage was

theirs. The enemy's objective was the same as it had been against the French — to separate the Americans from their source of firepower or to strike quickly and withdraw before incoming firepower shifted the odds against them.[1]

Throughout the century, "moving fire boxes" have been used to extricate units from difficult situations:

> With the battalion [in Korea] under "heavy pressure from three sides and with a road block to its rear, an artillery barrage was placed around the unit. At an opportune time, the curtain of fire in the rear of the unit was lifted and the friendly force fought a withdrawing action in that direction protected still by artillery fire on the other three sides."[2]

In Vietnam, company commanders often helped squad-sized patrols extricate themselves from enemy encirclements. The commander would place an artillery spotting round in the vicinity of the most likely avenue of escape and then ask his squad for adjustment instructions.

The modern-day patrol leader should call for fire "at his command" every time he makes enemy contact. By preplanning targets *beyond danger-close range* of his patrol route (instead of at checkpoints), he can bring this fire to bear both quickly and safety. As soon as the enemy force is spotted, the friendly patrol leader should initiate his chance-contact technique and send his call for fire. He will have no difficulty controlling both at once. If his opponent turns out to be too large, his artillery fire will keep that opponent occupied while his squad escapes. All the while, unit pride will be preserved. After all, hasn't the squad attacked and hurt a larger force? Some might say that the enemy force will be too close to be attacked safely with supporting arms. Well-trained squad leaders can bring the fire to within 50 yards of their position. The French did in Indochina, and Americans did in Vietnam:

> To break a final charge, a French aerial observer would have to call in light artillery and napalm to within 40 yards of French troops. . . . Bombs were dropped within 100 yards; strafing by a skilled pilot could be brought as close as a few feet from a position.[3]

> With care, a battery of light artillery could be fired [in Vietnam] to within 50 meters as long as friendlies were behind cover.[4]

## UNIQUE CIRCUMSTANCES REQUIRE UNIQUE WAYS OF CALLING AND ADJUSTING FIRE

In calling and adjusting fire, just as in tactics, standardization of procedure can create the impression that one way will work for all types of targets and conditions. The manuals do not make much differentiation between point and area targets, or moving and stationary targets. The standard indirect-fire procedure works best against stationary area targets. That there are three other combinations of the target variables suggests that a different procedure may be required for each of them.

Formal schools push highly accurate desktop procedures that might be employed by an artillery Forward Observer (FO) to engage a distant target from a bunkered observation post. Infantrymen do not always have that luxury. For this reason, they have developed alternative techniques for judging range, quickly establishing target location, avoiding mistakes in computation and transmission, adjusting onto a target with the fewest number of rounds, hitting a nearby target safely, and actually killing their target before it kills them.

## THE CASE FOR PREREGISTRATION

As interest in maneuver warfare has spread, so too has concern about preregistering targets with indirect fire. Many worry that preregistering "points of attack" on offensive objectives will forewarn the enemy, and that preregistering "close defensive fires" around defensive perimeters will compromise their locations. These concerns are both valid and reconcilable.

Offensive objectives can be preregistered *while* the attack is in progress. There are, after all, innumerable explosions on any battlefield. The enemy can be deceived as to the source of any particular explosion or group of explosions. There are scores of artillery or mortar barrages for every one that is followed up with a ground assault. For this reason, a few artillery rounds can still serve as a valuable deception prior to a ground assault.

On the other hand, keeping the whereabouts of a defensive position secret during preregistration of close defensive fires can be accomplished by firing High Explosive (HE) rounds at widely spaced intervals. They will look to the enemy like Harassing and Interdiction (H&I) fires:

> The registration of guns for a raid or attack "with limited objectives" [by German stormtroopers] could be disguised as routine harassing fire.[5]

The case for preregistration is particularly strong during the defense. Chesty Puller's appreciation of it helped to save the Marines' defensive position at Guadalcanal:

> At dusk, as usual, the artillerymen registered their guns, and shells exploded in the thick growth a few yards beyond Puller's lines. . . . At 9:30 the phone rang in the battalion CP. . . . "Colonel, there's about three thousand Japs between you and me." . . . The front erupted with blazing weap-

ons, and over their heads the artillery shells soughed through the rainstorm. Explosions farther back in the jungle halted Japanese columns before they could move [up]. . . . Captured documents revealed that his half-battalion had beaten off the suicidal attacks of the equivalent of a Japanese Division. . . . This burial detail counted 1462 bodies.[6]

(Sources: MCO P1550.14D (1983), p. 8-22; OPNAV P 34-03 (1960), p. 404)

Only by preregistering, can a defender surprise a mobile attacker with the initial volley. To find the mark, rounds produced any other way will have to be adjusted. This gives the attacker time to take evasive action. To have value as preregistered targets, chokepoints in the terrain need not be visible from the defensive perimeter. They can be monitored by sentry posts or makeshift listening devices. Imagine the blow to the momentum of an unsuspecting attacker, of 15 rounds of accurately placed artillery fire; imagine the boost to the confidence of the defender. Even when the opponent never actually crosses a preregistration point, he can still be hit with the first volley. After all, the observer can shift from the known point as if a round had just landed there. Or, just *one* round can produce a bracket (the other end of which is the preregistration point itself). And this bracket can be established without giving the enemy any warning that an accurate volley is on the way.

## COMPETING REQUIREMENTS IN THE INITIAL CALL FOR FIRE

When calling for fire, two requirements initially compete for the spotter's attention — accurately computing the target location and quickly transmitting this key information. Many formal schools attempt to maximize both at once. With climatic variations, map error, gun error, and ammunition error, one wonders what can be gained from eight-digit grid coordinates for the initial target location. The round is not going to land there even if the grid coordinates are computed perfectly. When there are no friendlies near a target, rapidly placing a round in that target's general vicinity helps to kill it more quickly. The rapid response will, by itself, be enough to silence some targets — no matter what the accuracy. For example, an enemy mortar will often fall silent after any semblance of return fire. Of course, just as important as computing a general target location *accurately,* is transmitting that location *correctly* over the radio. Whatever delays are required to do this are worthwhile.

To save time and to counter the electronic-warfare threat, formal schools often encourage aspiring forward observers to use only the four mandatory elements of the call for fire — *observer identification, warning order, target location,* and *description of target.* Still, the two nonmandatory elements — *method of engagement* and *method of control* — are crucial to firing safely in proximity to friendlies and hitting anything other than a stationary area target. The firing batteries can't always accurately guess what has been left out of a call for fire. Sometimes, a spotter's specifications on how to hit a particular target must take precedence over secrecy.

The *method of engagement* — the fifth element of the call for fire — offers "precision fire" (for firing at close range, killing a point target, and preregistering), "danger close" (for reminding the battery to doublecheck its data prior to firing for effect), and "high trajectory" (for minimizing the effect of elevation changes between adjustment rounds). It also gives the spotter the chance to specify "type of round and fuze." There's no way the Fire Direction Center (FDC) can ascertain, from a multiword target description, the subtle nuances of a tactical situation. The shell best suited for killing a target may also kill the observer. For example, when the target is enemy troops in an open trench, the FDC might choose variable-time fuzing, whereas an observer 100 yards away might prefer delay fuzing. Finally, the method of engagement offers several sizes of fire-for-effect sheaf. Without specifying otherwise, the observer agrees to a "standard" sheaf that can cover an area *300 meters* in diameter — 200 meters for the BCS (computer-generated) sheaf plus 100 meters for the margin of error on gun, ammunition, and operator. The standard sheaf will make plenty of noise, but it may not hurt anyone except the observer.

The *method of control,* or sixth and last element of the call for fire, also offers useful options. The at-my-command method of control is vital during a ground attack. It can provide *timely* masking of telltale sounds and deception. "At my command" can also provide a way to hit a moving target. Then, there's the Time on Target (TOT) option. It is useful for hitting a moving target that is not visible, but for which an initial location, route, and speed have been ascertained. Without "continuous illumination" and "continuous fire," an infantry leader trying to call for fire (while guiding his flock through a firefight) would have to keep saying "repeat" over his radio. Only with "coordinated illumination" can he easily adjust fire after dark. The method of control also provides ways to adjust a "fire for effect," to request artillery round ordinates (heights) while planning an airstrike, and to relay

Time to Target (TTT) information for an airstrike so a battery can coordinate the marking and suppression of enemy air defenses. By not specifying the method of control, the forward observer agrees the battery's time schedule.

## QUICKLY ARRIVING AT *TARGET LOCATION* WITH ACCEPTABLE ACCURACY

Parts of Western Europe have been fought over so many times that they've been accurately mapped. That means that a map grid coordinate can produce an artillery shell at the same location depicted. Other parts of the world have not been as well mapped. There, many target locations are only approximate. Under these circumstances, *precisely* measuring grid coordinates serves no useful purpose; and only the target locations beyond danger-close range of friendly units, can be safely used. A good way to arrive at a target location quickly is through the *one-point-intersection* method from land navigation. When one hears an enemy mortar popping in the distance, he can orient his map on the ground, run a finger from his own known location toward the noise, stop his finger at the terrain feature probably defilading the mortar, pick up his radio handset with the other hand, and read the grid coordinates under his finger as a part of the call for fire. With practice, this sequence can be accomplished before the first enemy mortar rounds hit the ground.

## *POLAR* MISSIONS

Polar missions are those for which the firing battery knows the observer's location ahead of time. As infantry units are often mobile and under the fan of more than one firing battery, seldom does the infantry know where the artillery is and vice versa. Normally, the polar method of target location is used only by infantry units that are collocated with artillery or mortars. Forward observers who don't realize this may be tempted to transmit friendly locations in the clear over uncovered nets or try to adjust fire along what they suppose to be the *gun-target* line instead of the Observer-Target (O-T) line.

## THE *SHIFT-FROM-A-KNOWN-POINT* MISSION

It is not difficult to describe a target's location by the shift-from-a-known-point method. It is the same as describing that target's location in relation to the known point. It is also the same as adjusting onto that target, an imaginary round that has just landed at the known point. The known point is usually a preregistered target. Most human beings are not good at guessing lateral distances. To determine how far the target is to the left or right of the known point, even seasoned observers must rely on the Width Equals Range times Mils (WERM) rule. Instead of the actual range, an O-T factor is used. It is 1 for every 1000 meters. Only for distances of less than 1000 meters do fractions come into play. Looking through binoculars to determine the angular deviation between known point and target distorts normal depth perception and sacrifices the peripheral vision so vital to heavily involved infantrymen. Assigning 30 mils to the base of *every* finger held at arm's length is a better alternative.

Shifting from a known point is a highly versatile way of engaging targets. If the target is moving close to the known point, firing for effect on the first volley can produce ample accuracy and complete surprise. If the target is moving at some distance from the known point, one round can produce a bracket without startling the intended victim. This bracket will produce enough of a frame of reference for the observer to hit the target with a fire for effect on the next volley. Even if he misses, he can quickly summon another fire for effect by simply transmitting an adjustment and the word "repeat."

## OBSERVER-TARGET (O-T) DIRECTION

An O-T direction accurate to within a few degrees is necessary to adjust fire onto most targets. For an infantryman, an O-T direction accurate to within 10 mils is a waste of valuable time. His compass is usually a little out of calibration anyway, and his wrist watch and ammunition magazines will further distort the reading.

If the adjustment rounds do not move in the way expected, it means that the O-T direction was either given incorrectly or not at all. To insure that it is transmitted accurately, it should be included in every initial adjustment transmission, *whether or not it has already been given in the call for fire*. Again, staying on the radio a few extra seconds does more good than harm.

One way to ruin an otherwise accurate compass reading is to err on its conversion to grid azimuth. Infantrymen should be encouraged to send their O-T directions in the measure with which they are most familiar — degrees magnetic. This will save them from having to do under duress, and periodically botch, the conversion computations. Of course, they must also be warned that forgetting to specify the unit of measure could result in a serious mishap (the battery will infer mils grid). In every call for fire, *all* units of measure should be specified.

## DISTANCE ESTIMATION TECHNIQUES

There are several techniques with which to estimate range. Perhaps the most useful is the *map inspection* method. First, the map is oriented. Then, one looks downrange for a terrain feature near the target that is also depicted on the map. The distance to the target can now be easily estimated. A variation on this theme is to choose a known object beyond the target, and then to estimate what fraction of the distance to that object is the range to the target.

Additionally, there is the *flash-bang* method. It is based on the speed of sound between target and observer (330 meters per second). There must only be a sharp noise corresponding with a visible action. Any combination will do; it need not be the report and muzzle flash of a weapon.

Another way of estimating range is to imagine how many multiples of a well-known distance would be needed to fill the void. The distances between firing lines at the rifle range are those most familiar to infantrymen.

Antitank gunners use a variation of the WERM rule to estimate range. They use the number of mils displaced by a target and what they guess to be the target's width. In other words, they insert a known angular deviation and a known width into the WERM formula to find an unknown range. All armor is about 3 meters wide and 10 meters long. If the base of an upright finger at arm's length covers the entire breadth of a sideways moving tank, the tank is approximately 330 meters away:

W (10) = Range x Mils (30)
1/3 = Range

This technique can be used under many circumstances. The height of a tree line can be estimated from the known size of a man standing at its base. The height or width of a building can be estimated from the standard dimensions of a door. In either case, however many fingers are needed to cover the height or width of the object will disclose its range. The number of mils that an enemy soldier is tall on the reticle pattern of standard binoculars will also reveal how far away he is.

## LATERAL DISTANCE SHOULD ALWAYS BE COMPUTED MATHEMATICALLY

For most observers, trying to guess at lateral distance between the last impact and the target can be a waste of valuable time. In their eagerness to hit the O-T line, they end up "ping-ponging" back and forth across it. More than one spotter has come close to the O-T line with his initial shot, overcorrected, and then been unable to get near the line again. Once the range to the target has been determined by whatever means, the WERM rule should always be utilized to compute lateral distance. It is also important to modify this distance slightly to keep one's rounds upwind of the O-T line. Whether or not the drifting smoke partially obscures the target is often the only clue to whether the last round in a bracketing sequence was long or short. Once the round is close enough to the O-T line for the smoke to drift across it, the spotter should not attempt to move the round any more laterally until the final adjustment. Then, he can move it just slightly to the left or right (usually no more than 50-75 meters) in conjunction with the fire for effect. (See figure 13.1.)

When the gun-target line is almost perpendicular to the O-T line, manual plotting boards distort (enlarge) the lateral distance. Then, trying to move the round over to the O-T line often results in ping-ponging, unless all lateral adjustments are *halved* in accordance with what has come to be known as the "Angle-T" rule.

## TARGETS AT CLOSE RANGE

The maneuver warfare specialist or guerrilla will not make his presence known until he's within 50-100 meters

(Sources: MCO P1500.44B, p. 12-65; FM 22-100 (1983), p. 30)

Techniques from the NCO Corps

THE FIRST TASK IN MOVING AN ARTILLERY ROUND ONTO A TARGET IS DETERMINING THE LATERAL DISTANCE. THERE IS ONLY ONE RELIABLE METHOD — THE "WERM" RULE. TO ESTIMATE THE ANGULAR DEVIATION, INFANTRYMEN PREFER THEIR FINGERS TO BINOCULARS. THEY CANNOT AFFORD TO LOSE PERIPHERAL VISION AND PERSPECTIVE. TO SIMPLIFY THE MATHEMATICS INVOLVED, INFANTRYMEN ALSO PREFER ASSIGNING 30 MILS TO THE BASE OF EVERY FINGER WHEN HELD AT ARMS LENGTH.

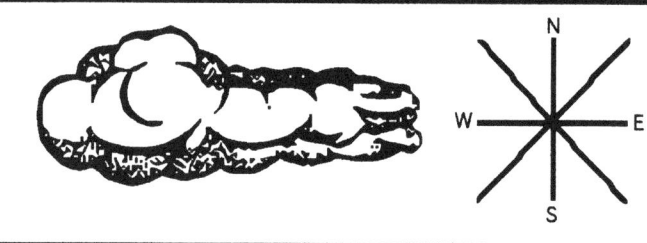

DON'T WASTE TIME TRYING TO MOVE THE ROUND RIGHT ON TOP OF THE O-T LINE AT FIRST. GET CLOSE ENOUGH FOR THE SMOKE TO DRIFT ACROSS IT. THEN, MAKE A SMALL LATERAL ADJUSTMENT RIGHT BEFORE THE KILL.

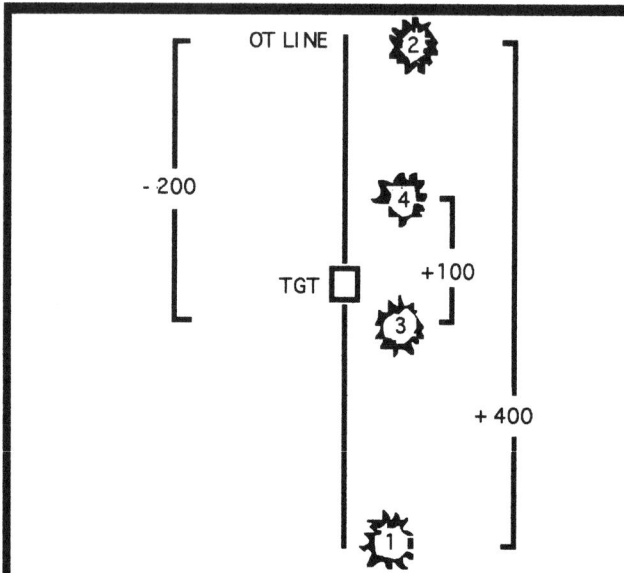

EXCEPT FOR DANGER-CLOSE TARGETS, ALWAYS USE SOME SORT OF BRACKETING ALONG THE OBSERVER-TARGET (O-T) LINE TO ARRIVE AT THE CORRECT DISTANCE. BEING FOOLED IN COMBAT BY THE OPTICAL ILLUSION THAT THE TARGET IS BEING HIT WHEN IT REALLY ISN'T CAN PROVE FATAL. INTENTIONALLY PLACING THE FIRST ROUND A LITTLE SHORT FACILITATES THE ALL-IMPORTANT FIRST "BOLD" ADJUSTMENT.

Figure 13.1: The Keys to Adjusting Indirect Fire
(Source: FM 6-30 (1991), pp. 3-11, 5-3, 6-15)

of an opponent. For this reason, U.S. infantrymen must be thoroughly proficient at calling for fire in close proximity to themselves. This takes a special technique.

First, the observer must understand the limitations of his weapons. If he is anywhere near the gun-target line, he shouldn't contemplate using naval gunfire. The M198 155mm howitzer is more accurate but still an area weapon. Its built-in margin of error is about 25 meters. Against point targets, the old 8-inch howitzer was more effective. How accurately an 81mm mortar can fire depends on how well its crew can "bubble up" between rounds.

Then, one should *not* "preplan" fires on top of any location he intends to occupy — whether patrol checkpoint, attack objective, or defensive perimeter. His target number may get used by accident. In Vietnam, H&I barrages hit friendly positions more than once.

Preplanning one's fires saves clearance time, but it does not insure that the rounds will land where expected. When calling for fire on a nearby enemy, one should *not* send (as target location) the enemy's actual grid coordinates. A better choice is the whereabouts of an imaginary target outside danger-close range. This will compensate for map error and for inadvertently getting a standard sheaf on the first volley. That sheaf can be 300 meters wide!

When the first round lands, it should be moved *just upwind* of the O-T line, and then walked no more than 100 meters at a time toward the target. Finally, the spotter can make minor lateral and distance adjustments (of no more than 50 meters each), specify *"converging sheaf"* or *"precision fire"* (for an extremely close target), and request "fire for effect." Rounds with normal fuzing can cause airbursts in trees; "delay fuzing" is safer. Without "high-trajectory" fire, a difference in elevation between spotter and target can cause short rounds. For a close-proximity mission, the spotter should really add several of these specifications to his method of adjustment.

## RADIO TRANSMISSION GUIDELINES

Surviving in war takes confidence; but, when calling for fire, misplaced confidence can produce mistakes. That's why "Know oneself" is one of the Leadership Principles. Unfortunately, as one's level of exhaustion under duress increases, so do his chances of making a mistake.

During calls for fire, there is the risk not only of computational errors, but also of communicative errors. In other words, the mouth does not always do what the brain tells it to, and the ears do not always pick up the difference. A communicative error can be disastrous when giving a target location, O-T direction, or adjustment. Often, the FDC has no way of knowing that a mistake has been made. Completely possible are the following: (1) juxtaposition of numbers, (2) losing track of how many zeros have been given, (3) failing to identify the applicable unit of measure, and (4) not giving a complete element of information. Just forgetting to say "over" after each transmission can jeopardize the request for support, because the FDC can't tell that the observer's transmission has been concluded.

There are ways to avoid communicative errors. The most foolproof is having another trained spotter monitor the call. If this isn't possible, one should write down what he intends to say ahead of time, or at least carefully listen to what he does say. It's a good idea to round off large numbers (like from "1925" to "nineteen hundred"); the latter is easier to say, easier to understand, and harder to jam. One should always specify the correct unit of measure for every number. This helps the FDC to keep the various numbers in the call for fire straight, and prevents the FDC from wrongly assuming that the standard unit of measure was intended. For example, while dodging bullets, a small-unit leader (who uses magnetic degrees to land navigate) could blurt out that the O-T direction was "180" (meaning that the target was to his south). Unfortunately, the artillery rounds would land to his north, because the battery would assume that his direction had been given in mils. Further, one must remember to unkey his radio handset after sending each element of information, and to listen carefully to the readback. Infantrymen should practice calls for fire until they can concentrate more on content than format.

Of the mistakes most commonly made while calling for fire, inadvertently saying "up" instead of "add" or "down" instead of "drop" is probably the most disastrous. No one is immune from this error. There is no telling how many *short rounds* have actually been self-inflicted. Saying "down 800" can cause the round from a low-trajectory artillery piece to land thousands of meters from the intended target, and potentially on top of a friendly unit. For infantrymen, the solution is to remove the terms "up" and "down" from their vocabulary when sending a call for fire. If the elevation of the target is different from that of the observer, he should either ask for high-trajectory fire or use other words to describe the difference in elevation.

## COMPETING FACTORS DURING ADJUSTMENT

In peacetime, one has no way of distinguishing between the visual and actual effects of indirect fire. In wartime, hurting an enemy is more often a function of ballistics than it is of visual effect. If the first round is short of the target but on the O-T line, and "add 50" produces a round that is long, saying "drop 25, precision fire, fire for effect" (with proper fuzing) will hurt the enemy no matter what the impact looks like.

After each impact, the spotter has roughly 15 seconds until the smoke dissipates. During this short period, he must determine four things: (1) the lateral orientation of round to target (right, left, or on line), (2) *the direction in which the smoke is drifting,* (3) the number of mils between round and O-T line, and (4) the range orientation of round to target ("long," "short," or "cannot be determined"). Because an infantryman may have difficulty finding both impact and target in the narrow field of vision afforded by binoculars, he has a better chance of quickly gathering all four elements of key information *without binoculars*. If unsure of a round's range orientation, he must *not* be tempted to guess at it. Guessing *incorrectly* that a round is either slightly long or slightly short, can forfeit his chance of ever killing the target, because the target now lies outside his bracket. Often, to discover whether a round is "long" or "short," he must *patiently* wait for its smoke to drift over the O-T line. If that smoke dissipates too soon, he must place another round closer to the line. Whenever unsure of range orientation, he must settle for "cannot be determined."

Once the infantryman has quickly acquired this key information, he can spend whatever time it takes to make accurate WERM-rule computations. If his first round is upwind of the O-T line, he must move it 50 meters less than what the WERM rule advises. If the first round is downwind of the line, he must move it 50 meters more than what the WERM rule says. Then, he won't have to waste time trying to hit the O-T line. Instead, the smoke will drift across the line and do the work for him. It's wiser to move one's round upwind of the O-T line and leave it there until ready to kill the target. For the final volley, one can add a slight adjustment to the right or left as needed.

Successive bracketing is the best way to insure — through ballistics — that a distant target will be killed. This is particularly true in hot climates, where heat shimmer can distort the size of a target. "Bracketing" is a term used to describe rounds that land on either side of a target *along the O-T line*. There is no such thing as sideways bracketing; that is ping-ponging. The "bold" adjustment recommended for creating the initial bracket is hard for former mortar men to learn. It often causes the second round to miss the target by a greater distance than the first one did. This additional distance melts away quickly as it is halved. How bold is bold? For a target 0-1000 meters out on flat terrain, an adjustment of 400 meters is bold. For one 1000-2000 meters out, one of 800 meters is bold. Beyond that range, one of 1600 meters is bold. Of course, it is safer to be bold while moving one's round downrange. For this reason, one should try to put the first round a little short. An accomplished observer will often intentionally miss a target with his first round to have a better chance (from the standpoint of ballistics) of ultimately killing it. (For how to kill a distant target, see figures 13.2 and 13.3.)

## IT DOESN'T TAKE A FRONTAL ASSAULT TO SILENCE A MACHINEGUN

Marines silenced machinegun nests by frontal assault in WWII only out of necessity. The Japanese automatic weapons were mutually supporting and crammed by the hundreds into spaces that defied maneuver. Many were so heavily bunkered that they could resist all but a direct hit from an artillery shell. In future wars, frontal assaults may not be required to silence machinegun emplacements. By then, there may be the technology and technique to silence them with indirect fire.

Adjustments of 25 meters or less were hard to compute using the old plotting board. Now, computers at the artillery battery FDC's make smaller adjustments possible. Still, FDC's ask observers if they want to fire for effect every time they request an adjustment of 50 meters or less. Small-unit infantry leaders must not be tempted to fire for effect prematurely. Or, when the smoke clears, they may find their targets still shooting back at them.

A more useful way to silence a machinegun is through the successive splitting of a small bracket. When the automatic weapon is only 50-100 meters from the observer, the artillery rounds must be placed long initially and then crept toward the target. This does not preclude slightly undershooting the enemy gun with the last creeping round, and then successively splitting the resulting bracket. Accuracy takes precedence over speed when a frontal assault is the penalty for failure. The observer can explain to the battery that this is a precision target, and that a 50 meter bracket must be split to hit it. Once on target, he must remember to ask for precision fire not only to protect himself, but also to increase his chances of killing the target. If the machinegun is bunkered, delay fuzing will also help from both standpoints. (See figure 13.4 for this counter-machinegun technique.)

## HITTING A MOVING TARGET

A moving target is difficult to hit. One way is to shift "at one's command" from a preregistration in the target's path. The time of flight for most rounds is between 30 and 60 seconds. When the moving target is 30-60 seconds away from the known point, the observer just says "fire."

If the target is traveling along an established road with a speed that can be estimated, a TOT method of control will also get the job done.

Hasty bracketing should only be used as a last resort. Merely to create a frame of reference, the spotter places one round short, and then another long. For his last adjustment, he attempts to predict where the target will be when the volley arrives. (See figure 13.5.)

## LOST ROUNDS

Sometimes a round will land in soft earth or behind a hill mass, and thus completely disappear from view. When this happens, "repeating" one's fire in the same place is a good initial course of action. Or, asking for a slightly different target location can sometimes bring the round into view. But, because the original target location

Evening Up the Odds with Indirect Fire

(Source: FM 7-8 (1984), p. E-10)

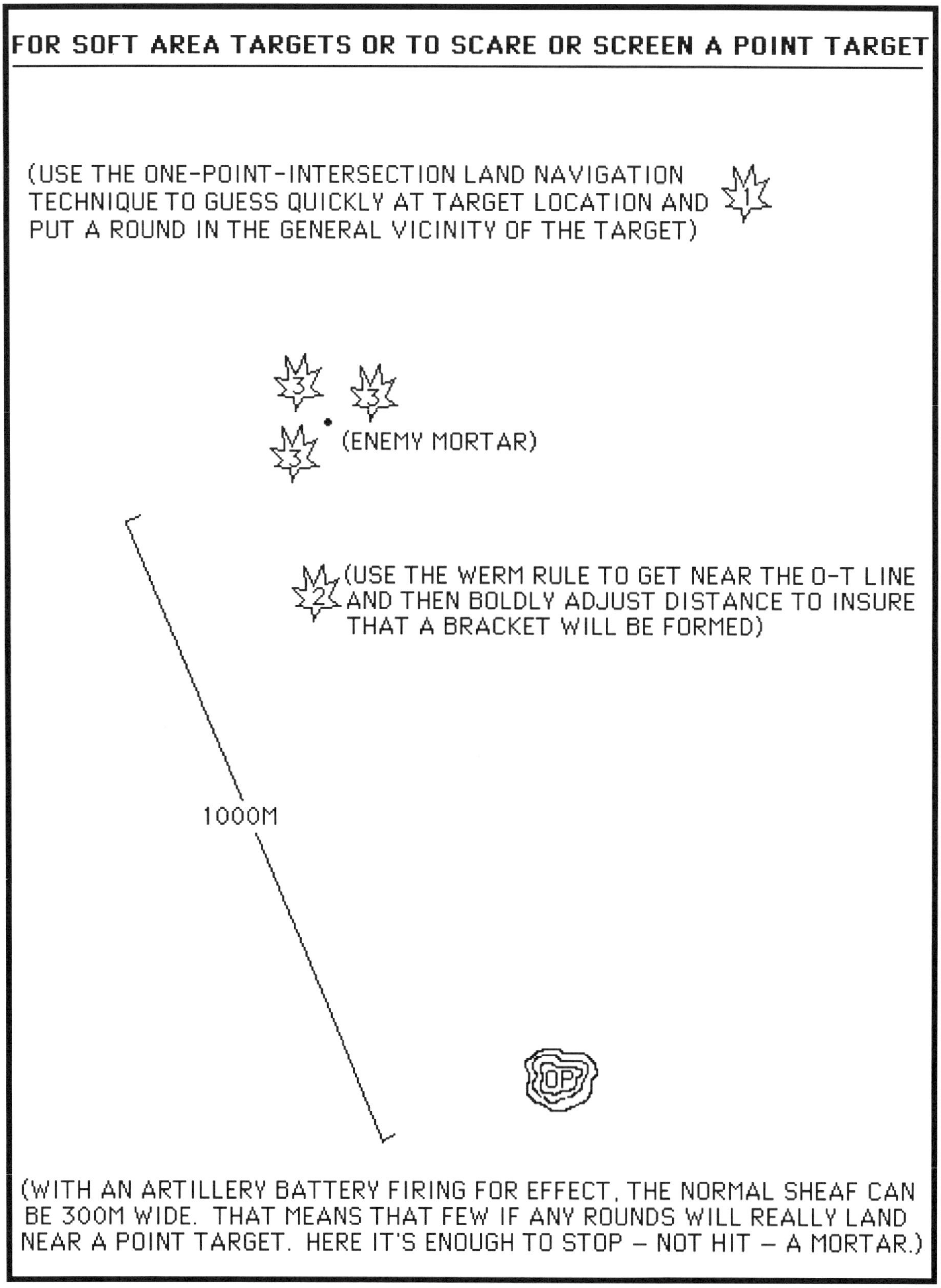

*Techniques from the NCO Corps*

---

**FOR SOFT AREA TARGETS OR TO SCARE OR SCREEN A POINT TARGET**

(USE THE ONE-POINT-INTERSECTION LAND NAVIGATION TECHNIQUE TO GUESS QUICKLY AT TARGET LOCATION AND PUT A ROUND IN THE GENERAL VICINITY OF THE TARGET) ※1

※3 ※3
※3 • (ENEMY MORTAR)

※2 (USE THE WERM RULE TO GET NEAR THE O-T LINE AND THEN BOLDLY ADJUST DISTANCE TO INSURE THAT A BRACKET WILL BE FORMED)

1000M

(OP)

(WITH AN ARTILLERY BATTERY FIRING FOR EFFECT, THE NORMAL SHEAF CAN BE 300M WIDE. THAT MEANS THAT FEW IF ANY ROUNDS WILL REALLY LAND NEAR A POINT TARGET. HERE IT'S ENOUGH TO STOP – NOT HIT – A MORTAR.)

*Figure 13.2: The Usual Firing Method Works Well Against Soft Area Targets*

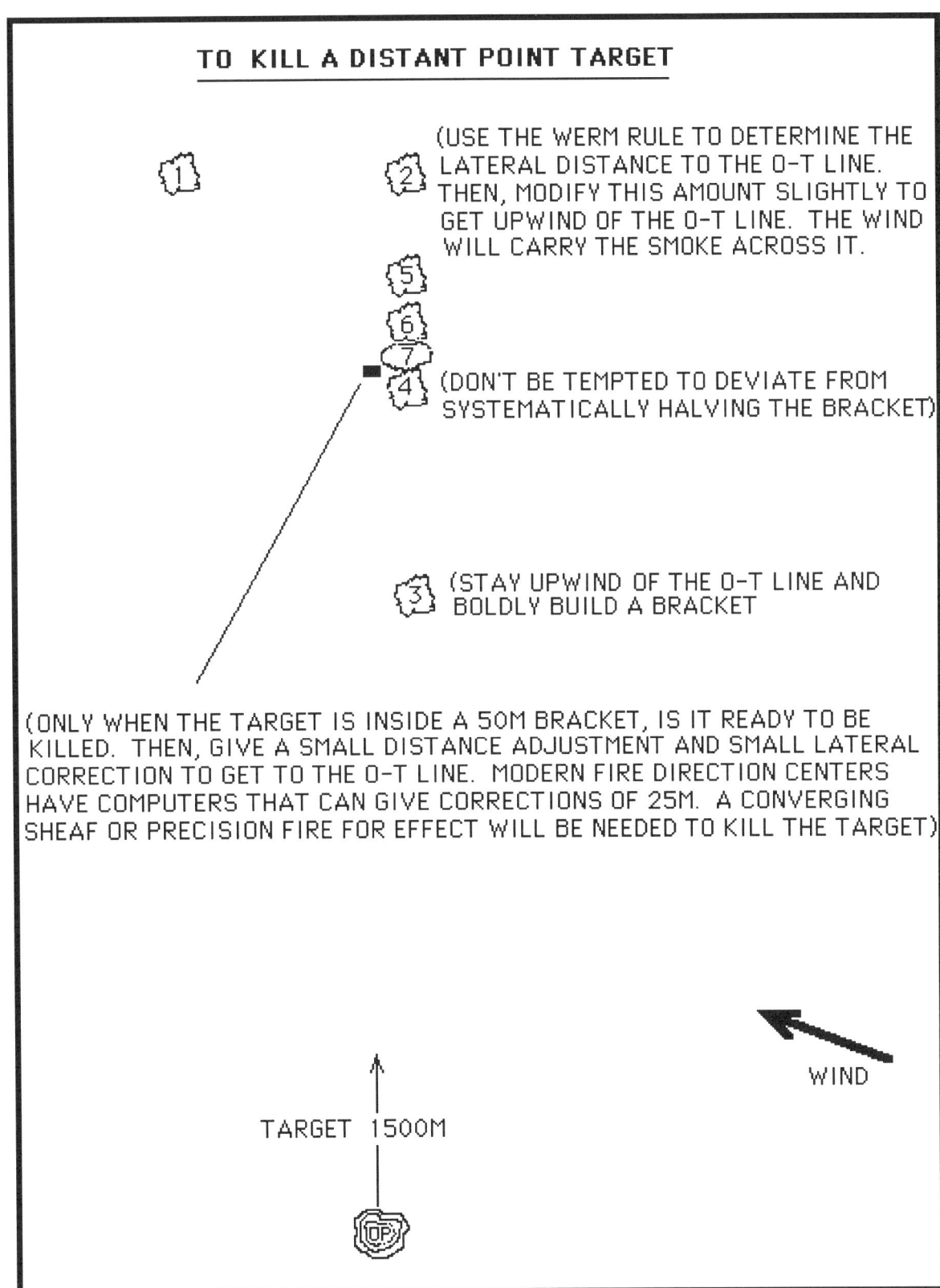

Figure 13.3: It Takes a Different Procedure to Hit a Distant Hardened Target

Techniques from the NCO Corps

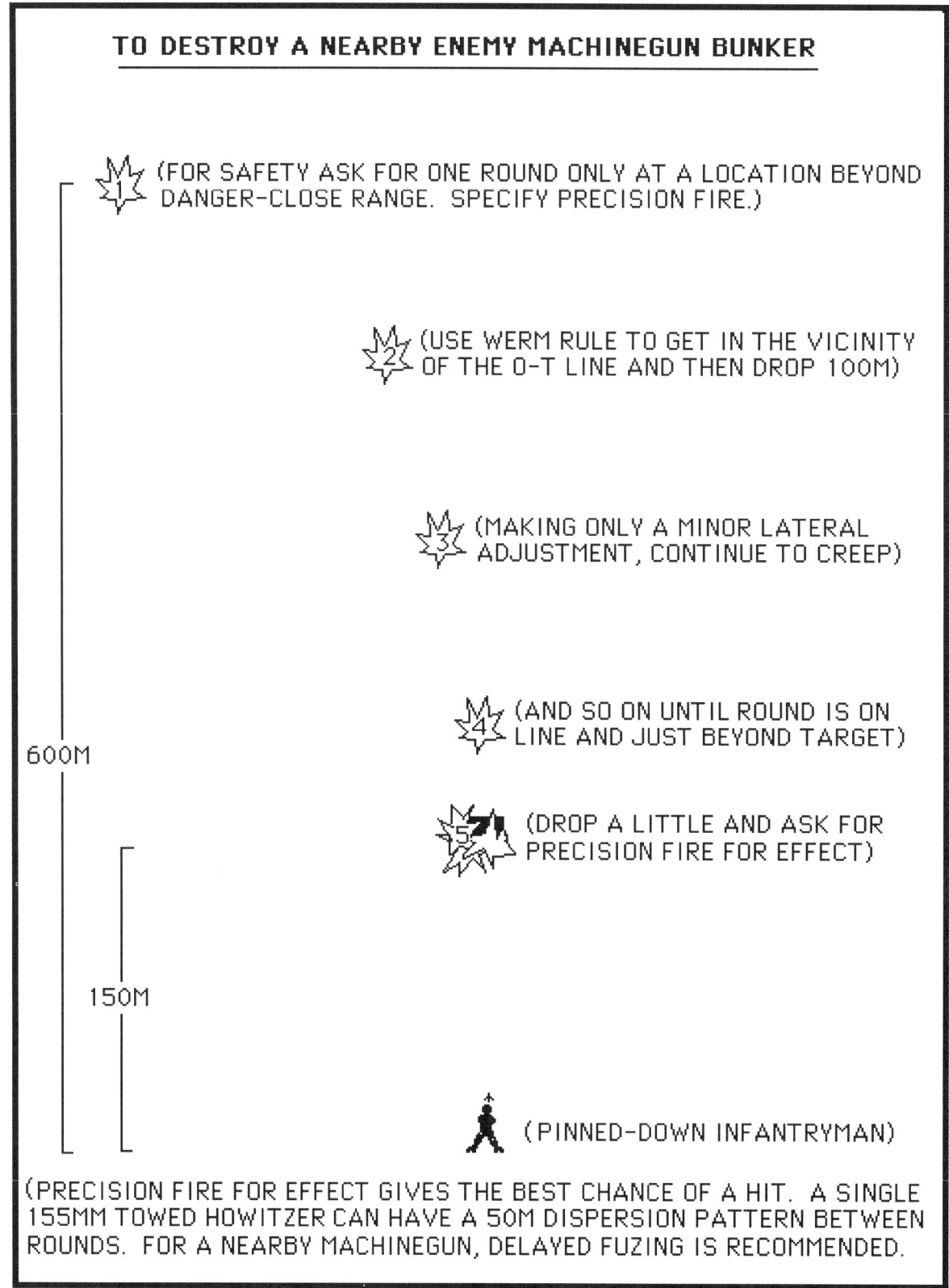

Figure 13.4: Precision Fire Could Replace Rushing Machinegun Bunkers

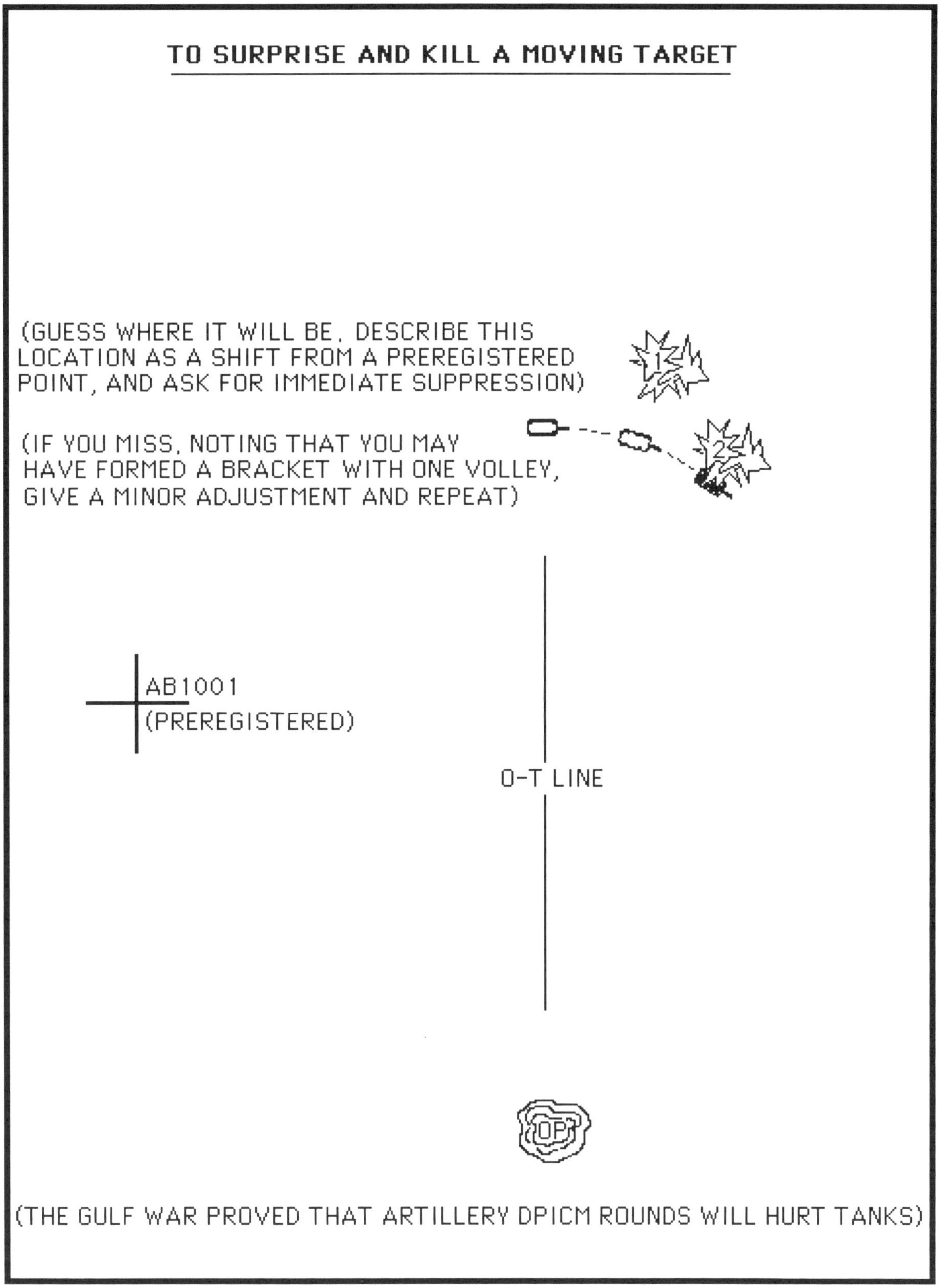

*Evening Up the Odds with Indirect Fire*

```
TO SURPRISE AND KILL A MOVING TARGET
```

(GUESS WHERE IT WILL BE, DESCRIBE THIS
LOCATION AS A SHIFT FROM A PREREGISTERED
POINT, AND ASK FOR IMMEDIATE SUPPRESSION)

(IF YOU MISS, NOTING THAT YOU MAY
HAVE FORMED A BRACKET WITH ONE VOLLEY,
GIVE A MINOR ADJUSTMENT AND REPEAT)

AB1001
(PREREGISTERED)

O-T LINE

OP

(THE GULF WAR PROVED THAT ARTILLERY DPICM ROUNDS WILL HURT TANKS)

*Figure 13.5: Still Another Technique Is Required to Hit a Moving Target*

may have been erroneous, a major adjustment (like "left 100, add 200") from that location can be dangerous. In precipitous or heavily vegetated terrain, an explosion 100 meters away may sound like one a mile away. It's not safe to adjust rounds that can't be seen.

For a round that gets lost in the middle of an adjustment procedure, one should ask for the exact opposite of the previous adjustment *without altering the O-T direction*. In other words, if "right 100, add 200" caused the round to disappear, "left 100, drop 200" will move it back to where it was visible before. Then, the O-T direction can be checked/changed, and the round moved toward the target by a different route — e.g., "right 150, add 300".

## PREVENTING MISTAKES

In combat, there are many ways to place fire onto one's own or another friendly unit by accident: (1) errors in computation or transmission, (2) an accurate target location that is too close to the observer, (3) too bold an adjustment toward the observer, (4) failing to ask for "precision fire" or a "converging sheaf" prior to firing for effect on a nearby target, and (5) calling for naval gunfire while on the gun-target line and near the target.

Marine NCO's used a wallet-sized fire support card to stop Iraqi tanks in the Gulf War. (See Figure 13.6.) The observer must also listen carefully to the FDC's readback.

Of course, the only foolproof way to prevent mistakes in combat, is to have another trained observer monitor every computation and radio transmission.

## TARGET LOCATION TECHNIQUES THAT DO NOT COMPROMISE THE SPOTTER'S LOCATION

Long-range reconnaissance elements and line infantry squads practicing maneuver warfare can wreak havoc behind enemy lines, simply by calling in supporting arms on targets of opportunity. Of course, they need special techniques. Standard methods of target location disclose, in varying degrees, the spotter's location to whoever may be monitoring his radio net. The grid mission reveals the exact target location and the direction of the spotter from that target. The polar mission gives both direction and range of the spotter from the target. The shift mission only discloses the spotter's direction from the target.

For the small unit trying to stay hidden, the answer at times might be (with the battery's permission) to adjust fire along the gun-target line, instead of O-T line. If the location of the firing battery is not known, the spotter can use a fictitious O-T direction. By choosing a direction 180 degrees out from the truth, he can adjust fire by substituting "right" for "left," and "add" for "drop." Then, his transmission will also serve as a deception. The controller of an airstrike has other ways of hiding his location.

```
                CALL FOR FIRE
OBSERVER ID             BOSSMAN, THIS IS SMALLFRY
WARNING ORDER           ADJUST FIRE (OR-FIRE MISSION-
                        FOR NGF), OVER
TARGET LOCATION         GRID 123456 (&ALTITUDE 1600 FT
                        AND DIRECTION 100 DEGREES MAG
                        .-FOR NGF) OVER
TARGET DESCRIPTION      BUNKER, (OVER-IF LAST ELEMENT)
METHOD OF ENGAGEMENT    PRECISION FIRE, HIGH TRAJECTORY
(CAN OMIT)              (OR REDUCED CHARGE-FOR NGF)
METHOD OF CONTROL       AT MY COMMAND, OVER

                 ADJUST FIRE
OT DIRECTION (IF NOT    DIRECTION 100 DEGREES MAGNETIC
ALREADY SENT)
METHOD OF ENGAGEMENT    DANGER CLOSE (WITH DISTANCE OF
CHANGE                  FRIENDLIES- FOR NGF)
                        CONVERGING SHEAF.
RIGHT/LEFT DEV.         LEFT 100
ADD/DROP DEV.           DROP 100
METHOD OF CONTROL       FIRE FOR EFFECT, REQUEST SPLASH,
CHANGE                  OVER

                  END MISSION
END MISSION             RECORD AS TARGET, END OF MISSION
                        BUNKER DESTROYED, OVER
```

```
              IMMEDIATE CAS REQUEST
UNIT CALLED:                BLUE BIRD THIS IS GOLF TWO
PRIORITY OF MISSION:        IMMEDIATE AIR
DESCRIPTION OF TARGET:      ENEMY TANKS
LOCATION OF TARGET:         GRID 123456
TIME ON TARGET:             ASAP OR WHAT TIME
DESIRED ORDNANCE/RESULTS    TOW COBRA
FINAL CONTROL
CALL SIGN:                  GOLF TWO
FREQUENCY:                  40.85
CONTACT POINT:              CP CHEVY
REMARKS                     ADDITIONAL INFO IF NEEDED
LOCATION OF FRIENDLIES      FRIENDLIES 600M EAST
DEGREE OF OBSERVATION/WEATHER CLEAR
THREATS:                    SAM MISSLE SITE TO NORTH
                     PILOT BRIEF
INITIAL POINT (ATK POS)     IP OR AP-FOR HELOS CHEVY
HEADING/OFFSET              HEADING 320 DEGREES MAGNETIC
DISTANCE                    DISTANCE 1600M
TARGET ELEVATION            ELEVATION 1200 FEET
TARGETDESCRIPT              TANKS
TARGET LOCATION             GRID 654321
MARKING TARGET              WILL MARK WITH WP
LOCATION OF FRIENDLIES      FRIENDLIES 900M SW
EGRESS                      EGRESS SOUTH
TIME TO TARGET/HACK         TTT 3+00, HACK OVER
             SUBSEQUENT TRANSMISSIONS
CONTINUE OR NOT         CONTINUE OR ABORT-ABORT, OVER
ADJUST OFF MARK         FROM THE MARK SOUTH 100 METERS OVER
WINGS LEVEL/NOT         CLEARED HOT OR ABORT-ABORT, OVER
REATTACK                CLEARED FOR IMMEDIATE REATTACK, OVER
                        END OF MISSION, BDA, OVER
```

*Figure 13.6: School of Infantry Fire Support Card Used by 2nd LAV Battalion in the Gulf War*

# 14 The Great Equalizer — Close Air Support

- *Is running an airstrike really all that difficult?*
- *Can one suppress enemy air defenses, mark, and still control a jet?*
- *To handle the dangerous final minute, what must one practice?*

(Sources: FM 90-3 (1977), p. 4-2; FM 6-30 (1991), p. 8-2; FM 7-11B3 (1976), p. 2-III-C-4.2)

## AIR SUPERIORITY CREATES THE CHANCE TO FIELD SMALLER MANEUVER ELEMENTS

With the air superiority that U.S. forces usually enjoy on the battlefield, American squad-sized units should be able to operate independently. Who could stop them? In concert with indirect fire, Close Air Support (CAS) can handcuff an opponent of any size or composition. As this chapter will show, squad leaders have ample ability to control both types of supporting arms at once. Even *fire teams* with state-of-the-art radios and training could patrol deep into enemy territory at acceptable risk. "Killer" reconnaissance and special-operations units have been doing it for years. During Operation Shining Brass in Vietnam, a small U.S. Army unit was inserted by helicopter near the Ho Chi Minh Trail complex, patrolled into the complex until finding an ammunition/fuel dump, called in an airstrike on the dump, and then hiked back out to a helicopter extraction point.[1] Marine reconnaissance "stingray" teams operated in much the same way. In heavily forested terrain, *any infantry squad* trained in maneuver warfare should be able to do this. The jungle is like a sea, and the patrol is like a submarine. During World War II, U.S. submarines managed to penetrate deep into the Japanese maritime empire without sustaining unacceptable losses; and they did so *without* any supporting-arms backup.

Cpl. Matthew Schott, a Marine sniper hiding in the deserted city of Khafji during the Gulf War when Iraqi armor rolled in, asserted later that with the authority to request and control his own close air support, he could have single-handedly stopped the tanks.[2] He and his partner did manage to put "metal on metal" with U.S. artillery fire. And city limits do constitute a common-sense control feature for airstrikes. Cpl. Schott could have simply told the pilots overhead that all armor north of the built-up area was fair game.

## SOME AIRCRAFT CAN PROVIDE BETTER CLOSE AIR SUPPORT THAN OTHERS

An aircraft that has been specifically designed to support operations on the ground can work wonders. In a defensive role, it can prevent a large enemy force from encircling a friendly patrol, stop a determined ground assault against an isolated outpost, or destroy a column of enemy tanks. With such an aircraft, the controller can be quite close to the enemy and still bomb safely. More than one Marine in Vietnam successfully bombed within 75 meters of his position.[3] All it took was an F-4 Phantom loaded with 250 pound bombs and a pilot willing to come in low and slow.

In an offensive role, a properly designed aircraft can soften up enemy tanks and *bunkers* prior to a ground assault. In this way, the heavily armored and mass-produced Russian Stormovik played a major role in turning the tide of WWII:

> On the morning of 22 June 1941, Hitler's Panzer legions rolled into the Soviet Union....
>
> ... Initially, the Soviet Air Force as well as the Russian ground forces had reeled and retreated before the Panzer onslaught, but as new equipment became available, the complexion of battle in the sky as well as on the ground began to change.
>
> The most significant challenge to the Germans from the Soviet Air Force came in the form of the most heavily armored, ground attack aircraft that would appear in World War II; the Ilyushin Il-2 *Shturmoviki*. The basic design of the aircraft was extraordinary. The forward fuselage surrounding the engine and the pilot was comprised of an armored shell which ranged in thickness from 5mm to 12mm. Armament consisted of two 7.62 machineguns, two 20mm cannons, and rails for eight 82mm rockets.
>
> ... Progressively, the 20mm cannon in the wings gave way to more powerful 37mm cannon. The awesome machine became known to the German Army as *Schwarz Tod* or "Black Death."
>
> The *Shturmoviki* met with immediate success against the German ground columns and even more so as a tank destroyer. Its cannon and rockets took a tremendous toll of armored equipment....
>
> On 20 November 1942, the Russian Army opened a great counterattack against the German forces in the southern salient of the Stalingrad front. Poor weather made air support difficult, but the [low-flying] Il-2 pilots continued to make life miserable for the enemy....
>
> The *Shturmoviki* pilots never let up throughout the war. Their tank destruction effort became legend and they proved to be the deciding factor in many tank battles. The "Black Death" more than lived up to its name and reputation.[4]

On offense, the right kind of aircraft can locate and eliminate the source of counterbattery fire. It can even permit ground troops to assault safely. After dropping bombs on several "wet" runs across an attack objective, it can make a "dry" run. The enemy soldiers will never see the ground troops coming. Now that maneuver has priority over firepower, this ploy may gain more legitimacy.

Americans have already embarked on a "fourth generation" of weapons technology. Targets that were previously invisible from the air can now be detected through heat signatures. Targets right next to friendly troops can be hit with "smart" bombs and missiles. All it takes is a laser tracker and a laser designator. The A-6 Intruder had both. To conduct maneuver warfare, squad-sized units require their own *portable* laser designators. Of course, close air support still has its limitations. Knowing what they are can enhance one's survivability in combat.

## RESPONSE TIME

In an active war zone, there are competing requirements for support, and aircraft can take a while to arrive overhead. Even in emergencies, those "scrambled" from strip alert can take 30 minutes, and those diverted from other missions 15 minutes. With planes already on station, it takes a controller a while to work up a pilot brief. So, while contemplating an airstrike, the infantry leader must ask himself whether he has the time to wait for one. Sometimes helicopter gunships on other business can keep the enemy occupied while the jets are en route.

There are two ways to control an airstrike: (1) the Running-Clock method, and (2) the Time to Target (TTT) alternative. To use the Running-Clock method, all controllers, pilots, marking units, and Suppression of Enemy Air Defense (SEAD) agencies must have their watches synchronized. To use the TTT procedure, the harried squad leader must only refer briefly to his mudcaked Timex. He has only to establish how many minutes the pilot will need to get bombs on target, and then relay this information to the artillery battery providing marking and SEAD support.

The only way to shorten this response time for close air support is to preplan it on a Joint Tactical Airstrike Request (JTAR) form or fire-support-plan overlay.

## COMMUNICATIONS PROBLEMS

At present, any platoon-sized unit or smaller operating away from its company headquarters *can't* ask for or control its own airstrike. It carries a Very High Frequency (VHF) radio that is not compatible with the communications equipment on all aircraft. This radio has limited range and cannot normally reach the Direct Air Support Center (DASC). If there's a mountain in the way, it may have difficulty reaching an aircraft at the closest Contact Point (CP). To make matters worse, the typical small unit does not carry the attachment that permits talking to the pilot over a covered net, as required by procedure.

If the small unit were to get overcommitted on the ground, its leader would have to request and control an airstrike through a Forward Air Controller (FAC) at his company headquarters. This unavoidable relay creates insurmountable problems. There's no guarantee that the FAC and pilot will even be monitoring the same covered net. Furthermore, it is virtually impossible to control the risky final 30 seconds of a modern airstrike through a relay. It takes uninterrupted communications between the observer, pilot, and artillery — simultaneously to mark, provide SEAD, and bomb. Additionally, if the marking or SEAD rounds are late, the pilot must be told immediately to abort.

When a squad in trouble cannot reach its company headquarters, it does have another way to request an airstrike. It can do so over the Tactical Air Control Party (TACP) Local net. This is the net used by the FAC's to talk to the air liaison officer at battalion. It's the only air frequency on the squad's VHF radio band.

On an extremely active battlefield, infantry squads should be allowed to talk directly to aircraft over uncovered tactical nets. To develop any momentum, they may have to. So much would be happening at the same time that the enemy could neither assimilate, nor act on, all the information. There were reports from the Gulf War that the normal rotation of encryption codes for Allied planes had to be abandoned. To unscramble communications, one U.S. Air Force FAC was instructed to use the same code for several days.[5]

## TO EMPLOY CONTROL FEATURES, ONE MUST KNOW THEIR LOCATIONS AND CODE NAMES

For an airstrike, the main control features are the Contact Point (CP) and the Initial Point (IP). The CP is where the plane circles awaiting instructions, and the IP is where the plane begins its bombing run. Both must be transmitted in code. If a small-unit leader is to request and control his own close air support, he must write down the locations and code names of all available CP's and IP's before leaving his parent-unit headquarters. While operating against a highly mobile enemy on a large battlefield, there is little chance that every target of opportunity will surface near a prearranged Attack Position (AP) — the attack helicopter equivalent of an IP. For an AP, the helicopter gunship needs a location behind an unoccupied hill mass and 2000-3000 yards from the target (the optimum range for its wire-guided missiles). To use an attack helicopter, the squad leader must temporarily create an AP in such a place, and then tell the pilot where it is in code. This can be done by using existing AP's as *thrust points*. The technique will be explained later.

## LIMITED VISIBILITY MAY NOT BE AN INSURMOUNTABLE PROBLEM

Many U.S. infantrymen believe that it takes an all-weather aircraft and an Ultra High Frequency (UHF) radio to hit a target at night. This is not true. Any plane can bomb at night. All it needs is some illumination:

> All night flares and illumination rounds lit up the battlefield [in 1939 in Manchuria] as Soviet aircraft bombed suspected Japanese fortifications.[6]

Bombing in the fog is what takes sophisticated equipment. Among other things, it takes a Radar Beacon Forward Air Controller (RABFAC) sending device. The pilot of the all-weather aircraft can tell where the device is positioned on the ground from the signals it sends up. The controller describes the target's location in terms of direction and distance from the beacon. Of course, he must also plan the flight path carefully. He must remember that the aircraft has a narrow field of vision with which to detect the beacon (55 degrees to either side of the nose for an A-6). He must also remember, for safety, to stay off the aircraft-target line. Finally, he must make sure that hills do not obscure the beacon from the plane on the way in. Of course, any garbling or jamming of the distance to target from the beacon could result in bombs too close for comfort. Interestingly, the AC-130 gunship can work off a RABFAC beacon with pinpoint accuracy.

## WITH FASTER AIRCRAFT, ACCURACY HAS BECOME MORE OF A PROBLEM

Modern war is hard on ground support aircraft. Although accurate, the slow AC-130 gunship is somewhat vulnerable to anti-aircraft fire. Even the fighter bombers have to fly faster and bomb from higher to keep from getting shot down. Although computerized targeting systems help to offset the resulting loss in accuracy, they *do not* permit pinpoint bombing with "dumb" ordnance. There are two solutions to the problem: (1) smart ordnance, and (2) large ordnance. Large bombs can kill a target from farther away, but also pose an additional threat to friendlies nearby. In the Gulf War, the "danger-close" range for an airstrike was 1000 meters.

Techniques from the NCO Corps

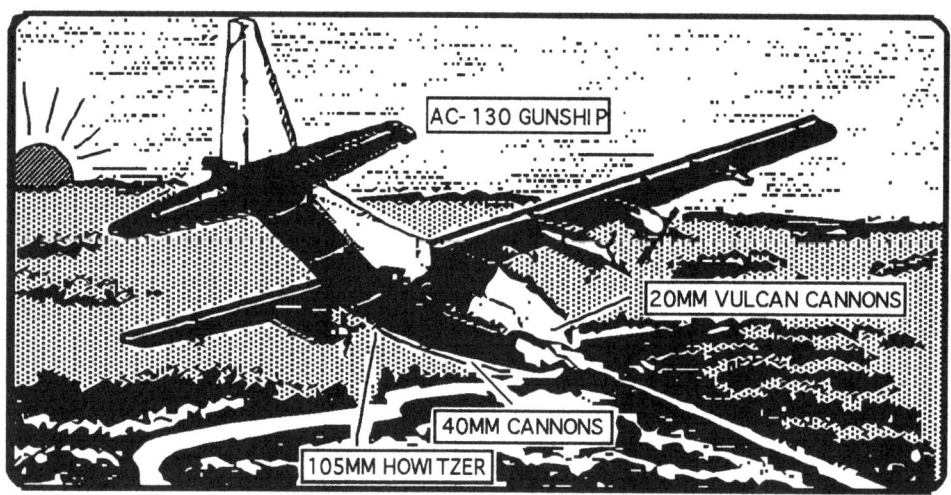

(Source: FM 7-85 (1987), p. 7-11)

(Source: FM 22-100 (1983), p. 3)

## MARKING FOR AN AIRSTRIKE IS NOT HARD

As contemporary aircraft fly faster and bomb from higher, there is more need to mark one's targets. Of course, there are pitfalls in marking. Grass huts burn white. A controller should not stand near a burning hut while the pilot of a fighter bomber attempts to locate a white marking round from 10,000 feet. Nor, should a controller allow a nearby unit to pop a white smoke grenade to screen its movement.

It does not overly complicate an airstrike to ask for marking from an outside agency, like an artillery or mortar battery. The battery assumes the responsibility for "splashing" the marking round 30 seconds before the end of the TTT. Then, all the controller must do is to relay to the battery the TTT confirmed by the pilot. Of course, if the round is late, the controller must also abort the plane.

The simplest way to mark for an airstrike is with a weapon organic to the infantry unit. The M203 grenade launcher has colored-smoke rounds that can reach beyond 200 meters. Machinegun tracers can mark a target thousands of meters away. Two widely separated guns can fire toward the same target, or one gun can fire at a target sitting astride a linear terrain feature visible from the air.

## SUPPRESSING ENEMY AIR DEFENSES IS SURPRISINGLY EASY

SEAD can take several forms, none of which are complicated: (1) choosing a flight path that will keep the plane away from anti-aircraft guns and missiles, (2) using organic weapons to neutralize those guns and missiles, and (3) suppressing the threat with supporting arms. More easily to accomplish concurrent marking and SEAD, one must allow an artillery or mortar battery to do all the timing. All required information can be easily transmitted to the gun battery using a slight variation to the traditional call for fire.

In the new format, the terms SEAD RED and SEAD GREEN represent discontinuous and continuous SEAD, respectively. For discontinuous SEAD, the suppression rounds cease as the marking round lands 30 seconds before the end of the TTT, and the suppression rounds recommence 60 seconds after the TTT (to allow the wing man through). For continuous SEAD, the controller keeps the aircraft away from the path of the suppression rounds, and the rounds continue throughout the bombing run. The controller can do so by telling the plane to stay to one side of a grid line, or above or below the level at which the rounds will cross the target (the ordinate). SEAD GREEN is perfectly suited for low-trajectory naval gunfire. Shown below is the required modification to the standard call for fire. For night work with a daylight bomber, "coordinated illumination" could be added to the last line.

```
CANNON, THIS IS SPOTTER,
    SUPPRESSION, SEAD RED,
GRID TO MARK _____, GRID(S) TO SUPPRESS _____,
DESCRIPTION OF TARGET _____,
STAND BY FOR TIME TO TARGET, OVER.
```

```
CANNON, THIS IS SPOTTER,
    SUPPRESSION, SEAD GREEN,
GRID TO MARK _____, GRID(S) TO SUPPRESS _____,
DESCRIPTION OF TARGET _____,
REQUEST ORDINATE ABOVE BOMBING TARGET,
STAND BY FOR TIME TO TARGET, OVER.
```

After the initial call for fire, subsequent transmissions to the firing battery and pilot are simple. It's not necessary to adjust the mark. Once the ordinate is acquired from the firing battery, the pilot is told to stay 500 feet above that ordinate or the 1200-foot bursting radius for shrapnel (whichever is higher). After getting the pilot's concurrence on the TTT, the controller must relay this information to the battery. To do so easily, he can subtract 30 or 60 seconds from the original TTT, send the modified TTT, and then say "hack" to the battery precisely 30 or 60 seconds after the one with the pilot.

Now the controller has only to tell the pilot where the target is in relation to the mark, and to abort him if something goes wrong. Sometimes, the plane aims at the wrong target or comes in on a dangerous attack heading. Other times, the support from the firing battery is late.

## OFTEN OVERLOOKED PRELIMINARIES

The small-unit leader won't usually have planes "stacked up" overhead waiting for something to do. If he hasn't submitted a JTAR or fire-support-plan overlay, he will have to use his radio for an Immediate CAS Request:

```
UNIT CALLED
PRIORITY OF MISSION
DESCRIPTION OF TARGET
LOCATION OF TARGET
TIME ON TARGET
DESIRED ORDNANCE/RESULTS
FINAL CONTROL
    CALL SIGN
    FREQUENCY
    CONTACT POINT
REMARKS
LOCATION OF FRIENDLIES
DEGREE OF OBSERVATION/WEATHER
THREATS
```

The format is self-explanatory. For *priority of mission,* "immediate air" will impart both priority and type of request. For *time on target,* "as soon as possible" will usually suffice. The *location of friendlies* can be deferred until the pilot brief.

By the time the plane arrives on station, the pilot brief should be ready. It is given in a "nine-line" sequence:

```
INITIAL POINT (IP)
  [ATTACK POSITION (AP) FOR HELO'S]
HEADING/OFFSET
DISTANCE
TARGET ELEVATION
TARGET DESCRIPTION
TARGET LOCATION
MARKING OF TARGET
LOCATION OF FRIENDLIES
EGRESS
  [REMARKS]
TIME TO TARGET/HACK
```

Again this format is straightforward, but to properly interpret its entries, one must envision a plane flying *all the way* to the target, whether this is the plan or not. For the aircraft that will release its ordnance early, the brief remains the same. One must not be confused by the fact that "distance" is measured from IP to target, while "TTT" is based on the entire flight path from CP through IP to target. This TTT is computed at one minute per 10,000 meters for fixed wing and per 1500 meters for helicopters, plus two minutes of administrative time. To select a route that will keep the plane away from both controller and SEAD threat, one must first know all available CP's and IP's. The "offset" is the permission to fly left or right of the IP-target line. The "egress" is the aircraft's exit instruction by cardinal direction. This guidance will help the plane to bomb parallel to friendly lines (to include those of adjacent units). For a variety of reasons, bombs sometimes release from their racks a few seconds early or late. At the speeds traveled by modern aircraft, seconds can translate into hundreds of meters. The controller must give the location of friendlies in relation to the target, not vice versa, and only in meters and cardinal direction. Additional remarks are permissible before proposing the TTT. For example, the pilot might appreciate hearing more about the enemy-air-defense threat, how to keep way from the SEAD rounds, a "final-attack" heading (different from the heading in line #2 of the brief), or a pullout direction (left/right). After suggesting a TTT and saying "hack," the controller must listen carefully to see if the pilot agrees with his recommendation. Not hearing a pilot's modification to that TTT could put the airplane and artillery rounds into the same airspace at the same time.

There are differences of opinion on how to transmit a pilot brief. Some pilots like to hear the line numbers followed by the key elements of information. Some want just the information in sequence without quantifiers. Almost all agree that the radio handset should be unkeyed after each line. Those who are close to where the half-ton loads of destruction will land, have a different point of view. They believe that, because no readback is required for a pilot brief, the information category should precede the actual information, much as a "preparatory command" precedes a "command of execution" on the drill field. They also believe that, as with calls for fire, rounding off numbers and adding quantifiers lessens the risk of the numbers being given incorrectly, jammed, or misinterpreted. The actively engaged infantryman prefers to give distances in meters, and target locations in grid coordinates. He doesn't have the time or experience to compute distances in nautical miles, and locations in longitude and latitude. The pilot should be able to make all the necessary conversions.

## THE CRUCIAL FINAL SIXTY SECONDS

The most important part of an airstrike is the final minute. Once the pilot "goes into the pop" (pulls up and rolls over to look for his target), he is only 60 seconds away from dropping his bombs. A controller's mistake at this point can result in friendly casualties. Knowing what to do is *not enough;* one must be able to do it within 60 seconds. What must be determined and then transmitted within this short period of time *cannot* be accomplished without continual practice. As was mentioned before, the chances of doing it through a relay at company headquarters are virtually nil.

When the pilot announces his arrival at the Pull-Up Point (PUP), the controller must initiate his "60-second drill." Because the plane overhead may be working for someone else and his own plane lost, he must first ascertain whether the pilot with whom he is talking is in the vicinity of the target. He does so by asking the pilot to corroborate major landmarks. Then, when the mark lands 30 seconds before the end of the TTT, he asks the pilot to confirm the mark and its color. The hard part — that which takes practice — is *quickly* describing the target location in relation to the mark, for example "300 meters SW of the mark." Finally, when the plane is pointed toward the target, the pilot should announce "wings level" and the controller send "cleared hot." This is the most critical part of the tricky final minute. If the plane has been given an offset, the controller won't know the final attack heading until the last few moments. If he sees the aircraft coming in over friendlies from front or back, he must abort the mission. A short story from the Vietnam War illustrates the point:

> Down the trail, Gunny Thomas stared up at the jets, wondering why they were coming in over their heads, instead of flying parallel to their

front. He didn't know about Fox Company.... Suddenly there was a tremendous roar and Harvey was slammed with a terrific concussion.... Harvey realized that two of the explosions had come from behind him. Oh no, he thought the pilot had pressed the button a second too soon.... On their flank, Fox Company was moving up to take the hill. They found twenty-one dead North Vietnamese in the demolished blockhouses, but that particular body count didn't mean much to the Hotel [Company] grunts.[7]

Some controllers like to signal to the plane with a mirror at the last second to further delineate friendly lines, in much the same way World War II Marines used colored air panels. Although the idea has some merit, talking about another signal with the pilot could consume valuable time and create unnecessary confusion. Most certainly, one should never resort to the word "mark" in the context of a friendly location.

If an outside agency is providing marking and SEAD support, the final minute becomes slightly more complicated. At 30 seconds before the end of the TTT, if the marking round has not yet landed or the discontinuous SEAD rounds have not yet stopped, the plane must be aborted. Generally, the wing man will come in 30 seconds behind the lead plane. If the lead plane misses the target, the wing man must be quickly apprised of the target location in relation to the miss — e.g., "200 meters NE of the lead plane's bombs." If the wing man is late during a discontinuous SEAD mission, he may have to be aborted to keep him away from the suppression rounds that will resume 60 seconds after the end of the TTT. Sometimes giving the wing man a different attack heading and pullout direction can also help him to avoid enemy fire.

## COMMON-SENSE CONTROL METHODS

Complicated pilot briefs are not always necessary. For example, if the friendly front lines are clearly visible from the air and all sentry posts are in, the pilot can be given a free-fire zone on one side of the lines, a no-fire zone on the other, and permission to bomb at will.

When a plane misses its target, the controller has only to describe where the target is in relation to the miss and to clear the plane for immediate reattack. If there is no SEAD coordination required, the pilot can choose his own route. Only if the plane subsequently runs in along the controller-target line, must it be aborted.

## CONTROLLING HELICOPTER GUNSHIPS

An attack helicopter is more vulnerable to ground fire than its fixed-wing counterpart. When it ascends from defilade to take its shot, any modern tank or antitank weapon can knock it down. For this reason, one must pay particular attention to all SEAD considerations while planning rotary-wing CAS.

A shortage of preestablished AP's near targets of opportunity can be rectified by using existing AP's as thrust points. To establish thrust points, a parent unit assigns code names (like colors) to intersections of grid lines within its area of responsibility. This gives subordinate elements a way to report their whereabouts in code. For example, if "red" were Grid Coordinate (GC) 1956, "from red, right 1.3, down 2.1" would describe the location at GC 203539. A helicopter pilot familiar with AP Chevy would have little difficulty finding a provisional AP at "from Chevy, right 5.2 and down 7.4."

One type of Aircraft Coordination Area (ACA) — an area through which artillery shells cannot be fired — also makes a good substitute for an AP. This is the ACA delineated by one quadrant of an intersection of grid lines — e.g., the NW quadrant of GC 2397. By mentioning this ACA instead of an AP, the controller tells the pilot that SEAD rounds may impact in the other three quadrants. The pilot can then reasonably assume that the direction and distance to the target are measured from GC 2397, and that the vacant quadrant is available for firing points.

Some attack helicopters are armed with Hellfire laser-guided missiles. With such missiles, gunships can shoot at targets from greater standoff distances. Of course, it can be dangerous to spotlight, with one's own laser designator, a target for any airstrike. There's always the chance the missile will veer off course and home in on the controller. A controller who is operating his own laser designator should ask the aircraft to approach (or fire at) the target from behind him on a diagonal. It's unwise to operate any type of laser source (to include a laser range finder) within view of a laser-guided munition or tracker. (See figures 14.1 and 14.2 to see how easy it is to tackle an enemy tank with a helicopter gunship, and then to finish off reinforcing armor with fixed-wing aircraft — any good infantry corporal could do it!)

(Source: Courtesy of Michael Leahy © 1994)

Techniques from the NCO Corps

(Sources: FM 7-11B4 (1976), p. 2-III-J-10.5; FM 22-100 (1983), p. 30; FM 7-11B3 (1976), p. 2-III-C-4.2)

*The Great Equalizer — Close Air Support*

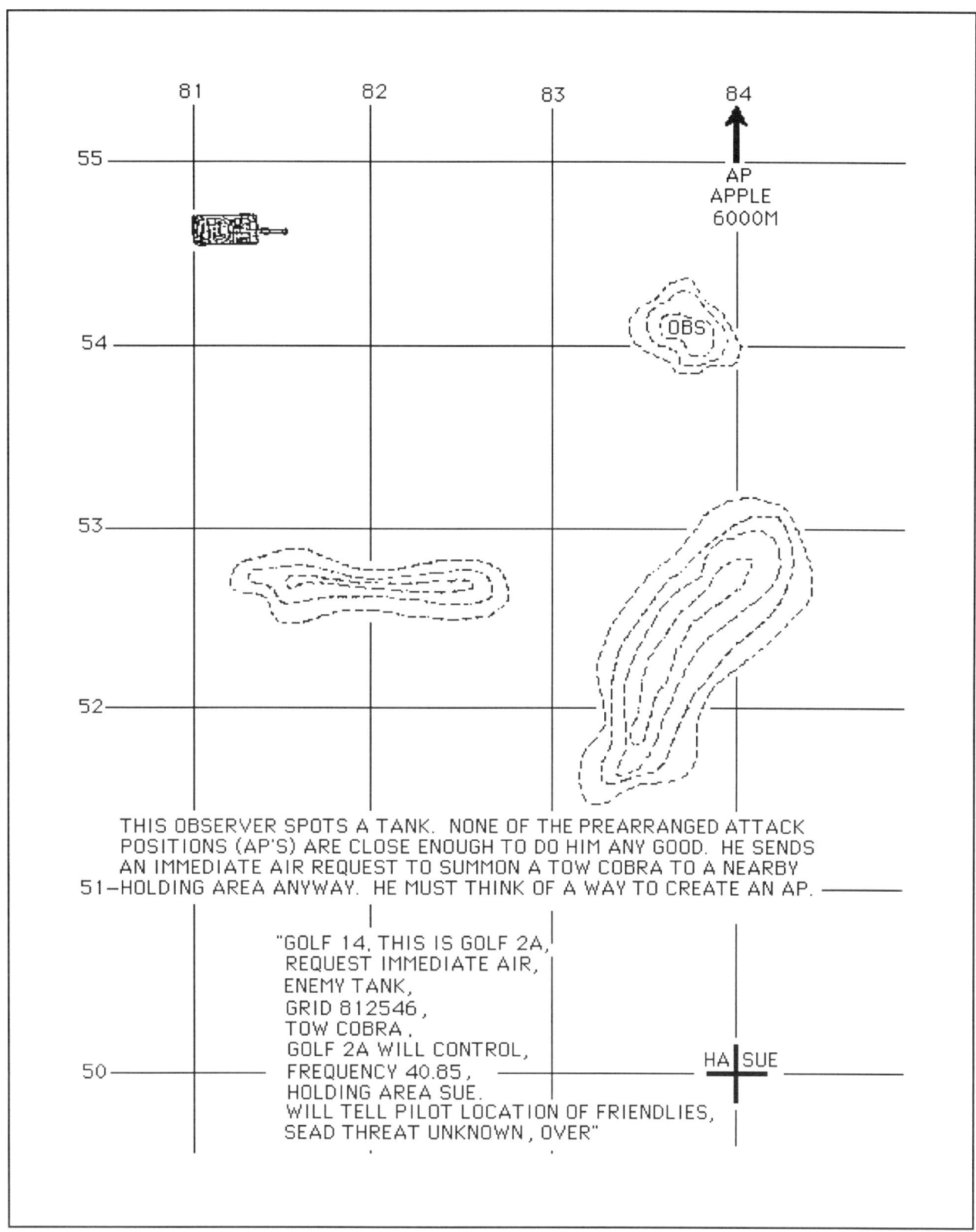

*Figure 14.1: Rotary-Wing Close Air Support*
(Source: FM 6-30 (1991), p. 5-7)

Techniques from the NCO Corps

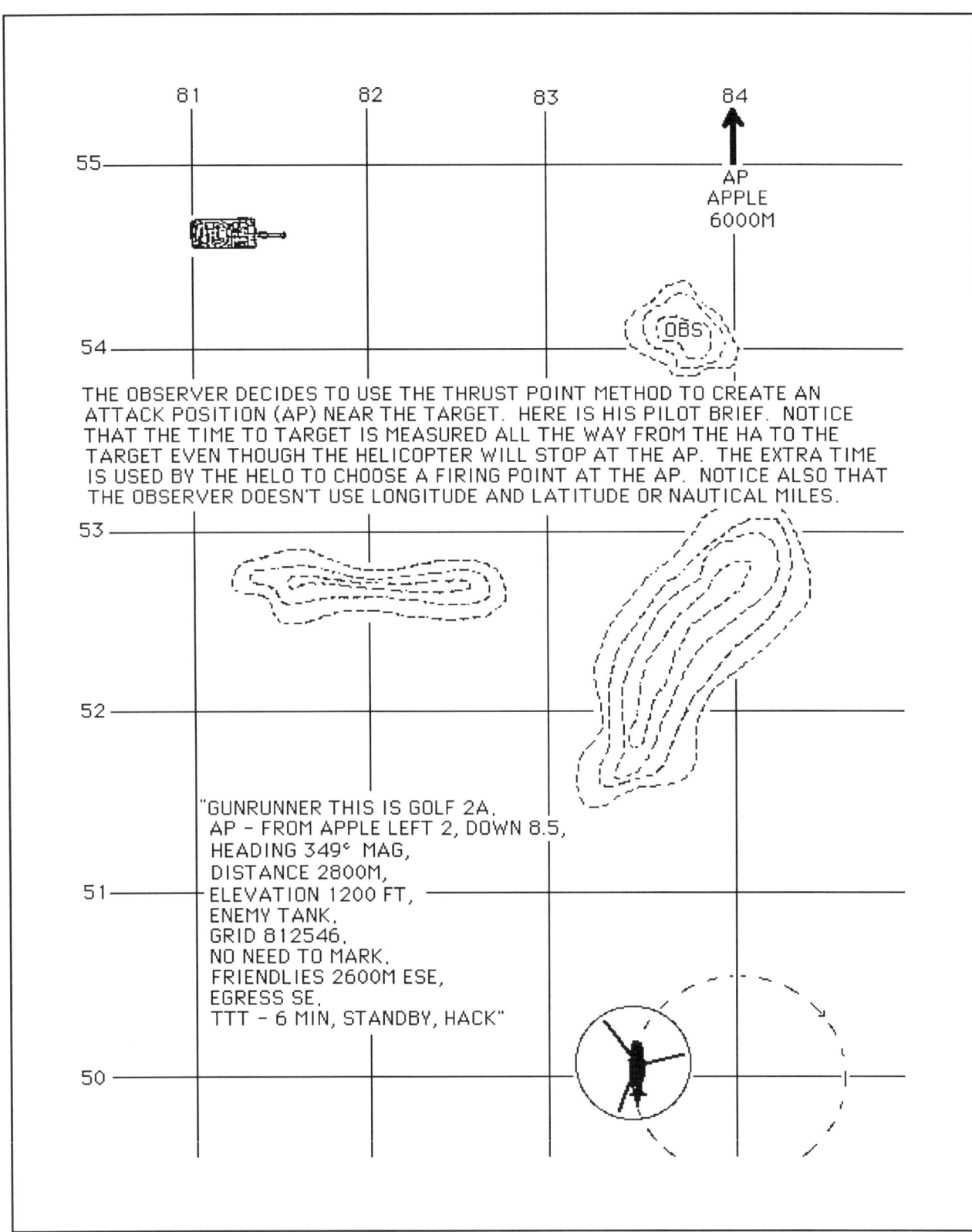

Figure 14.1: Rotary-Wing Close Air Support (Continued)
(Source: FM 6-30 (1991), p. 5-7)

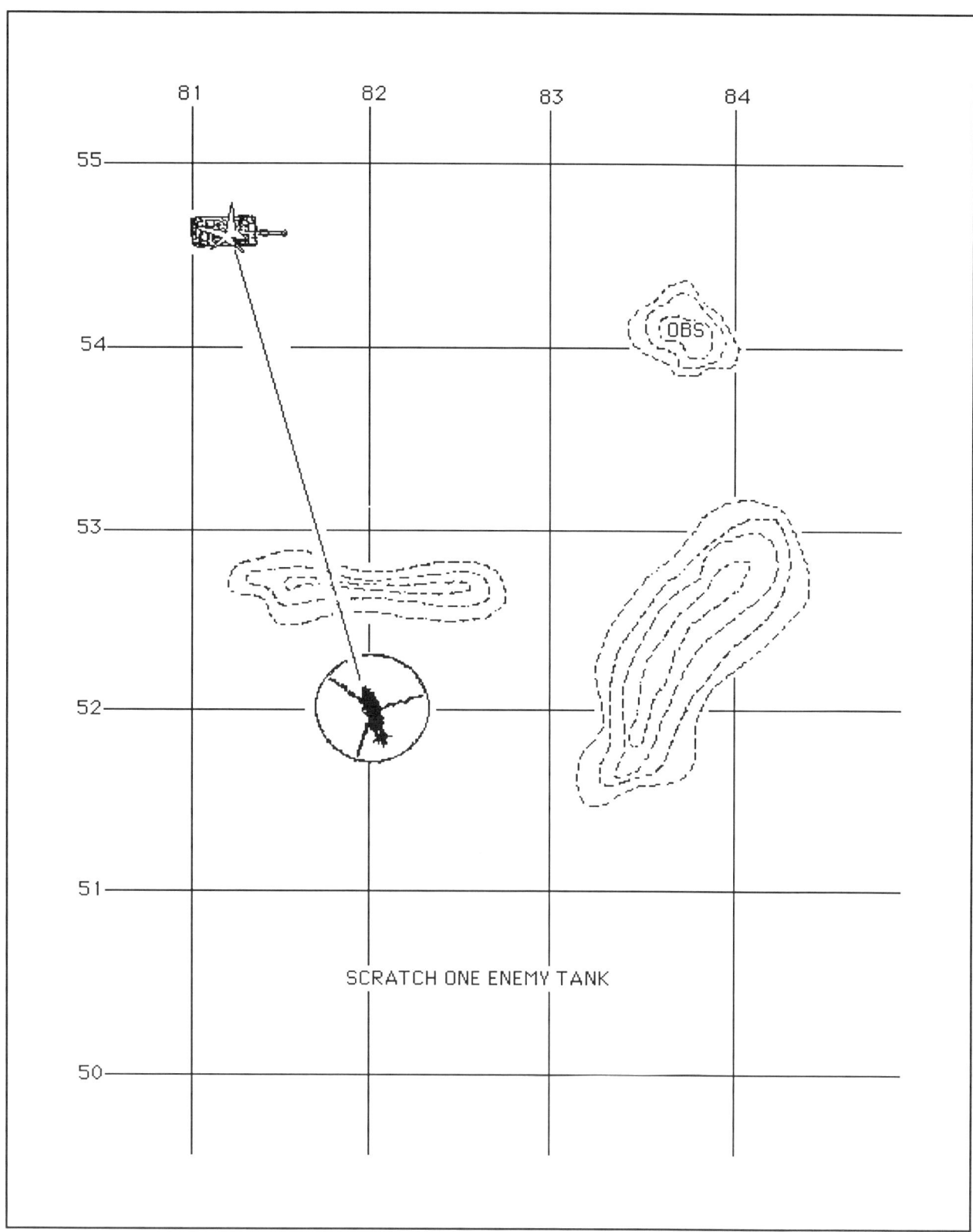

*Figure 14.1: Rotary-Wing Close Air Support (Continued)*
(Source: FM 6-30 (1991), p. 5-7)

Techniques from the NCO Corps

(Source: FM 7-85 (1987), p. 7-12)

(Source: FMFM 8-4 (1967), p. 91)

*The Great Equalizer — Close Air Support*

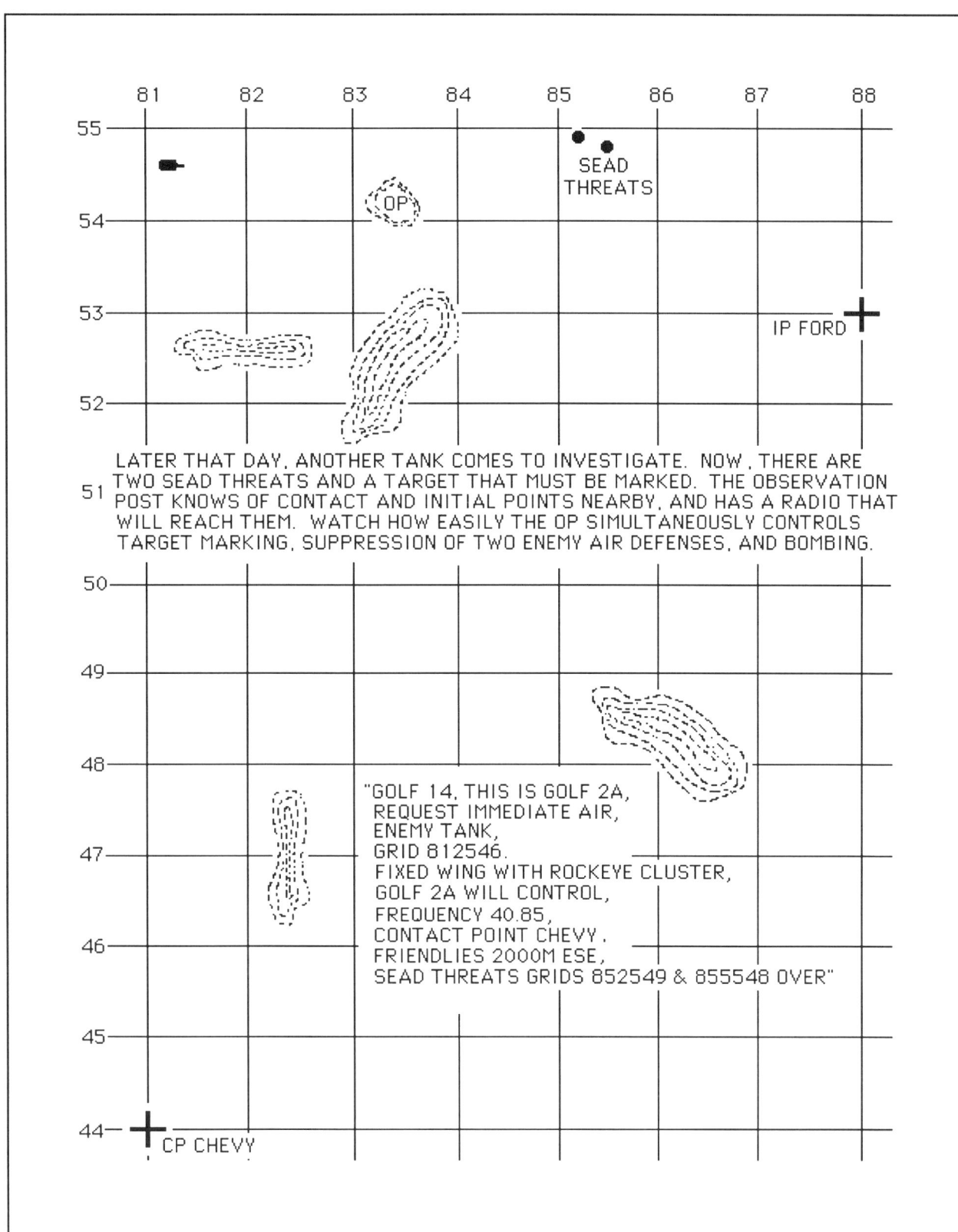

*Figure 14.2: Fixed-Wing Close Air Support*

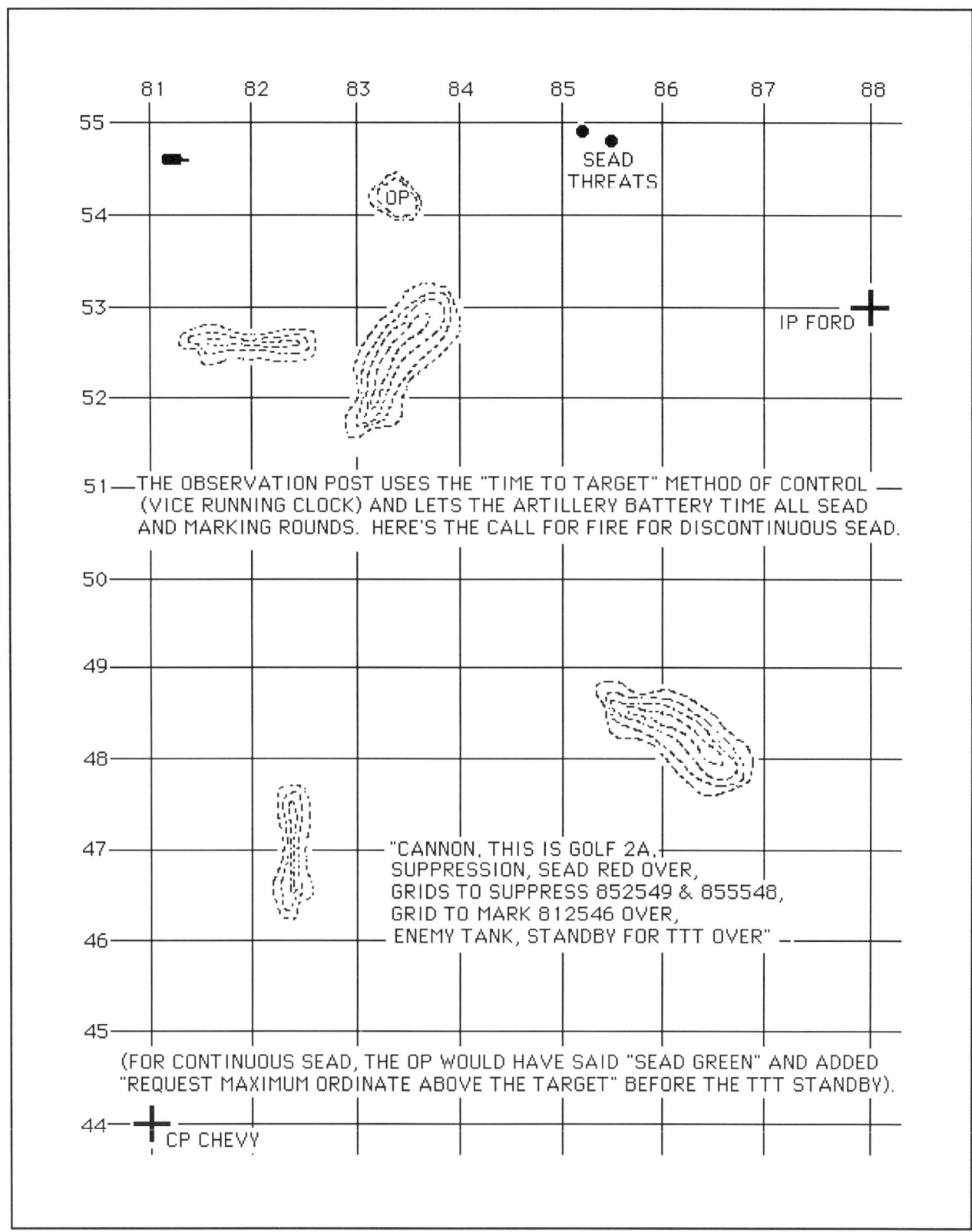

Figure 14.2: Fixed-Wing Close Air Support (Continued)

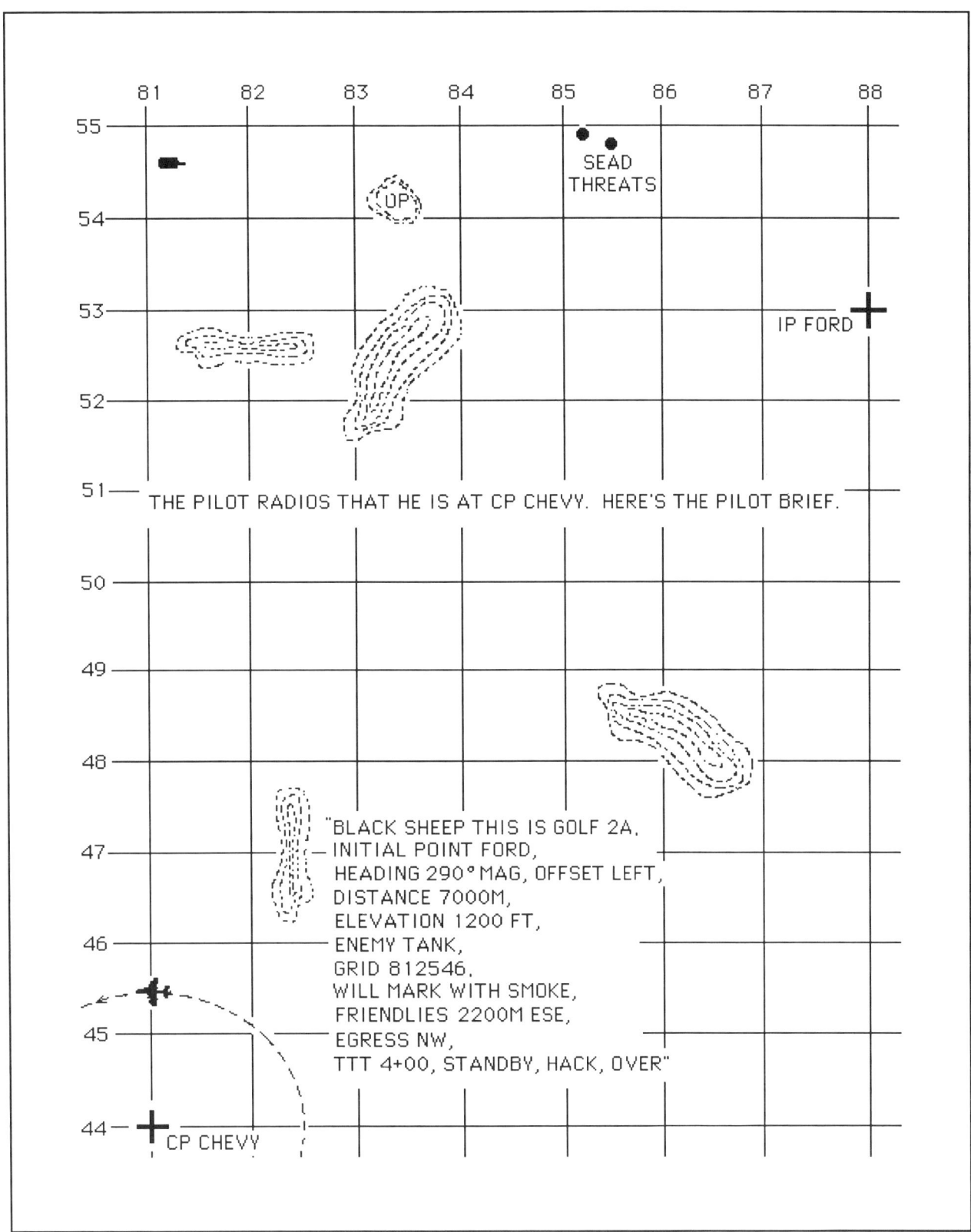

Figure 14.2: Fixed-Wing Close Air Support (Continued)

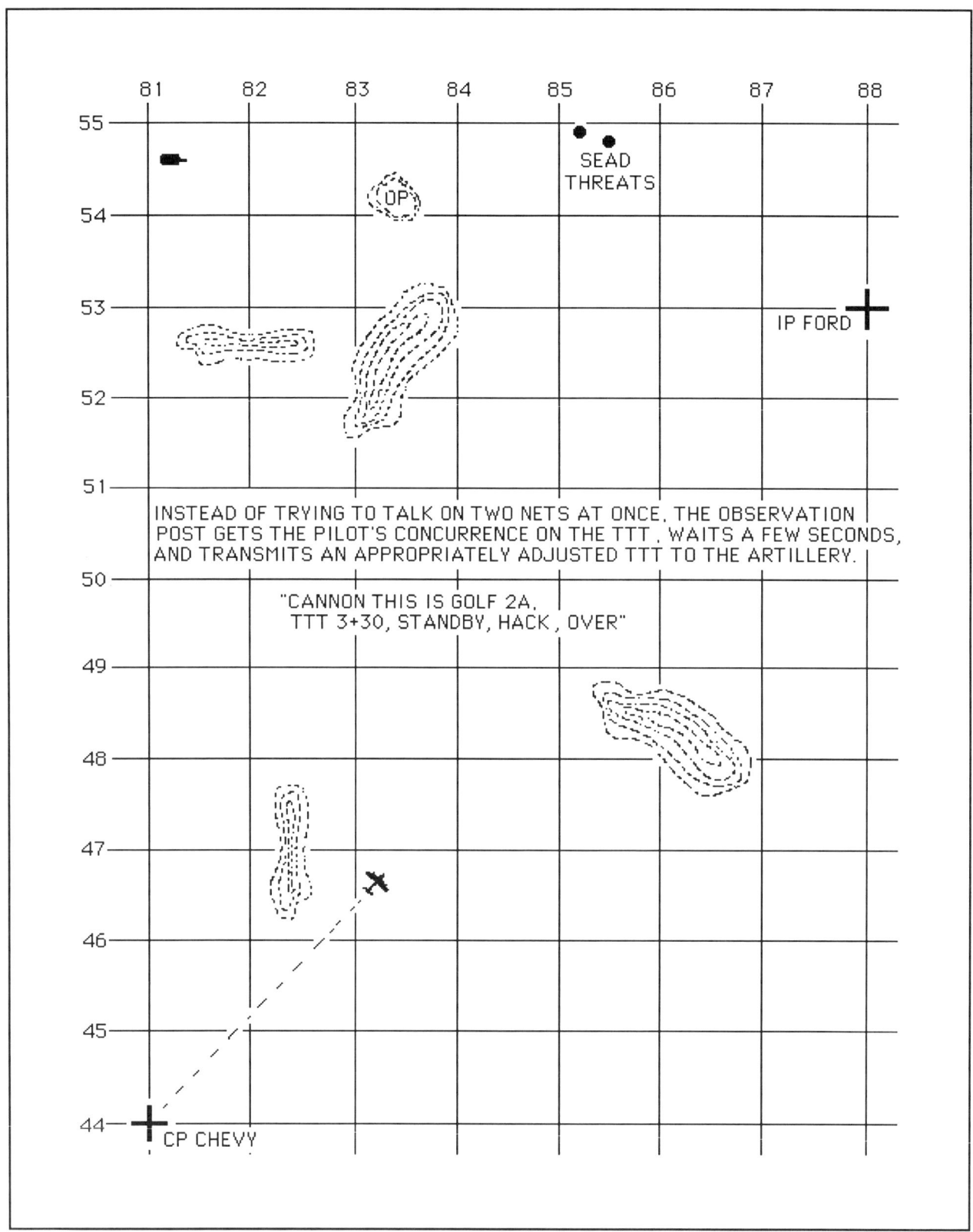

*Figure 14.2: Fixed-Wing Close Air Support (Continued)*

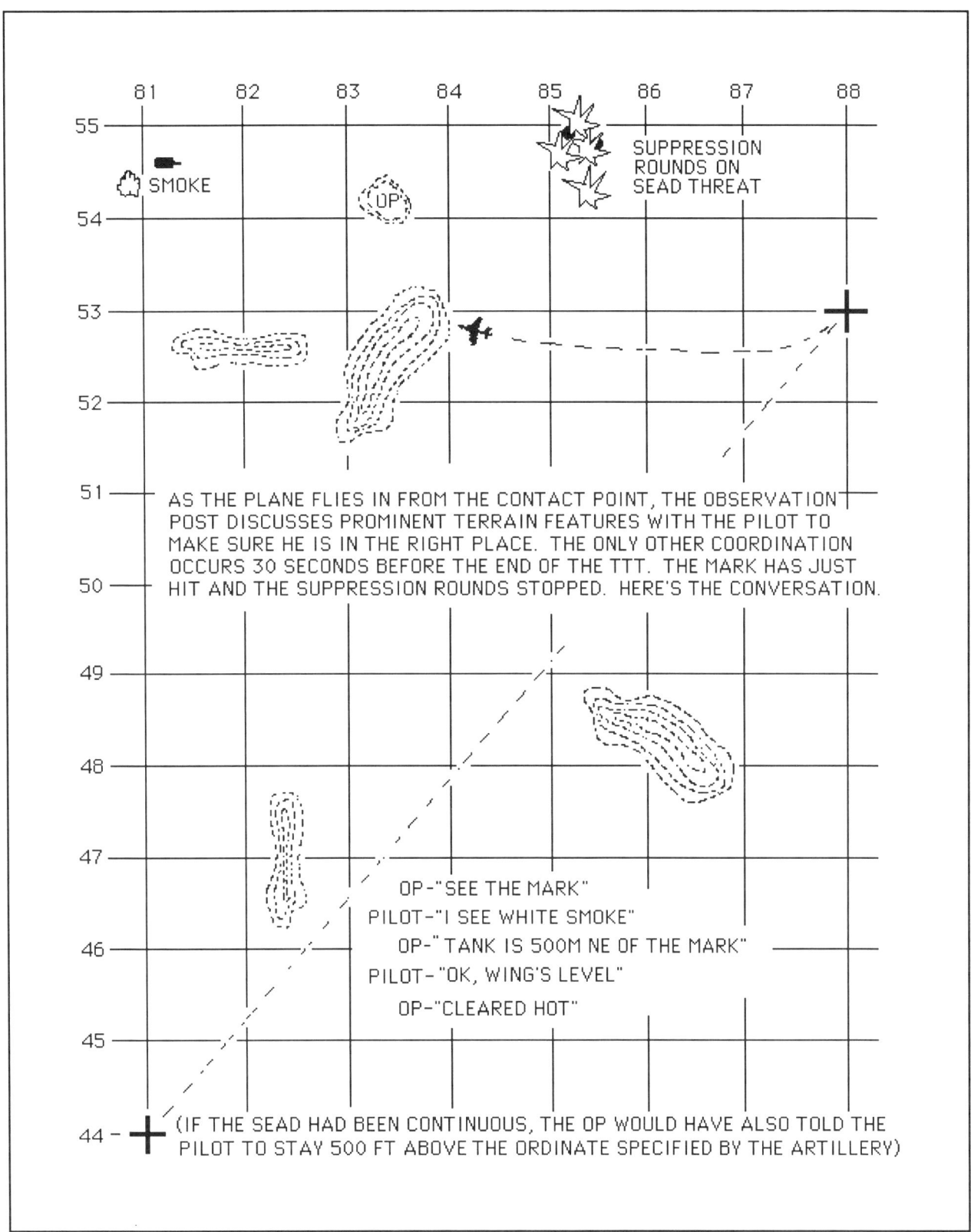

*Figure 14.2: Fixed-Wing Close Air Support (Continued)*

Techniques from the NCO Corps

## IT DOESN'T TAKE AIR SUPERIORITY TO PRACTICE MANEUVER WARFARE

In the early 1950's, the North Koreans, Chinese, and Viet Minh achieved some measure of success with their maneuver warfare ground initiatives. This was a milestone in the history of air power:

> For the first time in the history of modern warfare, an enemy force was able to conduct major ground campaigns successfully while never for a moment achieving air superiority.[8]

Twenty years later, the North Vietnamese repeated the same feat for almost a decade. What does this mean to the members of a U.S. rifle squad wanting to infiltrate deep into enemy territory? It means that, if they have been well enough trained, they won't need to stay within the protective umbrella of artillery. With the right kind of equipment, they can always summon an airstrike to handle the occasional target of opportunity or persistent pursuer.

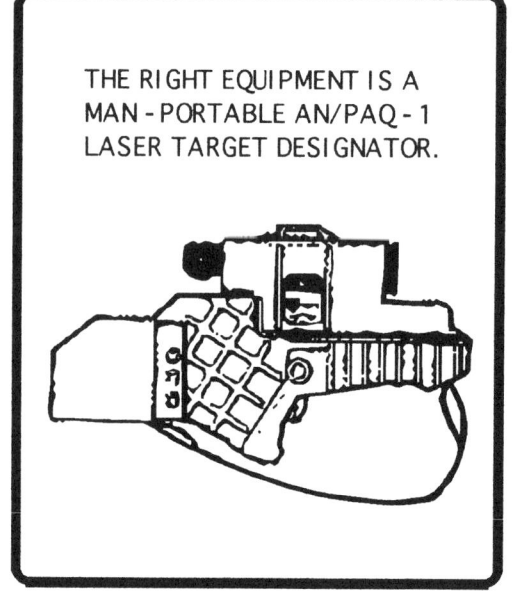

(Source: FM 7-85 (1987), p. 7-9)

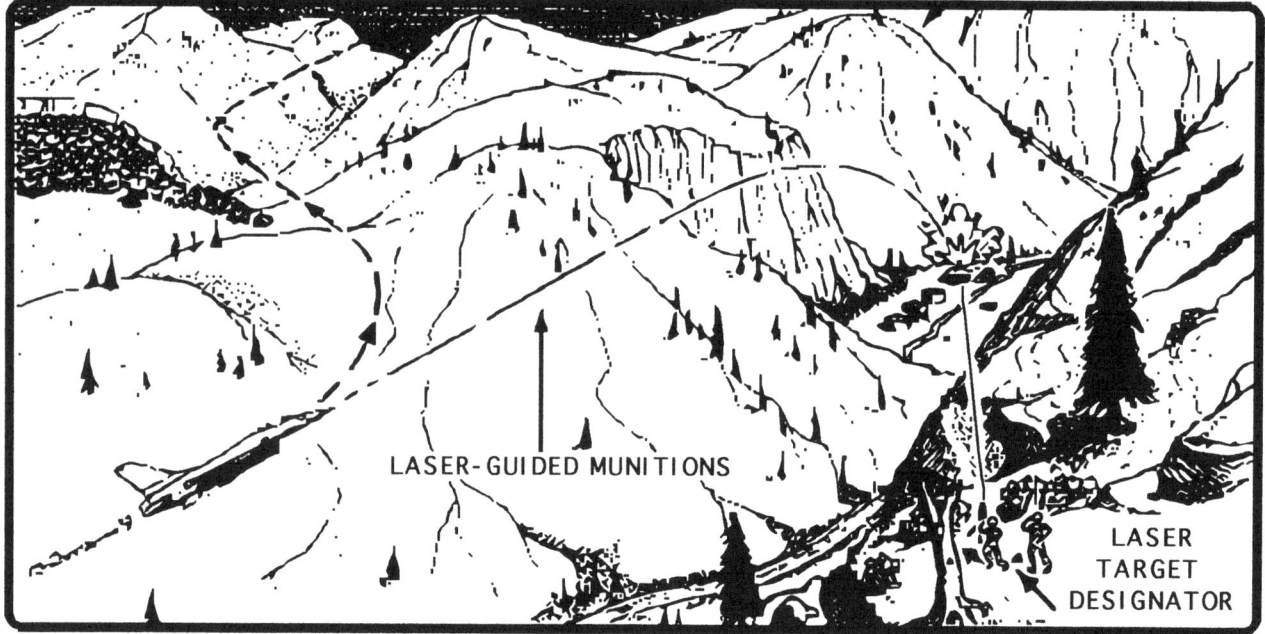

(Source: FM 7-85 (1987), p. 7-10)

150

# 15 Counterambushing

- *How can a unit's point men spot an impending ambush?*
- *With point men in the kill zone, how can a unit foil an ambush?*
- *After being ambushed, how can a unit minimize its casualties?*

(Source: FM 7-11B1/2 (1978), p. 2-II-A-4.2)

## DETECTING AN IMMINENT AMBUSH

An enemy ambush is difficult, but not impossible, to detect. Ambushers share a number of exploitable habits. Better to attack their quarry's main body, most will allow opposition security elements to get quite close to them. This can be the ambushers' undoing. Well-trained point men can detect them in many ways. At night, they can do so by sound. Invariably, a twig will snap. The adrenaline rush from seeing the long-awaited foe must cause a certain percentage of ambushers to shift their weight involuntarily. And there may be other muted but telltale sounds: (1) the faint rattling of an ammo canister, (2) the coming-off-safe of a rifle selector switch, (3) the bumping against ground or tree of a readied weapon. Or, the point men may detect fewer of the natural background noises. Properly to heed these warnings, they must travel silently and stop often. A few can also rely on a "sixth sense."

As important as hearing the inevitable warning is knowing what to do about it. Because instant death may be seconds away, point men must obey their natural survival instincts. That often means *getting down* fast, and motioning for those behind them to do likewise. As incoming fire will be high at night, taking cover without delay can make the difference between life and death:

> Night combat generally is characterized by a decrease in the ability to place aimed fire on the enemy.[1]
> — FMFM 6-4

Tsuji, still hoping to capitalize on the little element of surprise still his, ordered 3rd Platoon to assault. . . . Soviet heavy and light machineguns opened up an ear-shattering volume of fire. But, since the Japanese attackers continued up the hill in silence, most of the Soviet automatic-weapons fire sailed well over the crouching attackers' heads.[2]
— Leavenworth Papers No. 2

If the prone point men subsequently motion for those behind them to reverse direction and crawl away from the kill zone, and then follow suit, they may be able to defuse the ambush altogether. Often, it is only the enemy's sentries who have spotted the patrol. These sentries are surprised by the sighting and therefore indecisive. They don't have the authority to trigger the ambush themselves, so they must pass word of the sighting up the line to their superior. While this occurs, the patrol has a few seconds to move out of harm's way. Of course, without highly experienced or specially trained point men, no counterambushing ploy will work consistently.

### THE HASTY-FLANKING-ATTACK OPTION

Once the prone point men have signaled for those behind them to get down, they also have the option to initiate a variation of the "hasty flanking attack" discussed in chapter 12. Those within view of the enemy must function initially as a diversion and eventually as a "base of fire." Those out of sight of the enemy conduct a flanking attack that only vaguely resembles an Immediate-Action (IA) Drill. It differs from the IA Drill, in that it involves *thinking, deception, and stealth*.

Those who are to participate in the flanking attack crawl off into the bushes, confer briefly, leave the *senior man next to the trail*, form an assault line anchoring on him, and then guide on him as he moves toward the enemy. The senior man is careful to hug the edge of the trail so as to stay visible to his comrades in the kill zone, but invisible to the enemy. The maneuver force member who, because of the vegetation, can no longer see this senior man has only to stay slightly behind his on-line neighbor toward the trail side. What results is a ragged echelon formation moving toward the enemy. At first, those on line stalk their prey as described in chapter 12:

> Moving as intangibly as a ghost in the starlight, he is obscure, inaudible.[3]
> — Sun Tzu

As those in the maneuver force acquire confirmed targets, they begin to "fire and move." Then, the patrol members in or near the kill zone open fire as well. Because of the way the maneuver force leader is positioned, those in the base of fire can shift their aim automatically *without signals*. By keeping their fire ahead of the maneuver force leader, they can avoid hitting the (often obscured) personnel guiding on him. By not needing signals to shift the base of fire, the attacking force can achieve momentum. With practice, a unit can use this technique with devastating results. On dark nights, on-call mortar illumination must precede the move forward.

### WHEN THE ENEMY AMBUSHERS CANNOT BE DETECTED IN TIME

No training whatsoever on what to do when ambushed may be better than the wrong kind of training.

(Source: FMFM 0-1 (1979), p. 7-7)

When shot at unexpectedly, human beings react instinctively — they get down and crawl behind cover. If the personnel in the kill zone are not allowed to follow their natural instincts, their lives may be further endangered. The enemy leader will often use a closed-bolt weapon to initiate the ambush. His personnel will take a split second to react to this signal to open fire. That instant must be exploited by the friendly unit. Unless the ambushers are only a few steps away, the friendlies must get down.

It's doubtful that the IA drills in the patrolling manuals were ever intended to be used for counterambushing. Without the element of surprise, standup frontal assaults are discouraged by the attack manuals. To be sure, there may be times when flinging oneself against an enemy a few yards away is one's only chance to survive. But, for a cohesive unit, this last-resort maneuver takes neither practice nor commands. It is either kill or be killed, and the members of the unit will react as one without any prompting. On the other hand, if squads train to conduct upright frontal assaults every time they get ambushed from less than 50 meters, they are inviting disaster. In a tough situation, while most squad members may have better sense, some will blindly follow their training and certainly be killed. What keeps the ambushers from stringing a piece of communications wire at knee level across their front? Some would say that instantly moving toward one's ambusher is the best way to avoid the pellets from his claymores. Another way is to seek immediate cover in the folds of the ground. Claymores are difficult to aim and often fire high. One would prefer escaping both the claymore pellets and bullets. Doing this takes getting down.

After those caught in the kill zone have crawled behind cover, they are better positioned to lay down a base of fire. As soon as they assume a prone position, the rest of the patrol should do likewise. This creates the opportunity for deception. The ambushers won't know how many friendlies were in column initially, and they'll want to believe that someone was hurt by their wild (and usually high) firing. If those in the rear of the friendly column subsequently crawl back down and then off the trail, the ambushers won't have any way of detecting their presence. If, on the other hand, the untouched friendlies insist on remaining upright and shouting instructions to each other, they will inform their adversary not only of their existence, but also of their location. If they compound the error by charging into the bushes in column, they will not only expose themselves unnecessarily to fire, but also telegraph their intentions.

If the maneuver element succeeds in getting off the trail without being detected, it can use the same hasty flanking attack described in the last paragraph. Some may worry that those in the kill zone will unnecessarily suffer, because this procedure takes slightly longer than an IA drill. In all probability, whatever harm was destined for those up front has already occurred. The ones who should be concerned about further harm are those in the maneuver element. (See figures 15.1 through 15.4.)

(Source: FM 7-8 (1984), p. 5-22)

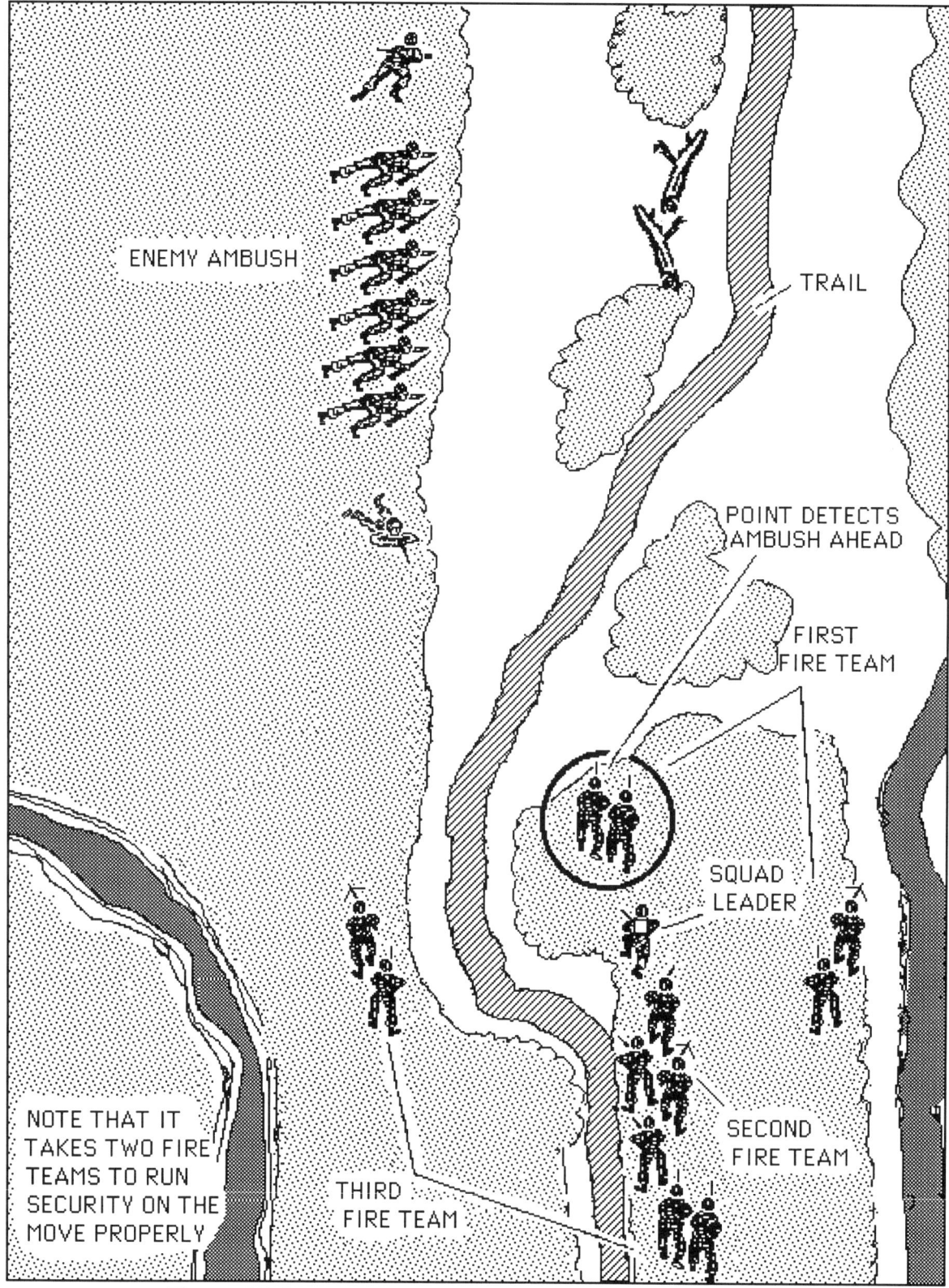

*Figure 15.1: A Typical Daytime Counterambush Scenario*
(Sources: FM 7-70 (1986), p. 4-20; FM 5-103 (1985), p. 4-6; FM 7-11B3 (1976), p. 2-VII-C-4.4)

Counterambushing

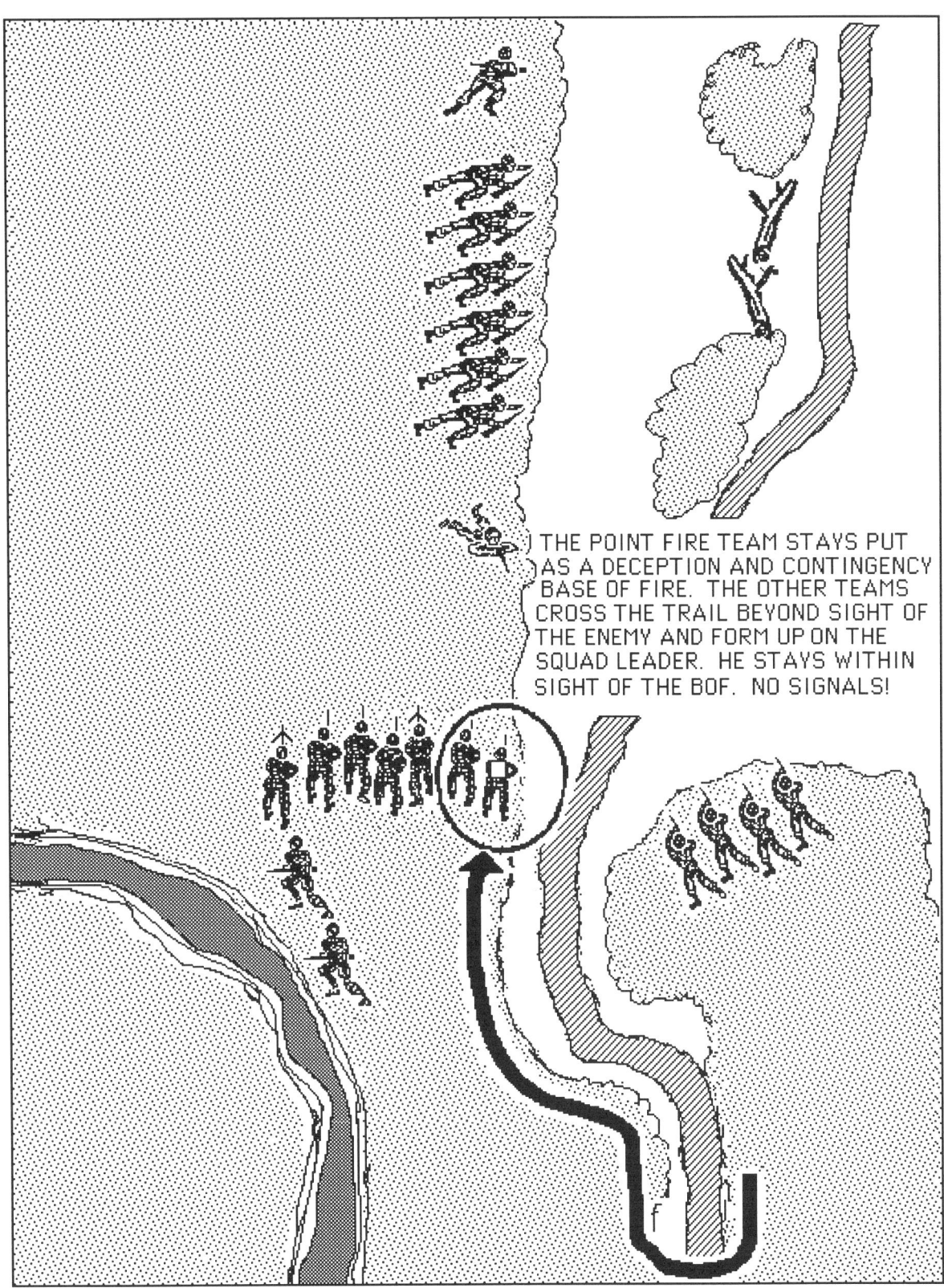

*Figure 15.2: The Counterambush Technique in the Daytime*
(Sources: FM 7-70 (1986), p. 4-20; FM 5-103 (1985), pp. 4-6, 4-38; FM 7-11B3 (1976), p. 2-VII-C-4.4)

Techniques from the NCO Corps

(Source: FM 7-8 (1984), p. B-4)

(Source: FM 7-8 (1984), p. B-3)

*Figure 15.3: A Common Nighttime Counterambush Opportunity*
(Sources: FM 7-70 (1986), p. 4-20; FM 5-103 (1985), p. 4-6; FM 7-11B3 (1976), p. 2-VII-C-4.4)

Techniques from the NCO Corps

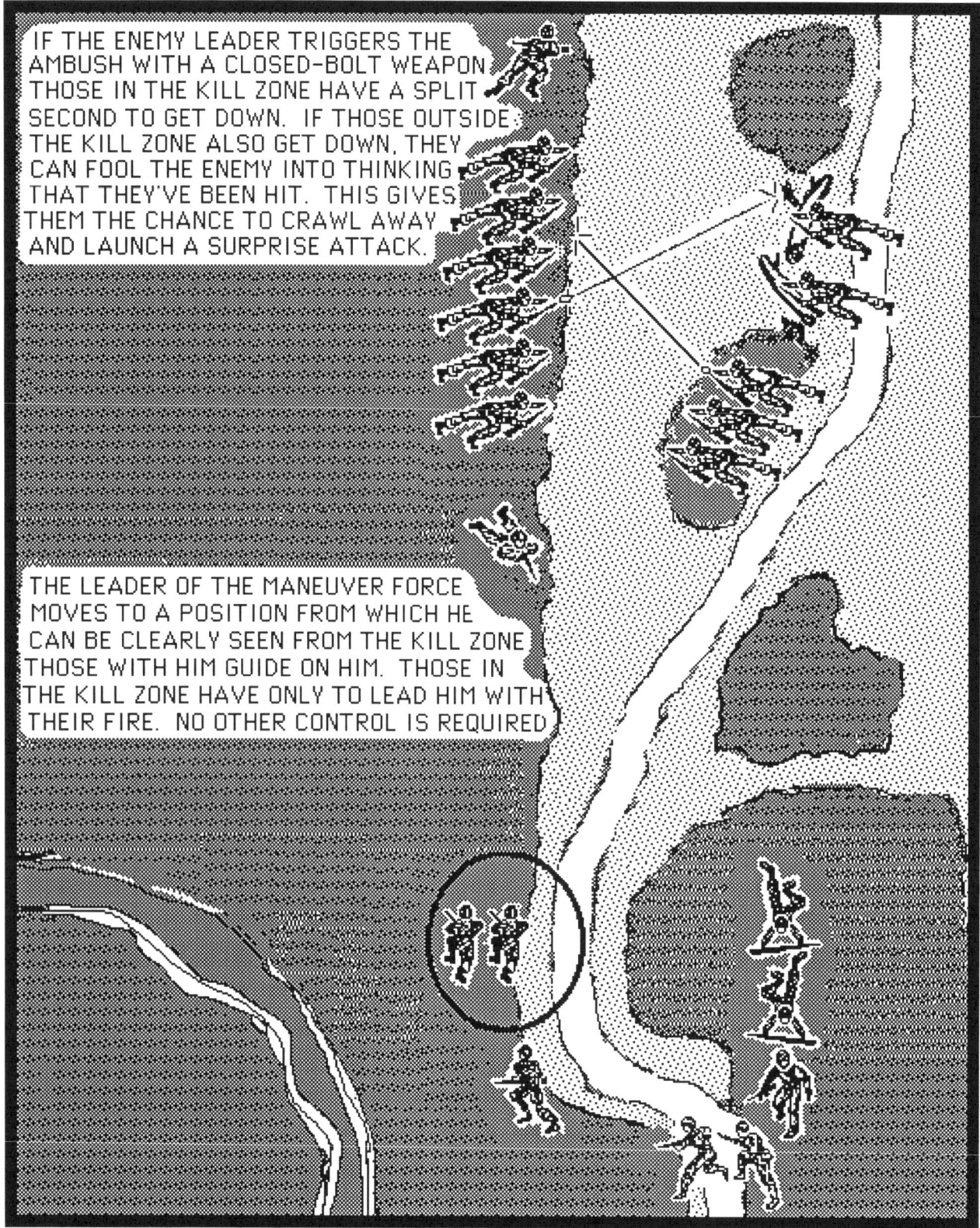

Figure 15.4: The Counterambush Technique at Night
(Sources: FM 7-70 (1986), p. 4-20; FM 5-103 (1985), pp. 4-6, 4-38, 5-10; FM 90-10-1 (1982), p. B-4; FM 7-11B3 (1976), p. 2-VII-C-4.4)

# 16 The Ultimate Ambush

- *How can a squad ambush a large enemy force without getting hurt?*
- *How important is this kind of ambush to maneuver warfare?*
- *What constitutes a good ambush site?*

(Source: FM 7-8 (1984), p. 5-22)

### THE PURPOSE OF AMBUSHING

Ambushing started out as a way to hurt one's enemy. Then, it became a way to gather intelligence. Now, it has evolved into a way to disrupt, channelize, and demoralize one's enemy. Ambush patrol leaders could easily misinterpret these mixed signals. Some might even believe themselves authorized to let numerically superior enemy forces pass through their ambush sites unmolested.

In combat, halfheartedly doing anything can be fatal. A rifle squad cannot accomplish any of the subsidiary missions of ambushing without first decimating its opponent. Furthermore, not getting kills on ambush erodes a squad's overall esprit de corps and ultimately its survivability in combat. An ambush patrol that would even consider granting free passage to a larger enemy force lacks confidence. After all, the ambush patrol is expected to operate alone in areas where it is always potentially outnumbered. It must find ways to hurt a larger opponent without getting hurt itself. It must develop an ambushing method so devastating that the opponent cannot react. It must do this, not to kill large numbers of enemy soldiers per se, but rather to operate safely where enemy soldiers abound. At the small-unit level, ambushing is a matter of kill or be killed. If the killing process is not efficient, the enemy will strike back. If even one enemy soldier survives the initial fusillade, he can single-handedly destroy anyone searching the kill zone for intelligence. Maneuver warfare has as its premier defense strategy, "killer" ambushes in series. They are intended progressively to weaken an attacker until he can be successfully counterattacked. Here again, the ambushers must kill efficiently to keep from being overpowered.

So, the inferred mission of any ambush (unless otherwise directed) is to kill as many enemy soldiers as possible without incurring friendly casualties. One wonders how well Americans have accomplished this inferred mission in the past?

## LESSONS FROM VIETNAM

Most American ambush patrols in Vietnam did *no* damage to the enemy. Since that time, U.S. ambushing procedures have changed little. An in-depth analysis of what happened then, may provide valuable insights into contemporary problems. Why did so many American ambushes fail in Vietnam? The courage of U.S. fighting men has never been at issue. There are only a few other possibilities: (1) too few small units to cover the likely infiltration routes, (2) faulty intelligence, (3) less than optimal training, or (4) an extremely proficient opponent.

To get within attacking distance of lucrative targets, the NVA had to cross large American Tactical Areas of Responsibility (TAOR's). To stay ahead of U.S. supporting arms while threading their way through the mazes of rice paddies and bamboo thickets, the NVA had to stay on the paths. These paths existed in limited number, so the "too-many-routes-to-cover" theory does not adequately explain why U.S. ambush patrols had so little success.

In Southeast Asia, the gathering and dissemination of intelligence was no easy task. Rifle companies spent 28 out of every 30 days in the field and often at some distance from their battalion headquarters. They had plenty to do without having to conduct their own intelligence effort. It would have taken someone knowledgeable in maneuver warfare properly to interpret the information anyway. Just to stage for an attack, the North Vietnamese had literally to *run* the gauntlet of U.S. supporting arms. In small columns, they ran long distances during periods of limited visibility. They could travel light, because they had stockpiled equipment and supplies in forward locations. Local Viet Cong units guarded these supply stashes and periodically took exception to American units poking around. Furthermore, NVA units moving along these provisioned routes periodically bumped into American forces coincidentally sweeping the area. Few U.S. commanders realized at the time that the enemy contacts and supply caches marked local infiltration routes, and that by backtracking along these routes, they could have found the larger conduits coming out of the mountains. The larger conduits were not identifiable by any other means, because most were camouflaged from the air and major cross trails. Simply by plotting on a map the caches discovered and contacts made near a lucrative target, and then connecting the dots radially outwards through navigable terrain, the commanders could have detected likely infiltration routes. An organized effort to ambush these routes might have met with more success.

The level of training varied from unit to unit in Vietnam. Ambush patrols went out at dusk and came back at dawn. Most made no other attempt to conceal their leaving or reentering of friendly lines. Headquarters elements generally picked the ambush sites without conferring with those who had previously patrolled into the same areas. The few ambushes that did produce results, often netted only one body. When an ambush is triggered with a closed-bolt weapon, all but one of the enemy soldiers in the kill zone have a split second to get down. As small-arms fire is usually high at night, very possibly the only enemy killed was the one at which the U.S. squad leader was aiming when he triggered the ambush. A typical U.S. ambush patrol didn't set in where obstacles would protect its front or flanks; it simply made the best of the assigned trail junction. Its occasional L-shaped ambush sometimes caused casualties from friendly fire on the short side of the "L."

(Source: MCOP1550.14D (1983), pp. 1-3, 10-8)

Perhaps the U.S. patrol's greatest oversight was its predictability. Moving at twilight may have helped the patrol to land navigate and to handle chance contact, but it concealed neither its passage through friendly lines, nor its intent. Local Viet Cong could have watched each U.S. perimeter, followed each patrol into position, and then marked (for the NVA forces moving through the area) the trails ambushed in much the same way a railroad signalman marks the tracks occupied by another train.

Of course, U.S. ambush patrols did many things right as well. While, they over-relied on the killing power of their small arms, they often added claymore mines to their heavy loads. Their flank security elements used tug ropes to warn of approaching enemy. Their favorite ambush formation was linear.

That the enemy was good needs little substantiation now. Waiting at major trail junctions might have worked against an adversary low on initiative. This enemy apparently learned how not only to skirt trail junctions, but also to get down and crawl away when shot at.

Of course, there were times when the enemy came up a little short. One night at Con Thien in the late spring of 1967, Alpha and Delta Companies of 1st Battalion, 4th Marines were hit by an estimated NVA regiment:

> At Con Thien, following a 250-round mortar barrage, two enemy battalions and a sapper unit assaulted the position of 1st Battalion, 4th Marines (Lieutenant Colonel Theodore J. Willis). The main thrust hit Company D. Forty-four Marines were killed and 100 wounded. But the enemy lost 197 killed and 10 taken prisoner, and over 100 weapons captured.[1]

Corporal Alvarez, LCpl Sam Briceno, LCpl Hodges and five others (all liberty risks and none taller than 5'8") ambushed at least part of the withdrawing NVA force. The next day, 30 enemy bodies were counted at the ambush site.[2] Many more may have crawled or been dragged away. Of note, the ambushing squad did not lose a single man. One can only speculate on how the squad could have been this successful. It is known that an attacking NVA force liked to depart its objective by an alternate route. Corporal Alvarez and the squad must have been waiting along the egress route. When they realized the size of the enemy force coming through their kill zone, they must have blown their claymores and summarily skedaddled. They were known to prefer the linear ambush formation, to rely on tug ropes for communication, and to initiate their ambushes with claymores. The thick hedgerows lining the trails in this part of Vietnam might have kept the enemy from overrunning or encircling the badly outnumbered Marines, or the explosions might have sounded to the NVA like artillery fire. Perhaps the Marines correctly deduced that shooting their small arms would disclose their location. At any rate, the simplicity of their plan, and their presence of mind to modify it under duress, produced astounding results with very little risk to themselves. In this historical example lies the seed for a good ambush technique.

## CONSISTENT SUCCESS AT AMBUSHING

Consistent success at anything takes motivation. Even to consider letting a numerically superior foe pass through one's ambush site unharmed is inconsistent with that level of motivation. Whether outnumbered or not, the squad must want to go where the enemy will be, and the squad leader must exercise enough initiative during the planning process to make it happen. To produce results, he must discover the opponent's probable whereabouts, a technique that will work well against a force of any size, and an ambush site that will permit that technique.

Then, the squad must get to the ambush site undetected. Once there, it must have a defensive alignment that provides adequate fields of fire, definitive communications and control, and ease of egress in more than one direction. Those manning the site must have a foolproof early warning system and a way of sharing subsequent information/instructions. The ambush must work equally well against an enemy approaching from any direction. Security elements must be deployed in such a way that they cannot be cut off from, or mask the fires of, the rest of the squad. Ideally, the technique must create the impression that the enemy has been mined or shelled, and not ambushed at all. At a minimum, it should disguise the direction from which the ambush came. Finally, the technique should allow the ambushers to defeat an all-out enemy assault from any direction.

## ACHIEVING THE PROPER LEVEL OF MOTIVATION

Only highly motivated squads can successfully ambush a good enemy. The squads must have a combination of self-confidence, commitment, and focus. Learning the fine points of ambushing can do wonders for their self-confidence. When they are further allowed to look for their own ambush sites during daylight patrols, they develop a vested interest in what happens there. The ambush patrols that come back empty-handed from areas infested with enemy should be reminded that they have failed at their mission. If the squads from any particular unit consistently fail, command and peer pressure should be *carefully* applied until at least one does what it takes to succeed. Then, the others will seek the satisfaction that can only come from mission accomplishment. When success becomes the norm, instead of the exception, the right level of motivation has been achieved.

It is important for squad members to maintain the "eye of the tiger" throughout the trip to the ambush site. When planning the route, the distance to be traveled should be balanced against the number of obstacles and danger areas to be negotiated. The squad should feel as highly motivated when they reach the site, as they did when they left the perimeter.

## WHAT CONSTITUTES A GOOD AMBUSH SITE?

A good ambush site must only satisfy two criteria: (1) it must be frequented by the enemy, and (2) it must be comprised of terrain favorable to the ambusher. The first condition can be most easily found deep in enemy territory or behind enemy lines. The second occurs when squads are allowed to choose terrain that is compatible with their ambushing techniques.

Finding the enemy is ultimately the responsibility of the small-unit leader. But, only when he is authorized to pick his own ambush sites can he adequately fulfill this responsibility. To determine what an enemy in any particular area is trying to accomplish, one must attempt to think like him. If he is believed to be watching the friendly perimeter, one must guess what route he uses to avoid detection. All patrol leaders within the same company must continually collect and share intelligence. A promising ambush site is one at which a daytime patrol has found fresh signs of enemy passage. The route may be one frequented by enemy reconnaissance elements, or scouted ahead of time for a subsequent night movement. In a guerrilla war, the juxtaposition on an S-2's map of enemy contacts and supply caches will reveal likely infiltration routes. Just one of these probable routes can provide many promising ambush sites. If no advance intelligence is available, "roving" ambush patrols can use real or artificial horizons to locate their enemy counterparts after dark. They can do this by moving through low ground or parallel to (but well away from) roads or bodies of water.

Ground that favors the ambusher is ground that is easy to defend. It must have good all-around observation and fields of fire, adequate cover and concealment, and natural obstacles to its front and flanks. A covered route (like a draw) to the rear of the ambush site will permit egress under fire. Gaps in the natural barriers to the flanks will facilitate exiting the site in another direction.

From the ambush site, someone in the squad must be able to see clearly in every direction to beyond grenade range. The squad leader must minimally have a narrow view of both front and rear kill zones. To use the ambushed trail as a navigational aid, the enemy unit need not travel down its center. It can walk along the edge of the trail, or roughly parallel to and just barely within sight of it. Of course, there is always the danger that an enemy point man will spot the ambush site and lead his companions around to the rear of it. Furthermore, an enemy with night vision goggles may be running flankers after dark. It was reported from Panama that the Cubans had the proficiency to do this. Finally, the enemy's route of march might be at right angles to the ambush formation. To be ready for any eventuality, the ambushers must have all-around security and highly responsive killing power in any direction.

Ideally, the ambush site should provide its occupants with some natural cover — e.g., a ditch, a series of holes, a small rise, or a fallen tree trunk. The site with natural barriers to the front and flanks (like large puddles, swampy areas, thick bushes, etc.) will not be as easily discovered by enemy flankers or overrun/encircled by their parent unit. Where natural obstacles don't exist, manmade ones can sometimes be *quickly* constructed. Something as simple as a stickered vine or strand of communications wire can discourage enemy passage through an area. In combination with the obstacles, Squad Automatic Weapons (SAW's) at the center and flanks of the formation should provide enough firepower to stop any number of attackers. Their ammunition canisters and high rate of fire give them this capability.

When a squad discovers its assigned ambush site to be inappropriate, it can announce its arrival at the general location and intention to look for a suitable place to set in. Invariably, there will be terrain close by that can at least be defended. To avoid unpleasant coincidences, the squad should apprise its headquarters of its distance and direction from the original site. To improve safety, most parent units would readily approve a slight shift in location.

## THE FORMATION AT THE AMBUSH SITE

For a squad on level ground, the strongest ambush formation is a straight line. The various "alphabetical" shapes complicate the issue and provide no advantage. The linear formation provides all-around security (when personnel alternately face outboard) and the massing of fires to either side (when half the personnel reverse their original direction). The linear formation is no longer vulnerable to attack at its ends when personnel with NVG's, automatic weapons, and claymores are stationed at those ends. Then, the automatic weapons can provide interlocking bands of grazing fire across both front and rear of the formation.

The Objective Rally Point (ORP) is only useful, when left *unmanned*. The route back to the ORP isn't secure, so how can manning the ORP serve any useful purpose? What if an enemy patrol gets between a manned ORP and the ambush site? Those at the site can no longer take the enemy under fire without endangering those at the ORP. Nor can the ambushers exit to the rear of the site to retrieve their ORP sentries.

Ambush security elements are most effectively *collocated* with everyone else. That goes for flank, as well as rear security personnel. Rear security can be accomplished by every other man facing backwards. Flank security can be achieved by the personnel at the ends of the linear formation watching the long axis. With NVG's, these closely deployed flank security people can provide plenty of advance warning to "main-body" personnel lying next to them. Then, when the enemy assaults from the side, the massed fires of the main body will keep the flank security men from being cut off; and when the enemy comes from the front or back, the crisscrossing automatic-weapons fire from the flankers will keep the main body from being overrun. When flank security and main-body personnel are all within touching distance, the patrol can more easily depart the ambush site in an alternate direction.

(Source: OPNAV P 34-03 (Revised 1960), p. 394)

## REACHING THE SITE UNDETECTED

To stand any chance of ambushing Third-World militia, former U.S. city dwellers must move into position without being detected. They cannot plan a route that crosses a road or open area, and they cannot be seen leaving their patrol base. To exit friendly lines, they must either crawl out as a unit after dark, exfiltrate a few at a time as fake Listening Posts (LP's), or secretly drop out of a platoon daylight foray. Whichever ruse they choose, they must remember that their proximity to friendly lines puts them in great danger. Only through concerted coordination can they escape accidental harm.

Then, the ambushers must remain inconspicuous en route to their site. When a road can't be avoided, they must go under it through a culvert. They must even avoid areas illuminated by bright moonlight.

Finally, after arrival at their destination, they must become all but invisible. Their leader can't walk the site prior to their setting in (he can only do that days ahead of time on another patrol). Further, their leader can't noisily position them, one at a time. En masse, they must quietly deploy on line, get down, crawl out to emplace claymores, reform, and then stay put until ordered to leave. Much of their security will depend on how well they are camouflaged. Here's how NVA units escaped discovery:

> In jungle bivouacs, the soldiers exercised care not to disturb the area or leave signs of their presence. Rather than digging fire pits, they built small stone fireplaces that they dispersed after the meal. They avoided stepping on plants....
>
> When they moved, the North Vietnamese generally marched in column formation without smoking or talking and without breaking branches or brush along the trail....

> ... The typical NVA soldier wore a circular frame on his back, to which he attached twigs and grass. When he crouched in a foxhole, the camouflage formed a cover; when he lay prone, it concealed his head and shoulders and allowed the soldier to turn his head without moving his camouflage.[3]

## IT TAKES STEALTH AND DECEPTION TO AMBUSH A LARGER FORCE

To ambush a larger opponent without risk of injury, one must conceal from that opponent what has really happened. The oversized quarry must be made to think that he has encountered supporting arms or mines. To create this deception, the ambushers must limit their response to *claymores* and *grenades*. Any firing of small arms will reveal the truth. By triggering the ambush with claymores, the friendly unit no longer gives its adversary the opportunity to get down.

## WHILE SETTING IN, WASTED MOTION MUST BE ELIMINATED

Because the claymore mines will do the killing, there is little reason for the squad leader to emplace his men one at a time. He needs only to position himself where he can clearly see the kill zones to front and rear. To operate secretly where the enemy abounds, his squad must occupy the site in one silent and fluid motion. Any sound or movement signature will give the unit away. The flank security teams should only fan out from the squad leader far enough to find unobstructed views to the sides. As long as the ambushers are deployed in a straight and compact line, they can defend themselves from any enemy threat, and still change locations in a hurry.

With the proper order of march, a squad column can easily assume the line formation just described. The squad leader walks into the ambush site right behind the point men. When the leader finds a location from which he can see both kill zones, he ties one end of a tug rope to a flexible twig, hands the other end to his point men, and dispatches them and half of the squad to one flank. Then, he repeats the process to the other flank with another tug rope, two more security guards, the rest of the squad. When the security teams reach locations affording good views to the flanks, they pull the tug ropes taut and secure them to flexible twigs of their own. Those behind them alternate facing outboard and get down *on top of* the tug ropes. Then, everyone crawls out simultaneously to clear the bottom foliage from the bushes and to emplace their claymores so the backblasts will be deflected. Finally, they crawl back, and all but the flank security personnel pass their claymore detonators up the line to the squad leader. Their role is now purely defensive, and they stay put until ordered to leave by tugs on the rope. However, they do have the prerogative to toss grenades with discretion before or after the ambush has been sprung, and to use small arms as a last resort in self-defense.

When any member of the squad spots enemy, he tugs on the rope to alert the squad leader and his side of the formation. Then, the squad leader relays the warning to the other side. Before any ambush patrol, combinations of tugs and pauses must be worked out for each of the following signals: "someone is coming from the," "left," "right," "back," "front," "they're on the inside track (parallel to the trail)," "they're the point element for a larger force," "they're running flankers," "they're friendly," "say again," "collect the claymores, we're pulling out to the," "move it out," and "we're not ready."

## SPRINGING THE AMBUSH

To the enemy, the ambush must sound like a mortar barrage or "daisy chain" of exploding mines. The claymores do the killing, with the grenades as a backup. All the claymores to the front and rear of the squad are controlled by the squad leader. By firing several at once, he eliminates the possibility that one misfire might compromise the element of surprise. The claymores on the flanks are controlled by the flank security teams. Those teams have authority to blow them prematurely, if an enemy column is coming directly toward them.

If, after the ambush has been sprung, a squad member must throw a grenade, he must do so without leaving a firing signature. He must carefully remove the spoon to prevent the telltale sound of the spoon ejecting normally. With the claymore wires reeled in, the enemy has no way of knowing that he has been ambushed, as long as *no small arms* have been fired. Even if he guesses correctly what has happened, he cannot tell from which direction the ambush came. He does not know which way to fire or to assault.

By the time the enemy realizes the truth, the ambushers should be long gone — providing, of course, they didn't have to search the bodies in the kill zone right away. Not all the enemy injured in the kill zone will die immediately. Some will crawl off behind cover. Once hidden, they will fire at anyone who comes into view. The odds of staying unharmed while searching the kill zone under these conditions, are not good. A better way to gather intelligence might be to leave the area, put airburst H&I munitions on the preregistered target near the ambush site until morning, and then search the entire area on line with one's parent unit.

## WHEN THE ENEMY COMES FROM AN UNEXPECTED DIRECTION OR HAS SECURITY ELEMENTS DEPLOYED

The enemy will probably not come down the center of the trail. If he does so on a modern battlefield, he will be running flankers wearing NVG's. That means that the ambush patrol has to be prepared for any eventuality. The technique just described works well no matter what the enemy does. It provides early warning, a comprehensive means of communication, and an all-around plan for defense. If the enemy patrol is approaching along the inside track, the flank security team can either blow its claymore to keep from being stepped on or let the enemy pass into the rear kill zone. If, on the other hand, the foe approaches on a diagonal, he will encounter the full force of at least one of the front or rear claymores.

If the enemy is running a point, the ambush leader must let that point pass unharmed through the kill zone to get at the main body. The enemy point becomes the responsibility of the flank security team on the far side of the formation. Once the claymores are detonated, this team can take out the point with grenades. If the enemy patrol is running flankers, friendly security guards may have to toss a grenade to keep from being discovered. Blowing all front and rear claymores should normally eliminate any enemy flankers along with their parent unit. The rear security element for the enemy patrol becomes the responsibility of the friendly flank security team that first spotted the patrol.

## IF THE AMBUSHED FORCE ATTEMPTS TO ASSAULT

By the time the opposition unit rallies for an assault, the ambushers should be long gone. In the unlikely event that the enemy soldiers guess correctly what has happened and instantly come storming out of the kill zone, they will still have to contend with grenades and barriers. As a last resort, the ambushers can fire their small arms before using the covered exit route. From the tight linear formation, their three automatic weapons can temporarily blunt any human-wave assault. With a little practice, this retrograde maneuver can be done in seconds.

If flank security men detect an enemy force trying to mount an assault from one end of the formation, they can

# The Ultimate Ambush

blow their claymore (or fire their automatic weapon as a last resort). They should also initiate the signal for the squad to pull out in the opposite direction.

## HOW THE WITHDRAWAL IS ORCHESTRATED

Artillery or mortar fire should be preregistered in front of the ambush site when it is chosen (days ahead of time). Indirect fire will further the deception and permit the squad to escape under heavy enemy pressure. If the fire is not preregistered, the squad leader can ask for a spotting round beyond danger-close range and walk it in. Either way, failing to say "precision fire" before "fire for effect" would be disastrous. Targets preplanned (but not preregistered) should not be hit until the unit is beyond danger-close range of them (400 meters for mortars).

Normally, the squad leader will decide when and in which direction to depart the ambush site. On receiving the signal to pull out after a sprung ambush, the flank guards blow their claymores and reel in their claymore wires. Then, each member of the squad becomes responsible for the whereabouts of the member behind him. He must either bring that person with him or signal that there will be a delay in the departure. In the linear formation, the squad can quickly exit the site through the covered route to the rear, or the gate in the obstacles to the flanks. In either case, by leaving the site last, the squad leader can count noses.

Following a different route home is the best hedge against calamity. After any ambush attempt, discipline is difficult to maintain. Elation over success is potentially more dangerous than despondency over failure. This is when the ambush patrol is the most vulnerable and when the patrol leader must work the hardest to earn his pay. (See figures 16.1 through 16.4 for how the "ultimate ambush" method might work in combat against a much larger enemy force.)

(Source: FM 7-8 (1984), p. B-2)

Techniques from the NCO Corps

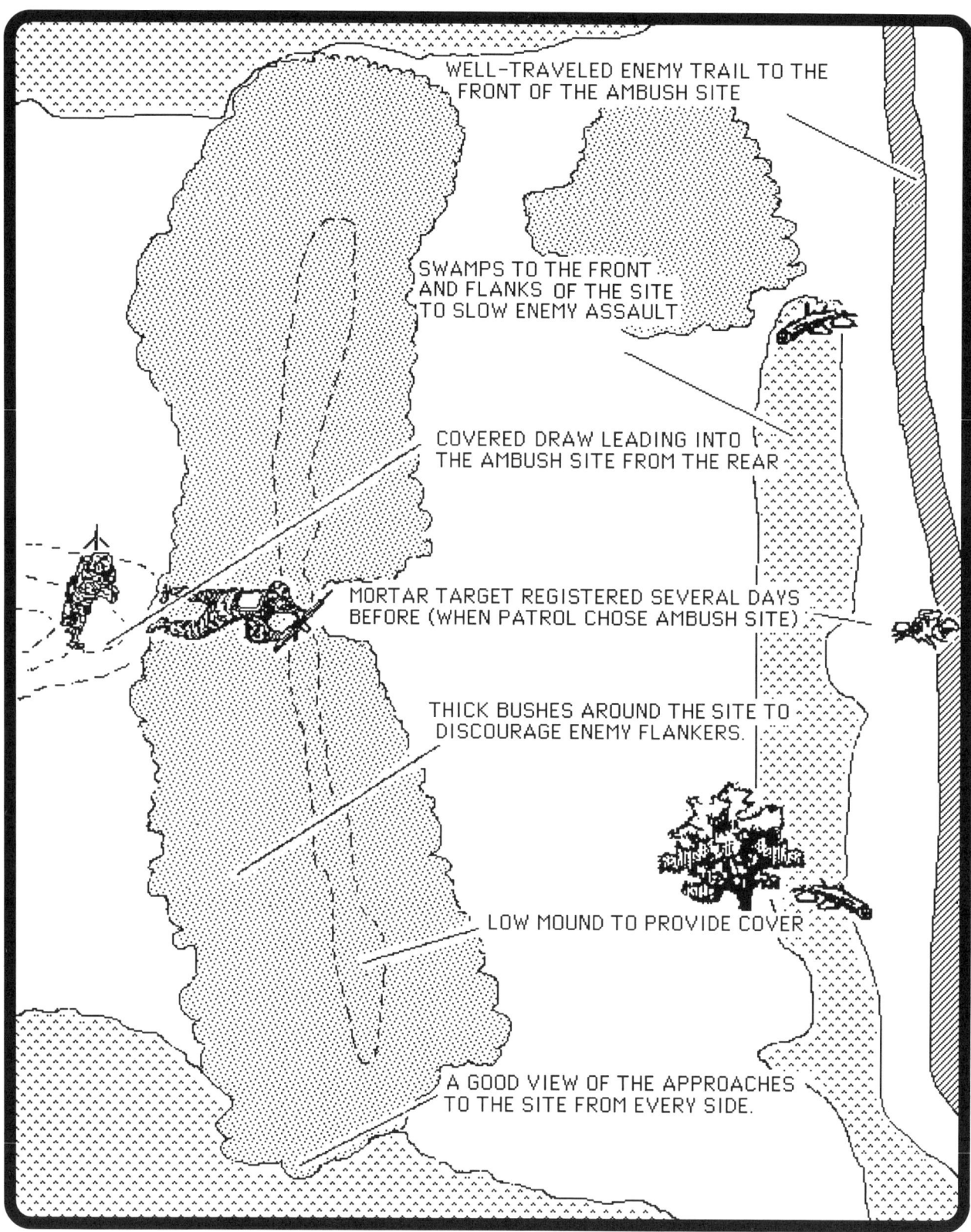

*Figure 16.1: Choosing a Good Ambush Site Is the Key*
(Sources: FM 22-100 (1983), p. 66; FM 7-70 (1986), p. 4-20; MCI 03.66 (1986), p. 2-8)

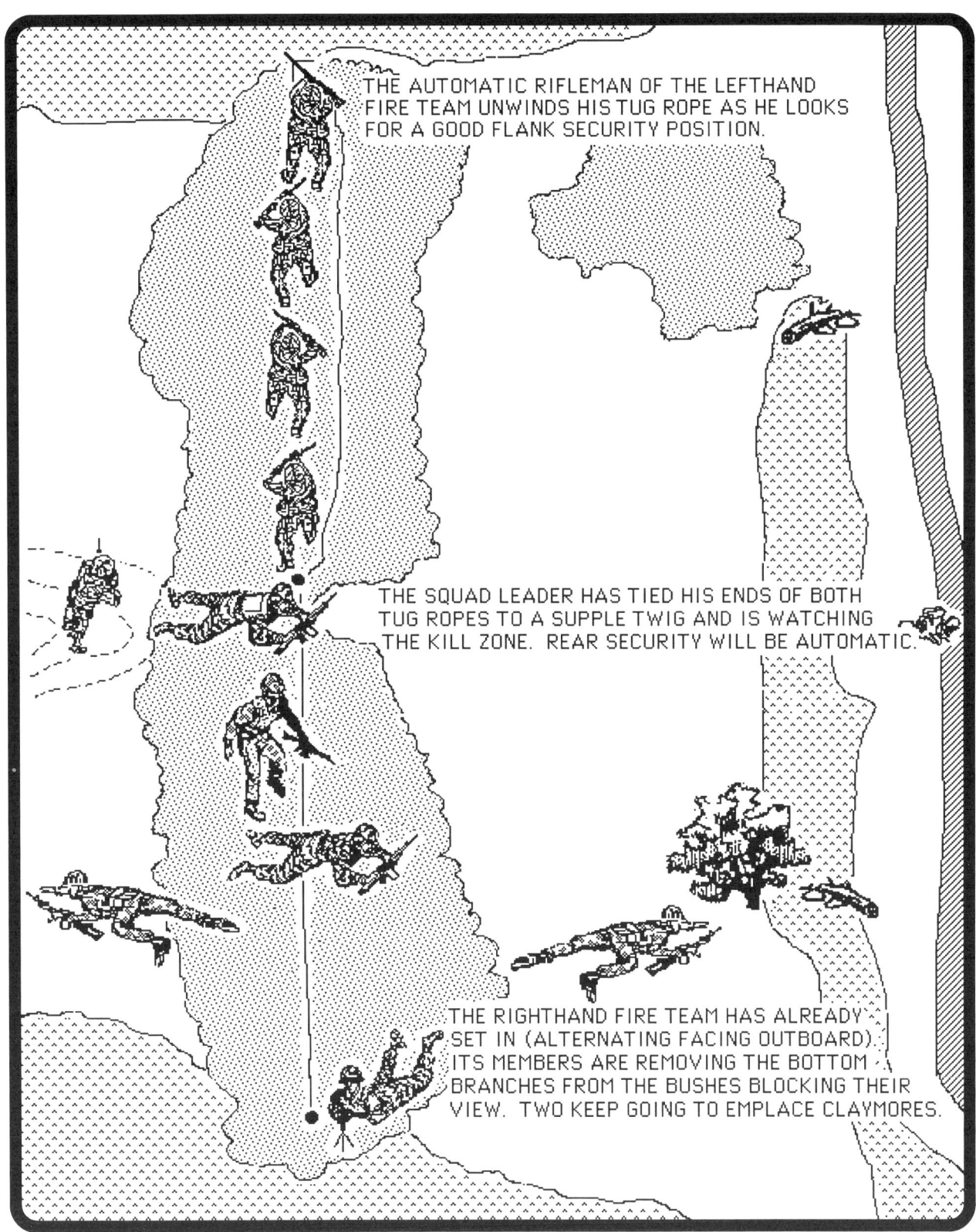

*Figure 16.2: Occupying the Ambush Site with No Wasted Motion*
(Sources: FM 22-100 (1983), p. 66; FM 7-70 (1986), p. 4-20; MCI 03.66a (1986), p. 2-8; FM 7-11B1/2 (1978), pp. 2-II-A-5.2, 2-III-E-8.2; FM 5-103 (1985), p. 4-6; FM 7-11B3 (1976), p. 2-VII-C-4.4)

## Techniques from the NCO Corps

*(Sources: FM 5-103 (1985), p. 5-2; FM 21-75 (1967), p. 67)*

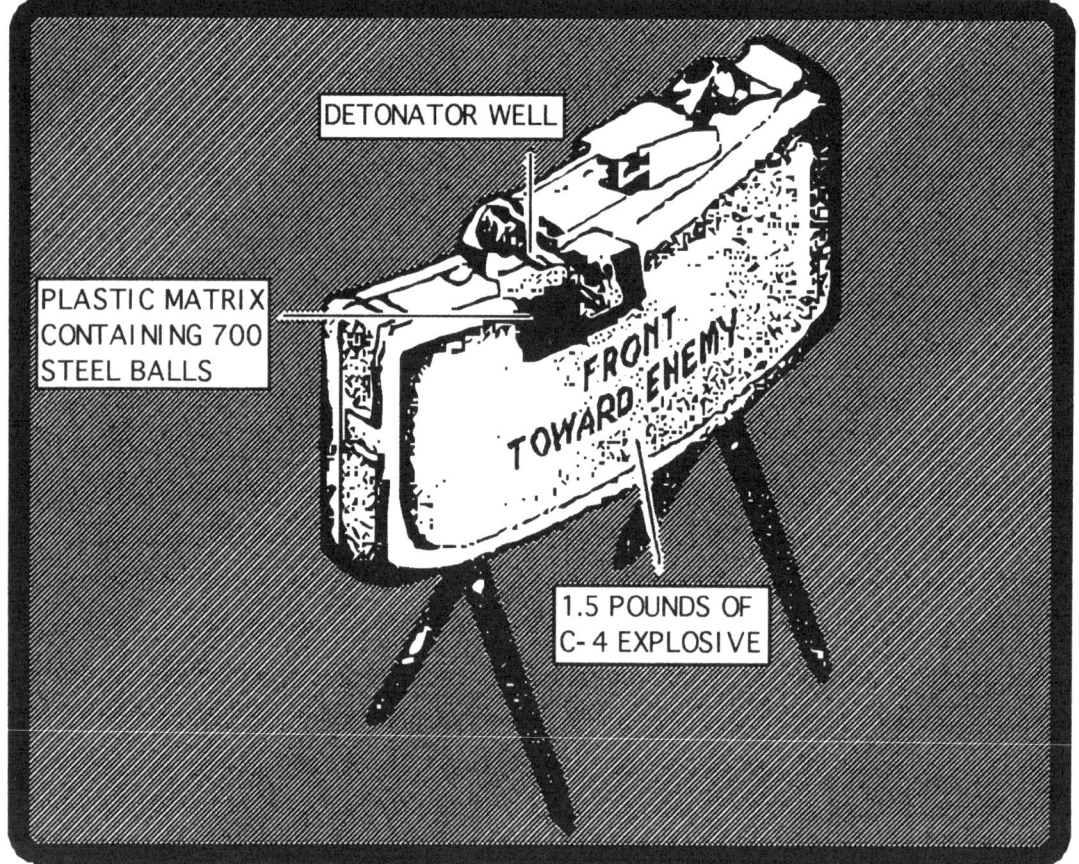

*(Source: FM 7-11B1/2 (1978), p. 2-IV-B-1.2)*

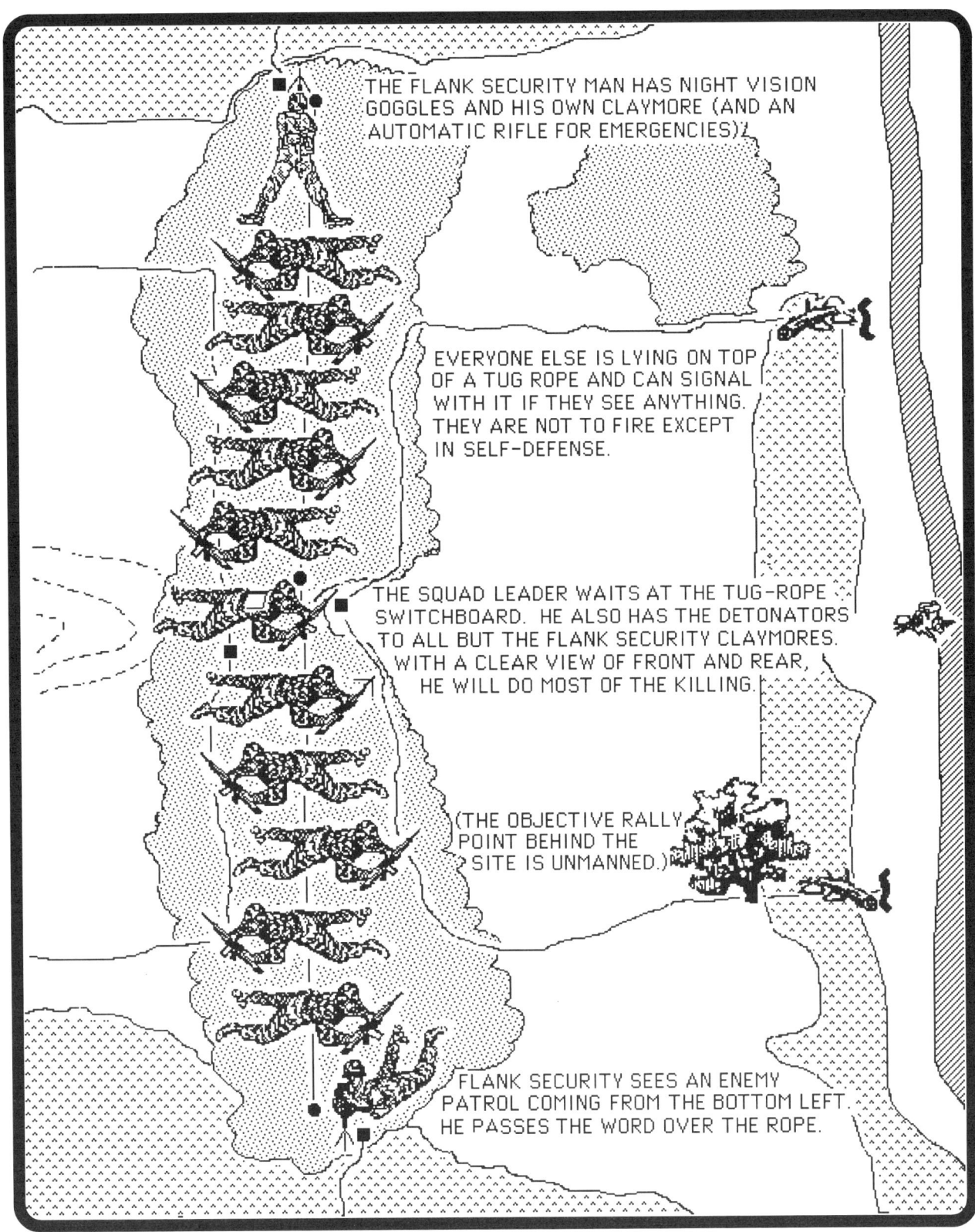

*Figure 16.3: The Ambush that Can Handle Any Force from Any Direction*
(Sources: FM 22-100 (1983), p. 66; FM 7-70 (1986), p. 4-20; MCI 03.66a (1986), p. 2-8; FM 7-11B1/2 (1978), pp. 2-II-A-5.2, 2-III-E-8.2)

Techniques from the NCO Corps

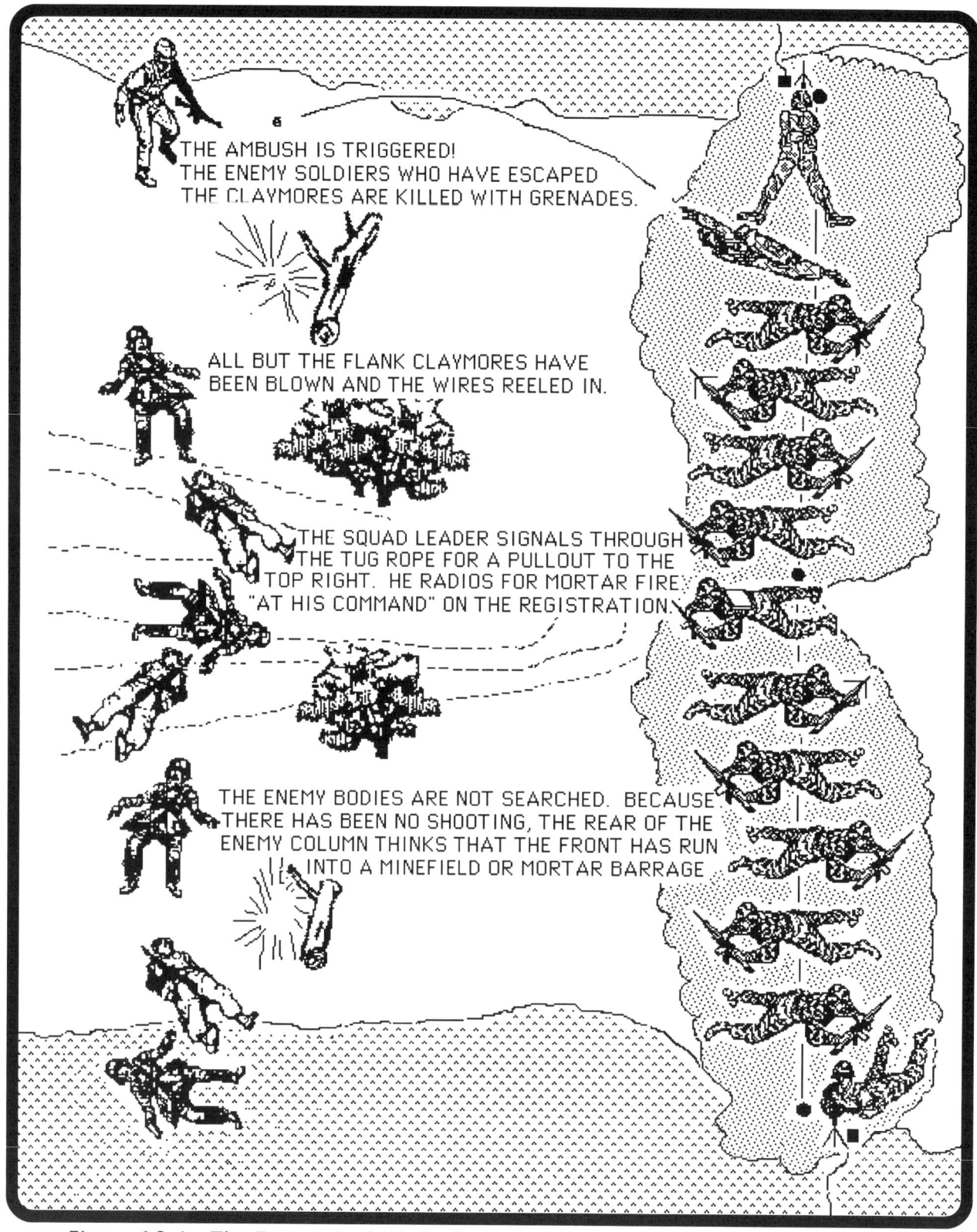

Figure 16.4: The Enemy Can't Tell What Happened, and the Ambushers Get Away
(Sources: FM 22-100 (1983), pp. 66, 84; FM 7-70 (1986), p. 4-20; MCI 03.66a (1986), p. 2-8; FM 7-11B1/2 (1978), pp. 2-II-A-5.2, 2-III-E-8.2; FM 23-30 (1988), p. 2-8)

The Ultimate Ambush

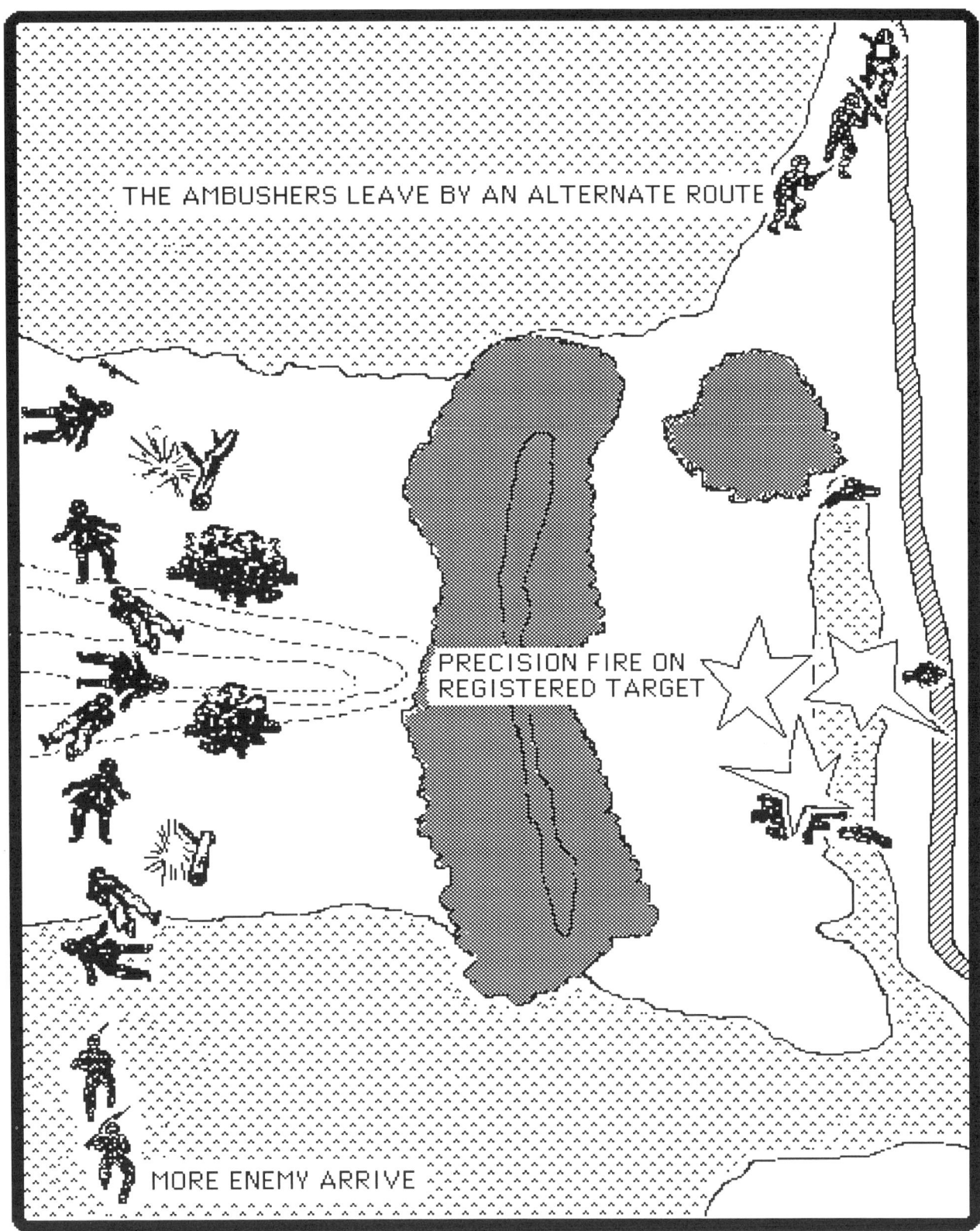

Figure 16.4: The Enemy Can't Tell What Happened, and the Ambushers Get Away
(Continued)
(Sources: FM 22-100 (1983), pp. 66, 84; FM 7-70 (1986), p. 4-20; MCI 03.66a (1986), p. 2-8; FM 7-11B1/2 (1978), pp. 2-II-A-5.2, 2-III-E-8.2; FM 23-30 (1988), p. 2-8; FM 5-103 (1985), p. 4-6)

## HOW TO TRAIN FOR THIS TECHNIQUE

What has been presented here is technique. It is only one way, among many, of getting the job done. While a technique must remain flexible, learning a technique requires attention to detail. There has been considerable detail presented in this chapter. Much of it does not exist in the manuals. It exists only in the collective experience of the NCO Corps.

To absorb this much detail without smothering individual initiative, a unit must practice the technique in a number of different situations. Only then, will the steps that must remain flexible become readily apparent. A detailed order and five-minute group discussion in the name of rehearsal cannot accomplish as much. Ideally, the "ultimate ambush" must be acted out to the last tug on the rope under expected conditions of terrain and visibility. It cannot be helped that so doing may insult the intelligence of some of the participants. Thorough rehearsal insures that everyone understands his job and how to function as part of the team. However, all must be continually reminded that everything (with the possible exception of the signals) can be changed to fit the situation. They must comply only with the spirit of what has been practiced and then inform the squad leader of necessary modifications when possible. A technique permits several people to function as a team, without squelching their personal initiative.

# 17 — When Prepared Enemy Positions Are Encountered

- *Why is it a bad idea to attack "hastily" a prepared enemy position?*
- *How could one's nearness to that position serve another purpose?*
- *What information about the position could come in handy later?*

(Sources: FM 5-103 (1985), p. 4-4; FM 7-11B/C/CM (1979), cover)

### HASTILY ATTACKING A PREPARED DEFENSIVE POSITION CAN BE COSTLY

A prepared defensive position is one that the enemy has improved with fighting holes, barbed wire, and claymores. Conducting a "hasty" attack against it is not only dangerous, but often futile. The enemy has had too long to study the ground, to position automatic weapons, to clear fields of fire, and to construct barriers. In the terminology of maneuver warfare, this is a "strongpoint" to be bypassed, if possible. A strongpoint can't be bowled over with size or momentum. This is the lesson of WWI.

There are only two ways to defeat a prepared position without getting hurt: (1) obliterate it with tons of explosives, or (2) *surprise* it. Revetments strong enough to absorb all but direct hits from heavy ordnance can preclude the first alternative. The second option requires time and planning. In other words, surprising a prepared defender takes a "deliberate" attack. When the members of a contact patrol encounter a *well-dug-in* adversary, they must not be tempted to "fire and move" against him:

> British doctrine in the 1920's taught the infantry to form squares against cavalry attacks, and until recently, Marine Corps doctrine included second-generation fire-and-movement tactics.[1]
> — MCI 7401

> Modern tactics are third-generation tactics.[2]
> — MCI 7401

In practice, the attack by "fire and movement" often failed miserably....

The fact is that open-order tactics of "fire and movement" were sometimes appropriate in mobile warfare, if the defender was caught unprepared and could not coordinate fire effectively.... However, in World War I, trench warfare on the Western Front proved that linear frontal attacks against prepared defenses did not work.[3]
— MCI 7401

A unit of any size takes a calculated risk when it "hastily" attacks after what appears to be an enemy ambush or chance contact. If the friendly unit subsequently finds its opponent to be dug in, it must resist the temptation to press home its attack. A dug-in adversary is at best part of a defensive position, and at worst part of a maneuver warfare "fire sack." Late one afternoon in early 1967, while moving west along the trail between Gio Linh and Con Thien, D Company, 1st Battalion, 4th Marines, suddenly encountered a large volume of enemy fire at the Three Gateways to Hell mentioned in chapters 3 and 10. Thinking themselves involved in an ambush or chance contact, the Marines quickly sent one platoon to the right. Though well led by 1st Lt. Jack Cox, the hasty flanking attack made little progress. When the beloved lieutenant was killed, his men had the sense to pull back, and his company commander had the sense to let them. After supporting arms and reinforcements were called in, two Marine companies assaulted to discover some communications wire and a double line of unimproved (and abandoned) fighting holes extending north from the trail. An NVA company or undersized battalion had probably stopped to rest while moving south along the well-hidden infiltration route that crossed the trail at that point.[4] Common sense had saved the Marines from overworking established procedure. This should serve as a warning to others. Hastily attacking a dug-in enemy is often futile.

If an elusive quarry stops to dig in, hunter beware. Eagerness to close with a skittish defender must give way to patient resolve. The attacker's pride can be restored later — while moving against the strongpoint (or, better yet, a soft target behind it) after proper preparation. The patrol that discovers a strongpoint must consider it both obstacle and potential deliberate-attack objective. From a distance, the patrol must spot a way secretly to circumnavigate or approach it. During this century, only the armies with an Oriental thought process have exercised enough respect for prepared defensive positions. They have attacked their enemy's defensive positions "deliberately," and have *lured* their enemy into attacking their own defensive positions "hastily":

> He who is well prepared and lies in wait for an enemy who is not well prepared will be victorious.[5]
> — Sun Tzu

## RECONNOITERING A PREPARED POSITION

Patrol members must learn to spot a prepared enemy position before that position can hurt them. They must also learn to reconnoiter such a position carefully. At stake is not only their safety, but also the safety of those who may have to attack the strongpoint deliberately. Indeed, the patrol members must avoid any action that would jeopardize their parent-unit's future options. Before doing any reconnaissance, they must establish the most promising schemes of maneuver for a deliberate attack. They cannot afford to be seen in the best avenues of approach to the objective. During the day, they must reconnoiter *from a distance only* with binoculars. Ideally, they should find an observation point that is *detached* from the draws and vegetation that form the main avenues of approach. In other words, one could not launch a daylight attack from there without being seen. Such a place would be ideal for a "base of fire." It would not normally be guarded by a sentry post. Additionally, the observation point *shouldn't* be on line with any promising night or infiltration attack route. There is a good reason for all of this deception. If the enemy spots those making the reconnaissance, he will be deceived as to the intended direction of attack.

If the deliberate attack can wait until nightfall or the next day, a few patrol members can move closer to the objective *after sundown*. If they can get by the enemy listening post, they can reconnoiter the daylight envelopment route right up to the probable FCL. If they can find enough watershed erosion or heavy vegetation, they can scout the night attack crawlways right up to the last piece of cover before reaching the barbed wire. Thermal imaging can't pick them up under these conditions. If the defenders don't have thermal imaging, trained sappers can reconnoiter the objective *from the inside*. Oriental "scouts" have been doing this to U.S. positions since 1941.

## GOALS OF THE RECONNAISSANCE

The reconnaissance party should look for enemy strengths that can be bypassed or neutralized, and enemy weaknesses that can be exploited. Typical strengths will be the following: thermal imaging, night vision goggles, sentry posts, barbed wire, claymores, machinegun bunkers, cleared fields of fire, level ground covered by grazing fire, etc. Weaknesses may be harder to spot. Sometimes, they will be nothing more than the absence of strengths — e.g., partially cleared fields of fire or a gate in the barbed wire. Or, they can be more subtle, like places where dampness discourages defender occupancy, where holes are positioned behind the military crest, where adjoining holes do not have an unobstructed view of the microterrain between them, where enemy soldiers have been observed sleeping on watch, etc. It takes special skills to spot these strengths and weaknesses through binoculars.

## DAYTIME BINOCULAR RECONNAISSANCE

At binocular range, even matching what appears in the distance to what shows on a map can be difficult. In fairly level and lightly forested terrain, the task can be particularly mind boggling. The problem is with depth perception. In other words, everything looks about the same distance away. Sometimes one can use the known size of a small object (like a man or fence post) to establish the dimensions of a larger object nearby (like a house or tree line), and thereby avail himself of the WERM-rule range estimation technique discussed in chapter 13.

Even with good depth perception, one can have difficulty studying the microterrain near an objective through binoculars. Unfortunately, ground that is fully cleared of vegetation but not pockmarked or eroded will *not* support a deliberate attack. For this reason, the observer should first study the contour lines on the map, and then take an educated guess at the watershed pattern for the objective. Shallow depressions are wetter than the ground around them, and for this reason support different varieties and sizes of vegetation. Through binoculars, subtle variations in the foliage may be the only clue to where this low ground lies. Cypresses and some deciduous trees prefer moist ground, whereas pines prefer well-drained ground. Furthermore, bushes are often thicker where there is more moisture. For example, a string of low bushes in a grassy field often delineates a shallow runoff ditch. Of course,

(Source: FM 7-8 (1984), pp. B-7, B-8)

(Source: FM 7-8 (1984), p. G-2)

other types of terrain require different observational techniques. They must be learned by trial and error for each locale. Infantry training must include "seeing exercises" in various types of terrain. Until infantrymen are specially trained to observe, they should carry cameras on patrol. On Guadalcanal, the legendary Col. Edson attempted to quantify the problem:

> There must be training in difficult observation, which is needed for the offense. It is my observation that only 5% of the men can really see while observing.[6]
>
> — Col. Merritt A. Edson
> (after Guadalcanal)

### TO DETERMINE HOW BEST TO ATTACK, WHAT ELEMENTS OF INFORMATION WILL THE PARENT UNIT NEED?

What the patrol sees, or fails to see, can impact greatly upon the plan of attack. Hasty impressions can lead to preconceived notions, and preconceived notions to inappropriate schemes of maneuver.

If the parent unit must attack the enemy position before dark, it will generally have more success with a "flanking attack" than with a "frontal attack." At least, the flanking attack aims at a gap. Most objectives will have a tree line or draw through which one can approach them closely from one side. Additionally, there will be microterrain and low foliage at the end of that tree line or draw. Ground contours, water-runoff ditches, and partially cleared fields of fire can hide prone infantrymen. Daylight attackers willing to do a little crawling can sometimes get quite close to their objective before having to mount their final assault.

The frontal attack is usually reserved for "cross-compartment" work — i.e., where elevated terrain near an objective permits the base of fire to shoot *over the top of* the maneuver element. For this type of attack to succeed, there should be abundant cover (like trees or rocks) in the low ground between this base-of-fire hill and the objective. The cover gives the members of the maneuver element the opportunity to fire and move, if necessary.

If the parent unit can wait until dark, it can launch a night attack from any one of several directions; a major envelopment route is not required. It can come across what appears from a distance to be relatively level and barren ground. Only required are some shellholes or erosion, and a couple of big trees or rocks near the enemy wire. Defensive sectors devoid of sentry posts, machineguns, and thermal imaging make the best points of attack.

Only with specially trained personnel, will a line infantry unit have the option of penetrating enemy barbed wire by stealth. But, if the objective is *not* protected by barbed wire, the average unit can attack by short-range infiltration to capitalize on more subtle defensive weaknesses (like the improper positioning of fighting holes relative to the military crest or spacing of holes relative to the microterrain). It takes close-in reconnaissance to discover every infiltration lane with promise.

### WITH SPECIALIZED TECHNIQUES, SMALL UNITS CAN SOMETIMES RUN DELIBERATE ATTACKS QUICKLY

During the Spring Offensive of 1918, German line infantry squads quickly launched attacks against successive Allied trench lines. Because, for each squad, every attack after the first was conducted without reconnaissance or rehearsal, some might conclude that they were hasty attacks. Actually, they were deliberate attacks made possible by unique circumstances. The German squads didn't need to reconnoiter, because they had detailed maps that had been made when their forces occupied the same ground earlier in the war. They didn't need to rehearse, because they had practiced a technique that the stormtroopers had thoroughly tested in combat.

With the techniques about to be presented, U.S. infantry squads could also conduct deliberate attacks in quick succession. After all, the Marines tackled mutually supporting machinegun bunkers in the Pacific. The key to successfully attacking an enemy position of any size is the relevance of one's technique to existing circumstances. Without highly specialized training, units should not attempt to attack prepared enemy positions until they have thoroughly reconnoitered the positions and heavily rehearsed their plans of attack.

# 18 The Daylight Attack Is the Hardest

- *Why is the day attack the most dangerous of the deliberate attacks?*
- *Is there any way to conduct one without getting hurt?*
- *What size of unit has the best chance?*

(Source: FM 7-8 (1984), pp. 3-14, 3-15)

### CONTRARY TO POPULAR OPINION, THE DAYLIGHT ATTACK IS THE RISKIEST OF THE DELIBERATE-ATTACK OPTIONS

It can be very dangerous to attack a prepared enemy position during the day. What a single daylight assault cost the British at the Somme during WWI boggles the imagination — over 60,000 casualties. Yet, to fully appreciate what that single assault cost, one must consider what it accomplished. By day's end, the British had occupied only one fourth of the *first* German defense line:

After an immense but useless bombardment, at 7:30 A.M. on July 1, 1916, the British Army went over the top and attacked the German trenches.[1]

The British Army's casualties on 1 July were the equivalent of seventy-five battalions or of more than six full divisions of fighting infantry.[2]

After centuries of refinement, the British Army of early 1916 probably considered itself tactically proficient. The parallels with U.S. infantry forces of today are sobering:

Infantry had not been able to walk across No Man's Land and take possession of the enemy ground; they had been overloaded and provided sitting targets. The NCO's of the new army had been inexperienced and knew little more than their private soldiers. And NCO's are the backbone of infantry. Out-of-date tactical formations had been used.... No attempts at concealment, surprise, initiative, or flexibility were called for; and with very few exceptions were not made.

Nothing had been left to the discretion of local commanders. Instructions were rigid, and were often adhered to even when obviously futile.[3]

When friendly troops attack during the day, they can better see what they are doing. Unfortunately, the defenders can also better see what those troops are doing. And, because the individual defender can remain stationary and hidden while the individual attacker can't, the defender has the edge not only in observing the battlefield, but also in avoiding harm. If an attacking unit brings all of its weaponry to bear against an objective, will doing so change all of this? Sometimes it will, and sometimes it won't. The massive fires directed against the defenders of Iwo Jima didn't stop them from taking a terrible toll. In Italy, the German defenses around the monastery at Monte Casino remained strong after being plastered by 600 tons of oversized bombs. Short of total obliteration, the only way to safely attack a prepared enemy position is through *surprise*. Of course, surprise is also more difficult to achieve in the daytime.

Defenders often appear more vulnerable to firepower than they actually are. Several factors contribute to the illusion. Occasionally, a military force with advanced weaponry can score a lopsided victory in war. When this happens, many conclude that more firepower is the solution to every problem. For example, in the Gulf War, strategy and the operational art were the deciding factors. Saddam Hussein had plenty of sophisticated weaponry of his own. Still, history will only record that the Allies had a technological advantage. Advanced weapon systems seem to enjoy a disproportionate amount of media attention in wartime, possibly because they are more visible and easily understood than strategy, campaigning, or tactics. Unfortunately, media interest only adds fuel to the ongoing barrage of advertising claims from the arms manufacturers. It's not difficult to see how a Western society could come to the mistaken conclusion that an advantage in weapons technology will always be the deciding factor in war. It wasn't in Southeast Asia twenty-five years ago, and it may not be again.

A weapon can have great visual effect during a controlled training evolution. Against an ancient armored hulk in the open, it can seem very proficient. Those watching could easily overestimate its effect on a hardened or moving target. Many weapons work well against exposed targets, but a defender is seldom exposed. If anything, daylight attacks have become more dangerous as the world's ordnance has improved. At the small-unit level, all nations share about the same sophistication in weapons technology. One tries not think about U.S. daylight attackers closing with an objective protected by the enemy equivalent of a MK-19 rapid-fire grenade launcher.

(Sources: MCOP1550.14D (1983), p. 1-2; FM 22-100 (1973), Studies-4)

How hard would it really be to stop a unit challenging one's defensive position in the daytime? Would a heavy volume of incoming small-arms fire preclude one from detecting and then hurting his attacker? When that attacker started shooting from close range in the assault, must a dug-in defender expose any vital organ to produce effective fire from a machinegun on a tripod with a Traversing and Elevation (T&E) mechanism, from an assault rifle held high overhead, from grenades, from claymores, from preregistered mortars? Or, does the sound and volume of that incoming fire merely help the defender to establish the exact time and direction of the final assault?

Sometimes special circumstances dictate that additional real estate must be taken during the daytime, but the cost of doing so must never be underestimated during the planning process. To minimize this cost, the attacker must somehow prevent his adversary from realizing, until the last moment, that a ground attack is underway.

## WHEN, IF EVER, IS A DAYLIGHT ATTACK APPROPRIATE?

Attacking units should try to bypass enemy strongpoints. When they cannot do so, they have the following options in *descending* order of relative risk: daylight attack, night attack, and short-range infiltration (or sapper) attack. In the daytime, the sapper attack should not be automatically ruled out. If the defenders have not adequately cleared fields of fire (as in the jungle), short-range infiltrators can get within grenade range of them.

Although more dangerous, conventional daylight attacks are sometimes necessary to achieve momentum. The relatively higher number of lives saved by keeping the enemy off balance, may sometimes justify the number of lives lost by attacking in the daytime. After all, like other complicated endeavors, war involves tradeoffs. It takes careful coordination to assault mutually supporting machinegun pits like the ones on Iwo Jima or in any defense in depth. It takes illumination to achieve this much coordination. On Iwo Jima, the defenders were well hidden in rock outcroppings. At night, the U.S. flares swinging from their parachutes in the ocean breeze probably created moving shadows. Perhaps, the flares couldn't throw off enough light for the Marines to properly consolidate a night attack objective.

Normally, the daylight attack should be attempted only when an objective can't be bypassed, and there is insufficient time for another type of attack. This most dangerous of attack options should be used only to seize a *gap* through which other forces can exploit softer targets. Because a daylight "envelopment" involves some deception, this maneuver is less costly than a "frontal" attack.

## WHAT THE DEFENDER HAS WAITING

Almost as detrimental as underestimating one's opponent, is overestimating him. Some will argue that attacking frontally across open ground is safer than attacking up a covered envelopment route. They assume that the envelopment route will be mined. Few opponents have the time or wherewithal to mine the length and breadth of the main avenue of approach to their position. In combat, the rifleman's first priority is getting away from the next piece of flying metal. He has a better chance of doing so, when he is in a ditch or behind a tree. If the defender has sufficient mines to fill every envelopment route as a hedge against "flanking attack," he also has enough mines to encircle his position as a hedge against "frontal attack." The envelopment route may contain one or two booby traps, but in the daytime the attacker should use it anyway. His overall casualty count will be lower.

The only mine that ordinarily guards the avenue of approach to an objective is a claymore just inside the defender's barbed wire. The defender does not plan to remain stationary, and does not need the aggravation of dismantling a mine field every time he moves. He relies on other means to guard this covered approach to his position. In the order that an attacker might encounter them, the defender has the following: a mortar preregistration, a Sentry Post (SP), barbed wire, a claymore, and a bunkered machinegun. By staying inside the woods or gully comprising the envelopment route, the attacker has a better chance of closing with his well-prepared adversary without being detected. In the open, not only will the attacker be spotted sooner, but he will come under fire from the very same weapons without the benefit of cover.

## COUNTERING THESE DEFENSIVE MEASURES

Massed preparatory fires cannot guarantee that all automatic weapons on an objective will be neutralized. The fires can only guarantee that the weapon operators will be awake for the attack. To overcome what the defender has waiting, the attacker must maintain the element of *surprise* until only a few feet away from the fighting holes of his foe. If the defender doesn't realize the attacker is there, he can't hurt him. It's not impossible to surprise someone during the day, just more difficult. The daylight attacker can achieve surprise through stealth, deception, and speed. When he gets too close to his quarry to rely on stealth, he must revert to deception and speed. He must create background noise to mask his sounds, and coincidental smoke or a diversion to veil his image.

To use stealth, the attacker must stay hidden and quiet. To do so initially, he must use a covered envelopment route. At the objective, he must utilize depressions in the microterrain. Where a deer can go, so can he:

> Since I have routinely observed this field at all hours of the day and night and have never seen a deer coming or going, I was curious as to how they did it.... On the south side of the field there was a small draw, no more than 12 inches deep, that originated at the edge of the field and meandered out towards the middle. It was bordered by somewhat thicker weeds than average and a few sagebrush plants, but not enough to be noticeable unless you knew what you were looking for. I found that the bottom of this little draw was well trampled by the deer.[4]
> —Maj. R.L. Dearth USMC

The real challenge during the day is staying hidden while breaching the enemy's barbed wire and crossing the open ground to his holes. One way is to screen with smoke. But the smoke must not look like a screening ploy, or it will only serve to announce the attack. The foe must be led to believe that the smoke exists for some other reason.

To stay quiet, the attacker must refrain from any noise. That means no *direct or indirect fire*. Here's how an attack without preparatory fires worked on Iwo Jima:

> Colonel Graham's 26th Regiment moved out at daybreak without artillery support, not as a tactic to surprise the enemy, but because Marine howitzers were short of shells from the previous day's bombardment. But the Japanese were caught off guard by the absence of pre-jump-off shelling, and the advance quickly made nearly two hundred yards, overrunning a defensive complex on a hill that had held up the previous day's advance.[5]

Firing must be limited to that which permits maneuver. No attacking unit can pinpoint every dug-in and camouflaged defender before its assault. With its firepower, it can't kill or suppress every enemy soldier. If just one surviving defender with an automatic weapon spots the maneuver force, he can stop the assault single-handedly.

Sometimes, the maneuver element cannot reach the end of the envelopment route silently. In heavy jungle, it may have to slosh up a streambed. In any type of terrain, it may bump into an enemy SP. SP's must be neutralized before they can alert their parent unit. Seldom can this be done both quickly and quietly. Until crossbows or silencers become standard issue, grenades or small arms may be required. Their sounds must be immediately *masked* so the parent unit won't hear them, or at least will be deceived as to their point of origin. Explosions in the envelopment route can be drowned out with artillery or mortar fire at another location. Unavoidable shots in the envelopment route can be covered over with firing from the Base of Fire (BOF). The masking noise should create a false alarm as in Oriental tradition:

> If my force is five times that of the enemy, I alarm him to the front, surprise him to the rear, create an uproar in the East and strike in the West.[6]
> — Chang Yu
> Sun Tzu Scholar

In the daytime, it takes a bangalore torpedo to breach an enemy's barbed wire without his knowledge. There is only one way to cover this much noise, and that is with artillery rounds on the objective. Of course, smoke will be needed to screen those emplacing the bangalore and subsequently passing through the hole in the barbed wire. When *just outside* an enemy position, an attacker has ways of creating screening smoke without divulging its purpose. He can start a grass fire (grass burns white), or he can call for an artillery barrage beyond danger-close range and then walk the smoke rounds up to his location. The defenders will think that their position is only one target out of many in a widespread artillery attack, and that the artillery spotter is so far away that he needs smoke to adjust. They will never suspect that the spotter is walking smoke rounds almost on top of himself. This type of deception was proposed by Sun Tzu long ago:

> When capable he feigns incapacity; when near he makes it appear that he is far away; when far away, that he is near.[7]

In summary, indirect fire can be used to mask the noise of moving up a swampy or bushy envelopment route, removing an SP with grenades, or bangaloring barbed wire. Artillery is used for many reasons on the battlefield other than softening up an objective for an impending ground attack. For this reason, without alerting the enemy, artillery can be used to mask the sounds of a daylight attack. If there is shooting in the envelopment route, the BOF must open up automatically to mask that sound. But it does so as a *deception,* not to suppress fire from the objective. For this reason, shooting at a target *other than* the objective should be seriously considered. This would further divert the defender's attention.

## THE VARIOUS IMPEDIMENTS TO MANEUVER MUST BE OVERCOME METHODICALLY AS THEY ARE ENCOUNTERED

The "deliberate attacker" must have steps in his technique for countering each of the enemy's principal threats. He must also have the leeway to perform these steps *selectively*. He wants to implement those for threats that materialize, and skip those for threats that don't. If he can remain silent while moving up the envelopment route, does not encounter an SP, and does not run into barbed wire, he has achieved total surprise and won't want to employ his artillery or small-arms BOF at all. He must deal only with what impedes his progress; but, as threats do materialize, he must overcome them *methodically*. That means one at a time, for as long as it takes, before going on to the next threat. His time schedule must be flexible. Speed must give way temporarily to thoroughness.

Methodically handling the threats encountered may resemble "systematic" or "attrition" warfare, but there is a fine distinction here. Its importance may have been lost in the rewriting of the lessons learned from past wars. With partially trained troops, all deliberate attacks must necessarily be combinations of attrition and maneuver warfare. The attacking unit requires maneuver tactics to get close enough to assault, and attrition tactics to concentrate enough force during the assault to win. Perhaps, traditional techniques should be streamlined to provide more stealth, deception, and speed. Maybe, those who must execute traditional techniques should be given more leeway (in the form of authority selectively to skip steps). For example, if additional cover and concealment were found at the end of an envelopment route, those in the maneuver force might welcome the chance to move the Final Coordination Line (FCL) forward. Crawling a little closer to the objective might give them a better chance of mounting a successful assault. After all, it is difficult (even with smoke) to cross more than 50 yards of open ground to the enemy's wire, and then another 30 yards to his holes. Additionally, the machinegunners in the BOF might appreciate the chance to leapfrog forward while the attack is in progress. This would divert the enemy's attention from the point of attack, and shorten the distance the guns must displace to fend off a counterattack. Finally, the opportunity to switch roles between maneuver and support elements in midattack might be enough to salvage an otherwise doomed effort.

## THE FIRE SUPPORT PLAN

If one's ground assault is to look like an artillery barrage, the firing and impact signatures from one's weapons and pyrotechnics must look like artillery explosions. "Smoking the wire" has to look like a spotting round from a distant observer. Knocking out the machinegun bunker with a SMAW has to resemble a lucky artillery hit. Blowing the wire with a bangalore has to look like an artillery round that landed long. Concentrated small-arms fire is *not* consistent with this deception. The BOF should only open up to mask the sound of unavoidable shooting in the envelopment route, and those in the final assault should limit their shots to "double taps" at well-defined human silhouettes.

It's almost impossible, from a distance, to preregister an objective accurately enough to pull off this illusion. However, the attacking-unit leader could do it easily from the FCL! Plus, the maneuver element would stand a better chance making it that far undetected, if the preregistration were postponed until then. Unless an SP has to be grenaded or barbed wire bangaloreed, there may be no reason for indirect fire at all. It should *not* be preregistered ahead of time. However, to save clearance time, it should be "preplanned"—*not* on the objective itself, but on a target beyond danger-close range of the objective. Then, as needed, it can be called for and adjusted while the attack is in progress. This will enhance both safety and deception. The enemy must not know until the last moment that someone is interested in his position. If the artillery can be preplanned on top of an adjacent enemy strongpoint or suspected SP, so much the better.

If the leader of the maneuver force sends the battery an "at-my-command" method of control as part of a "suppression mission" call for fire just before crossing the Line of Departure (LD), he can summon artillery or mortar support within one minute. If his men have to use explosives during some phase of the attack, he must only whisper "fire" over his radio to get a volley of HE rounds on the preplanned target. He can then walk single smoke rounds onto the objective to screen the assault. All the while, the defenders will be watching the fireworks with their backs to the impending ground attack. The maneuver force leader has only to move the rounds to a point where the smoke will *drift over* the part of the barbed wire he wishes to breach. The first smoke round will screen the personnel emplacing the bangalore, and the second smoke round will screen the assault. Then, when the second round is heard coming in, the SMAW man can destroy the machinegun bunker, and the bangalore man blow his torpedo. The defenders will think that the explosions are from High Explosive (HE) artillery shells, and that the inordinate amount of smoke is from a *single* prolific spotting round. Then, the target location can be *shifted* slightly, continuous precision HE fire requested, and rounds from the M203 grenade launchers used to keep up the deception at the point of attack.

Shifting the artillery is the job of the maneuver force leader. As long as his radio is working, he is in the best position to move the rounds to where they can do the most good. Of course, he must also be careful to give a valid direction and to say "add" instead of "drop" while shifting this fire. He must move the shells far enough forward to protect his men, but not so far that the defenders at the point of attack will want to take a peek at their wire. How far is that? "Delay fuzes" can shorten the distance. Only upon seeing the alternate signal to shift fires, should the senior man with the BOF try to shift the artillery. A good alternate signal for shifting fires is an M203 white-smoke round in another avenue of approach to the objective.

Once the indirect fire has shifted, the attacker must create the impression that the barrage is ongoing at the point of attack. At first, this can be accomplished from a distance with his M203 grenade launchers. The enemy will not hear their distinctive discharge sound over the noise of the artillery. Then, concussion grenades (homemade if necessary) must be thrown by the lead elements of the assault force. On one occasion, the NVA used satchel charges for this purpose.[8] The defenders should be too busy taking cover, from what they believe to be artillery and mortar shells, to notice the ground assault.

The white artillery smoke drifting over the wire can be augmented with M203 white-smoke-canopy rounds fired at the ground and High Concentration (HC) white-smoke grenades dropped by those first through the wire.

While the SMAW's should go on the assault, the machineguns should stay with the BOF. They are the hedge against trouble from an unexpected direction, and their operators must stay where they can overwatch the entire battlefield. They are too vital to risk on the assault.

## THE ROLE OF THE INDIVIDUAL WEAPONS

How the individual weapons are employed is central to the technique. Fragmentation hand grenades are too dangerous to throw as part of the initial deception; they should only be dropped from close range into enemy holes. However, their *intact* spoon-and-blasting-cap assemblies could, as a last resort, be *carefully* transferred into small blocks of C-4 or TNT to form concussion grenades. Some of the personnel first through the breach could toss these concussion grenades as part of the deception. Others could drop HC-smoke grenades as part of the screening. Small-arms fire must be reserved for confirmed targets only. Automatic riflemen should not shoot at all. Their role is one of contingency—to suppress enemy automatic-weapons fire if the assault is discovered prematurely. At that point, everyone has to "fire and move" anyway. But until then, even the riflemen must carefully ration their shots. They must only use double taps against visible opponents. While *running* in the assault, they must put one round near their target, and then "walk" the second round onto the enemy soldier's torso. This is not impossible to do. If there's enough surprise to justify a running standup assault, there should not be that many enemy soldiers visible. Every time a member of the assault line acquires a human silhouette, he can stop momentarily to "snap" shoot, and then catch up with the others. Perfect alignment is counterproductive during any assault because of the chance of enemy fire from the flank.

The North Vietnamese may have known of another way to fire a rifle on the run. The literature contains a photograph of an NVA assault on an Allied position in Vietnam.9 It was taken by a combat photographer at the left rear of the assault formation. It shows a ragged line of enemy infantrymen *running* closely behind what appears to be a rolling mortar barrage. Only a few are carrying their weapons at the ready! This may mean that the Allied defenders aren't yet aware of the ground assault, and that the NVA attackers are in no hurry to tell them — by shooting their weapons. One North Vietnamese soldier is holding his AK-47 out in front of him in a modified "eye-muzzle-target" mode where the rifle butt is *not* touching his shoulder. Perhaps, by so doing, he can maintain a steady firing platform while running. A famous Marine also chose to limit his small-arms fire while assaulting into a friendly artillery barrage:

> The final double-winner of the Medal of Honor [out of five enlisted Marines in World War I] was John Joseph Kelly, another member of the 6th Marines....
> As he and his unit charged the ridge [at Mont Blanc], a machinegun nest halted the Marines. Kelly charged into the barrage of artillery explosions with a .45 caliber pistol in one hand, and a grenade in the other.10

Why not just assault into what *appears to be* a friendly artillery barrage? The daylight attack method just described is safe enough to practice with live ammunition.

## THE ALL-IMPORTANT PREPARATION PHASE

Although not required by the BAMCIS preparation sequence, some reconnoitering of the objective usefully precedes arriving at an initial plan of attack. Erroneous preconceived notions can prove disastrous. During the day, a tactical solution must closely match its problem.

While an accurate perception of the problem can only be acquired through *reconnaissance,* a shared understanding of the mission can only be achieved through *rehearsal.* Thus, reconnaissance and rehearsal are the most important aspects of the preparation for an attack (short of the plan itself). For the team to function effectively during the operation, everyone must act out their roles ahead of time and under every conceivable circumstance. It cannot be helped that rehearsing every detail may insult someone's intelligence. As was the case for Marines in the Gulf War, rehearsal constitutes hard work. At the same time, everyone must be constantly reminded that what is being rehearsed can and will be modified in combat — to fit unforeseen circumstances.

The operations order is certainly important, but too much emphasis on order writing can produce so much detail that it even handcuffs those who understand it. In the classroom, "five-paragraph-order" writing helps infantrymen to memorize the factors affecting tactical decisions. But in the field, it's hard to issue even a short five-paragraph order. Terrain models that don't look exactly like the ground to be crossed mean little to an order recipient. Listing too many grid coordinates during an orientation talk can cause the entire first paragraph of the order to go unheard. The issuer of the order does not have perfect communication skills; and recipients of the order do not have perfect listening or note-taking skills. Because human beings may have an attention span of not much more than 10 minutes, five-paragraph orders are seldom used in protracted combat.

A "mission order" is easier to issue and understand. It contains only a brief situation and some general guidance on what to do. The leader can't normally foresee every aspect of a combat situation anyway. Only as the attack unfolds, will many of the situational details become apparent. If the leader issues his instructions in too much detail, his subordinates may opt for doing as told over properly reacting to the ever changing threat. The enemy is not going to cooperate. So, why devise a plan that takes over 10 minutes to present?

It takes many of the same skills to present a good mission order. Still vital are terrain models and brief orientation talks. On a good terrain model, terrain features are closely replicated in shape, color, and location (pine cone streams don't get it). However, relief should be exaggerated. During the orientation, the leader should only identify one or two control features on the terrain model by their grid coordinates. The whole idea is to get the order recipient off his map and onto a larger-scale facsimile of the battlefield. The issuer of the order must be enthusiastic and concise. He must maintain eye contact to sense who doesn't understand. He must enunciate his words. The listener can't copy down every word without missing the most important parts of the order. He should be encouraged to selectively ignore what doesn't apply to him or those who will be operating near him.

Without a rehearsal, the unit leader cannot assess how much of his operations order has been understood. After a mission order, many of the important details have yet to be worked out. A sketchy mission does not absolve the subordinate-unit leaders of their responsibility to develop enough detail to execute their portion of that mission. Much of this detail may already exist in their portfolio of practiced techniques, but the rest must be developed from scratch. Prior to the rehearsal, subordinate-unit leaders must be given time to pass the "word" to their men and to establish which additional techniques must be worked out. Attention to detail will still be vital to success. Problems occur when leaders not fully aware of their subordinates' training deficiencies, attempt to dictate detail. Then, what is directed, and what will work under the circumstances, don't match. The plan of attack is no longer feasible, and the subordinates may not be given enough leeway to make the necessary adjustments.

## ACTIONS EN ROUTE TO THE LINE OF DEPARTURE

At the assembly area, the unit leader requests advance clearance on (preplans) an artillery target *behind* his objective. He monitors the status of that request and records only the *approved* target designator. Then, just before reaching the LD, he insures that his artillery support will be available at a moment's notice. He uses the call-for-fire net to request a suppression mission on that preplanned target at his command.

Prior to crossing the LD, one last "radio check" with subordinates can pay big dividends. If anyone does not answer up immediately, he should be told to attach his radio handset to his helmet.

## ACTIONS AT THE LINE OF DEPARTURE

The maneuver element should pause at the LD to permit its leader to accompany the BOF element leader into position. There's no need to hurry yet, and the extra time can be well spent. By rehashing visible terrain, FCL location, and how far to shift fires on signal, the two leaders can resolve disparities in perception. They should also review the rules for opening small-arms fire and the procedures for shifting supporting-arms fire (if the alternate signal to do so becomes necessary).

The attack begins when the maneuver force departs the LD for the envelopment route. This force should be mentally prepared to shift speed as the situation dictates.

## WHAT TO DO EN ROUTE TO THE FINAL COORDINATION LINE

What happens from the LD forward cannot normally be based on time hacks. It depends on what the defender has waiting and how quickly each threat can be overcome:

> Your operations cannot be based on a clock. They must be based on the enemy. The enemy will never comply with your time schedule.[11]

WWI German stormtroopers could attack the Allied trench lines at night on a time hack, only because they had certain advantages that most daylight attackers don't have. They had precise large-scale maps of their objectives (having occupied the same ground earlier in the war), and they had customized firing tables for each artillery piece.[12] When the German artillery ceased at the scheduled time, the stormtroopers had just to bangalore the wire and jump into the Allied trench. To attack during the day on a time hack, one would have to preregister screening smoke days ahead of time and then secretly cut the enemy's barbed wire the night before. In Vietnam, the NVA were good at making severed wire look whole again.

If possible, the attacking unit should move between the LD and FCL before dawn. Doing so should allow the unit to bypass the enemy SP and reconnoiter the objective from close range.

During this phase of the attack, a *properly* selected/trained lead fire team can make all the difference. This fire team must be capable of either eluding, or quickly and silently neutralizing, an enemy SP. Only point men with quick-kill skills (or special weapons) can do this. If they can't remove the SP silently, they must do so with grenades only. On reaching the enemy wire, the lead fire team must have sapper and obstacle breaching expertise.

The attackers move slowly and stealthily up the envelopment route, until they encounter trouble. Then, time becomes a factor, and they must close with their objective quickly. Still, they cannot fall victim to their adrenaline rush, because upon reaching the FCL, they must again *slow down* to eliminate *deliberately* the various threats arrayed against them. As the lead fire team reaches the last covered position before the objective, the attacking column will grind to a halt. Its momentum will be jeopardized, unless the follow-on fire teams move quickly, quietly, and by the most direct route to their assigned places on line at the FCL. A column formation will eventually be needed to negotiate the breach in the wire, but this formation is too dangerous to maintain outside enemy lines in broad daylight. One well-placed burst of automatic-weapons fire could take out the whole unit. Deploying on line will give the SMAW man a clear backblast area and every M203 man a clear shot. If the objective is on an incline, daylight attackers in column cannot climb the slope fast enough to assault in unison. The accordion effect produces a slow or piecemeal assault.

If there's an insurmountable problem en route to the FCL, the focus of main effort can be shifted from maneuver element to BOF. In other words, the two can switch roles.

## THE ASSAULT TECHNIQUE

Whether or not the attack will succeed depends on what happens next. It's during the final assault that the unit is most vulnerable. During the day, dug-in defenders can defeat, or inflict heavy losses on, those who dare to openly challenge their position. The final assault must be accomplished without their knowledge. This takes covertly circumventing their final defensive measures: watchstanders, 80 yards of open ground, machinegun, barbed wire, and claymore. Because these threats are distinct, they must be handled sequentially with what will be called the "daylight assault sequence." At the FCL, the maneuver force must execute the sequence methodically, much as a football team would execute a play at the line of scrimmage. However, this sequence only *resembles* attrition warfare. Depending on the circumstances, its steps can be done concurrently, in a slightly different order, or not at all. (See table 18.1 and figures 18.1 through 18.6.)

WHEN THE FCL IS REACHED, THOSE IN THE LEAD FIRE TEAM BEGIN PLANNING HOW TO BREACH OBSTACLES PROTECTING THE OBJECTIVE.

AS SOON AS FCL ARRIVAL IS ANNOUNCED, OTHER FIRE TEAMS SPLIT OFF FROM THE MAIN COLUMN (IN OPPOSITE DIRECTIONS) TO GET ON LINE.

(THE UNIT LEADER MOVES THE FCL FORWARD IF POSSIBLE, AND THE FIRE TEAMS ALL CRAWL FORWARD TO THE NEW FCL.)

UNIT LEADER WHISPERS "FIRE" OVER ARTILLERY NET AND ADJUSTS WITH WHITE SMOKE UNTIL SOME DRIFTS OVER WIRE TO BE BREACHED.

TWO-MAN BREACH TEAM (IN LEAD FIRE TEAM) EMPLACES BANGALORE.

THE UNIT LEADER ASKS FOR ONE MORE SMOKE ROUND.

WHEN THE SMOKE ROUND IS HEARD COMING IN, THE SMAW MAN TAKES OUT THE ENEMY MACHINEGUN BUNKER.

THE BREACH TEAM BLOWS THE BANGALORE TO SIGNAL THE ASSAULT.

THE UNIT LEADER CONCURRENTLY SHIFTS THE ARTILLERY AND ASKS FOR "PRECISION, CONTINUOUS FIRE WITH DELAY FUZING."

(IF, AT THIS TIME, THE BOF IS SHOOTING AT THE OBJECTIVE, THE UNIT LEADER ALSO SHIFTS ITS FIRE TO A PREARRANGED LOCATION.)

AS THE ARTILLERY SHIFTS, THOSE WITH M203 GRENADE LAUNCHERS LOB "HE" ROUNDS AT THE ENEMY HOLES TO BE ASSAULTED, AND WHITE-SMOKE-CANOPY ROUNDS AT BARBED-WIRE BREACH TO BE SCREENED.

THE ATTACKERS DASH THROUGH THE BREACH IN SUCCESSIVE FIRE TEAM COLUMNS.

SOME THROW CONCUSSION GRENADES AT THE ENEMY HOLES AND OTHERS DROP "HC" WHITE SMOKE TO ENHANCE BREACH SCREENING.

FIRE TEAMS VEER OFF IN DIFFERENT DIRECTIONS TO EXECUTE THE "SPEED ASSAULT" TECHNIQUE (TO BE DESCRIBED LATER).

LEAD MAN IN EACH FIRE TEAM LOOKS FOR AND CLIPS CLAYMORE WIRES.

FIRE TEAMS ASSAULT UPRIGHT, RUNNING, ROUGHLY ON LINE (GUIDING ON UNIT LEADER IN CENTER), AND WITH MINIMAL SMALL-ARMS FIRE.

(WHEN WELL-DIRECTED AUTOMATIC-WEAPONS FIRE IS ENCOUNTERED INSIDE THE WIRE, FIRE TEAMS SHIFT TO PRONE "FIRE AND MOVEMENT.")

*Table 18.1: The Daylight Assault Sequence*

*The Daylight Attack Is the Hardest*

(Source: FM 7-8 (1984), p. 3-51)

Techniques from the NCO Corps

(Sources: FMFM 6-4 (1978), p. 356; FM 90-3 (1977), p. 4-70)

(Sources: MCO P1500.44B, pp. 12-74, 14-33; FM 90-10-1 (1982), p. 1-5)

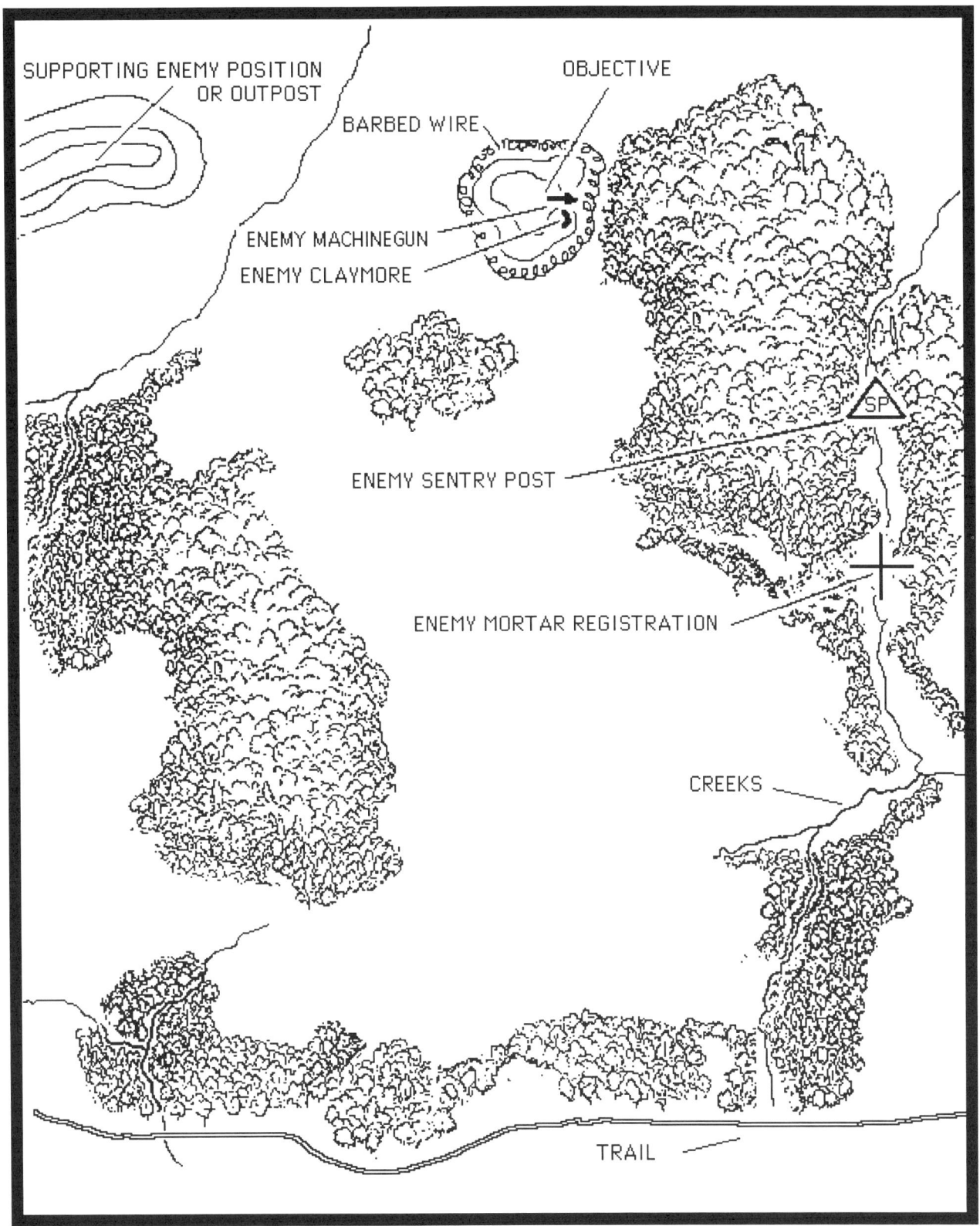

*Figure 18.1: The Situation Often Encountered during a Daylight Attack*
(Source: "Maps" by John Morris, from RICHMOND REDEEMED by Richard Sommers. Copyright © 1981 by Richard J. Sommers. Used by permission. See Notes.)

Techniques from the NCO Corps

*Figure 18.2: Preregistering the Objective is <u>Not</u> Part of the Plan of Attack*
(Source: "Maps" by John Morris, from RICHMOND REDEEMED by Richard Sommers. Copyright © 1981 by Richard J. Sommers. Used by permission. See Notes.)

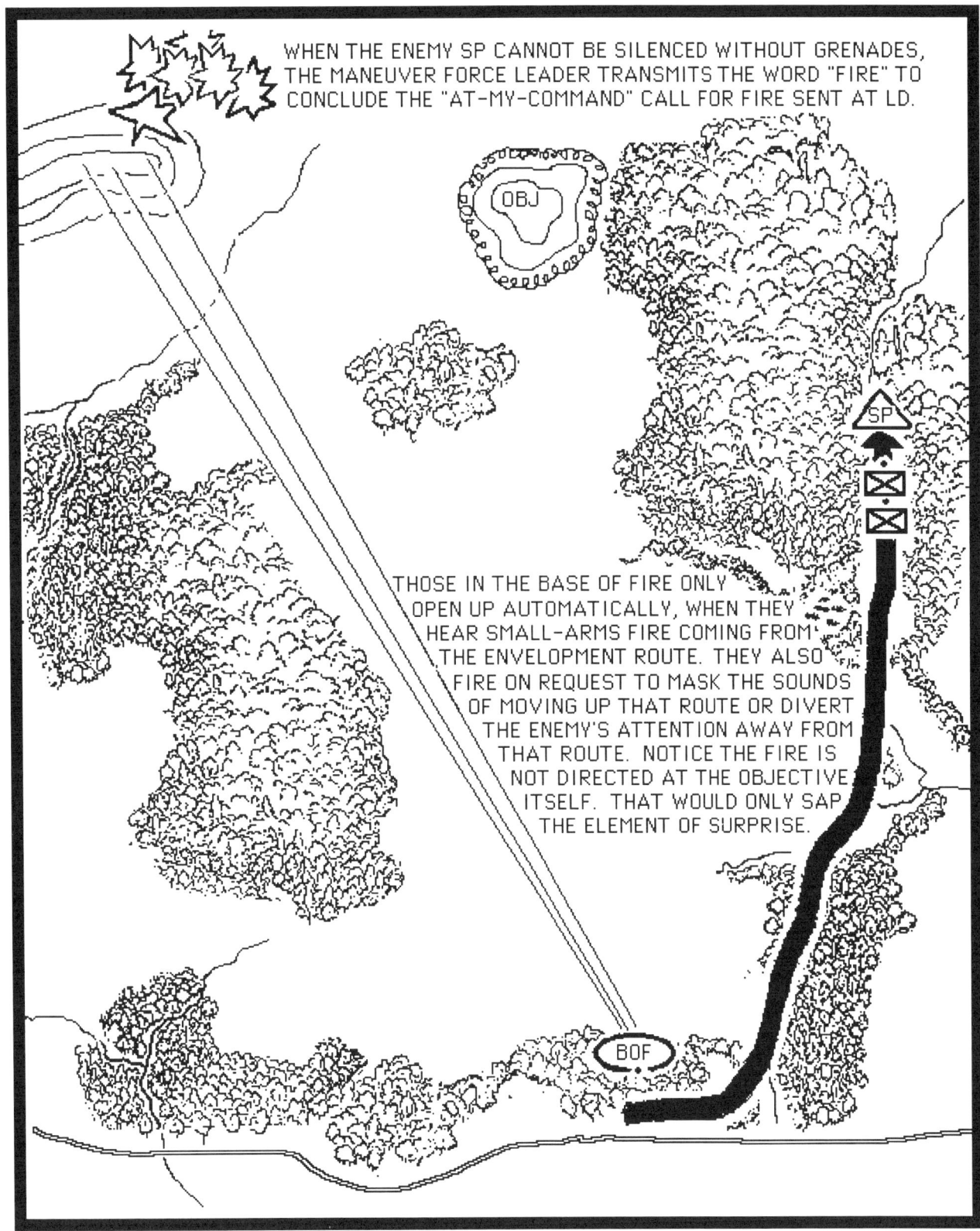

Figure 18.3: *Use the Artillery and Base of Fire Only to Mask Envelopment Noise*
(Source: "Maps" by John Morris, from RICHMOND REDEEMED by Richard Sommers. Copyright © 1981 by Richard J. Sommers. Used by permission. See Notes.)

Techniques from the NCO Corps

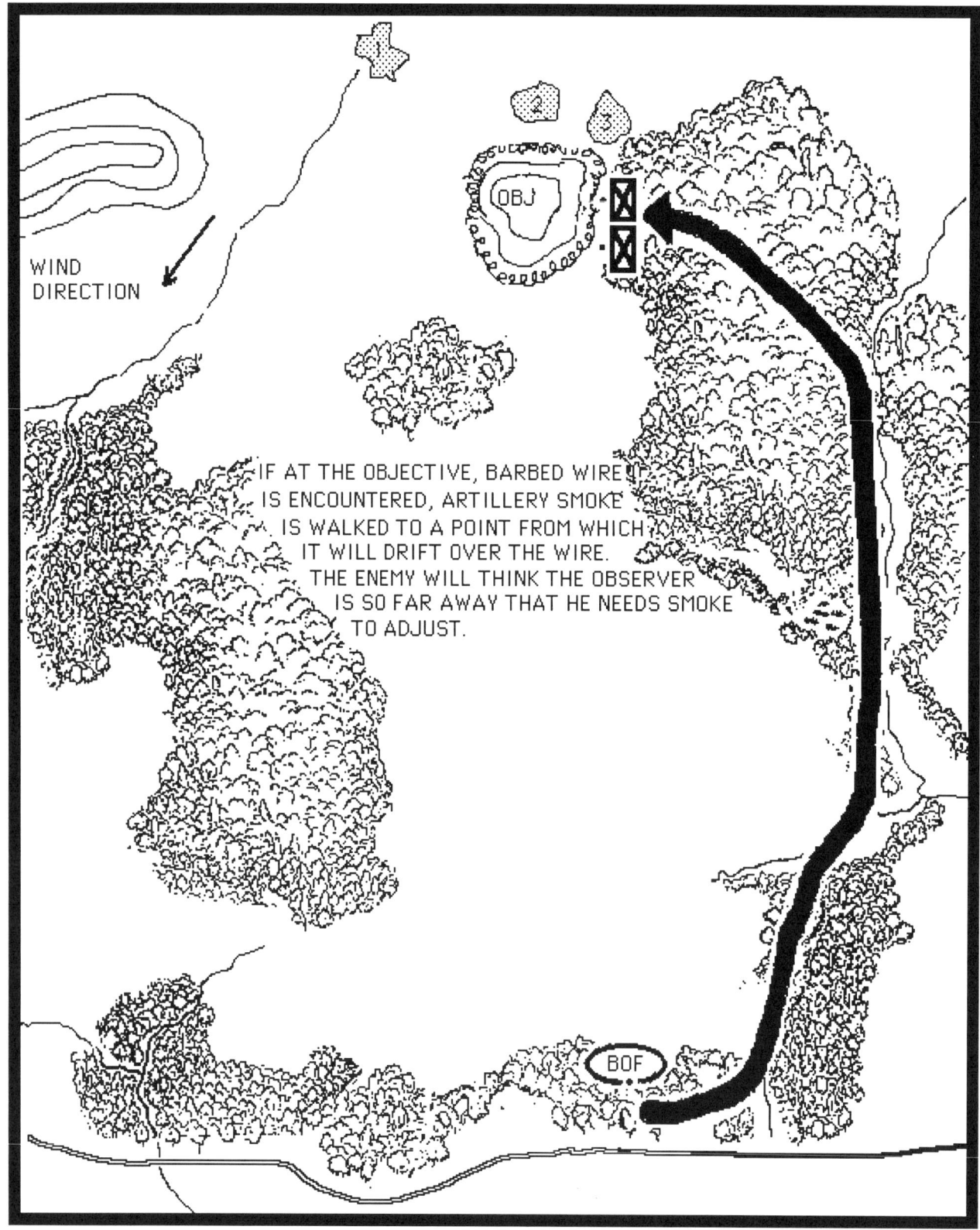

*Figure 18.4: When Facing Barbed Wire, Creep Smoke near the Intended Breach*
(Source: "Maps" by John Morris, from RICHMOND REDEEMED by Richard Sommers. Copyright © 1981 by Richard J. Sommers. Used by permission. See Notes.)

(Source: FM 7-11B1/2 (1978), p. 2-II-A-5.2)

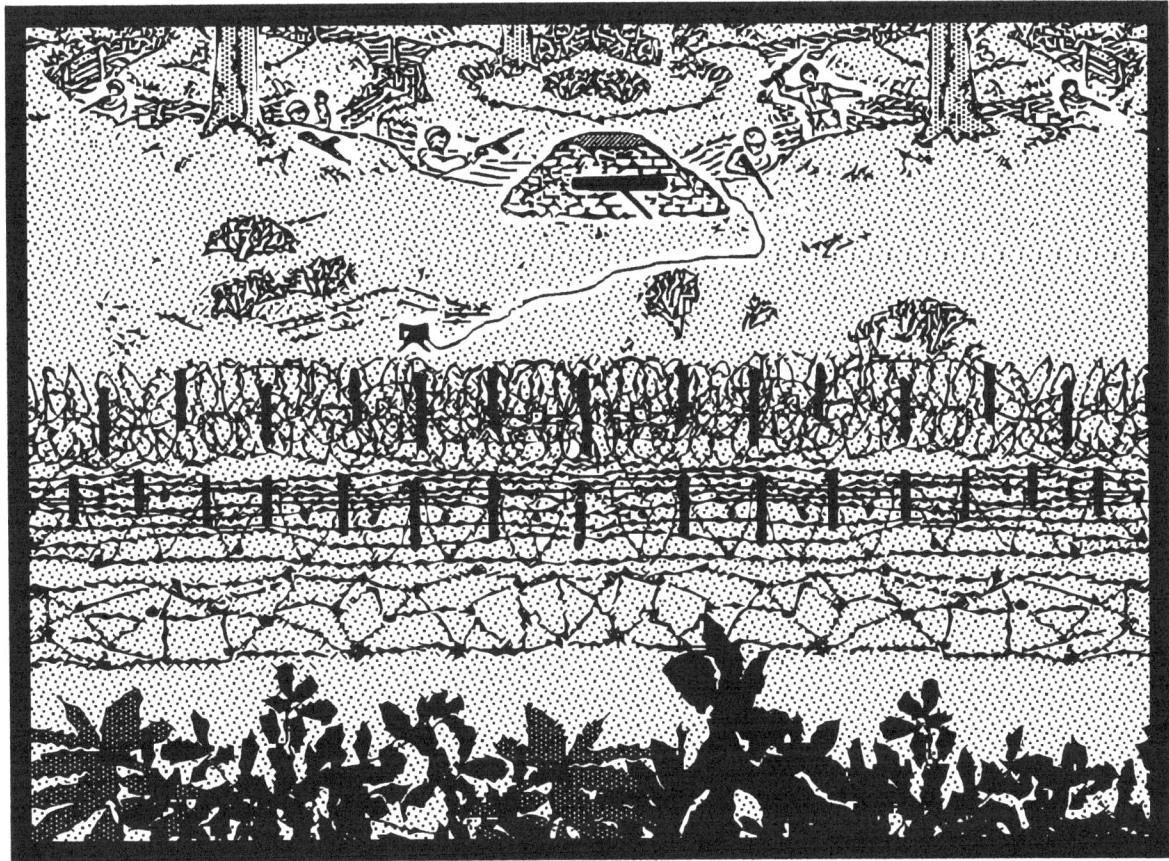

Figure 18.5: The Situation at the End of the Envelopment Route
(Sources: FM 7-8 (1984), p. 3-28; MCO P1500.44B, p. 14-18)

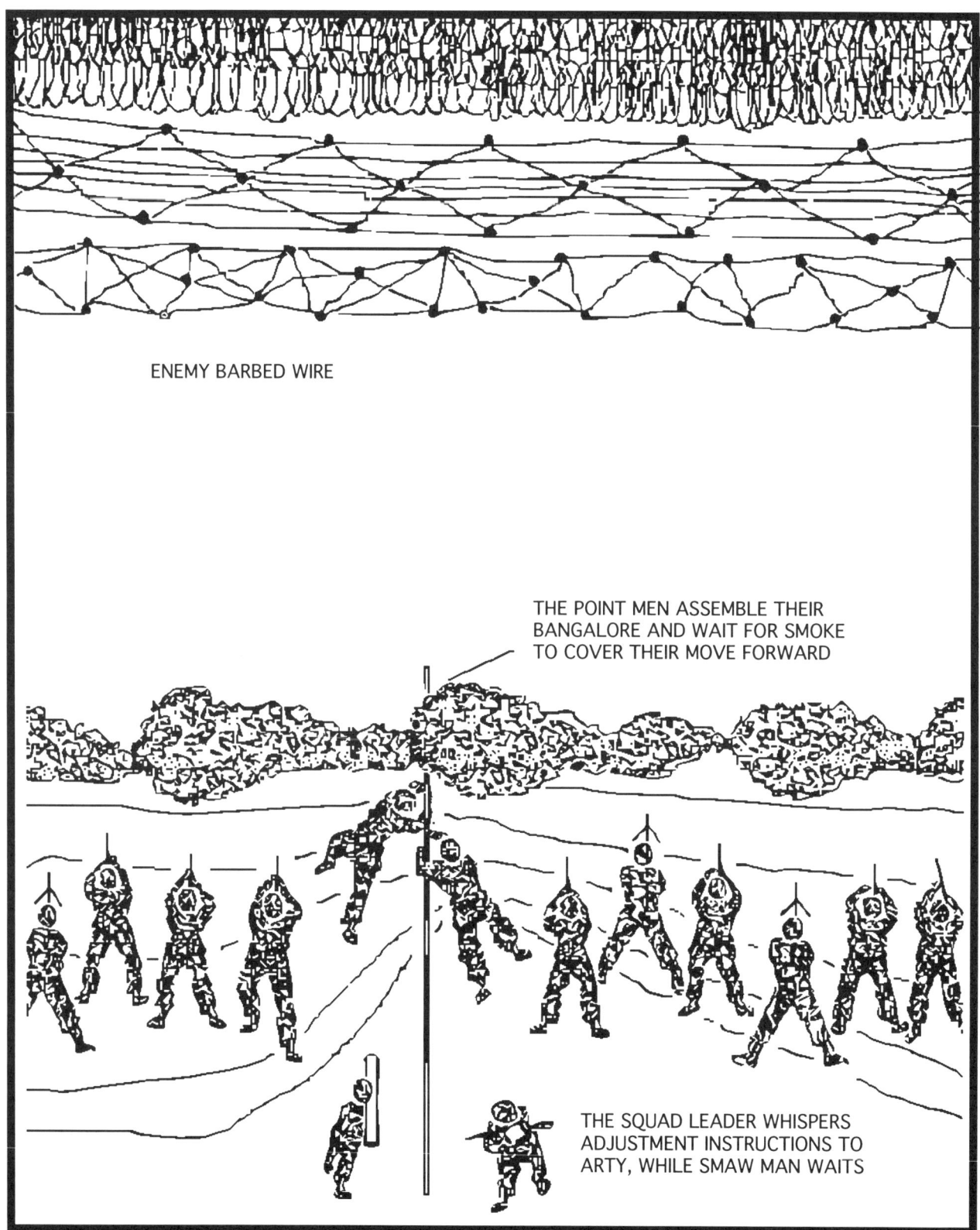

Figure 18.5: The Situation at the End of the Envelopment Route (Continued)
(Sources: FM 5-103 (1985), p. 4-6; TC 90-1 (1986), cover; FM 7-11B1/2, p. 2-III-E-8.2; FM 7-11B3 (1976), p. 2-VII-C-4.4)

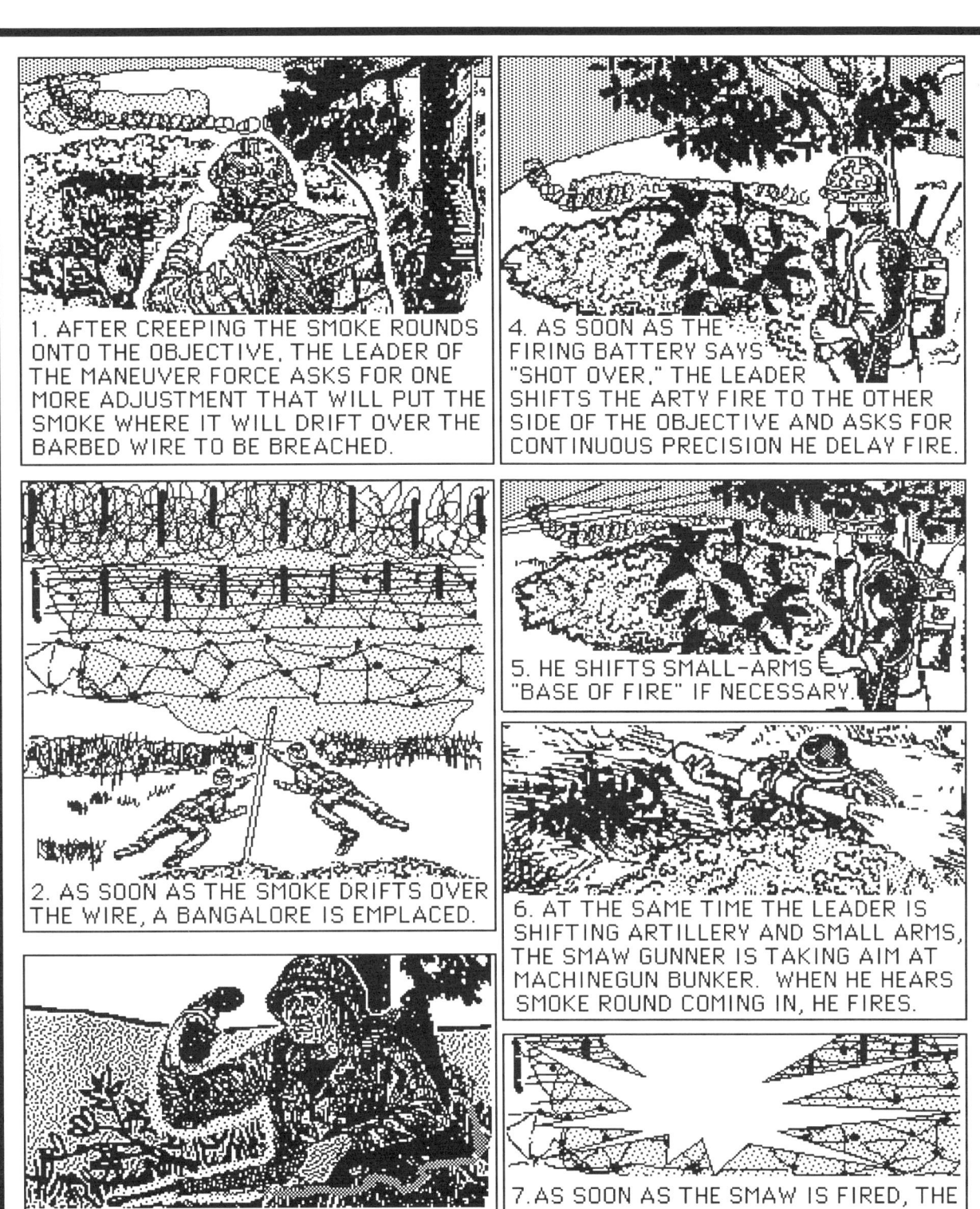

*Figure 18.6: The Daytime Assault Sequence*
(Sources: FM 22-100 (1983), pp. 22, 30; FM 24-1 (1976), p. 3-9; FM 5-103 (1985), p. 4-7; FM 7-11B3 (1976), p. 2-VII-C-4.4)

Techniques from the NCO Corps

*Figure 18.6: The Daytime Assault Sequence (Continued)*
(Sources: FM 23-30 (1988), p. 4-6; TC 90-1 (1986), cover; FM 5-103 (1985), pp. 4-4, 4-6)

## IF WHAT CAN GO WRONG, DOES GO WRONG

If it can go wrong in combat, it will. For starters, when the maneuver force leader decides to shift the BOF and artillery, he will invariably find a dead radio. To win consistently in war, one must consider worst-case scenarios without sacrificing his optimism. He must find ways to hedge against mistakes, without curtailing initiative. He must take the surprise out of misfortune, without losing the flexibility to handle the unexpected. Not all problems can be foreseen. Worrying too much about them breeds the micromanagement that precludes their solution. To overcome adversity, one must have a system of checks and balances, and alternate plans and signals. These should be developed and shared, as the unit rehearses for contingency situations.

Instead of issuing a complicated order, the leader should simply plan to station himself near any subordinate who has a pivotal role in the attack — e.g., near the man who will detonate the bangalore torpedo and thereby signal the assault. That way, misunderstandings can't jeopardize the mission. Even team efforts require some supervision.

## THE "SPEED ASSAULT" TECHNIQUE

While under the shadow of enemy guns, attackers must execute with precision their final movement forward. Without being detected, they must cross 50 yards of open ground to the enemy's wire, and then another 30 yards to his fighting holes. The drifting smoke will only partially obscure them. They must also rely on speed and silence. They must cover that dangerous 80 yards before the defenders can peek from their holes. If the assault is to succeed, the attackers can't wait for everyone to get on line after moving through the breach, or sacrifice speed to achieve better alignment and sight pictures, or fire and move when there is no reason. While surprise is intact, any hesitation on the part of an attacking unit gives the defending unit more time to react. It jeopardizes the power advantage needed to carry the position. One must remember what happened at Antietam to the jerky, loud, well-aligned, and piecemeal assaults of the numerically superior Union forces. Inside the enemy wire, the attacking force must rush the enemy holes at top speed, roughly on line, and with as little noise (shooting and shouting) as possible. General Thomas "Stonewall" Jackson advised "reserving your fire . . . until you get them (the enemy) to close quarters." Clausewitz also talked about speed in the assault:

> On no account should we overlook the moral effect of a rapid, running assault. It hardens the advancing soldier against danger, while the stationary soldier loses his presence of mind.[13]
> — Clausewitz

Squad members must change formations twice during the last hundred yards. From their line formation at the FCL, they must temporarily form a column to get through the narrow breach in the wire, and then re-form a ragged line to assault. Because they must make these changes in formation quickly, they need a technique. There's a way they can quickly funnel through the breach and then, without slowing down, fan out enough to keep from shooting each other. It's not new; something like it was tried successfully late in the Civil War to crack the Confederate lines around Richmond:

> A brigade commander in Wright's VI Corps, Upton had been preaching a new theory of attack — a hammer blow by a concentrated striking force advancing on a much narrower front than usual. Once this force had shattered a small segment of the enemy's line, a second wave of attackers would pour through the gap and strike the beleaguered Confederates in flank and rear.[14]

> The first line was to cross the Confederate earthworks and then split up, the 5th Maine swinging left, the 121st New York and the 96th Pennsylvania turning right to capture a Confederate battery. The second line would dash through the gap and head for Ewell's backup trenches. The third and fourth lines were to go into action wherever more Federal pressure was needed. If the plan was successful, Upton's novel assault would produce a narrow but deep fissure in the Confederate defenses. If the hole could be widened, Lee's entire front might collapse.[15]

> As more and more Federals got into the trenches, the Georgia troops broke and ran for the second line, which also gave way. The gap, meanwhile, was being widened by more waves of Upton's attackers. The plan had worked so far.[16]

Some of the world's best armies have already adopted (at the small-unit level) this tactic of fanning out after moving through the breach in an adversary's defensive barrier. The Chinese used it at the Chosin Reservoir in Korea. One Marine watched through the night vision scope on his tank while several Chinese assaults were initiated. He reported that the Chinese would quietly clip the barbed wire, slip through the breach two abreast, and then fan out to assault without ever stopping to align.[17]

To minimize the amount of time spent transiting the enemy's barbed wire, each squad in the attack force must make its own breach. The only way to get through a breach quickly is in column. Still, just a few men at a time must constitute this column, and then only for a few yards. Otherwise, there's too much risk from a single burst of automatic-weapons fire. With a little practice, the squad members can run to the breach by the most direct route from their positions on line at the FCL, form a column just long enough to get through the rows of barbed wire, and then immediately disperse again. As each fire team reaches the inner edge of the wire, it can veer off in a different direction or scatter. That way the enemy will only get a brief shot at *part* of the attacking force in column. If, once through the breach, the fire teams can somehow fan out and assault without ever stopping to align, they can again muster their full combat power quickly. This will be called the "speed assault" technique. With it in training, squads of U.S. Marines have been observed to cross the eighty yards between their FCL and enemy holes protected by barbed wire in *45 seconds.*[18] (See table 18.2 for the steps in the technique and figure 18.7 for a pictorial view of its execution.)

(Source: OPNAV P34-03 (1960), p. 406)

---

FIRST FIRE TEAM THROUGH THE BREACH TURNS HALF LEFT IN COLUMN.

SECOND FIRE TEAM THROUGH, TURNS HALF RIGHT IN COLUMN.

LAST FIRE TEAM THROUGH, FANS OUT IN THE MIDDLE.

SMAW GUNNER COMES THROUGH LAST AND STAYS BEHIND THE OTHERS.

CONCUSSION GRENADES ARE THROWN AND CLAYMORES DISARMED.

LEFT FIRE TEAM ECHELONS HALF RIGHT ON THE RUN.

RIGHT FIRE TEAM ECHELONS HALF LEFT ON THE RUN.

SIDE TEAMS PARTIALLY ALIGN WITH CENTER TEAM ON THE RUN.

(IF SURPRISE IS TOTAL, THE SQUAD CAN CONTINUE ACROSS OBJECTIVE.)

IF SURPRISE HAS BEEN COMPROMISED, THE SQUAD SHOULD STOP AT THE FIRST LINE OF ENEMY HOLES AND EXPLOIT SIDEWAYS.

---

*Table 18.2: The Speed Assault Technique*

*Figure 18.7: The Speed Assault Technique*
(Source: FM 5-103 (1985), p. 4-6)

Figure 18.7: The Speed Assault Technique (Continued)
(Sources: FM 5-103 (1985), p. 5-10; TC 90-1 (1986), cover)

## UNITS MUST ASSAULT AS QUIETLY AS POSSIBLE

During the "daylight assault sequence," the explosions — i.e., SMAW backblast, SMAW-round impact, and grenade bursts — all mesh with the artillery deception. The foe will have difficulty differentiating them from the explosions of artillery or mortar shells. The other sounds usually associated with a ground assault — i.e., yelling, whistle or bugle blowing, and small-arms shooting — must be minimized, because they will alert the enemy to what is really going on. While *any measure* of surprise is still intact, each infantryman must limit his shots to two per exposed enemy soldier.

Old habits are hard to break. Traditional ground assault noise has been known to scare rural militia. The enemy here is both well trained and courageous. The German infantrymen of WWI — the first Westerners to practice third-generation infantry tactics — had to break the bad habit of too much shooting. They learned that telltale noise in the assault did more harm than good:

> Sneaking up to an enemy position in the early morning darkness, without the emotional release of the traditional hurrah and with strict orders not to shoot until the French opened fire was not the way that these men had been taught to fight.[19]

The Germans had learned this lesson from the Japanese. The Japanese practiced what they preached when they took on the Russians in Manchuria in 1939:

> Tsuji, still hoping to capitalize on the little element of surprise still his, ordered 3rd Platoon to assault.... Soviet heavy and light machineguns opened up an ear-shattering volume of fire. But since the Japanese attackers continued up the hill in silence, most of the Soviet automatic-weapons fire sailed well over the crouching attackers' heads.[20]
> — Leavenworth Papers No. 2

Americans are trained not to give away their positions prematurely on defense. Why are some so eager to compromise their locations during an assault? Those who survived the first few weeks on Guadalcanal knew better:

> *We learned not to fire unless we had something to shoot at. Doing otherwise discloses your position and wastes ammunition* [italics from original].[21]
> — Corporal Fred Carter
> *Fighting on Guadalcanal*

There is only a slight chance of total surprise during a daylight attack, but whatever amount can be achieved must not be squandered. The attackers must keep to a minimum the number of defenders who realize that a ground assault is underway. If one enemy submachinegunner *to the side* of the point of attack hears the telltale sounds of a ground assault, he can single-handedly defeat that assault. If the attackers have too straight an assault line, he can knock them all down with one burst.

## WHAT THE ATTACKER FACES AFTER TAKING THE FIRST LINE OF ENEMY HOLES

The inside of a defensive perimeter or defense in depth is much tougher to capture than many infantrymen have been led to believe. Once an attacking unit has noisily taken the first line of holes at the point of attack, the unit becomes extremely vulnerable to fire from elsewhere. If it makes the mistake of trying to sweep on line across the entire breadth of a hilltop perimeter, it subjects itself to the massed firepower of every healthy defender along that perimeter. Furthermore, these defenders can all shoot uphill without any risk of hitting each other.

Unless the attackers can totally surprise the defenders in the first line of holes, they should not attempt an upright on-line sweep of the entire objective. There are safer ways to clear perimeters. Some don't require much light. Perhaps the safest is the trench warfare technique of setting up a base of fire at the point of penetration and then attacking sideways along the enemy's outer-perimeter holes. Although contrary to doctrine, working both ways at once gives each maneuver element the option of using the other's attack as a diversion. Of course, the two elements must coordinate as they approach each other on the far side of the perimeter.

To fire and move on line is a less controversial way for a unit to clear an objective, but good illumination is required. This would not be fire and movement in the normal sense. Because the ground would be swept by grazing fire, those wanting to move forward would probably have to crawl through depressions in the microterrain.

Of course, the initial standup assault can continue on across the objective as long as there is no firing of small arms. That's why the stormtroopers used only grenades and bayonets after jumping into an Allied trench. The same ploy would work against a string of enemy holes.

Once the objective has been crossed by whatever means, the attack is not over. Then comes pursuing the enemy by fire, displacing the BOF to meet a possible counterattack, consolidating, reorganizing, and exploiting (preferably at night).

## THE LESS COMPLICATED VARIATION

A defender will react fairly predictably when he sees an opposition plane bearing down on him with a load of 500-pound bombs and napalm *for the second time.* He'll start searching for an unexplored recess in his fighting hole. His natural reaction creates a perfect opportunity for a low-risk ground assault similar to the one just described.

After the first bombing strike, the pilot is asked to sandwich another "wet" run between two "dry" runs (no bombs dropped). During the first dry run, a bangalore is emplaced. During the wet run, the bangalore is blown — opening a hole in the wire. Then, during the final dry run, a squad runs a "speed assault" against very little opposition. This ruse was used in Vietnam. (See figure 18.8.)

Figure 18.8: It's Much Simpler to Use an Airstrike as the Deception
(Sources: MCI 03.10M, p. 5-10; FM 90-10-1 (1982), pp. B-3, B-4; FM 5-103 (1985), p. 4-38; FM 22-100 (1983), p. 22)

# 19 Attack at Night to Save Lives

- *Why are night attacks less dangerous than day attacks?*
- *To what extent have U.S. forces employed them in the past?*
- *How could the U.S. version be fine tuned to make it more effective?*

(Source: FM 7-11B1/2 (1978), p. 2-II-B-1.2)

## A WELL-EXECUTED NIGHT ATTACK IS LESS RISKY THAN ITS DAYTIME COUNTERPART

A well-known general once described the night attack as "a way to compensate for inferior force." This was an unfortunate choice of words, because no one wants to be associated with "inferior" force. Perhaps that's why those with "superior" force see so little reason to attack after dark.

What the general meant, of course, was that a unit can successfully attack at night while at a relative disadvantage in personnel and weaponry. Few would disagree. If one is willing to accept this deduction, he must also accept what it infers. If it takes fewer people to succeed at night, *fewer people can be subjected to harm by attacking at night*. In other words, by limiting the number of people committed and operating at night, an attacking unit can take fewer casualties.

It's no secret why the night attack is less costly at the small-unit level. After dark, attacking infantrymen enjoy more concealment. If they can't be seen as easily, they can't be hurt as easily. Assaulting at night has long been recognized as a way to reduce casualties:

> Soviet regulations before the outbreak of war in 1939 recognized that "night operations will be common under modern warfare conditions to exploit surprise, reduce losses, and disorganize the enemy."[1]
> — Leavenworth Papers No. 6

Darkness is a friend to the skilled infantryman.[2]
— Liddell Hart [1944]

Night combat has frequently been the recourse of . . . the army seeking . . . to reduce casualties in the face of great firepower.[3]
— Leavenworth Papers No. 6

Night attacks are a normal part of operations and become increasingly important as enemy firepower increases. Night attacks are employed . . . to avoid heavy losses which would likely result from daylight attacks conducted under the same conditions.[4]
— FMFM 6-4

American military leaders have never fully acknowledged the advantages of attacking after dark. During the Civil War, both sides liked to travel to the jumping-off places for their attacks before dawn. They used the low light and ground fog to obscure their movements. Yet, when the sun was setting, neither side saw much value in the same visibility conditions. It was as if their mutual weariness in the most obscene of all human endeavors had generated an unspoken truce. The Confederates would certainly have won the Battle of Shiloh, if General Beauregard had simply ordered an all-out attack when the Federal Hornet's Nest collapsed about four o'clock in the afternoon. Culp's Hill was there for the taking on the first evening at Gettysburg; and the pivotal battle of the Civil War might have ended differently, if General Ewell had simply complied with his commander's intent. It's difficult to understand why Americans attribute some value to partial light, but none to low light. While they occasionally risk an approach march in the semidarkness before dawn, they invariably "circle the wagons" during a full moon. Not all armies share this aversion to the dark.

On the modern battlefield, thermal imaging may partially erode the concealment that darkness provides, but few foes have thermal imaging below battalion level. A handful of night vision sights can't cover thousands of meters of battalion frontage. He who attacks at night can avoid well-defended sectors and doesn't have to use the obvious avenue of approach. He can overcome a partial loss of surprise, and his opponent cannot see well enough to take full advantage of the situation. Because the defender fears what he cannot clearly discern, he is slow to react to it and easily deceived as to its meaning. For one thing, the night attacker can more easily divert the defender's attention. Of course, there are exceptions to every rule. When new to an area or agitated, defenders trained only in attrition warfare can be so "trigger happy" as to pose a threat to their own kind.

Further, the night attacker capitalizes on human frailties. His opponent is only partially awake, has difficulty seeing anything with the naked eye, and even with thermal imaging cannot be sure of how many people he sees. This is an adversary who is reluctant to bother his superiors with an uncertain sighting, slow to compromise his location, and usually high with his aim when he fires.

## GETTING BEYOND THE MISCONCEPTION THAT NIGHT ATTACKS ARE HARD TO CONTROL

Some believe that attacking at night creates irreconcilable control problems. Control is a function of unit composition and method. Any commander would have difficulty pulling off a night attack with troops who are unaware of the finer points of nighttime moving and shooting, and with squads that haven't had the opportunity to develop their own approach and assault techniques. Yet, with self-assured subordinates, that commander would have no difficulty maintaining adequate control. Some U.S. infantrymen may be reluctant to trust night attacks, because they have only experienced the first variety. Most of the loss in control comes from moving too quickly. The standard U.S. night attack goes much smoother when the combatants crawl the last hundred yards. On a dark night, artillery illumination *behind* the objective can provide enough light to align the assault.

Some assume that it takes a large friendly force to conduct a night attack against a large enemy force. This is not true. A squad can sneak up on a heavily manned defensive position more easily than a company can; and, at night, one squad can accomplish almost as much as an entire company during the final assault. Picture a *single* fire team successfully capturing *one* enemy hole. Then, imagine its sister fire teams attacking sideways in opposite directions — *one* hole at a time. Hasn't the squad maintained a 3 to 1 combat power advantage throughout its attack? If only grenades are used, can't the enemy be deceived into thinking that only a mortar barrage is in progress? In this way, one squad can capture an entire perimeter, or at least seize a gap wide enough for its parent unit to pass through. The solution to the control dilemma is using *smaller maneuver elements*. At the root of the problem in America has been an unwillingness to decentralize control. Only a few U.S. commanders have strongly endorsed attacking at night:

> Soldiers must be taught to move and fight at night. This is becoming more and more imperative, and it does not mean to make an approach march at night. It means to conduct lethal operations in the dark.[5]
> — Gen. George S. Patton

## COMPARED TO OTHER NATIONS, HOW OFTEN HAS THE U.S. LAUNCHED NIGHT ATTACKS?

Night attacks played a crucial role in the birth of America. George Washington crossed the Delaware with token forces at Trenton to win one of first Colonial victories of the Revolutionary War. Then, two units — one French and one American under Alexander Hamilton — advanced under cover of darkness to seize the redoubts anchoring the British bastion at Yorktown. This forced Cornwallis to surrender in the decisive engagement of the war.

Night attacks also occurred during the Civil War. There was a successful attack by Union forces at Rappahannock Station in November of 1863:

> Spearheaded by the 6th Maine and the 5th Wisconsin, soldiers of the Federal VI Corps came out of the blackness, cheering as they charged the earthworks. Savage hand-to-hand fighting broke out; soldiers clubbed, stabbed and fired at close range along the line.[6]
>
> The battle surged back and forth until a second charge led by youthful Colonel Emery Upton gave the Union regiments a decisive edge. Broken, the Confederates fled across a bridge or tried to swim to the south bank of the river, having lost four cannon, eight battleflags and 1,303 men. In the South, the Battle of Rappahannock Station was called a "mortifying disaster." The Union celebrated a victory that marked the first successful night attack of the War.[7]

By the time the two sides locked up at Petersburg, both had learned to conduct approach marches before dawn:

> In the predawn darkness of September 29, he (Grant) quietly slipped Birney . . . and Ord's XVII Corps back across the James. . . . Ord successfully stormed heavily armed but badly undermanned Fort Harrison on the Varina Road.[8]

Then, in a valiant but ill-fated attempt to break through the deep layer of Confederate siege lines at Petersburg, Union forces finally attacked Fort Stedman one night:

> The ground in front of Fort Stedman was crisscrossed with picket trenches and covered ways and protected by what one Federal infantryman boasted "every . . . arrangement known to military science and art."
>
> Using all his innate guile and resourcefulness to overcome these formidable obstacles, Gordon devised one of the most methodical attack plans of the war. First, while it was still dark, special squads would open avenues through the Confederate defenses by quietly removing the obstructions that had been placed there. Then picked men (identified by strips of white cloth tied around their shoulders) would infiltrate forward to take out the advanced Union picket posts and open pathways through the Federal abatis. Behind this group would come fifty men with axes, who were to chop openings in the fraises protecting Stedman and its batteries.
>
> Right behind the ax men would be three storming parties of a hundred men apiece, whose job it was to rush and secure Fort Stedman and Batteries X, XI, and XII. After the storming parties had achieved their objective, three more groups of a hundred men each were to undertake a special mission . . . (seizing) several strongpoints well in the rear (that is, to the east) of Stedman. . . .
>
> As the special-mission groups headed toward their objectives, the bulk of Gordon's infantry would cross over the no man's land to widen the breach by sweeping north and south along the captured trenches. Once the infantry had secured the lodgement, a cavalry division would ride through the pocket to the enemy's rear, cutting communications and raising general havoc.
>
> Private Henry London, in Grimes's Division, [on 25 March about 3:30 A.M.] never forgot how the storming party, "with unloaded muskets and a profound silence, leaped over our breast works, and dashed across the open space in front." . . .
>
> Within minutes, Fort Stedman, too [along with the other Batteries], fell. . . .
>
> The first phase of Gordon's attack had secured nearly all of its goals. Fort Stedman and Batteries X and XI had been seized, along with the camps of the 29th and 57th Massachusetts regiments, and a hole nearly a thousand feet long had been opened in the Union line, with very small loss. First light was still forty-five minutes away.[9]

While U.S. night attacks during the nineteenth century were educational, they were by no means frequent. Czarist Russia was the first Western nation to rely heavily on offensive operations during the hours of darkness:

> Since their conflict with the Ottoman Turks in 1877-78, the Russians have shown both a predilection for night operations and considerable skill in conducting them.[10]
> — Leavenworth Papers No. 6

The Russo-Japanese War (1904-5) witnessed no fewer than 106 night attacks of company size or larger, as both sides relied on night to shield them from the increased lethality of firepower.[11]
— Leavenworth Papers No. 6

On the Eastern Front during WWI, both sides experimented heavily with night attacks. The Russians were slow to realize that without adequate artillery support masses of inadequately trained infantry did not fare well at night against defenses in depth.[12] The Germans became interested in short-range infiltration to counter the machinegun. By July of 1918, U.S. Marines had attempted at least one night attack at Belleau Wood.

By WWII, the Russians had improved their technique and often employed deception. With a ruse the Red Army had used against the White Army at the isthmus of Perekop in 1920, the Russians defeated fortified positions at Viborg, Finland in 1940, and Sakhalin Island in 1945. Their ploy was to conduct a frontal demonstration while closing with their opponent from the rear across a water obstacle.[13] As WWII progressed, the Russians honed their individual and small-unit infiltration skills. With these talents, they could either reconnoiter, or mass in sufficient strength to attack, any objective:

> During the fighting on the Kerch peninsula in the winter of 1942 the Germans captured Russian soldiers who had spent two nights and one day in the immediate vicinity of the German positions and who had been able to obtain a wealth of information during that time. In another instance . . . after the Russian attack had been beaten off, the German battalion commander found that a Russian rifle platoon had been left behind in the village after all other troops had withdrawn and that the men had concealed themselves in the dung hills near the farm buildings. Their mission was to observe the Germans after their entry into the village and communicate the information to the parent unit which was hiding in a nearby woods with the intention of launching a surprise [night] attack.[14]
> — DOA Pamphlet 20-236

By late in WWII, the Soviets had perfected their night attack technique. One prominent Soviet expert has estimated that 40 percent of all Soviet attacks in 1944-45 were at night.[15] There was no secret to their success:

> Most German officers who fought the Soviets on the Eastern Front acknowledged their "natural superiority in fighting during night, fog, rain or snow," and especially their skill in night infiltration tactics. . . . The success of [the] Soviet night operations was in large part due to intensive training and the ability to profit from mistakes and failures. . . . Although the Soviet combat leaders were acutely aware that "the success of any battle is determined . . . by the extent of preparation," *training standards for night operations were not uniform* [italics added].[16]
> — Leavenworth Papers No. 6

The Germans followed suit, and in North Africa both sides capitalized on the concealment that only darkness can provide. In Europe, a few U.S. outfits tried their luck:

> In Italy and France, the U.S. 3rd Infantry Division adopted night operations as a standard operating procedure and developed considerable skill in execution. . . . Specially trained for night operations by its commander in the United States, the U.S. 104th Infantry Division launched more than 100 successful night attacks in Holland and Germany. The U.S. 30th Infantry Division had similar successes in France, Belgium, Holland, and Germany. The Germans used night operations in the east more and more as the odds turned against them. . . . In the west, Allied air power and firepower forced a similar reversion to night operations on the part of the Germans.[17]
> — Leavenworth Papers No. 6

In the Pacific, the Japanese regularly attacked at night. To mass near U.S. lines, they relied on infiltration. Their success rate might have been higher, if they hadn't insisted on shouting "banzai" after being discovered. All the while, with only minimal experience in this type of operation, their opponent rarely attempted it. When the Marines used a night attack on Iwo Jima, its success surprised everyone:

> . . . The big E [General Erskine] had decided now was the time to spring the predawn attack on the Japanese. . . .
> Such a tactic hadn't been used on Iwo, and seldom had Marines employed it in earlier Pacific campaigns.
> It might work now, Erskine felt, as it had in France against the Germans in World War I. . . .
> Lieutenant Colonel Howard J. Turton, the . . . intelligence officer, . . . said the troops weren't trained in the demanding skills of night fighting. . . .
> Two companies from Colonel Boehm's Third Battalion of the 9th Marines began moving into the lines at 3:20 A.M. . . .
> Company commanders tried to orient themselves in the light of parachute flares, but the steady downpour and black night practically obliterated the landscape. . . .
> . . . They moved without detection for half an hour until a Japanese machinegun opened fire and gave the alarm. The position was silenced in seconds by a flamethrower. Now the enemy was aroused, but not before Marines had passed through the lines without being discovered and without suffering a casualty.
> . . . Many Japanese had been killed in their foxholes and pill boxes. Colonel Boehm reported that K Company was atop Hill 362C. But euphoria was brief. . . Boehm found that the Marines were on Hill 331 — not 362C. It was another 250 yards ahead.

...It was late afternoon before 362C was finally in American hands. Boehm's outfit wasn't alone in slipping through scores of slumbering Japanese before being detected. Lieutenant Colonel Robert E, Cushman's Second Battalion and Major William T. Glass's First gained several hundred yards before heavy fighting erupted around them at 7:30 A.M....

Two of Cushman's [rifle] companies — Easy and Fox — now were surrounded and in a roaring struggle for survival in an area that would quickly become known as Cushman's pocket....

Except for Cushman's pocket..., March 7 had been a gratifying day for the Third Division.... Colonel Boehm noted in his battle journal, "the strategy proved very sound, since it turned out that the open ground taken under cover of darkness was the most heavily fortified of all terrain captured.[18]

In Korea, the enemy again did much of his attacking in the dark, while U.S. forces continued to prefer the light of day. And again, North Korean and Chinese units called attention to themselves after being first detected — this time with bugles and whistles.

In Vietnam, the enemy still attacked mostly at night, but this time he refrained from telltale assault signals. How many of his night attacks actually succeeded may never be known. One thing is certain, few Vietnam veterans can deny having had enemy soldiers inside their wire at one time or another. At night, it is difficult to tell what is happening, when one is at the bottom of his hole trying to escape what he believes to be a mortar attack. When a command bunker or ammunition dump goes up, it's more comforting to think that a lucky mortar hit has caused the damage. If, instead, the perimeter has been penetrated by a small group of enemy sappers using mortars as a deception, defenders can easily miss this. The NVA may have so feared American supporting arms that they were reluctant to consolidate their objectives. Or, they may have never intended to kill every U.S. defender. Many U.S. camps were overrun, but few were totally destroyed. While the occupants were celebrating another successful defense, shipping out their damaged artillery pieces, and wondering where all the enemy bodies were, the intruders may have been back at their base camp celebrating another successful night attack.

Marines conducted a few night attacks in Vietnam. One was when badly outnumbered in the summer of 1968, during the Battle of Dai Do northeast of Dong Ha:

> Whenever possible, we operated during darkness and became quite effective in night operations. During April 1968, our night patrols and ambushes were particularly productive. Most of our kills were at night with very few friendly casualties. We even conducted a successful battalion night attack. We literally took the night away from the enemy.[19]
>
> — B.Gen. W. Weise USMC (Ret)

(Source: FM 7-8 (1984), p. 3-52)

More recently, the British conducted night attacks almost exclusively (no fewer than eight of them) in their final push on Port Stanley in the Falklands. By so doing in the open terrain, they minimized the effect of Argentinean direct and indirect fire. The British assaulted at night even when their objectives were protected by mine fields and *night vision devices*. They preferred their "noisy" night attack option partially because they believed the artillery fire would unnerve the Argentineans. British Marines and Paratroopers spearheaded the final push on Port Stanley with attacks against Mount Harriet, Two Sisters, and Mount Longdon. Then, the Scots Guards, Welsh Guards, and Gurkhas took Tumbledown Mountain and Mount William. Diversionary attacks preceded the efforts against Tumbledown Mountain and Wireless Ridge. Predictably, the world-renowned night stalkers — the Gurkhas — met only light resistance on Mount William and Sapper Hill.[20] Having witnessed firsthand what Gurkhas can accomplish, the British now have formal schools at which to train stalkers, trackers, and *sappers*.

At 4 o'clock one morning during the Gulf War, small contingents of U.S. Marines managed through stealth to breach the main Iraqi defense line and barrier system in two separate locations. Because of cloud cover, shortage of moonlight, and drifting oil smoke, the night had been unusually dark. These narrow breaches subsequently permitted large task forces to pass unmolested into the enemy's rear. While these recent successes at night are encouraging, the overall trend isn't. It's hard to estimate what percentage of all U.S. infantry attacks have been conducted at night. Still, their scarcity in the literature implies an *extremely low* percentage. This wouldn't mean that much if the world's other major armies — namely, the Russians, Germans, Japanese, North Koreans, Chinese, North Vietnamese, and now the British — had also underused the tactic.

## WHEN A NIGHT ATTACK IS MOST APPROPRIATE

Of course, bypassing an enemy strongpoint is always safer than confronting it. Only occasionally can it be obliterated with supporting arms. When it must be attacked on the ground, doing so at night will save lives. Short-range infiltration is the safest method. But, with only partially trained troops, short-range infiltration *won't work against a position protected by barbed wire*. The night attack about to be described, will.

Attacking after dark can accomplish many things: (1) minimizing casualties, (2) compensating for a shortfall in combat power, (3) maintaining momentum, (4) preventing the enemy from digging in, (5) making up for the absence of an adequate avenue of approach, (6) exploiting a gap that exists only after the sun goes down, (7) creating a breach that can be exploited at dawn, or (8) simply capitalizing on the size and shape of an objective.

## PROBLEMS ASSOCIATED WITH ATTACKING AFTER DARK

It takes longer to prepare for a night attack. If the unit commander rushes his reconnaissance effort, he may have to settle for incomplete information about the threat and microterrain near his objective. What results is a plan of attack that does *not* compensate for, or capitalize on, enough of the existing circumstances. Of course, even with a valid plan of attack, the commander must require his subordinates to rehearse diligently, or they will overreact to enemy countermeasures and deploy early.

Of course, it's harder to move and coordinate during periods of limited visibility. To conduct offensive night operations, one needs accomplished land navigators.

Too strict an interpretation of one's tactical doctrine can cause problems as well. The U.S. infantry manuals strongly discourage units from launching night attacks against *prepared* enemy positions (those with bunkers, barbed wire, and mines). While a foe's obstacles certainly deserve respect, they should not totally preclude a well-conceived night offensive against him. In truth, all defensive positions are partially fortified, and every attacking unit runs the risk of stumbling onto a claymore or a little barbed wire.

The U.S. manuals also require attacking strictly by *stealth* at night. Supporting arms cannot be used until surprise has been partially compromised. In truth, only specially trained sappers can attack prepared enemy positions without making any sound. If U.S. units are to have the night attack as an option, they must be permitted to use supporting arms for deception. With artillery impacts to mask the sound of bangalore explosions, the units will have little trouble getting through opposition barbed wire undetected. Although not quiet, artillery does not automatically forewarn the enemy of an impending ground attack. Here, too narrow an interpretation of doctrine could prevent the use of a very productive tactic:

> The non-illuminated attack is conducted by stealth. . . . A complete plan of fires and illumination is developed to support the attack. The fires and illumination are not employed until the attack is discovered by the enemy.[21]
> — FMFM 6-4

Although the manuals all agree that the psychological edge belongs to the attacker after dark, it's hard to convince the troops of this. Most have experienced doctrinal night attacks that made little provision for the peculiarities of the situation. Anyone who doesn't train much at night will feel uncomfortable operating at night. Most U.S. infantrymen don't receive enough nighttime training. Many view doctrinal night attacks as only slightly more promising than suicide. In short, they lack vital confidence.

Because of the higher level of psychological stress under which a night attacker must operate, he is also more likely to overreact to routine defensive procedures. When the first enemy ground flare goes off, he is tempted to believe that all is lost.

## RESOLVING TIME PROBLEMS

Vital to a successful night attack are many reconnaissance patrols and rehearsals. When time is limited, these activities must take priority. Before mounting an attack in WWI, the Germans closely studied the microterrain:

> In order to ensure that battle did not degenerate into a land navigation exercise, officers, NCO's, and men were oriented by means of large-scale maps (1:5000). To further ensure that all hands had a detailed knowledge of the battlefield, and, in particular, the location and characteristics of squad objectives, a full-scale model of the enemy position to be attacked, complete with trenches and barbed wire, would be built in a training area behind the line and used for full dress rehearsals, some of which even included the use of live ammunition.[22]

In battle, there may not always be time to prepare this thoroughly. But, if units practice appropriate techniques before entering the war zone, they won't need long to rehearse for any particular attack. German infantry squads proved that during the Spring Offensive of 1918. After practicing stormtrooper technique, they launched attacks in series against successive Allied trench lines.[23]

To what extent a foe has prepared his position must *not* be guessed at; it must be assessed from close range after dark. Until that information becomes available, there's little chance that any plan of attack will mesh sufficiently with its circumstances. In other words, the plan cannot be finalized until *after* the nighttime reconnaissance. There is one way to forge the necessary link between intentions and reality. *It is properly training and then trusting the Probable Line of Deployment (PLD) security guides.* They are the ones who will watch over the location from which the unit will assault. For this reason, they are the ones best qualified to spearhead the squad thrusts through the wire. If they are to lead the way through the wire, they should also be allowed choose where to do so. They should help the unit leader formulate his *tentative* plan of attack during the daylight (binocular) reconnaissance, perform the final (close-in) stages of the dusk and nighttime reconnaissance, and then propose necessary changes to the plan. In all probability, their spokesman — the senior PLD security guide — will *not* know the best point of attack, routes for each squad, and Squad Release Point (SRP) until inspecting the objective after dark. This does not create insurmountable problems. While the senior guide is performing his final reconnaissance, the leader can move the unit from the assembly area to the Point of Departure (PD). After conferring at the PD, the two can still launch a well-coordinated night attack. All that's required is passing some new "word," showing key personnel where the coordination features are on the ground, and then following those personnel forward. If the unit leader doesn't like the senior PLD security guide's advice, he can replace him and delay the attack long enough to reevaluate the situation.

How long it takes to prepare for a night attack can be halved by conducting reconnaissance and rehearsal concurrently. The platoon commander and platoon sergeant must take turns supervising concurrent events.

## RESOLVING LAND NAVIGATION AND COORDINATION PROBLEMS

With properly trained personnel, many of the challenges in land navigation and coordination disappear. Others must be resolved without jeopardizing the secrecy of the operation. It is ill advised to mark trails or coordination points with chemical lights. If the enemy has the right kind of night vision goggles, he can even detect infrared markers. Against rural militia, knocking down the grass twice in the same place invites ambush. The squad guides should be well enough trained as land navigators to use a different route for each of the three required trips to the PD. Using places where two linear terrain features cross as attack coordination points (PD, SRP, PLD) makes them easier to find later. After sundown, it's also easier to locate an objective that makes a distinctive silhouette against the sky — e.g., one with a watchtower. Then, on a dark night, firing artillery flares *far behind* the objective will provide a steering point.

One should bypass a position protected by thermal imaging whenever possible. However, there are ways to partially defeat this threat. For concealment, attackers can use camouflaged thermal blankets, deep folds in the ground, or thick foliage. In theory, they can achieve some parity between background and human temperatures. In the desert, they can attack as soon as the sand cools to 98.6 degrees Fahrenheit. Elsewhere, they can cool down in a stream before their attack. At a minimum, they must try to create a single image; they must crawl in column directly at that thermal-imaging device. Any lateral movement before an assault will destroy the illusion. With luck, the device operator will believe the image to be a wild animal or lone scout. Neither would evoke a full response from defenders with any fire discipline.

Approaching an enemy position in column need not be overly dangerous. If a ditch or series of depressions runs between SRP and objective, and if this covered route has a stout tree or rock at its terminus, the attacking force can *crawl* safely from the SRP forward. During WWI, German stormtroopers used shallow communications ditches to get within assaulting distance of Allied lines:

> An early solution to the problem of crossing fire-swept terrain was the use of *boyaux*, shallow ditches running across no man's land, that, because they had originally been dug as communications trenches, were roughly perpendicular to the fighting trenches. One such attack took place on February 28, 1915. Ensign August Hopp . . . led a group of 36 volunteers in single file through a *boyau* that ran up to (but not into) the enemy trench [italics from original throughout].[24]

(Sources: FM 7-11B1/2 (1978), p. 2-II-A-8.2; FM 7-11B3 (1976), p. 2-VII-C-4.4)

Because defenders prefer well-drained ground, most attack objectives have water-runoff ditches radiating outwards from them. For attackers willing to crawl, these ditches can provide cover. A string of shellholes worked for the Germans during their attack on Eban-Emael in 1940. With low vegetation and a big enough tree or rock at the end of a crawl lane, there would be less need for a depression in the microterrain.

## RESOLVING DOCTRINAL PROBLEMS

While U.S. doctrine discourages attacking a prepared enemy position at night, it also makes provision for placing the PLD on the enemy side of whatever obstacles exist:

> If the enemy has obstacles in front of his position, the probable line of deployment should be on the enemy side of the obstacle.[25]
> — FMFM 6-4

If the PLD were placed just *inside* the enemy's barbed wire, wouldn't doctrine be adequately served? After all, a unit must reach its PLD before it can assault. Requiring units to secretly breach the barbed wire around objectives accomplishes many of the same goals as requiring units to leave objectives surrounded by barbed wire alone. Without special assets, they won't be able to attack. Counting on unforeseen obstacles is a good way to limit casualties. Night attackers always run the risk of encountering hidden barriers. Any unit that does not plan for barriers may get a chance to relearn the lesson of Omaha Beach.

Some might say that it's not possible to move through a defender's barbed wire without being seen or heard. This is only partially true. *For all but specially trained sappers,* it's not possible to move through the *last row* of protective barbed wire *silently*. Ordinary troops can quietly cut their way through the outer rows of wire, but they have trouble with the inner row — the one that's only 30 yards in front of alert defenders. Until U.S. military planners decide formally to train sappers, U.S. units shouldn't expect to penetrate protective wire silently. Yet, they can still get through unnoticed! Establishing the PLD inside the enemy's wire virtually assures that the element of surprise will be compromised by ordinary troops. By doctrine, supporting arms are only disallowed while the surprise is intact. So, by placing the PLD just inside an enemy's protective wire, a unit can use supporting arms without violating doctrine. What better way to employ indirect fire than to mask the sound of bangalores? German stormtroopers used this trick in WWI.[26] The NVA used it again at Con Thien in 1967:

> ... At 0255, the morning of 8 May, ... [there was] a savage 300-round mortar and artillery attack. Concurrently, Camp Carroll, Gio Linh, and Dong Ha also came under fire.

> At Con Thien, enemy units maneuvering under cover of the barrage breached the defensive wire with bangalore torpedoes, and small elements moved inside. At approximately 0400, two NVA battalions ... attacked through the breach in the wire.[27]
> — U.S. Marines in Vietnam

The British have had a noisy night attack in their tactical inventory for years. If U.S. night attack doctrine lacks the flexibility to permit an artillery deception, perhaps the method just described should be called an infiltration attack. Then, the artillery ruse would be legal:

> Fires ... may be preplanned on call ... to provide deception [for infiltration attacks].[28]
> — FMFM 6-4

Throughout history, many nations have used indirect fire to mask the sounds of their night assaults:

> On 20 August 1939 Soviet gunners fired all along the Japanese front, but on 21 August they shelled Japanese strongpoints identified by [the] previous day's probing attacks. As artillery fire smashed these key positions ..., Soviet infantry silently infiltrated into the Japanese lines.[29]
> — Leavenworth Papers No. 2

A unit can obey radio silence and still coordinate the final stages of a night attack, as long as that radio silence is not interpreted too literally. The relative progress of the squads in a multisquad attack must be controlled by the keying of radio handsets in code. When the artillery has been preplanned beyond danger-close range of the PLD, it can be fired safely with a one-syllable radio transmission. Before the radio silence rule goes into effect, a call for fire with an "at-my-command-but-don't-load" method of control can be sent from the assembly area. Then, after the bangalores are emplaced, the commander has only to whisper "fire" over his radio to get the first round. Each impact will partially mask the next adjustment transmission. Then, the blowing of the bangalores will sound to the enemy watchstanders like an overadjustment by a distant artillery observer.

This is a reliable way to breach enemy wire. What if the attacking force is spotted crawling through the breach? U.S. night attacks must be frontal by doctrine, but the defender may not know this. When he starts receiving automatic-weapons fire from one side of his perimeter, he may expect to be assaulted from another. In level terrain, he will never expect the assault to come in *underneath* the machinegun fire. If the attackers are spotted crawling through the breach, machineguns mounted outside the wire and five feet off the ground can fire over their heads. Well-aimed return fire will also sail safely over their heads.

As part of the technique, the barrel of a machinegun will be strapped at eye level to a tree at the head of each squad's crawlway. If the squad members are spotted in the wire, the machinegunner can fire over their heads while they crawl either forward or backward. Overhead fire is authorized during a frontal attack. The Marines on Guadalcanal learned how to crawl in the assault:

> You crawl in the advance — unless you are to charge and make it. The reason for this is that all men are hit from the knees up, except for ricochets. We have crawled up to within 25 yards of a machinegun firing over our backs.[30]
> — Sergeant O.J. Marion
> *Fighting on Guadalcanal*

There must be some way to shut off the friendly machinegun and *roughly* align the assault (if the alignment is too perfect, the attackers will be vulnerable to fire from the side). On a dark night, there can be no semblance of alignment without artificial light. By firing an M203 illumination round at low trajectory behind the objective, the leader can signal both the assault and shutting off the machinegun(s). Such a flare should silhouette the defenders, while concealing the attackers in moving shadows. The defenders will believe the flare to be their own.

Then, the attackers must disarm the claymores and quickly cross the open area between the wire and the first line of enemy holes. The "speed assault" method in the last chapter will also work here. This time the attackers crawl through the initial steps of the technique. Then, when the illumination appears, they stand up and run through the remaining steps. Rehearsal of technique provides more than enough control for any assault.

## RESOLVING THE PSYCHOLOGICAL PROBLEMS

A night attack must have *properly trained* participants. Just spending more time operating after dark should give U.S. infantrymen the requisite skills to use this method. Once their fear of the dark is gone, they will only need practice in crawling, sound discipline, and snap shooting. Of course, squad guides will need additional training in close-in reconnaissance, night observation, land navigation, walking point, stalking, and obstacle breaching. Then, after rehearsing the technique, small U.S. units should be qualified to attack a prepared enemy position after dark.

Only through experience do troops realize that trip flares going off, defenders talking excitedly, aerial illumination popping overhead, and enemy machineguns firing, do not necessarily mean that their attack has been irretrievably compromised. As individuals, they must learn to resist the temptation to overreact to enemy initiatives. Only then will their parent unit be able to avoid deploying early.

All nighttime defenders occasionally put up artificial illumination, sometimes with little justification. When the "flash" occurs simultaneously with the "pop," the attacker must freeze in place. When there is a slight delay, he can dive for cover. Defenders eventually realize that rabbits will set off trip flares as easily as men, and they won't normally react to the first trip flare that goes off.

A burst of enemy small-arms fire does not necessarily mean that one's attack has been discovered. Novice defenders do a lot of shooting, with or without an excuse. Seasoned defenders will sometimes "recon by fire" to trick suspected attackers into deploying early. Yet, if the attacker can resist the temptation to return fire, he can still attack from an unexpected direction.

If a few defenders detect movement to their front and start talking about it, a good deception can divert their attention. For a night attack to succeed, absolute surprise is not necessary as long as most of the enemy soldiers are confused as to the final direction of attack.

## THE SLIGHTLY MODIFIED PREPARATION SEQUENCE

The chief cause for tactical failure is misreading the combat situation. As the situation around an enemy position often changes after dark, flexibility is the key to attacking that position at night. The unit leader can't be too eager to finalize his attack plan. Some details must wait until his unit has moved up to Line of Departure (LD). He must resign himself to possibly not knowing the precise direction of attack or locations of SRP, squad routes, and PLD, until *after* the senior PLD security guide has completed his nighttime reconnaissance.

The doctrinal requirement for three separate reconnoitering trips — daytime, dusk, and dark — is a blessing. Only through extensive reconnaissance can the subtle situational details be discovered. In open terrain, only at night can a reconnaissance element approach an enemy position closely enough to gather this type of intelligence.

Many elements of information contribute to a viable plan of attack. Enemy capabilities lead the list. Of these, thermal imaging is potentially the most dangerous. However, locations of enemy sentry posts and machineguns are also important. Both can have nighttime pullback positions. There are questions about the barbed wire: (1) how is it constructed, (2) are there antitampering devices, (3) where are the gates, (4) how often do patrols use these gates, and (5) what routes do patrols take after departing enemy lines? The attackers also need some idea of how many mines (namely, claymores) have been emplaced.

Finally, the approaches to the objective must be thoroughly reconnoitered. What cover and concealment exists in the microterrain? Do covered routes lead up to trees just outside the enemy wire? Ideally, one's attack route must bypass as many of the enemy threats as possible, and the enemy sentry posts for sure.

## CHOOSING THE GUIDES

Two guides are chosen from each squad: (1) one to watch the enemy's wire, and (2) one to lead the squad up to the enemy's wire. These guides should be fire team partners. The senior guide should be the platoon's most experienced fire team leader. The guides left behind at the objective must keep the PLD under close surveillance after dark. They must watch for the defender to shift backwards or to one side just before coming under assault. Under these circumstances, attackers reveal themselves without doing any damage, and become very vulnerable.

Who is more qualified to breach the enemy's wire than those who have been watching it since sundown? After dark, there's intermittent illumination around any defensive position. This light will help the PLD security guides to discover many details about the wire and claymores to their front. They can relay what they have learned to their spokesman during his final nighttime reconnaissance.

Well-trained PLD security guides can contribute much to a night attack. They can provide *a valid solution to the situation at the point of attack.* Because they conduct the all-important close-in reconnaissance of the objective, they should also establish the precise locations of all major control features: the PLD, wire-penetration points, covered routes to those points, and SRP. Squads need a frontage of 30 meters, while platoons need 90. As each squad's PLD security guide must breach the wire and precede his buddies through that breach, he is committed to performing his reconnaissance and planning roles well.

## THE TENTATIVE PLAN OF ATTACK

To be readily assimilated, a night attack method must be consistent with doctrine. The technique proposed here is the standard U.S. night attack with two minor modifications: (1) the PLD is placed just inside the enemy's barbed wire, and (2) the artillery is used as a deception to mask the sounds of breaching that wire.

Assaulting from inside the wire eliminates alignment problems. Until the attackers are well within assaulting distance, it also prevents telltale lateral movement.

While letting the PLD security guides pick the control features departs somewhat from established procedure, it should be viewed as the decentralization of control necessary to practice maneuver warfare. The unit will still subdivide into squads at the release point, and these squads will still approach the PLD abreast along roughly parallel lanes. The members of each squad will be in column, but now they will crawl from the SRP forward.

Not only stealth, but also speed and deception will be used to enhance surprise. Indirect fire will be preplanned, but only beyond danger-close range of, and across the objective from, the PLD. If barbed wire is encountered, this fire will be used to mask the sound of breaching and transiting the wire.

According to doctrine, a night attack should only be used against a distinctive and compact objective. That means the objective should be visible against the skyline and small enough for the attacking force to cover with one sweep. Too strict an interpretation of the second qualification can be counterproductive. Forces large enough to cover most objectives with one sweep are too large to get close enough undetected to assault. But the entire defense in depth need not be tackled all at once. Why not just capture a foothold in the enemy's front lines? A foothold can be expanded to the sides as the distances between holes are short and the enemy does not expect trouble from that quarter. Sweeping on line across a large perimeter can be costly. Under the illumination needed to align, the sweep is vulnerable to automatic-weapons fire from its flanks. Sweeping across the open areas between successive trench lines can be equally deadly. How far into a position to penetrate depends on how much surprise can be achieved initially. Of course, consolidating a large objective takes some illumination.

When to attack is also critical. Time must be allocated for properly reconnoitering the objective after dark, revising the plan of attack, disseminating the new "word," and then crawling up on the objective. The most opportune time for an attack is on a rainy night after the moon has set. The falling rain masks the sounds of movement and the complete darkness renders the enemy's night vision goggles useless.

The attack route must be carefully chosen. The whole reason to attack at night is to avoid the sentry post, mortar preregistration, machinegun, and claymores that guard the main avenue of approach. This covered route should be reconsidered only if the enemy has protected *every* sector of his lines with thermal imaging. Otherwise, the main avenue of approach should be avoided, and covered routes through the *microterrain* chosen instead. If each squad column crawls up a shallow linear depression to a tree (or stump or mound or rock) just outside the enemy's wire, it cannot be hurt by a burst of automatic-weapons fire. The German stormtroopers of WWI crawled in column right up to the Allied wire.

Ruses must be planned to counter predictable losses in surprise. First, there must be background noise to mask wire being clipped or bangalores being emplaced. What might sound to the enemy like tanks coming up the road from the opposite side of the objective would work nicely. Amphibious Tractors (Amtracs) and Armored Personnel Carriers (APC's) sound just like tanks from a distance, and their clanking carries well at night. An artillery barrage on an adjacent enemy unit worked for the British in the Falklands. If Amtracs and artillery are not available, defenders will often draw the wrong conclusions from the low cursing and breaking of twigs of "rear security" personnel left at a PD on another side of the objective.

To blow bangalore torpedoes without forewarning defenders of impending ground attack, the unit must use an artillery deception on top of the objective. Of course, only if the wire cannot be parted quietly, will this deception be necessary. After the rounds are walked onto the attack objective from a *distant preplanned target,* the bangalores are detonated one at a time. With any luck the foe will think that a distant observer has overadjusted. Then, the rounds can be shifted to another sector of the lines. The precision continuous fire at the other location will draw the enemy's attention away from the point of attack and also cover the sound of heavily armed men crawling through the wire. Although grenades are more difficult to control at night, they can't be seen coming and pose little danger to prone throwers. They shouldn't be ruled out for furthering the artillery deception, as long as they are only tossed by the lead elements of the maneuver force. Now, what about the rest of the fire plan?

Ideally, the machineguns (or more precisely their barrels) are strapped to stout tree trunks just outside the enemy wire. From there, they can provide overhead fire if necessary. If more than one squad is involved in the attack, the sectors of fire for their attached machineguns must be closely coordinated. Gunners must be warned *not to answer enemy reconnaissance by fire,* as doing so may prematurely compromise the element of surprise. If the maneuver element has been spotted, the enemy will put up ample illumination for the friendly gunner to fire accurately. The machineguns should stay outside the enemy wire until the objective is consolidated. Their job is to guard against defensive fires from an unexpected direction. These weapons are too valuable to risk on the assault.

A SMAW man should be positioned at the rear of each squad column. Then, as the squad fans out inside the enemy wire, he will have a clear backblast area and view of the enemy lines. His job is to neutralize automatic-weapons positions that can't be avoided. Once the artillery deception has begun, he must be allowed to fire his "bunker buster" at any clearly distinguishable emplacement.

SAW operators must *only* fire at *active* automatic weapons or in self-defense. Their fire must be regulated to reduce telltale small-arms noise.

Other types of fire support shouldn't be ruled out. In the Falklands, British patrols pinpointed the locations of Argentinean machineguns by intentionally drawing their fire. Attacking units then had the option to silence the machineguns with Milan missiles. The British also used overhead tracer fire as a night navigational aid.

The following technique is a variation of the standard U.S. night attack. It can be used by three rifle squads attacking in unison, or *one* squad attacking alone. To practice maneuver warfare, an infantry unit must sometimes punch a hole through enemy lines with a small maneuver element. It takes a small unit to get close enough to assault, anyway. Then, the parent unit can quickly move through the hole to exploit a softer target behind the lines.

## RECONNAISSANCE AND REHEARSAL DETAILS

How the three required rehearsals and reconnaissance patrols are accomplished can save many valuable hours. As the situation unfolds during the initial stages of attack, this time saved may come in handy for solving unforeseen problems.

During the initial daylight reconnaissance, the first location from which the objective is clearly visible from a distance should be designated as the PD. Subsequent reconnaissance patrols from the assembly area can usefully terminate here. Only the three specially trained PLD security guides should move forward of this location until just prior to the attack. At the PD, the senior PLD security guide can relay information about the situation to the "reconnaissance" patrols making the various round trips from the assembly area. As long as the PD is not directly on line with the final direction of attack, whatever activity the enemy detects at the PD will not fatally compromise the assault.

The initial reconnaissance patrol should consist of the commander, squad leaders, and two guides from each squad. This would leave the platoon sergeant at the assembly area to finalize individual training. During the initial patrol, one guide from each squad is left behind at the PD to function as a PLD security guide. The three PLD

(Sources: *FM 7-8* (1984), p. 5-51; *FM 7-70* (1986), p. 4-20)

security guides must have a *radio* to summon help in an emergency. A field phone won't get the job done; its wire may be noticed by an enemy patrol.

The dusk patrol could consist of the platoon sergeant and the three remaining squad guides. This would give the platoon commander and his squad leaders the opportunity to supervise all three rehearsals: daylight, dusk, and dark. Interspersed with rehearsals could be inspections of personnel and equipment.

Then, the unit's approach march can double as the first leg of the night reconnaissance patrol. When that unit reaches the PD, the senior PLD security guide can pass along situational details from his final reconnaissance and recommended changes to the plan of attack. Then, the senior guide can take the commander, squad leaders, and other guides forward to orient them just prior to the attack. All the while, the other two PLD security guides will be watching the PLD.

For the rehearsals, terrain like that in front of the objective must be used whenever possible. The German stormtroopers of WWI rehearsed in exact replicas of the trenches they were about to attack. The rehearsal is more important than the attack order, for it both instructs and assesses retention. What must be rehearsed in detail is not only the attack technique, but also the unit's reactions to enemy countermoves. Of the three rehearsals required, the ones at dusk and dark can be conducted back to back just before the unit steps off in the approach march. Whenever a reconnaissance patrol reports back to the assembly area, both the plan of attack and what is being rehearsed must be modified as necessary.

## WHAT IT WOULD BE LIKE TO BE ON AN ACTUAL ATTACK IN PLATOON STRENGTH

Before the platoon departs the assembly area, its leader calls for fire on a target beyond danger-close range of the tentative point of attack. His method-of-control transmission is "at my command, don't load." Then, while obeying radio silence, the platoon moves out in column with squad guides at the front of their respective squads. If the unit is blazing a new trail to the PD (as it should be for safety), it needs only point and rear security elements. Not running flankers gives the unit more speed. This speed enhances security, builds confidence, and saves valuable time that might be needed later.

When the unit reaches the PD, the senior PLD security guide should be almost done with his nighttime reconnaissance. If his changes to the plan of attack are approved, the new "word" is disseminated to the unit. Then, the senior guide takes the unit leaders and squad guides up to SRP. He shows the guides and leaders of the flank squads their respective crawlways, and dispatches them forward to link up with their PLD security guides. Then, he takes the platoon commander and the two members of his own squad up the center lane. Upon rendezvousing again at the SRP, the senior guide makes sure that all guides and leaders know the compass azimuth to the PLD.

Next, the leaders and guides return to the PD to lead the rest of the unit forward. The emphasis now (for everyone in the unit) is to *resist the temptation to overreact to enemy initiatives.* Any overreaction could disrupt the optimal sequence of events.

At the SRP, each squad goes into its respective lane and starts crawling in column toward the objective. The order of march is as follows: guide, squad leader, machinegunner, rest of the squad, and SMAW man.

When each squad links up with its respective PLD security guide just outside the enemy's barbed wire, the machinegunner *gets ready* to strap the barrel of his gun to the tree at the head of the infiltration lane. Then, the two guides crawl out to breach the wire silently. If they can't, they emplace a bangalore. When they return from their foray, the squad leader informs the platoon leader (by radio-handset-keying code) of their degree of success.

After all three breaching teams have been accounted for, the platoon leader decides whether or not to use artillery. If any bangalores have been emplaced, he whispers "fire" over his call-for-fire net and waits. Before the sound of each explosion dies away, he whispers an adjustment instruction into his radio handset. Carefully, he walks single HE rounds onto the objective.

When the rounds are roughly 100 yards away, the squad leaders blow their bangalores one at a time. As they are doing this, the platoon leader shifts the artillery away from the area he wishes to occupy, and asks for continuous precision fire for effect. Meanwhile the squads have started to crawl through their respective breaches in the wire. Only if they are discovered, do the machinegunners behind the trees open fire from five feet above the ground.

As each squad enters the enemy position through the wire, the lead fire team crawls in column to the half left, the next fire team crawls in column to the half right, and the last fire team spreads out the middle. All are looking for claymore wires to cut. When everyone is through the breach, the platoon leader has a nearby M203 man put up illumination behind the objective as the signal to assault. If surprise is intact, the "speed assault" technique from the last chapter is run upright. The alignment among fire teams and squads is achieved *as everyone moves forward.* There is no firing of small arms except at well-defined enemy soldiers, and then only "double taps." SAW's are fired only at *active* enemy automatic weapons.

If the crawling columns are spotted before the signal to assault, the machineguns open up automatically and cease fire on the assault signal. Then, the assault is conducted by "fire and movement." Flank fire teams echelon forward into the enemy lines, gaining alignment as they go with the center fire team and sister squads.

When surprise is total and the second line of enemy holes not too far ahead, the platoon leader motions for the assault to proceed. When the surprise has been compromised, he lets his men take cover in the first line of holes. If the defenders have baited a trap and moved to another location, those in the assault line *must not attempt, while upright, to wheel toward them.* They must hit the dirt, crawl into line facing the enemy, and then dispatch a flanking force during a lull in the illumination. Under illumination, daylight attack rules apply.

## EVERYONE MUST RESIST THE TEMPTATION TO OVERREACT TO APPARENT DISCOVERY

To attack at night, infantrymen must be comfortable operating at night. They must believe in themselves. They must understand that defenders are under more psychological stress than they are. Most importantly, they must resist the temptation to overreact to enemy illumination and firing. In 1939, the Japanese in Manchuria showed what could be accomplished by staying cool:

> Again the Soviets opened a violent storm of automatic-weapons and heavy-machinegun fire and flung grenades at flickering shadows. Both Japanese platoons again withheld any counterfire and continued to advance silently, guiding on their platoon leaders' backs. When they had closed to within a few meters of the Soviet front line . . . they leaped into the enemy trenches slashing and bayoneting the Soviet defenders there.[31]

## THE NIGHT ASSAULT SEQUENCE TO PRACTICE IN PEACETIME

For all but specially trained troops, prepared positions must be attacked systematically. That's why the Marines in WWII became so good at it. The steps for this night attack technique are all consistent with U.S. doctrine. Some are only necessary if the enemy has barbed wire, but those required must be executed in the proper sequence. This will be called the "night assault sequence." The technique is so strong that all U.S. infantry squads should be required to practice it in peacetime. Then, they will have it as one of their prerehearsed "plays" in combat.

This sequence will empower a single squad to establish a foothold in enemy lines, or several squads to attack in unison. Here, the steps for a platoon-sized attack are presented to show how squad coordination can be accomplished through a handset-keying code. (See table 19.1, and figures 19.1 through 19.3.)

(Source: FM 7-8 (1984), p. 3-57)

**BEFORE LEAVING THE ASSEMBLY AREA:**

THE PLATOON LEADER SENDS A CALL FOR FIRE "AT MY COMMAND, DON'T LOAD" ON A TARGET BEYOND DANGER-CLOSE RANGE OF, AND ACROSS THE OBJECTIVE FROM, THE TENTATIVE PROBABLE LINE OF DEPLOYMENT (PLD).

**AT THE SQUAD RELEASE POINT:**

(FOR EACH SQUAD, THE ORDER OF MARCH IN COLUMN FROM FRONT TO BACK SHOULD BE: GUIDE, SQUAD LEADER, MACHINEGUN MAN, REST OF THE SQUAD, AND SMAW MAN.)

EACH SQUAD CRAWLS UP THE DITCH TO THE TREE JUST OUTSIDE THE ENEMY'S WIRE.

EACH SQUAD LINKS UP WITH PLD SECURITY GUIDE ON WATCH.

**JUST OUTSIDE THE ENEMY WIRE:**

ALL SQUADS STAY IN DEFILADE IN SEPARATE COLUMNS.

IN EACH FLANK SQUAD, A MACHINEGUN IS *READIED* FOR LASHING TO A TREE (FIVE FEET UP).

A NOISY DECEPTION, LIKE A TRACKED-VEHICLE NOISE, IS CONDUCTED ON THE OPPOSITE SIDE OF THE OBJECTIVE FROM THE PLD.

AT THE SAME TIME, GUIDES FROM EACH SQUAD TRY SILENTLY TO BREACH ALL ROWS OF BARBED WIRE.

IF THEY ARE UNABLE TO DO SO, THEY INSERT BANGALORES.

THESE BREACH TEAMS CRAWL BACK TO INFORM THE SQUAD LEADERS OF THEIR PROGRESS; THE SQUAD LEADERS IN TURN NOTIFY THE PLATOON LEADER WITH HANDSET-KEYING CODE.

IF BANGALORES HAVE BEEN LAID, THE PLATOON LEADER WHISPERS "FIRE" OVER THE CALL-FOR-FIRE NET, USES THE EXPLOSIONS TO MASK HIS ADJUSTMENT TRANSMISSIONS, AND CREEPS THE FIRE ONTO THE OBJECTIVE.

THE SQUAD LEADERS BLOW THEIR BANGALORES ONE AT A TIME.

THE PLATOON LEADER SHIFTS THE ARTILLERY FIRE TO THE OPPOSITE SIDE OF OBJECTIVE AND ASKS FOR "CONTINUOUS PRECISION FIRE FOR EFFECT WITH DELAYED FUZING."

ALL SQUADS CRAWL IN SEPARATE COLUMNS THROUGH THEIR RESPECTIVE HOLES IN WIRE.

(IF LEAD ELEMENTS ARE SPOTTED, THE MACHINEGUN'S FIRE TO THEIR DIRECT FRONT.)

**JUST INSIDE THE ENEMY WIRE:**

THE LEAD FIRE TEAM FOR EACH SQUAD CRAWLS IN COLUMN TO THE HALF LEFT, LOOKING FOR (AND CLIPPING) CLAYMORE WIRES.

FOR EACH SQUAD, THE NEXT FIRE TEAM CRAWLS IN COLUMN TO THE HALF RIGHT, LOOKING FOR (AND CLIPPING) CLAYMORE WIRES.

FOR EACH SQUAD, THE FINAL FIRE TEAM FANS OUT IN THE CENTER, LOOKING FOR (AND DISARMING) CLAYMORES.

ON COMMAND BY THE PLATOON LEADER, AN M203 MAN FIRES AN ILLUMINATION ROUND BEHIND OBJECTIVE TO SIGNAL THE ASSAULT (AND TO TURN OFF THE BASE OF FIRE).

THE SMAW MAN WITH EACH SQUAD TAKES WELL-AIMED SHOT(S) AT ENEMY MACHINEGUN BUNKER(S) TO HIS DIRECT FRONT.

IF SURPRISE REMAINS INTACT, THE PLATOON ASSAULTS UPRIGHT (FLANK FIRE TEAMS OF EACH SQUAD ECHELON TOWARD THE ENEMY AND ALIGN WITH CENTER FIRE TEAMS AND SISTER SQUADS AS THEY GO).

(IF SURPRISE HAS BEEN LOST, THE PLATOON FIRES AND MOVES FORWARD AT THE CRAWL, ALIGNING AS IT GOES.)

*Table 19.1: The Night Assault Sequence*

Attack at Night to Save Lives

(Sources: FM 7-11B1/2 (1978), p. 2-II-C-4.2; FM 7-8 (1984), p. 3-28)

(Source: FM 7-11B/2 (1978), p. 2-IV-B-9.2)

Techniques from the NCO Corps

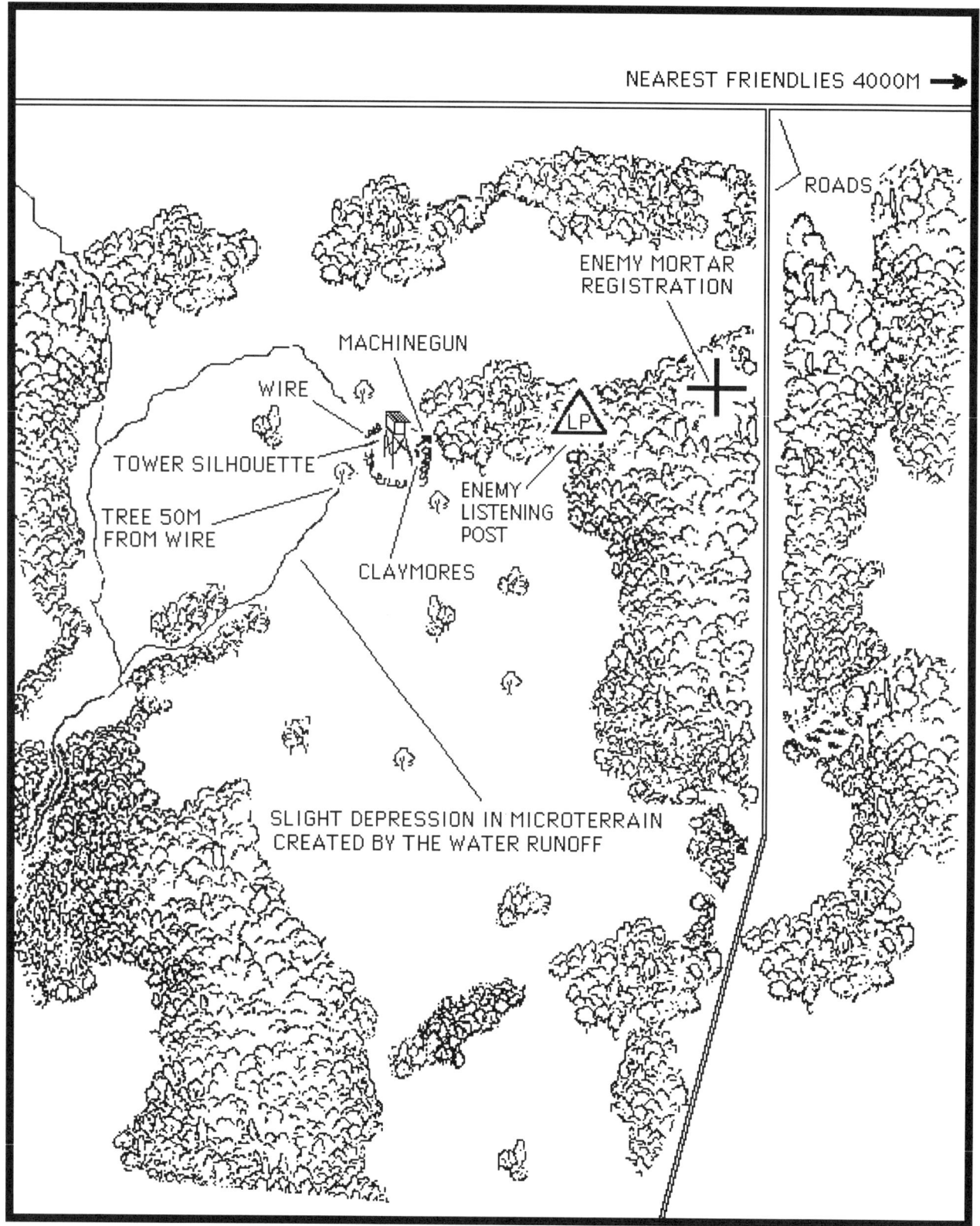

*Figure 19.1: The Situation Often Encountered during a Night Attack*
(Source: "Maps" by John Morris, from RICHMOND REDEEMED by Richard Sommers. Copyright © 1981 by Richard J. Sommers. Used by permission. See Notes.)

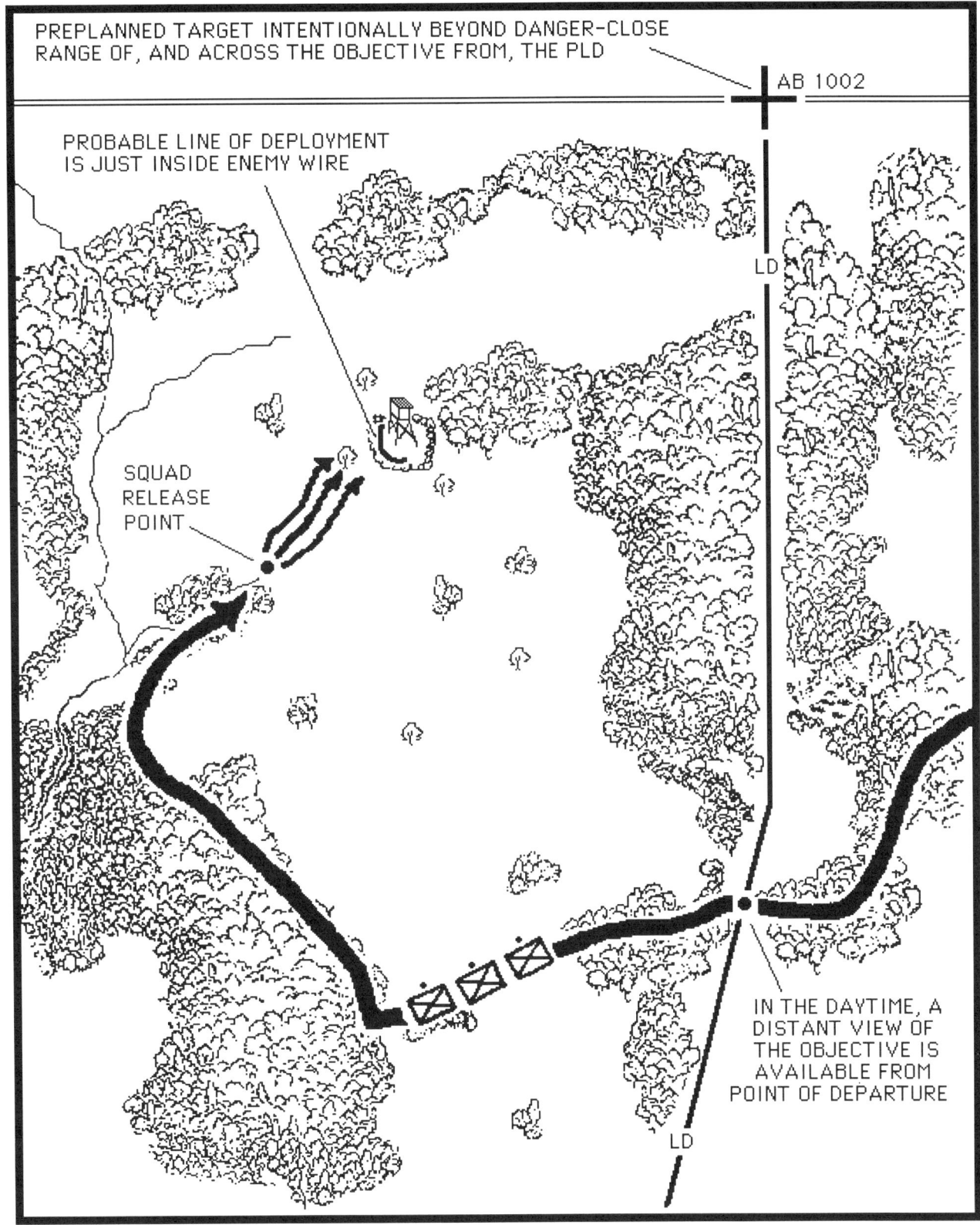

*Figure 19.2: The Inside Edge of the Barbed Wire Is the Probable Line of Deployment*
(Source: "Maps" by John Morris, from RICHMOND REDEEMED by Richard Sommers. Copyright © 1981 by Richard J. Sommers. Used by permission. See Notes.)

Techniques from the NCO Corps

(Source: FM 7-8 (1984), p. B-8)

1. FROM THE SQUAD RELEASE POINT, THE SQUADS CRAWL UP SEPARATE BUT PARALLEL COVERED ROUTES. THEY WERE CHOSEN BY PLD SECURITY GUIDES.

Figure 19.3: The Night Assault Sequence
(Source: FM 5-103 (1985), p. 4-4)

2. JUST OUTSIDE THE ENEMY'S WIRE, THE MACHINEGUNNERS WITH THE FLANK SQUADS MOUNT THEIR GUNS TO PROVIDE OVERHEAD FIRE IF THEIR COMRADES ARE SPOTTED IN THE WIRE. THEY MUST NOT ANSWER RECONNAISSANCE BY FIRE.

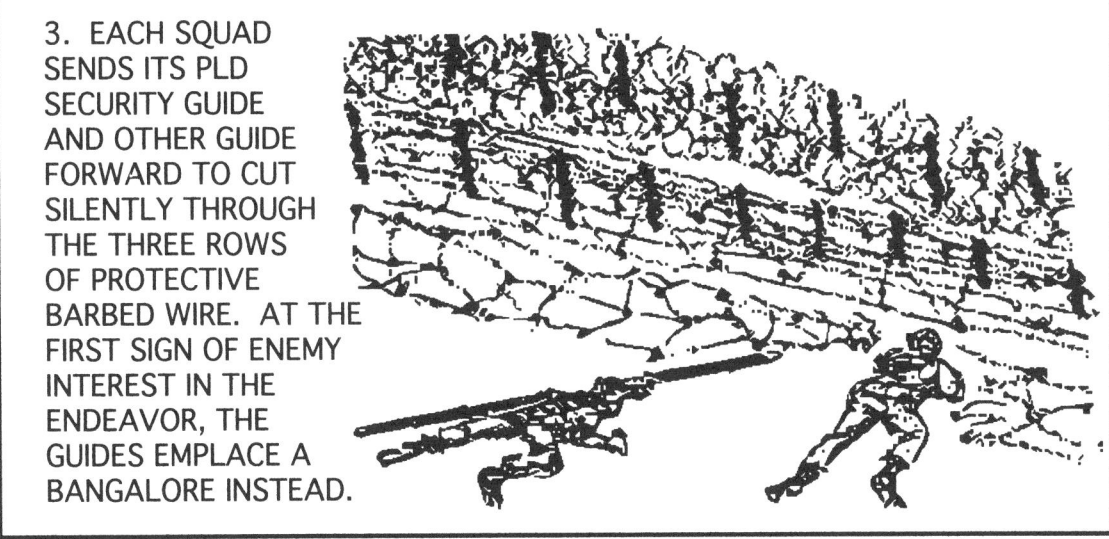

3. EACH SQUAD SENDS ITS PLD SECURITY GUIDE AND OTHER GUIDE FORWARD TO CUT SILENTLY THROUGH THE THREE ROWS OF PROTECTIVE BARBED WIRE. AT THE FIRST SIGN OF ENEMY INTEREST IN THE ENDEAVOR, THE GUIDES EMPLACE A BANGALORE INSTEAD.

*Figure 19.3: The Night Assault Sequence (Continued)*
(Sources: FM 90-10-1 (1982), p. B-44; FM 5-103 (1985), p. 4-4; FM 7-11B3 (1976), p. 2-VII-C-4.4)

Techniques from the NCO Corps

4. WITH RADIO-HANDSET-KEYING CODE, SQUAD LEADERS NOTIFY PLATOON LEADER OF SUCCESS IN SILENTLY BREACHING WIRE OR PLACING BANGALORE

*Figure 19.3: The Night Assault Sequence (Continued)*
(Sources: FM 5-103 (1985), p. 4-4; FM 22-100 (1983), p. 22)

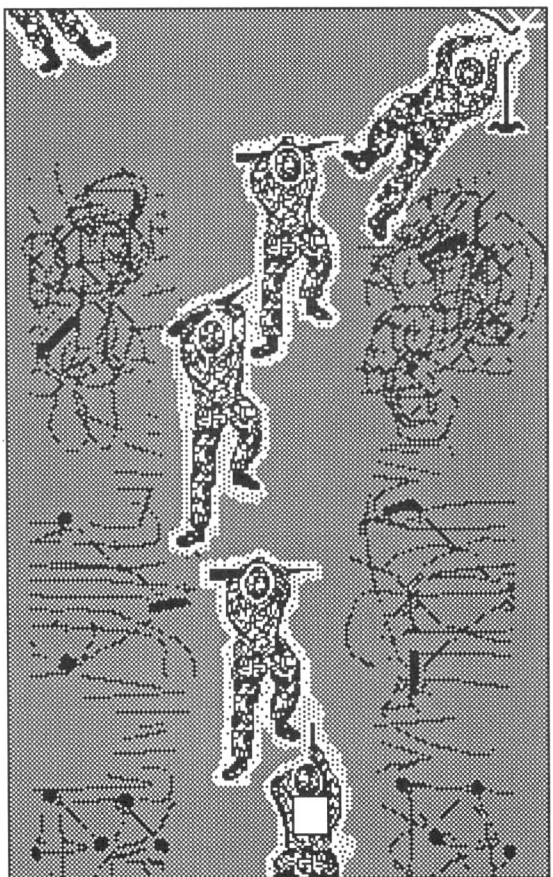

Figure 19.3: The Night Assault Sequence (Continued)
(Sources: FM 90-3 (1977), p. 4-9; FM 22-100 (1983), p. 30; FM 5-103 (1985), pp. 4-4, 4-6)

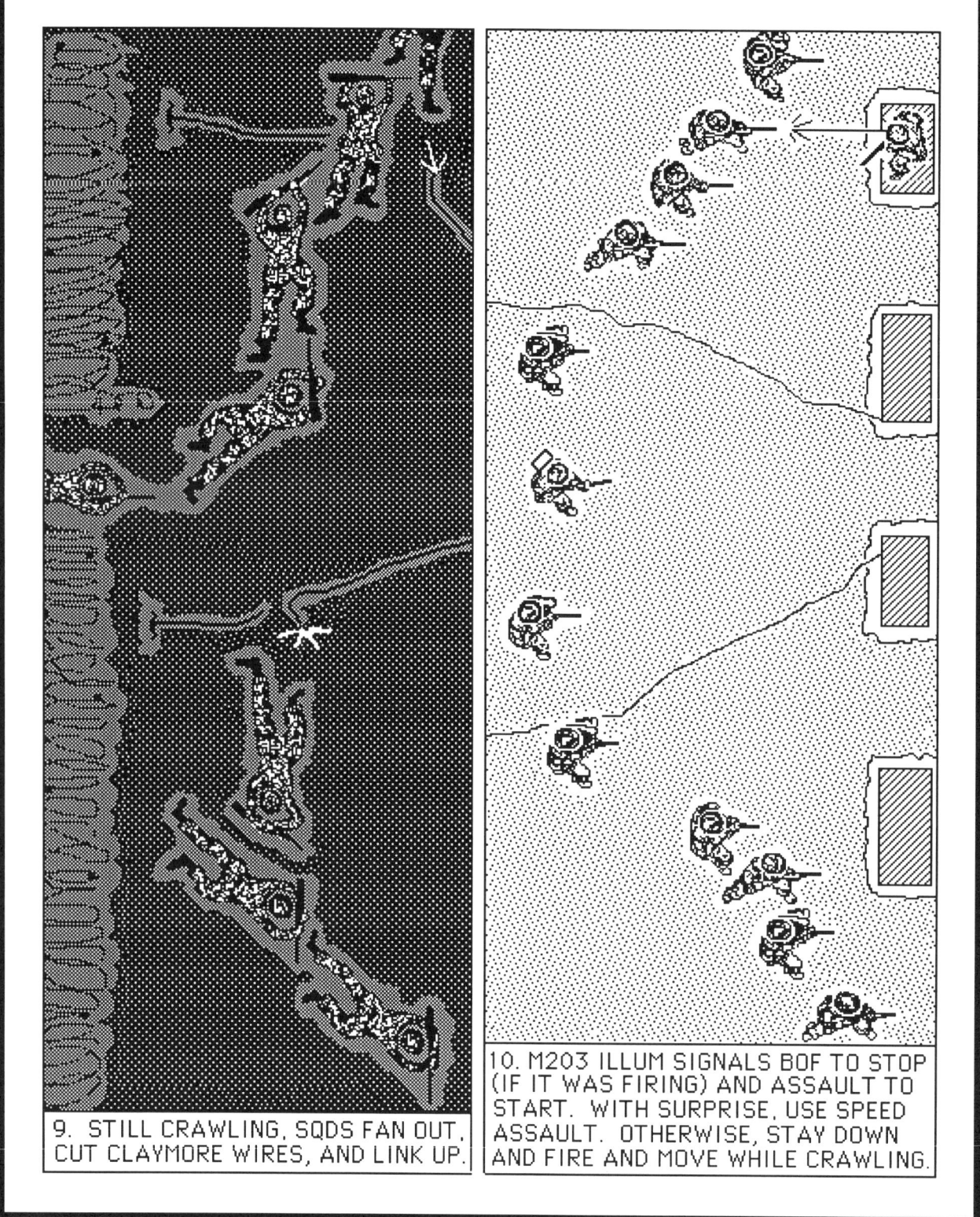

Figure 19.3: The Night Assault Sequence (Continued)
(Sources: FM 5-103 (1985), p. 4-6; TC 90-1 (1986), cover)

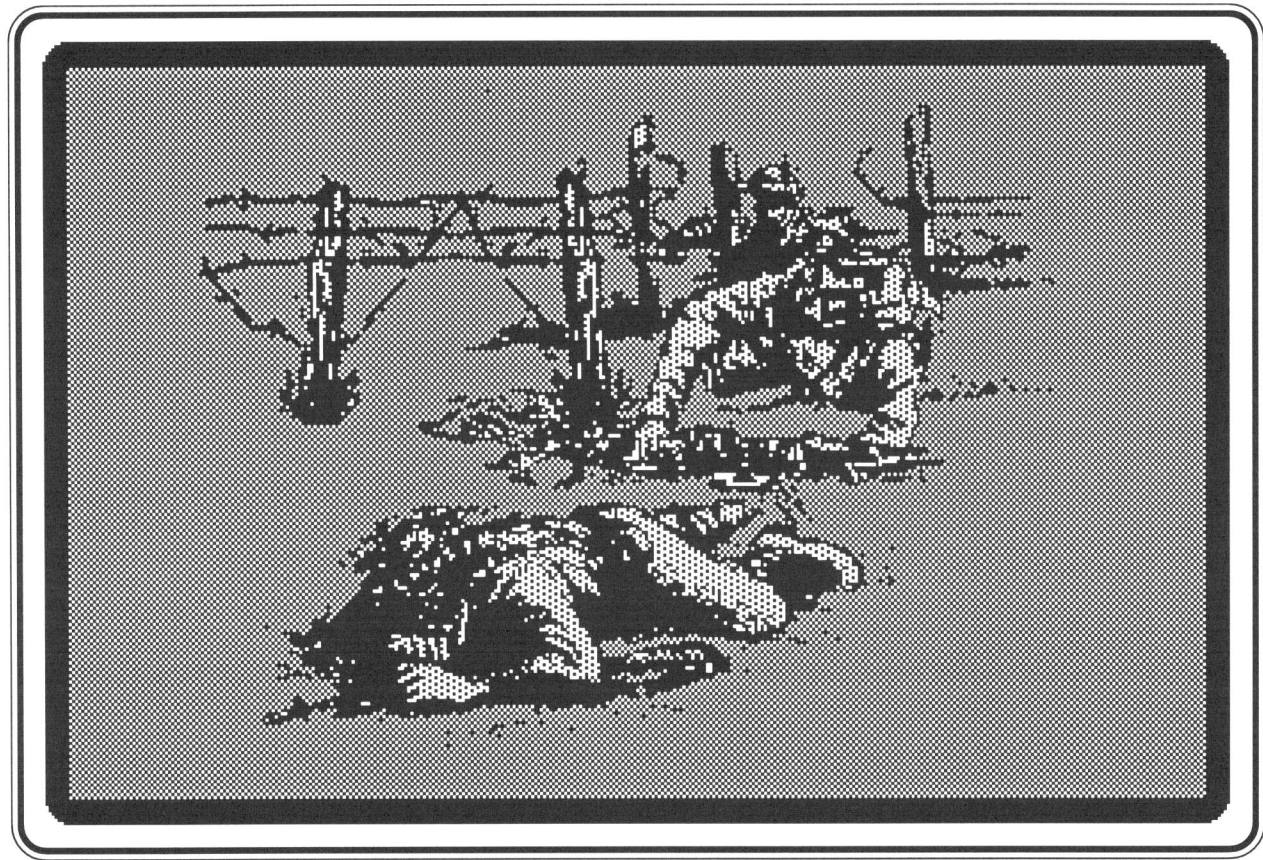

*(Sources: FMFM 0-1 (1979), p. 7-7; FM 21-75 (1967), p. 67)*

## OTHER NIGHT ATTACK POSSIBILITIES

The easiest alternative technique is the "Indian file" night attack. During this maneuver, the entire unit approaches an objective in single file much as a snake would approach its prey. As those in front close with the enemy position, they get lower to the ground and move more slowly. Then, the point men deliberately aim off to narrowly miss the mark. When the unit is centered on the target (or has been detected), everyone stands up in unison, faces the objective, and assaults roughly on line and in partial echelon. Because this technique involves dangerous lateral movement across an enemy's front, it only works on the darkest and wettest of nights against an enemy *without* thermal imaging. The danger of moving laterally can be lessened by finding a diagonal ridge or depression in the microterrain, and then using the wrinkle in the ground for cover. Of course, on such a night, the unit would need to illuminate during the final assault to maintain its alignment. This technique has few, if any, coordination problems. In fact, a unit could execute it without any preparation at all. The tactic might be appropriate for maintaining the momentum against an opposition unit that has already been beaten just before dark, and that has had little time to prepare an adequate defense. The method should *not* be used against an objective protected by barbed wire.

The *most promising* night attack alternative is the "grenade attack." It is also for an objective *without* barbed wire. The attackers crawl on line up to the enemy fighting holes, and then throw grenades on a time hack. Only those whose grenades find their mark actually assault, and they do so without ever standing up. Once safely in the neutralized holes, they use a signaling code to determine whether or not adjacent holes have been taken. If not, they can widen their footholds laterally with more grenades. With a little luck, a huge gap in the enemy's first line of defense could be opened at no cost. If the defenders had been led to believe that they were under a mortar attack all the while, they might never realize that a ground assault was in progress. (See figure 19.4 for a picture of this technique.) In its potential for surprise, lies the true value of any attack:

Defeat your enemy by a surprise move.[32]
— Sun Tzu

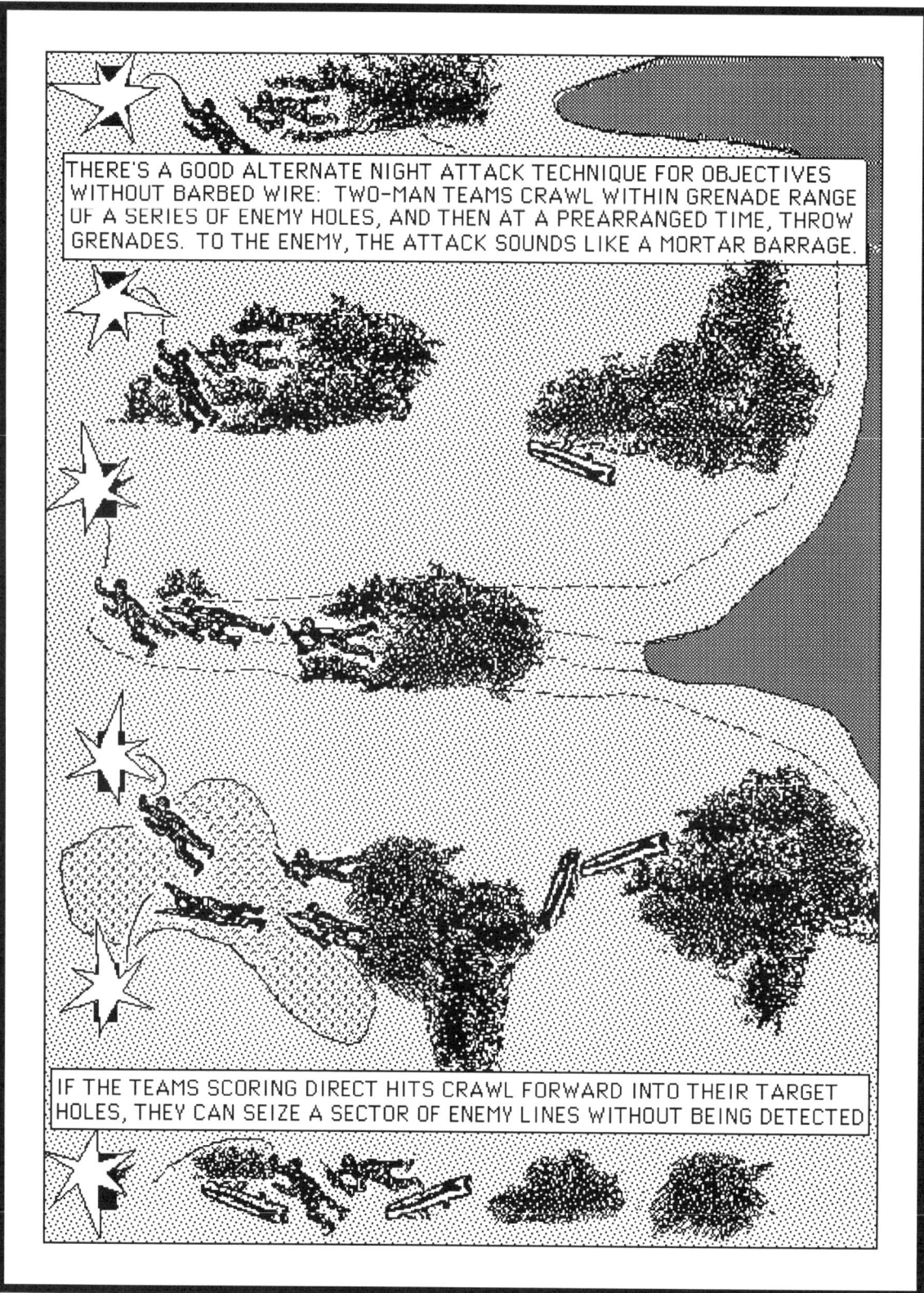

Figure 19.4: A Night Attack Alternative for an Objective without Barbed Wire
(Sources: FM 7-70 (1986), p. 4-20; FM 5-103 (1985), p. 4-6; MCI 03.66a (1986), p. 2-8; FM 23-30 (1988), p. 2-8; FM 7-11B3 (1976), p. 2-VII-C-4.4)

# 20 The Safest Way to Attack — Short-Range Infiltration

- *Why have Orientals always been such formidable infiltrators?*
- *To which skills can their success be attributed?*
- *How can employing these skills during an attack, reduce the risk?*

(Sources: FMFM1-3B(1981), p. 4-9; FM 5-103 (1985), p. 4-4)

### WHAT IT MEANS TO ATTACK BY INFILTRATION

Of the three deliberate attacks, the one by "infiltration" most closely resembles maneuver warfare. Because it initially targets an *undefended* sector of the enemy's lines, it's the best example of "soft-spot" tactics:

> Attack where the enemy is unguarded and catch him by surprise.[1]
> — Sun Tzu

To attack by infiltration, sister units move up roughly parallel "lanes" and attempt to bypass enemy strongpoints in those lanes. In other words, the units try to penetrate enemy lines *by stealth*. The ones that get through, rendezvous and strike a soft target to the rear. Each has been task organized to conduct the "subsequent operation" alone, if necessary. Prior to the rendezvous, each has been allowed to operate independently. Their parent unit has *decentralized control*. Perhaps that's why U.S. forces have had so little opportunity to conduct this form of attack.

At the infantry platoon level, there are two kinds of infiltration attack: (1) the "long-range" type where squads move between widely separated enemy strongpoints, and (2) the "short-range" type where two-man teams sneak between enemy fighting holes. Of course, to the individual rifleman, the long-range version doesn't constitute an attack at all, but rather an approach march or raid patrol.

Techniques from the NCO Corps

The Germans are generally credited with pioneering long-range infiltration tactics near the end of the First World War. Squad-sized columns of German infantry would attack simultaneously at slightly different locations. By not requiring the successful squads to wait for the slower ones, the parent units could drive deep wedges into the layered Allied defense system. This was not a penetration by stealth per se; the German squads needed artillery, bangalores, and grenades to accomplish the feat. Still, it was an infiltration attack in spirit, because the Allies couldn't tell that they were under ground assault. *With the day and night attack techniques described in the last two chapters, U.S. infantry squads could do the same thing in the next war.*

This facsimile of long-range infiltration was possible, because the Germans discovered a way to move through Allied barbed wire unnoticed. They could secretly breach the wire by masking bangalore blasts with artillery explosions. To emplace the bangalores, they used individual movement skills learned from the Japanese. One with such skills became known as a *"sapper."*

In the Orient, a sapper is more than just a military engineer with a bangalore torpedo. He is so skilled at camouflage and individual movement that he can reconnoiter an enemy position from close range during the day, and then build a spider hole within 75 yards of its barbed wire. After dark, he can either blow a hole in that wire, or sneak through it to reconnoiter the position *from the inside.*

Without formally trained sappers, infantry units *cannot* conduct short-range infiltration attacks against positions protected by barbed wire. As most U.S. infantry units have no trained sappers, this chapter will only discuss how to attack an objective *without protective barbed wire.*

## HAVE U.S. UNITS EVER USED INFILTRATION?

By the time the Pilgrims landed at Plymouth Rock, Native Americans had practiced short-range infiltration for centuries. They did so every time they donned buffalo robes to penetrate a buffalo herd, or white furs to sneak into an enemy's winter camp. When the Texans filtered out of the Alamo to spike Santa Anna's cannons in 1836, their attack might be loosely classified as one of short-range infiltration. And, when Merrill's Marauders rendezvoused behind Japanese lines to seize an airfield in Burma during WWII, their attack might be called one of long-range infiltration. But, in the annals of U.S. warfare, good examples of either are few and far between.

## HAVE U.S. FORCES EVER HAD TO DEFEND AGAINST SHORT-RANGE INFILTRATORS?

The Indian wars notwithstanding, U.S. forces have faced skilled short-range infiltrators since the turn of the century. To appreciate how pervasive this threat has been, one must study the wartime exploits of Germans, Russians, Japanese, North Koreans, Chinese, and North Vietnamese. Chapters 5-7 recount a few. The classic example of what short-range infiltration can accomplish occurred at Caporetto, Italy, during WWI. Here Central Power forces (including a young officer named Rommel) used infiltration to start a monumental rout of the Allies:

> Of the 2 million Italian soldiers arrayed against the Austro-Hungarian Empire, somewhere between 800,000 and 1,000,000 had been killed, wounded or captured [at Caporetto]. . . . France and Britain felt compelled to send 11 divisions to shore up their prostrate ally.[2]
>
> . . . One such [Italian] strongpoint was the battalion position on Hill 1114. . . .
> . . . [H]e [the Bavarian commander] sent two companies forward to attack from opposite directions. Each of these companies, in turn, infiltrated patrols through gaps in the Italian wire. . . .
> As darkness fell, a third company . . . infiltrated a platoon through yet another gap in the wire.[3]

Armies skilled in maneuver warfare use short-range infiltrators for many reasons: attacking, reconnoitering, and spotting for supporting arms. With sappers, the Russians probed Japanese lines regularly in Manchuria in 1939.[4] They were looking for defensive weaknesses:

(Source: FM 7-11B1/2 (1978), p. 2-II-A-5.2)

## The Safest Way to Attack — Short-Range Infiltration

Almost daily Soviet patrols poked and probed for weaknesses in the Japanese defenses. On 13 August [1939], for ex., at 0200 a squad of fifteen enemy crept to within fifty meters of the 6th Company [Japanese] front lines before grenade dischargers drove them off.[5]
— Leavenworth Papers No. 2

On another occasion, the Japanese defensive scouts were able to shadow Russian infiltrators.[6] Orientals have always been expert at this style of warfare. The morning after Chesty Puller's legendary defense at Guadalcanal, 250 dead Japanese were discovered *inside* Marine lines.[7] One of the earliest lessons learned from the Pacific War was that the Japanese relied heavily on infiltration:

Small groups of enemy that have infiltrated may appear anyplace. On Guadalcanal, a three-man enemy patrol attacked the First Marine Division CP.[8]
— FMFRP 12-9

This should have come as no surprise to anyone after what had just happened at Singapore. There, the Japanese had landed high on the Malay Peninsula, dispersed into small units, bypassed the road-bound British Commonwealth forces, paddled at night across the narrow Straits of Johore, and (though still outnumbered by at least two to one) forced the demoralized defenders to surrender.

In Korea, several Chinese divisions successfully infiltrated into the area around the Chosin Reservoir. Frozen Chosin veterans claim that small groups of Chinese were equally adept at crawling through U.S. lines at night.[9]

In Vietnam, the enemy was a master at both long and short-range infiltration. By different routes under cover of darkness, elements of the same unit could pass through U.S. TAOR's to rendezvous near a major installation. The reconstituted unit would stay hidden until the next night and then attack. The NVA units could strike quickly, because their objectives had already been reconnoitered from the inside. In some cases, they had been "paced out" by indigenous workers; but more often, they had been mapped by skilled sappers. One morning after seeing the silhouette of someone wriggling through the protective concertina at Dong Ha, a Marine lieutenant went outside the wire to look around in what resembled the sage brush country of southern Idaho. At a distance of 50 yards, he saw a blackened Vietnamese run behind a low rise.[10] In the time it took the lieutenant to cover that 50 yards, the small figure completely vanished. The young officer stomped around and tugged on every bush for 30 minutes, but to no avail. On another occasion, while walking to the billeting area in the 27th Marines base camp southwest of Da Nang, the same lieutenant came upon a friend who had just bumped into an infiltrator on the darkened path.[11] The intruder had bolted, clotheslined himself on somebody's wash, and then disappeared. Of course, the foe in Vietnam could do more than just reconnoiter an objective from the inside. Countless U.S. support personnel had the unpleasant experience of waking up to the sound of running feet and exploding satchel charges. The defenses were not lax, the enemy soldiers were just good at short-range infiltration. If they hadn't inherited this expertise from their ancestors, they had learned it from their Russian mentors:

Infiltration by small detachments, as well as by larger units up to an entire division, was probably the most effective Russian method of night combat [in WWII]. It was effective at all times

(Source: FM 21-76 (1970), p. 43)

## Techniques from the NCO Corps

1. DITCHES/DEPRESSIONS THAT LEAD INTO AN ENEMY CAMP, BUT INSIDE OF WHICH, THERE ARE NO DEFENDERS POSTED.

2. PLACES WHERE THE FIELDS OF FIRE HAVE NOT BEEN CLEARED.

4. WHERE WET AREAS EXTEND INSIDE THE ENEMY'S LINES.

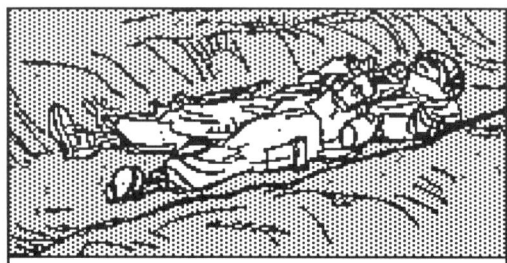

3. APPROACHES TO POSITIONS MANNED BY HABITUAL SLEEPERS.

5. AREAS IN DEEP SHADOW.

*Figure 20.1: Short-Range Infiltration Route Possibilities*
(Sources: FM 23-30 (1988), p. 2-8; FM 90-5 (1982), p. 1-5; FM 90-3 (1977), p. 4-9; FM 5-103 (1985), p. 4-4; FM 7-8 (1984), p. 69)

because the Russians were able to penetrate seemingly impassable terrain in any kind of weather.... Once the shortage of manpower had forced the German Army to resort to a system of defensive strongpoints rather than continuous lines, the Russians could employ their favorite night tactics to their greatest advantage. Time and time again their troops slipped through a lightly held sector during the night and were securely established behind the German front by the next morning.... Once established in the rear of the Division, the Russians lay low during the day, but came to life night after night. They sowed mines along the routes of communication, attacked columns bringing up rations and ammunition, and assaulted command posts and heavy-weapons positions.[12]

— DOA Pamphlet No. 20-236

### WHAT MAKES SHORT-RANGE INFILTRATION THE SAFEST TYPE OF DELIBERATE ATTACK

It's not hard to see why an attack by long-range infiltration costs less than a frontal assault. After all, completely bypassing enemy strongpoints is a good way to keep from getting hurt.

However, it's more difficult to see why *short-range infiltration is also safer*. Everyone can agree that *successfully* crawling between enemy fighting holes is safer than assaulting those holes. What must be explained is how one can crawl between those fighting holes without being detected in the first place. To achieve enough cover and concealment to accomplish this feat, an infantryman must know how to make the best use of microterrain and camouflage. And, to select a location at which to attempt this feat, he must know what constitutes a defensive weakness. But, that infantryman need *not* be specially trained as a sapper, as long as the objective is free of barbed wire. (See figure 20.1.)

### USING THE "MILITARY CREST" FOR COVER WHILE CRAWLING TO WITHIN GRENADE RANGE OF AN ENEMY FIGHTING HOLE

Where a defender's hole is positioned relative to the military crest establishes how easily an attacker can sneak up on its occupant. If the hole is above the place at which the slope falls away (as it usually is), an infiltrator can crawl up to the crest without being seen or shot. This is true whether or not the defender has thermal imaging. If the hole is also within grenade range of the crest (as it usually is), its occupant becomes extremely vulnerable. Countless Americans had to learn this lesson the hard way in Vietnam.

There will always be a few soldiers from any nation who won't learn where to position their fighting holes on sloping ground. In other words, there will always be opportunities for U.S. infiltrators to crawl within grenade range of enemy lines not protected by barbed wire. (See figure 20.2.)

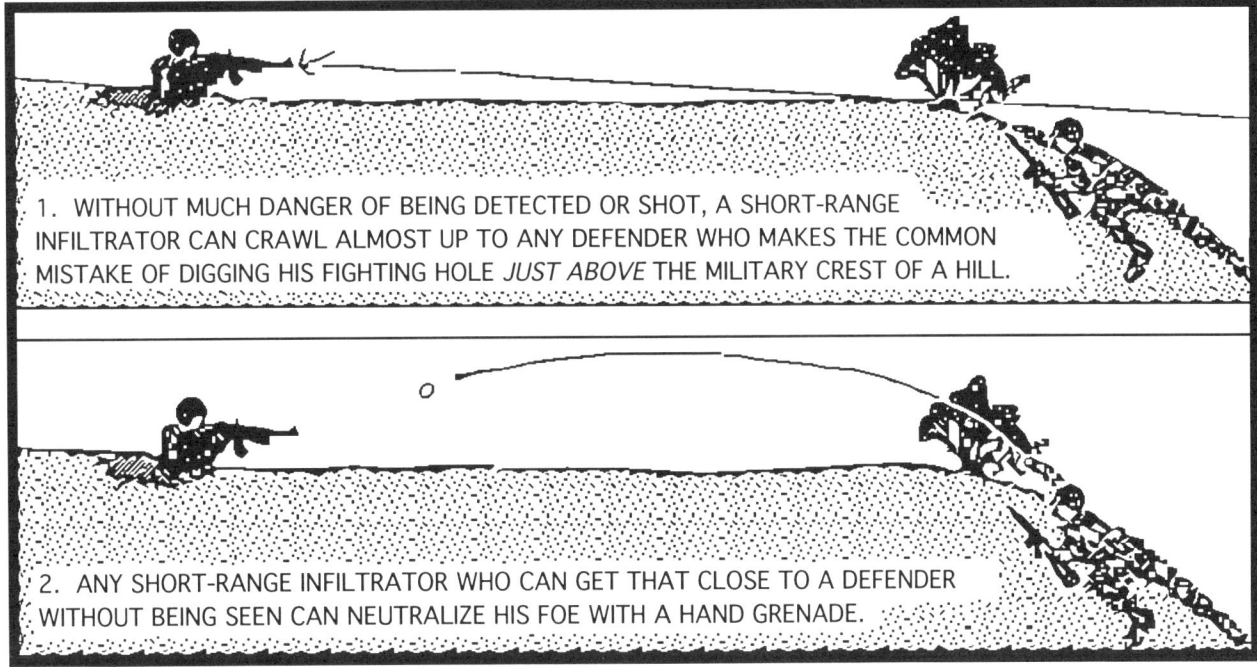

*Figure 20.2: How the Military Crest Helps the Short-Range Infiltrator*
(Sources: FM 7-8 (1984), p. 3-28; FM 7-11B1/2 (1978), p. 2-III-E-8.4; FM 7-11B3 (1976), p. 2-VII-C-4.4)

## USING VEGETATION FOR CONCEALMENT WHILE CRAWLING TO WITHIN GRENADE RANGE OF AN ENEMY FIGHTING HOLE

There are ways of sneaking to within grenade range of an alert defender across level ground. Unless that defender has cleared away every bit of vegetation to his front, he is vulnerable. Even in bright moonlight, a skilled infiltrator needs only a few isolated bushes for concealment. By keeping a bush between him and his quarry at all times, he can move forward without being seen. Of course, hard-pressed attackers learn quickly that lone trees and rocks provide valuable cover:

> About one hour after Kocak's act of valor which earned him two Medals of Honor [in WWI], Gunnery Sgt. Louis Cukela, a fellow member of the 66th Rifle Co., 5th Marines, crawled toward two machinegun positions. . . .
> Trying desperately to keep a tree between himself and the guns, Cukela inched forward. About 30 feet from the first pit he leaped, led by his fixed bayonet.
> He quickly killed two of the Germans occupying the pit, while the third made his way to the second German position. Cukela threw three grenades at the pit, and followed them with a charge.
> Four surviving Germans surrendered to Cukela. For this act he was awarded his Medals of Honor.[13]

## THE "ORIENTAL" INFILTRATION TECHNIQUE

The NVA had an infiltration technique that had to be seen to be believed. When the sun had set, enemy scouts camouflaged to look like bushes would start crawling toward a U.S. perimeter from different directions. They would move at whatever speed would make their arm and leg movements imperceptible to the naked eye under existing lighting conditions. Each would head for a fighting hole in his sector. By 3 o'clock in the morning, all would be within grenade range of their respective holes.

That a bush to the front of the lines was becoming larger over a matter of hours could be spotted by only the most discerning of U.S. defenders. Of course, there was no thermal imaging in those days. Now, even thermal imaging might have difficulty detecting an attacker covered with a camouflaged thermal blanket. (See figure 20.3.)

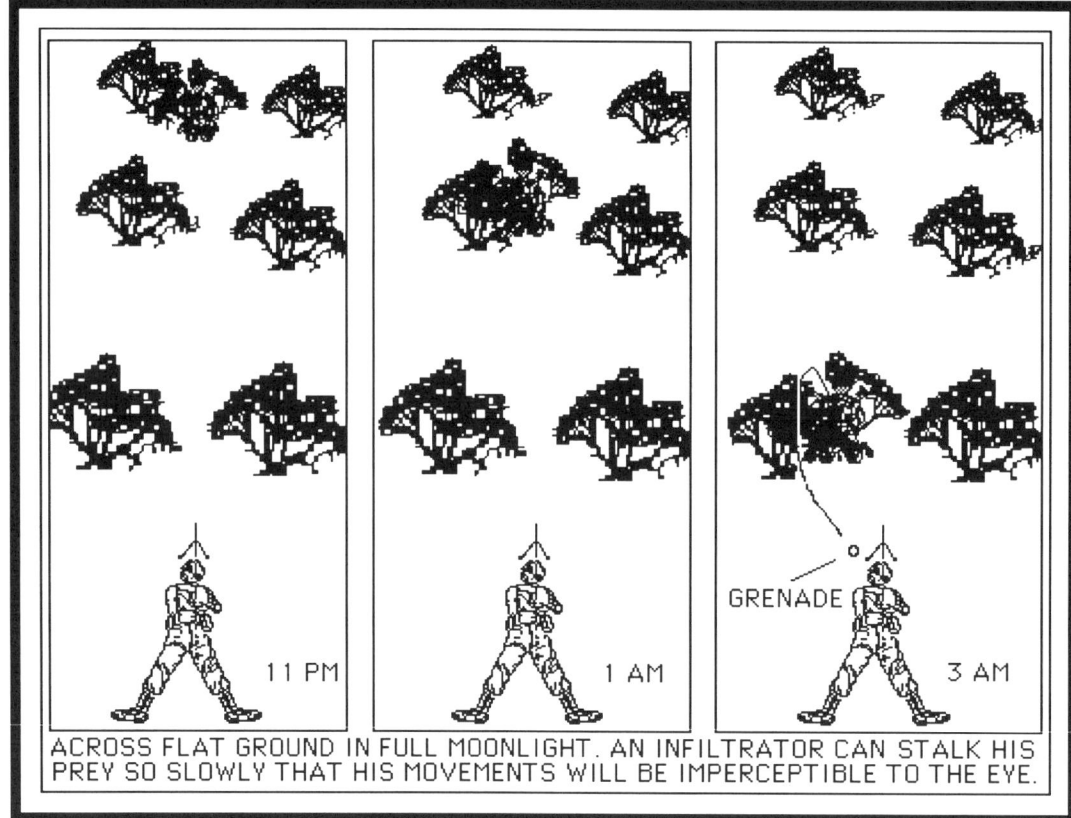

*Figure 20.3: The Oriental Infiltration Technique*
(Sources: FM 7-11B1/2 (1978), p. 2-iii-e-8.2; FM 7-8 (1984), p. 3-28)

## WHY NOT INFILTRATE TO THE ASSAULT POSITION DURING A DAY OR NIGHT ATTACK?

In the alternative night attack method described at the end of the last chapter, two-man teams crept up roughly parallel lanes to within grenade range of enemy emplacements. Some teams had a military crest to obscure their movements, and others had to rely on slow motion, vegetation, and low light. If the grenades missed their mark, the teams behind a military crest or some other form of cover did not have to assault.

If a few emplacements are captured in this manner, the whole enemy line becomes vulnerable. The new occupants can attack sideways without much difficulty. After all, the lateral distance between holes is seldom farther than grenade range, and defenders do not expect trouble from the side. With an identification signal (like the metal cricket used in Normandy), the attackers could consolidate their gains without illumination.

During a short-range infiltration attack, enemy lines are penetrated by stealth. Moving forward by stealth can also be useful prior to a traditional standup assault. If day or night attackers could secretly get within grenade range of their objective, their final assault would have a better chance of succeeding. One wonders why an attacking unit couldn't just infiltrate as close to an objective as possible, and then call that location the Final Coordination Line or Probable Line of Deployment.

## FOR POSITIONS WITHOUT BARBED WIRE, THERE'S ALSO AN ALTERNATIVE TO THE TRADITIONAL STANDUP ASSAULT

If two-man teams from the same squad were to crawl up roughly parallel lanes, and then quietly signal to each other upon finding a weakness in enemy lines, they would have an interesting alternative to the traditional upright assault. In all but totally barren terrain, this could work during the day. For example, if a buddy team were successfully to move through tall grass to within 20 yards of an enemy hole in their lane, could they not apprise the other teams of the potential "gap" through a radio-hand-set-keying code? The other teams could backtrack and fall in behind the successful team. Then, when the grenade was finally tossed, the whole squad could capitalize on the opportunity.

American Indians may have attacked this way. Instead of throwing a grenade, they may have waited for a distraction and then rushed their quarry. Instead of keying a radio handset, they may have used a distinctive bird call.

To develop a *detailed* plan of attack, leaders must have totally accurate and comprehensive information about the enemy's defenses. Seldom is this much information available before an attack, and the enemy can always modify his defensive posture after the attack gets underway. For these reasons, too much planning is counterproductive. When what had been planned didn't go as well as expected, Marines have often resorted to impromptu attacks by short-range infiltration:

(Source: FM 5-103 (1985), pp. 5-2, D-9)

Techniques from the NCO Corps

The second double-winner of the Medal of Honor [of five enlisted Marines in WWI] while fighting the Germans on the European battlefield was Sgt. Matej Kocak.

Combat was no stranger to Kocak, having served in various battles in the 10 years preceding World War I. . . .

In 1918, Kocak found himself as a member of the 66th Rifle Company, 5th Marines. Following the historic battle at Belleau Wood, Kocak and 70,000 French and American troops were tasked with crushing the last German offensive of the war. . . .

One machinegun nest posed a great threat to the Marines, though, as it sat cloaked and fortified nearly 200 yards away. . . .

Crawling through brush, Kocak listened to the firing of the gun, using the sound as his guide. Finally, he was upon the position. When he leaped at the nest, the startled Germans fled, leaving their machinegun. But also remaining was a supporting machinegun nest.

As the rounds of the second machinegun impacted all around him, Kocak crawled back into the safety of the woods. There, he joined with 25 French colonial troops — Moroccans who were notorious for their ability with knives. . . .

Together they were able to maneuver to the nest [and successfully assault it without firing a shot].[14]

Two problems have always plagued the daytime attacker: (1) he can't reconnoiter his objective from close range without revealing his intentions, and (2) he can't attack quickly without taking an unacceptable risk. Both problems can be resolved by using what will be called the "daylight infiltration technique." With it, there's no need for preliminary reconnaissance, because the movement forward is accomplished through *"recon pull."* And with it, the attack can be launched quickly with minimal risk, because it requires little or no rehearsal and takes the path of least resistance. (See figures 20.4 through 20.7 for what a daylight attack employing infiltration methods might look like.)

(Source: FM 7-8 (1984), p. 69)

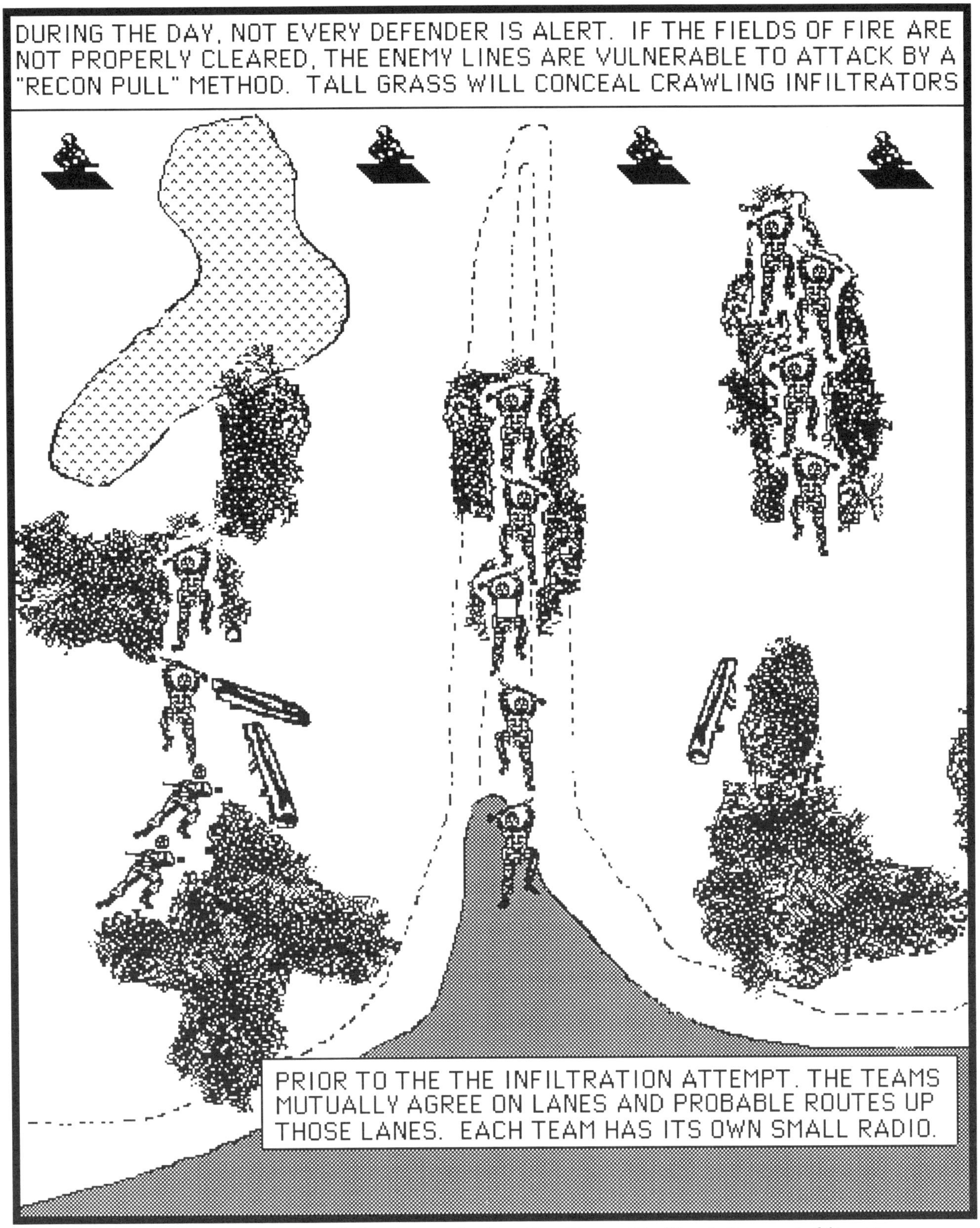

*The Safest Way to Attack — Short-Range Infiltration*

> DURING THE DAY, NOT EVERY DEFENDER IS ALERT. IF THE FIELDS OF FIRE ARE NOT PROPERLY CLEARED, THE ENEMY LINES ARE VULNERABLE TO ATTACK BY A "RECON PULL" METHOD. TALL GRASS WILL CONCEAL CRAWLING INFILTRATORS

> PRIOR TO THE THE INFILTRATION ATTEMPT, THE TEAMS MUTUALLY AGREE ON LANES AND PROBABLE ROUTES UP THOSE LANES. EACH TEAM HAS ITS OWN SMALL RADIO.

*Figure 20.4: Locating Soft Spots during the Day with Short-Range Infiltration*
(Sources: FM 7-11B3 (1976), p. 2-VII-C-4.4; FM 7-70 (1986), p. 4-20; FM 5-103 (1985), p. 4-6)

Techniques from the NCO Corps

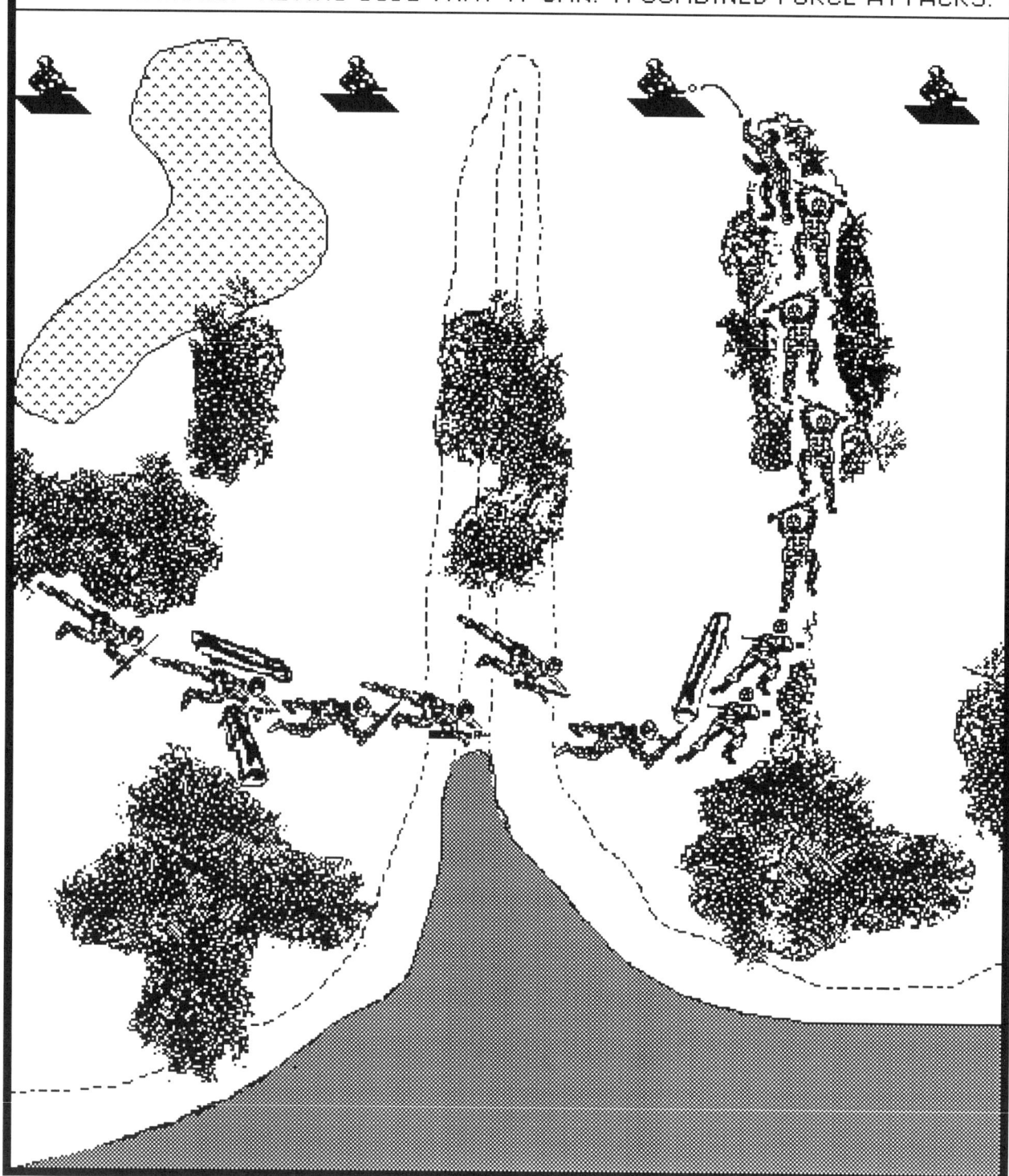

*Figure 20.5: The Teams That Can't Get Close, Fall In behind Those That Can*
(Sources: FM 7-11B3 (1976), p. 2-VII-C-4.4; FM 7-70 (1986), p. 4-20; MCI 03.66a (1986), p. 2-8; FM 5-103 (1985), p. 4-6)

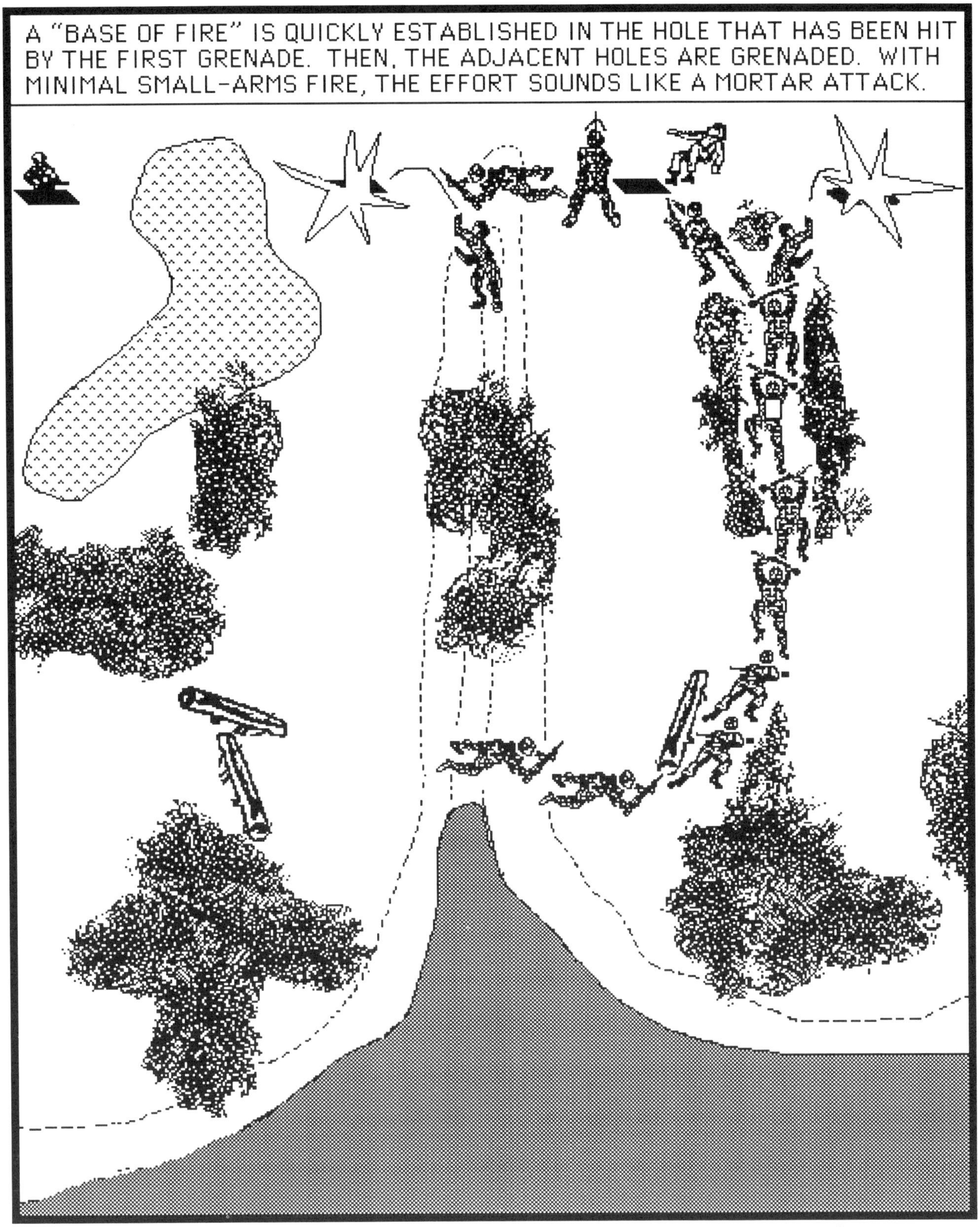

*The Safest Way to Attack — Short-Range Infiltration*

A "BASE OF FIRE" IS QUICKLY ESTABLISHED IN THE HOLE THAT HAS BEEN HIT BY THE FIRST GRENADE. THEN, THE ADJACENT HOLES ARE GRENADED. WITH MINIMAL SMALL-ARMS FIRE, THE EFFORT SOUNDS LIKE A MORTAR ATTACK.

*Figure 20.6: Once within Grenade Range, It's Easy to Force Open a Gap*
(Sources: FM 7-11B1/2 (1978), p. 2-III-E-8.2; FM 7-11B3 (1976), p. 2-VII-C-4.4; FM 7-70 (1986), p. 4-20; FM 5-103 (1985), p. 4-6; FM 22-100 (1983), p. 84)

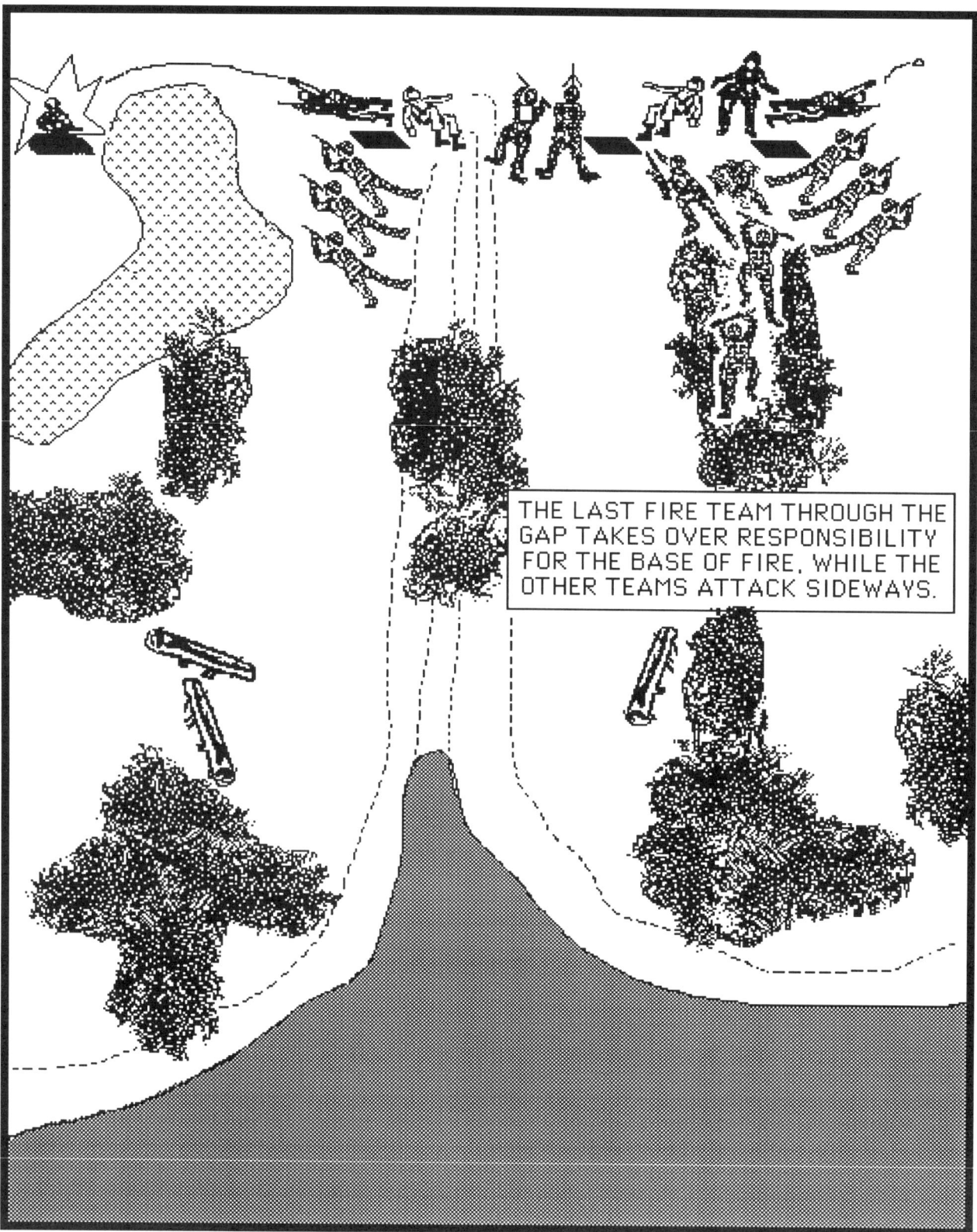

*Figure 20.7: The Gap Can Be Easily Widened*
(Sources: FM 7-11B1/2 (1978), pp. 2-III-E-8.2, 2-IV-B-1.3; FM 7-11B3 (1976), p. 2-VII-C-4.4; FM 7-70 (1986), p. 4-20; FM 5-103 (1985), p. 4-6; FM 22-100 (1983), p. 84; FM 23-30 (1988), p. 2-8)

## BACK TO THE PROBLEM OF PENETRATING ENEMY LINES STRICTLY BY STEALTH

To attack an objective by short-range infiltration, a unit should have as part of its mission "penetrating the enemy's lines by stealth." When *any portion* of this unit succeeds in sneaking through those lines undetected, the unit as a whole has accomplished that aspect of its mission. That's why the attack by short-range infiltration is not as difficult as it sounds. *Not all the infiltration teams have to get through.* Only in danger are those that try to pass between enemy fighting holes after realizing they have no chance. Preliminary reconnaissance can identify a promising gap for each team. Then, for the attack to succeed, only one team has to make it through its respective gap. One team can conduct the subsequent operation.

Over the course of several years, a Marine instructor watched as hundreds of NCO's tried to sneak through defensive lines carefully chosen and fully manned by their peers. About 15% got through undetected, and all but a few of the rest got to within grenade range of the defender in their lane.[15] These statistics are significant for a number of reasons. The defenders were encouraged to shoot MILES laser beams at suspected targets, and the attackers were forced to wear MILES laser sensors on their torsos and heads. The attackers had no formal sapper training, while the defenders had just received instruction in countersapper defensive techniques. The nights were not particularly dark, and the defenders knew precisely when and where the infiltrators would strike. These statistics infer that U.S. infantrymen have more than enough natural ability to do what Orientals have been doing for centuries. Still, one wonders what types of knowledge might enhance that ability.

## WHICH MICROTERRAIN OR VEGETATION GIVES ENOUGH COVER AND CONCEALMENT?

One's chances of entering enemy lines by stealth are enhanced by a thorough reconnaissance of the lines beforehand. Those responsible must know what to look for.

First, they should look for heavily foliated approaches to the objective. Here defenders cannot properly clear fields of fire. Where their lines abut thicket or jungle, they must often settle for "fire lanes." By moving slowly, prone humans can secretly cross fire lanes. On these bushy approaches to the objective, the reconnaissance team has only to determine whether or not the defenders have removed the bottom branches from the bushes to their direct front. Downrange of more typical sectors, defenders remove large obstructions, but ignore tall grass and weeds. Again, that's all the concealment an infiltrator needs.

Then, reconnaissance personnel should look for water-runoff ditches that intersect enemy lines. These are infiltration conduits, as long as defenders do not physically occupy them. If a linear depression is to be substituted, its bottom must be hidden from the defender on either side. Of course, what is hidden and what isn't, depends on the lighting conditions. As the moon is setting, a shadow from one lip of the depression may hide an infiltrator who would otherwise be visible.

Seldom are forces properly distributed along a defensive sector. This sector is often equally divided among subordinate units of the same size. For example, on a perimeter, one element may have 4-8 o'clock, another 8-12, and the third 12-4. On everything but perfectly level ground, what results is an imbalance in defensive effort — some sectors are overdefended, and others underdefended. To counter infiltration, the sector with the most diversity in microterrain would need more men. The attacker could conclude that the sector with the most wrinkled ground would probably be undermanned. It would be a prime target for short-range infiltration.

Any wet area is also ideal for infiltration. Defenders dislike sitting on damp ground for extended periods of time. Further, the sound of running water will mask the sound of a crawling man.

## OTHER CONDUITS FOR INFILTRATION

To discover more subtle infiltration routes through enemy lines, the reconnaissance team must first pinpoint the enemy emplacements. Given enough time, any defender will give away his location. He will either make a noise, sneak a cigarette, talk to his partner, or move against the horizon. Or, a well-meaning superior will walk up, silhouette himself, and start talking to him.

Some watchstanders get drowsy during the wee hours of the morning. If a sleeper is observed, his defensive sector becomes a promising infiltration lane.

Low light, by itself, constitutes an opportunity for short-range infiltration. On an overcast night *after the moon has set,* defenders can't see their hands in front of their faces. Standard night vision devices magnify existing light and aren't reliable at times like this. It's so dark that a column of attackers could pass upright between enemy holes. They would need luminous "cat eyes" on their headgear just to keep from becoming separated.

On a brightly moonlit night, trees cast shadows. These shadows lengthen and move as the moon moves. A shadow will hide a prone figure.

Various background noises will mask the sounds of a crawling human being. On a wet night, there's the incessant racket of rain and wind hitting vegetation and defenders' helmets. To move through dry underbrush or leaves, one needs only occasional helicopter, armor, or artillery noise. To operate silently, infiltrators must carry minimal equipment. An assault rifle with two magazines taped together is the largest weapon that should be contemplated, and a pistol is quieter. To create the deception that an objective was just under mortar attack, the German stormtroopers of WWI only carried grenades:

To facilitate crawling, the field uniform was reinforced with leather patches on the knees and elbows. As the hand grenade had eclipsed the rifle as the chief individual weapon of the stormtrooper, the leather belt and shoulder harness that had supported the rifle ammunition pouches were discarded in favor of a pair of over-the-shoulder bags to carry hand grenades.[16]

Artillery illumination can occasionally work to an infiltrator's advantage. In a stiff breeze, illumination canisters swing from their parachutes to create moving shadows in forested terrain. These moving shadows can hide moving men. The bright light also temporarily blinds the defenders wearing NVG's.

Enemy lines are not generally well guarded as the sun first warms the earth. The defenders who are not asleep, are eating or off on personal business. An infiltrator can use this lapse in vigilance to his advantage. In fact, he can capitalize on any pattern the defender sets in leaving or facing away from his defensive sector.

Finally, a deception can cause the defending unit to shift personnel out of the target sector. The Confederates won the Battle of Chickamauga after noticing a gap in Union lines that had been created when one unit went to the assistance of another. The possibilities for short-range infiltration are only limited by one's imagination.

## THE OPTIONS FOR ESCAPE AFTER A SUCCESSFUL INFILTRATION

There's not much said about what happens to those who succeed in penetrating enemy lines by stealth and then execute a follow-up strike. Nor is there much talk about a secondary mission for those who can't make it through enemy lines initially. Perhaps the second group could help the first group to get away. They could do so by forcing open an escape route.

Those who successfully penetrate by stealth only have a few ways to escape on their own. They can leave the same way they came in, force their way out, or hide and defend themselves until a major offensive can rescue them. While hiding until dawn might be possible, defending themselves until relieved seems a bit farfetched. If the enemy fire didn't get them, the friendly fire would. Only after conducting a subsequent operation with silenced weapons or explosives on a delay timer, would the infiltrators stand much chance of getting out on their own.

On the other hand, if the subsequent operation involved shooting or risk of discovery, the enemy lines would almost certainly become fully alerted and illuminated, and the infiltrators would have little chance of fighting their way out. However, this shooting might constitute a diversion of sorts. It would cause the frontline defenders to turn around. When they did, a grenade attack from just outside their lines might open an escape route.

## THE PLAN OF ATTACK

The phases of an attack by short-range infiltration must be planned in reverse order. First, one must consider the subsequent operation to be conducted by those who successfully infiltrate. If this operation can be accomplished silently (like with delayed explosions), those who stealthily get into the enemy camp, can get back out the same way. And those who can't get in, won't need a secondary mission. That's why two-man teams with satchel charges and timers stand the best chance. However, if those who penetrate enemy lines by stealth must make noise during their subsequent operation, they will need help escaping. And those who can't get through enemy lines are in a perfect position to provide that help.

Next, the planners must pick a covered and concealed place inside enemy lines and near the subsequent target. It will double as rendezvous point and assault position.

Then, to capitalize on what has been learned from the close-in reconnaissance, roughly parallel infiltration lanes must be chosen. Among other things, each lane must contain a promising gap and *no* barbed wire. This gap may be where an enemy emplacement is just above the military crest, fighting holes are too far apart, undefended ditches intersect enemy lines, areas are wet, fields of fire are improperly cleared, deep shade covers the area between holes, or sleepers man the lines.

Times must be chosen in reverse order as well. Two factors will affect "rendezvous time": (1) before dawn and after rendezvous, successful infiltrators will need at least an hour to conduct their subsequent mission and escape; (2) after the moon sets and the defenders tire (2:00 A.M.), prospective infiltrators will need *two* hours to transit the dangerous ground between enemy holes. That way each member of a two-man team can make the dangerous trip alone *while his partner covers*. The "time of departure" should permit teams ample opportunity to approach and study their preselected gaps while the moon is still out.

## PREPARING FOR WHAT NOW SEEMS POSSIBLE

As with the other types of deliberate attacks, this one takes extensive rehearsal. Of particular importance is the linkup between groups at the rendezvous point.

While part of the unit performs the preliminary reconnaissance, the others can train. They can take turns sneaking past each other. Before setting off on the actual attempt, team members should carefully camouflage themselves to match the scenery at the point of attack.

## THE INFILTRATION ATTACK THAT MAY MAKE NOISE DURING THE SUBSEQUENT OPERATION

To execute a short-range infiltration attack with a noisy subsequent operation, the unit must cross the line of departure and move to the release point shortly after dark. There the teams go off into their respective lanes, and advance like small patrols seeking to avoid enemy contact. They crawl within sight of their predetermined penetration points and prudently spend some time assessing the situation for themselves. As most will be observing their assigned gaps for the first time, they must also have the authority to decide whether or not to proceed.

*Those that don't think they can get through without being discovered, don't even try!* Instead, they dispatch one team member to within grenade range of a defensive hole in their lane. The easiest way for him to approach that hole is from the downhill side of a military crest. Another way is to keep a tree or rock directly between himself and his quarry. Still another way is to use the Oriental infiltration technique. In any case, his final destination should offer some cover, if possible.

The teams that decide to proceed should wait for an opportune time: a distraction, a changing of the guard, helicopter noise, a rain squall, ground fog, a shadow lengthening, the moon setting, or a cloud covering the moon. Each team member should make the attempt individually while the other covers. Once through enemy lines, teams go to the rendezvous point. At the rendezvous time, those assembled launch the subsequent operation.

Only if the subsequent operation *makes noise,* do the teams stuck just outside enemy lines perform their secondary mission. Under cover of darkness and while the frontline defenders are distracted, these outside teams throw grenades. The teams scoring direct hits on targeted holes crawl into them, but those failing to score direct hits stay outside the lines and wait for the pullback signal.

During a lull in the illumination, the sectors captured are widened enough to accommodate an escaping column of troops. Then, the friendlies manning those sectors send a *discreet* pullback signal to the inside group. To the enemy, a *white-star cluster* would look like a defective illumination pop-up, and a flashlight or cigarette lighter like a frontline defender surveying mortar damage.

Upon seeing the signal, the members of the inside group move toward the captured sector during lulls in the illumination. When they make good their escape, the friendly personnel manning the sector fall in behind them. Those still stuck outside the lines use this activity as a diversion to pull back themselves. The concurrent events should create competing demands on the defenders' attention. Then, all groups return to the line of departure along whichever lane they are in.

It takes a certain amount of patience to attack this way, but no more than the average Westerner can muster. The Germans used a similar procedure eighty years ago:

> [T]he Germans pioneered the development of . . . the infiltration attack. . . . [S]mall columns of stormtroopers used terrain to infiltrate the enemy's defense.[17]
> — MCI 7401

Rohr solved the problem of getting across no man's land. Through experience, he discovered that small columns of specially trained assault troops, using . . . terrain for cover, could cross no man's land and penetrate the enemy trench lines at several points. Then, trench lines were rolled up using hand grenades.[18]
— MCI 7401

Is this technique dangerous? Perhaps, but charging as a group into enemy machinegun fire is dangerous too. Courage has never been a problem for Americans; they exhibit it just as readily as individuals as they do in groups. To practice maneuver warfare, commanders must delegate some of their control to the lowest echelons. By thinking for themselves, individual infantrymen can better mesh their abilities with the threats they encounter. In other words, they have less chance of overcommitting themselves. Given the opportunity to choose whether or not to proceed forward, they have more survivability. Not only must they have the option to think, they must also have training on how to think:

> Untutored courage (is) useless in the face of educated bullets.[19]
> — Patton

## THE TECHNIQUE TO PRACTICE IN PEACETIME

This short-range infiltration technique involves sequential steps just as the day and night attack methods did. These steps give the technique the appearance of being methodical in nature, but here the unit as a whole does not have to wait for its slowest or unluckiest member. Only one infiltration team out of several has to get through enemy lines, and only one that can't get through has to score a direct hit with a grenade to capture the escape route. Here control is more *decentralized.* This is a better example of maneuver warfare. Of course, the best example is the infiltration attack that gives the enemy no clue that he has even been attacked on the ground. Unfortunately, against prepared enemy positions (those protected by barbed wire), this takes trained sappers.

It should now be clear why short-range infiltration is the safest of the three deliberate attacks. No one has to do more than he personally deems feasible, and fewer people are required to accomplish the mission. It just takes two "successful" infiltrators to do plenty of damage inside an enemy position, and two "frustrated" infiltrators to capture the escape route. That means that only four personnel were seriously endangered during the entire attack.

Because this infiltration technique is methodical in appearance, it can be practiced in peacetime. As with the day and night attack methods, those steps that don't strictly apply to existing circumstances can be skipped. (See table 20.1 and figures 20.8 through 20.15.)

## Techniques from the NCO Corps

*(Source: FM 21-75 (1967), p. 67)*

> IDENTIFIED (PROBABLY THE NIGHT BEFORE THROUGH CLOSE-RANGE RECONNAISSANCE) ARE PARALLEL LANES THAT EACH CONTAIN ONE GAP.
>
> AT DUSK, SEVERAL INFILTRATION TEAMS MOVE UP RESPECTIVE LANES.
>
> THOSE THAT CAN SNEAK THROUGH ENEMY LINES, DO SO ABOUT 2:00 A.M.
>
> THOSE THAT CAN'T SNEAK THROUGH, DISPATCH ONE MAN TO A COVERED LOCATION WITHIN GRENADE RANGE OF AN ENEMY HOLE IN THEIR LANE.
>
> AFTER RENDEZVOUS, THE INSIDE TEAMS RUN SUBSEQUENT OPERATION.
>
> WITH SILENCE OR EXPLOSIONS, INSIDE TEAMS SNEAK OUT SAME GAPS.
>
> IF THERE IS ANY SHOOTING, (DURING LULL IN ILLUMINATION AND WITH COMMOTION AS DIVERSION) OUTSIDE TEAMS GRENADE ENEMY HOLES.
>
> ONLY THE TEAMS SCORING DIRECT HITS CRAWL INTO THOSE HOLES.
>
> DURING ILLUMINATION LULL AND AFTER IDENTIFICATION CHECK, SEIZED SECTORS CAN BE EXPANDED BY ATTACKING SIDEWAYS WITH GRENADES.
>
> FROM FOOTHOLD CENTERS, ESCAPE ROUTE LOCATIONS ARE SIGNALLED TO INSIDE GROUP BY INFRARED FLASHLIGHT OR OTHER DISCREET MEANS.
>
> AFTER THE INSIDE GROUP ESCAPES THROUGH THE CENTER OF ONE FOOTHOLD, THOSE MANNING THAT FOOTHOLD FOLLOW IN TRACE.
>
> THOSE MANNING OTHER FOOTHOLDS OR STILL STUCK JUST OUTSIDE ENEMY LINES USE THIS ACTIVITY AS DIVERSION TO ESCAPE THEMSELVES.

*Table 20.1: The Short-Range Infiltration Sequence*

The Safest Way to Attack — Short-Range Infiltration

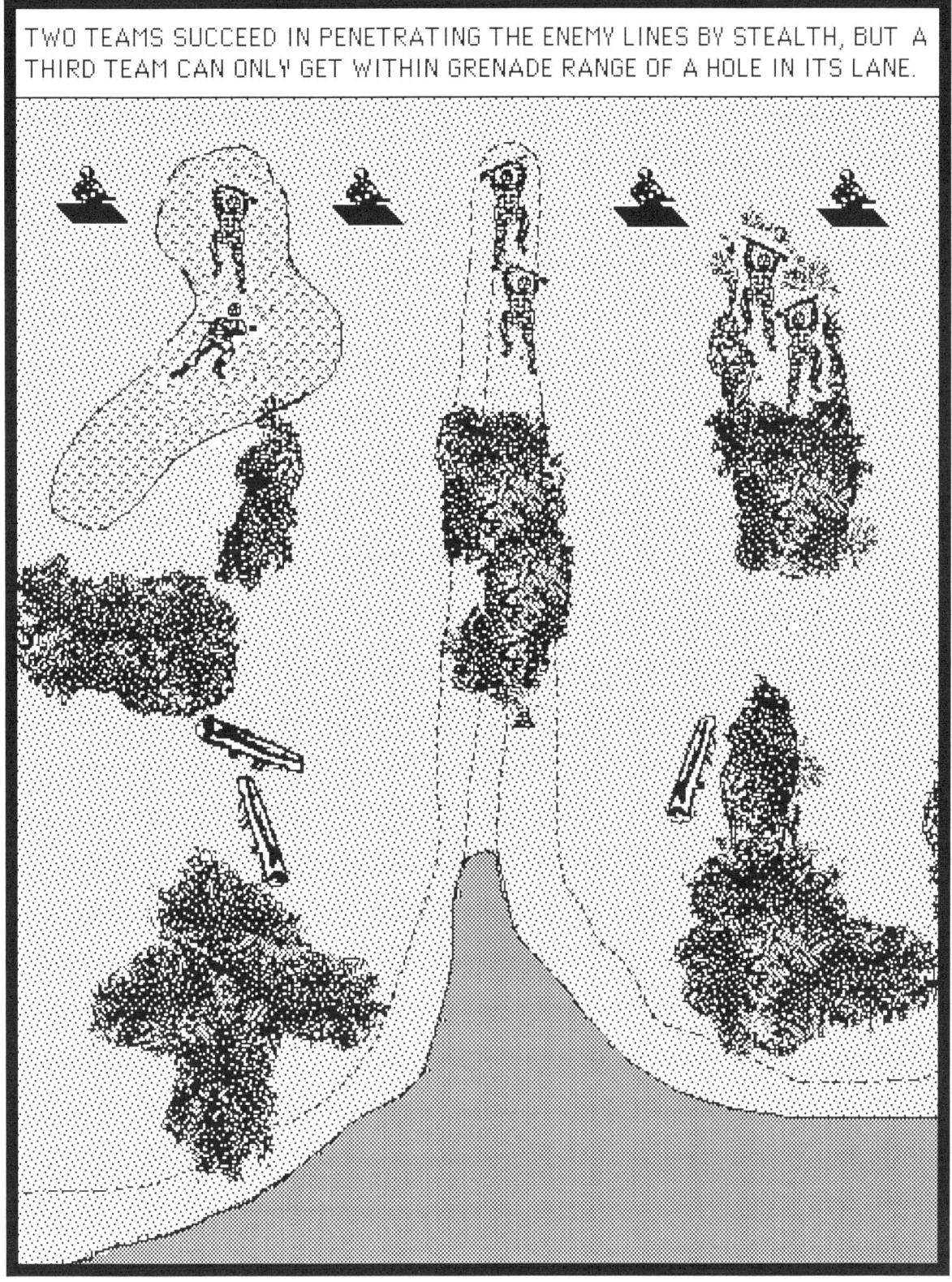

Figure 20.8: Unsuccessful Infiltration Teams Can Still Serve a Useful Purpose
(Sources: FM 5-103 (1985), p. 4-6; TC 90-1 (1986), p. 3-71; FM 7-70 (1986), p. 4-20)

Techniques from the NCO Corps

Figure 20.9: The Linkup at the Rendezvous Point between Successful Teams
(Sources: FM 5-103 (1985), p. 4-6; TC 90-1 (1986), p. 3-71, cover; FM 7-70 (1986), p. 4-20; MCI 03.66a (1986), p. 2-8)

Figure 20.10: If Possible, the Subsequent Attack Should Use Explosives Only
(Sources: FM 7-8 (1984), p. 3-1; TC 90-1 (1986), p. 3-71; FM 22-100 (1983), p. 84; FM 7-70 (1986), p. 4-20; FM 5-103 (1985), p. 4-6)

Techniques from the NCO Corps

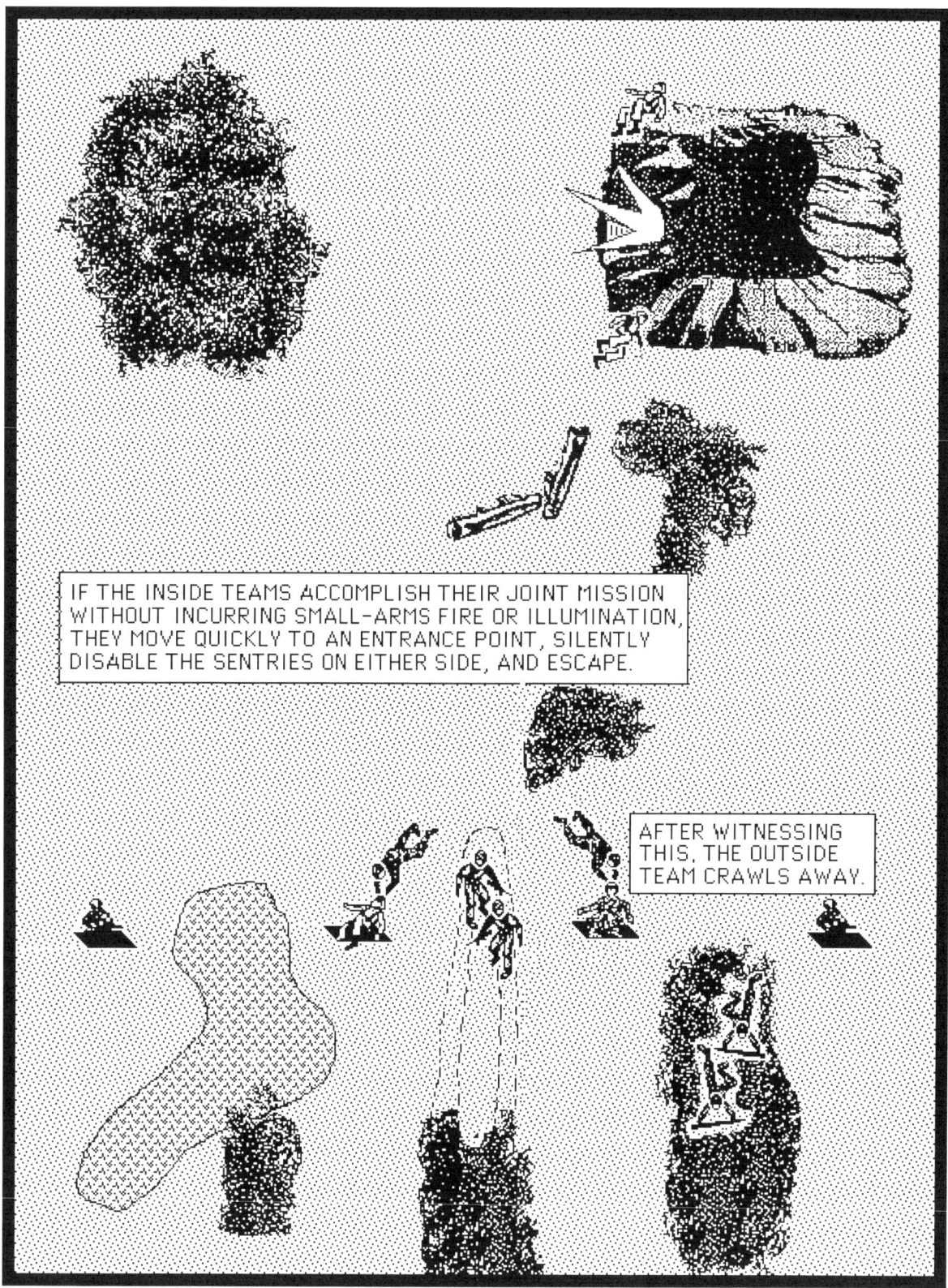

Figure 20.11: The Safest Way to Escape Is Silently
(Sources: FMFM 6-7 (1989), p. 1-13; TC 90-1 (1986), p. 3-71, cover; FM 22-100 (1983), p. 84; FM 7-70 (1986), p. 4-20; MCI 03.66a (1986), p. 2-8; FM 5-103 (1985), p. 4-6)

*The Safest Way to Attack — Short-Range Infiltration*

**IF THERE IS FIRING, THEY MUST ESCAPE ANOTHER WAY.**

(Source: FM 7-8 (1984), p. 5-24)

Techniques from the NCO Corps

Figure 20.12: The Sound of Small Arms Would Be the Signal for the Outside Teams to Act
(Sources: FM 7-8 (1984), p. 3-1; TC 90-1 (1986), p. 3-71; FM 22-100 (1983), p. 84; FM 7-70 (1986), p.4-20; MCI 03.66a (1986), p. 2-8, FM 5-103 (1985), p. 4-6)

*The Safest Way to Attack — Short-Range Infiltration*

*Figure 20.13: The Outside Team Is in a Good Position to Force Open a Gap in the Lines*
(Sources: FM 7-11B3 (1976), p. 2-VII-C-4.4; FM 7-8 (1984), p. 3-1; TC 90-1 (1986), p. 3-71; FM 22-100 (1983), p. 84; FM 7-70 (1986), p. 4-20; MCI 03.66a (1986), p. 2-8; FM 5-103 (1985), p. 4-6)

## Techniques from the NCO Corps

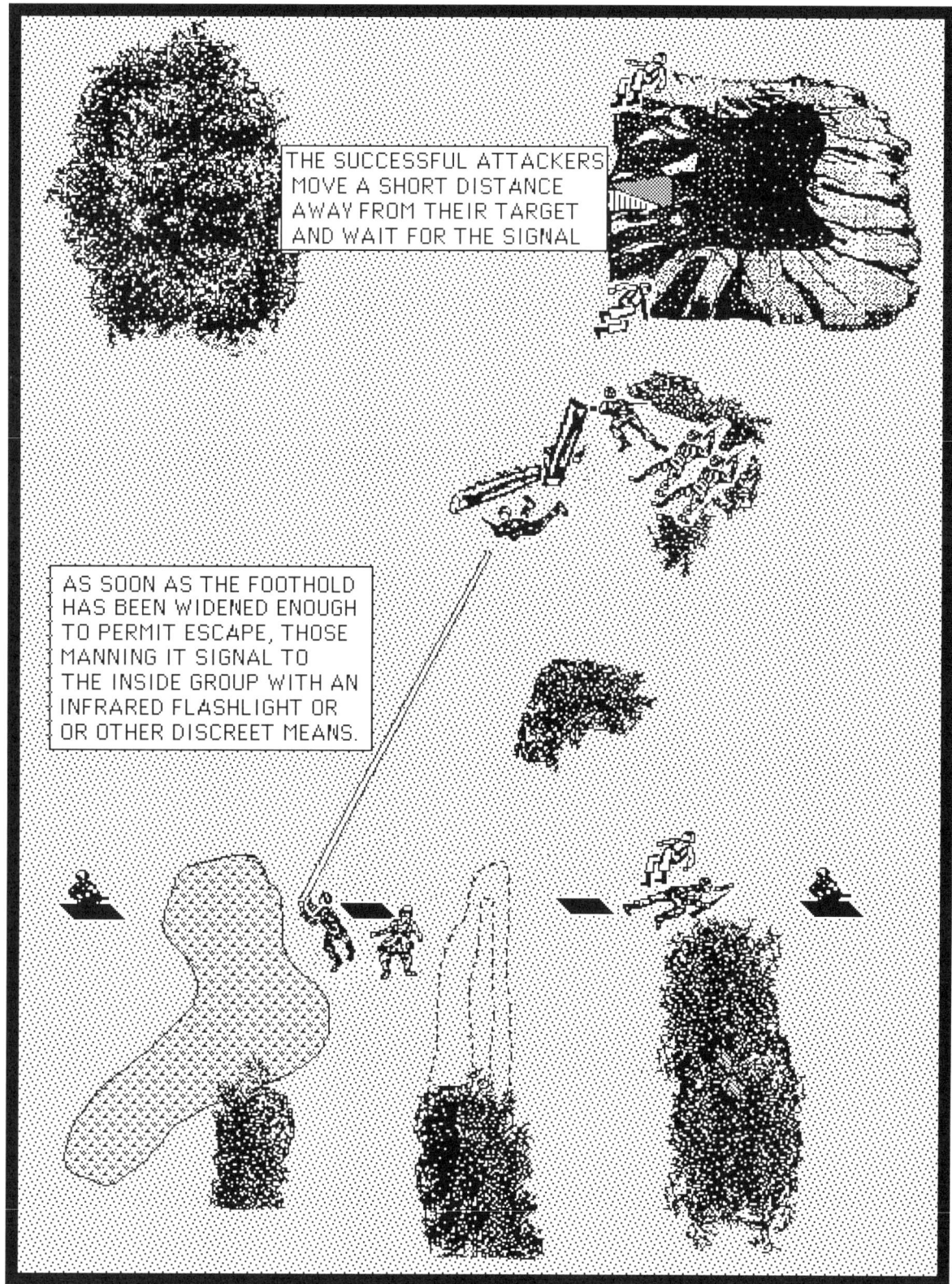

*Figure 20.14: Telling the Inside Group Where the Foothold Is Located*
(Sources: TC 90-1 (1986), p. 3-71; FM 7-11B1/2 (1978), pp. 2-II-A-5.2, 2-IV-B-1.3; FM 7-11B3 (1976), p. 2-VII-C-4.4; FM 22-100 (1983), p. 84; FM 7-70 (1986), p.4-20; MCI 03.66a (1986), p. 2-8; FM 5-103 (1985), p. 4-6)

The Safest Way to Attack — Short-Range Infiltration

Figure 20.15: The Entire Force Makes Good Its Escape
(Sources: TC 90-1 (1986), p. 3-71, cover; FM 7-11B1/2 (1978), p. 2-II-A-5.2; FM 22-100 (1983), p. 84; FM 7-70 (1986), p. 4-20; MCI 03.66a (1986), p. 2-8; FM 5-103 (1985), p. 4-6)

## OTHER INFILTRATION ATTACK POSSIBILITIES

The technique just described works best, when the subsequent mission can be accomplished quietly. Of course, some sounds can be masked with a noisy diversion.

In Vietnam, the NVA had a long-range infiltration technique that is well worth copying. Squad-sized elements of an American unit could move along different routes through hostile country at night, and then rendezvous near a lucrative target just before dawn. The reunited unit could watch and plan for a day, and then attack the next night. If the unit's objective had been previously reconnoitered *from the inside* by well-trained sappers, how could the attack fail? In fact, one wonders what it might take to stop a perfectly prepared sapper.

(Source: FM 7-8 (1984), p. B-8)

# 21     Defend Only to Reestablish Momentum

- On defense, why must both warfare styles be used simultaneusly?
- Which defensive procedure best counters each aspect of the threat?
- What are some ways to deceive an attacker?

(Sources: FM 5-103 (1985), pp. 4-4, 4-7; FM 7-11B3 (1976), p. 2-III-C-4.2)

## ATTACKING AND DEFENDING NEED NOT BE MUTUALLY EXCLUSIVE

"Attack, attack, attack" has been the message so far from the literature. Through attack, lies the shortest road to victory. But, to defend, an infantry unit does not have to stop attacking. "Providing for the security and integrity of the force" is one of the Fundamentals of the Offense. Just as a patrol can conduct security on the move, so too can an attacking force run flank and rear security during its assault.

If a unit can defend while attacking, maybe the converse is also true. After all, "making maximum use of offensive action" is one of the Fundamentals of the Defense. A defense need not be stationary; it can be mobile.

It may be counterproductive to draw too clear a distinction between attacking and defending. Throughout this chapter, an offensive thought process will be applied to the traditional static defense.

## HOW SELECTIVELY DEFENDING CAN ALSO CONTRIBUTE TO FINAL VICTORY

The literature recommends attacking *only when victory is assured*. Implicit in this qualification is a subtle warning — attacks should only be pressed home as long as winning (at acceptable cost) remains likely. Against a skilled opponent, not every attack will go as well as expected. Plus, there will be other unavoidable delays in any offense. Every time an attacking force stops to consolidate its gains or to plan its next strike, it must establish a hasty defense. In other words, whenever a unit stops attacking for any reason, it must defend. Its road to victory only lengthens when it becomes too comfortable during these stops — too satisfied with the status quo.

The static defense has a dangerous allure. Against a larger foe, a stationary defender can sometimes get lucky and do some real damage. Against an opponent who uses flawed or repetitive attack technique, he can become almost complacent. Still, by itself, no defense can achieve victory. The Confederates at Fredericksburg turned back no fewer than fourteen Union assaults on Marye's Heights. Yet, they did not inflict a mortal blow on the Union army; they succeeded only in forestalling that army's ultimate triumph later in the war.

It can be misleading to attribute too much significance to the lopsided casualty count that occasionally results from a successful static defense. By so doing, one might mistakenly conclude that the defense is always more productive than the offense. A tactic's real worth lies in its contribution to the overall outcome of the war. Some 5000 defenders were lost at Fredericksburg, compared to 13,000 attackers. Had the same 5000 been expended during an attack on Washington, D.C., after the First Battle of Bull Run, the war might have ended much sooner and hundreds of thousands of casualties been averted. Much of what nineteenth-century Americans thought a static defense could accomplish may have been an illusion. One wonders how productive the tactic might really be.

On a tiny island in the Pacific during WWII, the Marines almost looked forward to an all-out Japanese "banzai" attack. By defeating it, they could break the back of the resistance on the island. However, theirs was a unique situation — their opponents preferred death to surrender and could not be reinforced. After blunting such an attack, the Marines instinctively knew as well that they must attack themselves to capitalize on their temporary advantage. One could surmise from their exploits that the attrition warfare style of defense works well against human-wave assaults and short-range infiltration. However, history also makes clear that a successful defense cannot decisively win a battle. It can only lay the groundwork for the *counterattack* that does win the battle.

Maneuver warfare enthusiasts point out that the real value of the defense lies not in killing the enemy, but rather in *interrupting his momentum*. Only then, can friendly forces reestablish their own momentum to gain the ultimate victory at minimal cost. In other words, a defense is only as useful as the follow-up attack it facilitates. Military scholars from the Orient would add that a defense can function as the first phase of an offense. One alluded to this as early as twenty-five hundred years ago:

His [Sun Tzu's] principles of taking preemptive measures, of fighting a quick battle to force a quick decision, of bringing the enemy to the battlefield instead of being brought there by him, are all for the sake of gaining the initiative in a war.[1]

Invincibility lies in the defense; the possibility of victory in the attack.[2]
— Sun Tzu

## TO HAVE THE BEST CHANCE, THE DEFENDER MUST CHOOSE CIRCUMSTANCES TO HIS LIKING

To what extent any tactical technique will work in combat is greatly influenced by when and where it is tried. It depends on how closely the circumstances under which it is attempted can be matched to those for which it was designed. The defender has the best chance to study the ground before a battle. If he fully avails himself of this chance, and carefully chooses *where* to defend, he can win:

So it is that good warriors take their stand on ground where they cannot lose, and do not overlook conditions that make an opponent prone to defeat.[3]
— Sun Tzu

Central to the Oriental way of war, and thus to maneuver warfare, is luring the attacker into circumstances unfavorable to him:

Thus, one who is skilled at making the enemy move, does so by creating a situation, according to which the enemy will act. He entices the enemy with something he is certain to want. He keeps the enemy on the move by holding out bait and then attacks him with picked troops.[4]
— Sun Tzu

Hold out baits to lure the enemy. Strike the enemy when he is in disorder.[5]
— Sun Tzu

An Oriental defends not to preserve the status quo, but rather to seize the initiative. He sets a trap that cannot fail. By defending, he throws his adversary off balance or demoralizes him. He does so to make that adversary more vulnerable to subsequent attack. To the Oriental, the defense is a type of offense.

## THE DEFENSIVE STYLE MUST MATCH THE THREAT

The traditional or rigid defense is the most effective against human-wave assault. Interlocking machinegun fire along the outer edge of tactical triple concertina will stop any number of upright attackers. When carefully designed, this type of defense will also discourage short-range infiltrators.

However, the static defense cannot guarantee victory against an attacker with an armor or supporting-arms advantage. The traditional defender may kill every enemy tank before it reaches his lines, and then again he may not. If just one tank gets through, it can turn the tide of battle. Similarly, that defender may or may not be able to withstand a massive bombardment. Just the concussion alone from a large-caliber munition can kill every defender for many yards from the point of impact. What a Fuel Air Explosive (FAE) can do is better left unsaid.

It takes planning and flexibility to defend against an opponent with armor or supporting arms. One must pick favorable conditions, surprise his adversary, and then move away in a hurry. Maneuver warfare offers several ways to accomplish all three goals concurrently: *(1) ambushes in series, (2) strongpoints to channel tanks into preplanned killing zones, (3) reverse-slope defense, (4) soft or elastic defense in depth, and (5) not physically occupying the ground to be defended.* All are intended to lay the groundwork for an eventual *counterattack*.

## DEFENDING AGAINST VARIED THREATS TAKES A COMBINATION OF WARFARE STYLES

One cannot foretell the attack plans of an adversary. Even an underequipped enemy can muster an occasional localized advantage in supporting arms or armor. One did with artillery at Dien Bien Phu in 1953, and another did with tanks at Lang Vei in 1968. The best of both styles of warfare must therefore be integrated to meet what is usually a combined threat. At any given time, one must be prepared to defend against armor, air, artillery, Nuclear/Biological/Chemical (NBC) munitions, ground assault, or infiltration. Additionally, to exploit the shift in momentum that often results from defending successfully, one must have the capability to launch a timely counterattack.

On those tiny Pacific islands, the foe's lines were as formidable as the world has ever known. His separate emplacements were not only virtually invisible, but also mutually supporting. Every time the Marines tried to take one, they had to face fire from others behind it. Many of these emplacements were serviced by covered routes of resupply, reinforcement, and egress. The Japanese lost their strongholds not because they had poor defenses, but because the islands were small and the attacking infantrymen numerous.

## THE PROPER COMBINATION OF STYLES FOR AVERAGE CIRCUMSTANCES

Using both styles of warfare at the same time takes some doing. Some compromises have to be struck. The maneuver warfare style of defense relies heavily on surprise. But, surprising an attacker does not necessarily break his momentum in time. If he has already been allowed to mass too much combat power near the defensive position, he may overcome his surprise and still succeed. With the attrition warfare defense, organic weapons are fired as soon as the attacker comes into view. This prevents him from massing near friendly lines. It weakens him, disrupts his timing and synchronization, and causes him to deploy early. It also compromises the location of the main line of resistance, and gives the attacker a chance to employ his long-range weapons.

If the defender could somehow remain hidden while taking his opponent under fire, he could enjoy the best of both worlds. He could impede his opponent's forward progress, while preventing that opponent from properly organizing his deliberate attack or using his long-range ordnance. Furthermore, when the attacker finally stumbled onto the hidden defensive position, he couldn't use his supporting arms without risk of hitting his own men.

The way to combine styles of warfare to handle a multiple threat is to keep the location of the defensive position secret, while disrupting the enemy's forward motion with airstrikes or indirect fire from another location. The friendlies still use a fairly traditional defensive formation to stop human-wave and infiltration attacks, but now stay hidden and ready to move at a moment's notice to evade enemy armor and supporting arms.

## IT'S STILL CRUCIAL TO PREREGISTER ONE'S DEFENSIVE SECTOR OF RESPONSIBILITY

Preregistering to the front of a defensive position need not compromise that position's location. On any battlefield, there are scores of artillery barrages for every one that supports an impending ground action. Long-range reconnaissance, heavy spotter scopes, remote sensing devices, unmanned spotter aircraft, and now satellite photos provide many lucrative targets. For this reason, Harassing and Interdiction (H&I) fires are common. Registration can be made to look like H&I fire — simply by using HE rounds and delaying subsequent adjustments.

As soon as an approaching adversary comes under fire, he can take evasive action. Hurting that adversary with indirect fire takes surprise and accuracy — it takes preregistering the defensive frontage. By so doing, the defender can virtually guarantee a correct initial target location. When he spots his foe near one of his registrations, he can give the target location in terms of a short shift from a known point. Then, he must only ask for "fire for effect with a converging sheaf" (HE for ground troops and DPICM for armor) to get the job done. The enemy's momentum will almost certainly be disrupted. (See figures 21.1 and 21.2 for how preregistration and a fire support terrain sketch can strengthen any defense.)

Techniques from the NCO Corps

Figure 21.1: The Case for Preregistration in the Defense
(Sources: FM 24-1 (1976), p. 3-9; FM 7-70 (1986), p. 4-20; FM 90-6 (1980), p. 1-4)

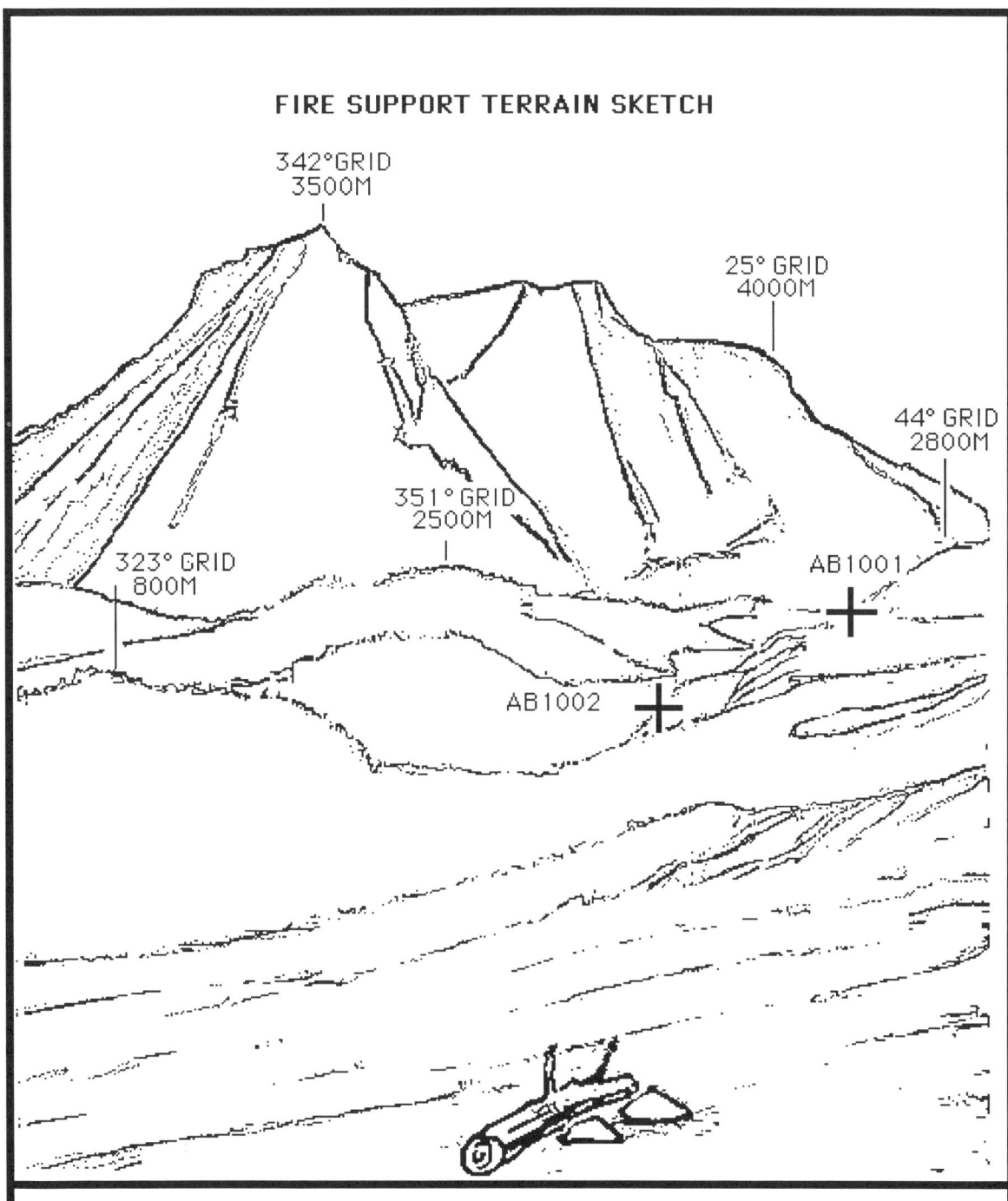

Figure 21.2: The Fire Support Terrain Sketch for the Defense
(Sources: FM 7-70 (1986), p. 4-20; FM 90-6 (1980), p. 1-4)

Through preregistration, a defender can also cover by fire a distant obstacle, or withdraw under pressure an ambush or forward security element. In the age of sophisticated counterbattery radar, preregistration continues to pay off. On defense, inaccurate fire serves little purpose. In Chesty Puller's classic defense at Guadalcanal, registration played a major role:

> At dusk, as usual, the artillerymen registered their guns, and shells exploded in the thick growth a few yards beyond Puller's lines.... The Colonel had the field phones opened down the line so that all companies and platoons could hear every message.... First Battalion, Seventh Marines was ready for its night of trial.... At 9:30 the phone rang in the Battalion... "Colonel, there's about three thousand Japs between you and me."... The front erupted with blazing weapons, and over their heads the artillery shells soughed through the rainstorm. Explosions farther back in the jungle halted Japanese columns before they could move but the vanguard pressed against the wire along a narrow front.... Puller had almost doubled the normal strength of machine-gun companies, picking up the weapons at every opportunity. Their weight was felt.... Sergeant Manila John Basilone's nest of guns was about the center of C Company.... Puller's casualties for the battle were nineteen dead, thirty wounded and twelve missing.... Puller's men found two hundred and fifty Japanese dead inside their lines.... Captured documents revealed that his half-battalion had beaten off the suicidal attack of... the equivalent of a Japanese division.... [A subsequent] burial detail counted 1462 bodies.[6]

## COMMAND-DETONATED CLAYMORES WILL SOUND TO AN ENEMY LIKE EXPLODING ARTILLERY SHELLS

To an enemy unit on the move, a string of command-detonated mines will seem like an artillery barrage. Claymores can be rigged in series with "detonating cord" and set off with a single electrical detonator. By reeling in one electrical wire, those manning a Sentry Post (SP) can remove the evidence that they have triggered a daisy chain of explosives. Even if the foe correctly guesses a claymore ambush, he has no way of knowing that there is a large defensive position nearby.

That means that not only supporting arms, but also claymore ambushes could be used to disrupt an attacking infantry force. After being hit by 700 well-aimed ball bearings from each claymore, even the most determined of infantry units might be tempted to reconsider its attack plan. One wonders if a tank column could be disrupted in a similar manner.

## ANTI-ARMOR AMBUSHES IN SERIES CAN DELAY ENEMY TANKS LONG ENOUGH FOR FRIENDLY AIRCRAFT TO COUNTERATTACK

Against enemy armor, there's only one totally reliable answer—close air. Unfortunately, after opposition armor shows up, many minutes may elapse before friendly aircraft can do anything about it. The enemy tanks may not be willing to wait.

Antitank mines can help to stop armor, but they can also compromise the whereabouts of one's defensive position. To be most effective, the mines must be sown far to the front of that position and then covered by fire. They should be used in concert with an anti-armor ambush. That way the enemy tanks will run into the mines just before or after encountering the ambush. If the site to be mined were also preregistered, the ambushers could cover their obstacles by indirect fire. Without setting off the mines, a few airbursts would discourage any enemy attempt at mine clearing.

If anti-armor ambushes were deployed in depth, enemy armor could almost certainly be delayed long enough for friendly air to arrive. An anti-armor ambush consists of a decoy and a killer team. The decoy picks a location with an antitank obstacle to its front and a covered route of egress to its rear. The decoy's role is to turn the tank long enough for the killer team to destroy it from the side. When anti-armor ambushes are employed in series, a little deception can sometimes compensate for a shortage in manpower. Only the first killer team needs its own decoy team. If the killer teams position themselves along alternating sides of a tank trail, they can serve as decoys for each other. Each successive shot will divert the enemy's attention and give the previous shooter a chance to escape. After shooting, each team can move over a rehearsed route to another anti-armor ambush site at the far end of the string. Until one of the teams gets tired, the enemy tank column will come under continuous attack.

Tanks are usually accompanied by dismounted infantry. In Vietnam, the NVA had a way of eluding that infantry, that Americans could usefully copy. Each U.S. killer team could hide until the enemy infantry passed *overhead,* pop up and fire when no one was watching, and then escape by either hiding again or falling back along a covered egress route. If sister teams were to launch subsequent attacks, they could create diversions for each other. Unless the shocked enemy could remember where each shot had come from and react immediately, the teams might avoid any retaliation whatsoever. If the team members could secretly move just a few yards to alternate "spider holes," they could successfully elude any enemy soldiers who quickly converged on the original firing site. For one or two men, it's much easier to evade enemy detection after an antitank ambush. (See figure 21.3 for the technique with which a small infantry force could delay an enemy tank column long enough for it to be counterattacked by close air.)

Defend Only to Reestablish Momentum

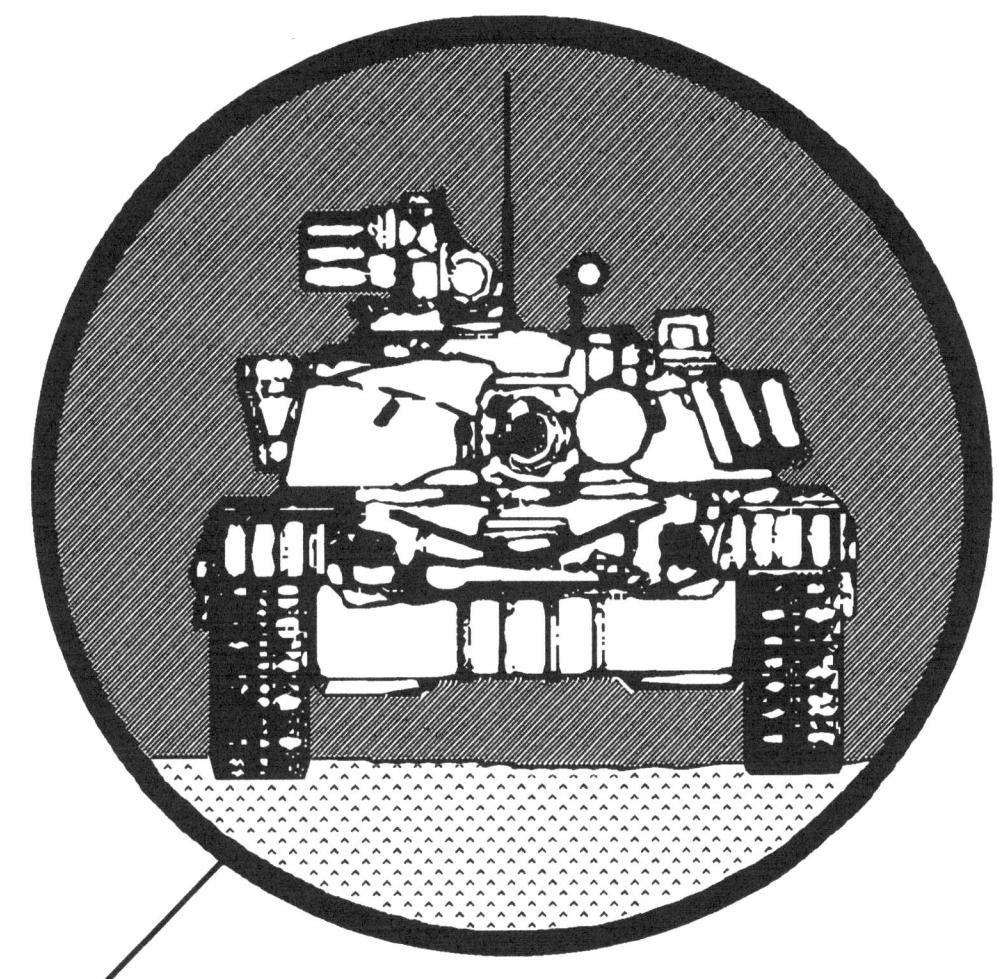

(Sources: FM 7-11B1/2 (1978), pp. 2-IV-B-1.3, 2-II-C-6.5; MCO P1500.44B, p. 12-67)

Techniques from the NCO Corps

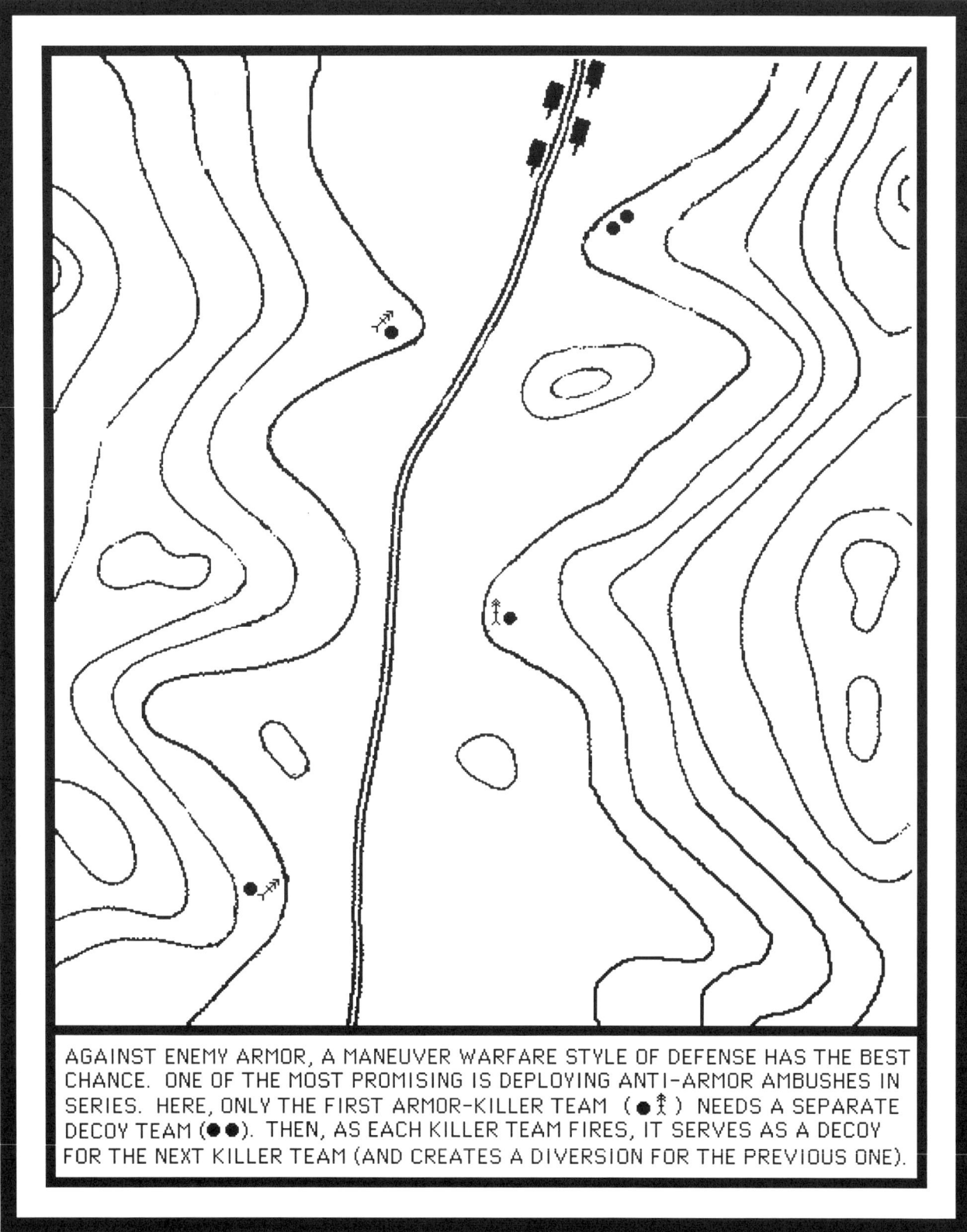

Figure 21.3: Anti-Armor Ambushes in Series to Delay Enemy Tanks

*Defend Only to Reestablish Momentum*

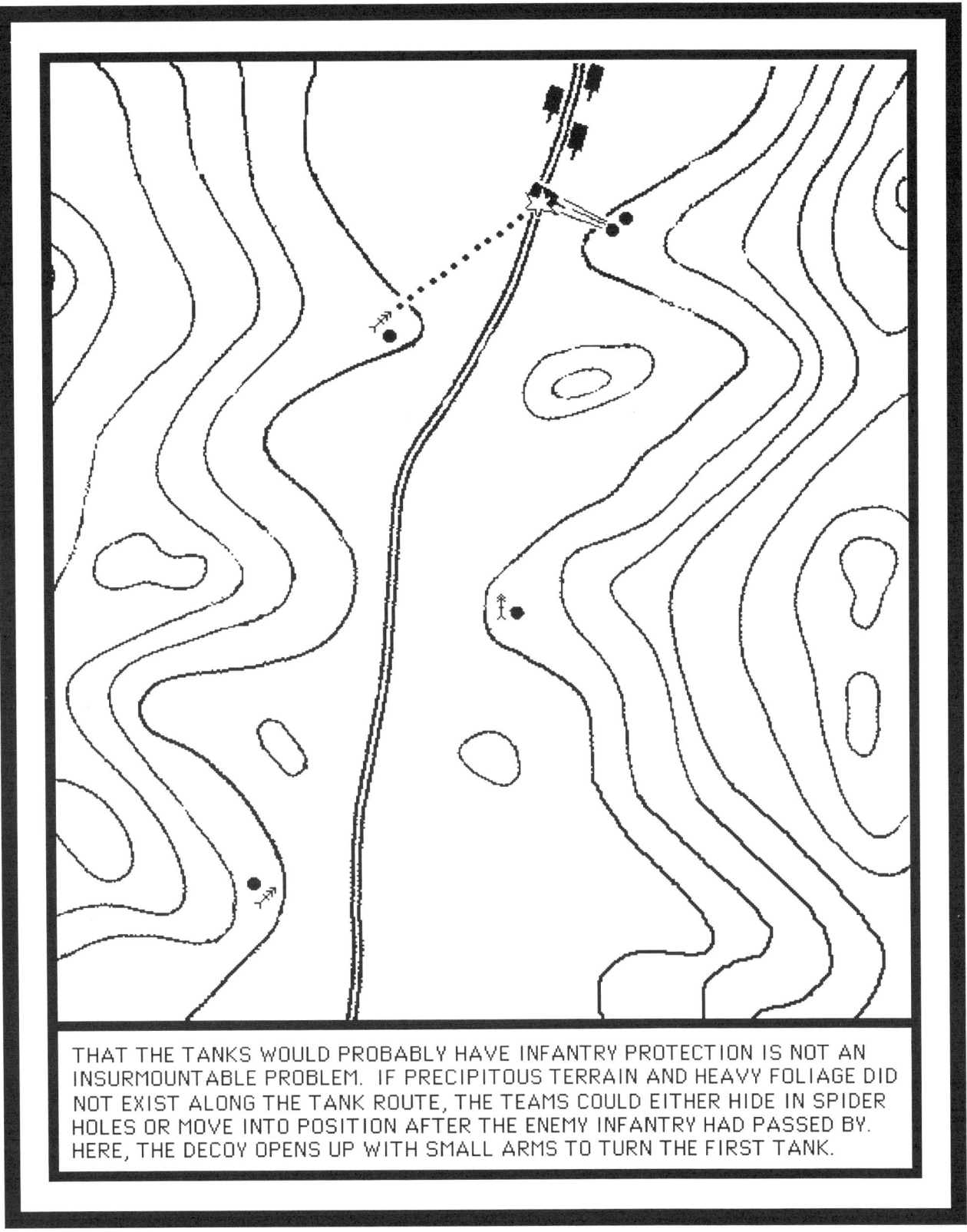

Figure 21.3: Anti-Armor Ambushes in Series to Delay Enemy Tanks (Continued)

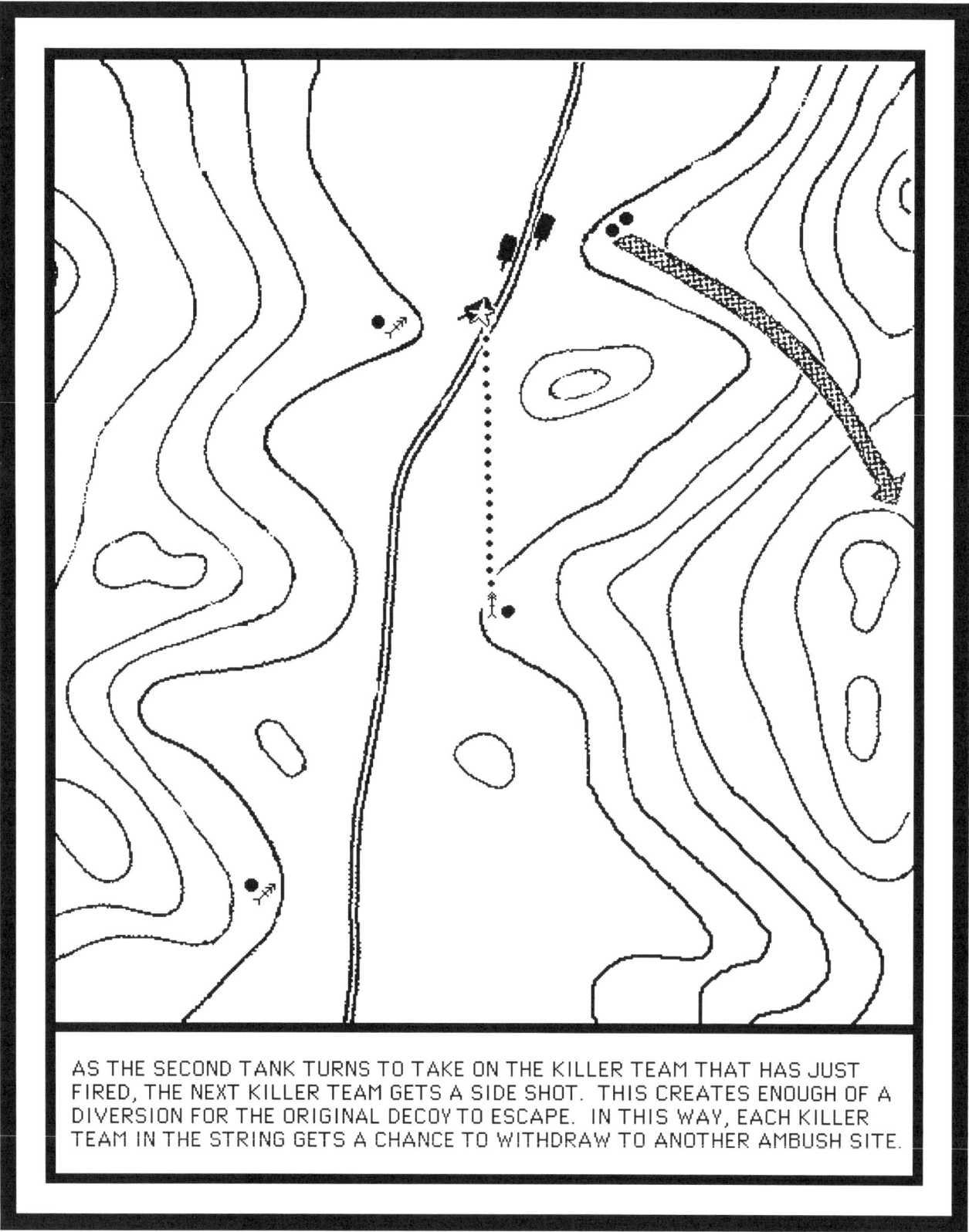

Figure 21.3: Anti-Armor Ambushes in Series to Delay Enemy Tanks (Continued)

## STRONGPOINTS CAN CHANNELIZE ENEMY TANKS

When a defending force has limited assets, it can place its infantry elements *forward* of its anti-armor elements. Then, the infantry units can establish strongpoints to channel opposition tanks into a prearranged killing zone. This is like forming a fire sack, but the surfaces on either side of the opening must be impervious to tank attack. For nonreinforced infantry units, only sites surrounded by antitank obstacles will work. Hilltops qualify. Tanks have trouble climbing steep hills and elevating their guns high enough to hit the tops. They also have difficulty negotiating venerable forests, bona fide swamps, several feet of snow, and deep water. If tanks can't physically overrun dug-in infantry, they can't hurt them. Here, the traditional hilltop position works, but for reasons other than observation and fields of fire. What matters is not the age of a technique but whether it solves a contemporary problem.

## OPPORTUNITIES FOR USING A REVERSE-SLOPE DEFENSE ARE FEW

When a defender occupies the reverse slope of a hill, he obscures his location from view and protects himself from direct long-range fire. The British positioned their infantry squares on the reverse slope at Waterloo to hide them from Napoleon's artillery spotters. Unfortunately, only gently rolling and lightly vegetated terrain usually lends itself to this type of defense.

Unless employed carefully, the reverse-slope defense can create more problems than it solves. Allowing the enemy to gain the high ground immediately to one's front is dangerous. If the defense is not positioned far enough back from the top of the hill, the enemy can achieve a tactical advantage by taking the crest. Because the defenders will need grazing fire all the way to the hill's highest point, terrain ideally suited for a reverse-slope defense is hard to find. On a more positive note, when an enemy tank crosses the topographical crest of a steep hill, it momentarily bares its lightly armored underbelly.

With this type of defense, the artillery and air observers should occupy the hill's top until the last moment. From there, they can disrupt the enemy's forward momentum without divulging the location of the main position.

## THE CONTROVERSIAL SOFT OR ELASTIC DEFENSE IN DEPTH

The defense in depth is an integral part of both styles of warfare. The defense that bends to keep from breaking is not. Even the thought of falling back is abhorrent to many attrition warfare enthusiasts. To them, unit pride is the overriding concern. While it's true that unit pride must be maintained, falling back does not have to permanently damage it. One way to fall back without losing face is to do some damage before leaving. Another is to lure the enemy into a fire sack or area laced with command-detonated explosives.

Flexible defenses have enjoyed legitimacy throughout history. In the American Civil War, both sides readily gave ground when confronted by a stronger opponent. No one disputes their courage. The only way the Russians could stop the German juggernauts of WWII was to employ soft defenses in depth. The German forces had to be slowed down before they could be stopped. After pushing through Russian lines, a few juggernauts were attacked from both flanks, cut off, and then encircled. After a while, it became difficult for the Germans to tell when the Russians were retreating out of fear, or to bait a trap.

This way of thinking can be applied at the small-unit level as well. When, at the last moment, a unit abandons the center of its defensive line, its antitank weapons at the ends of that line can more easily destroy the assaulting enemy tanks. Handheld antitank weapons can't stop modern tanks from the front. Furthermore, a sector suddenly abandoned by a token force of defenders can become a trap for enemy infantry as well. As the token force withdraws along covered escape routes, the whole area can be swept by machinegun fire from the rear. The Germans did this in WWI, and the Russians did it in Manchuria in 1939. In Vietnam, the enemy had a slightly different version of this ruse. A few Viet Cong would make a brief stand in a village and then "skedaddle" into a field of seven-foot-high elephant grass. Americans who too hastily pursued their gutless adversaries soon discovered that elephant grass will not stop machinegun bullets. After expending the effort to create a *fire sack,* it only makes sense to *lure* one's adversary into it.

Of course, falling back from one's defensive lines after dark is one of the oldest tricks *not* in the book. To complete the deception, one only needs a radio and spare uniforms stuffed with grass.

During WWI, the Germans discovered that small mutually supporting machinegun "forts" were more effective than trenches manned shoulder to shoulder. These forts were commanded by NCO's with authority to pull back on their own initiative. *Behind* each fort was a wall of sandbags or dirt. When a frontline fort came under ground attack, the forts to its rear would fire around it. If the covering fire did not sufficiently deter the attackers, the fort's occupants could use a trench to pull back to their fallback position. Of course, larger units were on standby behind this system of small forts to counterattack when necessary.

Veterans of the bloody Pacific campaigns may remember facing similar defenses. *This similarity is no coincidence.* Here's what the Marines found on Tarawa:

> Reconnaissance reveals a network of dugout, coral-block machinegun nests and interlocking

communication trenches. Lines of fire have been sighted so that every spot on the island can be crisscrossed with withering fire from many different angles.[7]

With a variation to this technique, U.S. forces might have fared better in Vietnam. Imagine a twenty-mile-deep network of miniature Tactical Areas of Responsibility (TAOR's) around every U.S. enclave like Da Nang. These TAOR's are off limits to Vietnamese nationals and clearly bounded by streams, roads, and rice paddy dikes. Picture U.S. infantrymen carefully selected and trained in secretly moving at night, building spider holes, firing bazookas, rigging claymores, throwing grenades, calling in supporting arms, and *not* shooting their rifles. Fire teams of these infantrymen could have easily controlled such TAOR's. Each team could have been secretly inserted and resupplied by night march, truck convoy, or helicopter. With hundreds of supporting-arms and claymore ambushes in the way, no North Vietnamese unit could have gotten to within rocket range of Da Nang without paying a terrible price. Gunships and rifle companies could have rescued within minutes any fire team having trouble evading enemy survivors.

**NOT OCCUPYING THE AREA TO BE DEFENDED**

To defend a piece of terrain, one does not need to occupy it. From an adjacent location, with direct and indirect fire, he can make that ground too costly for any attacker to take and surprise the attacker in the process. A fire sack's center is not occupied, yet still deadly.

There's a perimeter formation for a rifle squad that incorporates several fire sacks at once. The fire teams are deployed outwards from the squad leader like the three spokes of a wheel. At the end of each spoke is the operator of an automatic weapon. All sectors of fire are carefully coordinated. When the enemy attacks, he finds the least resistance between the spokes. As he moves forward, he incurs fire from both flanks. This may be similar to what the U.S. Army calls a "seamless-web" defense.

There are two categories of defensive deceptions: (1) those that discourage a foe from exploiting a gap, and (2) those that lure a foe into attacking a surface.

Obstacles, periodic illumination, or mannequins equipped with ringing field phones might help to stop infiltration through a lightly manned sector.

On the other hand, a "gate" or sloppily constructed segment of barbed wire might tempt an enemy force to assault a heavily defended sector. The apparent weaknesses could be secretly alleviated by aiming a machine-gun FPL through the gate and rigging the lousy wire with early-warning devices and claymores. Or, while the defenders of a recently vacated emplacement watch from a well-hidden alternate position, tape-recorded snoring sounds might be enough to lure short-range infiltrators.

**COMMON-SENSE WAYS OF ENHANCING THE TRADITIONAL DEFENSE**

During a traditional defense, most of the weapons organic to an infantry unit are fired as soon as the enemy comes into view. All, but the machineguns, are employed at maximum effective range. For example, enemy tanks are taken under fire by TOW missiles at 3750 meters, by Dragons at 1000 meters, and by AT-4's at 300 meters. Riflemen start shooting at enemy soldiers 550 meters away. This way of defending has some advantages. For one thing, it instantly disrupts the timing of all adversaries visible. Unfortunately, it also compromises the location of the defensive position.

If, in the traditional defense, the machineguns are kept quiet until the last moment, one wonders why the other weapons are not hidden as well. The adversary's timing can be adequately disrupted with artillery barrages, antitank ambushes, and claymore attacks — all without disclosing the location of the defensive position. Without firing a shot, those in the position can blend in perfectly with their natural surroundings. Holes can be dug so as not to disturb the microterrain, and fields of fire can be cleared so as not to change the pattern of foliage.

Unless the traditional defense is employed in depth, its rigidity constitutes another weakness. Any rupture in a single line of emplacements can forfeit the entire defensive mission. Commanders of companies and platoons must learn to defend in depth; they must deploy reserve personnel behind their front lines to nip enemy penetrations in the bud. These reserves should function both as a secondary defense line and mobile reaction force. On sloping ground, the reserves can easily shoot over the heads of frontline defenders. On level ground, they can provide covering fire as long as each frontline position is backed by a log, tree, rock, or mound of dirt. When positioned in depth, fighting holes can be mutually supporting and more difficult to capture.

**TO STOP SHORT-RANGE INFILTRATORS, ONE MUST CAREFULLY CHOOSE THE LOCATION OF EACH FIGHTING HOLE**

Where the fighting holes are placed in relation to the military crest and other undulations in the ground will establish whether or not they will stop infiltrators. First, from each hole, there must be a good view of anyone who might try to crawl within grenade range. Then, there must be a good view of anyone who might try to crawl between that hole and its adjacent holes. If holes are equidistant and form a perfect circle on anything but level ground, they will not perform either function.

In every sector, fighting holes must be placed either on a military crest or where grazing fire will be possible beyond grenade range. That means a platoon might have some holes near the top of its hill and others near the bottom. Nevertheless, the lines should remain linear or convex wherever possible. Otherwise, fields of fire must be carefully coordinated.

The spacing between fighting holes is also crucial. Obtaining an unobstructed view between holes is no easy matter. In level and unobstructed terrain, the holes can be 25 yards apart; but in ground covered with numerous obstructions and folds, the holes may have to be 5 yards apart. Additionally, all ditches, wet spots, or sectors with improperly cleared fields of fire must be fully manned.

Every hole must be situated, and *then the squad sectors established* — not the other way around. On nonlevel ground, subordinate-unit sectors will never be the same size. Only required is that the total responsibility for a major avenue of approach belong exclusively to one subunit. (See figures 21.4 through 21.7.)

### ONLY BY WALKING THE GROUND, CAN ONE ESTABLISH HOW TO DEFEND IT

Every time a unit stops for long, it should establish a deliberate defense. To do so, its leader and his immediate subordinates must walk the ground together. Whatever time this takes, is well spent. Where the fighting holes go is more important that how they are constructed.

*Figure 21.4: Stopping Infiltrators Requires Attention to Microterrain*
(Source: MCO P1500.44B, p. 12-63)

*Figure 21.5: How the Military Crest Affects the Placement of the Fighting Holes*

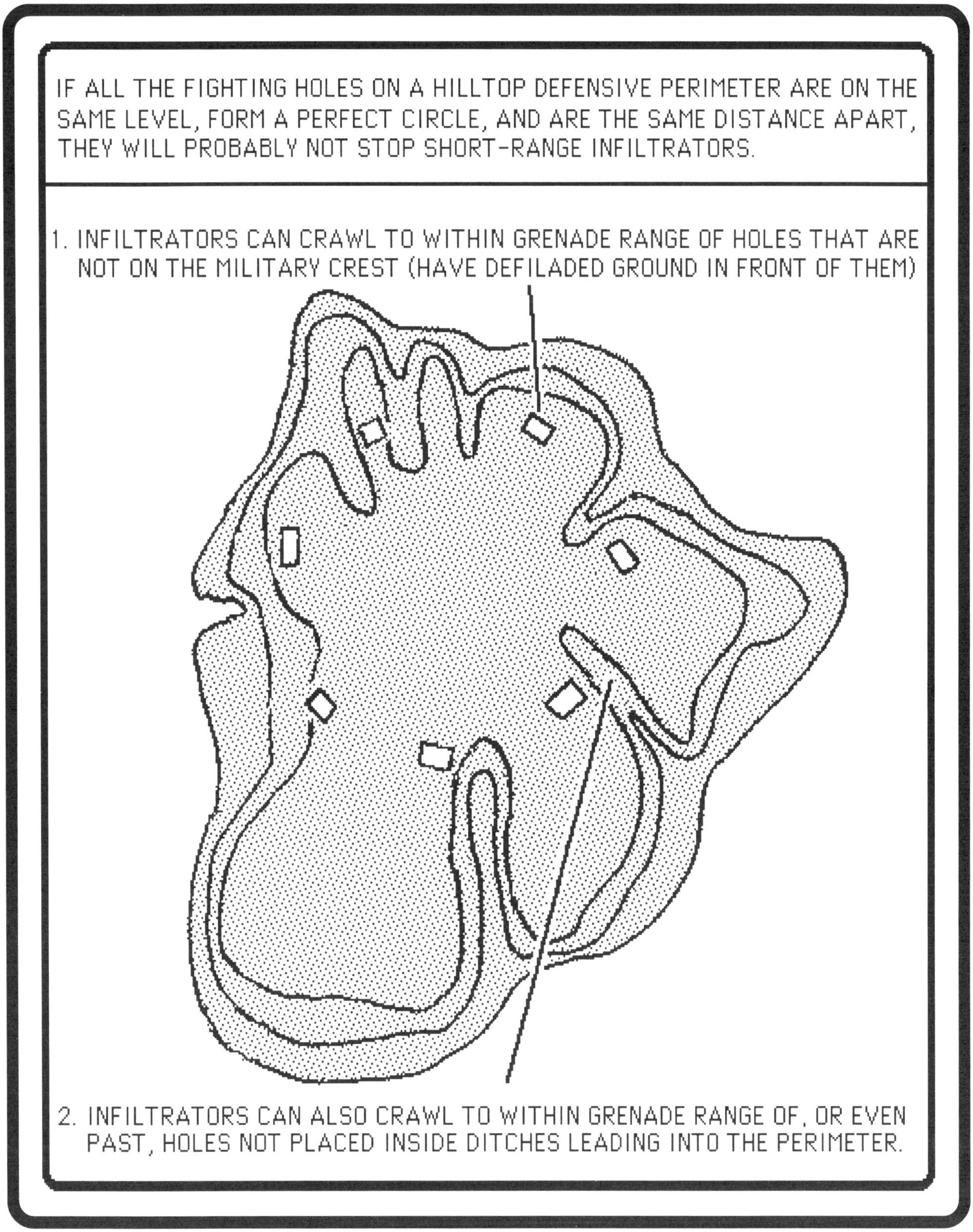

*Defend Only to Reestablish Momentum*

IF ALL THE FIGHTING HOLES ON A HILLTOP DEFENSIVE PERIMETER ARE ON THE SAME LEVEL, FORM A PERFECT CIRCLE, AND ARE THE SAME DISTANCE APART, THEY WILL PROBABLY NOT STOP SHORT-RANGE INFILTRATORS.

1. INFILTRATORS CAN CRAWL TO WITHIN GRENADE RANGE OF HOLES THAT ARE NOT ON THE MILITARY CREST (HAVE DEFILADED GROUND IN FRONT OF THEM)

2. INFILTRATORS CAN ALSO CRAWL TO WITHIN GRENADE RANGE OF, OR EVEN PAST, HOLES NOT PLACED INSIDE DITCHES LEADING INTO THE PERIMETER.

*Figure 21.6: The Wrong Way to Establish a Perimeter Defense*

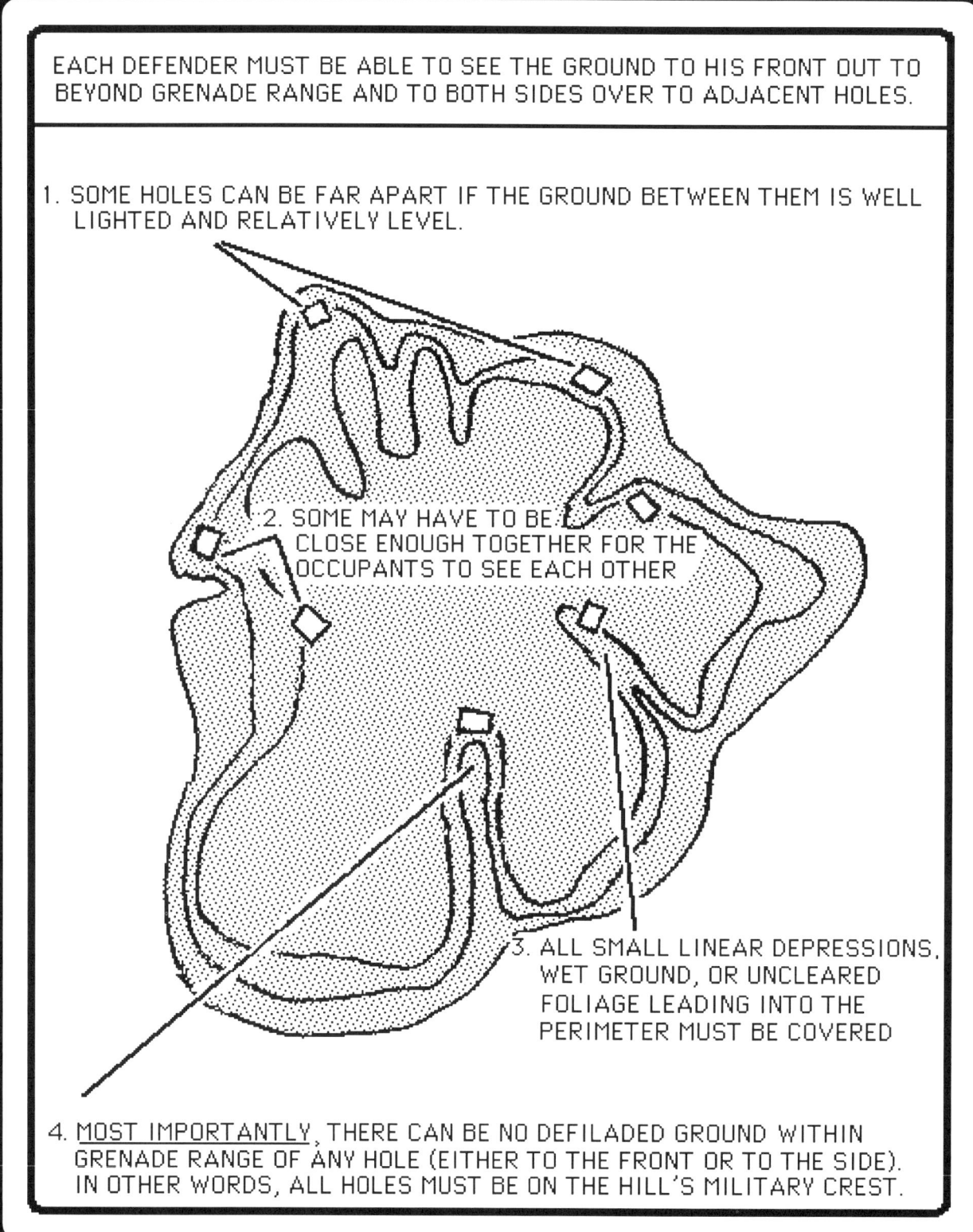

Figure 21.7: A Perimeter Defense That Will Stop Infiltrators

The most important part of this walk is to the front of the prospective position. To determine whether or not that position can even be defended, the leaders must view it from the enemy's perspective. They must envision enemy initiatives with armor/artillery, massed infantry, and sappers, and arrive at which deployment of their assets might blunt those initiatives.

First, they investigate the avenues of approach for armor. As they walk, they decide where the anti-armor ambushes, antitank mine fields, and artillery preregistrations must go. Then, they look at covered routes that might conceal enemy infantry. For each, they decide where the SP and preregistration must go. Next, they study the natural obstacles to the front of the position. Some may block or channelize the enemy; others may provide the enemy with cover. Those in the former category can be incorporated into the fire/barrier plan, but those in the latter category are counterproductive and must be preregistered. If there are too many, the unit may have to defend elsewhere.

Then, the leaders walk the position itself — to establish where the fighting holes should go. The front lines must run along the military crests. The holes must be spaced so as to block all infiltration lanes. They must blend in with the natural surroundings to provide both concealment and fields of fire. Interlocking machinegun fire and claymores must guard the covered approaches to the position. Sectors must be assigned so that no two subunits share responsibility for the same avenue of approach. Finally, a secondary line of holes should be contemplated for reserve forces.

## A CHANGE TO THE USUAL PRIORITY OF WORK

Traditionally, the defender doesn't preregister until he has dug in. That's like not setting up one's most effective weapon. If the enemy appears before the holes are dug, the defender may never get the opportunity to employ that weapon. Registration should occur before digging in; it should occur right after local security is deployed. Simply by relaying adjustments, the security personnel can place concentrations where they'll do the most good. Then, with indirect fire, they can either disrupt an enemy's attack or cover their own withdrawal.

## DEPLOYING A SENTRY POST

SP's have always been an integral part of the defense; they provide early warning of impending attack. If the SP's can be silenced prior to that attack, the defending unit can be defeated. Yet, very little has been written about SP's. Without specialized training, those manning an SP have about as much chance as those walking point. And, unless properly deployed, stationary sentries *cannot* accomplish their mission.

In Indian country, the SP's location must be kept secret. The sentries must go out, be relieved in place, and come back — *all without being observed* by the enemy. Often, units must deploy their SP's in broad daylight before optimal locations can be reconnoitered. A single security patrol can both find the best locations and drop of two-man teams. Without counting heads, the enemy would have no way of knowing what had happened. Or, the SP's can exfiltrate out of the perimeter using all available diversion, cover, and concealment.

With forward security teams, defending units must do the following: (1) nightly move them closer to friendly lines, (2) regularly relieve them to preserve their vigilance, and (3) periodically shift their locations to keep the enemy guessing. All of this entails movement. While concealed by low light, folds in the ground, and vegetation, the SP's can move on their own. To withdraw under pressure, they will need covered routes back to their perimeter anyway. Or, they can temporarily join a security patrol to accomplish both movement and reconnaissance. While the size of the patrol will grow by two every time an SP is in transit, the total number of personnel leaving and entering friendly lines will remain constant.

As important as keeping the enemy guessing at SP locations, is keeping the friendlies apprised of the same information. Because defensive lines often curve with ground relief, a two-man security team might become visible from more than one sector and get mistakenly shot. For sentries, the most dangerous time is leaving and reentering friendly lines. Those manning *every sector* of those lines must be continually reapprised of all SP locations, reentry routes, and signals. Of course, fire discipline must be strictly observed while SP's are inbound. After a large enemy force has been spotted, anyone reentering friendly lines is at extreme risk from friendly fire.

The parent unit and its SP's must have some way to communicate, for the safety of both hangs in the balance. The SP's need radios. With radios, they can not only alert the perimeter, but also adjust indirect fire, as necessary. These radios can be placed on squelch with the volume turned down. With a handset-keying code, there will be little talking required. If radios are in short supply, field phones are a poor substitute. Enemy scouts can backtrack along communications wire to silence SP's from behind. Commercial walky-talkies might be a better solution. Sounds from nature — e.g., bird calls, the tapping of a woodpecker, etc. — make good alternate signals. To facilitate withdrawal, SP's should position themselves between their preregistered targets and friendly lines.

## ADDITIONAL ROLES FOR SENTRY POSTS

Early warning of an attacker's approach does not guarantee success to the defender. In the defender's exuberance to surprise his opponent, he may take no action until that opponent has amassed a combat power

## Techniques from the NCO Corps

advantage just outside his lines. As soon as the aggressor force is detected, it must be attacked. This will interrupt its momentum and cause it to deploy early. The attack should be by supporting arms or a close facsimile, so as to disrupt the enemy's advance without giving away the defensive deployment.

Sentries must be allowed to do more than just alert their perimeter before withdrawing. Without disclosing their presence, they can disrupt enemy momentum. They can do so with either a claymore ambush or indirect fire. With a radio and preregistered target downrange from their hiding place, they can do some serious damage. Just by whispering a minor adjustment and request for precision fire for effect, they can surprise the enemy force with the first volley. With claymores rigged in tandem, they can accomplish even more. With the lone wire reeled in, the foe would have no way of knowing that the explosions had been command detonated.

When the location of a defensive position is common knowledge, the SP can adjust machinegun tracer fire onto an approaching enemy force as well. Doctrine requires only that the machinegun's final protective fires be withheld. Firing from an elevated position prior to an attack doesn't violate doctrine, as long as the gun is moved after that firing. One night in the spring of 1968, a Listening Post (LP) in front of the 27th Marines compound south of Da Nang reported an enemy force in transit. The LP was told to come in, the perimeter put on alert, and an artillery mission requested. Unfortunately, the area had never been preregistered, and the guns could not fire that close

(Sources: MCOP1550.14D (1983), p. 10-8; FM 22-100 (1983), p. 164)

to a friendly village. The NVA did not attack; they were probably just passing by on a long-range infiltration movement. If the officer in charge of perimeter security that night had carried his radio to the top of the tower containing the .50 caliber machinegun, he could have taken the enemy under fire.[8] He could have aimed at first into the rice paddy beyond the LP's location, and then asked the LP to adjust the tracer stream onto the target.

## EMPLACING THE MACHINEGUNS

In the deliberate defense, the role of the machinegun is to stop a human-wave assault. It does so most effectively *from a flank* of the main avenue of approach. From there, without being in harm's way, it can create a wall of lead through which attackers using that avenue must pass. When directed at a tight angle to friendly lines, a Final Protective Line (FPL) can cover an entire defensive frontage. This important part of doctrine has been often ignored, because in a *hasty* defense the machinegun is placed *in front of* the avenue of approach.

A machinegun should never be employed without its tripod and Traversing & Elevation (T&E) mechanism. Without them, the gun cannot fire accurately at distant targets. They also permit the gunner to record (for use after dark) his FPL and probable directions of attack. The operator simply aims the gun and then writes down the T&E reading on a range card. The tripod and T&E also help the gunner to fire accurately without a firing signature. He can do so by removing the tracers and shooting in short bursts through a tiny opening or cloth curtain.

Because short-range infiltrators will attempt to locate the machineguns prior to attacking, at the first sign of trouble, the guns should be moved to "alternate" positions nearby. From "supplementary" positions, machineguns can cover other sectors of the perimeter.

In a cigar-shaped defense, a unit with two machineguns can maximize their coverage over level ground. When placed at opposite ends of the elongated perimeter with supplementary positions nearby, *both* guns can engage an attacker almost anywhere along the perimeter.

## THE VARIOUS OPTIONS FOR CLEARING FIELDS OF FIRE

Fields of fire must be cleared without noticeably altering the environment. Otherwise, the element of surprise may be lost. Clearing away all the underbrush is seldom productive, as it compromises the location of the position. The individual defender should clear away only that which obstructs his vision or fields of fire. After the cuts are camouflaged and dead bushes discarded, the attacker will have no way of detecting the clearing effort.

Or, the defender can just remove some of the bottom foliage from the bushes to his front. An upright adversary can't detect the difference. Only his feet and legs may be visible at first, but once the shooting starts, he will have nowhere to hide.

In extremely thick vegetation, selective clearing may not be possible. Here the defender must cut "fire lanes." These are narrow openings that run diagonally outwards from his lines. They are particularly well suited for machinegun FPL's. Though more obvious than selective clearing, fire lanes are still very hard to detect by attackers who are most worried about the threat to their front.

In grasslands or dry underbrush, a controlled burn will provide the defender with more than enough observation and fields of fire. Of course, the area to be defended must be inconspicuous in a much larger burned area.

## EVEN ENTRENCHING TAKES COMMON SENSE

Each fighting hole must protect its occupant(s) from tanks passing overhead and grenades going off inside. Remembering these functions is more important to its builder than memorizing its dimensions. How much to dig, and whether to reinforce the sides, depends on local soil conditions and size of occupant(s). Side-by-side one-man holes provide more protection than a two-man hole.

In a one-man hole that will protect its occupant from a tank tread, there must be at least two feet of clearance above the occupant's head while he sits on the fire step. That's in average soil, when the tank doesn't swivel.

To construct a hole that protects its occupant(s) from grenades, one must deviate slightly from the manuals. When a grenade lands in one's fighting hole, there is no time to kick it into a grenade sump. It must roll into the sump by itself — *automatically*. That means the fire step and bottom surfaces of the hole must be *slanted,* and the mouth of the sump must point away from that portion of the hole that will probably be occupied. Until these criteria are satisfied, dummy grenades should be thrown into all fighting holes during their construction.

## THE BARRIER PLAN SHOULD BE AN INTEGRAL PART OF EVERY DEFENSE

Obstacles can impede an enemy at the main line of resistance, or force him into a prearranged killing zone before getting that close. Without being visible from the main position, these obstacles can still be covered by observation and fire. They can be watched through an SP or anti-armor ambush, and covered by indirect fire. Or, they can be monitored by homemade listening devices and covered by preregistrations.

Natural obstacles should be analyzed before choosing where to defend. They can't give away one's position. When they are available, fewer manmade obstacles are necessary. Whatever is manmade must either be camouflaged or placed in such profusion as to confuse the foe.

With proper technique, it's not hard to build a barrier. Once its purpose is clearly understood, there's no need to memorize construction particulars.

## AGAINST HUMAN WAVES AND INFILTRATORS, BARBED WIRE HAS ITS PLACE

"Tactical wire" slows human-wave assaults long enough to stop them with machinegun fire. It consists of straight rows of triple concertina along the *inner edges* of the machinegun FPL's. Triple concertina has a "soft" top that is difficult for attackers to bridge without becoming entangled. These straight rows of concertina would tell the enemy where the machineguns were positioned, if "supplementary wire" weren't used to confuse him. "Protective wire" is that which runs parallel to one's lines and keeps friendly fighting holes out of enemy grenade range. Its three rows of progressively taller wire — i.e., tanglefoot, double apron, and triple concertina — bring infiltrators up off the ground. Only trained sappers can get through this final maze of wire without making noise or being seen.

Tanglefoot is nothing more than strand barbed wire connected haphazardly in a horizontal plane six inches off the ground. Double apron looks like a long military pup tent. With proper technique, a work detail can string either configuration so quickly that the strand need not be cut off the spool. Furthermore, the detail can do so without ever leaving the friendly side of their construction. Triple concertina is built upon two parallel rows (one pace apart) of alternating long barbed-wire stakes (five paces apart). First, coils of concertina are spread out and bounced onto the outer row of stakes from the friendly side. Adjacent coils are joined by passing over the same stake the following: the bottom portion of one end loop, the other end loop, and finally the top portion of the first end loop. After the string of linked coils has been completed, a single strand of barbed wire is strung *over its top* to hold it down. Then, the whole process is repeated for the inner row of stakes.

(Source: FM 7-8 (1984), p. F-13)

Finally, a third string of concertina is placed over both rows of stakes. This top string of concertina does *not* have a lateral wire stretched over it. Its softness is what impedes enemy soldiers trying to cross it by ladder. A mass of barbed wire will also discourage tanks. The wire fouls their sprockets and causes their treads to come off.

## TO UTILIZE HASTY MINE FIELDS, CERTAIN RULES MUST BE FOLLOWED

It takes a battalion commander to authorize a hasty mine field. Only command-detonated mines are excluded; *booby traps are not*. This rule protects the friendly unit that must pass through an area after another unit has installed a mine field and then been forced out. A map of each mine field must be sent up the chain of command.

The mine-laying detail first chooses a reference point that exists on both map and ground. Then, they record the direction and pace count from this reference point to a local point of interest, like a tree. Stakes are temporarily placed in the ground at the ends of the prospective rows of mines. Next, the directions and pace counts to these stakes are ascertained and recorded. Finally, the mines are sown between the stakes, and the directions and pace counts between the mines again measured and recorded.

Once antitank mines are in place, "wands" must be affixed *before* safety collars are removed. Otherwise, the slightest movement of a wand will set off a mine. The same men who bury and arm the mines should retrieve them.

Units should never try to build booby traps out of grenades. Once the pin is out, an imperceptible jostle of the spoon can be enough to arm the grenade. Those who have nervously "milked" grenades are no longer around to talk about the experience.

## OTHER EASY-TO-BUILD ANTITANK OBSTACLES

With entrenching tools, a unit can build a dirt wall that will temporarily stop a tank. They do so by scooping a five-foot-deep cut out of sloping ground. This is another good reason to defend high ground.

With a saw, a unit can build a log hurdle out of tall pines or old telephone poles. The logs are piled one at a time between pairs of sturdy trees and tied in place with strand barbed wire. This structure must be only five feet high to impede tanks.

With demolitions, a unit can construct an abatis in minutes. A tree will fall toward the side on which a "cutting" charge has been placed. Pinpoint accuracy can be achieved by placing a small "pusher" charge higher up and on the opposite side of the tree. When the trees along a road are felled diagonally across it (toward the enemy), they form an abatis. The trees along opposite sides of the road are rigged in separate series with detonating cord, and then the sides are blown down a few minutes apart.

## A REMINDER ABOUT DEFENSIVE SECURITY PATROLLING

Defensive security patrols must seek out and make contact with any enemy force cohabiting their areas of responsibility. A mere warning may not save their defensive position. The patrols must disrupt the enemy's timing and synchronization to prevent him from massing near their parent unit's lines. The patrols must move along probable avenues of approach, follow whatever enemy sign they can find, and then attack. Aggressive security patrolling in no way compromises the parent unit's location.

## EARLY DETECTION OF ENEMY INFILTRATORS

To detect a short-range infiltrator, the defender must first thoroughly understand what a trained sapper can accomplish. Then, he must *stay hidden* and use special seeing and listening skills. (See figure 21.8.)

Peripheral vision can be of great value to a defender at night. By moving his head from side to side, he can bring an object alternately into both fields of his peripheral vision. When an intruder is present, what results is a dark shape that would not otherwise be discernible against its somewhat lighter background. A defender can also watch for changes in the size or shape of the objects to his front. Or, he can cup his fingers around each eye to concentrate whatever dim light may surround an object, while excluding the light reflecting from things around it. Finally, he has at his disposal both natural and artificial horizons. Even on relatively flat ground, he can sometimes create a *natural* horizon by holding his head near the earth and looking up. Wherever there is a slight rise in the terrain to his front, he can see silhouetted anyone crawling across it. If the ground has been cleared, it will be lighter in color than the background foliage and will serve as an *artificial* horizon against which dark objects will again be visible.

Infiltrators make a rustling sound as they crawl through dry leaves and a gurgling sound as they slither over swampy ground. By using an inverted megaphone made out of paper, a defender could better hear such sounds. Or, he could just put his ear to the ground:

> The recruit must learn that at best he can perceive only the outline of an object without any detail. Since he can observe better from below than from above, he must get down on the ground. . . . Sounds are transmitted most clearly at night, and the trainee must learn to differentiate between ordinary noises and those that should arouse suspicion. By putting his ear to the ground he will often be able to hear noises that are otherwise inaudible.[9]

## WHEN THE ENEMY ARRIVES

To execute one's defensive plan, thinking like the enemy again helps. For example, the traditional practice of walking the perimeter to check on one's men compromises their locations. Pulling on a series of tug-ropes might work better. If there's even a chance that the enemy has discovered the whereabouts of an emplacement, its occupants should move to an alternate position after dark.

The defending unit must rely on aggressive security patrols and SP's to detect and then disrupt its foe. Without giving away the whereabouts of the main line of resistance, these forward elements can keep the opposition force off balance with supporting-arms concentrations, anti-armor ambushes, and claymore attacks.

When the foe finally stumbles onto the main position, the senior defender must remember to put up *illumination*. Then, if his planning has been comprehensive, his subordinates will do the rest. Without illumination, those subordinates will only have a marginal chance of beating back a good attacker. Authority both to put up illumination and to signal for the final protective fires should be shared with subordinate leaders. Seconds count while under attack.

Once the final protective fires have been initiated, there will be a requirement to redistribute ammunition. Additionally, the *reserve* may have to retake a portion of the lines. This limited counterattack is one of the most dangerous of all infantry evolutions. When overrun, a infantryman will shoot anyone who gets near his fighting hole. It takes experienced NCO's and SNCO's to pull off this type of attack. It

Figure 21.8: Stopping Infiltrators Takes Staying Hidden
(Sources: FM 7-11B/C/CM (1979), p. 2-5; FM 5-20 (1968), p. 31)

was Gunnery Sergeant Winebar and Sergeant Price who counterattacked alone when A Company, 1st Battalion, 4th Marines was overrun by NVA at Cam Lo in August of 1966.[10] On their own initiative, they formed a two-man killer team to deal with the intruders one at a time. On Operation Maui Peak in late 1968, a pair of Hawaiian SNCO's pushed several NVA sappers off the crest of an almost conical hill. They did so by holding their rifles high overhead and utilizing the hill's *contour* as cover.[11] The last thing the enemy sappers saw was two rifles blazing away at them from just above the surface of the ground.

## WHEN ENEMY TANKS BREAK THROUGH

While bearing down on one's position, an enemy tank undoubtedly makes a fearsome spectacle. Yet, that tank is still vulnerable. There are so many ways to kill a tank "barehanded" that the German Army had a ribbon for it.

The defender's location is often the deciding factor. To kill an onrushing tank head-on with a shoulder-fired antitank weapon is difficult at best. To have any effect, the round must hit the narrow crevice below the tank turret.

The crest of a small hill will sometimes cause a tank momentarily to bare its lightly armored underbelly, but killing a tank usually takes either temporarily stopping or turning it. While a wall 5 feet high or ditch 13 feet wide may only cause a tank to hesitate, a few natural obstacles will prevent any further forward motion — e.g., several feet of water, 10 inches of mud, 3 feet of snow, hills with slopes of 45 degrees, or trees 10 inches in diameter. There's another way to turn a tank — with *flame*. Tanks are reluctant to drive through fire of unknown depth. To turn tanks in WWII, Russian defenders ignited bales of hay or ditches of fuel at the last moment. A mine field or jumble of barbed wire might accomplish the same thing.

As tanks are overrunning one's front lines, they become more vulnerable still. Now, there's the chance for a side shot with an antitank weapon. Furthermore, antitank mines can be pulled under tank treads. After small pathways have been cleared between fighting holes, flat bottomed mines (without wands attached) can be dragged back and forth between holes — *on strings*. The weight of the tank upon its tread will be enough to set off the mine.

Once tanks have passed over the first line of friendly fighting holes, they completely forfeit their invincibility. In one battle on the grassy steppes of Russia, Soviet infantry destroyed an entire German tank regiment and its accompanying armored infantry brigade while taking few casualties themselves. They did so by establishing a series of camouflaged dug-in positions, letting the Germans overrun them, and then firing handheld antitank weapons at them from the back. Each time a tank would turn to fire at one position, another position would open up causing the Germans to lose track of their initial target.

Most Soviet-made tanks have only coaxial or externally mounted machineguns. That means that, when a tank is "buttoned up," its machineguns can only shoot in the direction its main gun is pointing. Furthermore, its crew can't see or shoot at what is happening at its base. For the overrun defender, these weaknesses constitute opportunities.

If a tank can't be killed outright, it must be blinded, immobilized, and neutralized — often in that order. It can be blinded either by smoke grenades or by mud hurled against its periscope openings. Molotov cocktails will not only temporarily blind a tank, but also badly scare its occupants. Occasionally, the ignited ingredients will fry wiring or rubberized connections in the engine compartment. Scores of Russian tanks were disabled by molotov cocktails in the Hungarian Revolution of 1956. A log, metal stake, bangalore, or satchel charge between a tank's tread and sprocket will often cause that tread to come off.

Once a tank has been immobilized, it can more easily be neutralized. Placing a grenade or rock in the muzzle of the main gun may cause a round to detonate prematurely, thereby damaging the tube or breach assembly. Historically, infantrymen have defeated tanks by jumping on top of them. In WWII, someone destroyed a tank's machinegun with a sledge hammer. A Russian blacksmith created such a racket with his hammering that the tank's occupants had to surrender just to escape the noise. In Korea, Corporal Cross of the U.S. 9th Infantry Division earned the Distinguished Service Cross by pouring gasoline on a tank and then igniting it. Later in the war, an Irishman captured a tank by burning his shirt in front of the ventilation system. While opposition tanks now have filters to handle NBC contaminants, the opportunity to clog their ventilation systems still exists. Furthermore, most tanks are grounded. If an enemy tank came into contact with 220 volts of electricity, it would no longer have a functioning crew.

## THE FINAL REQUIREMENT FOR ANY DEFENSE

Lest any unit be lulled into a false sense of security by its defensive expertise, it must remain capable of shifting quickly over to the offense. For only by so doing, can it capture the momentum needed to win decisively. When Colonel Chamberlain's men ran out of ammunition on Little Round Top and counterattacked with bayonets, their "swinging-gate" maneuver captured the momentum in the Battle of Gettysburg (and ultimately in the Civil War) a full day before Pickett's charge. Much can be accomplished by counterattacking at the right moment.

However, this counterattack *shouldn't* always be launched at the very instant the foe's momentum seems blunted. Nor, should it always be conducted at top speed. Otherwise, it will become too predictable as were some of the German and Japanese counterattacks of WWII. It must often take the form of a carefully reconnoitered night attack, a tedious infiltration, or a flanking attack made possible by more bait and another fire sack.

# 22 Surviving the Unthinkable — NBC Attack

- Are U.S. "grunts" really prepared to survive a surprise NBC attack?
- Can more training prepare them to do so?
- What type of training is needed and by whom must it be conducted?

(Sources: FM 7-11B1/2 (1978), p. 2-I-B-10.2; FM 3-5 (1985), cover)

**THE NBC THREAT CONTINUES TO GROW**

How lethal are today's Nuclear, Biological, and Chemical (NBC) weapons? Most countries keep their capabilities secret, so no one knows for sure. It is known that on bare skin, one drop of nerve agent can kill within 60 seconds. Better left unsaid is what one cupful of a biological could do in a city's water supply.

To fully appreciate the magnitude of the NBC threat, one must consider both the proliferation of the weapons and the level of authority required to use them. Several potential adversaries (mostly former client states of the Soviet Union) already have the "bomb" and the missiles to deliver it. There is no telling how many other small nations or political groups have the capability to fabricate an oversized atomic explosive, or to simulate an atomic power plant meltdown. It doesn't take an airplane or missile to deliver an atomic device. Would that device do any less damage, if it were moved by rail or truck to a defensive sector about to be abandoned? Or, would it be any less devastating, if it were smuggled piece by piece through friendly lines, reassembled, and then command detonated? Unfortunately, nuclear proliferation is not the only problem. Many countries that do not yet have the bomb, believe that a chemical or biological arsenal will do just as much to upgrade their status in the world community.

How much authority does it take to use these weapons of mass destruction against U.S. troops? Prior to the breakup of the Soviet Union, the Soviet Army considered chemical munitions to be "conventional" weapons. In other words, chemical munitions could be unleashed at the whim of any field commander. To make matters worse, the Soviets considered biological toxins (concentrations of naturally occurring chemicals) to be chemical munitions. This means that U.S. troops might be subjected at any time to lethal agents that won't register on their *chemical detection kits:*

> Biological and chemical warfare was outlawed by the Geneva Protocol of 1925. More recently, the 1972 convention . . . (commonly called the Biological Weapons Convention) outlawed toxin warfare as well. . . . Unfortunately, recent evidence indicated that the Soviet Union, despite being a party to the 1972 Biological Weapons Convention, has not adopted this same posture in practice. United States Department of State Special Report No. 98 on chemical warfare in Southeast Asia and Afghanistan, dated 22 March 1982, outlines this evidence confirming the use of mycotoxins (widely publicized in the media as yellow rain) by Soviet-backed forces as early as 1974.[1]
> — FC 3-9-1

Experts no longer wonder if U.S. forces will again come under NBC attack; they just wonder when.

## N(O) B(ODY) C(ARES)

The thought of coming under an NBC attack is so nightmarish that many military men (and even their organizations) downplay its inevitability. Infantrymen often say, "It won't happen on my watch," "We'll all be killed instantly so why worry about it," or "The NBC specialists will take care of us." Of course, all of these arguments have holes in them.

There is substantial evidence to suggest that it just did happen on their watch during the Gulf War. If the Iraqis didn't do it to the Allies directly, the Allies did it to themselves when they bombed Iraqi ammunition dumps and factories.

Most human beings will pursue the slimmest of opportunities to avoid imminent death. Further, heavy exposure to NBC contamination is not always fatal. Reputedly, there's a firefighter from Chernobyl, who has suffered little effect from thousands of rads of radiation.

Finally, on an active battlefield, there will not be enough NBC personnel to go around. The few assigned to infantry regiments will be hard pressed to fulfill their responsibilities at battalion headquarters. They will not be with the subordinate units deployed at various distances from those headquarters, and subordinate units cannot all break contact with the enemy at once to move to centrally located decontamination sites. Small units will have to take turns decontaminating themselves.

## SOME UNANSWERED QUESTIONS

Realistically, infantrymen must not only plan to survive the unthinkable, but also to perform their mission during the unthinkable. A look at what might be required reveals oversights in established procedure. In fact, much of the *detail of execution* for NBC defense is missing from the manuals and block training packages.

There are many questions that still need to be answered. When is a unit most vulnerable to NBC attack? How can a unit prepare for such an attack without limiting its tactical mobility? How can it survive after enduring a surprise NBC attack? What if NBC and ground attacks occur simultaneously? Will the NBC gear work under extreme wartime conditions? Which tactics can be conducted by infantrymen in full NBC gear? How can those in small units perform deliberate decontamination on themselves? Again, the combined experience of the NCO corps provides the answers to these questions.

## WHEN A UNIT IS MOST VULNERABLE TO NUCLEAR ATTACK

Nuclear attack can take the form of a cataclysmic explosion or quiet leakage of radiation into the environment. Its destructive power can be immediate, borne by the wind for great distances, or present in the soil from long ago. At any given location, an atomic device can be delivered instantly from far away, or be already positioned from a smuggling effort or former occupation of the same area. It can explode on impact or be command detonated.

In modern war, infantrymen must be ready to survive a nuclear explosion. To minimize their injuries from such an eventuality, they must learn to keep their bare skin covered and to look away from bright flashes.

At risk on a modern battlefield, is any unit that does not periodically test for *residual* radiation. Exposure to four hundred and fifty (450) rads over a twenty-four (24) hour period is considered lethal; however, as little as fifty (50) cumulative rads can cause nausea. Any rapid jump of the needle on a radiac meter (even between relatively low readings) can mean that the next step may take the meter's operator into lethally high radiation.

## WHEN A UNIT IS MOST VULNERABLE TO CHEMICAL ATTACK

Chemical agents can take three forms: solid, liquid, or gas. The solids and liquids usually turn into dangerous gases before dissipating. There are four categories of agents: nerve, blister, blood, and choking. At normal temperatures, the first two are usually liquids, while the last two are gases.

The usual manmade delivery systems are aircraft, missiles, artillery shells, and mines. Liquids are generally sprayed from aircraft, whereas gases are dispensed from exploding artillery rounds, missile warheads, and mines. The chemical shells and mines make less noise than their high-explosive counterparts. Of course, the wind can also deliver both *solids* and gases. During the Gulf War, Allied forces were afraid that "dusty mustard" would be introduced into the sand storms that frequent the region.

While downwind of an adversary, units must be particularly watchful for NBC attack. The potency and life expectancy of the contaminant will establish its effectiveness. As heat causes all agents to evaporate, units are most at risk during the coolest times of the day. But, only in cool closed-in spaces, will those units usually encounter lethal doses of a blood agent. This is fortunate because heavy concentrations can break down gas mask filters in 15 minutes. Infantrymen should assume that most gases collect in low places, just as mustard gas did in WWI. After a gas attack, they may not want to jump into a hole to escape bullets and shrapnel. After a spray attack, they may not even want to move through heavy foliage. Liquid agents evaporate less quickly when protected from sun and wind. In freezing locales, solid agents can retain their potency for weeks.

## WHEN A UNIT IS MOST VULNERABLE TO BIOLOGICAL ATTACK

Some biologicals are nothing more than heavy concentrations of naturally occurring chemicals, but others consist of microscopic bacteria or viruses. While the toxins like "yellow rain" can be sprayed, the microscopic biologicals need vectors (like insects) for their distribution. None of the biologicals register on chemical detection kits.

To resist biological contamination, one must practice good personal hygiene and use insect protection — e.g., netting, clothing, and sprays or lotions.

## JUST DISCUSSING HOW TO SURVIVE AN NBC ATTACK IS NOT ENOUGH

A determined enemy could launch nuclear, chemical, and biological attacks simultaneously. Or, he could use NBC contaminants in support of an attack by aircraft, armor, and infantry. Even in full NBC protective equipment, friendly infantrymen might have difficulty weathering a combined nuclear and chemical attack; the radioactive dust would clog the filters on their protective masks. Further, because NBC gear is hot and restrictive of vision and movement, those wearing it would have a hard time fending off a conventional attack. And, for them, a counterattack would be out of the question.

Because nuclear blasts and nerve gases affect their victims almost immediately, being prepared to defend against these threats requires *more* than just knowing what to do. It requires taking the action *quickly*. Defending against a nerve agent is a complicated process. One must mask, sound the alarm, cover up with a poncho, unmask, decontaminate mask interior and all bare skin, and then remask. All must be done within 60 seconds — the time it takes for a drop of nerve agent to kill. To do all this while holding one's breath and keeping one's eyes closed, takes a great deal of manual dexterity. Professional athletes couldn't do it without weekly practice. An infantry unit is only ready to handle worst-case scenarios, when its NCO's run NBC drills every time a truck is late.

## JUST ISSUING THE PROPER EQUIPMENT IS NOT ENOUGH EITHER

Providing one's infantrymen with operational NBC gear involves more than just issuing it — it involves maintaining it. The equipment is fairly delicate, has a limited life span even in uncontaminated environments, and must function under very difficult conditions. There is only one way to assure its dependability — infantry NCO's must oversee its inspection and maintenance.

To insure readiness against NBC attack, platoon sergeants should carry extra M8 detection paper, M256 chemical test kits, pocket dosimeters (and a PP4276 to recharge and rezero them), M258A1 decontamination kits, and atropine. To maintain the equipment, platoon sergeants should have the wherewithal and authority to correct discrepancies. They must carry spare parts for gas masks (like the rubber valve disks and head-harness straps), extra collateral equipment (like carriers and hoods), extra boots and gloves, and extra Mission-Oriented Protective Posture (MOPP) suits. When the lighter MOPP suit becomes available, each rifleman should carry a change of protective clothing in his pack.

(Source: FM 3-100 (1985), cover)

## THE VITAL MAINTENANCE OF NBC GEAR

The modern infantryman values his gas mask. But, because the mask is expensive, it is reissued to many people over its lifetime. It gets some rough treatment under every conceivable condition. Just to change the *internal* filters on an M17, one must don another mask. Fortunately, the M17 is being replaced by the M40 with *external* screw-on filters. Yet, most of the problems that can render an M17 inoperable are universal to all masks.

The filters are the most important component of a gas mask. During inspection, any of the following discoveries can mean inoperable filters: (1) discoloration or clogging with dust, (2) black mildew spots from getting damp, (3) blue edges instead of green (on training models), or (4) a stock number indicating expired shelf life. There is no guarantee that the filters were even installed properly.

For the gas mask properly to seal, there can be no flaws in the rubber faceblank. One must watch for the following discrepancies: (1) tiny rips or dry rot in the rubber; (2) eye lenses cracked, loose, or not protected by eye-lens outserts; (3) inlet- or outlet-valve disks missing; (4) inlet-valve covers installed upside down (so that rain water can reach the filters); and (5) head-harness straps broken. There may be problems inside the faceblank as well: (1) nose-cup-valve disks missing; (2) nose-cup flaps tucked in by mistake upon reassembly; (3) buttons disengaged or missing; and (4) buttonholes ripped. A complete and properly assembled mask may still *not hold a seal*. To find out for sure, one must test each mask on a special machine. Of course, if the tested mask is subsequently bumped or slept on, it may lose its ability to hold a seal. Then, every infantryman must remember to enclose the mask in his waterproof bag and to snap the carrier on his thigh. Finally, each individual must have a serviceable hood and MOPP suit. Both must be free of tears and have functional zippers and velcro tabs. The existing MOPP suit is only good for two weeks after removal from its package and 6 hours in a contaminated environment; and it loses much of its effectiveness when wet. The new version will be light, compact, washable, and effective longer in a contaminated area.

## SURVIVING A *SURPRISE* NBC ATTACK

When surprised, an infantryman has trouble thinking. Yet, to survive an NBC attack, he must take certain actions instantly. That means he must practice those actions in advance until he can do them instinctively. In other words, *to stand any chance* of surviving a surprise NBC attack, he must regularly rehearse immediate-action NBC drills (perhaps as often as once a week). Most U.S. units aren't fully prepared to survive the inevitable.

## THE IMMEDIATE-ACTION DRILL FOR A NUCLEAR EXPLOSION

Coming under nuclear attack is mind numbing. The newsreels of Japanese survivors at Nagasaki attest to that. Yet, infantrymen must take certain immediate actions just to survive the flash, blast, and heat waves. When the bomb goes off, the appropriate responses must already be second nature to them. To be ready, U.S. units must practice the following drill *weekly*. (See table 22.1.)

---

WITHOUT LOOKING AT THE BLAST, GET DOWN WITH HEAD TOWARD IT (ONLY SEEK COVER IF IT IS A STEP OR TWO AWAY AND WON'T COLLAPSE).

COVER EXPOSED ARMS AND RIFLE WITH BODY.

(LEADER DETERMINES THE CARDINAL DIRECTION OF THE FLASH.)

(LEADER COUNTS SECONDS UNTIL HEARING BLAST AND COMPUTES BOMB LOCATION USING THE FLASH-BANG FORMULA — SOUND TRAVELS 330 METERS PER SECOND.)

AFTER 90 SECONDS (OR UNTIL BLAST WAVES FROM BOTH DIRECTIONS HAVE PASSED AND DEBRIS HAS STOPPED FALLING), STAND UP.

ROLL DOWN SHIRT SLEEVES, BRUSH OFF DUST, DON PONCHO WITH HOOD UP.

WRAP WET T-SHIRT AROUND NOSE AND MOUTH.

(LEADER CALLS IN LOCATION OF BLAST AS NBC REPORT.)

(LEADER WATCHES CLOUDS OR SHOOTS PYROTECHNIC TO FIND HIGH-LEVEL WIND DIRECTION.)

IF RADIATION CLOUD IS APPROACHING, MOVE OUT OF ITS WAY (IF TACTICALLY FEASIBLE).

*Table 22.1: The Immediate-Action Drill for Nuclear Attack*

## THE DRILL FOR RESIDUAL RADIATION

When there's latent nuclear contamination possible, units of all sizes should add another infantryman to their point security element. His job would be to monitor the radiation levels continuously with a dosimeter. When a low level of residual radiation is detected, a unit's very survival could depend on what is done about it. A seemingly insignificant jump from 5 to 15 rads on a pocket dosimeter, could mean the point element is only a few steps away from a lethally hot location. It doesn't take a telltale explosion to cover a sizable area with highly dangerous nuclear waste. The next drill should be rehearsed for residual radiation. (See table 22.2.)

---

ROLL DOWN SHIRT SLEEVES, BRUSH OFF DUST, DON PONCHO WITH HOOD UP.

WRAP WET T-SHIRT AROUND NOSE AND MOUTH.

(LEADER CALLS IN NBC REPORT WITH FRIENDLY LOCATION IN CODE ONLY.)

IF RADIAC METER SHOWS TURNBACK DOSAGE OR RAPID INCREASE IN INTENSITY, TURN AROUND OR TRY A DIFFERENT ROUTE.

DRINK WATER TO COUNTERACT NAUSEA.

---

Table 22.2: The Drill for Residual Radiation

(Source: FM 21-75 (1967), p. 67)

## THE IMMEDIATE-ACTION DRILL FOR AN UNKNOWN CHEMICAL/BIOLOGICAL AGENT

On a modern battlefield — *with precision and no warning* — chemicals can be delivered by artillery barrage, command-detonated booby trap, or supersonic jet at treetop level. The Allies got lucky against the Iraqis. Future opponents may be more willing to unleash their modern arsenals. For this reason, Americans must prepare more diligently.

To survive a surprise nerve agent attack without protective clothing, one must mask, unmask, decontaminate the mask's interior and all bare skin, and then remask — *all within 60 seconds*. This prodigious feat is *only* possible for those who regularly practice an appropriate immediate-action drill.

Which chemical or biological agent has been employed is seldom immediately apparent to its victim; all must be considered nerve agents until proven otherwise. Infantrymen who do not weekly practice an immediate-action drill similar to the one shown below are deluding themselves about their readiness to fight a modern war. All small-unit leaders must take the initiative to accomplish whatever NBC training their parent units can't, or they will compound the problem. (See table 22.3 and figure 22.1.)

(Sources: MCO P1500.44B, p. 15-26; MCI 7311B, p. 115)

HOLD BREATH AND SHUT EYES.

DON AND CLEAR GAS MASK IN 9 SECONDS; THEN, PULL DOWN HOOD IN THE NEXT 6 SECONDS.

SOUND THE ALARM.

FACE THE ENEMY, PUT RIFLE IN LAP, AND GET UNDER PONCHO (IF NO MANMADE STRUCTURE IS AVAILABLE).

OPEN PACKETS #1 AND #2 FROM M258A1 DECONTAMINATION KIT AND PLACE THEM AND AN OPEN CANTEEN WITHIN REACH.

CLOSE EYES, HOLD BREATH, AND REMOVE GAS MASK.

FLUSH EYES ONE AT A TIME BY CANTING HEAD TO THE SIDE AND HOLDING MOUTH OF CANTEEN TO LOWER EYE.

WHILE AVOIDING EYES, BLOT EXPOSED SKIN ON HEAD WITH PACKET #1.

BLOT SAME SKIN WITH PACKET #2 ANTIDOTE.

CLEAN INSIDE OF MASK AND HOOD WITH PACKET #2.

GO OVER INSIDE OF MASK AND HOOD WITH PACKET #1 (REVERSE ORDER NECESSARY TO KEEP FROM FOGGING LENSES).

REMASK.

BLOT BARE ARMS AND HANDS WITH PACKETS #1 AND #2.

DECONTAMINATE RIFLE WITH PACKETS #2 AND #1.

(LEADER DESIGNATES PERSONNEL TO KEEP WATCH OR REPEL ATTACKERS.)

(LEADER TESTS AGENT WITH M256 TEST KIT AND M8 PAPER.)

LAY PONCHO BACK CAREFULLY TO FORM A STERILE SURFACE OR SCRAPE OFF TOP LAYER OF SOIL WITH ENTRENCHING TOOL (AFTER DECONTAMINATING HANDLE).

DON MOPP SUIT WITHIN 15 MINUTES OF THE TIME OF THE ATTACK.

(LEADER SENDS AN NBC REPORT WITH FRIENDLY LOCATION IN CODE ONLY.)

IF TACTICALLY FEASIBLE, MOVE UPWIND OF CONTAMINATED AREA.

*Table 22.3: The Immediate-Action Drill for Chemical/Biological Attack*

## THE MODIFICATION TO THE DRILL FOR A BLOOD AGENT ALONE

MOPP suits take 10 minutes to put on. They are hot and restrict movement. In other words, they are inconsistent with outmaneuvering an opponent. When tests indicate that a blood agent alone has been used, "putting on the MOPP suit" can be completely omitted from the drill.[2] However, blood agents can also break down protective-mask filters in as little as 15 minutes. For this reason, "changing filters" must be added to the drill. In summary, when only a blood agent can be detected during the testing sequence, the unit can modify the end of the chemical agent drill. (See table 22.4.)

# Techniques from the NCO Corps

> DO THE MASKING AND DECONTAMINATION STEPS UP TO "CREATING STERILE SURFACE."
>
> DO *NOT* DON THE MOPP SUIT.
>
> CHANGE GAS MASK FILTERS EVERY 15 MINUTES.

Table 22.4: The Modification to the Drill for a Solitary Blood Agent

Figure 22.1: It Takes Practice to Counter a Surprise Chemical Attack
(Sources: MCO P1500.44B, p. 15-28; OPNAV P 34-03 (1960), p. 170)

## SIMULTANEOUSLY COUNTERING BOTH NBC AND GROUND ATTACK

There is no way to shoot at one's enemy and still decontaminate one's skin during the first 60 seconds of an attack. Luckily, even if that enemy were willing to use protective gear or specially ventilated armored vehicles to withstand his own chemical contaminants, he could not close with a defender in less than 60 seconds. *Therefore, the first 60 seconds must be solely dedicated to decontaminating one's skin.* Then, however many personnel are required to repel the assault, can do so. They won't need to don their MOPP suits for fifteen minutes. The outcome of the assault will be predestined before then.

The M16 rifle can be operated with the right arm alone — thumb on the selector switch, and index finger in the trigger well. That leaves the left arm to hold up the front of the poncho so that a bead can be drawn on the foe.

Pralidoxime chloride is the antidote for atropine. After receiving both, a nerve agent casualty can sometimes continue to perform his job. If the antidote is not available in a separate compartment on the atropine injector, it can be obtained from the battalion aid station.

It takes very little to break the seal on a protective mask. Either sweat or whiskers will do it. So too will contact with the butt of a rifle about to be fired. This is undoubtedly why NBC schools subject their students to CS riot-control agents as they run through obstacle courses. Perhaps the students should be required to conduct accurate live firing at the same time.

## WHICH TACTICS CAN BE CONDUCTED IN FULL NBC GEAR

Operating in full NBC gear has many drawbacks: (1) one can no longer use his peripheral vision; (2) one runs the risk of becoming a heat casualty; and (3), by just sweating or getting jostled, one can lose the seal on his mask. Standard rules on when to attack or defend generally apply; but, all things considered, most attacks should be by fire alone. Full-blown assaults should be avoided.

## HASTY DECONTAMINATION

Hasty decontamination should be accomplished approximately six hours after exposure (the life expectancy of the old MOPP suit in a contaminated environment). This procedure entails changing MOPP suits and brushing off individual equipment with a mixture of 2 parts Super Tropical Bleach (STB) and 3 parts dirt. Changing MOPP suits is a two-man job. First, one man decontaminates the other's hood with M258 packets. Then, he decontaminates his own gloves repeatedly as he rolls up the other's hood, helps the other to remove his suit, and finally helps the other to redress. At this point, the two switch roles. Not recontaminating each other takes practice. In training, they should use luminous dust to gauge their proficiency.

## HOW DELIBERATE DECONTAMINATION CAN BE SELF-ADMINISTERED

Deliberate decontamination is usually supervised by an NBC specialist, but there's no secret to doing it and no reason why a unit can't run its own decontamination site. A unit can easily carry enough lightweight gear to construct such a site: soap, powdered bleach, large plastic bags, sponges, brushes, gas mask filters, MOPP suits, chemical detection kits, and a radiac meter. With these few items, the members of any unit can rid themselves of both nuclear and chemical/biological contaminants.

The decontamination site contains eight separate stations arranged into the wind (to limit the spread of the contaminants). (See figure 22.2.) The site should have good drainage and a supply of clean water. Holes in the ground are lined with large plastic bags to hold solutions. Waste-water sumps are dug at stations #1 and #7. Engineer tape or string is used to fashion liquid and vapor control lines in front of stations #4 and #8 respectively. Each station is manned by a few men in full MOPP gear.

At station #1, the individual weapon and gear of the person to be decontaminated are immersed in 2 parts STB and 3 parts water, scrubbed in hot soapy water, and finally dipped in hot rinse water (all solutions are changed after every 10 sets of gear). Then, the equipment is tested with chemical detection paper and a radiac meter. Once decontaminated, it is sent up the equipment trail to station #8.

At station #2, the subject steps into a pit filled with 2 parts STB and 3 parts dirt. He kicks or brushes the mixture up on his boots. Then, those manning the station decontaminate his hood with M258 packets or hot soapy water, and then roll his hood.

At station #3, the subject's overgarments are taken off and discarded unless washable. At station #4, his overboots and gloves are removed to be decontaminated and reissued later. Overboot laces are only cut off if there are extras available. Care is taken not to let any contaminated article cross the liquid control line.

Station #5 is for monitoring the decontamination progress. With radiac equipment and chemical test kits, its operators test the man for residual contamination. A corpsman asks him how he feels, and if his suit had any leaks. Suspected contamination is cleansed on the spot.

Station #6 is for gas mask removal. After the man's mask is taken off, he holds his breath until crossing the vapor control line. If his mask has optical inserts, they are returned to him before he leaves the station.

At station #7 (connected to station #6), the subject's mask is decontaminated. First, the filters are removed. Then, the mask is immersed in hot soapy water, clear water, and finally a sanitizing solution. This solution can be made up of 1 part household bleach to 15 parts water, or four tubes of calcium hydrochlorite from the first aid packets to every gallon of water.

At station #8, masks are reassembled with new filters, and decontaminated gear reissued. Before redressing, each man can take a *cold* shower to wash off radioactive dust. After the last man has been decontaminated, the site's operators can close it down by moving from station #8 to #1. All nonretrievable items are buried in the sumps, and the sumps appropriately marked.

The key to survival in an active NBC environment is preparing *more than what is minimally required* by one's parent command, and then taking the initiative to protect and decontaminate oneself.

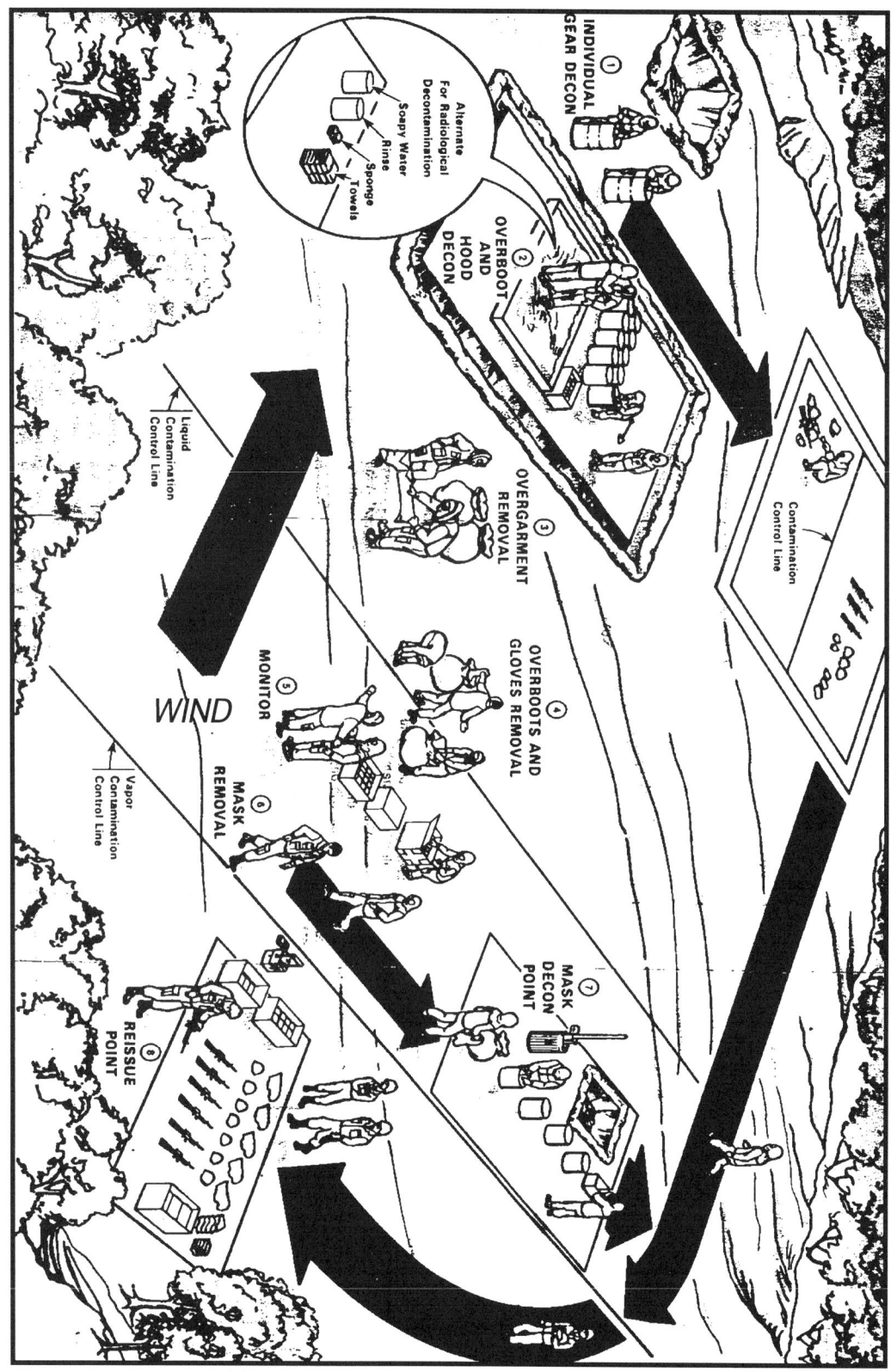

*Figure 22.2: The Deliberate-Decontamination Station*
(Source: FM 3-5 (1985), p. 6-3)

# 23 The Unbeatable Urban Defense

- What makes the urban defense potentially unbeatable?
- How can a small unit willing to pull back, defeat a much larger foe?
- What techniques can the unit employ to make this possible?

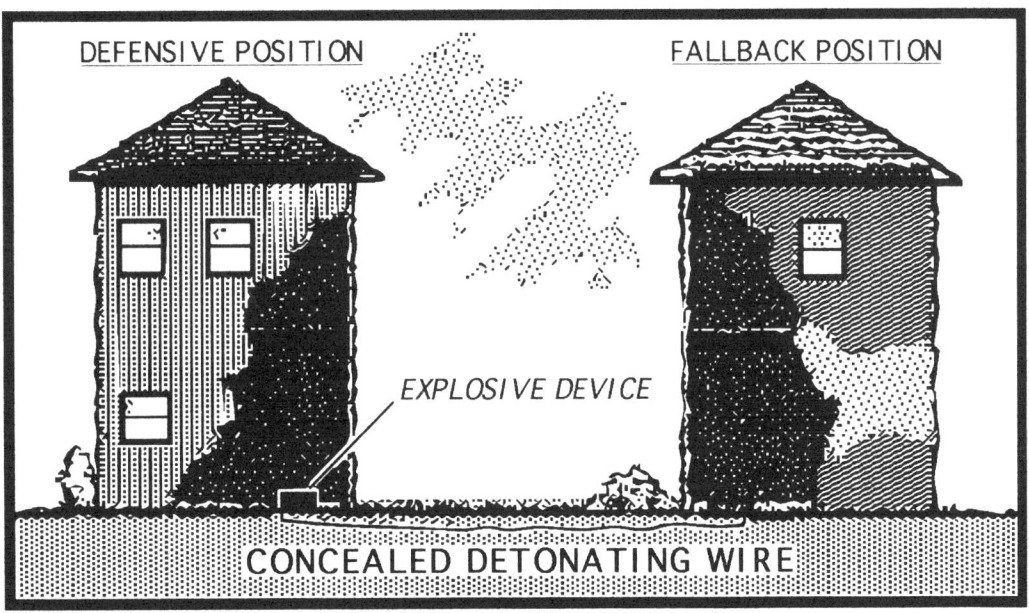

(Source: FM 90-10 (1979), p. D-3)

### ATTACKING THROUGH URBAN TERRAIN HAS NEVER BEEN POPULAR

Throughout history, military leaders have warned against attacking cities:

> The worst policy is to attack cities. Attack cities only when there is no alternative.[1]
> — Sun Tzu

Attacking through urban terrain can be slow and costly. In 1942, a few hundred Warsaw Ghetto Jews with pistols, grenades, and molotov cocktails fought an entire German army to a standstill. To break the deadlock, the Germans had to flood the sewers and burn down the ghetto:

> By January, when the fighters had their first baptism of fire, they had a store of 143 revolvers, one machine pistol and seven rounds of ammunition per weapon.... Their numbers increased to six hundred and fifty, divided into 22 groups.... The Ghetto fighters constructed an intricate network of underground cellars and tunnels. Concealed retreats and passages for shifting and distributing the defense forces were also devised....
> ...A hail of bullets, grenades, and bombs poured down on the Germans.... Tanks were brought in but the fighters aimed a barrage of gasoline-filled bottles.... The Germans quickly realized the Ghetto could not be cleared in one

burst of action. . . . At noon the Germans dammed up the sewers and flooded them. . . . Only fire could destroy the Ghetto. Stroop then decided to destroy the entire residential area by setting every block on fire.[2]

It was the urban defenders at Stalingrad who turned the tide of World War II. Two platoons of Russians in a grain elevator withstood the onslaught of three German divisions for a week. The elevator might never have fallen, if the drinking water had lasted:

> One fortress which had slowed the German timetable was the huge grain elevator. . . . For nearly a week, since September 14, a group of less than fifty able-bodied Russians had holed up in the corrugated-metal side tower, and defied the guns of three Nazi Divisions. . . . Reinforced on the night of September 17 by Lt. Andrei Khoyzyanov and a platoon of Marines . . . the garrison fought with renewed spirit. . . . For the next three days German artillery pounded the stronghold, set the grain on fire with incendiary shells, and riddled the tower itself with high explosives. German infantrymen broke in and crept up the stairs, but the defenders managed to drive them out with knives, fists, and bullets. Now, on the night of September 20, the exhausted garrison was almost out of ammunition, and the water supply had been used up completely. In a frantic search for something to drink Lt. Khoyzyanov led his men out.[3]

At one point in the battle for Stalingrad, the Russian enclaves west of the Volga were only 300 yards deep and defended by *roving* squads of infantrymen:

> But, the Russians, though still heavily outnumbered remained their [the Germans] masters in the technique of house-to-house fighting. They had perfected the use of "shock groups," small bodies of mixed arms — light and heavy machinegunners, tommy gunners, and grenadiers usually with antitank guns, who gave one another support in lightning counterattacks; and they had developed the creation of "killing zones," houses and squares heavily mined to which the defenders knew all the approach routes, where the German advance could be canalized. . . . By the end of October the Russian positions at Stalingrad had been reduced to a few pockets of stone, seldom more than three hundred yards deep, bordering on the right bank of the Volga. . . . But these last islets of resistance, hardened in the furnace of repeated attacks, were irreducible. Paulus's VI Army was spent.[4]
> — A.J.P. Taylor

By the Spring of 1945, the Russians had fought their way through many of the largest cities in Eastern Europe. Those who were still alive had learned a great deal about urban warfare. Yet, at Berlin, against old men and boys, the Russians suffered an additional *300,000* casualties:

> It had taken just sixteen days for the troops of three fronts — the First Byelorussian, the First Ukrainian and the Second Byelorussian — to crush enemy forces in the area of Berlin and to seize the German capital. . . . [T]he cost of the final battle in Soviet casualties — killed, wounded, missing — was enormous: 305,000 from April 16 to May 8.[5]

## THERE'S ONLY ONE WAY TO DEFEAT AN URBAN DEFENDER AT NO COST

To neutralize a contested built-up area at no cost, the attacker must obliterate it from a distance. The smaller the area, the easier this is to do. In sufficient quantity, fire, flood, artillery shells, missiles, and aerial bombs will all get the job done. Therein lies an important lesson for the urban defender. He cannot occupy rooms that might burn or buildings that might collapse under direct fire from standoff weaponry. In fact, against an opponent with close air support, he can't defend any ordinary structure for long. He must keep his location secret until the last moment and then move back after springing an ambush. Whenever responsible for key terrain, he must carefully decide where to set in. For example, the buildings around a key intersection (or rural crossroads) would always be at risk from aerial bombardment.

On the other hand, history confirms that the defenders of durable or *obscure* buildings have a slight edge over those who would attack them. At Stalingrad, a grain elevator and some factories (all framed in iron and covered with sheet metal) withstood every bomb and shell the Germans could throw at them. In the same battle, less durable structures were defended only briefly. From the standpoint of the *mobile* defender in a *large* urban area, the susceptibility of many structures to collapse creates more problems for his opponent. Rubble is easier for the defender to cover by fire, and rubble will impede attacking armor. Furthermore, it takes time and considerable ordnance to drop a reinforced-concrete building from a distance. The upper floors will normally insulate the lower floors from indirect fire and aerial bombs.

## IN THE CITY, THE DEFENDER HAS THE EDGE

How to attack has been the main thrust of this book so far. In rural terrain, a good attacker can often prevail. Yet, every rule has its exception. In the city, a good defender has the edge. This edge comes from the terrain, and what the defender does to enhance it. Three-dimensional terrain can greatly complicate someone's plan of attack — each block, building, floor, and room requires a different scheme of maneuver. This scheme of maneuver can't be ascertained ahead of time. It must be developed on the spot and then executed "deliberately." As a result, the attacker has trouble building momentum. He also has difficulty communicating. Radios prefer an unobstructed line of sight. Every time an attacker waves or calls to his companions, he telegraphs his intentions, and exposes himself to enemy fire. The defender can use a telephone.

For the defender, urban terrain provides better cover and concealment plus better observation and fields of fire. A city is nothing more than a maze of open spaces — i.e., streets, hallways, rooms, etc. To the individual attacker, these open spaces constitute danger areas. While passing through them, he can be shot not only from the side, but also from above or below. If that weren't enough, the partitions between open spaces are honeycombed with holes (some covered with glass, but holes just the same). The individual attacker can be shot through any one of these holes. Many of the walls, floors, and ceilings are so thin that, in the context of a high-powered rifle, they offer little more than concealment to the attacker. In other words, to change location, the attacker must risk injury. If he so much as temporarily takes cover in a doorway, he silhouettes himself to anyone inside. If he enters a building, he silhouettes himself every time he walks in front of a window. If he passes between the windows on opposite sides of a room, he can be shot from a building several blocks away. In short, there are more ways for the attacker to get killed in urban terrain. He can't even camouflage himself to blend in with his surroundings. Meanwhile, the defender can operate from any number of gun ports and mask his firing signature. The urban attacker has trouble figuring out who shot him.

In the city, even attackers willing to absorb massive losses must struggle to evict skilled defenders. Those defenders have to their advantage a virtual maze of obstacles that can be easily reinforced. These obstacles automatically channelize the attackers into kill zones. To maintain any semblance of mobility or security, attacking tanks must operate along spacious boulevards. To build any pretense of momentum, attacking infantrymen must move through vacant lots, streets, alleyways, stairwells, hallways, rooms, doors, and windows. In other words, the walls favor the defender. They can be breached, but only at great expense in time and logistics. By *blocking key passageways through these walls,* the defender can acquire a decided edge over his foe. He can prevent that foe from ever building momentum. In fact, he may bring the attacker to a virtual standstill.

Imagine what might happen to a squad of infantrymen trying to capture a contested multistory building surrounded by vacant lots. Establishing a foothold in that building might be the least of their problems. If those in the defending unit had a 360-degree barrier plan for each occupied room and concertina wire in the stairwells and hallways, they could hold out for quite some time. Further, if they had covered these barriers with observation and fire, they could win. With so much as a pinhole in wallpaper at the top of a flight of stairs, a defender could shoot anyone climbing those stairs right through the wallboard. By listening for footsteps on the floor above, he could shoot their maker through the ceiling. By watching through a tiny hole in an air-conditioning duct, he could shoot adversaries in the room below him through the floor. By positioning a small mirror outside an open door, he could accurately fire up a hallway without ever exposing his body. By booby trapping barriers and hiding command-detonated claymores where attackers might congregate, the defender could further shave the odds against him. In fact, if he really wanted to get ornery, he could rig the entire building to explode, dive down a laundry chute, and then escape into the sewer system.

In summary, it's difficult for the urban attacker to move *with momentum* through terrain comprised almost entirely of danger areas and obstacles. If he encounters a defender skilled in barrier construction, he won't be able to move forward at any price. That's the lesson of the Warsaw Ghetto, Stalingrad, and Berlin. Those who attack cities risk embarking on a no-win situation.

## URBAN TERRAIN ALSO SLIGHTLY HANDICAPS THE DEFENDER

A three-dimensional battlefield creates additional security problems for the defender. In the city, he can come under attack not only from any side, but also from above or below; he must watch the rooftops and sewers. In the sewers, jumbles of concertina, microphones, and 55-gallon drums of gasoline rigged for command detonation may suffice (under a loose interpretation of the Geneva Conventions). On the rooftops, sentries in tall buildings can prevail. With tracer bullets, they can ignite gas cans that, in turn, light fuzes to claymores.

Even at ground level in built-up areas, the defender has more security problems: (1) gutters make perfect infiltration lanes, (2) walls provide covered avenues of approach to his position, and (3) structures may collapse around him. He can't afford to get caught in a building that might burn or be knocked down by standoff weaponry. He must occupy framed buildings and construct fighting positions with overhead protection. Furthermore, rubbling can block his fields of fire. Machinegunners must have alternate positions from which to shoot their FPL's. To counteract the dust and smoke that will accompany a concerted attack, each defender must have aiming stakes for his weapon.

For the defender, the walls also create communications and mobility problems. They isolate him from his buddies; and they make him difficult to reinforce, resupply, and withdraw. Only with covered routes through the walls, can this crucial support be easily accomplished. And, only with a reliable means of communication to each two-man position, can control be exercised and stress be managed.

## WHAT THE URBAN DEFENDER MUST FACE

Before an attacker can systematically clear a built-up area of any size, he must *isolate* that area and then gain a *foothold*. For this reason, the defender (of a city, town, neighborhood, block, building, or room) does what he can to prevent isolation and penetration.

To keep from being isolated, the defender must protect his mobility, resources, and command/control network. At every level, he must cover phone, water, and electricity junction boxes by observation and fire. He must establish a dual means of communication and a covered route of reinforcement/egress to each defensive position.

Preventing an urban attacker from gaining a foothold presents more of a challenge. What constitutes an adequate urban defense during the day, may not work after dark. Then, the gutters and shadows create additional infiltration lanes. Unfortunately, with heavy explosives, the attacker can blow down almost anything in his path. That means the defender must refuse the edge of his built-up area without heavily manning it, and he must create barriers that will not telegraph his exact location.

For example, heavily manning the edge of a city will not prevent a skilled enemy from getting in. With armor and supporting arms, he can obliterate the buildings at the point of attack. Without heavy weapons, he can easily reach assaulting distance of the city limits — through a drainage ditch during the day, or across open ground at night. If he prefers, he can completely bypass the main line of resistance. He can send his entire force into the city's outskirts through a single sewer outlet, or separate detachments into the city's center along a variety of infiltration conduits. In the outskirts, his seizure of a tall durable building will give him an observation advantage. At the city's center, his capture of a government building or TV station will give him an advantage in morale.

## STOPPING SUPPORTED ARMOR

To stop armor backed by supporting arms, the urban defender must use a maneuver warfare technique. Initially, he must try to prevent an enemy foothold by positioning his artillery/air observers and antitank weapons teams at the edge of town. Then, he must weaken or channelize the opposing armor that does get in with strongpoints, soft/elastic defense, ambushes in series, or not occupying the ground to be defended. Finally, that armor must be expelled with a counterattack. Once inside a city, tanks can level almost any structure at which they can get a clear shot.

## HALTING ENEMY INFANTRY INSIDE THE CITY

On the other hand, the defender needs more traditional techniques to stop massed infantry. Only tactical wire and interlocking bands of grazing machinegun fire can do that. The machineguns must be positioned at ground level — e.g., in basement windows, under porches, or away from buildings altogether. If tactical or protective wire is to be used, supplementary wire must be placed in other streets to deceive the enemy as to the actual location of the main line of resistance. Stopping enemy sappers takes blocking infiltration lanes with additional nighttime positions, intermittent illumination, jumbles of barbed wire, homemade early-warning devices, and patrols.

The formation in the manuals works nicely. It's a rigid defense in depth that doubles as a perimeter when not under attack. It has two subordinate units up and one back. In a typical platoon sector, the two forward squads each defend a one-block frontage, and the rear squad provides defense in depth, rear security, and a reserve. Interestingly, this formation is the *same* as the one traditionally used for the *urban offense*. That means that a platoon of urban defenders could, in theory, shift quickly over to the offense.

## COURSES OF ACTION TO MEET THE COMBINED THREAT

To counter a combined threat, the defender could place a fairly rigid, yet still mobile, defense line a few blocks in from the edge of town. Forward of that line, he could have supporting-arms spotters and antitank teams to refuse armor, and patrols to discourage infiltrators. If the enemy still got in, the buildings at the edge of town could be command detonated, and the rubble either retaken or covered by fire.

Or, the defense might consist of a string of strongpoints to channel mechanized infantry into preplanned killing zones. By occupying buildings that were impervious to large-caliber ordnance, the defender could force attacking tanks to take streets that converged on areas that could be flooded, set afire, mined, collapsed, or saturated with anti-armor or supporting-arms fire.

Of course, the defender could also prevent the foe's occupation of one area, by shooting at him from another. The city offers perfect conditions for this type of defense. Its streets provide observation and fields of fire for great distances. For example, an antitank gun at one end of a street could prevent enemy tanks from crossing at any point along that street. A collocated machinegun could do the same thing to enemy infantry. As soon as the friendly weapons were targeted by enemy guns, they could move sideways one or two streets and repeat the process — all without manning the area directly in front of the opposition force. If the same street were also preregistered, the foe would pay a dear price to cross it. This type of defense could slow down an enemy force enough for a mobile reserve to move into position to block it. Most infantry organizations do not have enough personnel to man a continuous line of resistance across a large city anyway.

As another alternative, the defender could use a series of ambushes. In urban terrain, armor-killer teams can hide from enemy infantry, and still escape along covered routes. The counterattack could be launched by friendly aircraft with smart ordnance.

Still, the real key to defending a large city with limited forces is the final maneuver warfare option — *the soft or elastic defense in depth*. A defense that could move backwards with some semblance of order could bleed an attacker dry. After whittling a much larger opponent down to size across the breadth of a city, a defender could expel that attacker himself. The defense at Stalingrad consisted almost entirely of independent squads popping up here and there. Yet, clearing the city so weakened the Germans that they couldn't break out of the encirclement created by the counterattack.

## TO ACHIEVE MOBILITY, THE DEFENDER MUST FULLY UTILIZE COVERED ROUTES

There are many conduits for movement below the streets of a city: subways, sewers, electrical tunnels, water ducts, etc. As modern cities are built atop their predecessors, many have the equivalent of catacombs — e.g., there is an old city below the streets of Seattle. Through underground passageways, the defender can either pull back or move forward to conduct a spoiling attack.

In the urban setting, there are hidden passageways above ground as well: (1) air-conditioning ducts, (2) air shafts between buildings, (3) crawlways between upper-story walls and sloping roofs, and (4) spaces above suspended ceilings. All are promising routes of resupply, reinforcement, and egress. During WWII, Jews used covered routes in the Warsaw Ghetto to great advantage:

> Trenches and ditches were dug under pavements, behind walls and through sewers. Attics also became vital passageways.... [H]oles were cut in walls, making it possible for people to move from house to house and street to street.[6]

## TECHNIQUES AT THE EDGE OF TOWN

From the edge of town or top of a tall building, a supporting-arms spotter can start shooting as soon as enemy armor comes into view. He can greatly simplify this job by creating a free-fire zone beyond, and a no-fire zone inside, the town. Then, instead of having to work up complicated pilot briefs, he merely has to identify the built-up area as a no-fire zone, and then tell the pilots to bomb at will. The pilots can see where the fields stop and the buildings start. They would probably prefer planning their own flight paths anyway, and they can often provide their own SEAD support as well. On the approaches to a city, enemy armor doesn't need marking.

The antitank assets at the edge of town must shift their location after each shot. If they can't stop the opposition armor, those not assigned to an anti-armor ambush should fall back to the main line of resistance.

## THE "SCHEME OF MANEUVER" AT THE MAIN LINE OF RESISTANCE

Inside the city, the urban defender must keep his location secret until the last moment. Because enemy tanks will have trouble maneuvering and elevating their main guns, they'll prefer to lag behind their infantry and fire at pockets of resistance from several blocks away. For this reason, the defender should accomplish much of his local security with anti-armor ambushes. Those manning the ambushes must find some way to hide from the enemy infantry, and then escape to the main line of resistance after killing a tank. Places to hide include air-conditioning ducts, crawl spaces between walls and eaves, and "spider holes" in plantings or shrubbery. Escape options include the following: hiding until dark, moving along rooftops, and following sewers.

A rigid defense can't hold out for long against an opponent with substantial armor and supporting arms. The main line of resistance must be both invisible and mobile. To have the best chance of winning against superior combat power, the defender must surprise his adversary and then *fall back*.

## LOOSELY CONTROLLED AND WIDELY SEPARATED SMALL UNITS CAN EFFECTIVELY DEFEND CITIES

In WWI, the Germans replaced continuously manned trench lines with a network of small forts. Additionally, *they allowed those manning the forts to fall back on their own initiative*. The NCO's in charge had the authority to abandon their forts under pressure. Behind this network of forts, was a mobile reserve that could counterattack when necessary.

A city could be defended in the same way. Groups of durable buildings could serve as "forts," and the streets could function as the fire and observation lanes between forts. With a way temporarily to defend one or two blocks at a time, the facsimile would be complete. The defense would consist of a series of "moving pockets of resistance." These pockets could temporarily withstand any threat, cover unmanned areas between them by fire, and move backwards as necessary. Strongpoints covered by artillery fire from across the Volga worked well at Stalingrad.

Of ideal size for a moving pocket of resistance is the reinforced rifle platoon. Its traditional methods will work against any threat, as long as the defensive formation is hidden and *not required to remain stationary* against a stronger opponent. In other words, "two up and one back" will suffice as long as the squads can move rearward under pressure. The rigid defense can stop human-wave assaults and short-range infiltration, but it can't guarantee success against armor and supporting arms. It takes the flexibility to move rearward to prevent the breakthrough of an opponent with enough standoff weaponry to level anything in his path. If this movement rearward were orderly, what harm could it do? Prearranged routes and guidelines for when to pull back could provide adequate control. Because the relative positioning of the squads is the same for both offense and defense in the city, the platoon could just as easily move forward instead — to take advantage of a break in enemy momentum.

To handle any threat, the traditional formation only needs less rigidity. Its tactical wire and final protective fires can stay the same. After all, if barbed wire is placed in several streets at once, the enemy has no way of knowing which street is actually defended. All that must change is the *duration* of the stand at any particular location. Now, instead of having to defend urban ground to the death no matter what the odds, rifle squads and crew-served-gun teams can surprise a more powerful foe and then leapfrog backwards along covered routes to fallback positions.

Some might say that a unit moving rearward under pressure would uncover the flanks of its neighbors and thereby destroy the integrity of the defensive line. They would be correct, if this unit had any close neighbors. But the moving pocket of resistance doesn't. Its lack of neighbors and small size helps to it to hide. It has all the properties of a strongpoint.

Others might argue that the enemy would simply pour between the pockets of resistance. If each platoon had an independent maneuver partner, the area between the platoon and its neighbors could be defended *without physically occupying it*. A small force of antitank weapons and machineguns could cover this unmanned ground without ever compromising the platoon's location. That force could do so by operating a few blocks behind the platoon. That way it could enjoy some protection to its front, and still quickly dodge enemy fire from its flanks. Every time it was fired upon, it could shift to another street and continue to cover the same defensive sector. An opposition force taking fire from the side might be reluctant to leave its attack lane to silence that fire.

The unmanned part of the defense line could be considered a kill zone into which the enemy had been channelized by the pockets of resistance. In other words, the no-man's land between the platoon enclaves could be preregistered and turned into free-fire zones for friendly supporting arms. A highly mobile reserve could stay several blocks behind the loose network of forts to counter breakthroughs as necessary, and frontline platoons could be pulled back to realign as necessary.

There's no telling what a network of mobile platoons could accomplish. At first, they could be deployed roughly on line and in some depth. Each would be assigned only a *lane* to defend. *Control over the platoons would be loose.* One must admit that a line of widely separated units with the capability of protecting their own flanks, bends more easily than a traditional line. In other words, each unit is not automatically uncovered every time a neighbor is forced to fall back. Permitting smaller units to operate independently under decentralized control more closely follows the tenets of maneuver warfare. A platoon might occasionally get surrounded, but that is no more dangerous than being overrun. In the city after dark, an experienced unit should be able to exfiltrate out of almost any encirclement, particularly after it had pre-reconnoitered the route. (See figure 23.1 for how these moving pockets of resistance might stop a determined attacker.)

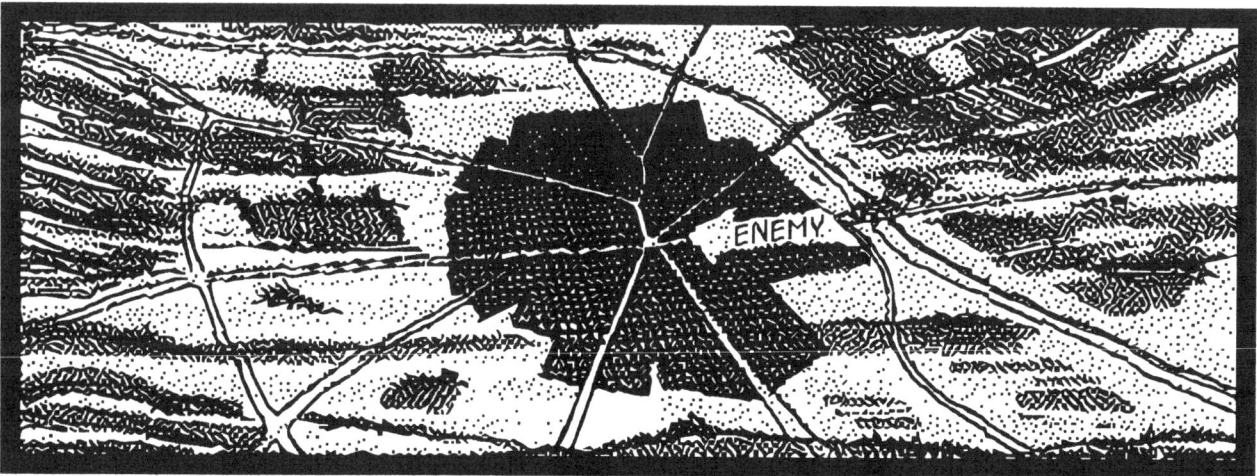

(Source: FM 90-10 (1979), p. 1-9)

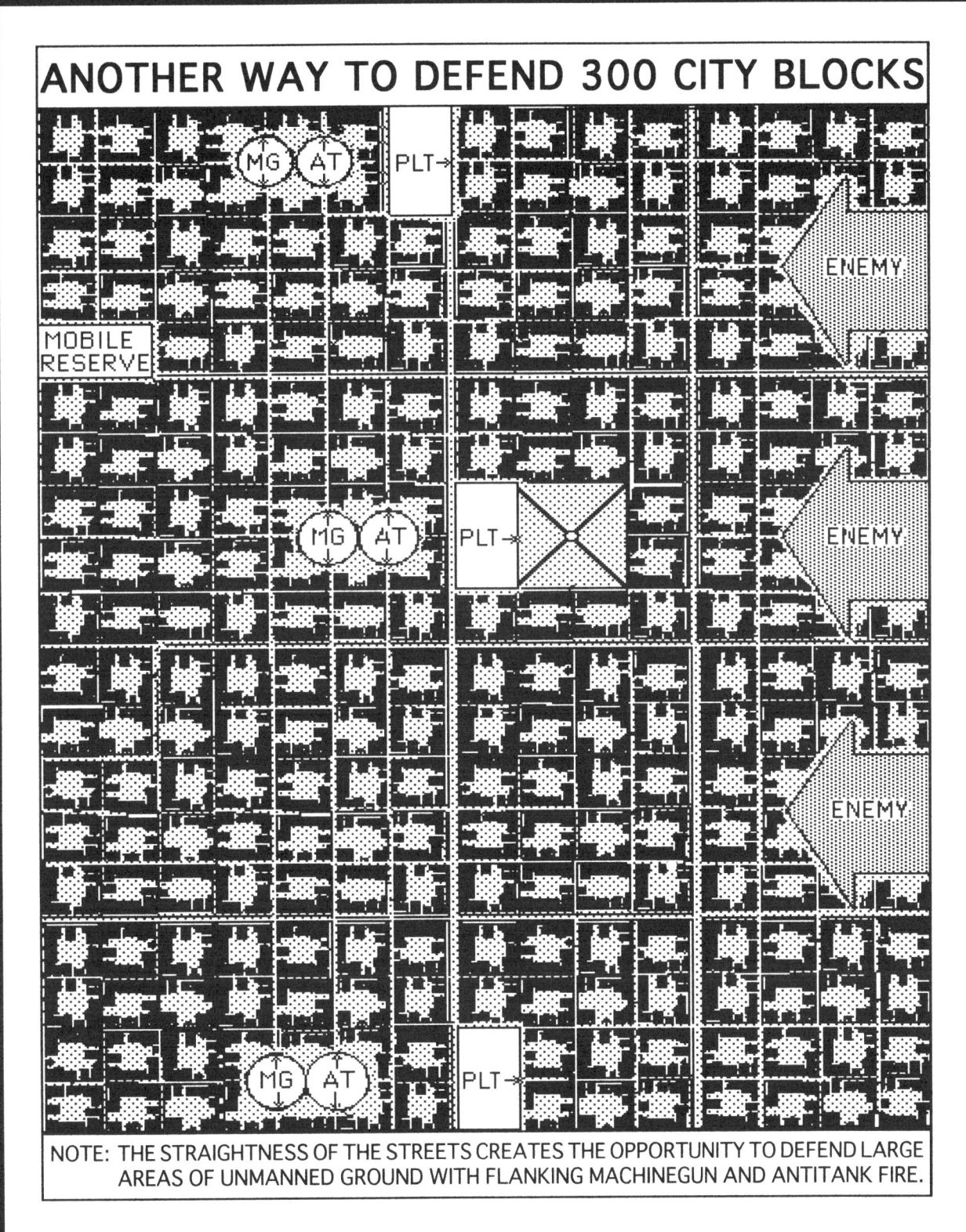

Figure 23.1: Moving Pockets of Resistance

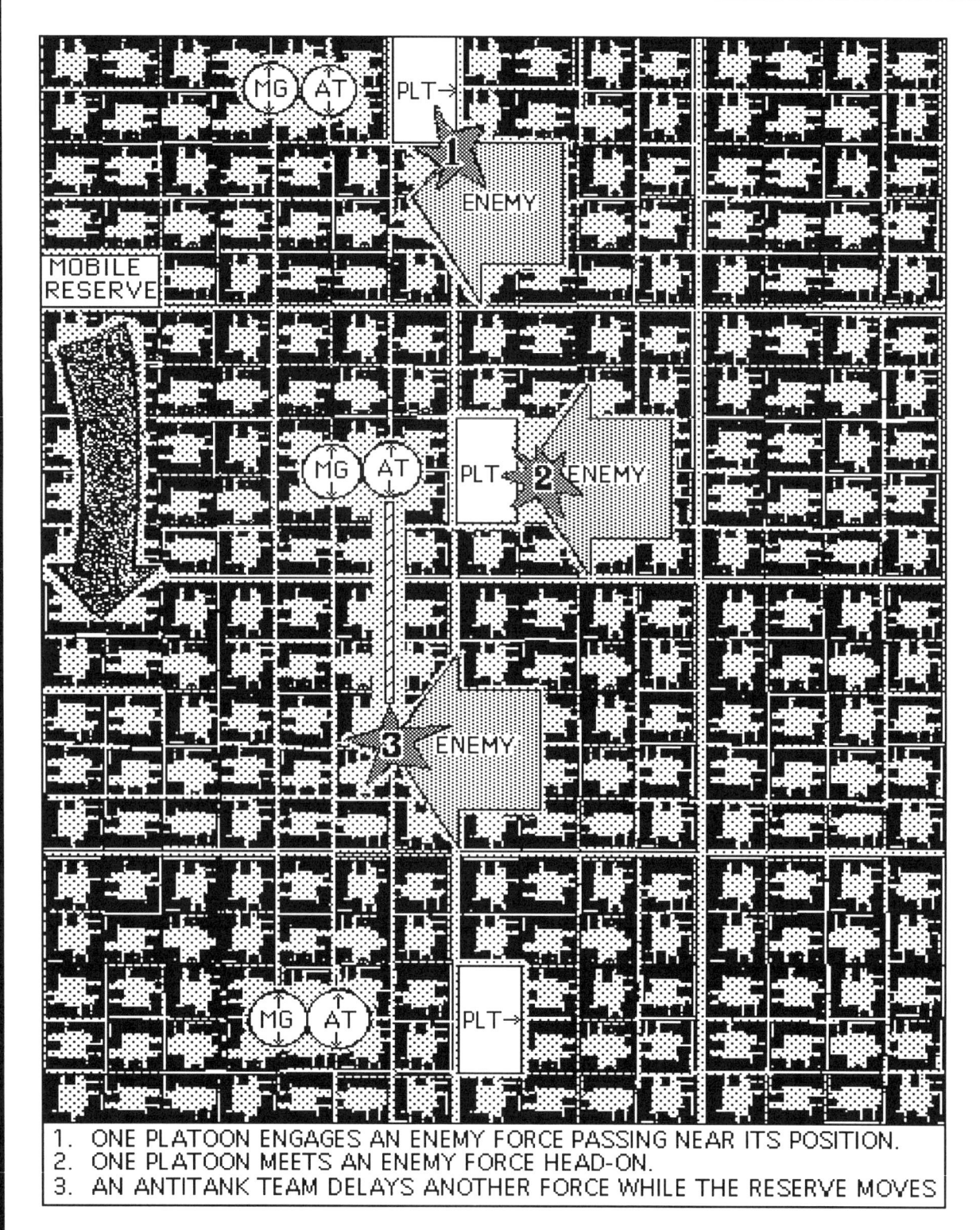

Figure 23.1: Moving Pockets of Resistance (Continued)

*The Unbeatable Urban Defense*

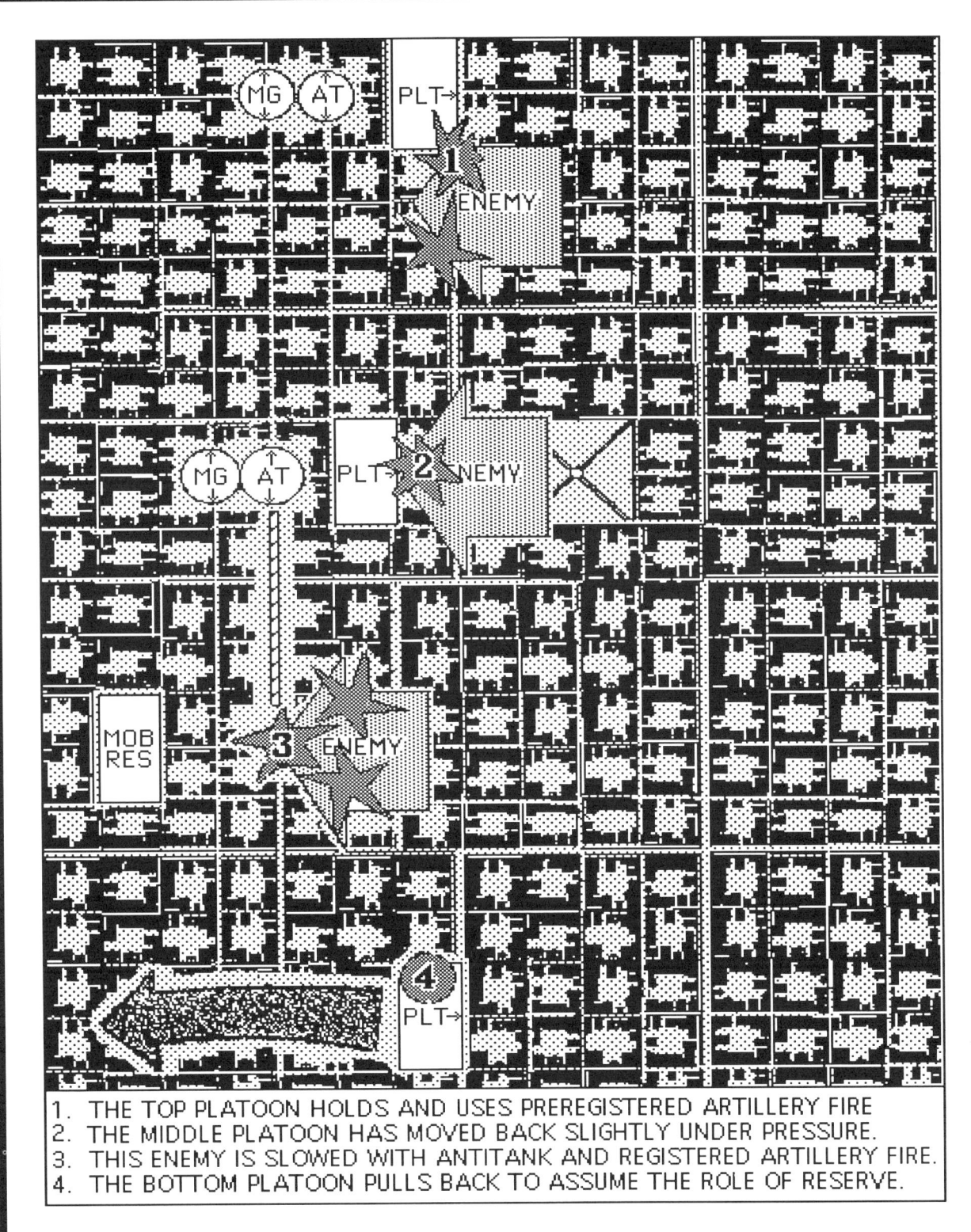

Figure 23.1: *Moving Pockets of Resistance (Continued)*

## CHANCES FOR DECEPTION

One of the best opportunities for deception in urban combat is to defend from some place other than the interior of a building. Unless this location is blatantly obvious (like a roadblock), the enemy won't expect it.

In a built-up area, the places to hide are many. While struggling to maintain some semblance of momentum during the clearing process, the attacker will look for clearly visible opposition and little else. He will not normally search an air-conditioning duct, the area between a wall and slanted roof, or a space above a suspended ceiling. He may even forget to look on a roof or in the trees overhanging it. If no one opposes him, he will assume that the area is empty. After being initially bypassed, defenders can do some real damage.

In urban terrain, there are also unique opportunities for the camouflaging of defensive positions. By dragging an abandoned car over an open manhole cover, one can easily create a machinegun nest with a perfect avenue of egress. Every cellar window, vent, protruding pipe, shellhole, missing brick, or crack in the side of a building can be made into a peephole or gun port. In some walls, there are so many existing bullet holes, that a new one would hardly be noticed. In other walls, a new opening can be concealed behind vines or stretched burlap.

Finally, traps are easier to bait in the city. Whole buildings can be command detonated after being intentionally abandoned. If there were a shortage of explosives, flammable buildings could be ignited by tracers fired into hidden gas cans. Of course, any use of flame crowds the Geneva Conventions.

## THE FIRE SUPPORT PLAN

Because the city provides the attacker with a greater proliferation of infiltration routes, the urban defender requires a more comprehensive illumination plan. Large structures cast deep shadows. Every gutter that is not manned, clogged with concertina, protected by an early-warning device, rigged with a trip flare, or occasionally patrolled, must either be watched through a night vision scope or randomly illuminated. Then, it takes additional light to expel suspected intruders. An illumination grenade can be tossed by a sentry from a rooftop, or a prepositioned flammable liquid can be released (and ignited) by an automatic rifleman with a tracer. In gutters, flaming liquids flow downhill.

In urban terrain, an ordinary rifleman can play an important role in the fire support plan. While positioned high in a building, he can provide final protective fire into what otherwise would have been dead space in the machinegun FPL's. Sometimes, he can do so either with plunging fire or grenades. With a few molotov cocktails, he can impede enemy tanks. (See figures 23.2 and 23.3.) Any self-respecting private can design a "foogas cannon" that will kill a tank at an antitank obstacle. Given the opportunity, that same private can also figure out how to drop a 220-volt electric line on an enemy tank from standoff distance.

Tanks and TOW-missile launchers can hide inside buildings and shoot through windows. Tanks should only try this in buildings without basements. All antitank weapons must move to alternate positions after each shot.

Over a city, most aircraft can operate more effectively with smart ordnance. However, even without target designation by laser, slow moving A-10 tank killers and TOW-Cobra helicopters can shoot accurately into boulevards and parks.

For the urban defender, the most useful of the indirect-fire weapons is the mortar. Because of its high trajectory, it can reach hard-to-get-at targets between buildings and on rooftops. Mortars are particularly effective when directly aligned on targets that are clearly visible up streets and alleyways. Low-trajectory artillery and naval gunfire are most useful for illumination. Still, if there are laser designators available, smart munitions should not be ruled out. Smart 155mm Copperheads can be used on any building that protrudes above its natural surroundings, as long as there are no tall structures along the gun-target line. Cruise missiles are expensive, but might nevertheless be available with adequate justification.

Machineguns are usually positioned at ground level to provide interlocking bands of grazing fire across an entire defensive frontage. One way to provide flash and dust suppression is to set each gun to the side of, and well away from, its gun port. When mounted on a tripod with a T&E, the gun can shoot its FPL through a thin slit in a window shutter. The only foe who can spot it then, won't live to tell about it. Because rubbling may block fields of fire, each machinegun should have an alternate position.

Shoulder-fired antitank weapons can be employed from any room large enough to absorb their backblast. Tanks are easier to kill from above.

Snipers are as good at gathering intelligence, as they are at shooting their rifles. From elevated positions within sight of the commander, they can easily pass along information. They should only fire to disrupt an enemy's command-and-control effort or to cover a distant obstacle.

The engineers should be used to build antitank obstacles, rig buildings for command detonation, and (mechanically) dig covered escape routes between buildings. Infantrymen can blow "mouseholes" in walls.

## THE BARRIER PLAN

When utilized in conjunction with covered escape routes, *interior* obstacles make the urban defense almost unbeatable. However, outside barriers are also important. These barriers must block the avenues of approach from above and below, as well as from the front.

*The Unbeatable Urban Defense*

To stop penetration from below, jumbles of barbed wire must be placed in subterranean passageways or at their surface exits.

To guard against attack at ground level, antitank obstacles must block the streets, tactical wire must follow the inside edges of machinegun FPL's, and protective wire must encircle buildings. In urban terrain, tangles of concertina will plug infiltration lanes and the *dead space in machinegun FPL's*. Concertina should fill the hallways around, and all the entrances to, defended rooms. Command-detonated explosives and (with proper authority) booby traps can further protect these avenues of approach.

To prevent an attacker from having the chance to clear a building from the top down, concertina should be placed in its stairwells and along the edges of its rooftop. A claymore can be command detonated to clean off an occupied roof. To discourage helicopter assault in Vietnam, the enemy used communications wire strung between tall bamboo poles. Something similar might discourage a helicopter assault onto a defended building.

To be effective, all obstacles must be covered by observation and fire. One could maintain observation over an obstacle inside a house with something as simple as a pinhole in wallpaper, or a carefully canted mirror. At street level, one could use a homemade listening device to detect tampering with a distant obstacle. Then, he could rely on snipers, mortar preregistrations, and command-detonated explosives to deal with the culprit.

Additionally, all obstacles that would give away the location of the defensive position must either be camouflaged or surrounded by enough supplementary obstacles to deceive the enemy.

IN URBAN TERRAIN, PLUNGING FIRE CAN BE USED TO COVER DEAD SPACE IN MACHINEGUN FINAL PROTECTIVE LINES.

*Figure 23.2: The M-16 Can Cover Machinegun Dead Space in Urban Terrain*
(Source: FM 90-10-1 (1982), p. E-6)

Techniques from the NCO Corps

Figure 23.3: Every Man Is A Tank Killer in an Urban Setting
(Sources: FM 90-10-1 (1986), p. H-7; MCI 03.66a (1986), p. 3-11)

## EARLY WARNING THAT WILL MAKE THE ENEMY DEPLOY PREMATURELY

*Within* the city, the attacker enjoys good cover and concealment all the way up to the main line of resistance. For this reason, the defender must have more than just early warning of his adversary's approach; he must have offensive action to disrupt that adversary's momentum. Aggressive patrolling can provide both. So too can sentries, antitank ambushers, and snipers. A conventional sentry post can command detonate mines and call in preregistered mortar rounds without compromising its location. An anti-armor team can kill a tank and then run back to the main line of resistance along rooftops or sewers. A sniper can disrupt the foe's command-and-control effort without disclosing his own position. He has only to mask his muzzle flash, smoke, and noise.

Because in the city everything manmade is connected, seismic-intrusion devices have limited utility for early warning. In other words, these devices can be mistakenly triggered by friendly activity several blocks away. Barriers rigged with field expedient listening devices may have to take their place. If electricity is available, commercial motion detectors can augment trip flares. Whenever the enemy is detected early, his progress can be disrupted with command-detonated explosives or preregistered mortars.

## THE MACHINEGUN SPOILING ATTACK

The spoiling attack has long been recognized as the way to disrupt the timing of a more powerful adversary:

> A fundamental principle is never to remain completely passive, but to attack the enemy frontally and from the flanks, even while he is attacking us.[7]
>
> — Clausewitz

On Tarawa, the Japanese employed a machinegun spoiling attack with devastating effect. Although the initial waves of Marines successfully cleared the approaches to the landing beaches, second-day reinforcements encountered heavy machinegun fire from *seaward*. Apparently, during the night, Japanese gunners had reached a shipwreck on the reef and an enclosed privy at the end of a wooden pier:

> [N]ow [on day two] one of our mortars discovers one of the machineguns that has been shooting at the Marines. It is not back of us, but is a couple of hundred yards west, out in one of the wooden privies the dysentery-fearing Japs built out over the water.... "The ... Japs must have swum out there last night and mounted a machinegun in that freighter," says an officer beside me.[8]

> This second day landing is worse than the first.... Machineguns smuggled at night aboard the grounded freighter cut down Marines in rows.[9]

While this Japanese spoiling attack bordered on suicide, its modern equivalent through the sewers of a city would not. Picture attackers checking a burned-out car, seeing nothing in it, and then moving on. If the defenders had moved that car over an open manhole, they could launching a machinegun attack from there later.

## A TECHNIQUE TO GIVE THE POCKET OF RESISTANCE SUFFICIENT MOBILITY

For a string of platoon-sized pockets of resistance to absorb the attack of a powerful opponent, each platoon must have the capability of pulling back under pressure. To do so, it needs a "soft-urban-defense" technique. This technique would have a high probability of success in combat, because it could be rehearsed (and further developed) in the very terrain in which it would be used. In other words, the procedure could be *tailored* to the exact layout of the buildings. This would allow the defender to do *beforehand* much of his tactical decision making.

To counter the threat of ground assault and infiltration, the soft urban defense must retain several of the characteristics of a traditional rigid defense. To counter the threat of armor and supporting arms, the technique must add secrecy, rearward mobility, and a potential for immediate offensive action. To meet both threats at once, the platoon must carefully select where to make its stand and then hide this location from the enemy. For forward security, it should rely heavily on two-man ambushes. While its defensive formation should be fairly traditional, its subunits must have the authority to pull back under pressure. They can do this along prerehearsed routes to pre-established positions. And their initial hideouts can be pre-rigged with explosives for command detonation. Finally, the platoon must be able to shift smoothly and rapidly over to the offense.

To employ this technique, unit leaders at every echelon must give their subordinates credit for having common sense. Control must be decentralized all the way down to the two-man teams at the individual fighting positions. In other words, these teams must be allowed to pull back on their own initiative. To do so under pressure, each will need a dual means of communication, covered route of egress, and at least one fallback position. Adequate control is maintained by requiring the teams to keep their superiors informed of all movements.

By the time the enemy reaches the main line of resistance, the anti-armor teams should be back from their security ambushes. Opposition forces must find each street in the platoon sector defended by an antitank weapon and the entire platoon frontage crisscrossed by grazing machinegun fire. This is only possible when the machineguns are mounted at ground level and at either end of the defensive sector.

For each building containing a crew-served weapon, there must be a fire team to protect that weapon. When this building comes under intense enemy pressure, the crew-served-weapon team pulls back first. It goes to a preplanned position in support of the reserve squad. Then, as the original structure becomes untenable, the fire team falls back to the next line of resistance *behind* the reserve squad. Depending on the configuration of the buildings, the leaders have several options at this point: (1) to command detonate the abandoned structure, (2) to counterattack, (3) to withdraw other frontline fire teams, or (4) to leave those fire teams in place. If the reserve squad has adequate fields of fire on both sides of the abandoned building, it can defend the vacated sector from behind. It must only prevent the enemy from moving to adjacent buildings from the captured building.

However, if the retrograde maneuver is to proceed, it must resemble orderly "fire and movement" backwards. Normally, the reserve squad covers the pullout by fire and temporarily inherits the responsibility for the defensive frontage. With fields of fire enhanced by rubbling and firepower improved with crew-served weapons, the reserve squad should be able to hold its own until the subsequent line of resistance is fully manned behind it. The pullback sequence will largely depend on the unique configuration of the buildings. The rehearsal should disclose the best options. Sometimes it works better for one squad at a time to pull back, leaving the other two squads in a staggered defensive formation. That way, the enemy must confront two squads at any given moment.

Once the "moving surfaces" have inflicted enough damage on the enemy, the platoon can shift over to the offense. The squads are already in position to counterattack up the street that bisects their defensive sector. The two squads closest to the enemy could leapfrog up the street, while the third follows in trace. That the unit already knows the terrain into which it is attacking, should greatly simplify the process. With slight realignment, the platoon could also attack sideways to outflank a passing enemy force or to break out of an encirclement. (See figures 23.4 through 23.7 for a pictorial display of how this technique might work. Normally, because of the threat posed by standoff weaponry, a unit would not defend the buildings at the edge of an open expanse. However, the park-front scene facilitates illustration.)

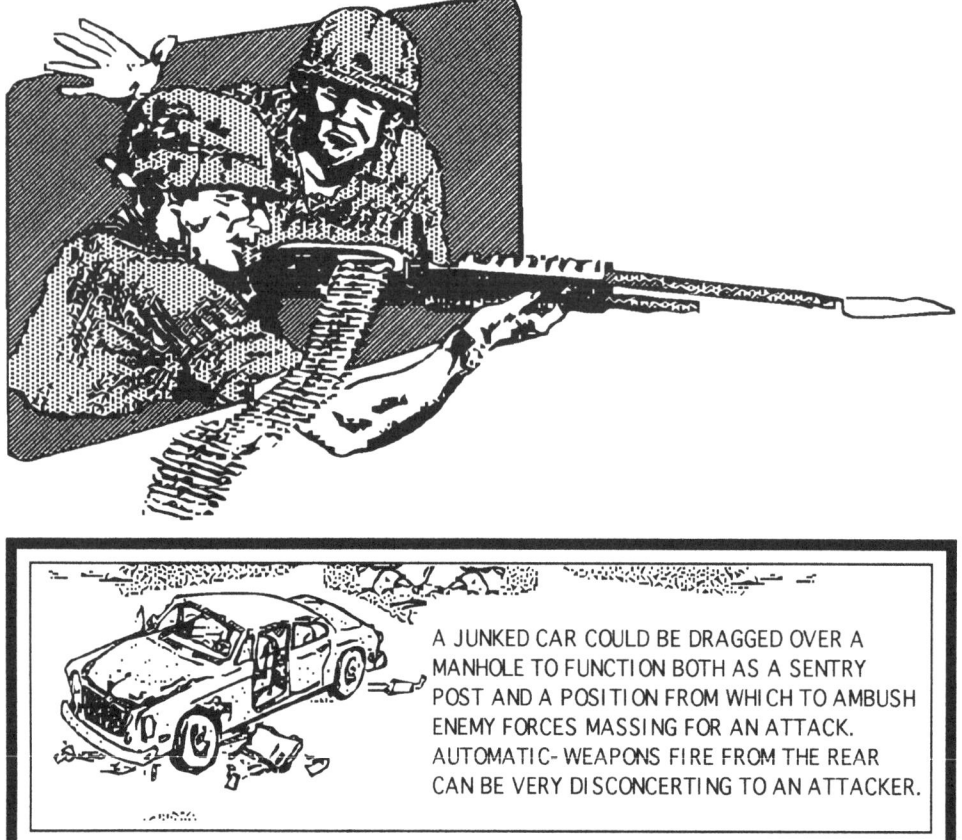

Figure 23.4: Maneuver Warfare Options for a City Defense Scenario
(Sources: TC 90-1 (1986), p. 3-23; FM 90-10-1 (1982), pp. 3-35, 5-7; FM 22-100 (1973), p. 2-4)

The Unbeatable Urban Defense

## WHAT THE ENEMY SEES AS HE NEARS THE BATTLEFIELD

LET'S LOOK AT THE MANEUVER WARFARE OPTIONS AVAILABLE TO A RIFLE PLATOON DEFENDING THE NORMAL TWO-CITY-BLOCK FRONTAGE. IN THIS PICTURE, THE PLATOON OCCUPIES THE BUILDINGS AT THE TOP OF THE PAGE FACING THE TOWN SQUARE. TO DEFEND AGAINST AN ENEMY WITH ARMOR AND SUPPORTING ARMS, THE PLATOON MUST BE AUTHORIZED TO GRADUALLY MOVE BACKWARDS. IF THE UNIT WERE TO DEFEND FROM A SERIES OF PRE-ESTABLISHED FALLBACK POSITIONS, THIS WOULD HAVE THE SAME EFFECT ON THE ENEMY AS AMBUSHES DEPLOYED IN DEPTH. SUBORDINATE UNITS COULD OCCASIONALLY ACT AS DECOYS TO LURE THE ATTACKERS INTO FIRE SACKS — LIKE BUILDINGS RIGGED FOR COMMAND DETONATION. WITH SUBTERRANEAN PASSAGEWAYS FOR EGRESS, SECURITY ELEMENTS COULD HIDE WHILE THE ENEMY FORCES PASS BY, AMBUSH THEM FROM THE REAR, AND THEN FALL BACK IN TIME TO DEFEND THE MAIN LINE OF RESISTANCE.

Figure 23.4: Maneuver Warfare Options for a City Defense Scenario (Continued)
(Sources: TC 90-1 (1986), p. 3-23; FM 90-10-1 (1982), pp. 3-35, 5-7)

Techniques from the NCO Corps

1. MACHINEGUNS WITH INTERLOCKING FIELDS OF FIRE AT GROUND LEVEL.
2. AT-4'S COVERING THE STREETS FROM UPPER FLOORS (ONE DEPLOYED FORWARD INITIALLY).
3. FIRE TEAMS FROM THE TWO SQUADS HOLDING THE INITIAL LINE OF DEFENSE.
4. FIRE TEAMS FROM THE RESERVE SQUAD HOLDING THE SECOND LINE OF DEFENSE.

Figure 23.4: Maneuver Warfare Options for a City Defense Scenario (Continued)
(Source: FM 90-10-1 (1982), pp. 3-14, 3-35)

*The Unbeatable Urban Defense*

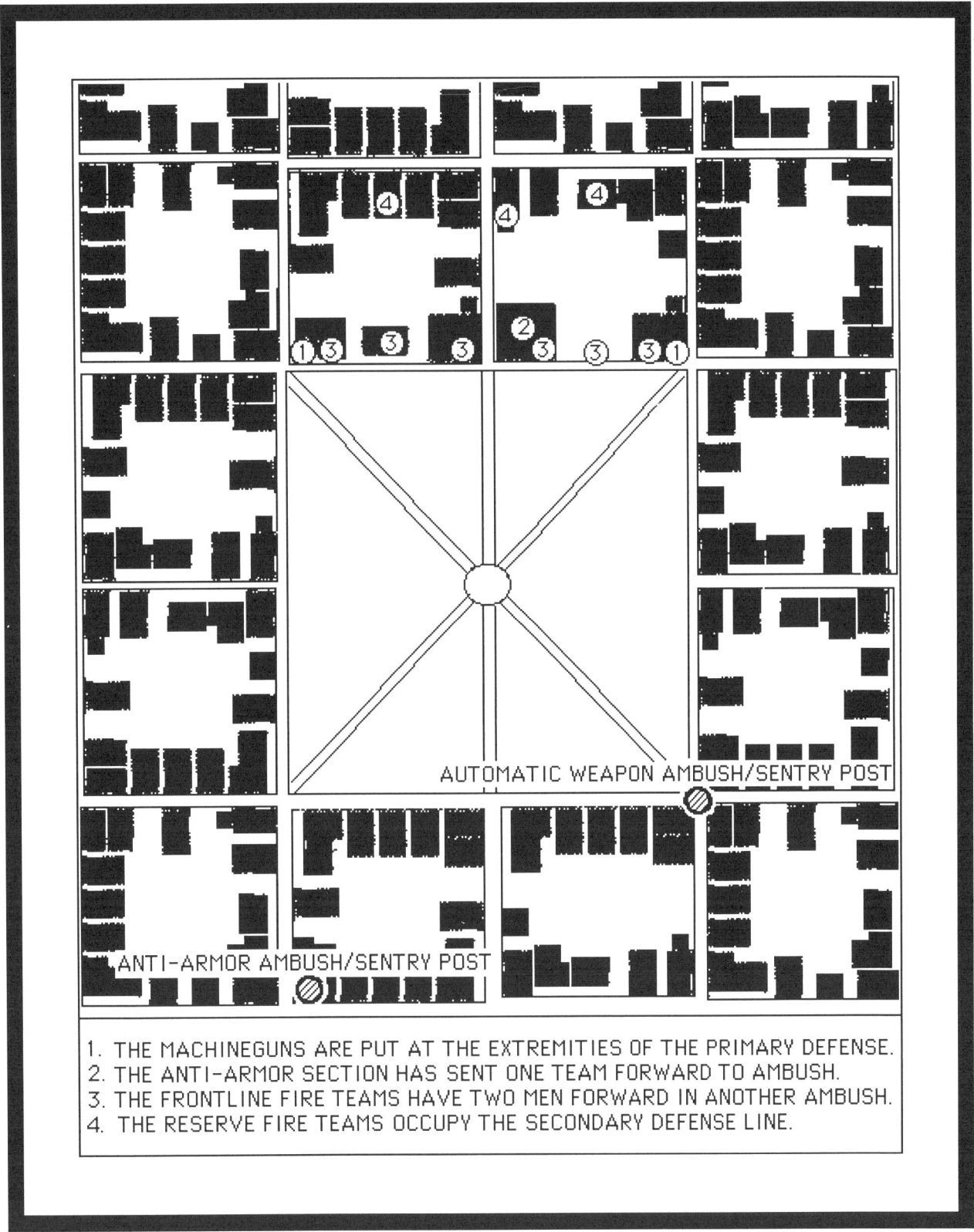

Figure 23.5: *The Soft-Urban-Defense Technique*

Techniques from the NCO Corps

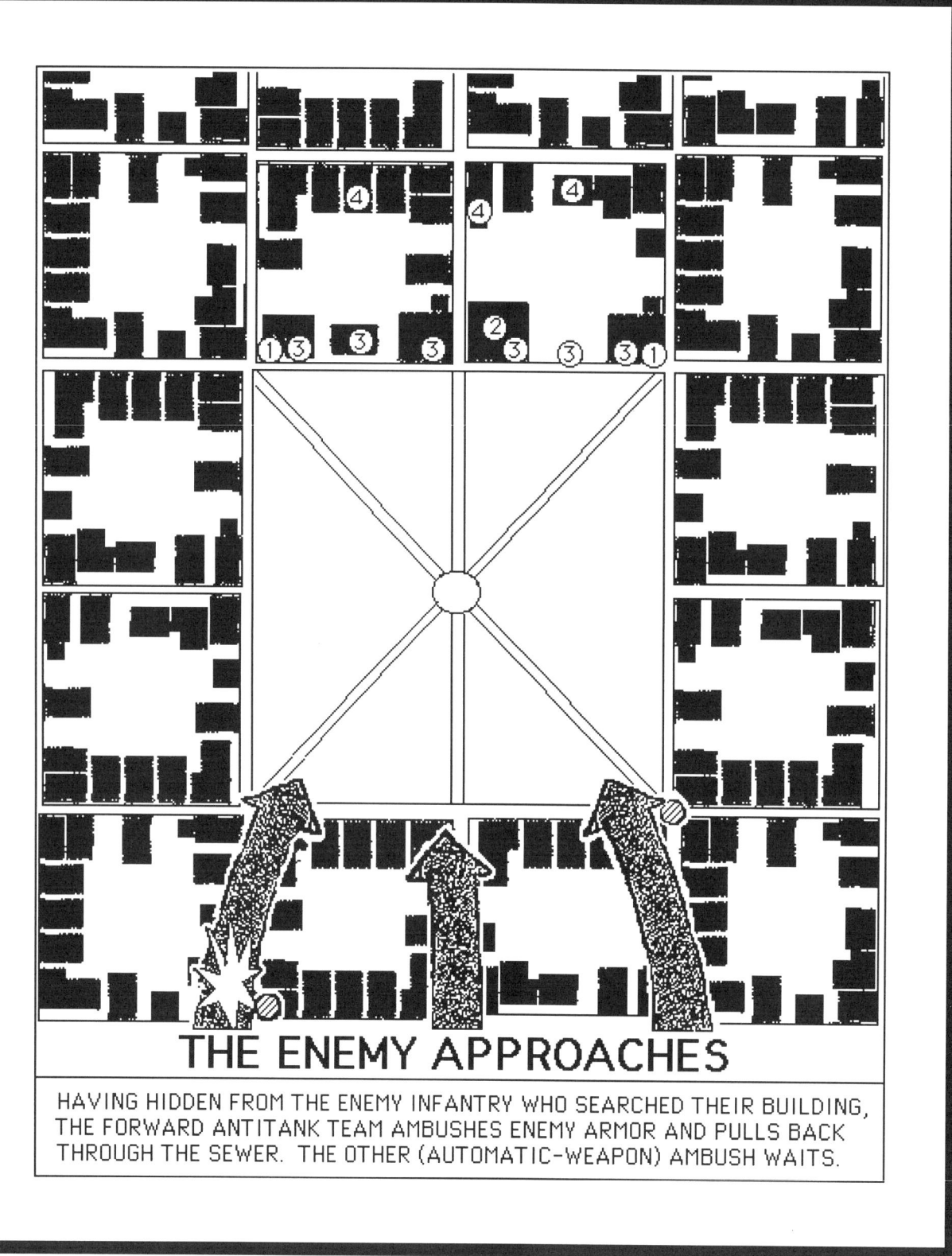

Figure 23.5: The Soft-Urban-Defense Technique (Continued)

The Unbeatable Urban Defense

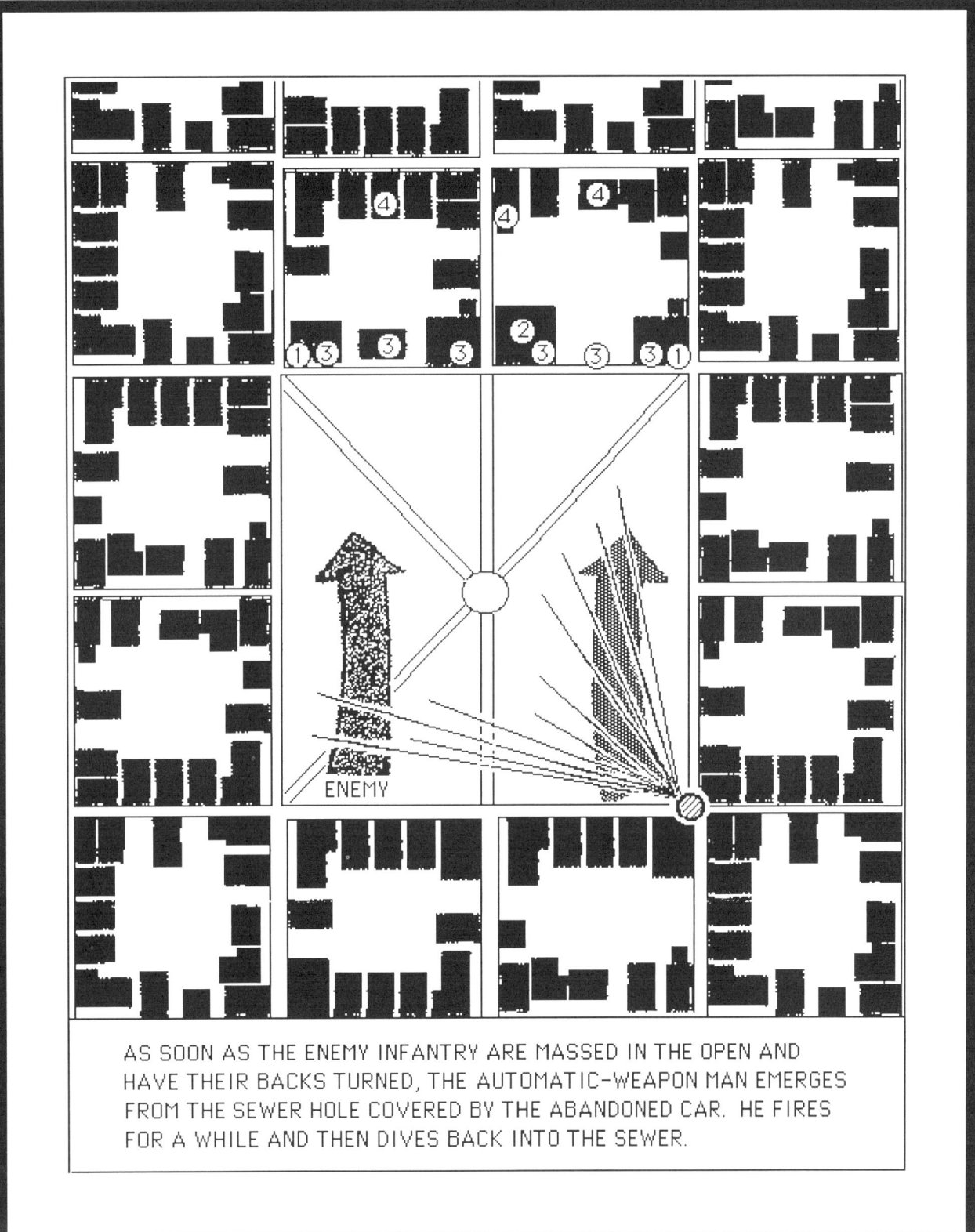

Figure 23.5: The Soft-Urban-Defense Technique (Continued)

Techniques from the NCO Corps

(Source: FM 90-10-1 (1982), pp. 3-14, 3-35)

WHEN THE ATTACKING FORCE STARTS TO CROSS THE STREET IN FRONT OF THE MAIN LINE OF RESISTANCE, THE DEFENDING PLATOON OPENS UP WITH ITS FINAL PROTECTIVE FIRES. ONE GUN CREW FIRES AS LONG AS IT CAN AND THEN MAKES A WISE TACTICAL DECISION — IT FALLS BACK TO A SECONDARY LINE.

(Source: FM 90-10-1 (1982), p. B-37)

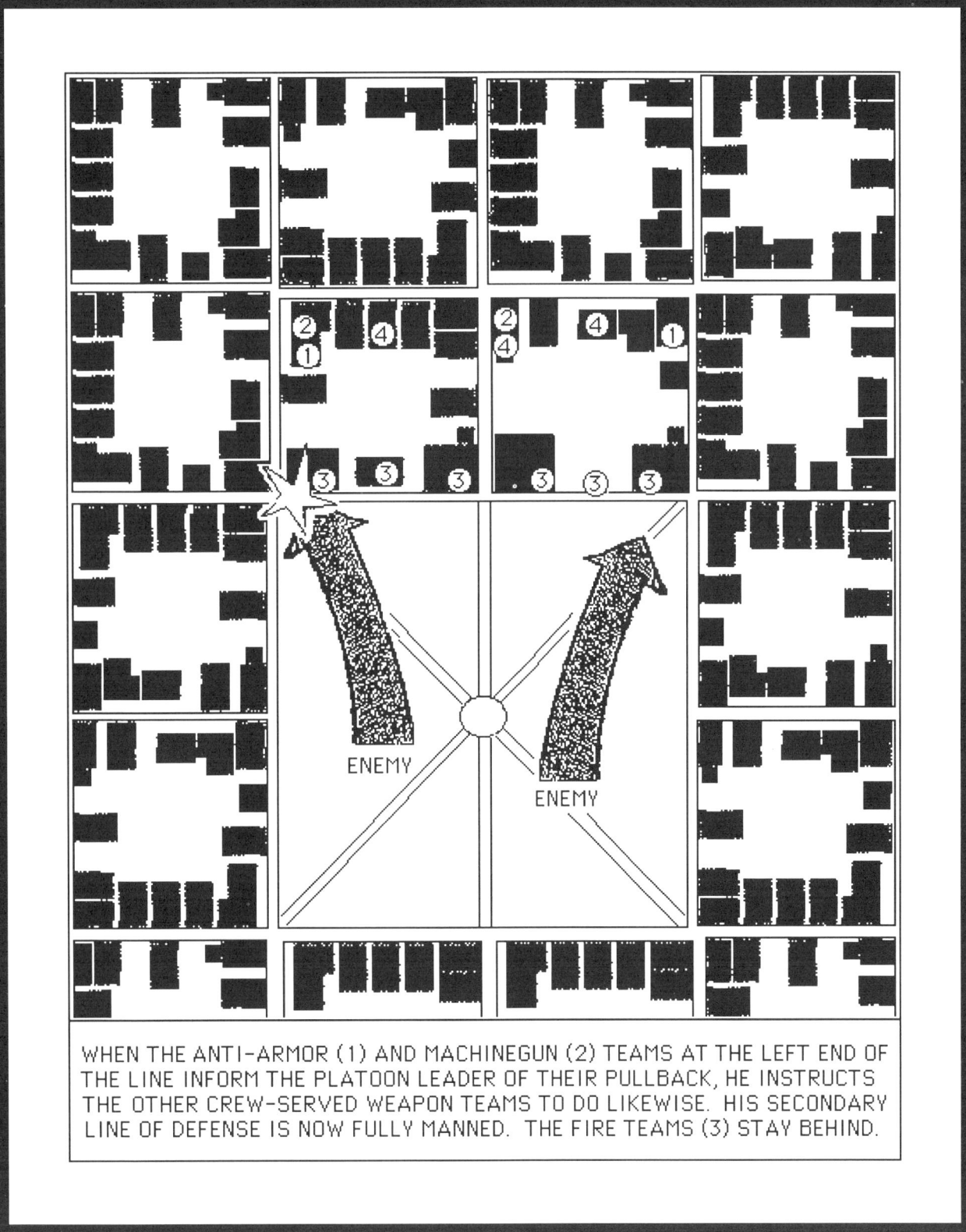

Figure 23.5: The Soft-Urban-Defense Technique (Continued)

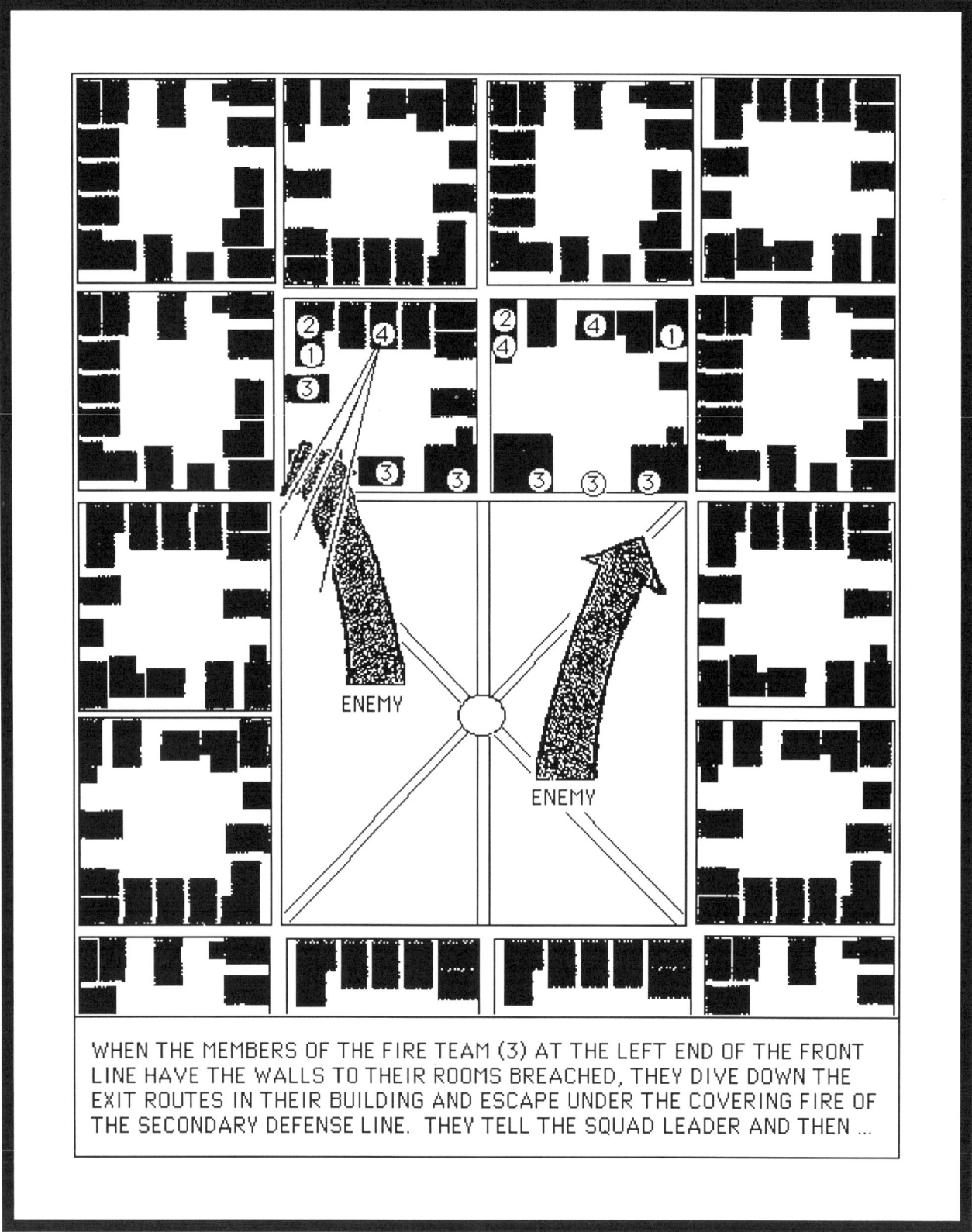

Figure 23.5: The Soft-Urban-Defense Technique (Continued)

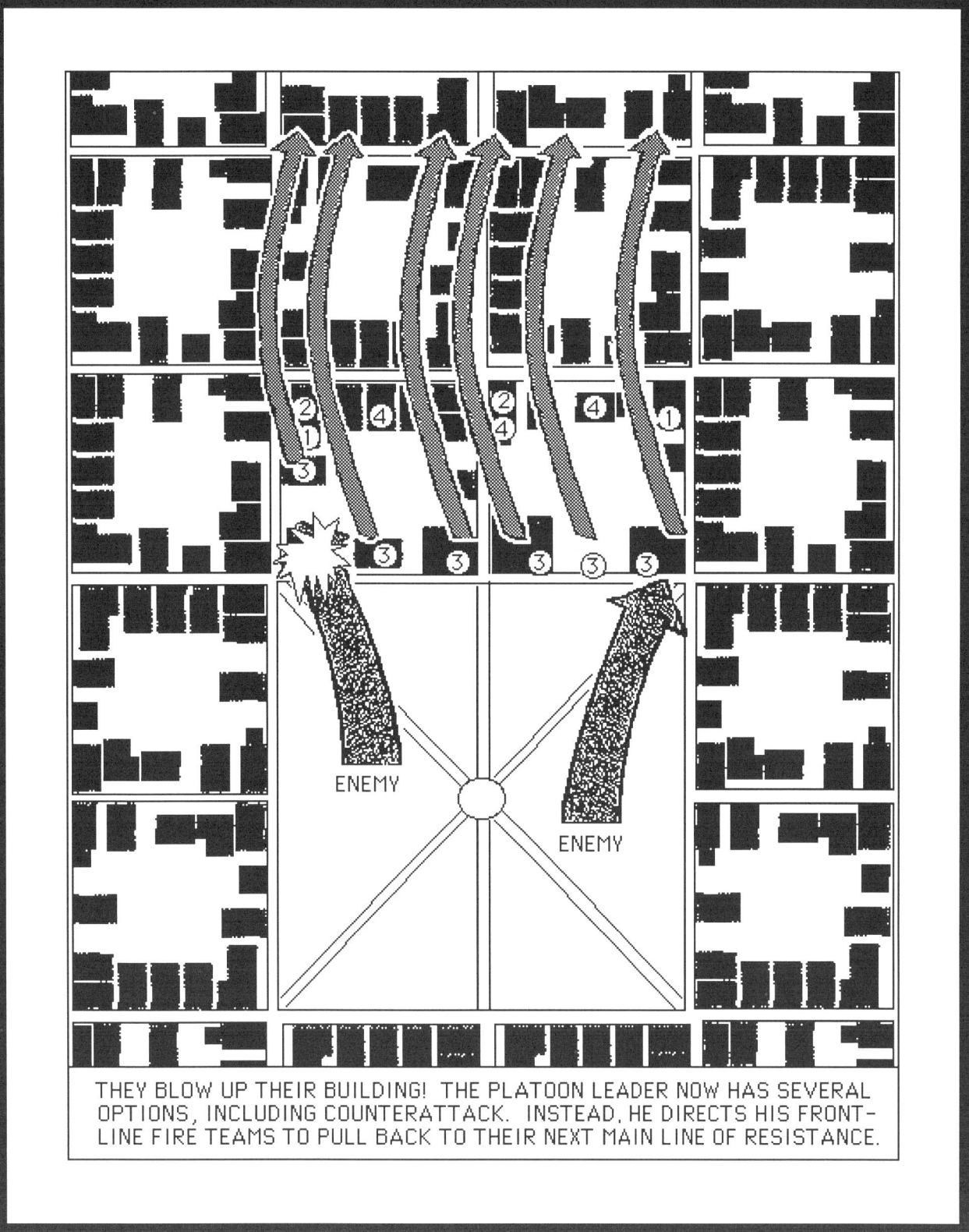

Figure 23.5: The Soft-Urban-Defense Technique (Continued)

Techniques from the NCO Corps

## WHEN THE DEFENDERS MUST FALL BACK QUICKLY

INFANTRY SQUADS CAN LEARN TO PERFORM RETROGRADE MOVEMENT UNDER FIRE IN URBAN TERRAIN IN MUCH THE SAME WAY THEY LEARN TO ATTACK — THE SQUADS TAKE TURNS COVERING FOR EACH OTHER AND MOVING. THIS PROCESS CAN BE EXPEDITED BY ASSIGNING FIELDS OF FIRE TO FIRE TEAMS IN ADVANCE. ALL SHOOTING MUST BE RESTRICTED TO CONFIRMED TARGETS.

Figure 23.6: Retrograde Movement along a City Street
(Sources: TC 90-1 (1986), p. E-2; FM 90-10-1 (1982), p. 3-14)

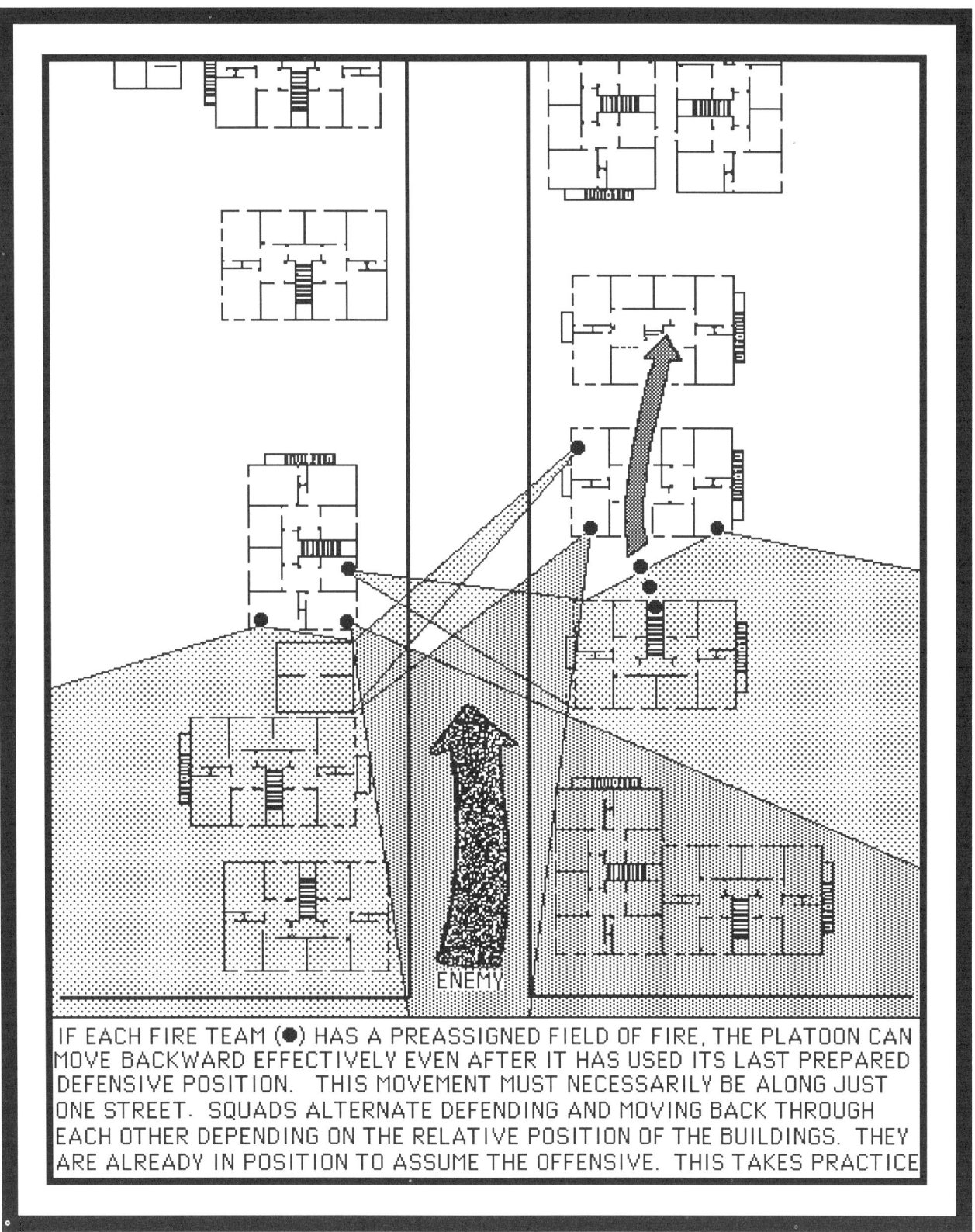

Figure 23.7: An Alternate Technique for Moving Backward in Urban Terrain
(Source: TC 90-1 (1986), p. 3-57)

## HOW TO DEFEND EACH TWO-MAN ROOM

It's not realistic to expect a pair of young Americans to defend an isolated room to the death. Wars are won with bravery, not foolhardiness. It's more productive to establish some loose pullback parameters, and then to let the riflemen defend the room as long as they can. This type of mission could only enhance their effectiveness. With a covered egress route, foolproof defense plan, and several ways to expel intruders, the pair of defenders could do some real damage before being forced to withdraw. Their "leaving" would not uncover their neighbors' flanks any worse than their "dying in place" would. At least, in a fallback position, they could still contribute to the defense. Just telling their superiors what occurred would enhance overall coordination. Armed with this information, the leaders could make appropriate changes to their plans.

Some might say that, after engaging the foe at close quarters, the two Americans couldn't get away. With a good escape plan, the pair would have little trouble devising a way to do some damage before leaving. What if they put barbed wire or furniture along the interior walls of their room? This would prevent the enemy from quickly entering that room through a breach in an interior wall. What if the defenders constructed their position *along an exterior wall* of that room? Then, sandbags or furniture could protect them from any grenade tossed through an interior-wall opening. With a sandbagged pathway to a "mousehole" in the wall or floor, the two could leave after tossing a fragmentation grenade of their own. Without a covered route, they would need a concussion grenade.

In the urban environment, the individual fighting position is isolated. For this reason, it must be self-sufficient. It should provide all-around (including bottom and top) protection from bullets, shrapnel, and falling debris. A strong wooden door and some sandbags are the only materials required. The position should be located in a room with a 360-degree barrier plan. Lined with barbed wire should be all doors, windows, and surfaces that could be breached by enemy explosives. (See figure 23.8.)

Each pair of defenders should have two means of communication with their chain of command. Commer-

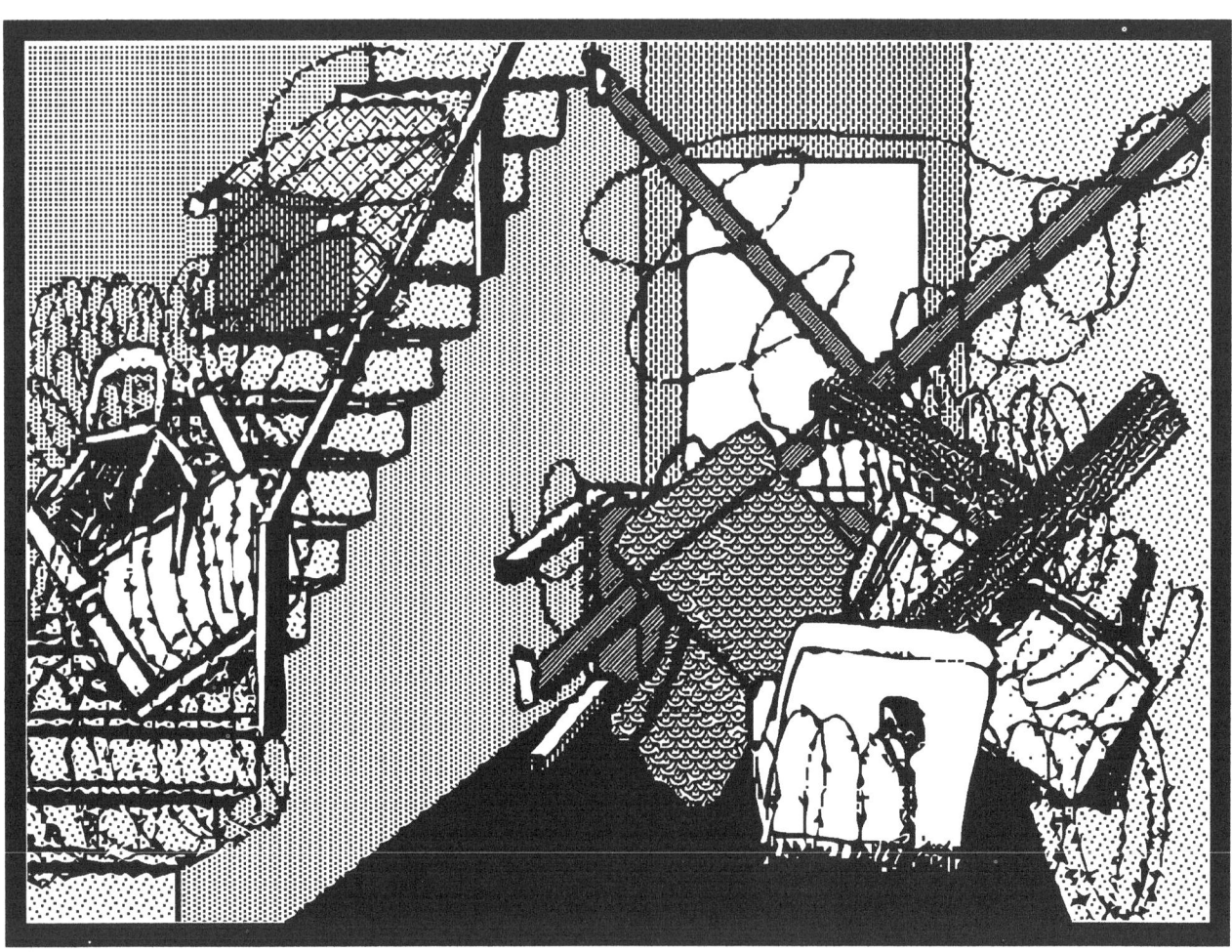

Figure 23.8: Inside Barriers Give the Defender an Edge
(Sources: FM 90-10-1 (1982), p. E-9; TC 90-1 (1986), p. E-9; MCI 03.66a (1986), p. 3-14)

cial telephones can often fulfill half of this requirement. For the other half, the defenders will need field phones, tug ropes, or visual signaling (flags, mirrors, or hand-and-arm signals during the day, and red/infrared signals at night). Within the building, a tapping code might suffice.

Each position must have a covered route of egress — e.g., a corridor of sandbags leading to a hole in the floor, a ladder reaching into the basement, a loose air vent in the basement wall, and then a gutter leading back to another building. Or, it might consist of a crawl space beneath the eaves of a house and the connecting rooftops beyond. To discourage pursuit, build the escape route through a maze of *authorized* booby traps. (See figure 23.9.)

The enemy must not have the opportunity to locate the position easily. That means the defenders need flash- and dust-suppression apparatus for their weapons. The enemy must not have the chance to lob a grenade into the room. That means screening or shutters on the windows. Additionally, the enemy must not be able to outlast the position. That means stockpiled water and ammunition.

If possible, the two-man teams should be positioned to cover each other. Every time an attacker goes after one, he should be subjected to the fire of another. Even inside a building, this type of mutual support is still possible. The interior walls of modern buildings are thin. After a tapped alert and seeing an intruder's image in a shard of mirror, one position could shoot right through a wall to cover another. (See figure 23.10 for what a pair of urban defenders might accomplish from a properly prepared position.)

## THE ALL-IMPORTANT CONDUCT PHASE

The key to properly executing a soft urban defense is rehearsing the pullback. However, there is nothing to rehearse until the covered routes of egress and the fall-back positions are prepared. While control is decentralized, communication will still make or break the effort. For this reason, subordinates should be instructed to report all pullbacks as soon as possible.

Prior to the attack, the emphasis should be on allaying psychological stress. The dual means of communication and covered routes of egress to each emplacement should be utilized frequently to check on its defenders without giving away their location. The mind-crippling effect of being a defender can be lessened by encouraging those manning each position to develop their plans for deception, *offensive action,* and escape. Stress can be further reduced by arranging for positions to be mutually

Figure 23.9: Escape Routes Permit the Defender to Win
(Source: FM 90-10-1 (1982), pp. B-4, E-11)

Techniques from the NCO Corps

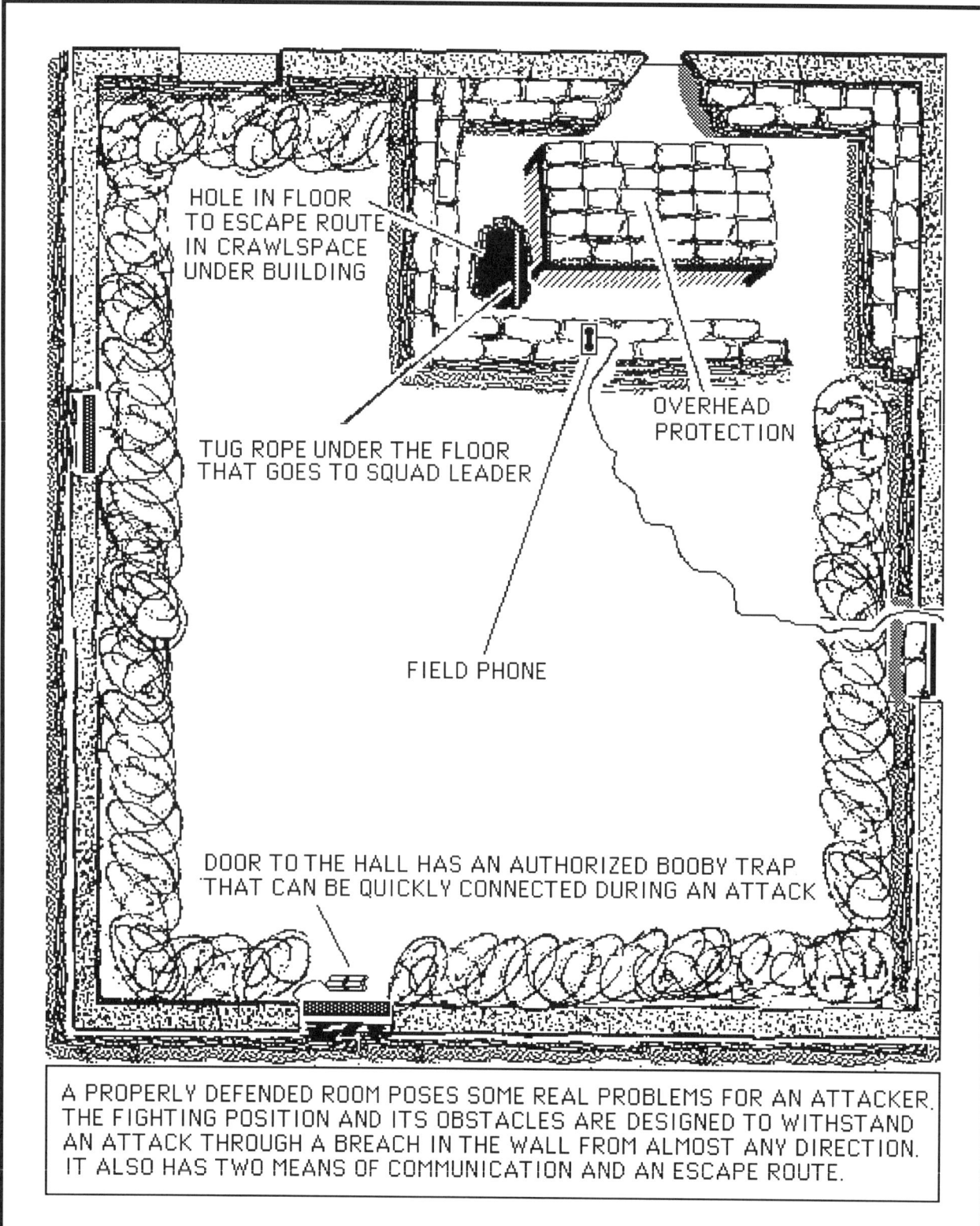

*Figure 23.10: The All-Around Room Defense*
(Source: FM 90-10 (1979), p. C-5)

# The Unbeatable Urban Defense

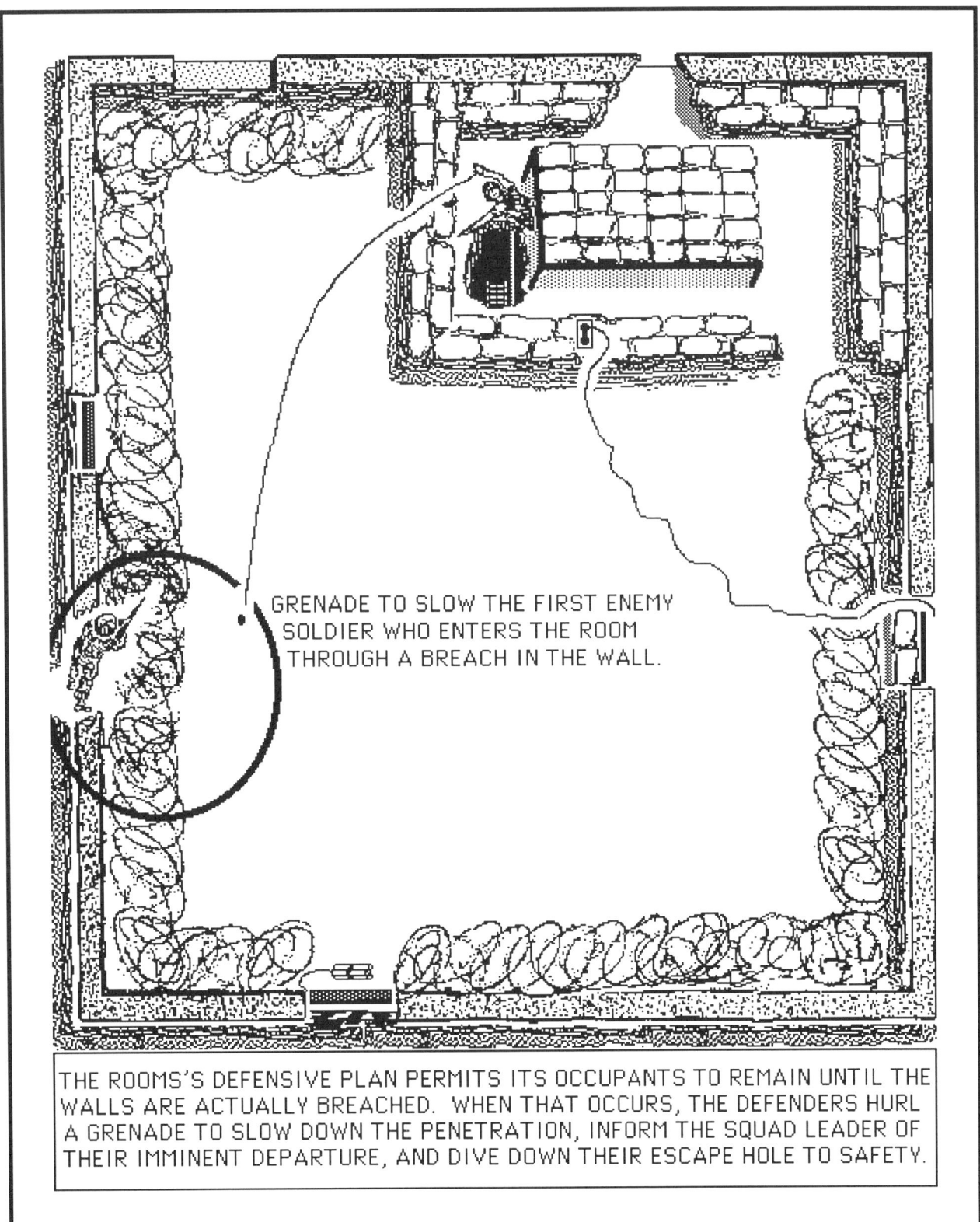

Figure 23.10: The All-Around Room Defense (Continued)
(Source: FM 90-10 (1979), p. C-5)

supporting and augmented by alternate or supplementary positions (like those needed to block infiltration lanes after dark).

When the enemy shows up, precious seconds can be saved, if the authority to signal for the final protective fires has been delegated. The attack will inevitably create rubbling and reduced visibility. To fire accurately, the defenders may need aiming stakes and T&E mechanism settings even during the day. If rubbling blocks their fields of fire, they must move to alternate positions.

As the street battle progresses, ammunition shortages will undoubtedly occur. The covered egress routes can be used for resupply. In all likelihood, there will be uneven pressure along the line. It can be handled by pulling back or reinforcing. With enough rehearsal, the reserve squad can provide the necessary covering fire either way. When all does not go as planned, the routes of egress can be used to rescue trapped defenders. The proper tone for the operation will be set when the first vacated building is allowed to fill with jubilant attackers, and then *command detonated*. This is a defensive technique with offensive potential. Such a break in enemy momentum should be exploited immediately with a counterattack.

# 24 What the Urban Attacker Must Know to Stay Alive

- What makes attacking along a city street so dangerous?
- What can the urban attacker do to minimize this danger?
- How can he clear the buildings as he goes and still enjoy momentum?

(Sources: FM 7-11B1/2 (1978), p. 1-I-A-8; FM 90-10-1 (1982), pp. 3-14, B-8)

### WHAT THE ATTACKING RIFLEMAN FACES IN THE CITY

In wartime, an infantryman must occasionally endure the nightmare of attacking through urban terrain. Because he can now be killed by fire from above, he has more trouble finding cover. Every time he moves between buildings, he risks getting shot from any number of openings in the walls. Even when his companions succeed in watching every opening, he can still fall victim to the first bullet. By entering a building, he encounters a whole new set of problems. Now, he can be shot not only through any window, but also through thin interior walls, ceilings, and floors. In short, the attacking rifleman has trouble surviving in the city. This should come as no surprise to anyone:

When troops attack cities, their strength will be exhausted.[1]
— Sun Tzu

### ONE MUST HAVE SPECIAL SKILLS TO LAST FOR LONG IN OFFENSIVE URBAN COMBAT

Moving through a hotly contested built-up area is the most dangerous of all infantry maneuvers. It takes special training and total focus. For those who want, through study, to increase their chances of surviving this experience, there is one small consolation. Possibly because all urban terrain consists of walls, holes in walls, and spaces between walls, the tactical fundamentals for taking cities also work for taking blocks, buildings, and rooms. This is lucky, because the annals of warfare only chronicle the taking of cities; and the manuals don't sufficiently detail the other procedures. Do not the methods for moving along streets work equally well for moving along hallways? Both are danger areas. One must avoid exposing himself for long in either. Just as it is safer to move parallel to a city street through the side entrances of buildings, so too is it safer to move parallel to a hallway through the doors between rooms.

## THE LESSONS OF HISTORY

During the World Wars, the Russians and Germans got the majority of experience in attacking and defending large cities. However, U.S. units got a good taste of urban combat as well — while moving through the towns of Western Europe and defending places like Bastogne. Toward the end of WWII, U.S. infantrymen conducted a three-month offensive for Manila. In the early fifties at Seoul, the Marines got their chance to attack a large city:

> The enemy fought at every intersection, from roadblocks of sand-filled rice bags, most of these defended by antitank guns. Snipers worked from houses, high and low.... They learned to cover each other and watch the windows and doors of houses and to handle the intersections.... Puller's order went out to the company commanders: "Keep the men moving; all buildings and rooftops are full of Reds.... Leave the snipers if they are beyond your reach. Let the Korean Marines mop up behind you. Circle to the side streets when you have trouble at the barricades. The important thing is to keep moving."[2]

Then, seventeen years later at Hue City, the Marines got another chance. Because the lands around strategic harbors are often heavily populated, Marines have always had a keen interest in offensive urban combat. One of their primary missions is capturing forward naval bases.

## THE BEST AVENUES OF APPROACH TO A CONTESTED URBAN AREA

A good avenue of approach to a built-up area must provide cover and concealment while exploiting a gap in enemy lines. A forested draw that extended into the outskirts of a town would certainly qualify. There is another avenue of approach unique to urban terrain — a sewage tunnel. However, the attacker is interested in more than just gaining access to the city as a whole, he also needs avenues of approach between buildings.

Cities are crisscrossed with a wide variety of subterranean passageways, but the smaller ones are extremely dangerous. Even natural gases can spontaneously explode in the confined spaces of a branch sewage tunnel. It's not hard to imagine how a remote listening device, open manhole, 55-gallon drum of gasoline, and tracer could seal the fate of a maneuver force in a feeder sewer. Larger spaces — e.g., underground shopping malls, subway tunnels, pedestrian passages, drainage canals, water ducts, catacombs — make better conduits of movement.

Paradoxically, heavily built-up areas make the best avenues of approach at ground level. That's because they offer the most cover. At street level, it is the open areas that pose the greatest threat to movement. To cross them safely, the attacking force must have the concealment of darkness or the cover of microterrain. At night, infiltrators can sometimes use shadows or gutters.

If the buildings on a block are close enough together in height and proximity, their rooftops provide another conduit of movement and a way to escape fire from the street. Of course, whenever an attacking unit enters its objective structure through the roof, it can more easily clear that objective.

## INITIAL OBJECTIVES IN A CITY

Transportation hubs and tall durable buildings constitute the "key terrain" in a city. The side that controls a transportation artery has the edge in resupply and reinforcement; the side that controls a tall structure has the edge in intelligence gathering and fire direction. Where there exists a tall durable building at the city's edge with a forested gully leading up to it, an attacking force has little difficulty choosing its initial objective.

To capture an urban area, the attacker must first isolate it. Among other things, this means cutting off the utilities. That's why utility junction stations also make good initial objectives. The defender will have fewer options after his telephones, electricity, and water have been shut off.

There are also "key buildings" in urban terrain — e.g., city hall, a radio or TV station, etc. Their capture can demoralize defenders throughout the city. Theoretically at least, a small force could convince an entire army to abandon a large metropolis simply by infiltrating through subterranean passageways to take a key building. By almost capturing the U.S. embassy in Saigon in 1968, the Viet Cong greatly damaged U.S. resolve in Vietnam.

## MINIMIZING THE PROBLEMS ASSOCIATED WITH OFFENSIVE URBAN COMBAT

While attacking through urban terrain, it's difficult to limit casualties, to maintain control, and to build momentum. It's virtually impossible to do all three at once.

To minimize the chances of getting shot, the individual attacker must find a way to evade the bullets that seek him out during every move. Unfortunately, in urban terrain, there are more locations from which these bullets can come. And, the buddies covering his movement with fire, can't always spot the shooter ahead of time. This means the attacking infantryman must rely on his individual movement skills to defeat the first bullet. Or, in other words, he must move in such a way than no enemy can acquire an adequate sight picture. Only then, will it do any good for his companions to suppress subsequent bullets. In summary, *individual movement and small-unit covering techniques are the keys to offensive urban combat.* But, not only must the individuals and small units be well trained, they must also stay well focused throughout the battle. The ones at the front must be continually rotated. Maneuver squads must be interchanged with reserve squads, search parties with cover parties, and search teams with cover teams. Infantrymen with personal problems should not be allowed anywhere near the fighting.

In a city, control is more difficult to maintain. The walls block the line of sight between leaders and subordinates; they also impede radio transmissions and visual signaling. On the other hand, the open areas preclude face-to-face coordination meetings, and expose to enemy fire anyone who would even risk a visual signal.

Furthermore, it's difficult to establish any momentum in a built-up area. Sister platoons can't move with both alignment and speed. Just choosing boundaries between adjacent units can be hard, because the streets are not always straight or parallel. Even when the zones of action are the same width, building and room configurations will still vary. For this reason, some units can always move faster than others. Keeping them on line, so as not to uncover their flanks, constitutes forcing them to move no faster than the slowest unit. In other words, *systematically clearing along a wide frontage automatically sacrifices momentum.*

Attacking across a wide frontage could initially help to identify soft spots in the defense. But then the forces slowed by stiff resistance should fall in behind those making headway. Only a force attacking along a narrow frontage would stand much chance of keeping the enemy off balance. If this force were to aim for a key building on a hilltop and then raise a U.S. flag, it might cause the entire city to be abandoned.

While attacking along a narrow frontage, the lead element would *not* need much control from higher headquarters. That type of control could only hamper momentum. Still, the "tip of the spear" might run out of ammunition or get cut off, unless its sister units fell in behind it to keep open a resupply corridor.

If the lead element were a platoon, it would advance along a single street. Two squads would attack up opposite sides of that street, while the third squad provided rear and flank security. By doctrine, the front two would take turns covering for each other during this advance. A few signals and rehearsed techniques would provide more than enough control to execute this simple maneuver; the squad leaders *would not* need recurring orders. In fact, with a well-thought-out assortment of techniques, the platoon could function as a team and accomplish its mission with *very little* further direction from its commander.

To build momentum in Seoul, Chesty Puller left hard-to-get-at snipers to follow-on forces. However, it doesn't always take speed to build momentum, it merely takes moving *more quickly than the enemy believes possible.* Just as important as clearing a building quickly, is doing so silently — or at least without unnecessary shooting or yelling. To make less noise, U.S. troops will need new techniques:

> The true speed of war is not headlong precipitancy, but the unremitting energy which wastes no time.[3]
>
> — Mahan

## THE PHASES OF OFFENSIVE URBAN COMBAT

An urban attack is normally accomplished in three phases: (1) isolating an objective, (2) gaining a foothold, and (3) systematically clearing that objective. This sequence works equally well for a town, block, building, or single room.

Isolating an urban area takes cutting off the utilities and preventing anyone from entering or leaving the area. An aerial observer with fixed-wing aircraft on call, can cut off a city from water, electricity, gas, telephone service, and reinforcement. An artillery spotter or tank commander on a hill, can do the same thing to a small town. To isolate a building, a platoon must cut off the utilities and cover all approaches by fire. To isolate a single room, a squad must clear the floor above it, capture the room next to it, and cover by fire the hallway that runs past it.

For large built-up areas, footholds can be established not only by force, but also through deception and stealth. For example, attackers can gain access to a town by disguising themselves as civilians, and to a building by entering through an undefended window on upper floor. However, to establish a foothold in a room, the attackers may have to blow a new hole in the wall.

Once the clearing of an urban area begins, surprise becomes more difficult to achieve. Because clearing must be systematic, it becomes somewhat predictable. By doctrine, units must attack frontally to keep from shooting adjacent units. Luckily, urban terrain provides plenty of chances for overhead supporting fire. Still, the offensive process is essentially one of fire and movement — or, more precisely covering and movement. In a type of "bounding overwatch," two squads move up opposite sides of a street. To clear a building along that street, each squad has two fire teams that cover and one that searches. To clear a room in that building, each fire team has two men that cover and two that search. It takes daylight or illumination to perform this clearing process. After dark, the attacker can only hope to gain a foothold.

It's hard to practice pure maneuver warfare while systematically clearing a built-up area. However, by clearing that area with stealth and speed, the attacker can still establish momentum.

## SCHEMES OF MANEUVER AVAILABLE

The central theme of maneuver warfare is to bypass and collapse one's enemy. Chesty Puller bypassed snipers in Seoul. Infiltrating or penetrating by force along a narrow corridor to seize a prominent municipal building, might demoralize the defenders of a city. Then, thinking themselves outflanked or isolated, the defenders might flee.

Maneuver warfare is also based on surprise. One way to maintain surprise is to keep the enemy off balance through speed. The attacker can generate more speed during his advance by wisely incorporating "hasty attacks." Such attacks work best against gaps. In the city, built-up areas constitute gaps, whereas open areas constitute surfaces. This means that a hasty attack might suffice between adjacent buildings at mid-block, but a deliberate attack would be needed at the cross street between blocks. In other words, it would normally take planning to negotiate a cross street safely. However, as the German stormtroopers proved in World War I, deliberate attacks can be launched in rapid succession. The main prerequisite is prerehearsed technique. Of course, whether to try a hasty or deliberate attack during the daylight hours ultimately depends on the circumstances. For example, an objective completely surrounded by vacant lots may require a deliberate attack, whereas a narrow cross street may only need a hasty attack. Of course, a particularly well defended building may call for a deliberate attack no matter where it is.

Surprise can also be achieved through stealth and deception. Urban attackers must learn to clear buildings without unnecessary shooting and yelling; they must develop ways to deceive their opponents.

Styles of warfare can be combined during systematic clearing, but the extent to which maneuver warfare can be practiced depends on the willingness of the unit to decentralize control. Because of the varying structural densities in a city, floor plans in a building, and furniture arrangements in a room, the scheme of maneuver must continually change. Each subsequent objective must be assessed by the infantrymen at the scene. To have any chance at achieving momentum at minimal cost, the authority to choose the scheme of maneuver must be *delegated to the leader of the forward element.* For a building, this is normally a squad leader; and for a room, it's the senior member of a search team. On seeing an objective for the first time, a subunit leader can't design (and rehearse) a new plan of attack quickly enough to maintain momentum. He must be allowed to choose and to modify *prerehearsed* schemes of maneuver.

In an urban setting, maneuver elements will often be out of sight or hearing from their parent unit. Yet, having watched techniques being rehearsed, superiors will always have a general idea of what their subordinates are doing. These superiors can also require subordinates to keep them informed of major decisions.

## SCREENING MOVEMENT ACROSS OPEN AREAS

There are three ways of screening troop movement across open and level ground in a city: darkness, smoke, and dust. For example, after dark, the deep shadow from a tall building might provide lanes up which to launch a deliberate short-range infiltration attack against a structure surrounded by vacant lots. Of course, within anything but a limited objective, the most that can normally be seized at night is a foothold.

Smoke and dust will also screen movement. However, in the city, white smoke often draws fire. At Hue City, the Marines learned *not* to toss white smoke before crossing a street. *Gray or black* smoke (like from burning tires) would probably work better. Dust is so prevalent during most urban battles that it provides a unique opportunity to screen movement. If the attacker could stir up this dust and at the same time force his opponent to blink, he could cross open areas more easily. Here's how the Marines did precisely that at Hue City:

> The grunts tossed smoke grenades into the street for cover, but the flanking [enemy] gun fired blindly through the smoke. Marines . . . decided to bring up a 106mm recoilless rifle to cover the street crossing. . . . The round flashed down the street, the back blast blew smoke [and dust] onto the road, and the NVA ducked their heads for a few seconds. The platoon got across the street.[4]

## THE MANY POSSIBILITIES FOR DECEPTION

To deceive an urban defender, a unit must pretend to assault at one location, and then actually assault at another. For example, a platoon must make a feint at one place on a street, and then send its maneuver element across at another. There are several sights and sounds normally associated with an assault: moving, shooting, yelling, and white smoke. In the city, white smoke works best as a *distant* diversion. It can be generated by either mortar or M203 grenade launcher. Unless masked by background noise, firing and yelling is counterproductive.

Another way to deceive a foe is to produce the sights and sounds of an assault in two places at once — one real and one fake. Then, the adversary is forced to watch both locations at once. This may cost him a second or two while trying to aim his weapon. That's all the edge young Americans need to cross a danger area.

## FIRE SUPPORT PLAN OPTIONS

The first priority of the urban attacker must always be to safeguard the city's civilian population. *That's why the warfare style that entails the least shooting is usually preferable.* Before shooting or tossing a grenade into a room, an attacker must be relatively sure that the room is occupied only by enemy soldiers.

Furthermore, urban warfare is dangerous enough without accidentally coming under friendly fire. Window glass won't stop bullets, and clearing a building can be like conducting concurrent attacks through a maze of plasterboard walls. Clearing several buildings at once across a wide frontage merely compounds the problem. Then, the chances of loss from friendly fire become unacceptable. Even if every attack were meticulously planned and executed in slow motion, the sheer number of simultaneous attacks would produce mistakes. One can only prevent these mistakes by attacking along a narrow frontage and *minimizing friendly fire.* Of course, to accomplish the latter, the attacker must also be expert in the use of his weapons.

Collapsing the buildings at the edge of town with standoff weaponry can make gaining a foothold much easier. However, this bombardment must be closely followed by ground assault. That's the lesson of Monte Casino in WWII. Of course, the Rules of Engagement will establish to what extent supporting arms can be employed. At Hue City, artillery barrages and airstrikes were disallowed for several days.

In the city, *direct fire* is more effective than indirect fire. The narrowness of the streets, protection of upper stories, and proximity of friendly units severely limits the use of indirect fire and close air support. Only direct fire can reach many strongpoints. Along the Eastern Front in WWII, both sides sent artillery pieces forward with their lead infantry elements to provide direct fire. Of course, too much rubbling can limit an attacker's mobility.

Over a populated city, only A-10 tank killers and helicopter gunships can provide conventional close air support. They could easily hit a target on a boulevard, at the edge of a park, or that protruded above the buildings around it. In support of a ground unit with a laser designator, any aircraft equipped with a laser tracker can accurately deliver "smart" ordnance.

If there's a tall durable building in the way, naval gunfire can solve the problem. Because of its low trajectory, it can be used like a direct-fire weapon. Even "long" rounds will still hit a tall building.

Normally, artillery does not have the trajectory or accuracy to hit a point target within a built-up area. However, high-trajectory smart rounds can get the job done. Again, the ground troops would need a laser designator.

In heavily built-up areas, mortars are the most effective of the indirect-fire weapons. They can hit enemy soldiers *atop* or *between* tall buildings. Mortars are most effective when they can be directly aligned on visible targets. To block enemy reinforcement or retreat, Hue City Marines dropped mortar rounds *behind* buildings they were assaulting.

(Source: Marine Corps "Battle Drill Guide," p. 3-17-17)

SMAW teams should be attached to the forward squads. That way, they can breach walls and neutralize enemy strongpoints. The holes they make may be small, but the dust and shock they create could help grunts to cross dangerous open ground.

Machinegun teams should be attached to the *reserve* squad. That way, by taking turns displacing between tall buildings, the gun teams can provide continuous support. With pre-established free-fire zones, they would not need signals to shift their fires. The street along which the platoon attacks can be a free-fire zone, because the lead squads never cross it. Plus, anyone firing from the area *beyond* the block being cleared, should be fair game. However, the gunners must remember that automatic-weapons fire compromises the element of surprise. They must employ single shots or short bursts when enemy fire masks the noise. (See figure 24.1.)

SAW's should be used primarily to suppress enemy automatic-weapons fire. They can also cover alleyways, hallways, and stairwells. Against a SAW, the enemy would have difficulty reinforcing or retreating.

Before entering a building, U.S. personnel are supposed to toss in a grenade. It would help, if the exterior walls were thick and the targeted room free of civilians. Unfortunately, tossing a grenade into every building sacrifices momentum. That many grenades are either too heavy to carry or too slow to resupply. If each man carried four grenades, and if each block contained ten buildings, a platoon could only advance eight *undefended* blocks before requiring resupply. Attackers should only throw grenades into rooms *known to be defended and free of civilians.*

Figure 24.1: How to Employ the Machineguns without Curtailing Momentum
(Source: FM 90-10-1 (1982), pp. 3-14, E-18)

The doctrinal procedure of shooting through every closed door also wastes ammunition, civilians, and surprise. Because an explosion won't automatically forewarn other defenders of an impending ground attack, a better solution might be a quarter-pound of C-4 under the latch. With the door open, the attacker has another option — the pieing-off technique. With it, he slowly scans the room over the sights of his rifle. Only when he spots enemy, does he fire. This saves both ammunition and innocent lives.

In short, relying too heavily on one's small arms in offensive urban combat has significant drawbacks: (1) running out of ammunition, (2) shooting friendlies or civilians by accident, (3) announcing one's presence prematurely to the enemy, (4) reducing one's mobility with heavy loads, and (5) creating resupply problems. Infantrymen should be told to use single shots or double taps against only confirmed targets. That is not to say that a frontal assault through a door should take the place of shooting a confirmed adversary through a thin wall or floor. Nor, is it to say that blindly firing a weapon on full automatic, is always a bad idea. Everyone has seen the picture of the urban resistance fighter sticking his AK-47 over a windowsill to spray a heavily contested room.

### INDIVIDUAL MOVEMENT TECHNIQUES

The infantryman's survivability in offensive urban combat depends largely on how well he can move through built-up terrain. He can be covered by fire perfectly, and still get killed by the first bullet. Only through practice, can he can acquire the movement skills he needs. In peacetime, this practice must come through "free play." Units must count "sight pictures" or MILES-laser hits for game points. That way, common sense will dictate which movement techniques work and which ones don't.

To move in the city, one must wait until properly covered by fire, pick a safe place no more than 3 seconds away, and then dash to that spot. This doesn't sound too difficult. However, en route, the runner must also make as small a target as possible and avoid openings in surfaces. He must choose whether to dive under, jump over, or quickly pass in front of these openings. All the while, he must resist the temptation to hug walls. Bullets fired at walls from an angle tend to follow those walls. In other words, it takes a *complicated* thought process to change location safely in urban terrain. It's not hard to see why partially trained combatants quickly become casualties.

Movement under these conditions is an art. The attacker must realize that not all cover is equally safe. A doorway helps him to escape fire from many directions, but it also silhouettes him to anyone inside the building. Because urban terrain offers less concealment than rural terrain, the urban attacker must take advantage of the limited concealment available. He must use shadows, drifting dust and smoke, and the projections of buildings.

To move, an attacker must keep his location secret and wait for the defenders to be distracted. He can't let part of his body or equipment give away his hiding place. Further, he can't shout "coming out" to a cover team every time he leaves a building. All coordination must be accomplished in code — and nonverbal code at that.

A street is a danger area. Only a few infantrymen at a time can cross one. They can't be on line or aimed in column at any given defender. The pictures in the manuals never show more that one fire team crossing a street at the same time. Its members are always running and never on line. Still, streets must be crossed by the most direct route. That means on a perpendicular, and not a diagonal. Of course, the best way to cross any open area is at night.

To cross a wall, one must quickly look over it to pick a covered location for which to head. Then, he must hit the wall running at another place, roll over it with his rifle in his strong hand, and scramble for the covered position.

These lessons can be learned under fire, but then the price for a mistake is higher. Until each rifleman can move well enough to evade the first bullet, there is little reason to practice offensive unit tactics.

## INDIVIDUAL FIRING TECHNIQUES

In urban warfare, just as in other types of combat, small-arms fire erodes surprise. That means that the attacker must shoot only when absolutely necessary. Explosions are the preferred alternative, because they occur for many reasons other than in support of a ground attack. Still, even explosions must be rationed — to preserve ammunition.

An important axiom of urban warfare is never letting an enemy prematurely see the muzzle of one's rifle. Certain carrying stances can help to accomplish this. An infantryman with his rifle in the "field-ready position" has its butt stock to his hip and its muzzle in his line of sight to the target. One with his rifle in the "ready" position, has the butt stock in the pocket of his shoulder, his elbow tucked in, and the muzzle pointed toward the ground. In the "alert" position, the rifleman brings the butt stock to his shoulder, and once again maintains a straight line between eye, muzzle, and target.

In urban warfare, pieing off is the most useful of the individual firing techniques. It can be used by one man to look around a corner, or by two men to scan a room. To use the procedure for room scanning, two men stand on opposite sides of a door or window. The man on the left holds his weapon in his right hand and then, exposing only his rifle and right eye, gradually scans the room from front to back. Meanwhile, the man on the right holds his rifle in his *left* hand and then, exposing only the rifle and his *left* eye, does the same thing. This permits the individual attacker to engage *only confirmed defenders,* and it permits him to do so while exposing only an eye and hand for a split second. Infantrymen must learn to shoot equally well from either hand. Then, if they can keep the muzzles of their rifles from announcing their presence, they may stand a chance.

Of course, there are other techniques as well. With a small mirror on a long stick, one can shoot defenders through thin walls, floors, and ceilings. And, by intentionally ricocheting bullets off a more durable surface, one can hit defenders who are not visible at all.

## A HASTY-ATTACK METHOD FOR MID-BLOCK

To move up a contested street with any degree of coordination and safety, one squad must attack while the other covers. Then, if structural density permits, they must shift roles. However, if the next building on the other side of the street is too distant, or if alternating roles has become too predictable, one squad may have to attack twice (or more) in a row. In other words, the squad leaders need a quick way to discuss who should attack next. Then, to build any momentum, their units must be able to perform their respective roles quickly and quietly.

Attacking squads can't always maintain absolute quiet. However, to maximize surprise, they must minimize shooting. Police SWAT teams routinely use concussion grenades before entering defended rooms. Grenades, breaching charges, and "bunker-busting" projectiles sound to the foe like mortar rounds, prematurely sprung booby traps, or defensive demolitions. The defender who hears a large volume of small-arms fire is forewarned that a ground assault is underway. Single shots are better than bursts of fire, because a building's acoustics will sometimes make a single shot sound like a small explosion.

Techniques from the NCO Corps

The loud shouting that doctrinally occurs while U.S. infantrymen systematically clear a building must be replaced with some other form of communication. Perhaps pounding on the walls in some sort of code could get the job done. For example, two loud raps could mean "room clear," and three could mean "cover party coming in." At a distance, pounding sounds like muffled explosions.

The cover squad must shift its supporting fires before the maneuver squad can launch its assault. Conventional signals take time. Why couldn't the cover squad merely shift its fires when the first member of the attacking squad nears the objective building? The cover squad leader can't always see this happening from his location; but he could delegate to every member of his squad, the responsibility to watch for it, and the authority to initiate the command to shift fire. As an additional safeguard and alternate signal, the first member of the attacking squad could display an upside-down object in the front window of his entry room.

Agreeing on which squad should attack next could be handled by signal as well. The spacing between buildings would normally be the determining factor. Still, when the buildings are equidistant, constantly alternating attacks is too predictable. Either way, the decision must be made on the spur of the moment by the person in the best position to assess the changing situation. That person is the squad leader about to attack. If both squad leaders agree, the platoon commander need not get involved.

How can this mutual decision be reached quickly? By doctrine, the squad leader who has just finished clearing his building must mark it as being clear. Why couldn't he indicate his preferred role in the next attack at the same time? Perhaps a white cloth in the window could mean "My building is clear, I'm ready to cover, and you attack next," and another color cloth could mean "My building is clear and I want to attack next." As long as different signals were displayed on opposite sides of the street, the squad leaders would agree on the next move.

If every fire team were permanently assigned a particular sector to cover, they could shift more quickly from their attack to cover roles. This is no different than preassigning consolidation sectors before a traditional attack in rural terrain.

If an occasional deception were needed, the cover squad could send two men forward to man a position behind a garden wall. To the defenders, this would look like the initial stages of an assault.

*By delegating both authority and responsibility, the platoon leader can better adapt his attack to the situation.* By rehearsing in all types of urban terrain and using events as signals, he can capture territory more quickly than the enemy deems possible. Even when an attack requires some shooting, the enemy should not be able to predict the next move quickly enough to do much about it. (See figures 24.2 through 24.4 for specifics of the technique.)

(Source: MCI 03.66a (1986), pp. 2-10, 2-19)

*What the Urban Attacker Must Know to Stay Alive*

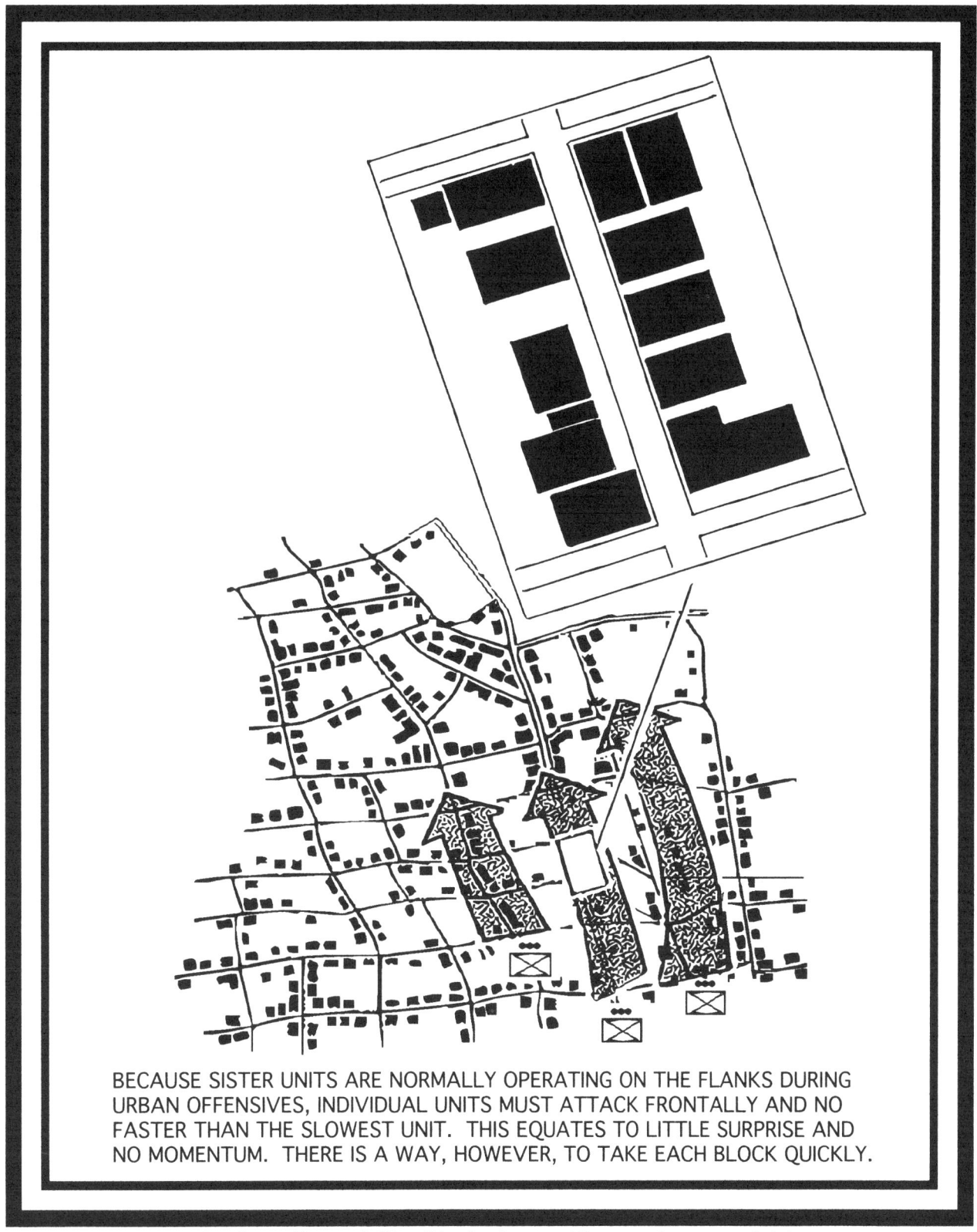

BECAUSE SISTER UNITS ARE NORMALLY OPERATING ON THE FLANKS DURING URBAN OFFENSIVES, INDIVIDUAL UNITS MUST ATTACK FRONTALLY AND NO FASTER THAN THE SLOWEST UNIT. THIS EQUATES TO LITTLE SURPRISE AND NO MOMENTUM. THERE IS A WAY, HOWEVER, TO TAKE EACH BLOCK QUICKLY.

Figure 24.2: A Typical City Block along a Platoon Avenue of Advance
(Source: FM 90-10-1 (1982), p. 4-11)

*Techniques from the NCO Corps*

### THE STREET DOWN WHICH THE PLATOON MUST ATTACK

THE PLATOON FACING A BLOCK OF CONTESTED, SEMI-DETACHED BUILDINGS, HAS DIFFICULTY USING SURPRISE/MOMENTUM WITHOUT SACRIFICING COORDINATION. THE VARYING HEIGHTS OF BUILDINGS AND DISTANCES BETWEEN THEM MAKES MOVING ACROSS ROOFTOPS IMPRACTICAL. AT GROUND LEVEL, THE UNIT MUST ADVANCE THROUGH SIDE AND REAR ENTRANCES OF ADJACENT STRUCTURES, INSTEAD OF ALONG STOREFRONTS. TO DEVELOP SURPRISE/MOMENTUM, TWO SQUADS MUST LEAPFROG QUICKLY UP OPPOSITE SIDES OF THE STREET. THAT TAKES TECHNIQUE! THE SQUADS MUST BE ABLE TO RAPIDLY SWAP ATTACK AND COVER RESPONSIBILITIES, COVER EVERY POSSIBLE SOURCE OF ENEMY FIRE, AND SHIFT THEIR FIRES AS NECESSARY. WITHOUT LONG DEBATE, THEY MUST BE ABLE TO ALTER THEIR ATTACK SEQUENCE TO FIT EXISTING CIRCUMSTANCES. FINALLY, THE ONE THAT ATTACKS MUST BE ABLE TO MODIFY DETAILS OF ENTERING AND CLEARING FOR EACH OBJECTIVE. ALL MUST OCCUR FASTER THAN EXPECTED.

*Figure 24.3: Options for Moving along a City Street with Momentum*
(Source: FM 90-10-1 (1982), p. B-9)

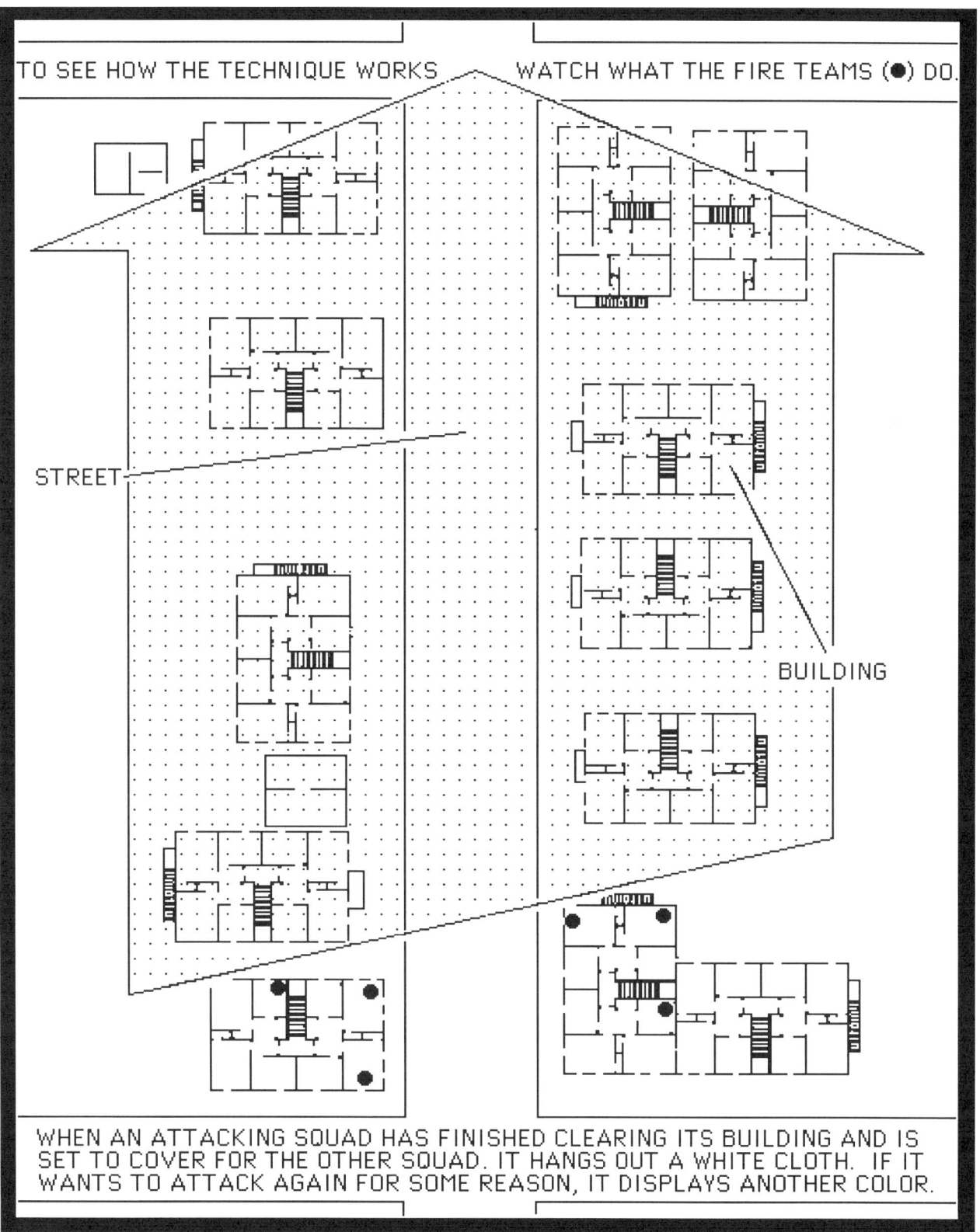

*Figure 24.4: The Mid-Block Technique*
(Source: TC 90-1 (1986), p. 3-53)

Techniques from the NCO Corps

**THE ONLY SIGNALING NECESSARY TO COORDINATE THE NEXT ATTACK IS A SINGLE PIECE OF CLOTH**

(Sources: FM 90-10-1 (1982), p. B-29; FM 3-4 (1985), p. 3-5)

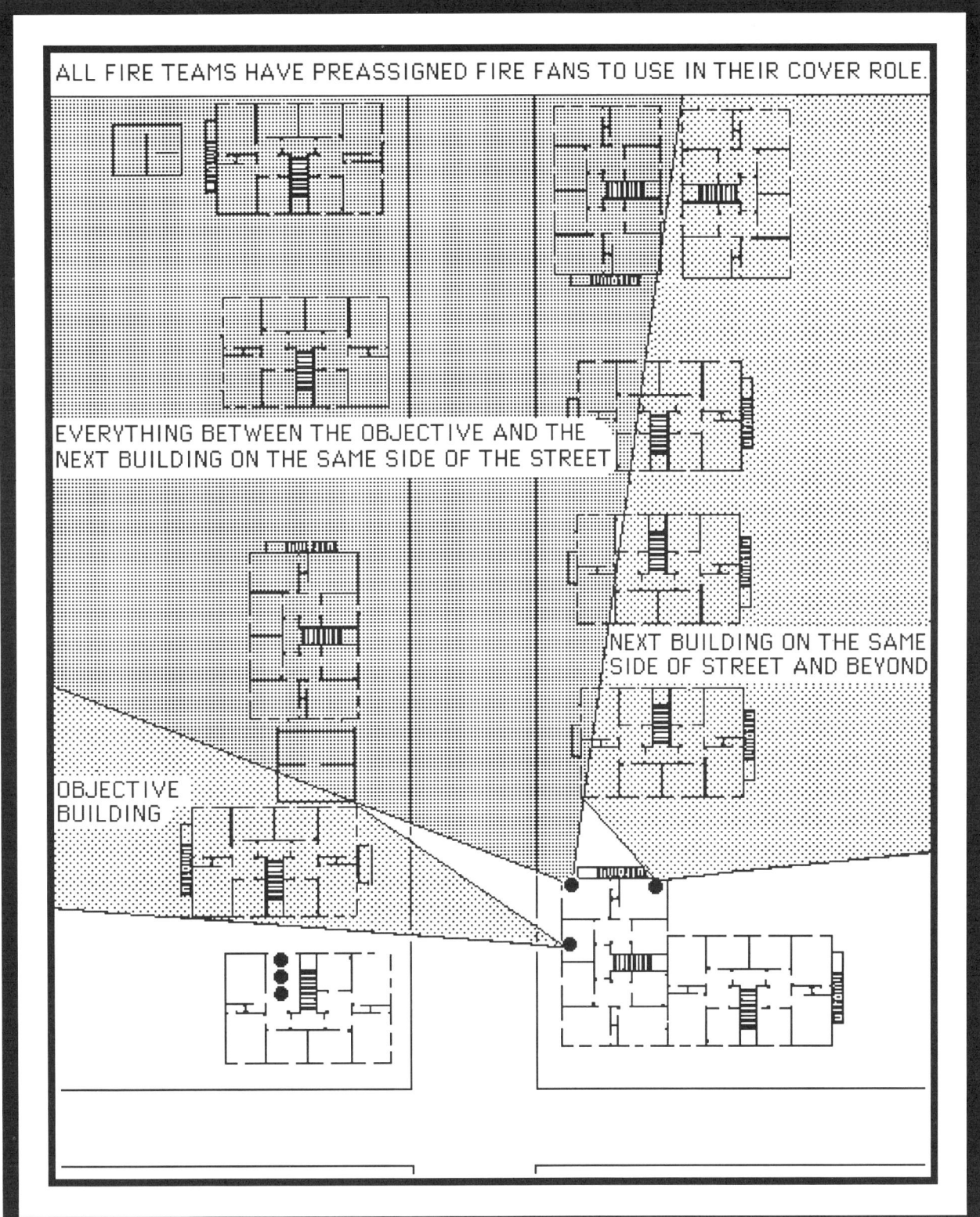

*Figure 24.4: The Mid-Block Technique (Continued)*
(Source: TC 90-1 (1986), p. 3-53)

Techniques from the NCO Corps

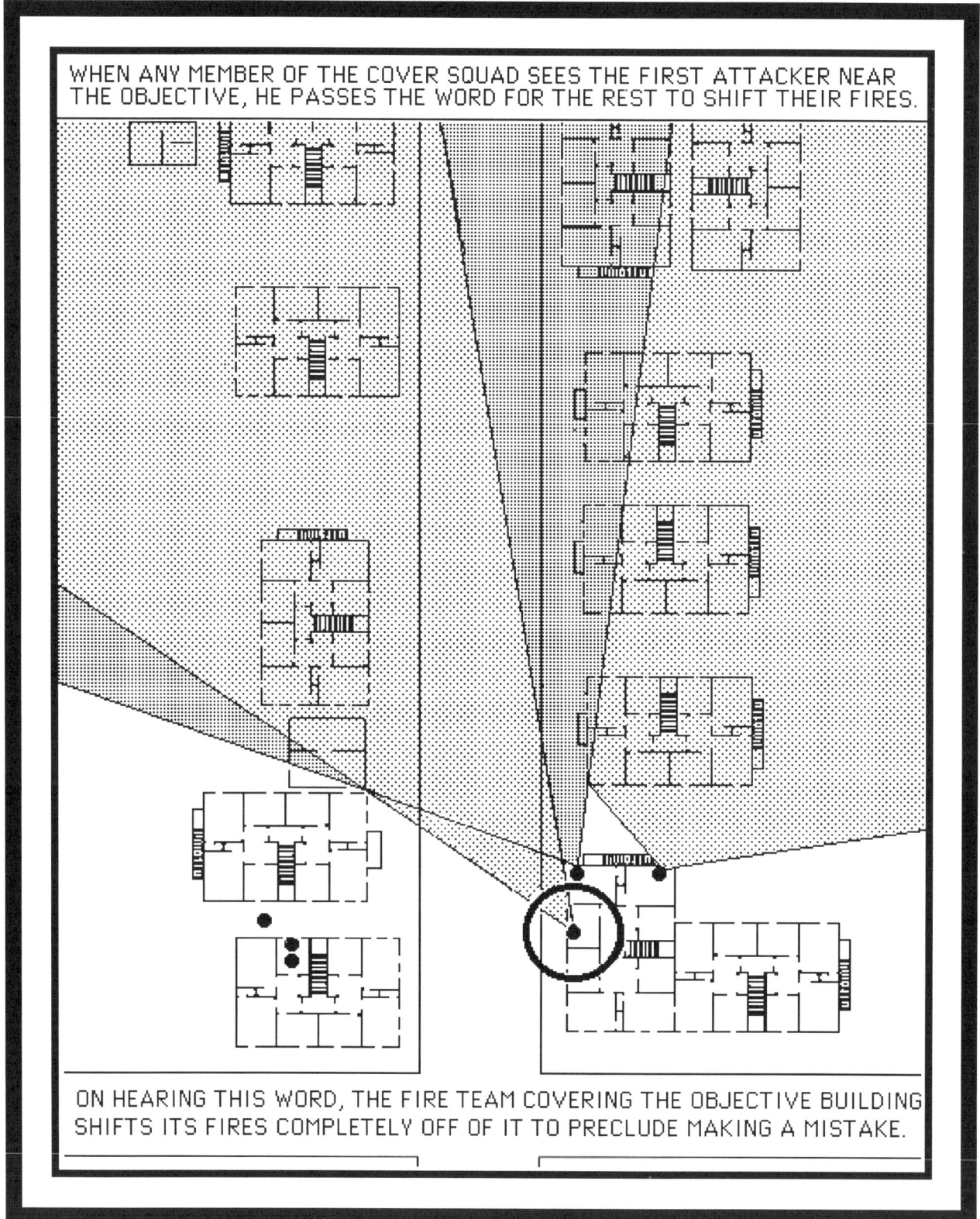

Figure 24.4: The Mid-Block Technique (Continued)
(Source: TC 90-1 (1986), p. 3-53)

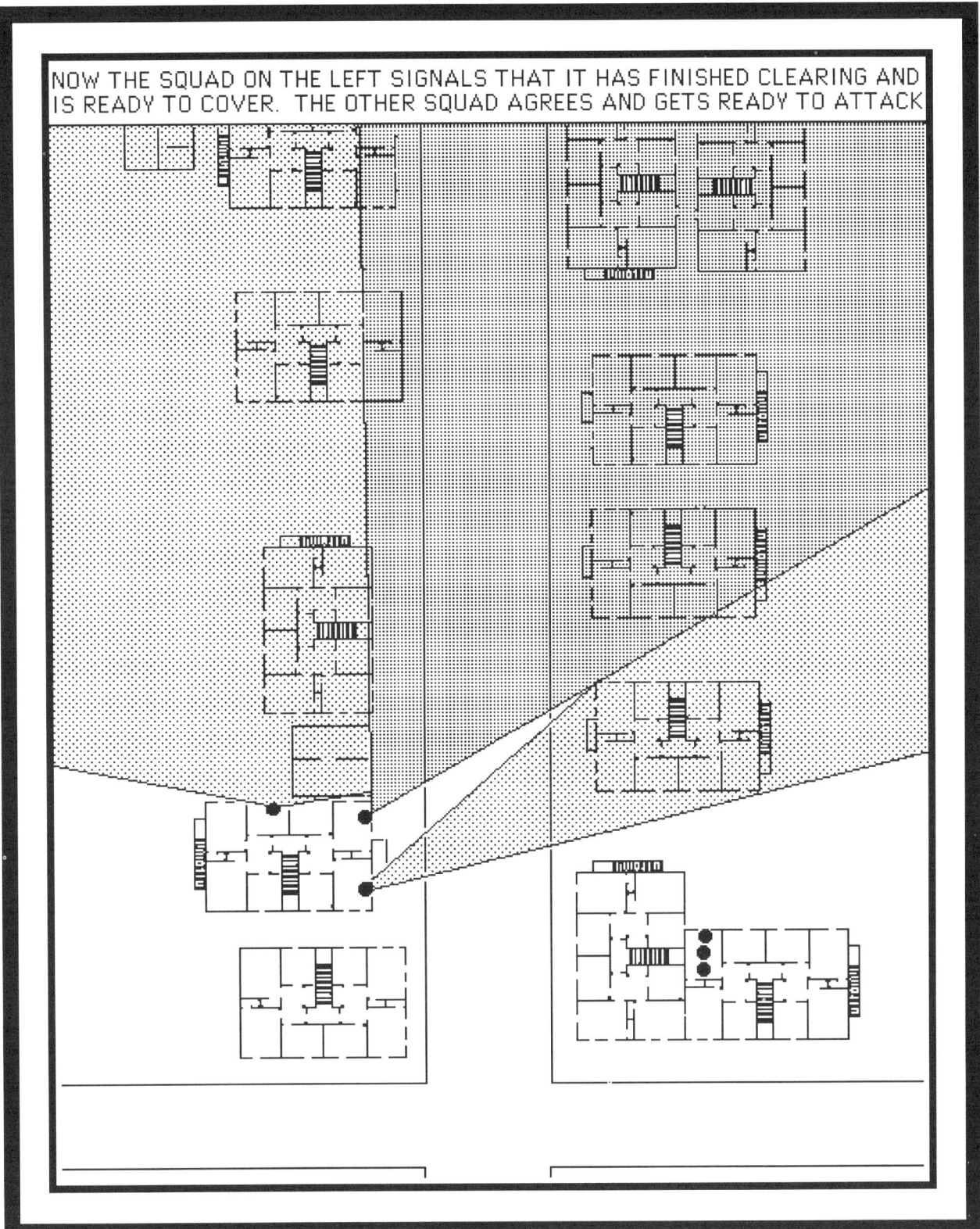

*Figure 24.4: The Mid-Block Technique (Continued)*
(Source: TC 90-1 (1986), p. 3-53)

Techniques from the NCO Corps

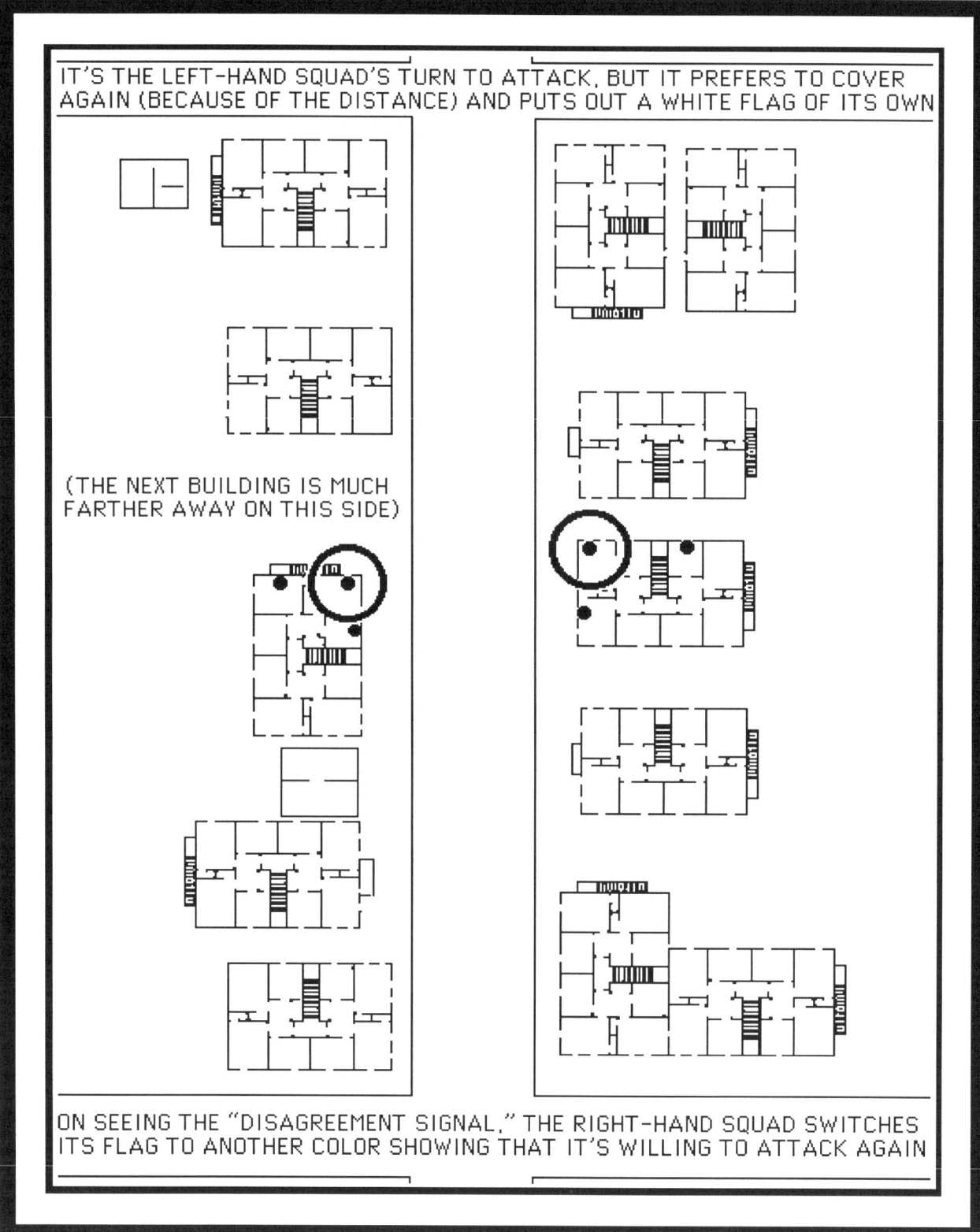

Figure 24.4: The Mid-Block Technique (Continued)
(Source: TC 90-1 (1986), p. 3-53)

## A DELIBERATE-ATTACK METHOD FOR THE CROSS STREET AT THE END OF THE BLOCK

More dangerous than moving between buildings at mid-block is negotiating the cross street at the end of the block. If there has been any fighting at mid-block, the defenders of the next block will be forewarned. Therefore, to negotiate the cross street safely, the attackers must regenerate surprise through deception and speed. They must launch a deliberate-attack technique *quickly*. To do so, they must have a prerehearsed technique that can be modified to fit the unique configuration of the buildings. There's a frontal attack method that will work. Although it is systematic in its execution, it keeps the location of the maneuver element secret until the last moment. Additionally, it provides a way to cover every possible source of enemy fire, to cross the street at minimal risk, and to coordinate the two.

As in a football play, each fire team must have a preassigned role. As soon as the lead squads have cleared the buildings facing the cross street at the end of the block, one fire team from each squad moves to the corner of its building to cover the ground floor of the structure diagonally across the intersection. Another fire team from each squad goes upstairs to cover the upper stories of the structure(s) directly across the street. The third fire team from each squad moves *secretly* to the closest edge of the platoon sector. Then, from opposite ends of that sector, one team can assault, while another creates a diversion.

If the covering fire teams never acquire an enemy target, they can maintain fire superiority *without shooting*. This helps to preserve both surprise and ammunition. Fire discipline can translate into valuable momentum. If, on the other hand, those covering fire teams are forced to fire, the assault can function as the signal to shift their fires. When they see the first member of the assaulting force reach the other side of the cross street, they can cease overhead fires and shift crisscross fires to confirmed targets *behind* target buildings. This should hamper enemy efforts at reinforcement or withdrawal.

Even with every possible source of enemy fire covered, the platoon still needs a procedure to launch its maneuver element by surprise. This method must provide for breaching the side of the objective building, causing the building's defenders to duck, screening the assault, and creating a diversion elsewhere. There's a way to accomplish all four goals at once — by having the lead squads fire their SMAW's in close succession. The SMAW with the cover squad could shoot first. Then, the one with the attack squad could fire to signal the assault. The objective buildings in both sectors would have holes punched in their walls, most of the defenders would be forced to duck, dust would be raised to screen the assault, and the exact point of attack would still be in doubt. Enemy soldiers defending the cross street at other locations would think that the explosions were from mortar rounds, and would not suspect that the street was being crossed. The full deception sequence would be as follows: (1) the SMAW with the cover squad fires, (2) a fire team with the cover squad fakes an assault, (3) the SMAW with the attack squad fires, and (4) a fire team with the attack squad actually assaults.

For the element feigning the assault, the diversion might take the form of a move forward to a parked car. Shooting and yelling would be appropriate only if there were other noise to mask the sound. White smoke might draw indiscriminate fire from the side.

For the actual maneuver element, the window of opportunity is narrow. To cross the street safely, the four infantrymen must use an assault formation that permits moving rapidly, dispersing in the face of frontal and flanking fire, and firing as a group into their objective building. *In column at the edge of the platoon sector, the*

(Sources: FM 7-8 (1984), p. B-8; FM 90-10-1 (1982), p. B-17)

infantrymen can accomplish all three. They can run at full speed, avoid enemy fire down their long axis, and shoot as a group (on a diagonal) into their objective building at the intersection. Furthermore, by crossing at the periphery of the sector, they are partially hidden by the signs protruding from the objective building.

For this technique to work, the squad leaders must quickly decide who will send a fire team across the street. The same coordination method that worked for the hasty-attack method at mid-block, will also work here. Pieces of cloth will be hung from the side windows of the buildings facing the intersection. The color of cloth will establish which squad will actually assault. No other signals are necessary. The covering fires are shifted automatically when the lead man of the maneuver element reaches the far side of the street. (See figures 24.5 and 24.6 for what might happen enemy soldiers attempting to pull back from such an attack.)

Figure 24.5: What the Platoon Often Faces at the End of the Block
(Sources: TC 90-1 (1986), p. E-6; FM 90-10-1 (1982), pp. 3-8, 3-30)

## What the Urban Attacker Must Know to Stay Alive

1. ONE FIRE TEAM FROM EACH SQUAD COVERS THE GROUND FLOOR OF THE CORNER BUILDING DIAGONALLY ACROSS THE INTERSECTION.
2. ANOTHER FIRE TEAM IN EACH SQUAD COVERS THE SECOND AND HIGHER FLOORS OF THE BUILDINGS DIRECTLY ACROSS THE STREET.
3. THE LAST FIRE TEAM IN EACH SQUAD PREPARES EITHER TO CONDUCT AN ASSAULT ACROSS THE STREET OR TO FEIGN ONE, AS DIRECTED.
4. THE SMAW TEAM ATTACHED TO EACH SQUAD POSITIONS ITSELF WHERE IT CAN BEST SUPPORT ITS ASSAULT FIRE TEAM. WITH ONE SHOT. IT CAN SIGNAL THE ASSAULT. FORCE THE FOE TO DUCK. SCREEN THE ASSAULT ELEMENT WITH DUST, AND BREACH THE OBJECTIVE WALL.
5. SQUADS DISPLAY RAGS IN WINDOWS OF THEIR RESPECTIVE BUILDINGS TO ASCERTAIN WHICH WILL ASSAULT AND WHICH WILL PRETEND.

Figure 24.6: The Intersection-Crossing Technique
(Sources: TC 90-1 (1986), p. E-6; FM 90-10-1 (1982), pp. 3-8, 3-30)

Techniques from the NCO Corps

1. THE SMAW TEAM ATTACHED TO THE COVER SQUAD FIRES FIRST.

2. THEN, IF MASKING NOISE PERMITS, THE FIRE TEAM TASKED WITH THE DIVERSIONARY ASSAULT BEGINS TO YELL AND SHOOT. SMOKE IS ANOTHER OPTION, BUT IT MAY DRAW FIRE FROM UP THE STREET (FIRE THROUGH WHICH THE MANEUVER ELEMENT MUST RUN).

3. THE FAKE ASSAULT IS THE CUE FOR THE SMAW TEAM SUPPORTING THE MANEUVER ELEMENT TO FIRE.

4. AT THE SAME INSTANT THE SMAW GOES OFF, THE MANEUVER FIRE TEAM DARTS ACROSS THE STREET WITHOUT FANFARE (ONLY SHOOTING AT CONFIRMED TARGETS).

Figure 24.6: The Intersection-Crossing Technique (Continued)
(Sources: TC 90-1 (1986), p. E-6; FM 90-10-1 (1982), pp. 3-8, 3-30)

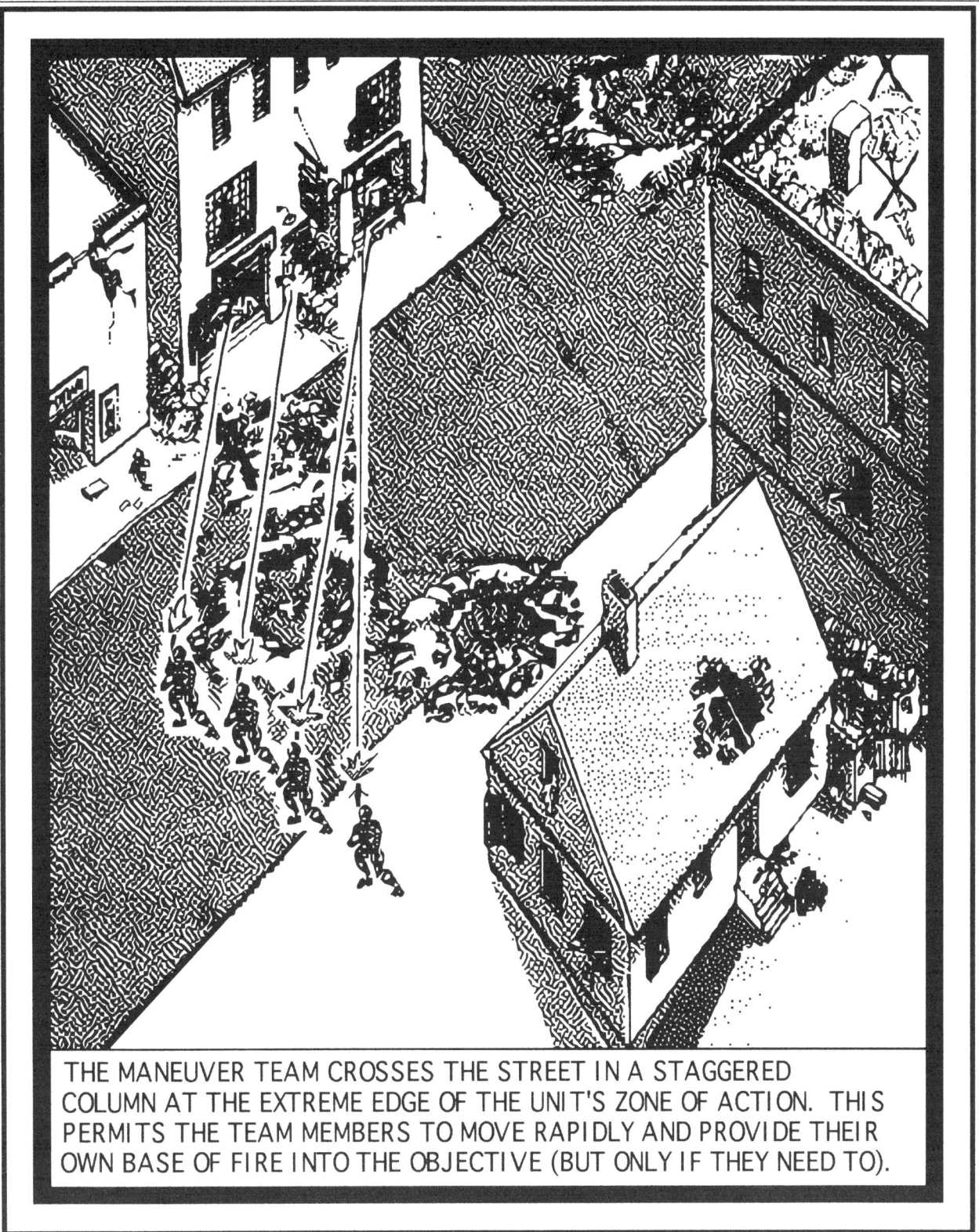

Figure 24.6: The Intersection-Crossing Technique (Continued)
(Sources: FM 5-103 (1985), p. 4-38; TC 90-1 (1986), p. E-8)

Techniques from the NCO Corps

Figure 24.6: The Intersection-Crossing Technique (Continued)
(Sources: TC 90-1 (1986), p. E-6; FM 90-10-1 (1982), pp. 3-8, 3-30)

## What the Urban Attacker Must Know to Stay Alive

### ALTERNATE WAYS TO NEGOTIATE SUBSEQUENT CROSS STREETS

To keep the enemy guessing, the attacker must use a slightly *different* attack play at the end of each block. Having more than one technique should also make possible adapting more quickly to unique circumstances.

By altering the *diversion* in the method just described, the attacker can formulate easy-to-learn alternate methods. For example, any of the following can replace the existing diversion: dropping a WP mortar round up the cross street, only firing the cover squad's SMAW, or waiting for a sister platoon to negotiate the cross street in another attack lane. In fact, for a narrow or lightly defended cross street, any coincidental diversion will work. For example, a passing helicopter will both divert enemy attention and mask small-arms noise.

### ESTABLISHING FOOTHOLDS IN BUILDINGS

Not all neighborhoods are heavily defended. But, to maintain surprise and momentum in one that is, the attacking squads may have to move parallel to their assigned street through the side entrances of the buildings facing that street. Doing so will protect them from both observation and fire. (See figure 24.7.)

When possible, a contested building should be entered through an opening near its roof. It is much easier to make a hole through some shingles and roofing plywood, than through foundation cement. From the top down, any building is easier to clear. There are various ways to reach the roof: from adjacent buildings, up fire escapes, by way of tree limbs, etc. Most platoons have a few personnel who can be trained to climb the drain pipe of a multistory building. Sold commercially are *folding*

FRONT ENTRANCES AND INTERIOR STAIRWELLS ARE DANGEROUS. WITH DRAINPIPE CLIMBER AND "BLOCK AND TACKLE," A UNIT CAN ENTER CONTESTED BUILDINGS AT ROOFTOP LEVEL FROM THE SIDE.

Figure 24.7: Move between Buildings without Facing Fire in the Street
(Sources: FM 90-10-1 (1982), p. E-14; FM 7-11B1/2 (1978), p. 2-IV-C-1.2)

grappling hooks that can be shot from crossbows like arrows. With a small pulley and double line attached, such an arrow could create the opportunity for a squad to *pull* a small man without gear to the top of a building. Next up could be a block and tackle rigged with heavier rope. Soon, fully armed men would be moving skyward, and the last member of the squad could pull himself up.

If the attackers must enter a contested building at ground level, their best chance is through an undefended room. Their next best chance is through a new hole in an exterior wall, but the wherewithal to make such a hole is not always available. Prior to entering through a door or window, the attackers must first check for booby traps. Then, for buildings known to be free of civilians, the attackers can throw in a grenade. However, this grenade should *not* be tossed through the same wall opening they plan to use. When civilians are possible, or grenades in short supply, the attackers should instead pie off the first room, and shoot only confirmed defenders with single shots. Only on rare occasions, should an attacker hold his weapon at arm's length and spray a room with automatic-weapons fire. To use this option, he must be sure that there are no civilians present, and that other firing will mask the telltale sound of his automatic weapon.

To enter an open window rapidly, the attacker leads with one knee while holding his shin horizontal, and then extends that leg as soon as his foot clears the opening. All of this is done while covering the room with his rifle held in the strong hand. Ways to enter a door will be discussed in a later paragraph.

Once the attackers have entered a building, they must capture the first room, and then move to the top floor. It's safer to move through holes in ceilings than up stairwells. When members of the search party must climb stairs, they do so in leapfrog fashion. One climbs, while the other three closely cover by fire preassigned sectors at the top of the stairs. Stairs are climbed several at a time to lessen the chance of stepping on a booby trap. When the search party reaches the top floor, forgetting to check the roof could prove embarrassing.

## BUILDING-CLEARING TECHNIQUES

A single squad has enough men to clear systematically anything up to a three-story building with one stairwell and one hallway on each floor.

The building should be cleared from the top down. Each floor should be worked by a different fire team consisting of a two-man search team and two-man cover team. After this fire team clears its floor, it should stay on that floor to cover the stairwell and hall. This prevents counterattacks from enemy soldiers who have hidden or shifted floors. After the bottom floor has been cleared, all floors must be rechecked simultaneously to make sure that no defenders have escaped detection. While this process may seem complicated, it can be easily (and quickly) accomplished after a little rehearsal.

## WORKING ALONG A CONTESTED HALLWAY

Each hall should be made into a free-fire zone for a cover party at the stairwell. (See figure 24.8.) This will prevent any defender from sticking his AK-47 out of a doorway to take out an entire search party. It will also prevent enemy soldiers from crossing the hallway to escape or reinforce each other. However, the hall can only be made into a free-fire zone, if the search party stays out

Figure 24.8: Hallways Are Kill Zones Too
(Source: FM 90-10-1 (1982), p. F-8)

of it. Unless the door openings are recessed, the hallway offers little cover anyway. Hugging walls doesn't help, because bullets ricochet along walls. Instead of using the hall, search-party members should move through openings between rooms. When they finally reach the last room on one side of the hall, they should move back to the cover party, and then tackle the rooms along other side.

Backtracking is important for another reason. The interior walls of a building are too thin for a maneuver element to be moving toward a cover element. Complicated schemes of maneuver could result in accidents. The search party should always work *away from* the cover party at the stairwell. Of course, both sides of a hallway can be cleared at the same time by separate fire teams, as long as the fire teams are careful not to fire inboard. This will cut floor-clearing time in half.

## TALL OR LONG BUILDINGS

It takes more people to clear a larger building. A tall, thin building may require an entire rifle company — one fire team to clear and guard each floor. After the last floor is captured, all floors must be re-searched simultaneously to make sure they're still empty.

For a long building with a central stairwell, the hallway on each floor could be cleared more rapidly by positioning a cover party at its center and sending separate search parties in opposite directions. Actually, any number of hallways could be searched simultaneously from the same starting point. However, parallel hallways must be cleared one at a time, and then all rechecked at once. (See figure 24.9.)

## ROOM CLEARING

When possible, the search party should avoid entering a contested room through an existing door or window. That entrance may be booby trapped. Instead, the search party should create another hole in the wall. Often, such a hole is only big enough to admit one person at a time. Before entering, that one person should still toss in a concussion grenade or pie off the room.

When the attackers must use an open doorway, they have four techniques from which to choose: the "buttonhook" where two people on opposite sides of the door enter the room without crossing in front of each other; the "crisscross" where two people on opposite sides of the door change sides while entering; the "high/low" where both go in at the same time at different levels; and the "stack" where more than two go in at once on different levels. These methods take practice. The idea is, while entering, to cover by fire all parts of a room.

WHEN CLEARING MULTISTORY BUILDINGS, LEAVE THE COVER FIRE TEAMS NEAR THE STAIRWELLS. THAT WAY, THEY CAN COVER THE STAIRS AND THE HALLS AT THE SAME TIME. WHEN DONE CLEARING THE BUILDING ONE FLOOR AT A TIME, HAVE ALL THE COVER TEAMS RECHECK THEIR FLOORS AT ONCE.

Figure 24.9: The Floors in Multistory Buildings Must Be Cleared Twice
(Sources: FM 90-10-1 (1982), p. C-8; FM 90-10 (1979), p. C-6)

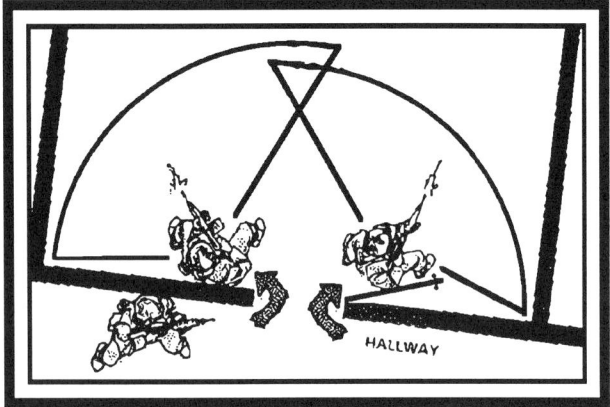

(Source: TC 90-1 (1986), p. E-4)

When the door to the room is closed, things become more complicated. Then, which way the door opens and familiarity with the latch become life-or-death issues for the search team. Closed doors are sometimes better opened with a small explosive charge.

L- and T-shaped rooms require special schemes of maneuver, and every rectangular room has a different furniture pattern. Prospective urban combatants must practice room clearing in a wide variety of settings. This will help them to resist being surprised by a new one.

## THE EXECUTION PHASE OF THE ATTACK

A platoon attacks up a street like a football team moves during its two-minute drill. The platoon leader does not issue any orders. He does not even convene huddles. All decisions are made by the subordinate-element leader who must execute the next attack. The platoon leader's role is to coordinate machineguns and supporting arms, to rotate the frontline squads with the reserve squad, and only occasionally to decide how to attack a particularly challenging objective. All hasty attacks in mid-block are essentially the same play. Yet, this one play produces less-than-predictable results, because the frontline squad leaders are permitted to choose who will attack, and the attacker is permitted to tailor his scheme of maneuver to the situation. Without leaving the protection of the cover squad, the lead squad still exploits whatever gaps exist. In other words, while systematically clearing, the platoon still maintains some momentum.

Control is decentralized within the squads as well. The leader of the attacking squad decides how to enter a building and reach the top floor, but the leader of the search party decides on how to seize that floor, and the senior member of the search team decides how to clear each room. When the building is secure, the squad leader decides which squad should attack next, quickly checks to see that his fire teams are covering preassigned fields of fire, and puts out the appropriate signal. Then, his fire team leaders assign the individual fields of fire within their pre-established sectors. While covering the maneuver element, each member of the support squad has the responsibility to watch for the lead man to enter the objective building, and the authority to pass the signal to shift fire. Then, the leader of the support squad decides how to attack next, and the process is repeated.

The alertness of those searching can be sustained by continually rotating them into less stressful jobs. That's why each fire team searches one floor and then assumes a covering role. Only when new men are in training, should any fire team use the same search team over and over.

The attackers must only shoot and throw grenades at confirmed enemy soldiers. This preserves ammunition, surprise, and lives (both civilian and friendly military).

At the end of the block, the platoon leader may reserve the right to veto the deliberate-attack variation chosen by his squad leaders. Still, his management by exception saves time. Just by employing techniques, the platoon achieves adequate coordination. The squad leaders are following their commander's intent, conducting something close to what has been rehearsed in his presence, announcing their decisions with color-coded rags that he can see, and watching (or listening) for him to veto any such decision. Further, they are keeping their schemes of maneuver simple to avoid accidental shootings. More control than that is hard to achieve in the city, even when the squads are slowed to a more traditional pace.

Security/consolidation must be continuous for the urban attacker, because of the ongoing threat of bypassed defenders or infiltrators. The reserve squad provides rear and flank security for the platoon. Cover parties and cover teams perform the same role for squads and fire teams respectively.

## WHAT PERMITS THIS ATTACK TO SUCCEED

The attack succeeds because it occurs quicker than expected. For momentum, there must be surprise; and for surprise, there must be stealth, speed, or deception.

Stealth has been achieved by limiting rifle fire and disallowing *shouting*. Objects in window openings have become the signals between buildings, and poundings on walls the signals between rooms.

Speed has been achieved by running plays that have been prerehearsed and slightly modified to mesh with the situation, and by announcing these plays through signals instead of formal orders or meetings.

Deception has been achieved by making various diversion options available within the same technique. The leeway to choose this option is part of what makes the attack unpredictable.

Still, no attack succeeds without fully prepared participants. Only with *concerted training* in peacetime, can infantrymen attack effectively through urban terrain in wartime. For the most risky of all offensive missions, only partially trained personnel have little chance.

# 25 Getting Ready to Meet the Test

- How can a small unit keep its tactics current with the threat?
- How can it learn the most about tactics and still have fun doing it?
- How can training be accomplished while waiting for another event?

(Source: FM 22-100 (1983), p. 217)

### IN SMALL-UNIT COMBAT, THERE'S NO SUBSTITUTE FOR TACTICAL TRAINING AND EXPERIENCE

At the *platoon* level, most nations have adequate weaponry, leadership, and personnel-assignment procedures to be victorious. It's the side with better *individual* and *small-unit* tactical training that wins more one-on-one and small-unit encounters and can therefore succeed at minimal cost. In Vietnam, the average enemy soldier was far better trained than his U.S. counterpart:

The typical North Vietnamese regular fighting in the South was twenty-three years old — four years older than his U.S. counterpart. . . . [H]e had already logged three years of compulsory service, undergoing military training and also instructing local militia.[1]

U.S. infantrymen in Vietnam did not set a precedent in this regard. After every war this century, returning Americans have talked about being thrown into combat with only minimal *tactical* training.

In peacetime, just as a society sometimes resists having a strong standing army, so too does an infantry leader resist having self-reliant subordinates. Of course, for both, there is a price to be paid later for their shortsightedness. To survive small-unit encounters with the enemy, subordinates need state-of-the-art training and the authority to do the unexpected:

Those who face the unprepared with preparation are victorious.[2]
— Sun Tzu

## KNOW YOURSELF, KNOW YOUR MEN, KNOW YOUR JOB

"Know yourself, know your men, know your job" was popularized during World War II as an abbreviated version of the eleven Leadership Principles. Its threefold message says it all. However, accomplishing these short tasks can be much harder than one might think. Perhaps the hardest is *to know oneself.* That takes keeping pride in perspective — pride in one's organization, in one's unit, and in oneself. Too much pride, after all, can cause a person to discount what might be learned from others. If he were really serious about minimizing his mistakes in combat, he would readily acknowledge his shortcomings and then try to do something about them. Any shortfall in knowledge, for whatever reason, carries with it a price tag in war:

If ignorant both of your enemy and of yourself, you are sure to be defeated in every battle.[3]
— Sun Tzu

For a leader *to know his men,* he must do more than just understand their personal problems and their human natures — he must recognize their tactical potential:

If I know that the enemy is vulnerable to attack, but do not know that my troops are incapable of striking him, my chance of victory is but half.[4]
— Sun Tzu

For a "grunt" *to know his job,* he must stay informed of advances in small-unit infantry tactics. As the weapons arrayed against him change, so must his tactics.

## ONE'S PERSONAL QUEST FOR TACTICAL KNOWLEDGE

Every professional infantryman possesses considerable tactical knowledge. He has studied the manuals, and he has been to the field to apply what's in the manuals. In fact, he's extremely knowledgeable on everything he has personally read, heard, or experienced.

Why, then, could most U.S. infantrymen benefit from more learning? The answer is simple — their *small-unit* tactics manuals are *not comprehensive.* Manuals like FM 7-8, FMFM 6-4, and FMFM 6-5 address, for the most part, just one style of warfare; and they contain techniques that work best under unique circumstances. However, there are two opposing styles of warfare, and every tactical situation is different. Most U.S. infantrymen have expertise in a series of *singular* ways to react to a *limited* collection of *unique* situations. The overall body of tactical knowledge is much larger than that.

As professional infantrymen rise through the ranks, their learning priorities change. They must now come to grips with the multifaceted chore of operating larger units. After all, it takes different types of knowledge to run different sizes of organizations. For example, knowing how to operate a fire team certainly doesn't qualify a person to run a battalion. What some have been slow to realize is that the converse is also true. Higher rank does not automatically infer a higher level of *overall* tactical knowledge. Personnel are promoted for many reasons, of which tactical knowledge is just one. Nor, does more time in service automatically infer more tactical knowledge. Experience is a good teacher, but not everyone is looking for additional answers. In fact, mistaking one's expertise in a few areas for comprehensive knowledge could be a considerable handicap. Suffice it to say that no one knows as much as they could about small-unit tactics. There are ways to correct this deficiency, but all require a little humility and a sincere hunger for more knowledge.

Tactical knowledge is an elusive goal. The closer one gets to it, the farther away it seems. With more knowledge also comes the uncomfortable realization of what one doesn't know. Yet, in this apparent paradox, lies the key. When men's lives are at stake, who solves any particular problem does not matter. When a leader freely admits what he doesn't know, he gives knowledgeable subordinates the chance to propose solutions. In combat, humility and an open mind are as important as knowledge. Not only will each combat situation be unique, but it will not fully reveal itself until the battle is well underway, and then it will change. Acquiring tactical knowledge involves *studying the questions,* as well as the answers. Only by identifying other combinations of circumstances, can one discover new ways to handle them.

When a leader doesn't have time to seek the advice of his subordinates in an emergency, he must rely on his own tactical knowledge. Still, ordinarily, whatever course of action he can dream up alone will be *less* feasible than one his subordinates can arrive at collectively — particularly when those subordinates are well trained and allowed to exercise initiative. To orchestrate a successful group effort, the leader must fully appreciate what his subordinates can contribute.

## UNLESS A LEADER HAS STUDIED THE BASICS, HIS TACTICAL DECISIONS MAY NOT WORK

To expand one's understanding of infantry tactics, one must study the "basics." Knowledge of the basics is like the foundation of a house — without it, everything else is an illusion. For infantrymen, the basics are "shoot," "move," and "communicate." Volumes could be written on each. To study these basics, one must identify some activity generally considered to be common knowledge, separate it into its major components, subdivide one component into its respective parts, and then try to learn something new about just one part. As what is common knowledge changes, important elements of the basics get lost. Throughout history, military leaders have said, "Study the basics":

> Lesson No. 1: From Fuller. To anticipate strategy, imagine. Lesson No. 2: Men, not weapons, will shape the future, so stick with fundamentals.[5]
>
> — S.L.A. Marshall

The basics are the foundation for every tactical decision. Without a firm grasp on the basics, and the intermediate knowledge they support, one can arrive logically at a tactical decision that *will not work*.

## GETTING THE MOST OUT OF THE MANUALS AND FORMAL SCHOOLS

Manuals and formal schools are easily accessible avenues of learning. They provide instruction on both doctrine and technique. Students must learn to differentiate one from the other, and to identify which circumstances each technique has been designed to handle.

*Doctrine* is an organization's tactical rules; it exists only in writing. A short edict like "The rifleman must . . ." or "A platoon is only authorized to . . ." usually precedes doctrine. What the manuals and student outlines contain is mostly *technique* — ways to handle specific situations. When an instructor says, "This is the only way to do something," he must be able to produce a quote to that effect from a manual. If he can't, his procedure is probably valid, but only under certain circumstances.

## HISTORICAL LITERATURE CONTAINS KNOWLEDGE OF CONTEMPORARY VALUE

Reading about past wars is an excellent way to prepare for the next war. After all, much of what goes on in combat hasn't changed for hundreds of years. Most informative are the narratives describing well-laid plans that went awry, and why. Regrettably, most books only detail the exploits of large units, and not the day-to-day actions of squads, fire teams, and individuals. Still, there are no new tactical ideas; some have just never been recorded. Many apply equally well to any size of unit. When one finds an idea he likes, he should test its applicability to his size of unit. Some historical advice actually gains relevance as time and weapons technology advance:

> [G]o back to the tactics of the French and Indian days. This is not meant facetiously. Study their tactics and fit in our modern weapons, and you have a solution. I refer to the tactics . . . of the days of ROGERS' RANGERS.[6]
>
> — Archibald Vandegrift

## THE POWER OF THE SPOKEN WORD

Much of what is known about individual and small-unit tactics has never been written down. To discover it, one must *talk to others*. About how to deal with any particular circumstance, one can learn just as much from a junior enlistee who has just experienced that circumstance, as from a seasoned veteran. What these experienced personnel collectively have to say, comprises much of the detail of execution for small-unit tactics. At first, the narrator may talk about which tactic worked. He may leave out, or not be aware of, the unique circumstances that facilitated it. If these circumstances were unusual, the technique might not work again for quite some time. Heroes will sometimes talk about how they won their medals. However, it can be risky to assume that their actions would have tactical value under ordinary circumstances. Desperate actions are sometimes required to salvage poorly conceived operations. Heroic actions often violate common sense. Real tactical insight can only be derived from the consensus opinions of many people. One must listen to their tactical advice, and then identify trends in what they say. These trends are the building blocks for valid techniques.

## BY BECOMING A TACTICS INSTRUCTOR, ONE CAN LEARN FROM HIS STUDENTS

Career infantrymen can enhance their overall tactical knowledge by becoming formal-school instructors. It's hard to tell others how to do things without first learning how to do them oneself. If an instructor is permitted to teach the same topic long enough, he can learn much of what there is to know about that topic from his students. If he is willing to ask those students for their *consensus* opinions, he can discover information about his topic that the manuals don't address.

The reliability of any particular consensus opinion will depend on the number of students participating and their collective level of experience. It will also depend on how well the instructor explains the situation and composes his question. He should cover the situation in detail, propose two ways to solve it, and ask for a show of hands.

## EXPERIMENTATION IS A GOOD TEACHER BECAUSE ONLY WHAT WORKS IS RETAINED

Research can be misinterpreted, and what one hears can be taken out of context; but what one learns through experimentation in the field is seldom wrong, particularly when its value has been quantified through consensus opinion or casualty assessment procedure.

One must duplicate as realistically as possible an interesting combat situation, and then challenge subordinates to come up with a technique to solve it. The subordinates can start with their principal options, and then gradually refine what works best. Each new attempt must be compared to the last from the standpoint of casualties incurred, because success at too high a cost is not success at all. Multiple Integrated Laser Engagement System (MILES) gear can greatly facilitate this process of casualty assessment.

## THE IMPACT ON LEARNING OF A ZERO-DEFECT MENTALITY

During field exercises, infantrymen must be allowed to make mistakes. Ordinarily, an adult can only assimilate new information that fits snugly into his existing frame of reference. A mistake permanently alters that frame of reference. For this reason, a mistake creates a valuable opportunity for learning. Most adults try not to make the same mistake twice.

For new infantrymen, errors committed in training equate to the same errors avoided in combat. However, these mistakes in training have no value unless they are immediately recognized as such. A unit leader can only see the major errors; he must rely on his subordinates to tell him about the minor ones. In training, that leader must create an environment in which his subordinates can admit to mistakes without fear of penalty. Only then, will *all* of their errors become catalysts for learning. If subordinates are afraid to "screw up," they will still make mistakes, but they will hide those mistakes from their leader. The leader won't discover the deficiencies until they are repeated in combat. Infantrymen who don't make mistakes are either perfect or not doing anything. Either way, they are not learning. The zero-defect mentality that is so easy to adopt in peacetime actually stifles improvement, and ultimately excellence. It may bolster unit prestige over the short term, but at what price later?

## AN INVENTORY TEST TO REASSESS TACTICAL KNOWLEDGE

To gauge how viewpoints on tactics change over time, one can employ an inventory test. Appendix A contains such a test. E-5 sergeants formally trained in maneuver warfare have scored in the high 90's on this test. A score of 80 or higher may be necessary to handle an enemy skilled in maneuver warfare at the small-unit level.

Readers may now want to retake this inventory test to see if any of their viewpoints have changed since starting the book.

## HELP SUBORDINATES TO MASTER THEIR JOBS, FOR THEY ARE THE ONES WHO WILL WIN OR LOSE THE BATTLE

It's what each rifleman does or fails to do, that will determine whether or not his unit can successfully cross "the last hundred yards" in combat. For the unit to prevail against a skilled enemy, each rifleman, fire team leader, and squad leader must know his job well. That's why the priority must go to individual training at the lowest echelons of the organization. When a unit lacks well-trained members, much of its apparent capability is an illusion. Subordinates at every level *(including privates)* will need help in two separate areas: alternative tactical techniques and *tactical decision making*. As these two areas of knowledge are distinct, they are *learned differently*. Where there are different ways of learning, there must also be different ways of training.

To acquire alternative tactical techniques, infantrymen must discover which circumstances to expect in combat and then use research and experimentation to solve those circumstances. To acquire tactical-decision-making ability, infantrymen must learn how to modify and combine those tactical techniques to solve unique combat situations. They can't be told how to do this, they must learn it through experience — through trial and error under battlefield conditions.

## HELPING SUBORDINATES TO ACQUIRE ALTERNATIVE TACTICAL TECHNIQUES

Invariably, a unit leader (or instructor) does not fully understand the job of each subordinate (or student). Yet, he has at his disposal countless experts, past and present, American and otherwise. His role is to conduct research and to present increasingly comprehensive information to his students in a way they can *accept, retain, and apply*.

Civilian cognitive research shows that convincing an adult to change his mind on an erroneous belief requires great effort and building upon the prior knowledge that led to that belief in the first place.[7] Apparently, what adults personally experience becomes hopelessly intertwined with what others have told them. Of course, in the retelling, even good ideas become abbreviated, stripped of their original intent, and detached from the circumstances that originally made them valid. In other words, what one understands or remembers may be only partially true. To teach tactics, an instructor must freely acknowledge the following: (1) his own tactical beliefs will not work under every circumstance; (2) individually, his students will possess valuable tactical experience; and (3) collectively, his students will have more common sense than he has.

Even with the proper frame of mind, the instructor has his work cut out for him, because students learn in different ways. Fortunately, there is an easy solution to this problem. The instructor can *teach the same concepts and over in a variety of ways.* Of all the ways, lecturing is probably the weakest. To pass the final exam for a lecture, students must simply memorize parts of the student outline. Showing generally works better than telling — hence the expression "A picture is worth a thousand words." Showing also tests the validity of what is being taught. If a tactical technique does not fare well in practice, it is probably in need of modification.

An instructor can verify a tactical technique at the same time he improves his "learning curve." He can do so by presenting the technique from several different perspectives: (1) having the students read about it before class; (2) using a historical example of it for an attention gainer; (3) stressing it during the lecture; (4) showcasing it during classroom demonstrations (on blackboard, overhead projector, sand table with miniature soldiers, and TACWAR board with unit designators); (5) letting students wargame it in the classroom; (6) analyzing it during the critique for a classroom practical-application test; (7) demonstrating it in the field; (8) talking about it during a field practical-application-test critique; (9) reviewing it while going over a written final exam; (10) making students incorporate it into written five-paragraph orders; (11) discussing it while critiquing those five-paragraph orders; (12) requiring students to prepare formal periods of instruction on it; and (13) insisting that students who don't understand it talk to those who do. That's a sufficiently wide assortment of teaching methods to reach every learning style. Tactics instructors must sometimes resort to *all* of these methods just to plant the seed of a *slight* variation to a standard procedure. Many students will not accept or retain a new technique without getting the opportunity to attempt it *on their own volition* in the field.

The instructor can create this opportunity by planning a *free-play* exercise during which the students are required to solve the exact situation for which the technique was designed. The students *should not be required* to perform the technique itself, only to solve the situation. There are good reasons for this roundabout approach to training: (1) it reminds everyone that the procedure is technique and nothing more, (2) it promotes retention of what is learned, and (3) it provides valuable feedback to the instructor. Once the students realize they need the technique to solve the situation, they will remember both. If they give the technique an honest try and fail, the instructor will still have valuable input on how to improve the procedure. To arrive at the *least costly* solution to a situation, the instructor must be allowed to modify his technique.

When one teaches (or leads) in this way, he moves inexorably toward the best solution to any given situation. He cares not whether the solution comes from peers, predecessors, or former enemies. Organizational knowledge grows in the process. The pioneers of the Western version of maneuver warfare proved that during World War I:

The same decentralization of authority that had permitted the development of stormtroop tactics in the first place also played an important role in its dissemination.... The freedom... resulted in the troops receiving training with a wide variety of emphases.[8]

## HELPING SUBORDINATES TO ACQUIRE ADDITIONAL DECISION-MAKING ABILITY

Too many non-infantry assignments or too much practice at blindly following orders may diminish a subordinate's ability to make tactical decisions. For him to perform maneuver warfare, this ability must be regenerated. Before each small-unit leader can exercise initiative, he must decide what to do. And, before each private can survive, he must outwit his immediate adversary. *Both* need practice at tactical decision making.

The unit leader (or instructor) should encourage his subordinates (or students) to experiment with a few of their own ideas in the field, even at the risk of making mistakes. If a student makes a mistake, the instructor should call it to his attention immediately, but not as an unpleasant reprimand. Otherwise, with the best of intentions, that instructor may be undermining his student's chances to learn and ultimately to survive in combat. While reprimand has its place, it can also discourage the voluntary disclosure of mistakes.

The instructor should periodically take his students to a specific location in the field, describe to them a combat situation, and then ask them to discuss a tactical solution. Or, he can stay in the classroom and, after *describing in detail the microterrain* on a large-scale map, ask his students to solve a "tactical-decision brief." Of course, before comparing answers, the students should solve each situation alone. Their tactical solutions can be presented verbally or in written five-paragraph-order format. But, for these solutions to have much value, the students must be able to picture the terrain down to the last bush and mound. Without knowledge of the microterrain, the students would be arriving at solutions to incomplete questions. That's about as useful as arriving at "4," without being asked what's "3 + 1."

Of course, for the most realistic practice in tactical decision making, there's no substitute for free play. During true free play, the students make all tactical decisions without interference. Their only guidelines are those to counteract cheating and overly aggressive behavior. Because the students now have a wily adversary, they put more thought into each decision. Because each decision must be executed, they incorporate techniques. During free play, the worth of each tactical decision can be measured through the outcome of an actual engagement. To determine this outcome, opposing forces can meet to agree on who "won," "lost," or "tied," or to compare numbers of hits from MILES (weak-laser) or paint guns.

(Source: FM 22-100 (1983), p. 177)

The unit trainer must *not* require his students to use any particular technique during free play. He can only require that the situation for which the technique was designed, be solved *at least twice*. For example, if he is interested in a night attack technique, he can require each side to attack the other's base camp twice during the hours of darkness. Each team will use its own method for the first attempt. But, if that method results in too many casualties, the trainer's method may be deemed the only way to catch up in the point standings during the final attempt. If the trainer's method works, every student involved on offense or defense will retain it for the rest of his career. If the method doesn't work, the trainer can see how to fix it. Free play is not a revolutionary idea; generations of Marine leaders have promoted it. Here's Col. Edson's advice after Guadalcanal:

> If I had to train my regiment over again, I would stress small-group training and the training of the individual....
> Our basic training is all right.... In your training put your time and emphasis on the squad and platoon rather than on the company, battalion and regiment.
> In your scouting and patrolling,... have the men work against each other. Same thing for squads and platoons in their problems....

> ... With proper training, our Americans are better [than the Japanese], as our people can think better as individuals. Encourage your individuals and bring them out.[9]
> — Col. Merritt A. Edson

As a side benefit, free play eliminates the boredom and discomfort normally associated with field infantry training. The participants aren't bored, because they're matching wits with each other. They aren't uncomfortable, because they're having too much fun to notice the dampness and insects. Appendix B has guidelines (which took years to perfect) for a platoon-sized "two-day war."

## ENLISTED SUBORDINATES MUST BE ALLOWED TO TRAIN THEIR OWN TROOPS

The combat readiness of any unit largely depends on the training status of its subunits and individuals. How prepared for war is a squad with expertise in standard patrolling procedure, but without trained point men?

It does little good to have squad members skilled in the basics, when their squad leader has yet to hear about "post-machinegun" tactics. If every squad leader were required to train his own squad, he and his subordinates could at least generate the missing knowledge together.

As long as the leader is told that there is much he doesn't know and shown how to conduct research and experimentation, he can learn as much from his men, as they can from him. This interaction can help him better *to know himself, his men, and his job* — it can help him to lead.

## FIRST PRIORITY IS "INDIVIDUAL TRAINING"

Individual training forms the foundation for all unit training. Its importance cannot be underestimated:

> Troops must receive a high degree of individual training.... Individuals must have thorough practice in throwing hand grenades in woods.[10]
> — Lessons Learned from
> *Fighting on Guadalcanal*

Before productive individual training can take place, training deficiencies must be identified through performance tests. For the members of an infantry squad, the tests should stress the basics. Under "how to move," a squad leader may want to find out which of his personnel can crawl 100 yards without making noise or getting tired, use all available cover while moving into enemy fire, and stalk an adversary. Under "how to shoot," he may want to discover who can throw a grenade 20 yards from the prone position, call and adjust mortars, and shoot holes in a human-silhouette target while running towards it.

Only those who cannot pass the performance test on any given activity, must be trained in that activity. This will save time and effort. Weapons training should be conducted in the following sequence: *explain, demonstrate, imitate, practice, test.* Tactical training should be conducted by trial and error in the field. How many casualties are assessed will establish which technique works best for each situation. If MILES gear is not available, consensus opinions will suffice. Even privates know when they would have become casualties, and privates aren't thoroughly indoctrinated in established procedure. In other words, they are more receptive to alternative techniques. They must be given the opportunity to direct their common sense toward the formulation of those techniques. After all, a private must make an instant tactical decision every time he confronts an opposition soldier on the battlefield. In combat, that private's survival will depend on his self-reliance.

After training comes retesting. For those who failed to learn, the training must be repeated. For those who still can't learn, reassignment may be necessary. Small-unit leaders must keep unofficial training records on their men; these leaders are the ones who are ultimately responsible for having the personnel assets to accomplish the mission.

Through individual training comes self-discipline, and through self-discipline comes the control necessary to conduct maneuver warfare:

> It is no less important to educate the soldier to think and act for himself. His self-reliance and sense of honor will then induce him to do his duty even when he is no longer under the eye of his commanding officer.[11]
> —German Fld.Serv.Regs.[1908]

## THEN, "UNIT TRAINING" MUST BE CONDUCTED FROM THE BOTTOM UP

Most U.S. infantry companies spend an inordinate amount of field time moving around en masse. Their subunits are expected to learn their roles in the process. With individual training under control, an infantry company has the opportunity to conduct "unit training" in a more productive manner — *from the bottom up.* To build on the foundation of individual expertise, the company logically trains progressively larger subunits: first the two-man teams, next the fire teams, then the squads, etc. Finally, the company as a whole can operate at full potential. At each echelon, the familiar training axiom — "Test first, train only those who need it, and then test again" — is followed.

First, riflemen pair up with their buddies to operate as two-man teams. They are shown a few techniques and asked to tailor those techniques to various circumstances. Possibilities are "how to fire and move," "how to operate a sentry post," "how to establish a two-man defensive position," "how to search a room," and "how to walk point." Every two-man team won't have what it takes to walk point. Only those having the natural ability should be trained, and then their training records so annotated.

Next, comes fire team training. The fire teams might work on capabilities like how to counterambush, how to shadow a decoy patrol, and how to clear the floor of a building. Then, the squads might investigate how to ambush, how to move up one side of a street, and how to breach enemy lines at night. The subunit leaders at each echelon are permitted to develop their own techniques. The leader of the next higher echelon provides only the situation for which the technique is required. This delegation of authority is the key to developing an infantry unit that can hold its own anywhere in the world.

*At each level, leaders/trainers must see themselves as learning facilitators instead of duty experts or enforcers of tactical doctrine.* To promote learning, each must enjoy researching his topic, experimenting in the field, and listening to his subordinates/students. *As a group,* subordinates must have a voice in how their techniques evolve. Otherwise, the techniques may neither obey common sense nor keep pace with the threat. Here's how German stormtroopers of World War I trained to penetrate Allied lines:

> The training programs of the [German] Assault Battalions were quite different.... Close

order drill . . . was largely, though not entirely, dispensed with. Its place was taken by exercises that cultivated rather than suppressed the initiative of the men. Half of each training day was usually devoted to sports. . . . [T]hese included obstacle courses and grenade-throwing contests.

The other half of the day was spent in the practice of various battle drills — crossing "no man's land," breaching barbed-wire obstacles, clearing trenches, cooperating with flame-throwers, following closely behind a barrage, and the like were all practiced. These battle drills were often supplemented by live-fire exercises.[12]

Leaders/trainers must resist the temptation to dictate tactical technique to their subordinates/students. They should offer organizational and historical methods only to stimulate further research and experimentation. They should limit their guidance to which situations must be solved and how much coordination (with other units) must be maintained. For example, a company commander might ask his gunnery sergeant to produce a company that can attack frontally up two parallel city streets, while clearing the buildings as it goes and moving faster than the enemy thinks possible. After this broad guidance had filtered down the enlisted "chain of command," fire team leaders might be told to start with what's in the manuals and then work on stealth, speed, and deception to develop three ways to clear a rectangular room. Not every fire team would come up with the same method. During building clearing, generally only one fire team assaults, so what would it matter? Slightly different methods would still work, and the fire teams might learn something from watching each other. Fire team leaders are group-oriented people. When allowed to develop optimal solutions, they will quickly adopt the most efficient methods of their peers. What results is technique that is not only outstanding, but also fairly uniform. Control is *not* sacrificed — the method does not matter as long as the leader of the next higher echelon knows what it is. Teamwork and cohesion are enhanced. These benefits are realized, because the unit training is generated *from the bottom up,* instead of from the top down. Many great leaders have realized instinctively that this is the way to train:

> Never tell people how to do things. Tell them what to do and they will surprise you with their ingenuity.[13]
> — Patton

## PUBLISHED TRAINING STANDARDS AND LEARNING OBJECTIVES ARE ONLY *MINIMUMS*

Leaders/trainers at every level must realize that published training standards and learning objectives are only what their military organization deems *minimally* essential to accomplish various tasks under ideal conditions. The list of tasks is not entirely comprehensive (there are other important infantry skills). For some tasks, the published standards/objectives don't even constitute an all-inclusive list of the steps required to accomplish that task. Common-sense and transition steps are often left out (possibly because they were originally considered to be tacitly understood). In other words, a task attempted in strict compliance with a manual or list of training standards can sometimes fail. Trainers should be encouraged to add as many common-sense and transition steps as deemed necessary. That is how the U.S. Marine Corps Instructional Management School teaches lesson writers to compose their lists of learning objectives — it encourages those writers to add common-sense steps to published Individual Training Standards.[14]

Similarly, leaders/trainers at every level must remember that established tactical procedures may represent predominantly one style of warfare and work best under specific circumstances (which may not be entirely clear). In short, the established procedures may not include all the common-sense ways to win at minimal cost. Just because squads measure up to published minimums, this does not guarantee that they will do well in battle. That's why small units must gain, through research and experimentation, knowledge on what may be missing from the various published lists of training standards and learning objectives.

## RIFLEMEN MUST HAVE A VOICE IN HOW THEY ARE TRAINED

With increased rank comes less time to ponder the challenges at the fire team level. As a group, privates and lance corporals possess considerable insight into how to keep from getting killed in combat. Their collective opinions may not only provide clues on how to keep them alive, but also on how to modify dated or inappropriate techniques. After every battle in Southeast Asia, North Vietnamese field commanders encouraged their junior enlisted personnel — during *Kiem thao* sessions — *publicly to criticize* the tactics used.[15]

## SOME SAY THERE'S NO TIME TO TRAIN

To conduct maneuver warfare, infantry organizations must have skilled personnel and small units. Much of the control for maneuver warfare comes from how well these elements are trained before entering the war zone. Lack of time and money are excuses normally given for shortfalls in U.S. infantry training. Yet, there is overwhelming evidence to suggest that maneuver warfare can reduce overall casualty levels. So what those who use the standard excuses are really saying is that they don't have the time or the money to minimize casualties.

Large headquarters could ease the competition for training man-days by conducting their field exercises *without troops*. Headquarters staff members could levy fewer requirements that interrupt field evolutions. But, whatever the staff does, there's no excuse for not training. If there isn't enough time on the training schedule, units must train while waiting for transportation or other events. Practical-application testing can be broken down into 20-minute increments and conducted on short notice. Because not everyone will need instruction on the same skills, the training sessions can be accomplished concurrently. The best format is the 20-minute "battle drill."

The battle drill has long been valued as a way to conduct individual and small-unit training. It consists of an attention gainer, a short lecture, a demonstration, a period of practical application (with everyone participating), and practical-application testing (again with all participating). The demonstration can be as simple as drawing a picture on a blackboard, the practical application as easy as replicating that picture on a piece of paper, and the testing as painless as evaluating the drawings.

Much of the unit training should be accomplished *after dark* — after normal working hours when the training schedule no longer applies. Most infantrymen won't object to working twenty-four hours a day — Monday through Thursday — as long as they are inspected on Friday morning and get the rest of the weekend off. Moreover, most commanders would be thrilled to have one of their squad leaders ask to conduct extra training in the field after hours. He must only provide blank ammunition, emergency vehicle, and corpsman. The unit that had already reserved the best training area wouldn't object to a small unit "piggybacking" in one corner, and it might welcome some aggressor support.

## TRAINING DOESN'T STOP IN A WAR ZONE

When a unit deploys, it cannot stop training. No unit is ever entirely ready for battle. It may be ready to defeat the enemy, but not ready to do so at minimal cost. The latter requires continual training, if for no other reason than to compensate for the normal turnover of personnel. Here's how hard the Japanese trained in Manchuria during their war with the Russians in 1939:

> [T]he *new conscripts* of the 7th [Japanese] Division underwent their advanced infantry training on the dusty plains near Tsitsihar [in Manchuria].... Most of the riflemen were just completing their first year of company training, a year that contained *thirty-eight weeks of night combat instruction*.... The men studied night attacks in various echelons, obstacle clearing, concealment, noise prevention, orientation at night, patrolling, and security [italics added throughout].[16]
> — Leavenworth Papers No. 2

In closely fought wars, ultimate victory belongs to the side that learns the most from its battlefield experiences. Did not Rommel attribute his early successes in North Africa to exactly that? Ideas generated from the bottom up, such as those from NVA *Kiem thao* sessions, could make a significant tactical difference against a powerful adversary.

## TEAMWORK IS STILL THE KEY TO SUCCESS

In small-unit combat, as in sports, teamwork can sometimes make up for individual-training deficiencies. A unit's cohesion establishes its will to fight. To develop teamwork and cohesion, an infantry organization depends on its NCO's. Those NCO's can best make that contribution when allowed to plan/conduct training, to determine personnel assignments, to lead, and to participate in tactical decisions. (For the contribution that a senior NCO can make to his unit, see appendix D.)

## SMALL UNITS MUST REHEARSE MORE THAN ONE TECHNIQUE FOR EACH RECURRING SITUATION

In the final analysis, it is how well fire teams and squads are trained that establishes to what extent an infantry organization can practice maneuver warfare. It will often take small units to force open the gaps through which follow-on forces can pass. But to perform this vital role without becoming predictable, small units need *several* rehearsed attack techniques for each category of situation.

Rehearsed techniques are as vital to infantry squads on the battlefield as rehearsed plays are to football teams on the gridiron — there's little momentum without them. In combat, as in football, the techniques need not be run precisely as rehearsed. Modifications can be "audibilized" by the leader as the situation unfolds. Still, it's the unit members' familiarity with the original technique that ensures enough teamwork to execute the modification.

These techniques need not be limited to one style of warfare. Traditional methods may be appropriate for some situations and maneuver warfare methods for others. Many techniques may take their inspiration from both styles of warfare. Penetrating a surface by force from close range requires a somewhat methodical procedure; whereas getting that close without being discovered, requires maneuver.

## ULTIMATELY, SURVIVAL IN COMBAT DEPENDS ON ALERTNESS AND FLEXIBILITY

Small-unit infantrymen must learn all they can now, but can't stop learning every time a firefight breaks out.

Techniques from the NCO Corps

No amount of knowledge will allow them to win, if they aren't alert to an ever changing situation, and willing to modify their plans accordingly. Just as an expert marksman can fall victim to a man-eating tiger, so too can a knowledgeable infantryman lose in war. Only by readily adapting to his adversary's countermoves, can either win.

Individuals and small units must strive to focus on the enemy. Their survivability depends on it. Leaders must rely heavily on common sense during tactical decision making, and must *allow subordinates of all ranks to do likewise:*

> Thus, one able to win victory by modifying his tactics in accordance with the enemy situation may be said to be divine.[17]
> — Sun Tzu

(Source: FM 7-8 (1984), pp. B-1, I-9)

348

# 26 What All of This May Mean to the Big Picture

- *To practice maneuver warfare, what capabilities must squads have?*
- *Why haven't U.S. squads reached this level of tactical proficiency?*
- *How must training management change?*

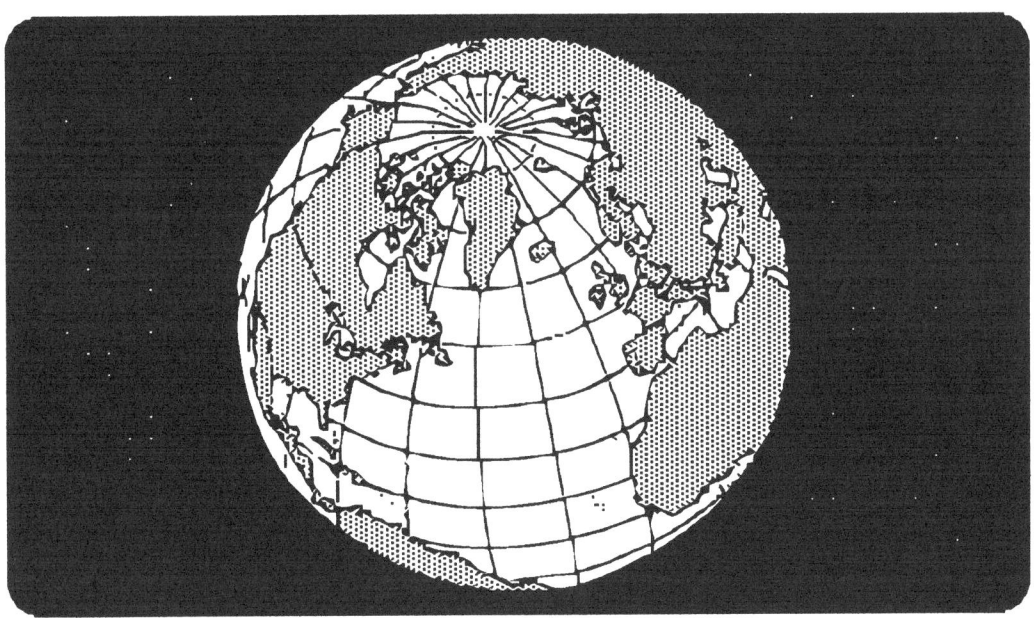

(Source: FMFM 0-1 (1979), p. 4-63)

### THE WORLD HAS LONG KNOWN HOW TO MINIMIZE BATTLEFIELD LOSSES THROUGH MANEUVER WARFARE

The tactical precepts with which to win battles at minimal cost have been published since *350 B.C.* The Western world has known how to apply these precepts to modern warfare at the small-unit level since the German Spring Offensive of *1918* — when every German infantry squad could operate independently on both offense and defense against a much larger opponent. Yet, to this day, *most* U.S. infantry squads are trained only in attrition warfare. They've been shown how to follow orders, shoot their weapons, and little else. They're still considered subunits to be closely controlled for greater fire power.

At the squad level, assaulting a powerful adversary from the front with guns blazing, violates the most basic of survival instincts. *Safely* attacking that adversary takes closing with him through patience and stealth, and then assaulting him from the blind side with deception and speed. *Safely* defending against him takes surprising him, and then counterattacking before he can regain his balance. And, *safely* finishing him off takes pursuing him until he loses interest in the fight. One wonders why U.S. squads have yet to learn how to operate this way in war.

Throughout history, U.S. military leaders — e.g., Washington, Lee, Jackson, MacArthur, Patton, Puller, Vandegrift, Gray, and Schwarzkopf — have preached using common sense on the battlefield. Shouldn't their advice also apply to what happens at the squad level?

## TAKING THE NEXT STEP TOWARD MANEUVER WARFARE

In the Gulf War, U.S. "task forces" skirted enemy strongpoints to demoralize an entire army. In narrower confines, it takes well-trained "small units" to bypass and collapse a larger opponent. *To fully embrace maneuver warfare,* U.S. forces must adopt common-sense tactics *at the small-unit level.* For each situational category, U.S. squads should have several common-sense techniques. Those in this book have come from the current generation of Marine SNCO's and NCO's. This is significant, because to practice common sense at the squad level, the squad leaders should agree on what constitutes common sense.

Of course, a much larger body of knowledge exists in the collective expertise of all the infantry NCO's worldwide. However, much of what their predecessors knew, may have already been lost. Of course, this knowledge is not permanently lost. It can be regenerated by simply encouraging small units to conduct historical research and to experiment with alternative methods. Through "free play," units can easily determine under which circumstances these methods will work.

## FOR AN ARMY TO USE MANEUVER WARFARE UNDER EVERY CIRCUMSTANCE, WHAT MUST ITS RIFLE SQUADS BE ABLE TO DO?

A small unit can more easily surprise and elude a powerful adversary. For this reason, it takes well-trained small units to conduct maneuver warfare under a wide variety of circumstances:

> Those who discern when to use many or few troops are victorious.[1]
> — Sun Tzu

A small unit can more easily force open a gap in enemy lines, because the large unit has trouble getting close enough to try. A small unit can also more easily ambush an enemy force, because the large unit has difficulty concealing itself and getting away. Of course, when units of lesser size can accomplish the same missions, fewer lives are jeopardized. In short, modern military organizations need infantry squads capable of operating as independent maneuver elements. Bill Lind makes this clear:

> Although combat experience should indicate otherwise, the rifle squad currently occupies a relatively minor place in . . . [U.S.] tactical thought. Squad level training and doctrine seem to suggest that the squad has little independent tactical value. The squad has been relegated to the role of subunit whose movements are closely controlled by the platoon commander. Considered in terms of maneuver warfare, this attitude is disastrous . . . (maneuver warfare demands that the squad assume a primary tactical role).[2]
> — Bill Lind

To operate independently, a squad must be capable of single-handedly tackling a more powerful opponent. Among other things, it must be able to do the following:

1. *Seek out and disrupt a large enemy force about to attack its parent unit.*

2. *Handle an adversary of greater size during a chance encounter.*

3. *Extricate itself from an ambush.*

4. *Ambush an enemy force of any size.*

5. *Perform short-range infiltration (penetrate enemy lines by stealth).*

6. *Single-handedly force open a gap in enemy lines at night.*

7. *As a last resort, single-handedly force open such a gap in the daytime.*

8. *Without support, defend against infiltration, tank, and NBC attacks.*

9. *Defend a one-block frontage of urban terrain from successive fallback positions.*

10. *In concert with another squad, attack along a city street (clearing the buildings as it goes) faster than an enemy thinks possible.*

This book has described in detail a few techniques with which lone infantry squads can acquire such capabilities.

## OTHER ARMIES HAVE HAD LINE INFANTRY SQUADS THAT COULD OPERATE ALONE

During WWI, each German infantry squad that participated in the Spring Offensive of 1918, could enter *by surprise* a fully manned Allied trench protected by barbed wire and machineguns. Further, it could clear any part of that trench without alerting other sectors that a ground assault was in progress. These weren't troops culturally endowed with the self-discipline and patience of the Orient; these were the relatives of U.S. immigrants.

One wonders what factors permitted the complete assimilation into the German Army of what Capt. Rohr had apparently learned from his enlisted subordinates. For the Germans, training was not standardized, and politics had little to do with promotion:

Free from all but the most general supervision and relieved, by a promotion system based on strict seniority, of the need to constantly please superiors, the German battalion or company commander was free to train his troops according to his own lights.[3]

## PERSONNEL MANAGEMENT PRACTICES AFFECT OVERALL TACTICAL EXPERTISE

A military organization's highest priority must be its *proficiency in combat*. Its personnel evaluation system should reward those who pursue this priority. What complicates the issue is that, at every echelon, tactical expertise is largely a function of flexibility to a changing threat. Furthermore, the threat and how to handle it can most easily be established *from the bottom up*. When a military organization has traditionally managed everything *from the top down,* its fitness report may be more a measure of who is the easiest to lead than of who knows what he's doing in war. In other words, its fitness report may have more indicators of personality than of tactical proficiency. This type of fitness report tempts service members to work harder on their personalities than on their warfighting skills. "Not rocking the boat" becomes their priority. Promotion becomes a function of how many people can be kept happy. Unfortunately, pushing for worthwhile change seldom makes everyone happy. In fact, it can easily be mistaken for "bucking the system." Only those who are exceptional can do it without jeopardizing their careers. What each individual has done to keep his unit's tactics *current with the threat* might make a better fitness report entry than his "military presence."

An organization's personnel assignment policies will also affect its tactical development. Some infantrymen have a better feel for tactics and teaching than others. Schools must be manned by those who have already displayed proficiency in both. Without highly qualified tactics instructors, new ideas are effectively squelched in a formal-school environment. Then, instead of producing state-of-the-art tactics, the schools can do little more than reinforce the status quo. When instructional billets are continually rotated among randomly selected novices, only so much tactical development can take place. It takes several months of teaching experience just to tell from a student's facial expressions when he doesn't understand. It takes considerably longer to research a subject thoroughly enough to discover what's not in the manuals, and then to tailor information to multiple learning styles.

## MISDIRECTED TRAINING MANAGEMENT CAN BE WORSE THAN NONE AT ALL

Tactical proficiency can only be pursued, it can never be totally achieved. It most certainly cannot be acquired by memorizing written tactical procedures or achieving minimal training standards. To become convinced that there is a "best" way of operating tactically is to become predictable and inflexible to changing situations. Conversely, to enter combat without first rehearsing procedures, is to ignore the importance of teamwork and to throw away the chance for surprise and momentum. The answer lies somewhere in between. Small units need not one, but *several* alternative techniques for each expected situation. These techniques must be developed and rehearsed at the one-man, two-man, fire team, and squad level. Then, they can be mixed and matched to fit whatever situation must be faced in combat. They can also be alternated to confuse the enemy. These methods can be drawn from historical writings, military manuals, or the collective opinions of subordinates or students. Of course, easiest to assimilate are slight variations to the methods already in the manuals. But, because the threat is ever changing, small-unit techniques must constantly evolve. Each method must be continually reevaluated and refined through experimentation in the field. To insure progress during this refinement process, a casualty assessment procedure will be necessary. Then, promising methods (and their supporting techniques) must be recorded for posterity. Otherwise, they may become lost at the expense of young Americans who must enter a future combat zone, thinking they have received the best training possible.

How much teamwork and cohesion contribute to a unit's tactical proficiency must never be underestimated. These crucial ingredients to "unit chemistry" cannot be directed from the top down; they must be generated from the bottom up. For any given unit, they will occur more often when NCO's are allowed to design and conduct the training, determine personnel assignments, and provide the majority of leadership. Of course, the NCO's potential cannot be fully realized until the bullets start flying. Then, the commander's success at "guiding his flock" toward shared goals will depend on the involvement of his NCO's. Furthermore, it's only through listening to their collective advice, that he will be able to avoid making tactical mistakes.

## WHY THE U.S. HAS NEVER PRODUCED SQUADS THAT CAN OPERATE ALONE

While it has been said that Vietnam was a squad leaders' war, one must understand in what context this was meant. It was a squad leaders' war in the sense that line infantry squads did a lot of patrolling and ambushing by themselves, and it was a squad leaders' war in the sense that one squad was the largest unit that could usually surprise an enemy force. However, it was not a squad leaders' war in the sense that squads were specially trained and then allowed to operate as an independent maneuver elements during attacks. The only small units that got special training and experience were "killer" reconnaissance and special-operations teams. Infantry squads rarely ventured more than 1000 meters from their company headquarters. They had difficulty handling chance contact and seldom ambushed a larger unit. They attacked a prepared enemy position by themselves only when there wasn't enough room for the rest of the company on the objective. Although the NCO's of that era were exceptional, much of what their squads knew about infantry tactics had to be learned the hard way. Perhaps, with specialized training, U.S. squads could have done more. Maybe, with stormtroop tactics, they could have *surprised* the defenders of more prepared enemy positions. After all, their opponents were using techniques that had originally inspired stormtroop tactics. This is all water under the bridge now. Yet, one wonders why other nations have had more success in developing squads that can operate alone. Did those nations have more training money? Did they screen their infantrymen more closely? Did they care more about minimizing casualties? Or, were they just more willing to *decentralize control?*

The privates are the ones who must ultimately close with the enemy in war. Have Americans seen so many photographs of their wartime commanders, that they have forgotten that the thin, weasel-eyed, slack-jawed, pimply, wonderful, brave, mortal privates standing behind them have been the ones rushing the machineguns? Have they failed to realize that giving these privates common-sense training and the authority to use it in an emergency, is the best way to help them to win without getting hurt? Can't they see that it is easier to win battles at minimal cost when fire teams and squads are allowed to use common sense? Succeeding on a modern battlefield takes delegating authority to develop and use common-sense tactics — it takes decentralization of control:

> The decentralization of tactical control forced on land forces has been one of the most significant features of modern war. In the confused and often chaotic environment of today, only the smallest groups are likely to keep together, particularly during critical moments.4

If individuals and small units are the key to modern war, shouldn't they also be the central focus for training? Granted, there are other considerations — e.g., political pressures, lack of funding, discipline problems, etc. But, which among them is more important than the final casualty count? Since the New York City Draft Riots of the Civil War era, Americans have had little patience with wars that produce too many casualties over too long a period. Are funds and time so limited that the rifleman, his fire team, and his squad cannot receive the type of training that will permit them both to win and to survive? Dynamic learning can do much for morale. He who sees inconsistencies in what has happened in the past, and does not try to do something about them in the present, *shares responsibility for what occurs in the future.*

## THE MANEUVER WAR THOUGHT PROCESS HAS YET TO REACH THE SQUAD LEVEL

Thanks to the integrity and foresight of the current generation of military leaders, this country again has the opportunity to adopt the small-unit tactics that will be needed on future battlefields. These are the tactics that permit units to disperse under the threat of modern weaponry, yet still to muster enough strength to defeat opposition forces. In the Gulf War, Americans saw what large maneuver elements can accomplish with common-sense tactics. It's time to find out what squad-sized maneuver elements can accomplish with those tactics. *Squads make smaller targets.*

This transition will not be easy. There are commanders who have been unable to convince their own subordinates to take this final step toward maneuver warfare. Their opposition has taken many forms. Because, for Americans, maneuver warfare is in many ways the opposite of the traditional style, many subordinates resist it out of misdirected loyalty to their heritage. Still others see decentralization of control as a threat to their traditional rank structure. Resistance at any point in the long chain of command can keep squads, fire teams, and privates from developing the self-reliance they need to survive in war.

To the consternation of those who have attempted to institute the change-over from the top down, maneuver warfare has never become widely practiced at the small-unit level in the U.S. military. If the new thought process had replaced the traditional one (if firepower had become subservient to maneuver), each infantryman would not still carry upwards of 60 pounds of ammunition into combat. Marines who understood the importance of surprise over firepower on Guadalcanal, carried very little ammunition as they searched for many times their number of highly skilled Japanese:

> The tendency is to overload the infantrymen with ammunition.... We soon found [on Guadalcanal] that 25 rounds was enough for two or three days.5
>
> — Col. Merritt A. Edson

American military men will know when the maneuver warfare thought process has finally reached the small-unit level — that will be the day small-unit leaders stop talking about fire superiority.

## OTHER WESTERN NATIONS HAVE EXPERIENCED SIMILAR PROBLEMS

Other nations have also had difficulty assimilating maneuver warfare at the small-unit level. The British unsuccessfully attempted to adopt the German system of elastic defense during WWI:

While the British [in WWI] were successful in copying the outward appearance of the German defensive system, they were unable to adopt its substance. The key to the German elastic defense was its reliance upon the initiative and good judgment of the man on the spot, whether he were a sergeant in command of a squad or a captain.... [S]uch reliance on junior commanders was an anathema to a system of command that valued, above all else, adherence to established procedure.[6]

When regulated by too many *established procedures,* it would appear that infantrymen have difficulty adapting to unique situations. The French also tried to adopt maneuver warfare during WWI, but to no avail:

The French, in particular, had a number of bright young officers who proposed tactical reforms similar to those being adopted by the Germans. While these proposals were warmly received by high-ranking officers, they got lost in the bureaucracy and had little effect on the way the French infantry actually fought.[7]

Here, it would seem that too *bureaucratic* a control structure might impede worthwhile change. Too many levels in a chain of command might tend to insulate people at the highest echelons from what people at the lowest echelons knew to be beneficial, and vice versa. In other words, intermediate-level leaders might sometimes take it upon themselves not only to "shortstop" improvements asked for from below, but also those directed from above. The longer the chain of command, the lower the probability that important information can be shared between its ends. The Italians of WWI had decentralized control enough to develop maneuver warfare tactics, but they couldn't or wouldn't disseminate what had been learned:

Decentralization alone, however, cannot explain the entire phenomenon of German successes with tactical innovation. The Italian Army of World War I, being like the German Army, a relatively recent amalgamation of the armies of subnational states, was also quite decentralized. While decentralization permitted the Italians to develop the *Arditi* [italics from original] units to such a high degree, it did not cause ordinary infantry units to change the way that they fought. The Italians thus had the means of developing new infantry tactics, but not of disseminating them.[8]

Another factor that set the German Army apart from the others was its willingness to let NCO's make tactical decisions. Perhaps to fully adopt maneuver warfare, a military organization must trust its NCO's. The French neither trusted their NCO's, nor did well in battle:

Neither the French NCO nor those company officers who had been commissioned after long service as NCO's were considered capable of the kind of independent action, that, by the end of the war, was universally expected of the German NCO's.[9]

It would seem that German NCO's, in turn, considered *privates* to be valuable tactical-decision makers:

[T]he social relations between officers, non-commissioned officers, and men . . . were the essence of stormtroop tactics.[10]

## THE WORTH OF ESTABLISHED PROCEDURE

An "established procedure" is a proven way to accomplish some activity. It usually consists of a series of steps to guide those performing that activity for the first time. Organizations create established procedures to insure smooth functioning during periods of heavy personnel turnover. Because U.S. military outfits struggle with heavy turnover even during peacetime, many of their established procedures provide a valuable service. But, others far outlive their usefulness. Military managers may often be tempted to mistake established procedures for manifestations of their proud heritage. Then, the procedures can take on lives of their own, and some be enforced to the detriment of the people they were originally designed to serve.

A military organization's heritage consists largely of its *combat* traditions. Many of these traditions grow out of the extraordinary efforts of only a few individuals. While "Uncommon valor was a common virtue" on Iwo Jima, it is doubtful that Tony Stein was following established procedure when he attacked every Japanese bunker in his sector with an aircraft machinegun he had spent months modifying. In fact, he may have been trying to save his friends from having to follow that procedure.

## TO FULLY ADOPT MANEUVER WARFARE, A MILITARY OUTFIT MAY HAVE TO RELINQUISH SOME OF ITS ESTABLISHED PROCEDURES

It stands to reason that an organization moving toward a style of warfare in many ways opposite to its traditional style, may have to modify some traditional procedures. One wouldn't expect this process to be easy.

Because the knowledge with which to perform maneuver warfare is best generated from the bottom up, the standard operating procedures for training may be the first to need modification. And, where training goes, personnel management and leadership cannot be far behind. To practice maneuver warfare, control must be decentralized. That means that the NCO "chain of command" must play a more significant role in the operation of each unit. It's the corporal or sergeant, after all, who must lead the key maneuver element — the rifle squad. Within the United States Marine Corps, decentralization of control is by no means a revolutionary idea. For over two years, the famous Marine Raider Battalions of WWII encouraged their junior enlisted men to take a more active role in decision making:

> Colonel Carlson had some very specific ideas about training his men, and one was to indoctrinate them with the same sort of democratic spirit as that practiced in the 8th Route Army. There was very little distinction between officers and men, and the slogan of the 2nd Marine Raider Battalion was "gung ho," or "work together," a slogan borrowed directly from the Chinese communists. In fact, later, when the methods of operation of the battalion became known to the public, this slogan and Carlson's techniques aroused a good deal of criticism in Congress and elsewhere, and some questioned Carlson's loyalties because he used techniques derived from the Chinese communists.[11]

Long before the birth of communism, Oriental armies realized that decentralizing control is the only way to minimize the chaos of battle:

> Those whose upper and lower ranks have the same desire are victorious.[12]
> — Sun Tzu

> Therefore, a skilled commander seeks victory from the situation and does not demand it of his subordinates. He selects suitable men and exploits the situation.[13]
> — Sun Tzu

To practice maneuver warfare at the small-unit level, American NCO's must also realize that today's privates are every bit as good as those of yesteryear (perhaps just in different ways), and that *these contemporary privates must be trusted and respected as decision makers.* Abraham Lincoln offered some valuable advice on how to work successfully with any segment of society:

> *If you would win a man to your cause, first convince him that you are his sincere friend. Therein is a drop of honey that catches his heart, which, say what he will, is the great high road to his reason and which, once gained, you will find but little trouble in convincing his judgment of the justice of your cause,* if indeed that cause be a just one. *On the contrary, assume to dictate to his judgment, or to command his action, or to mark him as one to be shunned and despised and he will retreat within himself, close all avenues to his head and his heart. . . . Such is man, and so must he be understood by those who would lead him, even to his own best interest* [all italics from original].[14]
> — Abraham Lincoln

## HOW MUST TRADITIONAL TRAINING MANAGEMENT CHANGE?

Established *tactical* procedures can often do more harm than good. Eager to comply with these procedures, recent inductees may try them at the wrong time. In other words, novice tacticians my be tempted to discount situational variables that would otherwise invalidate the procedures. By requiring small-unit leaders to follow tactical procedures, their commanders may be encouraging them to make illogical decisions. In war, common sense must take priority over preconceived notions:

> *Basic Field Manual* knowledge is fine, but it is useless without common sense. Common sense is of greater value than all the words in the book.[15]
> — Col. Amor Le R. Sims
> 7th Mar. CO on Guadalcanal

Before small units can fully contribute to maneuver warfare, their members may have to adopt a different way of learning. They may have to start viewing published training standards as minimal requirements rather than keys to victory, and manuals as collections of techniques for specific situations rather than pure doctrine. The members of the unit must learn to improve their effectiveness through ways *other than* memorizing established procedures. Two of the best ways are research and experimentation. Formal schools can help by expanding their curricula to include more classes on advanced infantry skills (like stalking, tracking, walking point, performing the role of a sapper, and ambushing armor from a "spider hole").

## RIFLE COMPANIES *CAN'T* BE TRAINED FOR MANEUVER WARFARE THE WAY THEY WERE TRAINED FOR ATTRITION WARFARE

Infantrymen can't learn how to exercise initiative through memorizing manuals, and small units can't learn how to operate independently by tagging along on joint exercises. Preparing for maneuver warfare will take something quite different from the traditional training process. One can discover how to train a unit for maneuver warfare from the tactics themselves. Basically, the training must be accomplished through "recon pull" instead of "command push." In other words, what should be learned must be generated *from the bottom up.* For, in the process, subunits at every echelon will get the chance to assess for themselves what it takes to operate alone, exercise initiative, and react to a changing situation.

What better way to teach riflemen, fire teams, and squads to exercise initiative, than to let them develop their own tactical techniques through research and experimentation? What better way to encourage officers, SNCO's, and NCO's to be responsive to ever changing situations than to let them make all their own decisions during free play. After all, it's through this research and experimentation that the lower echelons of a tall organization can most quickly learn about new weapon systems and tactics. Every time each squad discovers a new threat, it should reevaluate its tactics. When there are changes needed at the lower echelons, tall organizations *cannot* implement them from the top down fast enough anyway. Hiram Maxim developed the first machinegun in *1883*. It was not until late in WWI — some *35 years* and millions of casualties later — that any Western nation (Germany) began to practice small-unit infantry tactics that could effectively counter the machinegun.

## FOR MANEUVER WARFARE CAPABILITY, SMALL UNITS NEED BOTTOM-UP TRAINING THAT LEADERS CONTROL INDIRECTLY

To become proficient at maneuver war, leaders must step back from always being "in charge": company commanders must give mission-type training orders to company gunnery sergeants; platoon commanders must work through platoon sergeants; and platoon sergeants, squad leaders, and fire team leaders must allow subordinates to help to refine their own techniques. This can be accomplished *during delays* in the normal training schedule.

To initiate the planning process, the Commanding Officer (CO) gathers his platoon leaders to arrive at a few bottom-line goals — what squads should be able to do in combat (those on page 350 will suffice). After the CO hands this short list of goals to the company gunnery sergeant as training guidance, he and his lieutenants must assume supporting roles — indirectly controlling what happens next. Their only strict requirement is that tactical refinements obey doctrine and result in fewer casualties. They limit future "assistance" to locating historical techniques, reserving appropriate training areas, acquiring casualty assessment equipment, positioning aggressors, counting casualties, and recording what has been learned. Then, the gunnery sergeant assembles his SNCO's and NCO's to determine which squad, fire team, two-man, and individual techniques will be minimally required to accomplish the officers' goals. Each NCO must teach at least one 20-minute battledrill for established skills and *situational station* for transitional skills. Individual and buddy team techniques are assigned to fire team leaders, fire team techniques to squad leaders, and squad techniques to platoon sergeants or right guides. Subunit leaders stay with their men and retain authority to levy additional learning requirements. As squads are football-team size, squad training resembles football practice — procedural drills under progressively harder circumstances followed by scrimmaging.

The execution phase is accomplished sequentially. If there's 20 minutes of down time between other events, the NCO responsible for the next period of instruction divides the unit into 12-man groups and recruits/briefs enough of his peers to do the job. If there's more time available, several periods of instruction can be accomplished concurrently in "round-robin" format. The emphasis will be on movement rather than shooting — as that often only diminishes surprise. Success will be measured by whether stealth, speed, or deception (hence surprise) has been improved or personnel losses lessened, not by whether the book solution has been perfectly reenacted. If paint guns or MILES gear aren't available for casualty assessment, flour grenades within 10 feet of above-ground friendlies and 3-second sight pictures of upright opponents will suffice. Each tactical method will be practiced a second time in slightly different terrain to show that it can't be run in combat exactly as rehearsed. Elements will learn more than one technique for each category of wartime scenario. By having to choose between ways in combat, they'll be forced to think and less predictable. Their prerehearsed techniques are their "courses of action" — tactical options that can be numbered and polled quickly with subordinates by hand-and-arm signal.

First, individual riflemen are "trained" in the expanded list of basics for maneuver warfare — shooting, moving, communicating, seeing, hearing, not being seen, not being heard, self-defense, and tactical-decision making. Next, two-man teams, fire teams, and squads practice various techniques under simulated combat conditions.

Then, the NCO's conduct a *tactical demonstration* for their officers. To exactly recreate goal situations, the officers are encouraged to arrange all training support. After watching squads solve situations, the officers tell NCO's whether their expectations have been met.

(Source: MCO P1550.4C (1979), p. 43)

At this point, squads work against each other in a *free-play exercise*. Casualty counts will establish situational applicability of techniques. By watching how easily skills are combined, platoon leaders discover new platoon methods. (See appendix B for free-play guidelines.)

Then, the gunnery sergeant assembles the company for a *lessons-learned field day*. He asks for volunteers to reenact better tactical methods. After each demonstration, he requests a show of hands on the idea's worth. He and his enlisted panel now have what they need to improve the training. Their evolving portfolio of techniques constitutes the company's "corporate knowledge." While each company's skills are slightly different, their quality has been assured by doctrine and consensus opinion.

All the while, the commissioned officers have stayed in the background — accepting knowledge generated by subordinates as valid. Each has closely monitored the activities of his men — not only to better understand their capabilities, but also to decide what guidance, historical examples, and training support might best support the next training evolution. Realizing decentralization of control to be an absolute prerequisite of maneuver warfare, the CO and his officers have depended on *indirect* influence to enhance tactical techniques and decision-making ability throughout the company. They have only chosen problem scenarios, found proper terrain, positioned aggressors, and monitored casualty assessment. But, through their selfless management style, they've earned a valuable bonus. By studying *situations* and unit capabilities to handle them, they've learned when and where to prevail with minimal losses in combat. They've discovered how to win the next war before it gets fought!

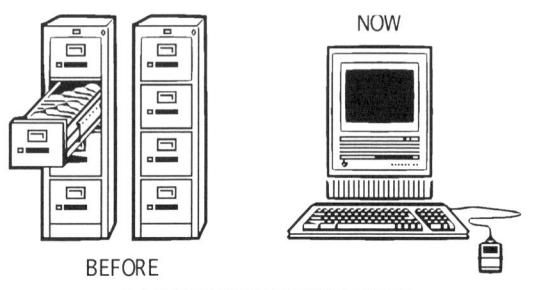

(Source: Click Art Business Images © 1987 T/Maker Co.)

## WHAT IS LEARNED THIS WAY DESERVES TO BE SHARED

The Italians couldn't duplicate the feats of the Germans during WWI, because they couldn't widely distribute the techniques developed by their own *Arditi*.

In this age of computerized information gathering, what can be relearned about small-unit infantry tactics through research and experimentation can easily build upon itself, be shared by all, and then be recorded for future generations. It wouldn't be doctrine, but merely a set of useful techniques to solve recurring situations.

## AN ANSWER TO THE QUESTION POSED AT THE BEGINNING OF THE BOOK

In the preface, there was posed a question — "After a succession of conscientious and knowledgeable military leaders, how could U.S. small-unit infantry tactics have failed to keep pace with the 'state of the art'?" After all, what is being discussed isn't recent tactical innovation.

It's clear that small-unit infantry knowledge doesn't build upon itself like other types of knowledge. Some of the nations that pioneered maneuver warfare have themselves at times discounted its precepts. The answer to the mystery must lie, not in the chain of custody for the knowledge, but rather in the way learning is accomplished within the military organization itself.

When the Germans developed their squad technique for forcing gaps through enemy lines in WWI, they did so not because they had just learned it from the Orientals, Boers, or whomever. Capt. Rohr might have just learned it from his students at the German NCO school for that matter. The real catalyst for this growth was the *decentralized control over training* that existed in the German Army at that time. In other words, the knowledge was generated *from the bottom up* instead of from the top down. German NCO's were considered to be tactical-decision makers, and company commanders could train anyway they wanted. Furthermore, German Army Headquarters had the foresight widely to disseminate what had been learned in this manner.

Military manuals and training standards can't adequately reflect the corporate knowledge of a great military organization anyway. Even if they could, the long chain of command creates too much opportunity for a subordinate-unit leader to misrepresent those standards. ***Until U.S. manuals are promoted as broad guidance instead of doctrine, training standards as partial minimums instead of all-inclusive panaceas, experimentation and free play as the preferred learning method instead of memorization, sharing what has been learned as the way to improve instead of enforcing doctrine, U.S. small-unit infantry tactics may never approach the state of the art.*** Until those in charge at every echelon within U.S. military organizations share the belief that infantry tactics at the small-unit level must continually evolve as weapons systems do, tactical decisions *that cost too much over the last hundred yards* may continue to haunt the American conscience:

> Prejudice against innovation is a typical characteristic of an Officer Corps which has grown up in a well-tried and proven system.[16]
> — Field Marshal Erwin Rommel

# Appendix A
# Inventory Test

1. HOW CAN LEADERSHIP BEST BE MEASURED?

    A. TRAITS.
    B. INDICATORS.
    C. PRINCIPLES.
    D. STYLES.

2. THERE IS ONE BEST LEADERSHIP STYLE FOR ALL LEADERS, GROUPS, AND SITUATIONS.

    A. TRUE.
    B. FALSE.

3. WHAT ARE THE INDICATORS OF LEADERSHIP?

    A. TACT, JUSTICE, JUDGMENT, ENTHUSIASM.
    B. AUTHORITARIAN AND DEMOCRATIC.
    C. MORALE, ESPRIT DE CORPS, PROFICIENCY, DISCIPLINE.

4. ESPRIT DE CORPS MEANS WHAT?

    A. SPIRIT OF THE MILITARY ORGANIZATION.
    B. PRIDE IN ONE'S UNIT.
    C. CAMARADERIE.
    D. POSITIVE ATTITUDE.

5. WHICH OF THE FOLLOWING IS A POPULAR SHORTENED VERSION OF THE LEADERSHIP PRINCIPLES?

    A. TACT, JUSTICE, JUDGMENT, ENTHUSIASM.
    B. AUTHORITARIAN AND DEMOCRATIC.
    C. MORALE, ESPRIT DE CORPS, PROFICIENCY, DISCIPLINE.
    D. KNOW YOURSELF, KNOW YOUR MEN, KNOW YOUR JOB.

6. FOR MANEUVER (COMMON-SENSE) WARFARE, AN AUTHORITARIAN LEADERSHIP STYLE IS USUALLY MORE EFFECTIVE THAN A PERMISSIVE LEADERSHIP STYLE.

    A. TRUE.
    B. FALSE.

7. WHAT IS THE GOAL OF MANEUVER WARFARE?

    A. MORE FIREPOWER THAN THE ENEMY.
    B. HIGHER TEMPO OF OPERATIONS THAN THE ENEMY.
    C. MORE PERSONNEL THAN THE ENEMY.
    D. BETTER CONTROL THAN THE ENEMY.

8. THE OFFENSIVE MISSION OF MANEUVER WARFARE IS WHICH OF THE FOLLOWING?

    A. LOCATE, CLOSE WITH, AND DESTROY THE ENEMY.
    B. USE SUPPORTING ARMS PRIMARILY TO KILL ENEMY.
    C. BYPASS AND COLLAPSE THE ENEMY.
    D. BREAK CONTACT WITH THE ENEMY.

*Appendix A*

9. MANEUVER WARFARE IS BETTER THAN ATTRITION WARFARE FOR ALL SITUATIONS.

    A. TRUE.
    B. FALSE.

10. THE DEFENSIVE MISSION OF MANEUVER WARFARE APPROXIMATES WHICH OF THE FOLLOWING?

    A. TO STOP THE ENEMY BY LONG-RANGE FIRE BEFORE HE REACHES THE FORWARD EDGE OF THE BATTLE AREA (FEBA), TO REPEL HIS ASSAULT BY CLOSE COMBAT IF HE REACHES THE FEBA, AND TO EXPEL HIM BY COUNTERATTACK IF HE CROSSES THE FEBA.
    B. TO SURPRISE/WEAKEN THE ENEMY SO HE CAN BE COUNTERATTACKED TO SEIZE THE MOMENTUM.
    C. TO BREAK CONTACT WITH THE ENEMY.
    D. TO NEVER DEFEND, BUT ALWAYS TO ATTACK.

11. MANEUVER WARFARE INVOLVES WHICH OF THE FOLLOWING ACTIONS DURING AN ATTACK?

    A. MOVING THROUGH GAPS TO GET BEHIND THE ENEMY IN AN EFFORT TO GET HIM TO SURRENDER.
    B. BEING CAREFUL OF ENEMY FIRE SACKS.
    C. ATTACKING SURFACES BY FORCE TO INFLICT MAXIMUM CASUALTIES ON THE ENEMY.
    D. BOTH A AND B.

12. FOR MANEUVER WARFARE, SUPPORTING-ARMS AND SMALL-ARMS BASES OF FIRE ARE UTILIZED TO PERMIT MANEUVER, AND NOT NECESSARILY TO KILL ENEMY.

    A. TRUE.
    B. FALSE.

13. THE TACTICAL CONTENT OF A MANUAL ON ANY GIVEN SUBJECT IS MOSTLY TECHNIQUE AND THEREFORE ONLY APPLICABLE TO SPECIFIC SETS OF CIRCUMSTANCES.

    A. TRUE.
    B. FALSE.

14. TECHNIQUES MUST BE DEVELOPED AND REHEARSED BEFORE COMBAT TO BUILD TEAMWORK, EVEN THOUGH THEY MUST INVARIABLY BE MODIFIED IN COMBAT TO MATCH THE CIRCUMSTANCES.

    A. TRUE.
    B. FALSE.

15. WHO MUST ACCEPT RESPONSIBILITY FOR MAKING SURE EACH SQUAD REHEARSES ENOUGH TECHNIQUES TO ESTABLISH MOMENTUM IN COMBAT?

    A. ITS PLATOON LEADER.
    B. ITS PLATOON SERGEANT.
    C. ITS SQUAD LEADER.
    D. ALL OF THE ABOVE.

16. A PFC RIGHT OUT OF BOOT CAMP CAN THINK FOR HIMSELF WELL ENOUGH TO SURVIVE ON "POINT" WITHOUT SPECIAL SCREENING OR TRAINING.

    A. TRUE.
    B. FALSE.

17. HOW CAN INFANTRY PERSONNEL BE TAUGHT TO THINK FOR THEMSELVES WHEN NECESSARY?

    A. FREE PLAY BETWEEN SMALL UNITS.
    B. DECISION BRIEFS REQUIRING SOLUTIONS FOR SPECIFIC SITUATIONS.
    C. WRITING ORDERS ON HOW TO SOLVE SPECIFIC SITUATIONS.
    D. ALL OF THE ABOVE.

18. HOW FEW PEOPLE SHOULD BE DEPLOYED IN ANY SECURITY ROLE?

    A. ONE.
    B. FOUR.

C. THREE.
D. TWO.

19. SECURITY ELEMENTS SHOULD NOT DEPLOY OUT OF SIGHT OF THE MAIN BODY WITHOUT SOME MEANS OF COMMUNICATION, LIKE A RADIO.

    A. TRUE.
    B. FALSE.

20. IF A UNIT ATTACKING A PREPARED ENEMY POSITION CANNOT MAINTAIN SOME SEMBLANCE OF SURPRISE BEFORE BREACHING THE BARBED WIRE, WHAT SHOULD IT DO?

    A. FIRE AND MOVE UP TO THE BARBED WIRE AND ATTACK AS ORIGINALLY PLANNED.
    B. SUPPLEMENT THE ORIGINAL PLAN WITH MORE FIRE SUPPORT.
    C. SUPPLEMENT THE ORIGINAL PLAN WITH MORE PERSONNEL.
    D. PULL BACK AND ATTACK FROM A DIFFERENT DIRECTION LATER (PREFERABLY AT NIGHT).

21. THE TWO MEN WALKING POINT HAVE BETTER SURVIVABILITY IF THEIR LAND NAVIGATION RESPONSIBILITIES ARE LIMITED TO CROSSING THE GROUND TO THEIR IMMEDIATE FRONT.

    A. TRUE.
    B. FALSE.

22. THOSE ON POINT IN A WAR ZONE MUST BE ALLOWED TO FIRE THEIR WEAPONS WHENEVER THEY DEEM IT NECESSARY TO SAVE THEIR LIVES.

    A. TRUE.
    B. FALSE.

23. THE SQUAD LEADER CAN CONTROL HIS SQUAD MORE EFFECTIVELY IF HE DOES NOT DELEGATE LAND NAVIGATION RESPONSIBILITY TO ANYONE ELSE.

    A. TRUE.
    B. FALSE.

24. ANYWHERE IN THE WORLD, A NAVIGATOR CAN TAKE AN AZIMUTH FROM HIS COMPASS AND PLOT IT DIRECTLY ONTO A MAP WITHOUT ANY CONVERSION.

    A. TRUE.
    B. FALSE.

25. LAND NAVIGATION TOOLS — E.G., MAPS AND COMPASSES — HAVE NO LIMITATIONS.

    A. TRUE.
    B. FALSE.

26. MAPS ALWAYS SHOW EXACTLY WHAT IS ON THE GROUND.

    A. TRUE.
    B. FALSE.

27. A WRIST WATCH OR AMMUNITION MAGAZINE WILL NOT AFFECT A COMPASS.

    A. TRUE.
    B. FALSE.

28. DEAD RECKONING (AZIMUTH AND PACE COUNT) IS ONLY ONE OF TWO MAIN LAND NAVIGATION TECHNIQUES.

    A. TRUE.
    B. FALSE.

*Appendix A*

29. IF MAGNETIC NORTH IS TO THE RIGHT OF GRID NORTH ON THE DECLINATION DIAGRAM OF A MAP, IT IS NECESSARY TO ADD THE G-M ANGLE TO CONVERT FROM MAGNETIC TO GRID AZIMUTH.

    A. TRUE.
    B. FALSE.

30. IN RELATIVELY FLAT AND HEAVILY VEGETATED TERRAIN, IT IS USUALLY POSSIBLE TO TELL HOW FAR ONE HAS TRAVELED ALONG A STRAIGHT LINE BY COUNTING HOW MANY DRAWS ARE CROSSED.

    A. TRUE.
    B. FALSE.

31. THE RESECTION TECHNIQUE FOR FINDING ONE'S OWN LOCATION WHEN LOST EMPLOYS WHAT?

    A. BACK AZIMUTHS PLOTTED FROM KNOWN TERRAIN FEATURES IN THE DISTANCE.
    B. FRONT AZIMUTHS PLOTTED FROM YOUR POSITION.
    C. NO CONVERSION FROM MAGNETIC TO GRID AZIMUTH.
    D. NONE OF THE ABOVE.

32. DRAWS AND FINGERS LOOK SIMILAR ON A MAP EXCEPT THAT THE TIPS OF FINGERS ARE USUALLY MORE POINTED AND AIM UPHILL.

    A. TRUE.
    B. FALSE.

33. WHEN PLOTTING OR READING GRID COORDINATES, THE RULE IS WHAT?

    A. LEFT AND UP.
    B. RIGHT AND DOWN.
    C. LEFT AND DOWN.
    D. RIGHT AND UP.

34. MAPS OF HEAVILY FORESTED TERRAIN ALWAYS CORRECTLY DEPICT LOW HILLS, AND THE LENGTHS OF FINGERS AND DRAWS.

    A. TRUE.
    B. FALSE.

35. A PACE COUNT CAN BE USED TO MEASURE ACCURATELY MAP DISTANCES OVER HEAVILY FORESTED AND UNEVEN TERRAIN.

    A. TRUE.
    B. FALSE.

36. ONE CAN ALWAYS DETERMINE HOW FAR UP A DRAW HE HAS MOVED BY COMPARING THE SIDE DRAWS ENCOUNTERED TO THOSE ON HIS MAP.

    A. TRUE.
    B. FALSE.

37. THE "ONE POINT" INTERSECTION TECHNIQUE IS OFTEN USED FOR ESTABLISHING THE ENEMY'S LOCATION IN A CALL FOR FIRE.

    A. TRUE.
    B. FALSE.

38. IN PATROLLING, SLOW CONTINUOUS MOVEMENT BY THE MAIN BODY PERMITS PROPER UTILIZATION OF SECURITY PERSONNEL IN EVERY SITUATION.

    A. TRUE.
    B. FALSE.

39. DURING NIGHT PATROLLING, SEEKING OUT ENEMY (WITHOUT BEING SEEN ONESELF) IS MADE EASIER BY MOVING ALONG WHICH TYPES OF LINEAR TERRAIN FEATURES?

   A. JUST ABOVE THE MILITARY CRESTS OF FINGERS.
   B. ALONG THE TOPOGRAPHICAL CRESTS OF FINGERS.
   C. ROUGHLY PARALLEL TO, BUT AT MAXIMUM VISUAL DISTANCE FROM ROADS.
   D. BOTH A AND C.

40. PATROL ROUTES SHOULD BE DESIGNED AROUND "ATTACK POINTS" THAT DON'T NECESSARILY LIE ON A STRAIGHT LINE BETWEEN PATROL OBJECTIVES.

   A. TRUE.
   B. FALSE.

41. WHICH OF THE BELOW TECHNIQUES DO NOT APPLY TO LAND NAVIGATION?

   A. AIMING OFF.
   B. USE OF COLLECTING AND LIMITING FEATURES.
   C. USE OF REFERENCE LINES AND POINTS.
   D. USE ON CONTACT POINTS AND HOLDING AREAS.

42. AN ATTACK POINT FOR LAND NAVIGATION IS WHAT?

   A. THE LAST COVERED POSITION BEFORE THE LINE OF DEPARTURE.
   B. A PLACE ON THE GROUND THAT ONE IS POSITIVE HE CAN FIND.
   C. THE LOCATION RIGHT BEFORE THE FINAL COORDINATION LINE AT WHICH LAST MINUTE COORDINATION IS MADE.
   D. A PLACE AT WHICH ONE EXPECTS TROUBLE FROM THE ENEMY.

43. WHICH OF THE FOLLOWING IS FAVORABLE TERRAIN FOR MAKING ENEMY CONTACT DURING DAYTIME PATROLLING?

   A. BOTTOMS OF DRAWS.
   B. MILITARY CRESTS OF FINGERS.
   C. TOPOGRAPHICAL CRESTS OF FINGERS.
   D. FIELDS CONTAINING HEAVY CONCEALMENT BUT LIGHT COVER.

44. WHEN USING THE TERRAIN ASSOCIATION TECHNIQUE TO ESTABLISH ROUTES, CHECKPOINTS ARE CHOSEN BEFORE THE LEGS.

   A. TRUE.
   B. FALSE.

45. A NAVIGATOR WHO USES A ROUTE CARD DOES NOT NEED TO LOOK AT HIS MAP, AND HAS MORE TIME TO LOOK FOR THE ENEMY.

   A. TRUE.
   B. FALSE.

46. A DIFFERENT LAND NAVIGATION TECHNIQUE MIGHT BE NECESSARY FOR EACH LEG OF A PATROL.

   A. TRUE.
   B. FALSE.

47. A DEFENSIVE SECURITY PATROL THAT RETURNS WITHOUT MAKING CONTACT FROM AN AREA INFESTED WITH ENEMY, HAS NEVERTHELESS ACCOMPLISHED ITS MISSION.

   A. TRUE.
   B. FALSE.

48. THE MOST LOGICAL FORMATION FOR A POINT, FLANK, OR REAR SECURITY TEAM IS WHAT?

   A. SIDE BY SIDE, ONE WATCHING TO THE LEFT AND ONE WATCHING TO THE RIGHT.
   B. IN STAGGERED COLUMN, ONE WATCHING FAR AND ONE NEAR.

Appendix A

      C. 100 METERS APART AND NOT NECESSARILY WITHIN VIEW OF EACH OTHER.
      D. NONE OF THE ABOVE.

49. WHICH AMBUSH TECHNIQUE MIGHT BE MOST SUCCESSFUL AGAINST A NUMERICALLY SUPERIOR FORCE?

      A. L-SHAPED AMBUSH WITH MACHINEGUN DEPLOYED ON THE SHORT LEG.
      B. STANDARD LINEAR AMBUSH WITH MANNED OBJECTIVE RALLY POINT 200 METERS AWAY.
      C. LINEAR AMBUSH WITH NATURAL BARRIERS TO THE FRONT AND SIDES, A COVERED ROUTE OF EGRESS, AND CLAYMORES TO DO THE KILLING.
      D. STANDARD LINEAR AMBUSH INITIATED BY A CLOSED-BOLT WEAPON.

50. WHICH TECHNIQUE FOR HANDLING CHANCE CONTACT GIVES THE FRIENDLY UNIT A BETTER CHANCE OF GETTING AT LEAST ONE CONFIRMED ENEMY KILL?

      A. COMING ON LINE FACING THE ENEMY, STALKING THAT ENEMY ON LINE UNTIL SPOTTED, THEN ADVANCING BY "FIRE AND MOVEMENT" UNTIL COVER OR FIRE SUPERIORITY IS LOST.
      B. SETTING UP A HASTY AMBUSH.
      C. IMMEDIATELY ENVELOPING THE ENEMY.
      D. CALLING IN SUPPORTING ARMS ON THE ENEMY.

51. "IMMEDIATE-ACTION" DRILLS FOR PATROLLING ARE REALLY JUST TECHNIQUES TO BUILD TEAMWORK; THEY WERE PROBABLY NEVER INTENDED TO BE EXECUTED THE SAME WAY EVERY TIME.

      A. TRUE.
      B. FALSE.

52. WHEN A UNIT ON THE MOVE ENCOUNTERS A PREPARED ENEMY POSITION FOR THE FIRST TIME, WHAT IS THE WISEST ACTION FOR IT TO TAKE?

      A. ATTACK IMMEDIATELY BY FIRE AND MOVEMENT.
      B. REPORT ITS LOCATION TO HEADQUARTERS AND THEN RECOMMEND THAT THE POSITION EITHER BE BYPASSED, DEMOLISHED BY SUPPORTING ARMS, OR DELIBERATELY ATTACKED.
      C. RUN A HASTY ENVELOPMENT.
      D. NONE OF THE ABOVE.

53. AS WEAPONS HAVE BECOME MORE DEADLY, MANEUVER ELEMENTS HAVE HAD TO BECOME SMALLER IN SIZE.

      A. TRUE.
      B. FALSE.

54. WHEN SURPRISE IS PARTIALLY LOST DURING A DELIBERATE ATTACK (AS IT ALMOST ALWAYS WILL BE), WHAT SHOULD BE DONE?

      A. USE MORE PERSONNEL.
      B. FIRE AND MOVE.
      C. USE DECEPTION TO TRY TO REESTABLISH SURPRISE.
      D. USE MORE FIREPOWER.

55. A COLORED POP-UP FLARE OR SMOKE GRENADE IS A GOOD ALTERNATE SIGNAL FROM THE ENVELOPMENT ROUTE TO SHIFT OR CEASE THE BASE OF FIRE.

      A. TRUE.
      B. FALSE.

56. CEASING THE BASE OF FIRE IS BETTER THAN SHIFTING IT.

      A. TRUE.
      B. FALSE.

57. U.S. DOCTRINE ALLOWS ONLY FRONTAL ATTACKS WITH OVERHEAD MACHINEGUN FIRE AT NIGHT, NO ENVELOPMENTS.

      A. TRUE.
      B. FALSE.

## Inventory Test

58. U.S. DOCTRINE AUTHORIZES FIRING SUPPORTING ARMS DURING A NIGHT ATTACK ONLY AFTER THE ATTACKING FORCE HAS BEEN DETECTED.

    A. TRUE.
    B. FALSE.

59. TO MAXIMIZE SURPRISE ON THE DAY ATTACK, WHEN IS THE BEST TIME FOR THE BASE OF FIRE TO OPEN UP?

    A. AUTOMATICALLY, AS SOON AS THE MANEUVER FORCE HEADS UP THE ENVELOPMENT ROUTE FROM THE LINE OF DEPARTURE.
    B. AUTOMATICALLY, ONLY TO COVER THE SOUND OF GUNSHOTS IN THE ENVELOPMENT ROUTE.
    C. AUTOMATICALLY, AS THE ENVELOPING FORCE ASSAULTS.
    D. NONE OF THE ABOVE.

60. TO MAXIMIZE SURPRISE IN THE DAYLIGHT ATTACK, WHAT IS THE BEST TIME FOR THE SUPPORTING ARMS TO OPEN UP?

    A. TO COVER THE SOUNDS OF EXPLOSIONS IN THE ENVELOPMENT ROUTE.
    B. AS SOON AS THE ENVELOPING FORCE LEAVES THE LINE OF DEPARTURE.
    C. TO COVER THE SIGHTS AND SOUNDS OF BREACHING BARBED WIRE.
    D. EITHER OR BOTH A AND C.

61. IF STILL UNDISCOVERED AFTER TRANSITING THE ENEMY BARBED WIRE IN THE DAYLIGHT ATTACK, THE ASSAULTING UNIT SHOULD PROBABLY DO WHAT TO MAINTAIN SURPRISE?

    A. MOVE FORWARD QUICKLY IN A RAGGED LINE USING ONLY "DOUBLE TAPS" AGAINST CONFIRMED ENEMY SOLDIERS.
    B. FIRE AND MOVE.
    C. MOVE FORWARD SLOWLY IN A RAGGED LINE FIRING ALL WEAPONS AT THE MAXIMUM SUSTAINED RATE.
    D. NONE OF THE ABOVE.

62. WHEN FIRE SUPERIORITY IS LOST WHILE ASSAULTING INSIDE ENEMY WIRE, WHAT IS THE PROPER COURSE OF ACTION?

    A. MOVE FORWARD IN A RAGGED LINE USING ONLY "DOUBLE TAPS" AGAINST CONFIRMED ENEMY SOLDIERS.
    B. FIRE AND MOVE IN THE PRONE POSITION.
    C. MOVE FORWARD IN A RAGGED LINE FIRING ALL WEAPONS AT THE MAXIMUM SUSTAINED RATE.
    D. NONE OF THE ABOVE.

63. IF AN ENEMY DEFENDER IS SITTING JUST ABOVE THE MILITARY CREST, IT IS EASY TO CRAWL WITHIN GRENADE RANGE OF HIM.

    A. TRUE.
    B. FALSE.

64. IF AN ENEMY DEFENDER IS SITTING ON THE MILITARY CREST, BUT DOES NOT HAVE THERMAL IMAGING, IT IS SOMETIMES STILL POSSIBLE TO CRAWL UNDETECTED TO WITHIN GRENADE RANGE OF HIM.

    A. TRUE.
    B. FALSE.

65. IT IS VIRTUALLY IMPOSSIBLE TO CRAWL UNDETECTED PAST ALERT DEFENDERS.

    A. TRUE.
    B. FALSE.

66. IT IS EASIER TO ATTACK THAN TO DEFEND IN URBAN TERRAIN.

    A. TRUE.
    B. FALSE.

Appendix A

67. IN URBAN TERRAIN, ONE SHOULD ALWAYS HUG WALLS.

    A. TRUE.
    B. FALSE.

68. IN URBAN TERRAIN, A UNIT SHOULD WORK FROM THE BOTTOM UP WHILE CLEARING A BUILDING.

    A. TRUE.
    B. FALSE.

69. IN URBAN TERRAIN, STAY OUT OF STREETS AND HALLWAYS IF POSSIBLE.

    A. TRUE.
    B. FALSE.

70. EACH TIME SOMEONE MOVES IN URBAN TERRAIN, EVERY POSSIBLE SOURCE OF ENEMY FIRE MUST BE COVERED BY FRIENDLY FIRE.

    A. TRUE.
    B. FALSE.

71. WHICH URBAN DEFENSE TECHNIQUE CAN PREVENT EVEN AN ENEMY WILLING TO TAKE HEAVY LOSSES FROM BUILDING MOMENTUM.

    A. A BARRIER PLAN.
    B. COVERED ROUTES OF EGRESS.
    C. MUTUALLY SUPPORTING POSITIONS.
    D. NONE OF THE ABOVE.

72. A DEFENSIVE FIGHTING POSITION IN URBAN TERRAIN SHOULD HAVE WHICH OF THE FOLLOWING CHARACTERISTICS?

    A. BE DEFENDABLE FROM 360 DEGREES.
    B. HAVE A COVERED ROUTE OF EGRESS.
    C. HAVE TWO MEANS OF COMMUNICATION WITH SUPERIORS.
    D. ALL OF THE ABOVE.

73. FRONTAL ATTACKS ARE BEST EMPLOYED IN WHAT TYPE OF TERRAIN?

    A. LEVEL WITH NO COVER.
    B. CROSS COMPARTMENT (FROM ONE PIECE OF HIGH GROUND TO ANOTHER ACROSS THE LOW GROUND BETWEEN).
    C. LEVEL WITH COVER.
    D. NONE OF THE ABOVE.

74. WHEN ESTABLISHING A DEFENSE IN RURAL TERRAIN, WHICH OF THE FOLLOWING SHOULD BE DONE AT THE SAME TIME SECURITY IS SENT OUT?

    A. ENTRENCHING.
    B. PREREGISTERING SUPPORTING ARMS.
    C. BUILDING ALTERNATE POSITIONS.
    D. BUILDING BARRIERS.

75. TO ESTABLISH A DEFENSIVE POSITION THAT WILL STOP SHORT-RANGE INFILTRATORS, IT IS NOT NECESSARY TO WALK THE GROUND AHEAD OF TIME.

    A. TRUE.
    B. FALSE.

76. DEFENSIVE HOLES ON UNEVEN SLOPING GROUND SHOULD BE POSITIONED HOW?

    A. ON THE TOPOGRAPHICAL CREST.
    B. ON THE MILITARY CREST.

C. ALWAYS EQUIDISTANT FROM EACH OTHER.
D. BOTH B AND C.

77. TO ADJUST AN ARTILLERY OR MORTAR ROUND, WHAT INFORMATION SHOULD BE GATHERED BEFORE THE SMOKE DISSIPATES?

A. WIND DIRECTION.
B. ON WHICH SIDE OF THE TARGET THE IMPACT IS, AND HOW MANY FINGERS FIT BETWEEN IT AND THE TARGET.
C. WHETHER IT IS LONG, SHORT, OR "CAN'T TELL" FROM THE TARGET.
D. ALL OF THE ABOVE.

78. DURING THE DANGEROUS FINAL SECOND OF AN AIRSTRIKE, HOW IS THE PILOT USUALLY TOLD WHERE THE TARGET IS?

A. CARDINAL DIRECTION AND DISTANCE FROM THE MARKING ROUND.
B. AZIMUTH AND DISTANCE FROM THE OBSERVER.
C. ADD/DROP AND LEFT/RIGHT FROM THE MARKING ROUND.
D. NONE OF THE ABOVE.

79. AFTER WALKING THE ADJUSTMENT ROUNDS ONTO A TARGET 150 METERS AWAY, ONE CAN ASK FOR A STANDARD "FIRE FOR EFFECT" FROM ARTILLERY WITHOUT ANY DANGER TO HIMSELF.

A. TRUE.
B. FALSE.

80. TO HIT A DISTANT STATIONARY *POINT* TARGET WITH ARTILLERY OR MORTARS, ONE MUST USE WHICH TYPE OF ADJUSTMENT?

A. CREEPING.
B. SYSTEMATIC BRACKETING.
C. ONE-ROUND ADJUSTMENT.
D. FIRE FOR EFFECT.

81. WHAT TRANSMISSION SHOULD BE SENT BY THE CONTROLLER TO A FIXED-WING AIRCRAFT COMING IN LOW OVER ONE'S SHOULDER TO BOMB A TARGET?

A. CONTINUE.
B. ABORT, ABORT, ABORT.
C. CLEARED HOT.
D. NONE OF THE ABOVE.

82. WHEN TRYING TO HIT, WITH INDIRECT FIRE, A MOVING TARGET THAT MUST BE SURPRISED TO KILL IT, ONE HAS A BETTER CHANCE WITH WHICH METHOD OF TARGET LOCATION?

A. POLAR.
B. GRID.
C. SHIFT FROM A KNOWN POINT (PREREGISTERED TARGET).
D. NONE OF THE ABOVE.

83. HOW CLOSE SHOULD ONE APPROACH ON THE GROUND TO A PREPLANNED (CLEARED BUT NEVER FIRED) TARGET, BEFORE FIRING ON THAT TARGET?

A. 100 METERS.
B. 200 METERS.
C. DANGER CLOSE FOR THE WEAPONS SYSTEM INVOLVED.
D. 50 METERS.

84. WHICH METHOD OF ADJUSTMENT MUST ONE USE TO KILL A TARGET IN CLOSE PROXIMITY TO HIMSELF?

A. CREEPING.
B. SYSTEMATIC BRACKETING.

Appendix A

   C. ONE-ROUND ADJUSTMENT.
   D. FIRE FOR EFFECT.

85. ONCE INSIDE DANGER-CLOSE RANGE, WHAT IS THE MAXIMUM DISTANCE AN OBSERVER CAN "CREEP" AN ADJUSTMENT ROUND TOWARD HIMSELF?

   A. 200 METERS.
   B. 50 METERS.
   C. 100 METERS.
   D. 300 METERS.

86. WHAT MUST ONE REQUEST TO "FIRE FOR EFFECT" SAFELY AFTER WALKING ADJUSTMENT ROUNDS TO JUST WITHIN 150 METERS OF HIS LOCATION?

   A. PARALLEL SHEAF.
   B. PRECISION FIRE.
   C. CONVERGING SHEAF.
   D. EITHER B OR C.

87. WHEN SHIFTING FROM A KNOWN POINT, ONE CAN MAKE A BRACKET AROUND A TARGET WITH JUST ONE ROUND.

   A. TRUE.
   B. FALSE.

88. BRACKETS ARE ONLY MEASURED ALONG THE OBSERVER-TARGET LINE, SO THE SIZE OF THE BRACKET AT ANY GIVEN TIME IS NOT NECESSARILY THE EXACT DISTANCE BETWEEN THE LAST LONG AND SHORT ROUNDS.

   A. TRUE.
   B. FALSE.

89. WHICH OF THE FOLLOWING ARE MISTAKES OFTEN MADE BY NOVICE OBSERVERS?

   A. TRYING TO GET AN ADJUSTMENT ROUND EXACTLY ON THE OBSERVER-TARGET LINE BEFORE BRACKETING TO ESTABLISH RANGE.
   B. TRYING TO GUESS WHETHER THE FIRST ROUND IS LONG OR SHORT, INSTEAD OF MOVING THE ROUNDS CLOSER TO THE OBSERVER-TARGET LINE BEFORE MAKING THE DETERMINATION.
   C. BRACKETING TOO OFTEN.
   D. BOTH A AND B.

90. FOR A SHIFT MISSION, DIRECTION IS THE AZIMUTH FROM THE KNOWN POINT TO THE TARGET.

   A. TRUE.
   B. FALSE.

91. FOR CLOSE AIR SUPPORT THAT IS NOT YET AIRBORNE, THE PILOT BRIEF IS THE FIRST FORMATTED TRANSMISSION THAT MUST BE SENT OVER THE RADIO.

   A. TRUE.
   B. FALSE.

92. IN THE PILOT BRIEF, "DISTANCE" IS MEASURED FROM WHERE TO WHERE?

   A. CONTACT POINT THROUGH INITIAL POINT TO TARGET.
   B. INITIAL POINT TO TARGET.
   C. ATTACK POSITION TO TARGET.
   D. NONE OF THE ABOVE.

93. HOW IS "TIME TO TARGET" FOR FIXED WING COMPUTED?

   A. 1500 METERS PER MINUTE.
   B. 1000 METERS PER MINUTE.
   C. 5000 METERS PER MINUTE.
   D. 10000 METERS PER MINUTE PLUS TWO MINUTES ADMIN. TIME.

94. THE FRONT SIGHTPOST OF THE RIFLE ALSO FUNCTIONS AS THE FRONT SIGHTPOST FOR THE QUADRANT SIGHT ON THE M203 GRENADE LAUNCHER ATTACHMENT TO THE RIFLE.

  A. TRUE.
  B. FALSE.

95. THERE IS NO M203 ROUND THAT WILL ARM AND CAN DETONATE ONLY 3-5 METERS FROM THE MUZZLE.

  A. TRUE.
  B. FALSE.

96. FOR ZEROING ALL WEAPONS, MOVING THE FRONT SIGHTPOST WILL MOVE THE ROUND IN THE SAME DIRECTION; MOVING A REAR SIGHTPOST WILL MOVE THE ROUND IN THE OPPOSITE DIRECTION.

  A. TRUE.
  B. FALSE.

97. IT IS PERFECTLY SAFE TO BE ON THE GUN-TARGET LINE WHEN FIRING NAVAL GUNS.

  A. TRUE.
  B. FALSE.

98. A SENTRY POST CAN BE USED TO AMBUSH OR TO ADJUST SUPPORTING ARMS ONTO AN ATTACKING ENEMY WITHOUT GIVING AWAY ITS POSITION.

  A. TRUE.
  B. FALSE.

99. IN AN ANTI-ARMOR AMBUSH, A DECOY SHOULD TRY TO TURN THE ENEMY TANK SIDEWAYS TO ANOTHER TEAM CARRYING THE ANTITANK GUN.

  A. TRUE.
  B. FALSE.

100. WHICH OF THE FOLLOWING FIELD EXPEDIENT ORDNANCE CAN BE USED TO KILL/DISABLE TANKS AS A LAST RESORT?

  A. MOLOTOV COCKTAILS, POLE CHARGES, SATCHEL CHARGES.
  B. FIRING SMALL ARMS DOWN THE MUZZLE.
  C. M21 ANTITANK MINES PULLED ON STRINGS BETWEEN FIGHTING HOLES.
  D. BOTH A AND C.

## ANSWER KEY

| | | | |
|---|---|---|---|
| 1. A | 26. B | 51. A | 76. B |
| 2. B | 27. B | 52. B | 77. D |
| 3. C | 28. A | 53. A | 78. A |
| 4. B | 29. A | 54. C | 79. B |
| 5. D | 30. B | 55. B | 80. B |
| 6. B | 31. A | 56. B | 81. B |
| 7. B | 32. B | 57. A | 82. C |
| 8. C | 33. D | 58. A | 83. C |
| 9. B | 34. B | 59. B | 84. A |
| 10. B | 35. B | 60. D | 85. C |
| 11. D | 36. B | 61. A | 86. D |
| 12. A | 37. A | 62. B | 87. A |
| 13. A | 38. B | 63. A | 88. A |
| 14. A | 39. D | 64. B | 89. D |
| 15. D | 40. A | 65. B | 90. B |
| 16. B | 41. D | 66. B | 91. B |
| 17. D | 42. B | 67. B | 92. B |
| 18. D | 43. B | 68. B | 93. D |
| 19. A | 44. B | 69. A | 94. B |
| 20. D | 45. A | 70. A | 95. B |
| 21. A | 46. A | 71. A | 96. B |
| 22. A | 47. B | 72. D | 97. B |
| 23. A | 48. B | 73. B | 98. A |
| 24. B | 49. C | 74. B | 99. A |
| 25. B | 50. A | 75. B | 100. D |

# Appendix B
# Guidelines for a Free-Play Exercise

**CONCEPT:**

In a free-play exercise, participants use any tactics they want *without interference* from their superiors or instructors. Umpires exist only to enforce rules of engagement and assess casualties. If paint guns or MILES equipment aren't available, participants can count flour grenades within 10 feet of themselves or 3-second sight pictures of upright opponents. Below is described an exercise that will give infantrymen practice at making tactical decisions that get the job done at minimal cost.

Opposing forces are assigned base camp locations no farther than 500 yards apart. They must continually defend these locations with one third of their strength. They must conduct a series of deliberate attacks with remaining personnel against the other side's position within the allotted time frame — *at least two* in the daytime and *two more* during hours of darkness. The dual requirement gives participants the opportunity to try a recently learned attack technique on their own volition.

The idea is then to statistically determine which side accomplishes its mission *at minimal cost*. One demerit is assessed for every casualty suffered. There are also blocks of demerits for not running the prescribed number of attacks and for violating the rules of engagement. On the other hand, a large block of bonus points is awarded for successfully executing a deliberate short-range infiltration attack to capture a colored flag (which must be prominently displayed no higher than six feet off the ground). At the end of the allotted time, the war is declared over and the team with the lowest number of demerits wins.

**PROBLEMS THAT MAY OCCUR:**

Real combat has few, if any, rules. Because good discipline must always be maintained during peacetime training exercises, free play must have a few rules. Participants are continually tempted to break these rules to try to win. Furthermore, they invariably become convinced that the other side is breaking the rules. Some of this friction will persist no matter what the umpires do. Who wins the free-play exercise is not really important. What is important is that both sides continue to attack throughout the allotted period. That means attacking whether behind after an unpopular call by the umpires, or ahead after all mandatory attacks are completed. Only then will the value of momentum, and the difficulty of capturing it, become apparent to the participants. Having each participant keeping a running total of what he personally experiences with flour grenades and 3-second sight pictures seems to defuse the friction.

**DUTIES OF UMPIRES WHEN MILES GEAR IS USED:**

An umpire with a radio is positioned inside each defensive perimeter. His job is to ensure that all of the MILES equipment is fully functional before and after every engagement. Both umpires must make sure that their respective units zero their MILES gear before the start of the war. Doing so will minimize the complaints of cheating. Umpires should tell their personnel to wear helmets with MILES apparatus attached while under attack in their own perimeters, or suffer a demerit for each man who does not. Both sides are further told that it is their responsibility to keep their MILES gear operational, and that they will lose a point every time an improperly functioning set is found. The umpires must hold frequent but unannounced inspections. When fired at with a controller gun, each man's gear should "beep." For that man's MILES gear properly to signal a kill, the flat surface inside the key hole on his suspender strap must be vertical.

The umpires also keep track of the overall score. Their job *is not* to give tactical advice or to require that proper tactical procedure is followed. Umpires allow all encounters at which they are present *to run their full course*. Then, they assemble all participants, separate them into opposing groups, move the groups out of earshot of each other, and inspect each group for beeping or dysfunctional MILES gear. Before leaving each group, the umpire also asks, on the honor system, if anyone would have become a casualty if his MILES gear had worked properly. Finally, he computes the score for the engagement.

When patrols return from a contact not witnessed by an umpire, they undergo the same inspection procedure. Their umpires inspect them and modify as necessary over the radio the scores agreed upon by the participants at the time of the contact. The times and locations of each event must be carefully recorded in a log book, as there may be several contacts near the same time, and the final score may be very close.

The umpires compare notes frequently over the radio so that their running totals will be identical. The opposing groups will remain more motivated by staying apprised of umpire decisions and the cumulative score.

When there is no umpire present, the engagements will last exactly 10 minutes or until one side breaks contact. Each group must then muster in a slightly different location and submit to inspection by the commander of the opposing group. Both commanders then meet to arrive at a mutually agreeable score. They record the time and the location of the contact, and return to their respective defensive perimeters as time permits to confirm these scores with their umpires.

Appendix B

**DUTIES OF UMPIRES WHEN MILES GEAR NOT USED:**

If flour grenades and 3-second sight pictures are to be used to assess casualties, the umpires have only to remind participants to keep an accurate count of how many of each they personally experience and then tally the overall score at the end of the exercise.

**HOW DEMERITS ARE ASSESSED:**

1 DEMERIT — A CONTINUAL "BEEP" EMANATING FROM A PARTICIPANT'S MILES GEAR.

1 DEMERIT — PARTICIPANT CAUGHT WITH NON-OPERATIONAL MILES GEAR.

5 DEMERITS — UNIT NOT MANNING ASSIGNED DEFENSIVE PERIMETER WITH ONE-THIRD OF PERSONNEL.

10 DEMERITS — USING A VEHICLE FOR ANY REASON.

10 DEMERITS — PER INSTANCE OF HOSTAGE TAKING OR BODILY CONTACT.

5 DEMERITS — NOT RETURNING TO OWN POSITION BEFORE REENTERING PLAY AS REPLACEMENT OR NOT KEEPING QUIET ON ENEMY DISPOSITIONS.

5 DEMERITS — NOT MOVING COMPLETELY OUT OF VIEW OF OTHER SIDE AFTER CONTACT DECLARED OVER.

10 DEMERITS — PER OCCURRENCE OF NOT RUNNING REQUIRED NUMBER OF DELIBERATE ATTACKS WITH TWO-THIRDS STRENGTH.

10 DEMERITS — SITTING ON A LEAD BY NOT CONTINUALLY PATROLLING.

**HOW BONUS POINTS ARE EARNED:**

30 POINTS — SEIZING OPPONENT'S FLAG BY STEALTH.

**EXECUTION:**

A group of 40-80 men is split in half. Slight differences in uniform are agreed upon — e.g., one team may wear their shirts inside out. Blank ammunition, radios, other equipment, chow and water are equally distributed. The teams are told that any blank ammunition found must be equally distributed between them. They are given a reasonable amount of time to move to their assigned positions. The umpires take their place and establish radio contact. The teams are given time to zero their MILES gear and to be inspected. Then, war is declared and a time established as the cutoff for all hostilities.

**THE PRIZE:**

Promising some prize to the winner of the war provides an additional incentive to its participants. This prize can be as simple as recognition at a formation or a picnic hosted by the losing team. Ties are not uncommon and should not be ruled out. The real prize for both sides is hours of exciting and effective training that required very little preparation. Adults will retain the tactics that they can freely choose and personally observe to work.

**CRITIQUE:**

No free-play exercise would be complete without a critique. But, this critique must wait until the participants are rested. Two-man teams, fire teams, and squads should get the chance to demonstrate useful methods that they have developed. To establish technique value, the critique leader asks for a show of hands.

# Appendix C
# Eulogy to a Fallen Platoon Leader

On 27 February 1991, Captain W.L. Roach USMCR (Ret.) finally succumbed to complications from war wounds suffered twenty-four years earlier at a place called Con Thien. Before he was hit in the small of his back by a fist sized piece of recoilless rifle shrapnel, then Lieutenant Roach had been one of the most highly revered platoon leaders in 1st Battalion, 4th Marines. He instinctively knew how to hurt the enemy without suffering casualties himself. A brief look at his life and times may give platoon leaders of today some valuable insight into what it takes to succeed in combat.

Bill was the son of an Irish father, who had seen desperate action during WWII as an enlisted Army infantryman, and a wonderfully compassionate Italian mother. He was also the product of the mean streets of the south side of Chicago, and as such was a born leader. He and several of his buddies had even worked in the Gary steel mills before joining the Marine Corps in 1965, much as the heroes of the movie "The Deer Hunter" had. At Quantico, he roomed with an All-American from Georgia who would give anyone the shirt off his back — Jack "the Georgia Peach" Cox. Then, both Marines embarked for the Far East to meet their destiny.

Bill joined A Company just in time to help 1st Lt. Don Campbell's Marines repulse the large NVA force that partially overran Cam Lo in August of 1966. Jack joined D Company and went on to get killed in December of that year trying single-handedly to outflank a dug-in NVA battalion at the Three Gateways to Hell portion of the trail between Gio Linh and Con Thien. As the Georgia Peach had been unabashedly loved by all ranks in the Battalion, his passing was deeply felt by all. But, Bill suppressed his grief and continued to happily guide his flock through many engagements along the DMZ until the early summer of 1967. Then, his turn to "ante up" came. What made Lt. Roach such an outstanding combat leader?

*Quiet Aggressiveness:* Unaffected by the mixed signals of the Vietnam era, Lt. Roach knew instinctively to attack. But uniquely, he did it without bravado. One night on the Deck House VI Operation south of Chu Lai, Lt. Roach without fanfare decided to take his whole platoon on what could best be described as a tiger hunt (complete with beaters) around the periphery of an abandoned village. They made good contact that night. The other platoon leaders followed standard operating procedure, and each dispatched one squad to ambush a trail junction within their respective sectors. These squads made no contact.

*Coolness under Fire:* If Lt. Roach ever knew a day of fear in his life, he hid it well. He could sleep soundly until the last second before an opposed landing by the Special Landing Force. Meanwhile, his peers would nervously pace the bowels of the ship.

*Self-Perspective:* Lt. Roach never pulled rank on anyone. He was so well respected by his men that he didn't have to. He considered himself to be nothing more that a quarterback on a platoon football team, and was never the least bit self-serving in his actions. He must have gained insight into the importance of the team concept in combat from his father and his buddies in Chicago. His SNCO's were his equals and friends, he valued their advice, and he was deeply hurt when their professionalism would cost them their lives. He talked until his death about his platoon sergeant S.Sgt. "Gus" Gustafson who loved his troops to the point of almost mothering them. A couple of weeks after Bill was hit, Gus died as he had lived — with his troops — facing an NVA flamethrower at the mouth of the troop compartment to his Amtrac.

Now Capt. Roach belongs to the ages. The full depth of his character did not reveal itself until after Vietnam. The severity of his wounds should have killed him outright, and most certainly should have permanently sapped his drive. But as a paraplegic with a permanent colostomy, Bill never saw any reason to complain or to quit. With the encouragement of his lovely wife Betty and adopted daughter Susan, he went on in 1990 to earn a Ph.D. in English and then to land a job as a college professor. Even after he was sent home for the last time and he knew that his lungs were slowly filling with fluid, Bill couldn't relinquish his humor or quietly putting others first. One wonders if it was coincidental that he died on the very day the Gulf War was won, or if he held back death just long enough to cheer on his beloved Marines one last time.

*SEMPER FI, CAPTAIN ROACH, WE HAVE LEARNED FROM YOUR EXAMPLE.*

# Appendix D
# Eulogy to a Fallen Staff Sergeant

"Wee Willy" Williams was a Marine Staff Sergeant who served in Vietnam almost thirty years ago. He was mild mannered, red-headed, slender, 5'9" tall, and from Flat Rock, Alabama. His story may help contemporary infantrymen to appreciate the SNCO's role in combat.

By the summer of 1968, S.Sgt. Williams had some eighteen years in service, and an untold number of years in grade. No one knew exactly why he was called "Wee Willy," but he was rumored to be at his terminal rank because of being somewhat of a liberty risk.

When the Gunnery Sergeant of G Company, 2nd Battalion, 5th Marines made the fatal mistake of too quickly checking the crater from an incoming mortar round, S.Sgt. Williams was the odds-on favorite to fill his billet. To every enlisted man in the company, he was a leader; and to every officer, he was a friend. He and the company commander enjoyed so much rapport that they could communicate at distances of up to 100 yards without ever resorting to words or gestures — they did so by thoughts and expressions alone. One time, when the company was in An Hoa for an overnight refitting, all the SNCO's and officers decided to visit the club for a little liquid refreshment. The company commander stayed behind to do some last minute coordination for the next day's return to Indian country. Shortly after dark, S.Sgt. Williams came back from the club with several SNCO's and officers in tow. He was carefully balancing a cardboard box full of partially consumed drinks. When asked, by the company commander, why he was back so early, S.Sgt. Williams politely posed a question of his own — "Did you think we'd forget you, sir?"

Later, he announced that "this was his night." Of course, the company commander didn't understand what he meant at the time. Nor, did he understand the significance of what occurred two days later south of Liberty Bridge — an indescribably beautiful evening in which everyone and everything in nature seemed in perfect harmony.

The next day, the company commander found out what this all meant. While the first squad of the lead platoon crossed a rickety bridge into a small hamlet, the "s— hit the fan." The company commander knew instinctively to move toward the front of the company. He swam the small river, disarmed an enemy claymore, and married up with the lead platoon commander and part of his first squad. Then, he looked back for his friend Willy. He spotted him at the center of the company giving directions much as a traffic cop would. Their eyes met and the company commander beckoned for S.Sgt. Williams to join him. While at their maximum range for visual communication, the two still conferred. Willy explained that his place was there and that he could not come. Then, both expressed their deep respect and affection for each other and the communication ended.

Sometime before the F-4 Phantom came in to bomb from fifty feet above the objective, Willy graduated with honors from the school of hard knocks. The story told later was that he had stepped in front of a lieutenant who would not get down. Today, that lieutenant is an active-duty Marine Corps general.

*STAFF SERGEANT WILLIAMS, THE GIVING OF YOUR LIFE FOR A FRIEND HAS NOT GONE UNNOTICED.*

# Notes

**SOURCE NOTES**

Reprinted with permission of Film Australia, from its documentary series — *ASIAN INSIGHTS*. Protected by U.S. copyright.

Reprinted with permission of Scribner, a division of Simon & Schuster, Inc., from *THE WORLD CRISIS*, by Winston S. Churchill. Copyright © 1923, 1927, 1929, 1931 by Charles Scribner's Sons; copyright © renewed 1951, 1955, 1957, 1959 by Winston Churchill.

Reprinted with permission of Doubleday, a division of Bantam Doubleday Dell Publishing Group, Inc., from "Maps" by John Morris, in *RICHMOND REDEEMED*, by Richard J. Sommers. Copyright © 1981 by Richard J. Sommers.

Reprinted with permission of Presidio Press, 505 B San Marin Drive, Novato, CA 94945, from *BRINGING UP THE REAR*, by S.L.A. Marshall. Copyright © 1978 by Presidio Press.

Reprinted with permission of Presidio Press, 505 B San Marin Drive, Novato, CA 94945, from *BATTLE FOR HUE — TET 1968*, by Keith William Nolan. Copyright © 1983 by Presidio Press.

Reprinted with permission of Presidio Press, 505 B San Marin Drive, Novato, CA 94945, from *FORWARD INTO BATTLE*, by Paddy Griffith. Copyright © 1981, 1990 by Paddy Griffith.

Reprinted with permission of Presidio Press, 505 B San Marin Drive, Novato, CA 94945, from *THE ART OF MANEUVER*, by Robert Leonhard. Copyright © 1991 by Robert Leonhard.

Reprinted with permission of Presidio Press, 505 B San Marin Drive, Novato, CA 94945, from *COMMON SENSE TRAINING*, by Lt.Gen. Arthur S. Collins Jr. Copyright © 1978 by Presidio Press.

Reprinted with permission of Naval Institute Press, from *A DICTIONARY OF MILITARY AND NAVAL QUOTATIONS*, by Col. Robert Debs Heinl Jr. Copyright © 1966 by the United States Naval Institute, Annapolis, MD.

Reprinted with permission of Naval Institute Press, from *HANDBOOK FOR MARINE NCOs*, by Col. Robert Debs Heinl Jr. Copyright © 1970 by the United States Naval Institute, Annapolis, MD.

Reprinted with permission of *THE NEW YORK TIMES COMPANY*, from "Mao's Primer on Guerrilla Warfare," by Mao Tse-tung. Translated by B.Gen. Samuel B. Griffith. Copyright © 1961 by The New York Times Company.

Reprinted with permission of Harper Collins Publishers, from *MARSHAL ZHUKOV'S GREATEST BATTLES*, edited by Harrison E. Salisbury. Introduction and editorial-comments copyright © 1969 by Harrison E. Salisbury. Translation and maps copyright © 1969 by Harper and Row Publishers, Inc.

Reprinted with permission of the publishers of the *SMITHSONIAN*, from "'. . . heavy fire . . . unable to land . . . issue in doubt,'" by Michael Kernan, November 1993. Copyright © 1993 by the Smithsonian Institution.

Reprinted with permission of the Admiral Nimitz Foundation, from *TARAWA — THE STORY OF A BATTLE*, by Robert Sherrod. Copyright © 1944, 1954, 1973 by Robert Sherrod.

Reprinted with permission of Westview Press, Boulder, CO, from *MANEUVER WARFARE HANDBOOK*, by William S. Lind. Copyright © 1985 by Westview Press.

Reprinted with permission of W.W. Norton & Co., Inc., from *SWORDS AND PLOUGHSHARES*, by Maxwell D. Taylor. Copyright © 1972 by Maxwell D. Taylor.

## Source Notes

Reprinted with permission of W.W. Norton & Co., Inc., from *THE FIRST DAY ON THE SOMME,* by Martin Middlebrook. Copyright © 1972 by Martin Middlebrook.

Reprinted with permission of W.W. Norton & Co., Inc., from *THE BATTLE FOR THE FALKLANDS,* by Max Hastings and Simon Jenkins. Copyright © 1983 by Simon Jenkins.

Reprinted with permission of Random House, Inc., from *THE CIVIL WAR,* by Geoffrey C. Ward. Copyright © 1990 by American Documentaries Inc.

Reprinted with permission of the Greenwood Publishing Group Inc., Westport, CT, from *STORMTROOP TACTICS — INNOVATION IN THE GERMAN ARMY 1914-1918,* by Bruce I. Gudmundsson. Copyright © 1989 by Bruce I. Gudmundsson.

Reprinted with permission of the Greenwood Publishing Group Inc., Westport, CT, from *ON INFANTRY,* by John English. Copyright © 1981 and 1984 by Praeger Publishers.

Reprinted with permission of University of California Press, from *MODERN LAW OF LAND WARFARE,* by Morris Greenspan. Copyright © 1959 by the Regents of the University of California.

Reprinted with permission of Boston Publishing Company, from *VIETNAM EXPERIENCE: PASSING THE TORCH,* by Edward Doyle, Samuel Lipsman, and Stephen Weiss. Copyright © 1981 by Boston Publishing Company.

Reprinted with permission of Boston Publishing Company, from *VIETNAM EXPERIENCE: A CONTAGION OF WAR,* by Terrence Maitland and Peter McInerny. Copyright © 1983 by Boston Publishing Company.

Reprinted with permission of the publishers of *MARINES MAGAZINE,* from "There Were More Than Two," by Cpl. Lance Bacon, February 1994.

Reprinted with permission of Gene Duncan Books, 715 6th St., Boonville, MO 65233, from *GREEN SIDE OUT,* by Maj. H.G. Duncan and Capt. W.T. Moore Jr. Copyright © 1980 by H.G. Duncan.

Reprinted with permission of National Defense Univ. Press, from *FIREPOWER IN LIMITED WAR,* by Robert H. Scales, 1990.

Reprinted with permission of Recon Publications, P.O. Box 14602, Philadelphia, PA 19134-0602, from *HOW WE WON THE WAR,* by Gens. Vo Nguyen Giap and Van Tien Dung. Copyright © 1976 by Recon Publications.

Reprinted with permission of the publishers of *PACIFIC STARS AND STRIPES,* from "Recalling the Jungle Battles of Guadalcanal" by Hal Drake, 2 August 1992. Copyright © 1992 by Pacific Stars and Stripes.

Reprinted with permission of Krieger Publishing Company, Malabar, FL, from *THE HOLOCAUST YEARS: NAZI DESTRUCTION OF EUROPEAN JEWRY,* by Nora Levin, 1990. Copyright © 1968 by Nora Levin.

Reprinted with permission of Harold Matson Company, Inc., from *ENEMY AT THE GATES,* by William Craig. Previously published by Dutton Books. Copyright © 1973 by William Craig.

Reprinted with permission of Peters Fraser & Dunlop Group Ltd., from *AND WE SHALL SHOCK THEM,* by Sir David Fraser. Copyright © 1983 by David Fraser.

Reprinted with permission of Vanguard Press, a division of Random House, Inc., from *IWO JIMA — LEGACY OF VALOR,* by Bill D. Ross. Copyright © 1985 by Bill D. Ross.

Reprinted with permission of Time Life Inc., from *GREAT AGES OF MAN: HISTORIC INDIA,* by Lucille Schulberg and the editors of Time-Life Books. Copyright © 1968 by Time-Life Books Inc.

Reprinted with permission of Time Life Inc., from *THE CIVIL WAR: THE KILLING GROUND,* by Gregory Jaynes and the editors of Time-Life Books. Copyright © 1986 by Time-Life Books Inc.

Reprinted with permission of Shambhala Publications, Inc., P.O. Box 308, Boston, MA 02117, from *THE ART OF WAR,* by Sun Tzu. Translated by Thomas Cleary. Copyright © 1988 by Thomas Cleary.

Reprinted with permission of Sterling Publishing Co., Inc., 387 Park Ave. S., New York, NY 10016, from *SUN TZU'S ART OF WAR: THE MODERN CHINESE INTERPRETATION,* by Gen. Tao Hanzhang. Copyright © 1987 by Gen. Tao Hanzhang.

Reprinted with permission of Oxford University Press, from *THE ART OF WAR,* by Sun Tzu. Translated and with an introduction by Samuel B. Griffith. Foreword by B.H. Liddell Hart. Copyright © 1963 by Oxford University Press.

Source Notes

Reprinted with permission of Andre Deutsch Ltd. and the Mikes Estate, from *THE HUNGARIAN REVOLUTION,* by George Mikes. Copyright © 1957 by Andre Deutsch Ltd.

Reprinted with permission of the Bavousett Estate, from *MORE WORLD WAR II AIRCRAFT IN COMBAT,* by Glen B. Bavousett. Originally published by Arco Publishing. Copyright © 1981 by Glen B. Bavousett.

Reprinted with permission of Pocket Books, a division of Simon & Schuster, Inc., from *THE MARINE RAIDERS,* by Edwin P. Hoyt. Copyright © 1989 by Edwin P. Hoyt.

Reprinted with permission of Henry Holt and Company, Inc., from *PEOPLES WAR — PEOPLES ARMY,* by Vo Nguyen Giap. Copyright © 1962 by Frederick A. Praeger.

Reprinted with permission of Simon & Schuster, from *A DICTIONARY OF MILITARY QUOTATIONS,* by Trevor Royale. Copyright © 1990 by Trevor Royale.

Reprinted with permission of Simon & Schuster, from *ABOUT FACE,* by David Hackworth and Julie Sherman. Copyright © 1989 by David Hackworth and Julie Sherman.

Reprinted with permission of Simon & Schuster, from *THE BIG PUSH,* by Brian Gardner. Copyright © 1961 by Brian Gardner.

Reprinted with permission of Macmillan Publishing, from *GREAT BATTLES OF THE CIVIL WAR,* by John MacDonald. Copyright © 1988 by Marshall Editions Ltd.

Reprinted with permission of David McKay Publishing, a subsidiary of Random House, Inc., from *DEFEAT INTO VICTORY,* by Sir William Slim. Copyright © 1961 by Field Marshal Sir William Slim.

Reprinted with permission of Werner Soderstrom Osakeyhtio — WSOY — from *MEMOIRS OF MARSHAL ZHUKOV,* by Georgi Zhukov. Copyright © 1971.

Reprinted with permission of Alfred A. Knopf Inc., from *CROSSING THE THRESHOLD OF HOPE,* by His Holiness John Paul II. Original copyright © 1994 by Arnoldo Mondadori Editore. Translation copyright © 1994 by Alfred A. Knopf Inc.

Reprinted with permission of the publishers of *SEARCH AND RESCUE MAGAZINE,* from *MANTRACKING* by Roland Robbins. Copyright © 1977 by Dennis E. Kelley.

Reprinted with permission of the publishers of *CIVIL WAR TIMES,* from *BATTLE CHRONICLES OF THE CIVIL WAR,* edited by James M. McPherson. Copyright © 1989 by Civil War Times Illustrations, a division of Cowles Magazines, Inc., P.O. Box 8200, Harrisburg, PA 17105.

Reprinted with permission of Little, Brown and Company, from *THE LAST CITADEL,* by Noah Trudeau. Copyright © 1991 by Noah Andre Trudeau.

Reprinted with permission of Little, Brown and Company, from *MARINE,* by Burke Davis. Copyright © 1962 by Burke Davis.

Reprinted with permission of the Marine Corps Association, from *SOLDIER'S LOAD AND THE MOBILITY OF A NATION,* by S.L.A. Marshall. Copyright © 1950 by the Association of the United States Army.

Reprinted with permission of the publishers of the *MARINE CORPS GAZETTE,* from the following: "Mao's Primer on Guerrilla Warfare," by Mao Tse-tung, 1941; "Tactics in Maneuver Warfare," by William S. Lind, September 1981; "Memories of Dai Do," by B.Gen. William Weiss, September 1987; "Ideas for Changing Doctrine," by Col. Michael D. Wyly, August 1988; "The Legacy and the Lessons of Tarawa," by Maj. Jon T. Hoffman, November 1993; and "Microterrain — A Small-Unit Leader's Ally," by Maj. Rodney L. Dearth, December 1993. Copyright © by the Marine Corps Association.

Reprinted with permission of Harcourt Brace & Company, from *THE ROMMEL PAPERS,* by Lucie-Maria Rommel, B.H. Liddell Hart, Manfred Rommel, Fritz Bayerlein-Dittmar, and Paul Findley. Copyright © 1953 by B.H. Liddell Hart and renewed 1981 by Lady Kathleen Liddell Hart, Fritz Bayerlein-Dittmar, and Manfred Rommel.

Reprinted with permission of Houghton Mifflin Company (all rights reserved), from *WAR AS I KNEW IT,* by Gen. George S. Patton. Copyright © 1947 by Beatrice Patton Walters, Ruth Patton Totten and George Smith Totten. Copyright © renewed 1975 by Maj.Gen. George Patton, Ruth Patton Totten, John K. Waters Jr., and George P. Waters.

Reprinted with permission of Putnam Publishing Group, from *THE SECOND WORLD WAR — AN ILLUSTRATED HISTORY,* by A.J.P. Taylor. Copyright © 1975 by A.J.P. Taylor.

*Endnotes to Chapter 2*

**ENDNOTES**

**Preface**

1. Unidentified American general, as quoted by Maj.Gen. O.K. Steele USMC, in the graduation speech for a Camp Lejeune Platoon Sergeants' Course about 1990.
2. Lt.Gen. Arthur S. Collins Jr. U.S. Army (Ret.), *Common Sense Training — A Working Philosophy for Leaders* (Novato, CA: Presidio Press, 1978), p. 15.
3. Bruce I. Gudmundsson, *Stormtroop Tactics — Innovation in the German Army 1914-1918* (New York: Praeger, 1989), pp. 146, 147.
4. Ibid., p. 94.
5. Georgi K. Zhukov, Marshal of the Soviet Union, *Reminiscences and Reflections*, 1974, in *Warriors' Words — A Quotation Book*, by Peter G. Tsouras (London: Cassel Arms & Armour, 1992), p. 282.
6. Burke Davis, *Marine* (New York: Bantam Books, 1964), pp. 69, 70.
7. Col. David H. Hackworth U.S. Army (Ret.) and Julie Sherman, *About Face* (New York: Simon & Schuster, 1989), p. 818.
8. Col. Amor Le R. Simms, CO of 7th Marines, in *Fighting on Guadalcanal,* from U.S.A. War Office (Washington, D.C.: U.S. Govt. Printing Office, 1942), p. 30.
9. Maj.Gen. J.F.C. Fuller, *The Foundations of Science of War*, 1926, in *Warriors' Words — A Quotation Book*, by Peter G. Tsouras (London: Cassel Arms & Armour, 1992), p. 146.
10. Erwin Rommel, *The Rommel Papers,* ed. B.H. Liddell Hart, 1953, in *A Dictionary of Military Quotations,* by Trevor Royale (New York: Simon & Schuster, 1989), p. 60.
11. Sun Tzu, *The Art of War,* trans. and with an introduction by Samuel B. Griffith, foreword by B.H. Liddell Hart (New York: Oxford Univ. Press, 1963), p. 82.

**Part One:** *The Shortfall in Recorded Knowledge*

**Chapter 1:** *The Anatomy of Small-Unit Victory*

1. Sun Tzu, *The Art of War,* trans. Samuel B. Griffith, p. 39.
2. Robert H. Scales, *Firepower in Limited War* (Washington, D.C.: National Defense Univ. Press, 1990), p. 4.
3. Collins, *Common Sense Training,* p. 102.
4. Ibid., pp. 2, 3.
5. Ibid., p. 8.
6. Ibid., p. 214.
7. Col. Michael D. Wyly, "Ideas for Changing Doctrine," *Marine Corps Gazette,* August 1988, p. 42.
8. Basil H. Liddell Hart, *Thoughts on War,* 1944, in *Warriors' Words — A Quotation Book,* by Peter G. Tsouras (London: Cassel Arms & Armour, 1992), p. 430.
9. Winston Churchill, in a telegram to Anthony Eden, 3 Nov 1940, in *Dictionary of Military and Naval Quotations,* by Col. Robert Debs Heinl Jr. USMC (Ret.) (Annapolis, MD: U.S. Naval Inst., 1966), p. 35.
10. Collins, *Common Sense Training,* pp. 215, 216.
11. Ibid., p. 120.
12. Ibid., p. 201.
13. FMFM 6-4, *Marine Rifle Company/Platoon,* from Marine Corps Develop. & Educ. Cmd. (Washington, D.C.: Hdqts. U.S. Marine Corps, 1978), p. 5.
14. Col. Robert Debs Heinl Jr., *Handbook for Marine NCOs* (Annapolis, MD: U.S. Naval Inst., 1970), p. 308.
15. Gen. George Washington, letter to Henry Knox, 21 Oct 1798, in *Warriors' Words — A Quotation Book,* by Peter G. Tsouras (London: Cassel Arms & Armour, 1992), p. 82.
16. Gen. Maxwell Taylor, *Swords and Ploughshares,* 1972, in *Warriors' Words — A Quotation Book,* by Peter G. Tsouras (London: Cassel Arms & Armour, 1992), p. 82.
17. S.L.A. Marshall, in *The Story of the Non-Commissioned Officer,* by Arnold G. Fisch Jr., and Robert K. Wright Jr., and the general editors (Washington, D.C.: Center of Military Hist., U.S. Army, 1989), pp. 16-18.
18. Bruce I. Gudmundsson, *The Forlorn Hope: Tactical Innovation in the German Army 1914-1918* [renamed "Stormtroop Tactics"], pp. 43-50, in MCI 7401, *Tactical Fundamentals,* 1st course in Warfighting Skills Program (Washington, D.C.: Marine Corps Inst., 1989), p. 46.
19. Collins, *Common Sense Training,* p. 90.
20. Ibid., p. 90.

**Chapter 2:** *Operate on Blind Luck or Win Consistently*

1. Frederick the Great, *Instructions for His Generals,* 1747, in *Warriors' Words — A Quotation Book,* by Peter G. Tsouras (London: Cassel Arms & Armour, 1992), p. 243.

Endnotes to Chapter 3

2. Field Marshal Helmuth Graf von Moltke (1800-1891), in *Warriors' Words — A Quotation Book,* by Peter G. Tsouras (London: Cassel Arms & Armour, 1992), p. 243.
3. Collins, *Common Sense Training,* p. 214.
4. Ibid., p. 214.
5. FMFM 1-1, *Campaigning,* from Marine Corps Combat Develop. Cmd. (Washington, D.C.: Hdqts. U.S. Marine Corps, 1990), p. 7.
6. Robert Leonhard, *The Art of Maneuver* (Novato, CA: Presidio Press, 1991), p. 10.
7. Gen. John J. "Blackjack" Pershing, Commander of the AEF in WWI, in *The Story of the Non-Commissioned Officer,* by Arnold G. Fisch Jr., and Robert K. Wright Jr., and the general editors (Washington, D.C.: Center of Military Hist., U.S. Army, 1989), p. 15.
8. Dwight D. Eisenhower, 17 January 1961, farewell address as President, in *Warriors' Words — A Quotation Book,* by Peter G. Tsouras (London: Cassel Arms & Armour, 1992), p. 104.
9. Gudmundsson, *Stormtroop Tactics,* p. 18.
10. Ibid., p. 177.
11. John S. Mosby, *War Reminiscences,* 1887, in *Dictionary of Military and Naval Quotations,* by Col. Robert Debs Heinl Jr. USMC (Ret.) (Annapolis, MD: U.S. Naval Inst., 1966), p. 139.
12. John F. Kennedy, address to the graduating class of the U.S. Naval Academy, 6 June 1962, in *Dictionary of Military and Naval Quotations,* by Col. Robert Debs Heinl Jr. USMC (Ret.) (Annapolis, MD: U.S. Naval Inst., 1966), p. 140.
13. His Holiness John Paul II, *Crossing the Threshold of Hope* (New York: Alfred A. Knopf, 1995), pp. 205, 206.
14. Morris Greenspan, *Law of Land Warfare* (Berkeley, CA: Univ. of California Press, 1959), pp. 318, 319.
15. Ibid., p. 317.
16. Lt.Col. Chandler USMC (Ret.) (attributed).
17. Greenspan, *Law of Land Warfare,* p. 355.
18. Sun Tzu, *The Art of War,* trans. Samuel B. Griffith, pp. 41, 42.
19. Sun Tzu, *The Art of War,* in *Sun Tzu's Art of War: The Modern Chinese Interpretation,* by Gen. Tao Hanzhang, trans. Yuan Shibing (New York: Sterling Publishing, 1990), p. 71.
20. Sun Tzu, *The Art of War,* trans. Thomas Cleary (Boston, MA: Shambhala Publications, 1988), p. 89.
21. Gen. Vo Nguyen Giap, *Peoples War — Peoples Army,* 1961, in *A Dictionary of Military Quotations,* by Trevor Royale (New York: Simon & Schuster, 1989), p. 60.

**Chapter 3: *Improving One's Chances for Success***

1. Bill D. Ross, *Iwo Jima — Legacy of Valor* (New York: Vintage Books, 1986), p. 135.
2. Ibid., p. 13.
3. Sun Tzu, *The Art of War,* trans. Thomas Cleary, p. 91.
4. Erwin Rommel, *The Rommel Papers,* ed. B. H. Liddell Hart, trans. P. Findlay (New York: Da Capo Press, 1953), p. 523.
5. Ibid., pp. 225, 226.
6. Ibid., p. 130.
7. Sir William Slim, *Defeat into Victory* (New York: David McKay Publishing, 1961), p. 120.
8. MCI 7401, *Tactical Fundamentals,* 1st course in Warfighting Skills Program (Washington, D.C.: Marine Corps Inst., 1989), pp. 37-39.
9. Paddy Griffith, *Forward Into Battle* (Novato, CA: Presidio Press, 1991), p. 50, in MCI 7401, *Tactical Fundamentals,* 1st course in Warfighting Skills Program (Washington, D.C.: Marine Corps Inst., 1989), pp. 37-39.
10. Ibid., p. 49.
11. Scales, *Firepower in Limited War,* p. 180.
12. Maj. Jon T. Hoffman USMCR, "The Legacy and the Lessons of Tarawa," *Marine Corps Gazette,* November 1993, p. 64.
13. Sun Tzu, *The Art of War,* in *Sun Tzu's Art of War: The Modern Chinese Interpretation,* by Gen. Tao Hanzhang, trans. Yuan Shibing (New York: Sterling Publishing, 1990), pp. 99, 100.
14. Ibid., p. 17.
15. Ibid., p. 97.
16. Memo for the record by H.J. Poole.
17. Col. Merritt A. Edson, in *Fighting on Guadalcanal,* from U.S.A. War Office (Washington, D.C.: U.S. Govt. Printing Office, 1942), p. 14.
18. MCI 7401, *Tactical Fundamentals,* p. 70.
19. Sun Tzu, *The Art of War,* trans. Samuel B. Griffith, p. 82.
20. Memo for the record by H.J. Poole.
21. Frederick the Great, *Instructions for His Generals,* 1747, in *Dictionary of Military and Naval Quotations,* by Col. Robert Debs Heinl Jr. USMC (Ret.) (Annapolis, MD: U.S. Naval Inst., 1966), p. 20.
22. Sir William Slim, *Defeat into Victory* (London: Cassel, 1956), pp. 550, 551.
23. Gen. Holland M. "Howlin' Mad" Smith, *Coral and Brass,* 1949, in *Warriors' Words — A Quotation Book,* by Peter G. Tsouras (London: Cassel Arms & Armour, 1992), p. 293.
24. Sun Tzu, *The Art of War,* in *Sun Tzu's Art of War: The Modern Chinese Interpretation,* by Gen. Tao Hanzhang, trans. Yuan Shibing (New York: Sterling Publishing, 1990), p. 95.

*Endnotes to Chapter 5*

25. FMFM 1-3, *Tactics,* from Marine Corps Combat Develop. Cmd. (Washington, D.C.: Hdqts. U.S. Marine Corps, 1991), p. 77.
26. Ibid., pp. 9, 10.
27. Nathan Bedford Forrest (1821-1877), in *Dictionary of Military and Naval Quotations,* by Col. Robert Debs Heinl Jr. USMC (Ret.) (Annapolis, MD: U.S. Naval Inst., 1966), p. 63.
28. Basil H. Liddell Hart, *Thoughts on War,* 1944, in *Dictionary of Military and Naval Quotations,* by Col. Robert Debs Heinl Jr. USMC (Ret.) (Annapolis, MD: U.S. Naval Inst., 1966), p. 63.

**Chapter 4: *Old Habits May Get in the Way***

1. Sun Tzu, *The Art of War,* trans. Samuel B. Griffith, p. 84.
2. Col. M.D. Wyly USMC (Ret.) (attributed).
3. Col. Merritt A. Edson, in *Fighting on Guadalcanal,* from U.S.A. War Office (Washington, D.C.: U.S. Govt. Printing Office, 1942), pp. 14-19.
4. Sun Tzu, *The Art of War,* trans. Samuel B. Griffith, p. 43.
5. Sun Tzu, *The Art of War,* in *Sun Tzu's Art of War: The Modern Chinese Interpretation,* by Gen. Tao Hanzhang, trans. Yuan Shibing (New York: Sterling Publishing, 1990), p. 99.

**Chapter 5: *A Different Style of Warfare May Be Necessary***

1. Scales, *Firepower in Limited War,* pp. 4, 5.
2. *Random House Encyclopedia,* electronic ed., s.v. "Buddhism."
3. Sun Tzu, *The Art of War,* trans. Samuel B. Griffith, p. vii.
4. Ibid.
5. Lucille Schulberg and the editors of Time-Life Books, *Historic India* (New York: Time-Life Books, 1968), p. 61.
6. Ibid., pp. 58, 59.
7. *Random House Encyclopedia,* electronic ed., s.v. "Taoism."
8. Thomas Cleary, in preface to *The Art of War,* by Sun Tzu trans. Thomas Cleary (Boston, MA: Shambhala Publications, 1988), pp. vii, viii.
9. Gudmundsson, *Stormtroop Tactics,* p. 21.
10. Ibid., pp. 161, 162.
11. Ibid., pp. 147-149.
12. Ibid., p. 49.
13. Edward J. Drea, Leavenworth Papers No. 2, *Nomanhan: Japanese — Soviet Tactical Combat, 1939* (Fort Leavenworth, KS: Combat Studies Inst., U.S. Army Cmd. & Gen. Staff College, 1981), p. 45.
14. Gudmundsson, *Stormtroop Tactics,* pp. xi, xii.
15. Ibid., p. 94.
16. Drea, Leavenworth Papers No. 2, *Nomanhan: Japanese — Soviet Tactical Combat, 1939,* pp. 18, 19.
17. Lt.Col. David M. Glantz, Curriculum Supervisor, in foreword to Leavenworth Papers No. 6, *Soviet Night Operations in World War II,* by Maj. Claude R. Sasso (Fort Leavenworth, KS: Combat Studies Inst., U.S. Army Cmd. & Gen. Staff College, 1982), p. viii.
18. Winston S. Churchill, *The World Crisis* (New York: Charles Scribner's Sons, 1923), vol. II, p. 5, in FMFM 1, *Warfighting,* from Marine Corps Combat Develop. Cmd. (Washington, D.C.: Hdqts. U.S. Marine Corps, 1989), p. 17.
19. Sun Tzu, *The Art of War,* trans. Samuel B. Griffith, p. 103.
20. William S. Lind (attributed).
21. Gudmundsson, *Stormtroop Tactics,* p. 84.
22. Ibid., p. 147.
23. Ibid., pp. 147-149.
24. Ibid.
25. Ibid., p. 21.
26. Ibid.
27. Drea, Leavenworth Papers No. 2, *Nomanhan: Japanese — Soviet Tactical Combat, 1939,* p. 88.
28. *Japan/Hong Kong — Singapore,* narrated by John Temple, vol. 1 of "Asian Insights Series" (Lindfield NSW, Australia: Film Australia), distributed by Films Inc. of Chicago, IL, as videocassette 0188-9019.
29. *Random House Encyclopedia,* electronic ed., s.v. "T'ang Dynasty."
30. Samuel B. Griffith, in the introduction to *The Art of War,* by Sun Tzu, trans. Samuel B. Griffith (New York: Oxford Univ. Press, 1963), p. ix.
31. *Random House Encyclopedia,* electronic ed., s.v. "Sung Dynasty."
32. Sun Tzu, *The Art of War,* trans. Thomas Cleary, p. 105.
33. Ibid., p. 54.
34. Sun Tzu, *The Art of War,* in *Sun Tzu's Art of War: The Modern Chinese Interpretation,* by Gen. Tao Hanzhang, trans. Yuan Shibing (New York: Sterling Publishing, 1990), p. 97.

## Endnotes to Chapter 5

35. Sun Tzu, *The Art of War,* trans. Thomas Cleary, p. 96.
36. *Sun Tzu's Art of War: The Modern Chinese Interpretation,* by Gen. Tao Hanzhang, trans. Yuan Shibing (New York: Sterling Publishing, 1990), p. 28.
37. Gudmundsson, *Stormtroop Tactics,* pp. 191, 192.
38. Ibid., p. 104.
39. MCI 7401, *Tactical Fundamentals,* p. 55.
40. Gudmundsson, *Stormtroop Tactics,* p. 94.
41. Drea, Leavenworth Papers No. 2, *Nomonhan: Japanese — Soviet Tactical Combat, 1939,* p. 17.
42. Gudmundsson, *Stormtroop Tactics,* p. 88.
43. Boeicho boeikenshujo senshishitsu, ed., *Senshi sosho Kantogun (1) Tai So senbi Nomonhan jiken* [Official War Hist. Series: The Kwantung Army, vol. 1, Preparations for the War against the USSR and the Nomonhan Incident] (Tokyo: Asagumo shimbunsha, 1969), p. 36, in Edward J. Drea, Leavenworth Papers No. 2, *Nomonhan: Japanese — Soviet Tactical Combat, 1939* (Fort Leavenworth, KS: Combat Studies Inst., U.S. Army Cmd. & Gen. Staff College, 1981), p. 19.
44. Drea, Leavenworth Papers No. 2, *Nomonhan: Japanese — Soviet Tactical Combat, 1939,* p. 19.
45. Boeicho boeikenshujo senshishitsu, ed., *Senshi sosho Kantogun (1) Tai So senbi Nomonhan jiken* [Official War Hist. Series: The Kwantung Army, vol. 1, Preparations for the War against the USSR and the Nomonhan Incident] (Tokyo: Asagumo shimbunsha, 1969), p. 36, in Edward J. Drea, Leavenworth Papers No. 2, *Nomonhan: Japanese — Soviet Tactical Combat, 1939* (Fort Leavenworth, KS: Combat Studies Inst., U.S. Army Cmd. & Gen. Staff College, 1981), p. 19.
46. Drea, Leavenworth Papers No. 2, *Nomonhan: Japanese — Soviet Tactical Combat, 1939,* pp. 17-20.
47. Marshal of the Soviet Union Mikhail N. Tukhachevsky (1893-1937) (attributed), *Red Army 1936 Field Service Regulations,* in *Warriors' Words — A Quotation Book,* by Peter G. Tsouras (London: Cassel Arms & Armour, 1992), p. 417.
48. Drea, Leavenworth Papers No. 2, *Nomonhan: Japanese — Soviet Tactical Combat, 1939,* p. 87.
49. Ibid., pp. 67-69.
50. DOA Pamphlet No. 20-236, *Historical Study — Night Combat,* from U.S. Army Center of Military Hist. (Washington, D.C.: Hdqts. Dept. of the Army, 1953), pp. 19-21.
51. Gudmundsson, *Stormtroop Tactics,* p. 21.
52. Unidentified NCO to Chesty Puller, in *Fighting on Guadalcanal,* from U.S.A. War Office (Washington, D.C.: U.S. Govt. Printing Office, 1942), p. 37.
53. Col. G.C. Thomas USMC, Maj.Gen. Vandegrift's Chief of Staff, in *Fighting on Guadalcanal,* from U.S.A. War Office (Washington, D.C.: U.S. Govt. Printing Office, 1942), p. 65.
54. Unidentified NCO to Chesty Puller, in *Fighting on Guadalcanal,* from U.S.A. War Office (Washington, D.C.: U.S. Govt. Printing Office, 1942), p. 35.
55. Unidentified NCO to Chesty Puller, in *Fighting on Guadalcanal,* from U.S.A. War Office (Washington, D.C.: U.S. Govt. Printing Office, 1942), p. 37.
56. FMFRP 12-9, *Jungle Warfare,* from Marine Corps Combat Develop. Cmd. (Washington, D.C.: Hdqts. U.S. Marine Corps, 1989), p. 41.
57. Col. G.C. Thomas USMC, Maj.Gen. Vandegrift's Chief of Staff, in *Fighting on Guadalcanal,* from U.S.A. War Office (Washington, D.C.: U.S. Govt. Printing Office, 1942), p. 64.
58. Platoon Sgt. F.T. O'Fara, in *Fighting on Guadalcanal,* from U.S.A. War Office (Washington, D.C.: U.S. Govt. Printing Office, 1942), p. 3.
59. Col. Merritt A. Edson, in *Fighting on Guadalcanal,* from U.S.A. War Office (Washington, D.C.: U.S. Govt. Printing Office, 1942), pp. 14, 15.
60. Capt. H.L. Crook, in *Fighting on Guadalcanal,* from U.S.A. War Office (Washington, D.C.: U.S. Govt. Printing Office, 1942), p. 53.
61. Sgt. O.J. Marion, Platoon Guide in Company L, Fifth Marines, in *Fighting on Guadalcanal,* from U.S.A. War Office (Washington, D.C.: U.S. Govt. Printing Office, 1942), p. 12.
62. Drea, Leavenworth Papers No. 2, *Nomonhan: Japanese — Soviet Tactical Combat, 1939,* p. 17.
63. Maj.Gen. Vandegrift, in *Fighting on Guadalcanal,* from U.S.A. War Office (Washington, D.C.: U.S. Govt. Printing Office, 1942), p. v.
64. Hal Drake, "Recalling the Jungle Battles of Guadalcanal," *Pacific Stars and Stripes,* 2 August 1992, pp. 8, 9.
65. Davis, *Marine,* p. 390.
66. Ibid., p. 325.
67. Mao Tse-tung, "Mao's Primer on Guerrilla War," trans. B.Gen. Samuel B. Griffith, in FMFRP 19-9, *The Guerrilla and How to Fight Him,* from Marine Corps Combat Develop. Cmd. (Washington, D.C.: Hdqts. U.S. Marine Corps, 1990), p. 7. Also in the *Marine Corps Gazette,* January 1962 [and a 1941 issue].
68. Edward Doyle, Samuel Lipsman, and Stephen Weiss, *Vietnam Experience: Passing the Torch* (Boston, MA: Boston Publishing, 1981), picture caption on p. 45.
69. Terrence Maitland and Peter McInerney, *Vietnam Experience: A Contagion of War* (Boston, MA: Boston Publishing, 1968), pp. 100, 101.
70. Memo for the record by H.J. Poole.
71. Maitland and McInerney, *Vietnam Experience: A Contagion of War,* p. 9.
72. Gens. Vo Nguyen Giap and Van Tien Dung, *How We Won the War* (Philadelphia, PA: Recon Publications, 1976), pp. 52-54.
73. Hackworth and Sherman, *About Face,* pp. 680, 681.

Endnotes to Chapter 8

74. MCI 7401, *Tactical Fundamentals,* p. 50 [the idea of modern warfare in three distinct generations was originated by William S. Lind].

75. Liddell Hart, in foreword to *The Art of War,* by Sun Tzu, trans. Samuel B. Griffith (New York: Oxford Univ. Press, 1963), p. vii.

76. Samuel B. Griffith, in the introduction to *The Art of War,* by Sun Tzu, trans. Samuel B. Griffith (New York: Oxford Univ. Press, 1963), p. xi.

**Chapter 6: *Perhaps the Role of the Small Unit Must Change***

1. *Fighting on Guadalcanal,* from U.S.A. War Office (Washington, D.C.: U.S. Govt. Printing Office, 1942), p. 68.
2. Gudmundsson, *Stormtroop Tactics,* p. 143.
3. Bill Lind, *Maneuver Warfare Handbook* (Boulder, CO: Westview Press, 1985), p. 25.
4. Ibid., p. 25
5. Basil H. Liddell Hart, *Strategy,* 1954, in *Warriors' Words — A Quotation Book,* by Peter G. Tsouras (London: Cassel Arms & Armour, 1992), p. 179.
6. William S. Lind, "Tactics in Maneuver Warfare," *Marine Corps Gazette,* September 1981, in MCI 7401, *Tactical Fundamentals,* 1st course in Warfighting Skills Program (Washington, D.C.: Marine Corps Inst., 1989), p. C-7.
7. Maitland and McInerney, *Vietnam Experience: A Contagion of War,* p. 97.
8. Vo Nguyen Giap, *Peoples War — Peoples Army* (New York: Frederick A. Praeger, 1962), p. xx.
9. Maitland and McInerney, *Vietnam Experience: A Contagion of War,* p. 101.
10. Ibid., pp. 100-102.

**Chapter 7: *Another Outlook on When to Advance and When to Hold***

1. Sun Tzu, *The Art of War,* trans. Samuel B. Griffith, p. 85.
2. *Webster's New Twentieth Century Dictionary,* unabridged 2nd ed., s.v. "momentum."
3. Gen. Sir David Fraser, *And We Shall Shock Them,* 1983, in *Warriors' Words — A Quotation Book,* by Peter G. Tsouras (London: Cassel Arms & Armour, 1992), p. 24.
4. Sun Tzu, *The Art of War,* trans. Samuel B. Griffith (New York: Oxford Univ. Press, 1963), p. 134, in FMFM 1, *Warfighting,* from Marine Corps Combat Develop. Cmd. (Washington, D.C.: Hdqts. U.S. Marine Corps, 1989), p. 55.
5. Stonewall Jackson, in a letter of April 1863, in *Dictionary of Military and Naval Quotations,* by Col. Robert Debs Heinl Jr. USMC (Ret.) (Annapolis, MD: U.S. Naval Inst., 1966), p. 1, in FMFM 1-1, *Campaigning,* from Marine Corps Combat Develop. Cmd. (Washington, D.C.: Hdqts. U.S. Marine Corps, 1990), p. 53.
6. Gudmundsson, *Stormtroop Tactics,* p. 94.
7. Timothy T. Lupfer, Leavenworth Papers No. 4, *The Dynamics of Doctrine: The Changes in German Tactical Doctrine During the First World War* (Fort Leavenworth, KS: Combat Studies Inst., U.S. Army Cmd. & Gen. Staff College, 1981), in MCI 7401, *Tactical Fundamentals,* 1st course in Warfighting Skills Program (Washington, D.C.: Marine Corps Inst., 1989), p. 43.
8. John MacDonald, *Great Battles of the Civil War* (New York: Macmillan, 1988), p. 106.
9. A.J.P. Taylor, *The Second World War — An Illustrated History* (New York: G.P. Putnam's Sons, 1975), pp. 144-146.
10. Geoffrey C. Ward with Ric Burns and Ken Burns, *The Civil War* (New York: Alfred A. Knopf, 1990), pp. 219-221.
11. Col. Merritt A. Edson, in *Fighting on Guadalcanal,* from U.S.A. War Office (Washington, D.C.: U.S. Govt. Printing Office, 1942), p. 18.
12. Memo for the record by H.J. Poole.
13. Lt.Col. Jack Westerman, in *U.S. Marines in Vietnam: An Expanding War — 1966,* by Jack Shulimson (Washington, D.C.: Hist. & Museums Div., Hdqts. U.S. Marine Corps, 1982), p. 186.

**Chapter 8: *Reassessing the Role of the Weapons***

1. John A. Cash, "Battle of Lang Vei," in *Seven Firefights in Vietnam,* by John A. Cash, John Albright, and Allan W. Sandstrum (Washington, D.C.: Center of Military Hist., U.S. Army, 1985), pp. 109-138.
2. Gudmundsson, *Stormtroop Tactics,* p. 52.
3. Hal Drake, "Recalling the Jungle Battles of Guadalcanal," *Pacific Stars and Stripes,* 2 August 1992, p. 8.
4. Michael Kernan, "'... heavy fire ... unable to land ... issue in doubt,'" *Smithsonian,* November 1993, p. 124.
5. Ross, *Iwo Jima,* p. 294.
6. Scales, *Firepower in Limited War,* p. 180.
7. Max Hastings and Simon Jenkins, *The Battle for the Falklands* (New York: W.W. Norton & Co., 1983), p. 244.
8. Ibid., p. 246.
9. Davis, *Marine,* p. 146.
10. Gudmundsson, *Stormtroop Tactics,* pp. 161, 162.
11. Ross, *Iwo Jima,* pp. 70, 71.

12. George Mikes, *The Hungarian Revolution* (London: Andre Deutsch Ltd., 1957), p. 97.
13. Hackworth and Sherman, *About Face,* p. 594.
14. Sun Tzu, *The Art of War,* trans. Thomas Cleary, p. 67.
15. Drea, Leavenworth Papers No. 2, *Nomanhan: Japanese — Soviet Tactical Combat, 1939,* pp. 64, 65.
16. Gudmundsson, *Stormtroop Tactics,* p. 191.
17. Unidentified NCO to Chesty Puller, in *Fighting on Guadalcanal,* from U.S.A. War Office (Washington, D.C.: U.S. Govt. Printing Office, 1942), p. 35.
18. B.Gen. William Weiss, "Memories of Dai Do," *Marine Corps Gazette,* September 1987, p. 52.
19. S.L.A. Marshall, *Soldier's Load and the Mobility of a Nation* (Quantico, VA: Marine Corps Assoc., 1980), pp. 69, 70.
20. Ibid., pp. 44-46.

**Part Two:** *Techniques from the NCO Corps*

**Chapter 9:** *Successfully Traversing a Battlefield*

1. Sun Tzu, *The Art of War,* in *Sun Tzu's Art of War: The Modern Chinese Interpretation,* by Gen. Tao Hanzhang, trans. Yuan Shibing (New York: Sterling Publishing, 1990), p. 118.
2. Davis, *Marine,* p. 98.
3. Maj.Gen. Vandegrift, in *Fighting on Guadalcanal,* from U.S.A. War Office (Washington, D.C.: U.S. Govt. Printing Office, 1942), p. v.
4. S.L.A. Marshall, *Soldier's Load and the Mobility of a Nation,* pp. 45, 46.
5. Scales, *Firepower in Limited War,* p. 88.
6. FMFM 6-7, *Scouting and Patrolling for Infantry Units,* from Marine Corps Combat Develop. Cmd. (Washington, D.C.: Hdqts. U.S. Marine Corps, 1989), p. E-2.

**Chapter 10:** *Point Men*

1. Unidentified "old" NCO of 2nd Bn./7th Mar., in *Fighting on Guadalcanal,* from U.S.A. War Office (Washington, D.C.: U.S. Govt. Printing Office, 1942), p. 47.
2. Maitland and McInerney, *Vietnam Experience: A Contagion of War,* pp. 96, 97.
3. Platoon Sgt. J.C.L. Hollingsworth, Company H, Fifth Marines, in *Fighting on Guadalcanal,* from U.S.A. War Office (Washington, D.C.: U.S. Govt. Printing Office, 1942), p. 5.
4. Maitland and McInerney, *Vietnam Experience: A Contagion of War,* p. 98.
5. Memo for the record by H.J. Poole.
6. Roland Robbins, *Mantracking* (Montrose, CA: Publishers of *Search and Rescue Magazine,* 1977), pp. 9-20.
7. R.C.B. Haking, *Company Training,* 1917, in *Common Sense Training — A Working Philosophy for Leaders,* by Lt.Gen. Arthur S. Collins Jr. U.S. Army (Ret.) (Novato, CA: Presidio Press, 1978), p. 156.

**Chapter 11:** *Patrols That Look for Trouble*

1. FMFRP 12-9, *Jungle Warfare,* p. 61.
2. Robert E. Lee (1807-1870) (attributed), in *Warriors' Words — A Quotation Book,* by Peter G. Tsouras (London: Cassel Arms & Armour, 1992), p. 36.
3. Drea, Leavenworth Papers No. 2, *Nomanhan: Japanese — Soviet Tactical Combat, 1939,* p. 62.
4. Kyoiku sokanbu [Insp. Gen. of Military Educ.], ed., *Nomanhan Jiken Shosen reishu* [Collected Examples of Skirmishes during the Nomonhan Incident] (Tokyo: 1940), fig. 21, in Leavenworth Papers No. 2, *Nomanhan: Japanese — Soviet Tactical Combat, 1939,* by Edward J. Drea (Fort Leavenworth, KS: Combat Studies Inst., U.S. Army Cmd. & Gen. Staff College, 1981), p. 64.
5. Hackworth and Sherman, *About Face,* pp. 683-703.
6. Field Marshal Aleksandr V. Surorov (1729-1800), in *Warriors' Words — A Quotation Book,* by Peter G. Tsouras (London: Cassel Arms & Armour, 1992), p. 432.

**Chapter 12:** *Winning Chance Contact*

1. Gen. Al Gray USMC (Ret.) (attributed).
2. Sun Tzu, *The Art of War,* in *Sun Tzu's Art of War: The Modern Chinese Interpretation,* by Gen. Tao Hanzhang, trans. Yuan Shibing (New York: Sterling Publishing, 1990), p. 50.
3. MCI 7401, *Tactical Fundamentals,* p. 68.
4. Col.Gen. Heinz Guderian (1888-1954) (attributed), in *Warriors' Words — A Quotation Book,* by Peter G. Tsouras (London: Cassel Arms & Armour, 1992), p. 37.

Endnotes to Chapter 18

    5. Adm. Andrew Browne Cunningham, 11 November 1940 [before attacking the Italian Fleet at Taranto], in *Warriors' Words — A Quotation Book,* by Peter G. Tsouras (London: Cassel Arms & Armour, 1992), p. 37.
    6. Stonewall Jackson, 1863, in *Dictionary of Military and Naval Quotations,* by Col. Robert Debs Heinl Jr. USMC (Ret.) (Annapolis, MD: U.S. Naval Inst., 1966), p. 19.
    7. Davis, *Marine,* p. 29.
    8. Ibid., p. 112.
    9. Dwight D. Eisenhower at the Republican National Convention, in *Warriors' Words — A Quotation Book,* by Peter G. Tsouras (London: Cassel Arms & Armour, 1992), p. 24.
    10. Gudmundsson, *Stormtroop Tactics,* p. 21.

### Chapter 13: *Evening Up the Odds with Indirect Fire*

    1. Scales, *Firepower in Limited War,* p. 74.
    2. Ibid., p. 17.
    3. Ibid., p. 46.
    4. Ibid., p. 89.
    5. Gudmundsson, *Stormtroop Tactics,* p. 161.
    6. Davis, *Marine,* pp. 154-162.

### Chapter 14: *The Great Equalizer — Close Air Support*

    1. Maitland and McInerney, *Vietnam Experience: A Contagion of War,* p. 124.
    2. Memo for the record by H.J. Poole.
    3. Memo for the record by H.J. Poole.
    4. Glen B. Bavousett, *More World War II Aircraft in Combat* (New York: Arco Publishing, 1981), pp. 90, 91.
    5. Memo for the record by H.J. Poole.
    6. Drea, Leavenworth Papers No. 2, *Nomanhan: Japanese — Soviet Tactical Combat, 1939,* p. 77.
    7. Keith William Nolan, *Battle for Hue — Tet 1968* (Novato, CA: Presidio Press, 1983), p. 177.
    8. Scales, *Firepower in Limited War,* p. 16.

### Chapter 15: *Counterambushing*

    1. FMFM 6-4, *Marine Rifle Company/Platoon,* p. 152.
    2. Drea, Leavenworth Papers No. 2, *Nomanhan: Japanese — Soviet Tactical Combat, 1939,* p. 67.
    3. Sun Tzu, *The Art of War,* trans. Samuel B. Griffith, p. 41.

### Chapter 16: *The Ultimate Ambush*

    1. *The Marines in Vietnam 1954-1973: An Anthology and Annotated Bibliography,* from Marine Corps Hist. & Museums Div. (Washington, D.C.: Hdqts U.S. Marine Corps, 1974), p. 73.
    2. Memo for the record by H.J. Poole.
    3. Maitland and McInerney, *Vietnam Experience: A Contagion of War,* p. 100.

### Chapter 17: *When Prepared Enemy Positions are Encountered*

    1. MCI 7401, *Tactical Fundamentals,* p. 51.
    2. Ibid., p. 50.
    3. Ibid., pp. 37, 38.
    4. Memo for the record by H.J. Poole.
    5. Sun Tzu, *The Art of War,* in *Sun Tzu's Art of War: The Modern Chinese Interpretation,* by Gen. Tao Hanzhang, trans. Yuan Shibing (New York: Sterling Publishing, 1990), p. 100.
    6. Col. Merritt A. Edson, in *Fighting on Guadalcanal,* from U.S.A. War Office (Washington, D.C.: U.S. Govt. Printing Office, 1942), p. 14.

### Chapter 18: *The Daylight Attack is the Hardest*

    1. Martin Middlebrook, *The First Day on the Somme* (New York: W.W. Norton & Co., 1972), front cover flap.

2. Ibid., p. 301.
3. Brian Gardner, *The Big Push,* (New York: William Morrow & Co. Inc., 1963), p. 92.
4. Maj. Rodney L. Dearth, "Microterrain — A Small-Unit Leader's Ally," *Marine Corps Gazette,* December 1993, p. 63.
5. Ross, *Iwo Jima,* p. 305.
6. Chang Yu, in *The Art of War,* by Sun Tzu, trans. Samuel B. Griffith (New York: Oxford Univ. Press, 1963), pp. 79, 80.
7. Sun Tzu, *The Art of War,* trans. Samuel B. Griffith, p. 41.
8. Memo for the record by H.J. Poole.
9. Maitland and McInerney, *Vietnam Experience: A Contagion of War,* p. 101.
10. Cpl. Lance Bacon, "There Were More Than Two," *Marines Magazine,* February 1994, pp. 31-33.
11. Col. M.D. Wyly (attributed).
12. Gudmundsson, *Stormtroop Tactics,* pp. 161, 162.
13. Karl von Clausewitz, *Principles of War,* 1812, in *Dictionary of Military and Naval Quotations,* by Col. Robert Debs Heinl Jr. USMC (Ret.) (Annapolis, MD: U.S. Naval Inst., 1966), p. 19.
14. Gregory Jaynes and the editors of Time-Life Books, *The Civil War: The Killing Ground — Wilderness to Cold Harbor* (Alexandria, VA: Time-Life Books, 1986), pp. 89, 90.
15. Ibid., p. 91.
16. Ibid.
17. Memo for the record by H.J. Poole.
18. Memo for the record by H.J. Poole.
19. Gudmundsson, *Stormtroop Tactics,* p. 34.
20. Drea, Leavenworth Papers No. 2, *Nomanhan: Japanese — Soviet Tactical Combat, 1939,* p. 67.
21. Cpl. Fred Carter, Company I, 5th Marines, in *Fighting on Guadalcanal,* from U.S.A. War Office (Washington, D.C.: U.S. Govt. Printing Office, 1942), p. 10.

**Chapter 19**: *Attack at Night to Save Lives*

1. Lt.Col. David M. Glantz, Curriculum Supervisor, in foreword to Leavenworth Papers No. 6, *Soviet Night Operations in World War II,* by Maj. Claude R. Sasso (Fort Leavenworth, KS: Combat Studies Inst., U.S. Army Cmd. & Gen. Staff College, 1982), p. viii.
2. Basil H. Liddell Hart, *Thoughts on War,* 1944, in *Warriors' Words — A Quotation Book,* by Peter G. Tsouras (London: Cassel Arms & Armour, 1992), p. 280.
3. Maj. Claude R. Sasso, Leavenworth Papers No. 6, *Soviet Night Operations in World War II* (Fort Leavenworth, KS: Combat Studies Inst., U.S. Army Cmd. & Gen. Staff College, 1982), p. ix.
4. FMFM 6-4, *Marine Rifle Company/Platoon,* p. 152.
5. Gen. George S. Patton Jr., *War as I Knew It,* 1947, in *Warriors' Words — A Quotation Book,* by Peter G. Tsouras (London: Cassel Arms & Armour, 1992), p. 280.
6. Jaynes, *The Civil War: The Killing Ground — Wilderness to Cold Harbor,* p. 33.
7. Ibid.
8. James M. McPherson, ed., and Richard Gottlief, managing ed., *Battle Chronicles of the Civil War 1864* (New York: Grey Castle Press, 1989), p. 68.
9. Noah Andre Trudeau, *The Last Citadel* (Boston, MA: Little, Brown & Co., 1991), pp. 332-341.
10. *Night Fighting,* 2nd ed. (London: William Clowes & Sons, 1893), p. 9, photocopy of published pamphlet containing translation of articles from *Svoennei Sbornik* [Russian military magazine], December 1885. CARL 355.422 5968n2, in Leavenworth Papers No. 6, *Soviet Night Operations in World War II,* by Maj. Claude R. Sasso (Fort Leavenworth, KS: Combat Studies Inst., U.S. Army Cmd. & Gen. Staff College, 1982), p. ix.
11. Gorman C. Smith, "Division Night Attack Doctrine," (Master's thesis, 1964), pp. 80-81, in Leavenworth Papers No. 6, *Soviet Night Operations in World War II,* by Maj. Claude R. Sasso (Fort Leavenworth, KS: Combat Studies Inst., U.S. Army Cmd. & Gen. Staff College, 1982), p. ix.
12. DOA Pamphlet No. 20-236, *Historical Study — Night Combat,* p. 27.
13. Sasso, Leavenworth Papers No. 6, *Soviet Night Operations in World War II,* p. 43.
14. DOA Pamphlet No. 20-236, *Historical Study — Night Combat,* p. 22.
15. John Erickson, "Combined Arms: Theory and Practice," photocopy of typescript (Edinburgh, Scotland: Univ. of Edinburgh, September 1979), p. 51, in Leavenworth Papers No. 6, *Soviet Night Operations in World War II,* by Maj. Claude R. Sasso (Fort Leavenworth, KS: Combat Studies Inst., U.S. Army Cmd. & Gen. Staff College, 1982), p. 14.
16. Ibid., pp. 35, 36.
17. Ibid., p. 33.
18. Ross, *Iwo Jima,* pp. 297-300.
19. FMFM 6-4, *Marine Rifle Company/Platoon,* p. 153.
20. Hastings and Jenkins, *The Battle for the Falklands,* pp. 285-305.
21. B.Gen. William Weiss, "Memories of Dai Do," *Marine Corps Gazette,* September 1987, p. 44.
22. Gudmundsson, *Stormtroop Tactics,* p. 50.

Endnotes to Chapter 22

23. Ibid., pp. 162-166.
24. Ibid., pp. 32, 33.
25. FMFM 6-4, *Marine Rifle Company/Platoon,* p. 154.
26. Gudmundsson, *Stormtroop Tactics,* p. 191.
27. Maj. Gary L. Telfer, Lt.Col. Lane Rogers, and V. Keith Fleming Jr., *U.S. Marines in Vietnam: Fighting the North Vietnamese — 1967* (Washington, D.C.: Hist. & Museums Div., Hdqts. U.S. Marine Corps, 1984), p. 21.
28. FMFM 6-4, *Marine Rifle Company/Platoon,* p. 188.
29. Drea, Leavenworth Papers No. 2, *Nomanhan: Japanese — Soviet Tactical Combat, 1939,* p. 75.
30. Sgt. O.J. Marion, Platoon Guide in Company L, Fifth Marines, *Fighting on Guadalcanal,* from U.S.A. War Office (Washington, D.C.: U.S. Govt. Printing Office, 1942), pp. 11, 12.
31. Drea, Leavenworth Papers No. 2, *Nomanhan: Japanese — Soviet Tactical Combat, 1939,* p. 69.
32. Sun Tzu, *The Art of War,* in *Sun Tzu's Art of War: The Modern Chinese Interpretation,* by Gen. Tao Hanzhang, trans. Yuan Shibing (New York: Sterling Publishing, 1990), p. 33.

**Chapter 20: *The Safest Way to Attack — Short-Range Infiltration***

1. Sun Tzu, *The Art of War,* in *Sun Tzu's Art of War: The Modern Chinese Interpretation,* by Gen. Tao Hanzhang, trans. Yuan Shibing (New York: Sterling Publishing, 1990), p. 33.
2. Gudmundsson, *Stormtroop Tactics,* p. 136.
3. Ibid., p. 134.
4. Drea, Leavenworth Papers No. 2, *Nomanhan: Japanese — Soviet Tactical Combat, 1939,* p. 57.
5. Ibid., pp. 64, 65.
6. Ibid., p. 62.
7. Davis, *Marine,* pp. 154-162.
8. FMFRP 12-9, *Jungle Warfare,* p. 41.
9. Memo for the record by H.J. Poole.
10. Memo for the record by H.J. Poole.
11. Memo for the record by H.J. Poole.
12. DOA Pamphlet No. 20-236, *Historical Study — Night Combat,* pp. 22, 23.
13. Cpl. Lance Bacon, "There Were More Than Two," *Marines Magazine,* February 1994, pp. 31-33.
14. Ibid.
15. Memo for the record by H.J. Poole.
16. Gudmundsson, *Stormtroop Tactics,* p. 51.
17. MCI 7401, *Tactical Fundamentals,* p. 49.
18. Bruce I. Gudmundsson, *The Forlorn Hope: Tactical Innovation in the German Army 1914-1918* [renamed "Stormtroop Tactics"], p. 43-50, in MCI 7401, *Tactical Fundamentals,* 1st course in Warfighting Skills Program (Washington, D.C.: Marine Corps Inst., 1989), p. 46.
19. George S. Patton, *Cavalry Journal,* April 1922, p. 167, in FMFM 1, *Warfighting,* from Marine Corps Combat Develop. Cmd. (Washington, D.C.: Hdqts. U.S. Marine Corps, 1989), p. 39.

**Chapter 21: *Defend Only to Reestablish Momentum***

1. Sun Tzu, *The Art of War,* in *Sun Tzu's Art of War: The Modern Chinese Interpretation,* by Gen. Tao Hanzhang, trans. Yuan Shibing (New York: Sterling Publishing, 1990), p. 50.
2. Sun Tzu, *The Art of War,* trans. Samuel B. Griffith, p. 85.
3. Sun Tzu, *The Art of War,* trans. Thomas Cleary, p. 90.
4. Sun Tzu, *The Art of War,* in *Sun Tzu's Art of War: The Modern Chinese Interpretation,* by Gen. Tao Hanzhang, trans. Yuan Shibing (New York: Sterling Publishing, 1990), p. 104.
5. Ibid., p. 95.
6. Davis, *Marine,* pp. 159-162.
7. Michael Kernan, "'... heavy fire ... unable to land ... issue in doubt,'" *Smithsonian,* November 1993, p. 121.
8. Memo for the record by H.J. Poole.
9. DOA Pamphlet No. 20-236, *Historical Study — Night Combat,* p. 43.
10. Memo for the record by H.J. Poole.
11. Ibid.

**Chapter 22: *Surviving the Unthinkable — NBC Attack***

1. FC 3-9-1, *Toxins,* from U.S. Army Chemical School (Fort Monroe, VA: TRADOC Cmdr., 1986), p. 1.
2. FM 3-5, *NBC Decontamination,* from U.S. Army Chemical School (Washington, D.C.: Hdqts. Dept. of the Army, 1985), p. C-4.

## Endnotes to Chapter 26

**Chapter 23: *The Unbeatable Urban Defense***

1. Sun Tzu, *The Art of War,* trans. Samuel B. Griffith, p. 78.
2. Nora Levin, *The Holocaust* (New York: Thomas Y. Crowell Co., 1968), pp. 343-352.
3. William Craig, *The Enemy at the Gates — The Battle for Stalingrad* (New York: Readers Digest Press, 1973), pp. 102, 103.
4. Taylor, *The Second World War — An Illustrated History,* p. 146.
5. Georgi K. Zhukov, *Marshal Zhukov's Greatest Battles,* ed. Harrison E. Salisbury, trans. Theodore Shabad (New York: Harper & Row Publishers, 1969), p. 288.
6. Levin, *The Holocaust,* p. 346.
7. Karl von Clausewitz, *On War,* 1832, in *Dictionary of Military Quotations,* by Trevor Royale (New York: Simon & Schuster, 1989), p. 14.
8. Robert Sherrod, *Tarawa — The Story of a Battle* (Fredericksburg, TX: Admiral Nimitz Foundation, 1944), pp. 89, 90.
9. Michael Kernan, "'... heavy fire ... unable to land ... issue in doubt,'" *Smithsonian,* November 1993, p. 128.

**Chapter 24: *What the Urban Attacker Must Know to Stay Alive***

1. Sun Tzu, *The Art of War,* trans. Samuel B. Griffith, p. 73.
2. Davis, *Marine,* p. 275.
3. Mahan, *Lessons of War with Spain,* 1899, *Dictionary of Military and Naval Quotations,* by Col. Robert Debs Heinl Jr. USMC (Ret.) (Annapolis, MD: U.S. Naval Inst., 1966), p. 306.
4. Nolan, *Battle for Hue,* pp. 46, 47.

**Chapter 25: *Getting Ready to Meet the Test***

1. Maitland and McInerney, *Vietnam Experience: A Contagion of War,* p. 94.
2. Sun Tzu, *The Art of War,* trans. Thomas Cleary, pp. 80, 81.
3. Sun Tzu, *The Art of War,* in *Sun Tzu's Art of War: The Modern Chinese Interpretation,* by Gen. Tao Hanzhang, trans. Yuan Shibing (New York: Sterling Publishing, 1990), p. 100.
4. Ibid., p. 118.
5. S.L.A. Marshall, *Bringing Up the Rear,* 1978, in *Warriors' Words — A Quotation Book,* by Peter G. Tsouras (London: Cassel Arms & Armour, 1992), p. 238.
6. Maj.Gen. Vandegrift, in *Fighting on Guadalcanal,* from U.S.A. War Office (Washington, D.C.: U.S. Govt. Printing Office, 1942), p. v.
7. Robert J. Marzano, *A Different Kind of Classroom* (Alexandria, VA: Assoc. for Supervision and Curriculum Develop. (ASCD), 1992), pp. 67, 68; and ASCD staff, *Learning About Learning* (Alexandria, VA: ASCD, 1992), pp. 21-28.
8. Gudmundsson, *Stormtroop Tactics,* pp. 146, 147.
9. Col. Merritt A. Edson, in *Fighting on Guadalcanal,* from U.S.A. War Office (Washington, D.C.: U.S. Govt. Printing Office, 1942), pp. 14-19.
10. *Fighting on Guadalcanal,* from U.S.A. War Office, pp. 66, 67.
11. Gudmundsson, *Stormtroop Tactics,* p. 1.
12. Ibid., p. 87.
13. George S. Patton, *War as I Knew It,* 1947, in *A Dictionary of Military Quotations,* by Trevor Royale (New York: Simon & Schuster, 1989), p. 108.
14. *Unites States Marine Corps Systems Approach to Training,* chapt. 2, from Marine Corps Combat Develop. Cmd. (Washington, D.C. Hdqts. U.S. Marine Corps, 1993); also "Write a Learning Objective," training support package no. 15, task #9806.11, from East Coast Instructional Management School (Camp Lejeune, NC: Base Cmdr., 1993).
15. Maitland and McInerney, *Vietnam Experience: A Contagion of War,* p. 97.
16. Japanese Research Div., Military Hist. Sect., Hdqts. U.S. Army Forces Far East, "Japanese Night Combat," pt. 1, *Principles of Night Combat,* 1955, charts 1-a-d, 2-1-f, and 3-a-e, respectively, in Leavenworth Papers No. 2, *Nomanhan: Japanese — Soviet Tactical Combat, 1939,* by Edward J. Drea (Fort Leavenworth, KS: Combat Studies Inst., U.S. Army Cmd. & Gen. Staff College, 1981), p. 20.
17. Sun Tzu, *The Art of War,* in *Sun Tzu's Art of War: The Modern Chinese Interpretation,* by Gen. Tao Hanzhang, trans. Yuan Shibing (New York: Sterling Publishing, 1990), p. 107.

**Chapter 26: *What All of This May Mean to the Big Picture***

1. Sun Tzu, *The Art of War,* trans. Thomas Cleary, pp. 80, 81.
2. Lind, *Maneuver Warfare Handbook,* p. 25.
3. Gudmundsson, *Stormtroop Tactics,* p. 18.
4. John A. English, *On Infantry* (New York: Praeger, 1981), p. 217.

## Endnotes to Chapter 26

5. Col. Merritt A. Edson, in *Fighting on Guadalcanal,* from U.S.A. War Office (Washington, D.C.: U.S. Govt. Printing Office, 1942), pp. 14, 15.
6. Gudmundsson, *Stormtroop Tactics,* p. 157.
7. Ibid., p. 173.
8. Ibid., p. 173.
9. Ibid., p. 175.
10. Ibid., p. xiii.
11. Edwin P. Hoyt, *The Marine Raiders* (New York: Pocket Books, 1989), p. 16.
12. Sun Tzu, *The Art of War,* trans. Thomas Cleary, pp. 80, 81.
13. Sun Tzu, *The Art of War,* in *Sun Tzu's Art of War: The Modern Chinese Interpretation,* by Gen. Tao Hanzhang, trans. Yuan Shibing (New York: Sterling Publishing, 1990), p. 104.
14. Abraham Lincoln, from a speech to temperance workers in 1842, in "Lincoln," *Life Magazine,* February 1991, p. 27.
15. Col. Amor Le R. Simms, CO of 7th Marines, in *Fighting on Guadalcanal,* from U.S.A. War Office (Washington, D.C.: U.S. Govt. Printing Office, 1942), p. 30.
16. Field Marshal Erwin Rommel, *The Rommel Papers,* 1953 in *Warriors' Words — A Quotation Book,* by Peter G. Tsouras (London: Cassel Arms & Armour, 1992), p. 224.

# Glossary

| | | |
|---|---|---|
| A-6 | Aircraft | Fixed-wing jet from the Vietnam era that had all-weather close-air-support capability. |
| A-10 | Aircraft | Slow moving fixed-wing jet designed to kill tanks. |
| AC-130 | Aircraft | Propeller-driven fixed-wing aircraft that carries a rapid firing Vulcan cannon, a 105mm howitzer, and other weapons. By circling a target, it can deliver extremely accurate fire. |
| ACA | Airspace Coordination Area | An area through which indirect-fire weapons cannot shoot. |
| AK-47 | Assault rifle | Communist Bloc assault rifle using 7.62mm ammunition. |
| AP | Attack Point | A location that a land navigator knows beyond any shadow of a doubt that he can find. |
| AP | Attack Position | A maneuver area that contains the firing points for a helicopter gunship. It's the equivalent of the Initial Point (IP) for fixed-wing aircraft. |
| AT-4 | Antitank (weapon) | Shoulder-fired antitank weapon organic to the infantry company. |
| BAMCIS | Management acronym | Troop Leading Procedures: Begin planning (make estimate of situation and analyze mission, plan how to use time and issue warning order, continue to estimate situation, make final plan); Arrange for (movement of unit, reconnaissance, issuance of order, coordination); Make reconnaissance; Complete plan; Issue order; Supervise. |
| BCS | Battery Computer System | Computer at the artillery battery fire direction center that allows artillery pieces in any configuration on the ground to fire their rounds in a circle with a 100-meter radius (standard sheaf). |
| BOF | Base of Fire | The traditional mission for the support element in an attack. It provides covering fire as needed for the maneuver element. |
| CAS | Close Air Support | Airstrikes by aircraft in support of ground forces. |
| CP | Command Post | Headquarters for a unit. |
| CP | Contact Point | Where a fixed-wing aircraft circles to receive the pilot brief for a close-air-support mission. |
| CS | Choking agent | Riot-control agent. |
| DASC | Direct Air Support Center | Coordination agency for air support. |
| DMZ | De-Militarized Zone | The buffer zone between North and South Vietnam. |
| DPICM | Dual-Purpose Improved Conventional Munitions | Antitank bomblets. |
| F-4 | Aircraft | Extremely durable fixed-wing jet of the Vietnam era. |

## Glossary

| | | |
|---|---|---|
| F/A-18 | Aircraft | Modern fixed-wing jet with some all-weather close-air-support capability. |
| FAC | Forward Air Controller | Person tasked with controlling airstrikes. |
| FAE | Fuel Air Explosive | A fire bomb that explodes above the earth, sucking up all the oxygen beneath it. |
| FCL | Final Coordination Line | Last covered position before a daylight attack objective. This is where the unit forms for the assault. |
| FDC | Fire Direction Center | Coordination agency for indirect-fire support. |
| FEBA | Forward Edge of the Battle Area | The line being defended. |
| FM | Field Manual | Military manual. |
| FMFM | Fleet Marine Force Manual | Manual used by the Marines. |
| FO | Forward Observer | Person tasked with controlling artillery or mortar attacks. |
| FPL | Final Protective Line | Direction of fire for a machinegun in the final protective fires for a defensive position. It extends across the entire front of a defensive sector. |
| GC | Grid Coordinate | Location on a map. |
| HA | Holding Area | Location at which a helicopter gunship receives a pilot brief. |
| HC | High Concentration | A type of white-smoke hand grenade. |
| HE | High Explosive | Type of artillery or mortar round. |
| HF | High Frequency | Range of radio bands. |
| H&I | Harassing and Interdiction | Category of artillery fires. |
| IP | Initial Point | Point from which a fixed-wing aircraft starts his final run on the target. |
| LAAW | Light Assault Antitank Weapon | Vietnam era antitank missile that comes packed in its own firing tube. |
| LD | Line of Departure | The location at which an attack starts. Sometimes the maneuver and support elements part company at the LD. |
| LDR | Leader | Person in charge of a unit. |
| LP | Listening Post | Two-man security post deployed forward of a defensive position at night. |
| M8 | Chemical detection paper | Detects type of chemical attack from liquids present. |
| M16A2 | Rifle | Rifle carried by U.S. infantrymen. |
| M17 | Gas mask | Gas mask with internal filters. This mask is currently being phased out. |
| M40 | Gas mask | Gas mask with external screw-on filters. |
| M72 | Antitank missile | Light Assault Antitank Weapon (LAAW) used during the Vietnam War. |
| M79 | Grenade launcher | 40mm grenade launcher from the Vietnam era. |
| M203 | Grenade launcher | 40mm grenade launcher attachment for the M16A2 rifle. Each fire team has one. |

| | | |
|---|---|---|
| M256 | Chemical detection kit | Detects type of chemical attack from vapors present. |
| M258A1 | Decontamination kit. | Packets for decontaminating bare skin and individual weapons after a chemical attack. |
| METT-TSL | Acronym describing a combat situation | Mission, Enemy, Terrain and Weather, Troops and Fire Support Available — Time, Space, Logistics. |
| MG | Machinegun | Heavy automatic small arm organic to the Marine infantry company. |
| MILES | Multiple Integrated Laser Engagement System | Casualty assessment equipment. A weapon attachment shoots a laser beam every time a blank is fired. This beam can cause the laser detectors on an opponent's body harness and headgear to "beep." |
| MK-19 | Grenade launcher | 40mm-grenade-launching machinegun organic to the Marine infantry battalion. |
| MOPP | Mission-Oriented Protective Posture | Suit for protection against Nuclear, Chemical, Biological (NBC) attack. |
| MOUT | Military Operations in Urban Terrain | Military operations in cities. |
| MULE | Modular Universal Laser Equipment | Laser designator. |
| NCO | Non-Commissioned Officer | Enlisted man of grade E-4 or above. |
| NBC | Nuclear, Biological, Chemical | A type of nonconventional warfare. |
| NVA | North Vietnamese Army | The enemy during the Vietnam War. |
| NVG | Night Vision Goggles | Goggles that enhance existing light at night. |
| OBJ | Objective | Target for a ground assault. |
| OP | Observation Post | Two-man security post deployed forward of a defensive position in the daytime. |
| ORP | Objective Rally Point | Rally location behind an ambush site. |
| O-T | Observer-Target (line) | Line between an artillery observer and his target. |
| PD | Point of Departure | The point at which a force attacking at night crosses the line of departure. |
| PLD | Probable Line of Deployment | The line at which a force attacking at night forms for the assault. |
| PLT | Platoon | Infantry unit comprised of three squads. |
| PP4276 | Recharger | Recharges and rezeroes the pocket dosimeter (radiation detector). |
| PT-76 | Tank | Lightly armored amphibious tank used by the North Vietnamese. |
| RABFAC | Radar Beacon Forward Air Controller | Radio signal transmitter with which to run an airstrike during periods of reduced visibility. |
| S-2 | Intelligence officer | Staff officer on the battalion staff. |
| SAW | Squad Automatic Weapon | M249 automatic weapon carried by each fire team. |
| SEAD | Suppression of Enemy Air Defenses | Suppression of anti-aircraft fire during an airstrike. |
| SMAW | Shoulder-launched Multipurpose Assault Weapon | Bunker buster organic to the Marine infantry company. |
| SNCO | Staff Non-Commissioned Officer | Enlisted man of grade E-6 and above. |

## Glossary

| | | |
|---|---|---|
| SP | Sentry Post | Two-man security post deployed forward of a defensive position. |
| SQD | Squad | Infantry unit comprised of three fire teams. |
| SRP | Squad Release Point | The point at which the squads in a night attack separate. |
| STB | Super Tropical Bleach | Powder used in liquid and solid slurries to decontaminate gear after chemical attack. |
| TACP | Tactical Air Control Party | Those tasked with controlling airstrikes. |
| TACWAR | Wargaming board | Board simulating relief and vegetation at a scale of 100 yards per inch. |
| TAOR | Tactical Area of Responsibility | A large unit's defensive security sector. |
| T&E | Traversing and Elevation | Adjustable mechanism to steady a machinegun on its tripod. |
| TOT | Time on Target | Time that ordnance is scheduled to hit a target. |
| TOW | Tube-launched, Optically tracked, Wire-guided | Antitank missile. |
| TTT | Time to Target | Time an aircraft takes to run in on his target. |
| UHF | Ultra High Frequency | Range of radio bands. |
| VHF | Very High Frequency | Range of radio bands. |
| VC | Viet Cong | Enemy irregulars in Vietnam. |
| VT | Variable Time | Fuze that causes an artillery round to explode above the ground. |
| WP | White Phosphorus | Type of artillery round. |

# Bibliography

**Military Research, Historical Studies, Manuals, and Course Materials:**

DOA Pamphlet No. 20-236. *Historical Study — Night Combat.* From U.S. Army Center of Military Hist. Washington, D.C.: Dept. of the Army, 1953.
Drea, Edward J. *Nomanhan: Japanese — Soviet Tactical Combat, 1939.* Leavenworth Papers No. 2. Fort Leavenworth, KS: Combat Studies Inst., U.S. Cmd. & Gen. Staff College, 1981.
FC 3-9-1. *Toxins.* From U.S. Army Chemical School. Fort Monroe, VA: TRADOC Cmdr., 1986.
*Fighting on Guadalcanal.* From U.S.A. War Office. Washington, D.C.: U.S. Govt. Printing Office, 1942.
FM 3-5. *NBC Decontamination.* From U.S. Army Chemical School. Washington, D.C.: Hdqts. Dept. of the Army, 1985.
FMFM 1. *Warfighting.* From Marine Corps Combat Develop. Cmd. Washington, D.C.: Hdqts. U.S. Marine Corps, 1989.
FMFM 1-1. *Campaigning.* From Marine Corps Combat Develop. Cmd. Washington, D.C.: Hdqts. U.S. Marine Corps, 1990.
FMFM 1-3. *Tactics.* From Marine Corps Combat Develop. Cmd. Washington, D.C.: Hdqts. U.S. Marine Corps, 1991.
FMFM 6-4. *Marine Rifle Company/Platoon.* From Marine Corps Develop. & Educ. Cmd. Washington, D.C.: Hdqts. U.S. Marine Corps, 1978.
FMFM 6-7. *Scouting and Patrolling for Infantry Units.* From Marine Corps Combat Develop. Cmd. Washington, D.C.: Hdqts. U.S. Marine Corps, 1989.
FMFRP 12-9. *Jungle Warfare.* From Marine Corps Combat Develop. Cmd. Washington, D.C.: Hdqts. U.S. Marine Corps, 1989.
Lupfer, Timothy T. *The Dynamics of Doctrine: The Changes in German Tactical Doctrine During the First World War.* Leavenworth Papers No. 4. Fort Leavenworth, KS: Combat Studies Inst., U.S. Army Cmd. & Gen. Staff College, 1981.
MCI 7401. *Tactical Fundamentals.* 1st course in Warfighting Skills Program. Washington, D.C.: Marine Corps Inst., 1989.
Sasso, Maj. Claud R. *Soviet Night Operations in World War II.* Leavenworth Papers No. 6. Fort Leavenworth, KS: Combat Studies Inst., U.S. Army Cmd. & Gen. Staff College, 1982.
Shulimson, Jack. *U.S. Marines in Vietnam: An Expanding War — 1966.* Washington, D.C.: Hist. & Museums Div., Hdqts. U.S. Marine Corps, 1982.
Telfer, Gary L., Lane Rogers, and V. Keith Fleming Jr. *U.S. Marines in Vietnam: Fighting the North Vietnamese — 1967.* Washington, D.C.: Hist. and Museums Div., Hdqts. U.S. Marine Corps, 1984.
*The Marines in Vietnam 1954-1973: An Anthology and Annotated Bibliography.* From Marine Corps Hist. & Museums Div. Washington, D.C.: Hdqts. U.S. Marine Corps, 1974.
*United States Marine Corps Systems Approach to Training.* Chapt. 2. From Marine Corps Combat Develop. Cmd. Washington, D.C.: Hdqts. U.S. Marine Corps, 1993. Also "Write a Learning Objective." Training support package no. 15, task #9806.11. From East Coast Instructional Management School. Camp Lejeune, NC: Base Cmdr., 1993.

**Books and Magazine Articles:**

Bacon, Cpl. Lance. "There Were More Than Two." *Marines*, February 1994.
Bavousett, Glen B. *More World War II Aircraft in Combat.* New York: Arco Publishing, 1981.
Cash, John A.; John Albright; and Allan W. Sandstrum. *Seven Firefights in Vietnam.* Washington, D.C.: Center of Military Hist., U.S. Army, 1985.
Collins, Lt.Gen. Arthur S., Jr. *Common Sense Training — A Working Philosophy for Leaders.* Novato, CA: Presidio Press, 1978.
Craig, William. *The Enemy at the Gates — The Battle for Stalingrad.* New York: Readers Digest Press, 1973.
Davis, Burke. *Marine.* New York: Bantam Books, 1964.
Dearth, Maj. Rodney L. "Microterrain — A Small Unit Leader's Ally." *Marine Corps Gazette*, December 1993.
Doyle, Edward; Samuel Lipsman; and Stephen Weiss. *Vietnam Experience: Passing the Torch.* Boston, MA: Boston Publishing, 1981.
Drake, Hal. "Recalling the Jungle Battles of Guadalcanal." *Pacific Stars and Stripes*, 2 August 1992.
Duncan, Maj. H.G., and Capt. W.T. Moore Jr. *Green Side Out.* Clearwater, FL: D&S Publishers, 1980.
English, John A. *On Infantry.* New York: Praeger, 1981.

# Bibliography

Fisch, Arnold G., Jr.; Robert K. Wright Jr.; and the general editors. *The Story of the Non-Commissioned Officer.* Washington, D.C.: Center of Military Hist., U.S. Army, 1989.

Fraser, Sir David. *And We Shall Shock Them.* London: Hodder & Stoughton, 1983.

Gardner, Brian. *The Big Push.* New York: William Morrow & Co. Inc., 1963.

Giap, Gen. Vo Nguyen, and Gen. Van Tien Dung. *How We Won the War.* Philadelphia, PA: Recon Publications, 1976.

Giap, Vo Nguyen. *Peoples War — Peoples Army.* New York: Frederick A. Praeger, 1961.

Greenspan, Morris. *Law of Land Warfare.* Berkeley, CA: Univ. of California Press, 1959.

Gudmundsson, Bruce I. *Stormtroop Tactics — Innovation in the German Army 1914-1918.* New York: Praeger, 1989.

Hackworth, David H., and Julie Sherman. *About Face.* New York: Simon & Schuster, 1989.

Hanzhang, Gen. Tao. *Sun Tzu's Art of War — The Modern Chinese Interpretation.* Trans. Yuan Shibing. New York: Sterling Publishing, 1990.

Hastings, Max, and Simon Jenkins. *The Battle for the Falklands.* New York: W.W. Norton & Co., 1983.

Heinl, Col. Robert Debs, Jr. *Dictionary of Military and Naval Quotations.* Annapolis, MD: U.S. Naval Inst., 1966.

Heinl, Col. Robert Debs, Jr. *Handbook for Marine NCOs.* Annapolis, MD: U.S. Naval Inst., 1979.

Hoffman, Maj. Jon T. "The Legacy and the Lessons of Tarawa." *Marine Corps Gazette*, November 1993.

Hoyt, Edwin P. *The Marine Raiders.* New York: Pocket Books, 1989.

John Paul II. *Crossing the Threshold of Hope.* New York: Alfred A. Knopf Inc., 1995.

Kernan, Michael. "'...heavy fire...unable to land...issue in doubt.'" *Smithsonian*, November 1993.

Leonhard, Robert. *The Art of Maneuver.* Novato, CA: Presidio Press, 1991.

Levin, Nora. *The Holocaust.* New York: Thomas Y. Crowell Co., 1968.

Lincoln, Abraham. "Lincoln." *Life Magazine*, February 1991.

Lind, William S. *Maneuver Warfare Handbook.* Boulder, CO: Westview Press, 1984.

Lind, William S. "Tactics in Maneuver Warfare." *Marine Corps Gazette*, September 1981.

MacDonald, John. *Great Battles of the Civil War.* New York: Macmillan, 1988.

Maitland, Terrence, and Peter McInerney. *Vietnam Experience: A Contagion of War.* Boston, MA: Boston Publishing, 1983.

Mao Tse-tung. "Mao's Primer on Guerrilla War." Trans. B.Gen. Samuel B. Griffith. In FMFRP 19-9, *The Guerrilla and How to Fight Him.* From Marine Corps Combat Develop. Cmd. Washington, D.C.: Hdqts U.S. Marine Corps, 1990. Also in the *Marine Corps Gazette*, January 1962 [and a 1941 issue].

Marshall, S.L.A. *Soldiers Load and the Mobility of a Nation.* Quantico, VA: Marine Corps Assoc., 1980.

Marzano, Robert J. *A Different Kind of Classroom.* Alexandria, VA: Assoc. for Supervision and Curriculum Develop. (ASCD), 1992. Also ASCD staff. *Learning About Learning.* Alexandria, VA: ASCD, 1992.

McPherson, James M., ed., and Richard Gottlief, managing ed. *Battle Chronicles of the Civil War 1864.* New York: Grey Castle Press, 1989.

Middlebrook, Martin. *The First Day on the Somme.* New York: W.W. Norton & Co., 1972.

Mikes, George. *The Hungarian Revolution.* London: Andre Deutsch Ltd., 1957.

Nolan, Keith William. *Battle for Hue — Tet 1968.* Novato, CA: Presidio Press, 1983.

Patton, Gen. George S. *War As I Knew It.* New York: Houghton Mifflin Co., 1947.

Robbins, Roland. *Mantracking.* Montrose, CA: Publishers of *Search and Rescue Magazine*, 1977.

Rommel, Erwin. *The Rommel Papers.* Ed. by B. H. Liddell Hart. Trans. P. Findlay. New York: Da Capo Press, 1953.

Ross, Bill D. *Iwo Jima — Legacy of Valor.* New York: Vintage Books, 1986.

Royale, Trevor. *A Dictionary of Military Quotations.* New York: Simon & Schuster, 1989.

Scales, Robert H. *Firepower in Limited War.* Washington, D.C.: National Defense Univ. Press, 1990.

Schulberg, Lucille, and the editors of Time-Life Books. *Historic India.* New York: Time-Life Books, 1968.

Sherrod, Robert. *Tarawa — the Story of a Battle.* Fredericksburg, TX: Admiral Nimitz Foundation, 1944.

Slim, Sir William. *Defeat into Victory.* New York: David McKay Co., 1961.

Sun Tzu. *The Art of War.* Trans. and with an introduction by Samuel B. Griffith. Foreword by B.H. Liddell Hart. New York: Oxford Univ. Press, 1963.

Sun Tzu. *The Art of War.* Trans. Thomas Cleary. Boston, MA: Shambhala Publications, 1988.

Taylor, A.J.P. *The Second World War — An Illustrated History.* New York: G.P. Putnam's Sons, 1975.

Taylor, Maxwell. *Swords and Ploughshares.* New York: W.W. Norton & Co., 1983.

Trudeau, Noah Andre. *The Last Citadel.* Boston: Little, Brown & Co., 1991.

Tsouras, Peter G. *Warriors Words — A Quotation Book.* London: Cassel Arms & Armour, 1992.

Ward, Geoffrey C., with Ric Burns and Ken Burns. *The Civil War.* New York: Alfred A. Knopf Inc., 1990.

Weiss, B.Gen. William. "Memories of Dai Do." *Marine Corps Gazette*, September 1987.

Wyly, Col. Michael D. "Ideas for Changing Doctrine." *Marine Corps Gazette*, August 1988.

Zhukov, Georgi K. *Marshal Zhukov's Greatest Battles.* Ed. Harrison E. Salisbury. Trans. Theodore Shabad. New York: Harper & Row Publishers, 1969.

Zhukov, Georgi K. *Memoirs of Marshal Zhukov.* New York: Delacourt, 1971.

**Videotapes:**

*Japan/Hong Kong — Singapore.* Narrated by John Temple. Vol. 1 of "Asian Insights Series" from Film Australia of Linfield NSW, Australia. Distributed by Films Inc. of Chicago, IL, as videocassette 0188-9019.

# About the Author

After almost twenty-eight years as a commissioned and non-commissioned infantry officer, H.J. Poole retired from the United States Marine Corps on 1 April 1993. On active duty, he studied small-unit tactics for nine years: 6 months at the Basic School in Quantico (1966), 7 months as a platoon commander in Vietnam (1966-67), 3 months as a rifle company commander at Camp Pendleton (1967), 5 months as a regimental headquarters company commander in Vietnam (1968), 8 months as a rifle company commander in Vietnam (1968-69), five and a half years as an instructor with the Advanced Infantry Training Company (AITC) at Camp Lejeune (1986-92), and one year as the SNCOIC of the 3rd Marine Division Combat Squad Leaders Course (CSLC) on Okinawa (1992-93).

While at AITC, he developed, taught, and refined courses of instruction on maneuver warfare, land navigation, fire support coordination, call for fire, adjust fire, close air support, M203 grenade launcher, movement to contact, daylight attack, night attack, infiltration, defense, offensive Military Operations in Urban Terrain (MOUT), defensive MOUT, NBC defense, and leadership. While with 3rd Marine Division CSLC, he further refined the same periods of instruction and developed others on patrolling.

He has completed all of the correspondence school requirements for the Marine Corps Command and Staff College, Naval War College (1000-hour curriculum), and Marine Corps Warfighting Skills Program. He is a graduate of the Camp Lejeune Instructional Management Course, the 2nd Marine Division Skill Leaders in Advanced Marksmanship (SLAM) Course, and the East-Coast School of Infantry Platoon Sergeants Course.

# Name Index

**A**

Afghanistan 17, 274
Alamo 26, 226
Alvarez 161
American Revolution 26, 31
An Hoa 373
Antietam 3, 195

**B**

Basilone 52, 56, 121, 256
Bastogne 314
Beauregard 202
Belleau Wood 204, 232
Berlin 28, 284, 285
Boehm 204, 205
Boer War 27, 31, 356
Briceno 161
Budapest Uprising 56
Buford 63
Bull Run 252
Burma 17, 226

**C**

Cam Lo 50, 272, 371
Cambrai 39
Camp Carroll 208
Campbell 371
Caporetto 226
Carlson 35, 354
Carter 199
Chamberlain 48, 49, 272
Chancellorsville 26
Cheatham 14
Chiang Kai-shek 38
Chickamauga 238
Chosin Reservoir 28, 35, 55, 57, 103, 119, 195, 227
Chu Lai 93, 371
Churchill 6, 29
Civil War 12, 16, 26, 44, 47, 48, 63, 195, 202, 203, 261, 352
Clausewitz 31, 195, 295
Collins xv, 5, 6, 8, 10
Con Thien 31, 161, 174, 208, 371
Couplet 52
Cox 174, 371
Cross 272

Cukela 230
Cushman 205

**D**

Da Nang 36, 227, 262, 268
Dai Do 58, 205
Dearth 179
Dien Bien Phu 28
Dong Ha 36, 205, 208, 227

**E**

Edson 19, 23, 34, 48, 176, 344, 352
Eisenhower 11, 103
Erskine 204
Europe 13, 34, 204, 284, 314
Ewell 195, 202

**F**

Falklands 28, 38, 54, 57, 205, 210, 211
Forest 20
Franco-Prussian War 10
Frederick the Great 9, 19
Fredericksburg 44, 252
French and Indian Wars 35, 65, 341
Fuller xvii, 341

**G**

Gettysburg 44, 48, 49, 63, 202, 272
Giap 14, 36, 38, 42
Gio Linh 19, 174, 208, 371
Glass 205
Gordon 203
Graham 179
Grant 16
Gray xix, 102, 349
Griffith 32, 38
Guadalcanal xvii, 19, 23, 34, 35, 39, 52, 57, 63, 65, 66, 87, 89, 120, 176, 199, 227, 256, 344, 352, 354
Gudmundsson 7
Gulf War xix, 6, 23, 26, 29, 44, 48, 54, 132, 133, 135, 178, 182, 205, 274, 275, 350, 352
Gustafson 371

## H

Hackworth xvi, 38
Haiti xvi, 103
Hamburger Hill 3
Hamilton 203
Hart 6, 20, 38, 40, 202
Harvey 139
Ho Chi Minh Trail 19
Hodges 161
Hollingsworth 89
Hue 38, 314, 316, 317
Hungarian Revolution 272

## I

Ia Drang 66, 119
Inchon 26
India 17
Indian wars 226
Indochina 120
Iwo Jima 15, 46, 52, 56, 177, 179, 204, 353

## J

Jackson 26, 44, 103, 195, 349
John Paul II 12

## K

Kasserine Pass 23
Kelly 182
Kennedy 12
Khafji 133
Kocak 230, 232
Korea xvi, 7, 18, 26, 28, 35, 38, 48, 52, 55, 86, 87, 119, 120, 150, 195, 205, 226, 227, 272, 314

## L

Lang Vei 52
Lee 26, 92, 195, 349
Lincoln 16, 44, 354
Lind xix, 40, 41, 350
Ludendorff 31, 46

## M

MacArthur 26, 349
Mahan 315
Malay Peninsula 227
Malaysia 89, 92
Manchuria 28, 33, 57, 92, 135, 199, 213, 226, 261, 347
Manila 314
Mao Tse-tung 35, 36, 38
Marion 34, 209
Marshall 7, 58, 341
McClellan 20

Meade 44
Merrill 226
Moltke 10
Mont Blanc 182
Monte Casino 178, 317
Mosby 12, 26

## N

Napoleon 31, 46, 261
Nicaragua xvi, 103
Normandy 26, 231
North Africa 16, 23, 204

## O

O'Fara 34
Omaha Beach 208

## P

Pacific War xix, 13, 33, 34, 45, 46, 48, 52, 92, 176, 204, 227, 252, 253
Patton 26, 202, 239, 346, 349
Pershing 11
Petersburg 203
Pickett 48, 49, 272
Price 272
Puller xvi, 34, 35, 54, 57, 63, 102, 103, 115, 120, 121, 227, 256, 315, 316, 349

## Q

*no entries*

## R

Rappahannock Station 203
Revolutionary War 203
Roach 93, 371
Rogers 65, 341
Rohr 27, 31, 52, 350, 356
Rommel xvii, 16, 17, 23, 102, 226, 356
Russo-Japanese War 31, 33, 35, 204

## S

Saigon xvi, 314
Savage 56
Schmid 52
Schott 133
Schwarzkopf 26, 349
Seoul 314, 315, 316
Shenandoah Valley 26
Shiloh 202
Sims xvii, 354
Singapore 227

Slim 17, 19
Smith 19
Soissons 52
Solomons 92
Somme 29, 47, 55, 177
Stalingrad 28, 48, 134, 284, 285, 287
Stein 56, 353
Sun Tzu xviii, 13, 14, 16, 18, 19, 22, 23, 24, 26, 27, 29, 31, 32, 38, 43, 44, 57, 62, 102, 152, 174, 180, 223, 225, 252, 283, 313, 340, 348, 350, 354

**T**

Tarawa 18, 52, 261, 295
Taylor 7, 284
Thomas 138
Trenton 203
Turton 204

**U**

Upton 195, 203

**V**

Vandegrift 34, 35, 341, 349
Vargas 58
Vietnam xv, xvi, 5, 6, 14, 17, 19, 28, 29, 30, 35, 36, 38, 41, 42, 48, 49, 50, 51, 52, 56, 58, 65, 66, 68, 82, 87, 89, 93, 101, 120, 125, 133, 134, 138, 139, 150, 160, 161, 163, 182, 183, 200, 205, 208, 226, 227, 229, 230, 250, 256, 261, 293, 314, 339, 351, 371

**W**

Walt 63
Warren 63
Warsaw Ghetto 283, 285, 287
Washington 7, 26, 202, 349
Waterloo 46, 261
Weise 58, 205
Westerman 50
Williams 373
Willis 161
Winebar 272
World War I 7, 11, 17, 27, 28, 31, 32, 34, 39, 45, 46, 47, 52, 54, 55, 102, 173, 174, 177, 182, 199, 204, 207, 208, 210, 212, 226, 230, 232, 237, 253, 261, 275, 287, 316, 343, 345, 350, 352, 353, 355, 356
World War II xix, 7, 12, 24, 26, 28, 34, 35, 48, 49, 102, 126, 133, 134, 204, 213, 226, 227, 252, 261, 272, 284, 287, 314, 317, 340, 354
Wright 195

**X**

*no entries*

**Y**

York 24
Yorktown 203

**Z**

Zhukov xvi, 28

To: Posterity Press, P.O. Box 5360, Emerald Isle, NC 28594
From: _____
         _____
         _____

Subject: *The Last Hundred Yards;* request for

1. Send me this large, fully illustrated book.
2. Enclosed is proof of active-duty, reserve, retired, or veteran status in the U.S. military and check/money order for this total:

| | |
|---|---|
| Price | $19.95 |
| Shipping Charges | 2.80 |
| Tax (North Carolina residents only) | <u>1.20</u> |
| Total | $23.95 |

3. I understand that delivery could take up to three weeks.

                            Signature _____

---

To: Posterity Press, P.O. Box 5360, Emerald Isle, NC 28594
From: _____
         _____
         _____

Subject: *The Last Hundred Yards;* request for

1. Send me this large, fully illustrated book.
2. Enclosed is proof of active-duty, reserve, retired, or veteran status in the U.S. military and check/money order for the total:

| | |
|---|---|
| Price | $19.95 |
| Shipping Charges | 2.80 |
| Tax (North Carolina residents only) | <u>1.20</u> |
| Total | $23.95 |

3. I understand that delivery could take up to three weeks.

                            Signature _____

---

To: Posterity Press, P.O. Box 5360, Emerald Isle, NC 28594
From: _____
         _____
         _____

Subject: *The Last Hundred Yards;* request for

1. Send me this large, fully illustrated book.
2. Enclosed is proof of active-duty, reserve, retired, or veteran status in the U.S. military and check/money order for the total:

| | |
|---|---|
| Price | $19.95 |
| Shipping Charges | 2.80 |
| Tax (North Carolina residents only) | <u>1.20</u> |
| Total | $23.95 |

3. I understand that delivery could take up to three weeks.

                            Signature _____